MEDIUM ÆVUM

MONOGRAPHS XXXIX

OVID IN THE VERNACULAR

TRANSLATIONS OF THE *METAMORPHOSES* IN THE MIDDLE AGES & RENAISSANCE

EDITED BY

GEMMA PELLISSA PRADES

&

MARTA BALZI

THE SOCIETY FOR THE STUDY OF MEDIEVAL
LANGUAGES AND LITERATURE

OXFORD · MMXXI

THE SOCIETY FOR THE STUDY OF MEDIEVAL LANGUAGES AND
LITERATURE
OXFORD, 2021

http://aevum.space/monographs

ISBN:
978-1-911694-00-7 (PB)
978-1-911694-01-4 (HB)

British Library Cataloguing in Publication Data
A catalogue record for this book is available
from the British Library

Published with the support of

The Institute of Greece, Rome and the Classical Tradition (University of Bristol)

Secretary for Universities and Research of the Ministry of Economy and Knowledge of the Government of Catalonia

Ministry of Science and Innovation of the Spanish Government

Departament of Culture of the Government of Catalonia

Universitat de Barcelona, Departament de Filologia Catalana i Lingüística General

CONTENTS

LIST OF ABBREVIATIONS

ATILF	*Dictionnaire du Moyen Français en ligne*
BITECA	*Bibliografia de Textos Antics Catalans, Valencians i Balears*
BMC	*Catalogue of Books Printed in the XVth century now in the British Library*
BL	*British Library*
BnF	*Bibliothèque nationale de France*
DBI	*Dizionario Biografico degli Italiani*
ESTC	*English Short Title Catalogue*
FEW	*Französisches Etymologisches Wörterbuch*
STC	*Short Title Catalogue*
STCN	*Short Title Catalogue, Netherlands*
STCV	*Short Title Catalogue Vlaanderen*
TL	*Tobler-Lommatzsch: Altfranzosisches Wörterbuch*
USTC	*Universal Short Title Catalogue*

LIST OF ILLUSTRATIONS

MARTA BALZI

INTRODUCTION

> quaque patet domitis Romana potentia terris,
> ore legar populi, perque omnia saecula fama,
> siquid habent veri vatum praesagia, vivam.[1]

(Ovid, Metamorphoses, xv. 877–79)

[Wherever Rome's power extends over the conquered world, I shall be read on the lips of the people, and, if the prophecies of bards have any truth, through all the ages shall I live in fame.]

Publius Ovidius Naso (43 BCE–17 CE) began his poetic career around the age of eighteen and went on to establish his fame by successfully reinventing the Latin elegiac tradition.[2] In the *Amores*, *Heroides*, *Ars amatoria* and *Remedia amoris*, Ovid gave new shape to known characters and conventional situations.[3] The theme of transformation is also central in Ovid's most important literary work: the *Metamorphoses*. The fifteen books of Ovid's *Metamorphoses* narrate the creation of all things through stories of transformation. Animals and plants, men and women, minerals and gods are the protagonists of the changes that gave birth to our world. Ovid gathered these tales from an extensive corpus of Greek and Roman mythology, interweaving them to form a continuous narrative thread from

---

[1] Throughout this Introduction, quotations from the Latin text and the translation are taken from the Loeb edition, see Ovidius 1916.

[2] Ovid was born in Sulmo (modern Sulmona, Abruzzo) on 20 March 43 BCE from a wealthy equestrian family, moving to Rome as the young Augustus consolidated his power as 'Princeps' of the Roman Empire. After a brief political service, he decided to abandon the *cursus honorum* (ladder of offices) and fully dedicated himself to poetry: see Liveley 2011: 1–2.

[3] Ovid's *Amores* was first published in 20 BCE and then reissued in 10 BCE. In the meantime, he worked on the *Heroides*, a collection of love letters and epistles from the heroines of classical myths to their lovers, and on the first two books of the *Ars amatoria*, a didactic poem on seduction and sex. Shortly afterwards, he published the third book of the *Ars amatoria* together with his *Remedia amoris*, a collection of anecdotes for unhappy lovers: see Liveley 2011: 2–3.

the original chaos to the deification of Julius Caesar.[4] Amongst its many themes, the *Metamorphoses* examines creation and destruction, anger and love, violence and politics, morality and monstrosity. The length and content of the poem make it an ambitious and daring poetical undertaking from which Ovid hoped to win eternal recognition. At the end of Book xv, after Pythagoras's lesson about the continuous flux and mutability of all things, Ovid proposed that as long as Rome holds its power, this poem would live forever (*Metamorphoses*, XV. 877–79). Ovid predicted an eternity in which he 'shall be read on the lips of the people' (*Metamorphoses*, XV. 878). This sentence hints at two transformations: the first is the metamorphosis of the poet into poetry (Liveley 2011: 153–54). Ovid, in fact, is the one who shall be read, not the poem. The second transformation is the re-embodiment of Ovid in future poets and readers. The Latin words 'ore legar populi' can be translated as 'I [i.e. my soul] will be gathered on the lips of the people', implying that Ovid's soul shall be found in the re-telling and re-writing of future poets and readers (Hardie 1999: 268, n. 44; 2002: 3). This epilogue embraces Pythagoras's doctrine of endless mutability.

Two thousand years after Ovid's death, this bold claim made in the epilogue of the *Metamorphoses* has proved to be justified. The poem has continued to exert an enduring influence on Western culture, and this volume explores new aspects of its afterlife. The object of study of this volume are the vernacular translations of the *Metamorphoses* written in Europe in the Middle Ages and the Renaissance. *Ovid in the Vernacular* covers eight linguistic areas (English, Spanish, Catalan, French, German, Italian, Dutch, and Greek) and offers new insights about the way in which each of these emerging vernacular cultures appropriated and transformed this Latin poem through words and images. At the same time, this book looks beyond national and linguistic borders and retraces the circulation of textual and visual elements of the vernacular Ovid across Europe, connecting different literary traditions. This volume overcomes any perceived division between Middle Ages and Renaissance, and charts continuities and discontinuities between these two historical periods, addressing the influence of manuscript culture and print culture on the re-fashioning of Ovid. The scope of this publication is to bear witness to the transformative ability of Ovid's *Metamorphoses* and unveil how the transformations to which this poem lent itself allowed this work to become a constitutive part of the literary and artistic life of Western Europe.

---

[4]   We do not know with certainty the exact date or year in which Ovid began to write this poem. In 8 CE, as Ovid received news that Augustus had decided to banish him from Rome to Tomis on the Black Sea coast (Romania), the *Metamorphoses* was still incomplete, and it is possible that Ovid continued working on the poem until his death in 17 CE; see Liveley 2011: 4.

Ovid in the Vernacular situates itself in the tradition of edited volumes addressing the reception of the *Metamorphoses* and other Ovidian works in the Western World. In the 1960s and 1970s, the first studies on reception stressed the idea that texts do not have a univocal meaning. On the contrary, meaning is variable and it is established by readers.[5] In Classical Studies, this concept shifted the focus from the text and its author and gave place to the idea that present and future literary criticism could not prescind from the study of the influence that classical texts exerted on subsequent historical times. Ovidian scholarship, according to Hardie, Barchiesi and Hinds (1999: 1), benefited from the study of reception: the investigation of Ovid's afterlives shed new light on the features of the *Metamorphoses* that have continued to exert their power on Western culture and reappraised the standing of Ovid, who – at the beginning of the twentieth century – dropped out of the central canon of classical poets. The edited volume *Ovidian Transformations: Essays on Ovid's Metamorphoses and its Reception* (Hardie, Barchiesi and Hinds 1999) reflects the new importance given to the reception of the poem by joining together modern criticism of the Ovidian texts and essays on established authors, such as Petrarch and Drayton, and their understanding and imitation of this classical poem (Lyne 1999; Hardie 1999). The union of modern criticism and reception also lies at the heart of the *The Cambridge Companion to Ovid* (Hardie 2002), which dedicates the final section of the volume to essays on the reception of this work from the Middle Ages to the present time. The enthusiasm and vibrancy surrounding the topic of Ovid's afterlife is also evident in a series of ambitious edited volumes published in the past fifteen years that concentrate exclusively on issues of reception. The contributions relative to the Middle and Early Modern Ages include *Metamorphoses: The Changing Face of Ovid in Medieval and Early Modern Europe* (2007); *Ovid in the Middle Ages* (2011); and *A Handbook to Ovid's Reception* (2014).

As specified in the title of this volume, the focus of the study rests on the vernacular Ovid. This is the first element that distinguishes *Ovid in the Vernacular* from the aforementioned publications, all of which combine articles on the Ovidian reception in Latin and the vernaculars. As we shall see in the individual articles in this volume, the relationship between Latin and the vernaculars changes significantly from one European linguistic group to the other and from the Middle Ages to the Renaissance. In recent years, medieval and early modern scholars alike have recognised the impossibility of fully understanding Ovid's reception without considering the vernacular cultures of Europe (Hexter 2002: 416). This volume stresses the importance of this vernacular tradition by giving it the pride of place.

---

[5] For the first conceptualisations of reception see Jauss 1982 and Iser 1978.

Some of the articles in this volume analyse linguistic areas that have not been explored in previous edited volumes, such as the translations of the *Metamorphoses* in German and Dutch, for example, and it also concentrates on previously neglected translators, such as Francesco Pona, Francesc Alegre and Ioannis Makolas.

Another element that distinguishes *Ovid in the Vernacular* from previous volumes is that it focuses on the vernacular translations of the full text of Ovid's *Metamorphoses*. The articles published in the volume deal with the translations of the fifteen books of Ovid's poem rather than dealing with authorial imitations of Ovidian themes and narrative strategies or with translations of single episodes taken from the poem's books. This decision allowed us to reflect on how medieval and early modern translators engaged with the work as a whole. How were Ovid's narratorial strategies and self-reflexivity dealt with throughout the book? How were the link between individual myths and separate books treated by translators? Which sets of illustrations decorating the poem travelled through Europe and how? There is a substantial difference between partial translations and complete translations. Complete translations, in fact, engage differently with the departure text. An important point to consider, for example, is the fact that a whole translation was often conceived as an improved text that could substitute the departure text. It may suffice to think about the *Ovide moralisé* or the *Ovidius moralizatus* which offered a moralised and enriched version of the *Metamorphoses* to be read as an alternative to the 'original' text (Fumo 2014: 120). The fact that the vernacular translation could potentially substitute the Latin poem engenders a complex relationship between author and translator, source and destination culture, that are not repeated in translations of individual myths of the *Metamorphoses* and also in commentaries – such as Arnulf's or John of Garland's – which could circulate independently from the *Metamorphoses* but in most cases would accompany Ovid's poem (Coulson 2011: 51, 64).

The articles in this volume are literary-historical studies that combine philological and book-historical approaches with translation history. This interdisciplinary methodological framework is situated within the field of Translation Studies. In the past forty years, the scope of the discipline has been substantially redefined in order to move from a principal focus on the linguistic transfer from one text to another, to an understanding that it is a more complex phenomenon which must be studied within its cultural context(s) (Bassnett and Lefevere 1990). This so-called 'cultural turn' within Translation Studies opened up the field to an exchange and encounter with neighbouring disciplines.[6] Particularly important for the articles in this book is the cross-fertilisation between Translation Studies and Media Studies.[7] In the last decade, Translation Studies has looked with increasing interest at the ways in which we articulate ideas in material forms and how the technical aspects of communication have influenced the production and dissemination of translations. Michael Cronin (2003), for example, contends that scholars should diversify their approach to translation. Although the linguistic and sociological aspects of translation are pivotal, more emphasis should be given to 'translations as things' (Cronin 2003: 10). Similarly, Christine Mitchell (2010) has stressed the materiality of translated texts. In 2015, Brenda Hosington published a ground-breaking article on the importance of working at the crossroads between Translation Studies and Book History in order to gain a fuller sense of the ways in which translation became such a pivotal and ubiquitous component of the European Renaissance. The acknowledgement of the importance of media in the understanding of translation production and dissemination, argues Karin Littau (2016: 87), is not relevant only to the discipline of Translation Studies, but it is part of a new phase in the humanities.[8] This turn towards the material is spurred by today's society, which is experiencing a technological change that makes media and technologies exceptionally visible (Littau 2016: 86). This material turn is a timely one, continues Littau (2016: 83), because it is impossible to think about intellectual history – and therefore translation – only in terms of abstract ideas, languages and meanings without taking into account the media entities that made the dissemination of these ideas possible at all. At the core of this new synergy is the idea that the intellectual world cannot be separated from the material technologies through which we express our ideas. This concept gives new importance to the material objects in which translations were written and transmitted and to the paratexts that accompany the translation. In *Ovid in the Vernacular*, for example, manuscript and printed illustrations in the margins of the text constitute a key object of investigation, as well as letters to the readers and commentaries that are part of the paratextual environment of a book.

---

[6]   In her introduction to *Rethinking Methods in Translation History*, Carol O'Sullivan (2012: 136) has underlined the importance of interdisciplinary and multidisciplinary research in Translation Studies. For the importance of interdisciplinarity in Translation Studies see also Snell-Hornby, Pöchhacker and Kaindl 1994; Kuhiwczak and Littau 2007 stresses the interdisciplinarity of the discipline by presenting essays which address the encounter of Translation Studies with other disciplines.

[7]   For an overview of the material turn in Translation Studies see Armstrong 2020.

[8]   See also the responses in the same issue to Littau's article by Armstrong 2016: 102–06, and Coldiron 2016: 96-102.

The aim of the following section of this Introduction is to present the content and original contribution of the individual chapters of the volume, and at the same time also to establish the literary-historical contexts for the translations of the *Metamorphoses* that will be the focus of the rest of the volume. Our volume is divided in five parts that address different linguistic areas (English; Catalan and Spanish; French; Italian; German and Dutch, and Greek). This subdivision does not follow a chronological or hierarchical pattern of any sort, and it is designed to give equal relevance to each linguistic tradition. In the following section of this Introduction, the individual 16 chapters that form the volume will not be presented in the order in which they appear in the volume, but they will rather form a chronological narrative. We will discuss the history of the translation of the *Metamorphoses* from the Middle Ages to the Renaissance in Europe, and the cultural and historical events that marked the emergence of new ideas of what should constitute a translation of a classical text. This Introduction does not provide a comprehensive list of all the vernacular translations of the *Metamorphoses* written in the period under investigation, and scholars specialised in specific linguistic areas must forgive the exclusion of important works attaining to that tradition. The Introduction, in fact, rather than aiming to present a full list of translations, is focused on tracing wider trends in the history of the vernacular Ovid and bringing to light previously unseen correspondences between different translatorial traditions.

The Vernacular Metamorphoses in Medieval and Early Modern Europe

The composition of the first vernacular translations of Ovid's *Metamorphoses* in Europe is linked to the changing status of Ovid in the Middle Ages as well as to the gradual emergence of vernacular literary cultures. The absence of Ovidian writings in manuscripts written between the sixth and eighth centuries suggests that familiarity with Ovid – one of the most visible literary authors in the fourth century CE – had gradually diminished in the early Middle Ages (Richmond 2002: 447; Clark 2011: 6).[9] Only in the ninth century is it possible to find the first hints of a resurgence of interest towards this author.[10] During the period of monastic

---

9   For the reception of Ovid's poetry in Late Antiquity see Ian Fielding (2014), who has shown the influence of Ovid's treatment of the themes of exile and eros in Latin poets working between the fourth and the sixth centuries.

10   For a study of the manuscript tradition of the Ovidian works and the evolution of the stemma codicum see also Buttenwieser 1940; Kenney 1962; Tarrant 1983. According to Richmond (2002: 450), the earliest direct tradition of the *Metamorphoses* includes substantial fragments from the ninth and tenth centuries, and the earliest extant complete texts of the poem date to the eleventh century. One of the earliest complete

expansion, between *c.* 950 and *c.* 1150, scriptoria of Italy and Western France became the main centre for the restoration and transmission of ancient authors, including Ovid, who became an established presence in Benedictine monasteries (Clark 2011b: 177–79). Gradually, the enthusiasm for the Ovidian works spread in extra-ecclesiastical environments such as the schoolroom of secular cathedrals and imperial and royal courts, so much so that by the second half of the twelfth century this author was a common presence in medieval libraries (Richmond 2002: 452; Clark 2011: 6–7). The glosses recorded in twelfth-century schoolbooks suggest that Ovid's works were read as repositories of grammatical, metrical and stylistic knowledge. At the same time, Ovid was also looked upon as a guide on loftier matters concerning astrology, history and theology. Thomas of Perseigne (d. 1119), for example, turned to Ovid's exile poetry to expound the Song of Songs (Clark 2011: 11). Alain de Lille (*c.* 1128–1202/1203) in France and later also Henry of Settimello (fl. 1191) in Italy used Ovidian amorous, epic and exile poetry to elaborate philosophical themes (Black 2011: 123).

As emerges from these few examples, in the high Middle Ages the Ovidian corpus lent itself to different readings. Medieval school masters took upon themselves to gather these interpretations in a succession of commentaries that became indispensable resources for medieval and early modern translators. As remarked by Alison Cornish (2011: 6) in her study on medieval translation in the Italian vernacular, there was no clear distinction between the act of translating and that of commenting in the Middle Ages: both these activities worked towards the same end, which was to keep ancient authors up to date. As we shall see in this volume, medieval and early modern translators relied on previous interpretations to amplify obscure passages in the text of departure and to add moral observations on the events narrated by Ovid. The commentary tradition on the *Metamorphoses* that began to flourish in twelfth-century France was complex and diverse in its form. Although there is still a general tendency to associate medieval commentaries with allegories, the medieval exegesis was literal as well as allegorical (Fumo 2014: 116). The Orleanais master Arnulf wrote two commentaries on the *Metamorphoses* (*c.* 1180).[11] One explanation was a grammatical and mythological gloss introduced by an accessus. The other was an allegorical exposition in which the stories were explained historically, morally and allegorically. The Vulgate commentary, the most authoritative reading of the *Metamorphoses* in the high Middle Ages, compiled in the

---

manuscript of the *Metamorphoses* came from Montecassino (Naples, Biblioteca Nazionale, MS IV F 3; late eleventh-century).

[11]   For an introduction to the commentaries composed in the Orléanais see Coulson 2011: 50–59; 65–70. Arnulf's commentaries are partially edited by Ghisalberti 1932.

Orléans area around 1250–1260, show the same combination of moral exegesis and linguistic excavation.[12] The fourteenth-century lectures on the *Metamorphoses* written by the Italian university master Giovanni del Virgilio are also divided in two separate commentaries which were supposed to be read in tandem: the philological explanation and the allegories.[13] Medieval commentaries existed in various formats and were in constant transformation. The allegorical commentary written by Arnulf, for example, was often transmitted with John of Garland's *Integumenta Ovidii* (*c.* 1234), a verse commentary written to uncover the hidden truths of the Ovidian fables.[14] The *Versus bursarii*, a philological gloss by William of Orléans (fl. 1200), was incorporated in the Vulgate commentary.[15] Copied as self-standing texts or transmitted together with the Latin poem, medieval commentaries spread in Europe and created a set of knowledge that put in connection vernacular translations from different linguistic areas. In Chapter 3 of this volume, for example, Irene Salvo shows how the international circulation of medieval commentaries created intertextual links in vernacular translations composed in different linguistic areas of Europe: the *General estoria*, a historiographical work commissioned by King Alfonso X (1256–1284) that contains Spanish translations of numerous tales taken from Ovid's *Metamorphoses*, and the *Ovide moralisé*, a fourteenth-century French translation of which we will talk at length later in this Introduction.[16]

In the period that goes from the end of the twelfth century to the first half of the thirteenth century the French speaking area had pride of place in the interpretation of the Ovidian texts, with the majority of important commentaries coming from the Orleanais area. The first French translations of individual myths extrapolated from Ovid's *Metamorphoses* date back to the third quarter of the twelfth century (Narcissus, Pyramus and Thisbe,

---

[12] Only small portions of the Vulgate Commentary have been critically edited up to date by Coulson (1991, 2015), who is working on the complete edition of the commentary (with French translation), projected for publication with Garnier.

[13] Ghisalberti (1933a) published the *accessus* to the *expositio* (13–19) and the *Allegorie* (43–110). For an introduction to Giovanni del Virgilio's commentary on Ovid see Black 2011: 127.

[14] For the different formats in which Arnulf's commentaries were transmitted in the Middle Ages see Coulson 2011: 54–55. The *Integumenta Ovidii* is edited by Ghisalberti 1933b and by Born 1929.

[15] For the edited text of William of Orléans's commentary see Engelbrecht 2003. For an introduction to this commentary and relative bibliography see also Coulson 2011: 55–59.

[16] According to Cristóbal (2011: 239) the *General estoria* constitutes 'the most important chapter of Spanish Ovidianism in the Middle Ages'.

Philomela).[17] Interestingly, considering the centrality of the French speaking world in Ovidian reception, the first extant vernacular translations of the complete *Metamorphoses* were written in languages other than French and came from two areas that had 'no direct influence on the course of vernacular translations of Ovid' (Hexter 2007: 1318): Thuringia and Byzantium.

As shown by Anna Cappellotto in Chapter 14 of this volume, a few fragments belonging to a single parchment dating back to the second half of the thirteenth century present extracts of translation written by the Saxon cleric Albrecht von Halberstadt (*c.* 1180–after 1251) in Middle High German.[18] According to Cappellotto, these fragments were with all probability part of a complete translation of the fifteen books of the Ovidian poem, and the project to translate this text was likely undertaken at the court of Hermann I (1155–1217) which was the most prominent literary *milieu* for the reception of classical Antiquity in Germany. As we gather from the few extant fragments, this medieval translator engaged directly with the Latin text, often simplifying it – and occasionally also moralising it – in order to adapt Ovid's epic to the taste of courtly readers. As shown by Cappellotto, textual evidence supports the hypothesis that Albrecht might have employed twelfth-century medieval commentaries such as the *Narrationes fabularum ovidianarum* and to Arnulf d'Orléans's *glosulae* and *allegoriae*. Interestingly, however, this translation does not present the systematic conjunction of translation and allegory typical of later fourteenth-century vernacular translations such as the French *Ovide moralisé* and the Italian *Ovidio metamorphoseos vulgare* (which we shall address later).

Similarly, also the twelfth-century Greek translation of Ovid's poem lacks moralisations and allegories deriving from previous commentaries. The Byzantine monk Maximos Planoudes (*c.* 1255–*c.* 1305) worked in the chancery for the Emperor in Byzantium and translated numerous Latin texts in Greek.[19] The diplomatic posting he covered in Byzantium required him to know Latin as the language of exchange between Greek East and

---

[17] Courtly poets in the French speaking area wrote original poems in the vernacular inspired by Ovidian erotic narratives, as emerges from the famous example of the *Roman de la Rose* (written before 1230). The *Ars Amatoria* was translated no less than four times in Old French verse during this century (Desmond 2011). Literature in French also played a pivotal role in the circulation of Ovidian re-writings in Europe and it provided vernacular poets in other linguistic areas with high standard literary models and sources which had already undergone cultural transfer and recodification (Segre 1996: 12–44).

[18] A new edition of the Middle High German fragments along with an Italian translation has been published by Cappellotto 2019.

[19] According to John Richmond (2002: 455) Planoudes' literal translations enabled philologists to reconstruct the reading of an old Latin manuscript transmitting classical texts.

Latin West. The purpose of his translation was probably to afford new and elegant epic material in Greek for courtly readers. In fact, according to Fisher (2011: 45), Planoudes envisioned a sophisticated readership well versed in classical mythology, and the translation served as a sample of Western culture.

As emerges from this initial enquiry, at the turn of the thirteenth century Ovid's *Metamorphoses* was already circulating in different forms and languages. This diversity of readings of the Ovidian canon shows that medieval readers did not understand Ovid as a monolithic figure, but rather as plural, elusive and transgressive (Desmond 1987: 3, Dimmick 2002: 264; Hexter 2002: 439; Clark 2011: 16; Newlands and Miller 2014: 6). In the fourteenth century, Ovid was considered an *auctoritas*, a person whose prestige and value could not be contested, and he was part of formal studies in schools and universities. In the Italian territory, for example, Ovid's *Metamorphoses* gained a leading position in the fourteenth-century syllabus, surpassing the popularity of Lucan and Virgil (Black 2001: 206-08). At the same time, he was also a controversial figure on multiple levels: political, theological, poetical and sexual. Ovid was banished from Rome for a poem and a mysterious crime ('carmen et error', *Trist.*, 2. 1. 207), and his love poetry was not easily contextualised within Christian doctrine and morality. The medieval author of the pseudo-Ovidian *De vetula* (*c.* 1222–1268), for example, expressed his anxieties regarding Ovid's status by presenting a sanitised version of the poet's persona.[20] Ovid is here represented as the exile poet who is conscious of his moral shortcomings and decides to abandon his love poetry to focus on philosophy. The plurality of Ovid's status favoured the re-writing of his work. Ovid's verse, in fact, continued to be relevant only as long as it was explained: this tension between preservation and change is at the heart of the first complete French translation of Ovid's *Metamorphoses* that came down to us, the *Ovide moralisé*.[21]

The anonymous author of this fourteenth-century French version of Ovid's *Metamorphoses* made the act of transformation the core of his poetic agenda. Transformation, in fact, is not only the central theme of Ovid's *Metamorphoses*, but is also one of the objectives of this medieval translator, who, as shown by Miranda Griffin (2015: 38), skilfully dismembered the Ovidian tales and artfully re-wrote them through the Christian tradition of

---

[20] For a study of *De Vetula* as the perfect representation of Ovid's plurality in the Middle Ages see Hexter 2002: 440–42; Hexter 2011: 284–92.

[21] The bibliography on the *Ovide moralisé* is vast. For an introduction, see Possamaï-Pérez 2006; Griffin 2012; Griffin 2015; Pairet 2011. For an up-to-date list of scientific publications and critical editions on the *Ovide moralisé*, see the *OEF* project (*Ovid in French: Genesis, Transformation, and Reception of the Ovide moralisé*), www.agence-nationale–recherche. fr/Project–ANR–12–FRAL–0001 [accessed 10 January 2018].

glossing and commenting. Recently, the complex genesis and transmission of this work has come under investigation by the international research group 'Ovid en Français' (*OEF*).[22] This volume reflects the rising academic interest towards this translation by presenting four different articles dealing with this work. In Chapter 7, Marylène Possamaï-Pérez focuses on the genesis of the *Ovide moralisé* and tries to uncover the translating techniques of the anonymous author of this medieval translation. The article deals with the text in Old French transmitted in the early fourteenth-century manuscript Rouen, Bibliothèque municipal, MS O.4., and takes as a case study the myth of Callisto. This Ovidian episode was greatly amplified in the translation in Old French. This amplification, according to Possamaï-Pérez, is a direct result of the translator's use of secondary sources, such as the medieval commentaries that were copied together with the Latin text. An example of manuscripts joining together Latin poem and commentary are Rome, Biblioteca Apostolica Vaticana, MS *Vaticanus latinus 1479* and Rome, Biblioteca Apostolica Vaticana, MS *Vaticanus latinus 1598*, for example, which the translator might have used for his work. Possamaï-Pérez also shows that this work of amplification is not only the result of the translator's reliance on secondary sources. Crucial are the intellect and imagination of this medieval translator, who expanded Ovid's verse with outstanding audacity and originality. Particularly interesting, for example, is the translator's meticulous description of Callisto's changing body, which was not an object of interest in medieval commentaries, and also the daring exegetical reading of the fable of Callisto as a metaphor of the relationship between Christianity and Judaism, which was erased in subsequent manuscript and printed copies of the *Ovide moralisé*.

As we learn from Possamaï-Pérez's article, the *Ovide moralisé* has a complex reception history and only a thorough philological work can unveil the various forms taken by this translation. Three chapters in this volume focus on aspects dealing with the reception of this work (Chapters 6, 7, 8). In Chapter 6, Mattia Cavagna argues that it is not possible to study the *Ovide moralisé* only in relation to a unique and stable source text. The translator, in fact, followed the Latin *Metamorphoses* as well as other intermediary texts (commentaries, sermons, and vernacular works among other things). Furthermore, the *Ovide moralisé* is a complex poem that does not exist – or it cannot be reduced to exist – in a single and unitary form. It was transmitted by 20 manuscripts dated from the early fourteenth century to the late fifteenth century (Baker and others 2018: 13–15). All these re-writings (in prose and verse, in manuscript and print) superimposed new meanings and purposes on the source text and they must be studied as

---

[22] See previous footnote.

works of art that have their own artistic and literary value. This article
illustrates the ways in which the various extant versions of the *Ovide
moralisé* make reference to each other: their networks. Sometimes a rewriter
made reference to another manuscript that transmitted the *Ovide moralisé*,
thus creating a connection between different material objects. In other
instances, the link between different readings of the same tale existed within
the same manuscript codex. In all instances, the tradition ensuing from the
Ovide moralisé continues to challenge the primacy of the Latin
Metamorphoses as a model of imitation and Ovid continues to be present,
but not as the unique author. As shown by Cavagna, multiple authorities,
including translator, copyist, printer and editor implicitly or explicitly
assumed an authorial role in the history of the *Ovide moralisé*.

The issue of the conflicting co-existence of different authorities in the
Ovide moralisé is further explored in Chapter 8. Prunelle Deleville examines
two late manuscripts of the *Ovide moralisé*: Paris, BnF, français 870 (*Z³*) *c.*
1410 and Paris, BnF, 19121 (*Z⁴*) *c.* 1390–1410. *Z³* and *Z⁴* stand out from
the tradition of the *Ovide moralisé* because they both omit the spiritual
allegories that originally constituted a significant part of the work. As shown
by Deleville, however, the author of the manuscripts *Z* does much more
than simply omitting parts of the *Ovide moralisé*. Through a comparative
textual analysis of the narration of Callisto's myth, it is possible to see how
the author of *Z³* and *Z⁴* borrowed the translatorial strategies devised by the
author of the *Ovide moralisé* and used them to a different end, offering a
new interpretation of the female character he is presenting. While in the
Ovide moralisé Callisto was condemned as a sinner for having succumbed to
Jupiter's sexual assault, the author of the *Z* manuscripts subverts this
perspective. He condemns Jupiter's assault and the deceitfulness of men in
general. This new interpretation of the myth and this new exegesis of the
role of women in the Ovidian myths, as shown by Deleville, became influential among medieval female writers such as Christine de Pizan Therefore,
this article shows how later re-writings of the *Ovide moralisé* could gain their
own readership thanks to their unique take on ancient mythology.

Not unlike medieval commentaries, medieval translations were often
transmitted together with other Ovidian materials. A late fifteenth-century
manuscript of the *Ovide moralisé*, for example, contains as a preface the 'De
formis figurisque deorum', Pierre Beruire's introduction to Book XV of his
Reductorium morale (*c.* 1340–1362).[23] Book XV of the *Reductorium morale* is
an allegorical commentary in Latin prose on Ovid's *Metamorphoses* that had

---

[23]   This is the manuscript Copenhagen, Det Kongelige Bibliotek, MS Thott 399 (c. 1480),
       see Chapter 6 of this volume for a discussion of this manuscript and the relative
       bibliography. Ghisalberti 1933c was the first complete study of Bersuire's treatise. It was
       followed by Engels 1966 and 1971, and Kretschmer 2016.

an immense fortune in all Europe and it is known as the *Ovidius moralizatus*. The first complete translation of the Ovidian poem in the Iberian Peninsula, for example, is a translation of Bersuire's *moralizatus*: the *Morales de Ovidio* (Hexter 2007: 1317–18).[24] Book I of Bersuire's *Ovidius moralizatus* was also rendered into French prose in 1480 (Copenhagen, ms. Thott 388) (Hexter 2007: 1314).

In Chapter 9 of this volume, Pablo Piqueras Yagüe examines some of the affinities and differences between the *Ovide moralisé* and the *Ovidius moralizatus*, two fourteenth-century works that had a great fortune in the Middle Ages, and whose reception – as we have seen – was often entwined. Piqueras Yagüe explains that the *Ovide moralisé* was written with the primary intention of creating a vernacular compendium of classical mythography. The anonymous author gave equal importance to the readability and beauty of the narrative discourse and to the moral and educational aspects of the tales. In addition, he chose a theme for each book of his poem and he selected what mythological tales to include or to exclude in order to give better shape to his authorial view of a certain topic. Unlike the *moralisé*, the *Ovidius moralizatus* privileged the educational and formative aspects of the narration. Bersuire narrated and moralised all the myths in his *Metamorphoses*, including those that Ovid mentioned only in passing such as, for example, the myth of the Palici and Marea. He lacked a narrative agenda comparable to that of the *moralisé* and saw beneath each myth a useful moral example. However, as shown by Piqueras Yagüe, despite their narrative and structural differences, these two very influential re-writings of Ovid's poem crossed paths and the *Ovide moralisé* occasionally became a source of inspiration for Bersuire. In the second version of the *Ovidius moralizatus* (version *P*), for example, Bersuire added two myths told by Ovid in the *Heroides*. The inspiration for these later additions, according to Piqueras Yague, probably came to Bersuire after reading the retelling of these episodes in the *Ovide moralisé*.

As in the French-speaking area, the first complete translation of the *Metamorphoses* in the Italian vernacular dates back to the fourteenth century. In contrast to the French tradition, however, the Italian one is more heterogeneous in nature, offering examples of 'allegorical' translation on the line of the *Ovide moralisé* and translations that engage more closely to the Latin source text. According to Bodo Guthmüller (2008: 114), Arrigo Simintendi da Prato (d. 1345/1356) translated Ovid's poem into vernacular prose almost certainly before 1334.[25] This is the first complete vernacular

---

[24] For the relevant bibliography on the *Morales de Ovidio* and its relationship to Bersuire's *Ovidius moralizatus* see also Chapter 4 in this volume.

[25] In the field of Ovid's reception in the Italian vernacular in the Middle Ages, Bodo Guthmüller's *Ovidio metamorphoseos vulgare* (2008) remains a fundamental reference

translation of the *Metamorphoses* of which we have record, and it was written at a time in which translation activities were flourishing in northern and central Italy.[26] The development of wealthy municipalities stimulated a lively cultural climate. An emerging vernacular society required notaries, preachers and other institutional figures to mediate and translate a set of knowledge that was previously transmitted only in Latin. Simintendi was probably a notary, like many other translators in the fourteenth century, and was active in the political life of his town, Prato (in Tuscany).[27] His juridical education allowed him sufficient knowledge to gain direct access to a Latin version of Ovid's poem, which, according to Guthmüller, he translated literally (Guthmüller 2008: 114). The second extant translation of the *Metamorphoses* was written in the second half of the fourteenth century. The translator, Giovanni dei Bonsignori da Città di Castello, was also a member of a wealthy family and covered political offices in his municipality (Città da Castello, Perugia).[28] His Ovidian translation, the *Ovidio metamorphoseos vulgare*, dated between 1375 and 1377, was not entirely based on a Latin version of Ovid's poem. As shown by Guthmüller, only the first book of Bonsignori's work is a translation of the Latin source text. The rest is a translation of the commentary written by Giovanni del Virgilio (Guthmüller 2008: 79). Giovanni del Virgilio's work is at the same time a summary and an allegorical commentary on the myths of Ovid's poem. Unlike Simintendi's work, Bonsignori's translation takes into account and incorporates the exegetical tradition developed in the course of the Middle Ages and offers a moralised reading of Ovid's poem, which is presented as a collection of useful moral exempla. Bonsignori's translation continued to be read in the years to follow inside and outside Italy. An early

point. This study, first published in 1981, follows the changing styles and fortunes of the translations of Ovid's *Metamorphoses* from 1333 to 1561, and his emphasis rests on the influence and afterlife of medieval translations and Ovidian readings in the Renaissance. This research has a linguistic and comparative approach and illuminates the changing strategies of translation and the cultural contexts in which these translations were written and read. On the influence of Ovid's poetry on medieval and Renaissance literature see Anselmi and Guerra 2006.

[26] For the importance of the socio-economical reconfiguration of Italy to the development of vernacular translation, see Segre 1996: 14 (this study was first published in 1953); Folena 1991: 29–31 (this essay was printed for the first time in *La traduzione: saggi e studi*, ed. by B. Malmberg (Trieste: Lint, 1973), pp. 57–120). Cornish 2011: 2.

[27] Guthmüller 2008: 119. See also Cristiano Lorenzi, 'Arrigo Simintendi', in *DBI*, www.treccani.it/enciclopedia/arrigo–simintendi_(Dizionario-Biografico)/ [accessed 12 December 2019].

[28] Guthmüller 2008: 119–25; Gianni Ballistreri, 'Giovanni Bonsignori', *DBI*, www.treccani.it/enciclopedia/giovanni-bonsignori_%28Dizionario-Biografico%29/ [accessed 12 December 2019].

fifteenth-century manuscript contains a translation by the otherwise unknown Gerolamo da Siena, which is a paraphrased version of Bonsignori's text: *Le fabole di Ovidi*.[29] According to Gemma Pellissa Prades (2017: 444), the *Ovidio metamorphoseos vulgare* also had a large readership in the Iberian Peninsula, where it became the source text of two translations that are now lost; one in Spanish and the other in Catalan (allegedly written by Francesc Galceran de Pinós, *c.* 1416–1475).[30]

The flourishing of vernacular translations of Ovid's poem in the fourteenth century testifies not only to the popularity of the Ovidian poem, but it also reflects a desire to acquire for the vernacular culture a set of knowledge belonging to the classical culture. This desire to speak, write and think like the Ancients eventually encouraged a rising number of men of letters to set aside vernacular translations and privilege a direct encounter with the Latin text and language. In the fourteenth and fifteenth centuries, the majority of manuscripts of Ovid's *Metamorphoses* were copied in the Italian Peninsula, where humanist scholars devoted themselves to a programme of recovery of ancient manuscripts often negligently housed in monasteries (Richmond 2002: 455). This new encounter with the past set in motion a movement that gradually changed the face of the Latin text of the *Metamorphoses*, and also the idea about what should constitute a vernacular translation of a classical text.

Latin Humanists in Italy gradually began to understand Latin as a living language that could be improved through the encounter with Greek literature. Like their Roman antecedents, humanist writers embarked on the daunting task of translating Greek into Latin, and Leonardo Bruni (1370–1444) was the first to dedicate a treatise on how to perform this task correctly: the *De interpretatione recta* (*c.* 1424–1426).[31] The understanding of the historicity of languages, including Latin, was the necessary pre-condition for the development of philology, mastered by humanists like Lorenzo Valla (1407–1457) and Angelo Poliziano (1454–1494) (Wyatt 2014: 7). These scholars understood the importance of establishing an authentic text and began to develop methods to bring a text to its pristine form. Following their example, the scholar-publisher Aldus Manutius

---

[29] The manuscript (Rome, Vatican Library, Ross. 1102) is probably an autograph; see Guthmüller 2008: 141.

[30] According to Pellissa Prades (2019: 25), there was probably a third fifteenth-century translator that relied on Bonsignori's medieval translation: Joan Roís de Corrella. See also Chapter 4 for more information about the relationship between the Italian and Catalan tradition.

[31] For the critical edition of the tract and its translation in Italian see Bruni 2004. For a discussion of Bruni's tract see Botley 2004: 5–41; Cornish 2011: 169–74; Bistuè 2013: 21–22.

(1449–1515) made an effort to restore ancient texts while also revolution-
ising the nascent printing industry. The second Aldine edition of Ovid's
works edited by A. Naugerius (Venice 1515–1516) brought significant
improvements on the Ovidian works and set a standard for subsequent
sixteenth-century editions of the *Metamorphoses* (Richmond 2002: 457).

The invention of the printing press had a contrasting effect on the
development of Latin Humanism. On the one hand, it 'perfectioned' the
restoration of classical texts by producing multiple copies of newly edited
texts.[32] Humanist printed commentaries became the repositories of
philological debates and speculations making available to a wider audience
the wisdom of Latin writers and teachers. On the other hand, the
development of the printing industry gradually contributed to strengthening
vernacular Humanism. The printing press created the conditions for the rise
of a new readership interested in the reception of Latin and Greek texts in
the vernacular (Pérez Fernández and Wilson-Lee 2015: 6). The translations
published in the first years of printing – including those of the
Metamorphoses – were not based on the texts critically edited by humanists
and were not in line with the ideas on translation developed in the field of
Latin translation. On the contrary, the first translations of the
Metamorphoses to be printed in Europe were translations written in the
Middle Ages or translations still based upon medieval translations.

As shown by Cappellotto in Chapter 14 of this volume, the early modern
translator Jörg Wickram (*c.* 1505–before 1562) translated Ovid's
Metamorphoses from Albrecht's thirteenth-century version of the *Metamorphoses*.[33] This early modern translation was printed for the first time in 1545
in Mainz by Ivo Schöffer.[34] Albrecht adapted the language and style of the
medieval translation for a new readership. With the help of the printer, the
medieval translation was also made more palatable by the addition to the
text of a new set of interpretations and moralizations written by the
Catholic theologian Gerhanrd Lorichius (1485–before 1553). According to
Cappellotto, this printed edition was noteworthy because it was 'the first
attempt to moralize the *Metamorphoses* in the German speaking area more

---

[32] Baker (2015: 184–233) has studied how the humanist agenda was influenced by the
     development of the industry of the printing press. Specifically, he has focused on Marco
     Antonio Sabellico, who proved to be particularly precocious in his understanding of the
     potential of the printing press as an instrument that could give continuity and resonance
     to the scholarly advancement made by humanist scholars. The idea that the printing
     press stabilised the humanist Renaissance is also expressed in Eisenstein (1979; 2005:
     123–63).

[33] Modern editions of Wickram's adaptation are Bolte 1905–1906 and Roloff 1990.

[34] It was then printed in 1551 (Mainz, by Ivo Schöffer); 1581 (Frankfurt am Main, by
     Sigmunt Feyerabendts); 1609 (Frankfurt am Main, by Johann Saurn); 1631 (Frankfurt
     am Main, Gottfried Tampach).

than two centuries after the paramount French undertaking, the *Ovide moralisé* (1309–1320)'. Schöffer's is an illustrated edition. In the first edition the woodcuts were 47 in total and made by Wickram himself. This series was later substituted by 178 woodcuts created by the Nuremberg master Virgil Solis. This set of illustrations had an international circulation, and, as we will see later in this Introduction, it was re-used in the editions of Florianus's Dutch translation of Ovid's poem and also in the Antwerp edition (1595) of Bustamante's Spanish Ovid (see Chapters 5 and 15). This example suggests how the connection between different traditions of the vernacular Ovid could be forged by the circulation of paratextual elements of visual nature, which could easily cross linguistic borders.

In Italy, Bonsignori's fourteenth-century translation of Ovid's *Metamorphoses* was printed for the first time in 1497 in Venice (and edited again in 1501; 1508; 1517; 1519; 1520; and 1523).[35] This medieval prose translation was subsequently re-worked and written in verse by Niccolò degli Agostini (d. *c.*1526) and printed for the first time in Venice in 1522 (and edited again in 1533; 1537; 1538; 1547; 1548).[36] Bonsignori's prose translation also became a source text for the first extant Catalan translation of Ovid's poem: the *Trasformacions* by Francesc Alegre written between 1472 and 1482. This translation was printed in 1494 in Barcelona by Pere Miquel (Pellissa Prades 2017 and 2019; Hexter 2007: 1318) and it is composed of two parts: the first is the translation of Ovid's poem in prose and the second is a commentary to the myths authored by Alegre himself. As shown by Pellissa Prades in Chapter 4 of this volume, not only the prose translation, but also the commentary was indebted to Italian medieval readings of Ovid's poem. Focusing on the first book of Alegre's commentary, in fact, it is possible to see how the translator purposefully created a fictional dialogue between himself and other medieval commentators to validate his view on ancient mythology. Alegre's primary interlocutor was Giovanni Boccaccio, an *auctoritas* in the mythological field thanks to his *Genealogia deorum gentilium*, whose prominence in the commentary shows just how much Alegre's translation, although disseminated through the new medium, was rooted within medieval culture.

For what concerns the French tradition, the versified version of the *Ovide moralisé* was never printed. However, as we learn in Mattia Cavagna's article in Chapter 6, the second prose redaction – which was preserved in Paris, Bibliothèque nationale de France (BnF), MS français 137, in London, British Library, MS Royal 17. E. IV and Saint Petersburg, National Library

---

[35] For the list of reprints and details of publication of Bonsignori's translation see Guthmüller: 302–10.

[36] For the list of reprints and details of publication of Agostini's translation see Guthmüller 2008: 302–10.

of Russia, MS F. v. XIV. 1. – found its way within the 'Gutenberg Galaxy'. In 1484, the Belgian Colard Mansion printed a new edition of Prose II in Bruges. His vernacular Ovid contained woodcuts and handmade illustrations, and it also featured a new set of annotations translated by Mansion himself from Bersuire's *Ovidius moralizatus*. Hence, this early modern printed edition presents itself as an impressive vernacular pastiche of two of the most influential medieval rewritings of Ovid's poem. The second prose redaction' of the *Ovide moralisé* (in the version published by Mansion) was also the start text for *La Bible des poëtes*, another re-writing printed by the Parisian printer Antoine Vérard (1493, 1499, 1503).[37] In turn, Vérard's printed edition became the source text for other Ovidian re-writings printed in the first half of the sixteenth century by Michel Le Noir and his son Philippe le Noir in Paris, and by Romain Morin in Lyon (see Chapter 6).

Prose II is also the departure text employed by the English printer and translator William Caxton (*c*. 1422–*c*. 1491) for his influential Middle English translation of Ovid's *Metamorphoses*: the *Booke of Ovyde Named Methamorphose* (*c*. 1480) (Lyne 2002: 249–51). Once again, Mansion's Bruges printing shop is the centre of the dissemination of Prose II, as it is often suggested that Caxton came across a manuscript version of Prose II while he was employed in Mansion's workshop (Lyne 2002: 250). The English translation of the *Metamorphoses* written by Caxton survives only in a manuscript copy found in the 1960s. Although it is still debated whether this translation was given to the press or not, it is undoubtable that it originated within the context of early print culture. In Chapter 1 of this volume, Marie-Alice Belle shows how the translator carefully crafted intertextual relationships between his *Booke of Ovyde* and other texts that were translated or printed by Caxton himself. This complex intertextual network set the translation within a precise literary genre and placed the *Booke of Ovyde* among other Ovidian texts, such as those written by Chaucer and Gower, and that were familiar to Caxton's English readership. Belle's 'horizontal reading' demonstrates that Caxton's translation programme involved much more than a mechanical transposition of words from one language to another. The translator knew the reading habits of his contemporaries and harnessed the popularity of Ovidian themes and characters within the *Ovide moralisé* and their later re-writings in English to meet the taste of contemporary readers, who enjoyed reading well known themes set in different forms. Caxton, as emerges from Belle's insightful article, is not only an expert writer and reader who is able to combine his

---

[37] For further insights into the fortune of Mansions' version of Prose II in subsequent printed editions see Chapter 6.

translatorial and printerly activities, but he is also an impressive cultural mediator between French and English culture.

In Europe, starting from the 1530s, there is a rise of translations seeking to distance themselves from the medieval tradition. These translations, however, are initially only partial translations of the *Metamorphoses*. Clément Marot (1496-1544), for example, translated only the first two books of the *Metamorphoses*. The first one was printed in 1534 and the second one in 1543. Barthelemy Aneau wrote a translation of the third book that accompanied Marot's translation starting from 1556. In 1547, Jaques Colines (1457) published a close rendering of the debate between Ulysses and Ajax over Achille's arms. François Habert (fl. 1540-1560) published the first six books of the *Metamorphoses* in 1549 and the complete translation in 1557 (Hexter 2007: 1315).

As in France, also in the English-speaking world we see a gradual emergence of 'Ovidian episodes' based on close readings pf Ovid's Latin text (T. Hedleys's *Midas* in 1552; T. Howell's *Narcissus* in 1560; T. Peend *Hermaphroditus and Salmacis* in 1565). The first complete translation of the *Metamorphoses* in English based on a direct encounter with the Latin text is the famous translation by Arthur Golding (*c.* 1536–*c.* 1606). The first part of Golding's translation (Books I-IV) was printed in 1565 and the complete version in 1567 (Hexter 2007: 1326). In Chapter 2 of this volume, Genevieve Liveley explores a subsequent Renaissance translation of Ovid's poem written by George Sandys (1578–1644). Sandys published his translation of Ovid's *Metamorphoses* (Books I-V) in English verse in 1621. He completed the rest of the translation during the outward journey to the New World and his stay in Jamestown (Virginia), where he served as a treasurer and councillor for the British colony. As he returned to England, he published the complete translation of the fifteen books of Ovid's poem: *Ovid's Metamorphosis Englished* (1626). This edition was shortly followed by a second one in 1632, this time enriched with illustrations and commentaries to each book, and also Sandys' translation of the first book of the *Aeneid*. The addition of this other translation was meant to create a parallel between Aeneas's journey to start a new civilization in Italy and England's expansion towards the New World. The importance that Sandy's adventure in Virginia played in the making of this translation has often led scholars to consider the *Ovid Englished* one of the first examples of American English vernacular literature. However, as shown by Liveley, the rich paratextual apparatus of Sandys' 1632 translation suggests that the translator's interpretation of Ovid's poem derived from Sandys's European – rather than New World – cultural background. The translation was infused with the knowledge that Sandys derived from his extensive readings of European authors, his travels to Europe and his desire to create a new

Ovid in English that could compete with the translations published in the continent, especially in Italy and France.

Like France and England, from the 1530s Italy saw a rise of literal translations of single books or episodes of the *Metamorphoses*.[38] In 1539, Bindoni and Pasini printed Lodovico Dolce's vernacular translation in blank hendecasyllables of the first book of Ovid's poem (Dolce 1539). In 1540, the printer Andrea Arrivabene printed Alessandro Piccolomini's partial translation of Book XIII of the *Metamorphoses* (Piccolomini 1540). In 1556, an unidentified Venetian printing house published Pietro Sirena's translation of the first book of the *Metamorphoses* (Sirena 1556). It is not by chance that all the above-mentioned translations of the *Metamorphoses* were printed in Venice. In the fifteenth century, this city printed more books than any other in Europe (4,500 titles), and in the sixteenth century, it remained the most important printing centre in Italy: half of the 64,500 sixteenth-century books remaining in Italy today were printed there.[39] Ephemera and cheap recreational literature contributed to shaping a thriving vernacular readership to which a growing number of printing houses in Venice became increasingly attentive.[40] Entrepreneurial printers, such as Gabriele Giolito for example, invested growing proportions of their capital in order to capture the market for vernacular literature.[41] They surrounded themselves with editors to publish 'correct' and widely readable texts, and co-operated with typesetters, woodcutters and other artisans of the book to publish book-objects that looked fashionable and appealing.[42]

The evolution of the market in vernacular books in Venice paved the way for the publication of two influential vernacular translations of the *Metamorphoses*: the *Trasformationi* by Dolce (1553) and the *Metamorfosi* by Anguillara (1561). These were ambitious literary projects developed through the co-operation of translators and printers, and they easily differentiated themselves from earlier sixteenth-century printed translations. Dolce and Anguillara knew Latin, and their work resulted from a direct encounter

---

[38] Guthmüller 2008: 269.

[39] For an account of the central role played by Venice as a centre of communication and information see McNeill 1974; Burke 2000; and Infelise 2013.

[40] For the printing of ephemera in Renaissance Venice, see Salzberg 2014. Laura Carnelos (2016) has investigated the trade agents and distribution conditions of news and small printed material within the Republic of Venice in the sixteenth and seventeenth century.

[41] On the rise of Gabriele Giolito as one of the most prominent Venetian printers of vernacular literature see Nuovo and Coppens 2005: 67–101.

[42] For an insight into the collaboration between editors and printers in sixteenth-century Italy see Richardson 1994: 1–18; and Trovato 1991: 51–71.

between the translator and the Latin source text.[43] They translated all fifteen books of the poem, engaging with the structure of the *Metamorphoses* and with Ovid's narratorial voice in a more profound and extensive manner than the translators of single episodes, or individual books, of the same poem. Language, style and metre of these translations were modelled on the vernacular authors that were held as models of imitation in the late-sixteenth century, in particular Petrarch and Ariosto.[44] The unprecedented ambition and originality of these translations was matched by the presentation of the printed editions, in which numerous editorial trappings heightened the readability of the translations while associating them with the classics of vernacular literature. The layout, the illustrations and the narrative structure of the *Trasformationi* by Dolce, the translator-portraits in the *Metamorfosi* by Anguillara, for example, were all consciously designed to recall the sixteenth-century editions of Ludovico Ariosto's chivalric epic, the *Orlando furioso*.

Part IV of this volume deals with various aspects concerning the translations written by Dolce and Anguillara and the Italian tradition of the vernacular *Metamorphoses* in the late sixteenth century. In Chapter 10, Giuseppe Capriotti studies the relationship between text and images in the first printed editions of Dolce's *Trasformationi*. The printer Giolito commissioned to the architect Giovanni Antonio Rusconi a set of illustrations to decorate his vernacular Ovid. Rusconi, however, instead of

---

[43] The identification of the Latin edition of Ovid's *Metamorphoses* employed by these translators has not been addressed by previous scholars. Identifying the source edition is a complex task because of Dolce and Anguillara's creative approach towards translation, which led them to frequent omissions and amplifications. Dolce worked in Venice and – as we learn from his letters – he was a friend of the printer Paolo Manuzio, who occasionally sent him printed books (Dolce 2015: 86–87). This fact suggests that Dolce might have had access to a copy of the edition of Ovid's *Metamorphoses* first printed by Aldo Manuzio in 1502. According to Gabriele Bucchi, Raphael Regius's commentary to Ovid's *Metamorphoses* was a fundamental exegetical instrument for sixteenth-century translators of the *Metamorphoses* (Bucchi 2011: 57–60). Hence, it is likely that all three translators consulted an edition of Ovid's poem printed with this commentary. The first edition was printed in Venice in 1493 by Bernardino Benali. Regius's revised version of his commentary was printed by Giovanni Taccuino in 1513 in Venice.

[44] Pietro Bembo argued that in order to master the use of Latin and vernacular one should imitate a single excellent model. He chose Cicero and Virgil for Latin prose and poetry. For the vernacular, he indicated Petrarch for poetry, and Boccaccio for prose. Bembo's theory of imitation proved to be highly influential in the sixteenth century, setting the path towards the standardisation of the Italian vernacular. See McLaughlin 1995; and Trovato 1994. In the sixteenth century, many intellectuals saw Ariosto's *Orlando furioso* as a model for imitation upon which it was possible to build a modern epic genre theory. Although this position was highly contested by the neo–Aristotelians, the Italian translators of the *Metamorphoses* heavily relied on Ariosto's poem to re-write Ovid. See Javitch 1998; 1991: 71–80.

working on the Latin *Metamorphoses* followed the illustrated editions of the *Metamorphoses* printed in the early sixteenth century, which were based on earlier medieval versions of the Ovidian poem. This created numerous discrepancies between Rusconi's woodcuts and Dolce's translation. Furthermore, Rusconi's set of illustrations was not fully complete at the time of the first edition of the *Trasformationi*. Hence, the printer and his collaborators occasionally decided to fill the blank spaces by using the same illustration multiple times within the same volume. According to Capriotti, it would be a grievous error to dismiss the re-use of these woodcuts as a mere mistake. In fact, by looking more closely at the relationship between illustrations and text it is possible to see that the disposition of the illustrations always followed a method. Although the re-used woodcut does not visually describe the myth it is supposed to illustrate, it still deals with a theme that is related to that myth. Hence, the combined reading of text and images puts a strong emphasis on a particular thematic understanding of the given myth, and it also implicitly links different myths from the Ovidian poem. In conclusion, according to Capriotti, it is important that we read Dolce's translation in its material setting. By looking at the way in which text and illustrations are combined we can begin to understand the complex ways in which classical texts were read and understood in the printing house and more generally in the late Renaissance.

Chapter 11 and 12 of this volume address the set of illustrations printed in Bernardo Giunti's editions (1584 and 1992) of Giovanni Andrea dell'Anguillara's *Metamorfosi*. Thirty editions (including those left incomplete) of the *Metamorfosi* by Anguillara were printed in the sixteenth century, and more than seventy editions have been printed up until today.[45] This high numbers testify to the enormous success enjoyed by this translation in Italy and beyond. The popularity of this translation was not only due to Anguillara's undisputed translatorial skills, but it was also made possible by the combined efforts of printers, editors, illustrators and the other book agents who co-operated to establish this translation as a new classic of the vernacular language. Focusing on the translator and author portraits printed in the Giunti editions of the *Metamorfosi*, Marta Balzi (Chapter 11) shows how Renaissance book agents presented the *Metamorfosi* as a canonical text comparable to other novelties of the vernacular literature (beginning with the *Orlando furioso*), and also re-framed Anguillara's image and authority by illustrating him as the new Ovid. Francesca Casamassima (Chapter 12) sheds light on another element of Giunti's 1584 edition that

---

[45] Bucchi (2011: 335–45) argues that twenty–nine editions of the *Metamorfosi* were printed in the sixteenth century. According to Balzi (2020: 146–47), taking into consideration Cartolari's edition of the first book of the *Metamorfosi*, however, the number rises to 30.

contributed to the establishment of Anguillara's reputation: the fifteen full-page copperplates made by the artist Giacomo Franco and set at the opening of each book of the *Metamorfosi*. This series of engravings represents an important novelty in the tradition of the illustrated *Metamorphoses*. In fact, thanks to the increased dimension of the illustrations, each copperplate introduces almost all the myths narrated in the book that follows. As shown by Casamassima, Franco studied Anguillara's translation very closely. However, he was not so constrained to his source that he did not stir a foot from it. On the contrary, in his visual translations he often followed trends that were established in the artistic tradition that preceded him rather than following the version of a myth chosen by Anguillara. Occasionally, Franco also modified the narrative sequence of the myths to create visual connections between tales that were thematically linked. Hence, as shown by Casamassima, Franco's artistry and intellect pervade the *Metamorfosi* and render the set of illustrations a work of art to be enjoyed in itself and in conjunction with Anguillara's verse.

The editorial history of the sixteenth-century translations of Ovid's poem in the Italian vernacular is indissoluble from that of another great classic of the Italian literary tradition: the *Orlando furioso* by Ludovico Ariosto, first printed in 1516 in Ferrara. As shown by Andrea Torre in Chapter 13, Ovid's epic poetry was one of the main sources of inspiration for Ariosto's narrative, and Renaissance critics wanted to legitimize the *Furioso* as a new classic by pointing out its affinity with this authoritative Latin model. This affinity was also furthered in sixteenth-century printing houses, where editors and printers worked in synergy to publish vernacular translations of Ovid's poem with the same editorial trappings and layout of the editions of the *Furioso*. As shown by Torre, an analysis of the text and illustrations of the editions of these two works shows how they remained deeply interconnected throughout the Renaissance. The visual representation of certain themes within the *Furioso*, for example, influenced the representation of similar themes and episodes within the Italian *Metamorphoses*, and vice versa. Through numerous examples of textual and iconographic borrowings, Torre effectively shows how Renaissance books were not static objects. Instead, they were designed to stimulate the reader's memory, help him to navigate different textual and non-textual paratexts, and occasionally draw him out of the material space of the book to shape connection with other works of art.

The study of the paratextual environment of sixteenth-century translations of the *Metamorphoses* is also at the centre of Chapter 15. In this section, John Tholen studies the first translation of the *Metamorphoses* in Dutch by the humanist Johannes Florianus, head of a Latin school in Antwerp. This translation was printed in Antwerp – another European epicentre of the nascent print industry – by Hans de Laet in 1552 and from its initial publication it appeared in no less than sixteen reprints up through the seventeenth century, mostly in Antwerp and Amsterdam. Florianus's translation, according to Tholen, is a perfect example of vernacular humanism and it is representative of the second wave of vernacular translations of the *Metamorphoses* in the later sixteenth century. In fact, the translator exhibits a humanistic education and openly engages with an erudite public that would come to the translation to enjoy the changes made by the translator to the source text. Like other vernacular translations printed in the second half of the sixteenth century, Florianus's work was the product of a co-operation between translator and book agents and it was introduced to the book market with an intricate paratextual infrastructure that supported the use of the book and determined its readership. As shown by Tholen, the Dutch Ovid was presented as a necessary tool for painters, and it is highly possible that it came to the attention of artists of the standing of Pieter Bruegel.

In Chapter 5, Barry Taylor focuses on the allegorical readings in translations, commentaries and imitations of Ovid's poem in Golden Age Spain. Although it is possible to detect a move away from allegories and moralizations in lofty cultural circles, this renewal happened more slowly for translations, commentaries and imitations of classical texts. The first Spanish translation of Ovid's *Metamorphoses* was written by Jorge de Bustamante (whose first dated edition is from 1542), considered to be the most influential Spanish prose version of the *Metamorphoses* (Hexter 2007: 1318). The second Spanish Ovid is the verse of Antonio Pérez Sigler (1580). Contrarily to Bustamante, who included some moralising annotations in the prefatory matter to his translation, Pérez Sigler added allegories at the end of each book. In numerous instances, as shown by Taylor, these annotations were copied from the *Metamorfosi* by Anguillara's Italian translation, whose work, thanks also to the beauty of Franco's illustrations, enjoyed an immense fortune among Spanish painters of the Golden Age.[46] The intersection between different European vernacular traditions intensified in the re-editions of Bustamante's translation. In the 1595 Antwerp edition, for example, the translation was accompanied by a woodcut series made by Virgil Solis (a series already in use in the German and Dutch translations of the *Metamorphoses*, see Chapters 14 and 15), and it was also complemented by a series of allegories copied from Pérez Sigler (and therefore from Anguillara's Italian Ovid). Anguillara, together with Dolce, is also mentioned in the following Spanish translation of the

---

[46] On the sets of illustrations accompanying Anguillara's translation see Francesca Casamassima's article in this volume (Chapter 12).

Metamorphoses (Books I–VII) by Felipe Mey (1586), and each book of the subsequent Spanish translation by Pedro Sánchez de Viana (1589) opens with an illustration taken from Anguillara's *Metamorfosi*. As in the Italian and French translation, also these late sixteenth-century Spanish translations present allegories that are greatly simplified in comparison to those found in medieval translations and commentaries. The focus rests on providing moral examples that can be useful to the reader. Hence, through this survey Taylor effectively demonstrates how translations (and their paratexts) crossed national and linguistic borders to meet neighbouring vernacular traditions.

The closing article in this volume deals with a linguistic area that has been neglected in previous volumes on the Ovidian reception in Europe. Specifically, in Chapter 16, Andreas N. Michalopoulos presents Ioannis Makolas's prose translation in vernacular Greek (1686) of eleven stories from Ovid's *Metamorphoses*. The genesis of this Greek translation is linked to a cultural environment that saw the production of some of the most influential vernacular Ovids in Europe: Venice. After the fall of Constantinople, Venice became an important intellectual and cultural centre for the free Greeks, and Makolas (1661–), a merchant from Athens, published his translation in this city in 1686 in the printing shop of Michelangelo Barboni. Through a thorough textual analysis, Michalopoulos shows how Makolas's flowing, lively, and attractive style contributed to creating a simple and easily understandable Greek Ovid. This translation constituted not only an enjoyable text for the scattered Greek communities of Europe, but also a pivotal contribution to the development of Greek vernacular literature in the post-Byzantine era.

I

OVID ENGLISHED

1

MARIE-ALICE BELLE

CAXTON'S *OVYDE* AND OTHER BOOKS OF TROY: READING THE *METAMORPHOSES* IN THE EARLY AGE OF PRINT[1]

Beyond the initial scholarly excitement and mobilisation surrounding the recovery in the 1960s of the Phillipps manuscript of William Caxton's *Booke of Ovyde Named Methamorphose*, studies of the translation have long been dominated by questions relating to its sources. This is hardly surprising given the exceptionally complex textual genealogy of the work. Caxton's *Booke of Ovyde*, translated *c.* 1480, is in fact a translation of a Middle-French prose version of the *Ovide moralisé*, most probably composed in Bruges in the 1470s.[2] While Caxton's original does not appear to be extant, the Middle-French prose version, now surviving in three manuscripts of Burgundian extraction, constitutes but an offshoot of a long and multi-faceted history of 'moralized' rewritings of the Ovidian poem, both in verse and in prose.

Recent editions of Caxton's translation by Richard Moll (2013), Diane Rumrich (2011), and Wolfgang Mager (2016) thus naturally devote significant room to the complex ramifications of the *Ovide moralisé* tradition. Their discussions of the translation as such similarly focus on its relationship to its (putative) French source. They highlight Caxton's indebtedness to French syntax and word order, note his characteristic use of French loanwords and doublets, and generally label the text as a literal, 'stencil' translation – despite a number of reading or interpretive 'mistakes' (see Moll 2013: 36; Rumrich 2011: xvi-xviii; Mager 2016: xxi-xxix). The material history of the manuscript also raises questions as to its origins, with Moll in

[1] Research for this article was supported by the Social Sciences and Humanities Research Council of Canada. I am deeply grateful to Anne E. B. Coldiron for her generous comments on a previous version of this essay.

[2] A full description of the *Ovide moralisé en prose* tradition is to be found in Moll's introduction to Caxton's *Booke of Ovyde* (2013); see especially p. 22. All quotations are taken from this edition. On the many delineations of the *Ovide moralisé* tradition, see the international project, *Ovid in French. Genesis, transformation and reception of Ovide moralisé*, funded by the French Agence Nationale de la Recherche, online: https://anr.fr/Project-ANR-12-FRAL-0001.

particular discussing at length the possibility that it was actually copied from a printed book, since the paper on which it was written was traced to Caxton's Westminster print shop, and shown to have been also used for his 1483 edition of Gower's *Confessio amantis* (2013: 42-45; see also Rumrich 2011: xvii-xviii, and Mager 2016: xi-xii).[3]

Whether Caxton's *Booke of Ovyde* was ever printed remains an open question, but the issue draws attention to the relationship that exists between the manuscript and other productions of Caxton's in the period– both as a translator and a printer . As has often been noted, Caxton includes his *Ovyde* among the 'works & hystoryes translated out of frensshe in to englysshe' listed in his prologue to the *Golden Legend* (*c*. 1484), alongside the 1473 *Recuyell*, the 1477 *Historie of Jason*, and the 1481 *Godefrey of Boloyne*, among others (quoted in Moll 2013: 43). The *Booke of Ovyde*, in turn, offers a number of cross-references to Caxton's other productions. In Book XII, he interpolates a reference to Chaucer's *House of Fame* – which he happened to issue in print in the same year 1483 as the manuscript was copied. In the epilogue to Book XIII, Caxton explicitly directs his readers to the *Recuyell*, 'which I translated in prose al alonge' (quoted in Moll 2013: 35). Other intertextual links have been recently highlighted, notably with Chaucer's *Canterbury Tales* (Fumo 2004: 368), which was one of the first books to be produced by Caxton in England (*c*. 1477), and with Gower's *Confessio amantis*, also printed by Caxton in 1483 (see Oakley-Brown 2016: 171-72 and Moll 2013: 35). Such connections are certainly to be read as part of Caxton's advertising strategies. Yet they also point, as Liz Oakley-Brown (2016: 172) has suggested, to the intra-lingual, as well as inter-lingual, nature of the translation process in which he was self-consciously engaging.

In this essay, I propose to pay specific attention to these intertextual connections, and to approach the *Booke of Ovyde*, not as an 'anomaly', as it has sometimes been labelled (see Martin 2009: 474), but instead as part of a 'family', or 'cluster' of texts then available – or made available through print – to Caxton's readership. Recent scholarship points in that direction. In a context of increased scholarly interest for Caxton's relationship with his readers, Jenny Adams, for instance, has identified common strategies of social and political self-promotion across a 'family of books' including the *Recuyell* and the *Book of the Chess* (2006: 124). Similarly, Jennifer Goodman (2006: 112) has invited us to consider Caxton's output of French translations in terms of 'family resemblances' between the variety of works he imported from the Continent. Drawing on Paul Needham's study of the

---

[3]   All dates for Caxton's publications here follow those in BMC xi (British Library 2007: 86–87). See also Hellinga 2009: 205–06.

presence of Caxton's translations in early modern *Sammelbände*, Seth Lerer (1999: 728) similarly suggests that such 'clusters of books' be examined as indicators of contemporary reading habits. This allows him to create connections between the early *Recuyell* and the late, 1490 *Eneydos* – and also to position the latter in relationship to other works, in particular the 1481 *Godefrey of Boloyne* translation.

Of course, the language of 'clusters' and 'family resemblances' is inherited from Wittgenstein's *Philosophical Investigations*, in which he urges to approach certain conceptual categories, not according to usual binary distinctions, but as 'clusters':

> if you look at them you will not see something that is common to all, but similarities, relationships, and a whole series of them at that. [...] And the result of this examination is: we see a complicated network of similarities overlapping and criss-crossing: sometimes overall similarities, sometimes similarities of detail. I can think of no better expression to characterize these similarities than 'family resemblances'. (1958: 18)

The 'observation' of 'complex networks of similarities' has been recently put forward by translation theorist Maria Tymoczko, among others, as an important way of re-thinking categories of translation that have been traditionally determined on the basis of a priori, top-down distinctions (2007: 83-100). This precedent informs my approach here, as I seek to revisit Caxton's *Booke of Ovyde*, not from the traditional perspectives of source/target comparisons, or considerations of faithfulness vs. originality, but by focusing on the 'overlapping and criss-crossing' literary connections that relate this work to other productions with which it bears 'family resemblances'.

The inclusion of the *Booke of Ovyde* in Caxton's own list of translations from the French clearly warrants such a 'cluster'-based approach. This form of reading also seems particularly congruent with late-mediaeval/early modern literary engagements with classical material. The *Ovide moralisé en prose* may itself in many ways be read as a 'cluster' of ancient and mythological stories, a textual network extending into other vernacular works. Examples of French re-workings of the *Ovide moralisé* are well documented – including, among others, Christine de Pizan's *Cité des dames* and her *Epistre Othea* (see e.g. Dulac 2002; Conklin Akbari 2007; Parussa 2008; Griffin 2015; Veilleux 2017). The English ramifications of the network are also well known, with Chaucer's and Gower's works as prime examples of sampling, re-writing, and expanding Ovidian material into vernacular poetry.[4] Late fifteenth-century habits of textual 'gathering' in the

---

[4] This is a vast body of critical literature, see for example Desmond 1987; Martindale 1990; Keith and Rupp 2007; Clark et al. 2011; and a full bibliography in Fumo 2017.

forms of manuscript or print collections also testify to the 'family' connections established by copyists, patrons and readers between certain re-writings of ancient material. A case in point is the British Library's Royal MS 17 E IV, one of the three extant versions of Caxton's source. The manuscript, copied in Bruges in the 1470s and acquired by Edward IV, one of Caxton's main dedicatees, equally contains works by Christine de Pizan and Alain Chartier, among other responses to the Ovidian, and more generally classical, literary imagination.

The benefits of a 'horizontal', so to speak, approach to Caxton's works – as opposed to the traditional, source-oriented accounts – have already been highlighted. Most recently, Anne Coldiron's work on 'patterns' of translation and textual transmission has eloquently shown how important and fruitful it is to step back from the linear logic of source-to-target *translatio* (2015: 20–21). Her 'catenary Caxtons' are instead conceptualised in terms of the 'recursive loops' and layered logic of the *recueil* as a mode of textual and imaginative 'gathering' (2015: 40, 45, respectively). Jamie Fumo (2011) has also recently explored the connections between the illustrated initials at the beginning of the *Booke of Ovyde* manuscript and other illustrated versions of the *Ovide moralisé* produced on the Continent. Previously, Patricia Ingham (2006) had drawn from Deleuze and Guattari's model of the rhizome to interrogate the politics of Caxton's relationship to the French language. She importantly noted that 'refusing to privilege a primary direction, rhizomatic histories interrogate horizontal multiplicities, varieties of possible (and simultaneous) outcomes where dormant connections can revive to revivify the organism' (2006: 277). Such 'horizontal multiplicities' are precisely what I offer to explore here – whether the connections revealed in the process be 'dormant', or instead, overtly acknowledged by Caxton and his readers.

In the following pages, I shall concentrate on the Troy narratives contained in Caxton's *Booke of Ovyde*, mainly because of their strong generic and intertextual ties with the *recueil* tradition imported from the Continent. Focusing more specifically on the treatment of the Dido episode famously contained in *Metamorphoses* XIV, I shall explore the parallel interpretive and literary traditions, both English and French, that the translation reactivates. This in turn will allow me to shed new light on Caxton's later translation of the *Livre des Eneydes* (1490), and to reassess its place, not only in Caxton's own literary output, but also in the English reception of *histoire ancienne* material in the early age of print.

One may take as a starting point the interpretive makeup of the specific version of the *Ovide moralisé en prose* translated by Caxton (also usually called the *Ovide moralisé en prose II*).[5] As is well known, this version differs from other prose 'moralisations' of Ovid in that it does not include the allegorical commentaries inherited from the twelfth-century verse poem, or those composed by Pierre Bersuire in the fourteenth century. According to Marc-René Jung (2009: 121), the elimination of Christian allegories in Caxton's source and other extant copies of this version is to be explained by the tastes and demands of their commissioners – all of whom (at least all those we know of) appear to be closely related to the Burgundian court and the crown of England. The Paris manuscript (BnF MS fonds fr. 137) was originally owned by Louis de Bruges, who arranged the marriage between the future Charles the Bold and Margaret of York (Rumrich 2011: xxxi). He was exceptionally granted the hereditary title of Earl of Winchester in return of his assistance to Edward IV during the war of the Roses (Blake 1991: 2). The copy now at the St Petersburg library (MS F.v.XIV.1) was commissioned by Louis de Bruges' brother-in-law, Wolfart of Borssele, a Burgundian courtier and knight of the Order of the Golden Fleece (Rumrich 2011: xxxiv). Finally, the British Library manuscript (Royal MS 17 E IV) was most probably acquired by Edward IV during his stay in Burgundy in 1470/71, his project to develop a royal library being itself most probably influenced by the examples of Charles the Bold and Louis de Bruges (Blake 1991: 2, Rumrich 2011: xxxvi).

While Caxton's exact source text is unknown, it is usually suggested that he came across the prose manuscript while employed in the workshop of Colard Mansion at Bruges (see e.g. Lyne 2002: 250). Significantly enough, Colard Mansion was to issue a printed *Ovide moralisé* in 1484, but his version includes the allegorical material precisely left out from the Bruges manuscripts – as does the volume published in 1493 by Antoine Vérard as *La Bible des poètes* (see Jung 2009: 121). Caxton's *Booke of Ovyde* thus belongs to a specific, non-allegorical strand in the transmission of the *Ovide moralisé en prose* – one which is directly related to the houses of Burgundy and York, and which, stripped of its allegorical commentaries, lends itself to amalgamation with other prose narratives in the *histoire ancienne* tradition.

Caxton's own description of the *Booke of Ovyde* in the prologue to his 1483 translation of the *Golden Legend* appears to confirm such associations.

---

[5]   There are two specific traditions of prose transmission of the *Ovide moralisé*, as explained for example in Rumrich 2011: xi–xiv. The second prose rendition, usually referred to as *Ovide moralisé en prose II*, distinguishes itself from the first (*Ovide moralisé en prose I*) in that it does not include allegorical commentaries on the Ovidian myths. See also Mattia Cavagna's article in Chapter 6 for an analysis of Prose I and Prose II.

The translation is mentioned among other 'hystoryes', and its label as a collection of 'fables' tends to align it with the tradition of the *recueil*:[6]

> dyvers works & hystoryes translated out of frensshe in to englysshe at the requeste of certeyn lordes | ladyes and gentylmen as thystorye of the recuyel of Troye | the book of the chesse | the hystorye of Jason : the hystorye of the Worlde | the xv bookes of Metamorphoseos in whyche be conteyned the fables of ouyde | and the hystorye of goddefoye of boloyne the conqueste of Jerusalem wythe other dyverse workes and books. (Chaucer 1483: unpaginated)

The 'family resemblances' established by Caxton through this catalogue of books are thus at once generic ('hystoryes translated out of frensshe') and related to patronage ('at the requeste of certeyn lordes | ladyes and gentylmen'). These links become particularly visible if one reads together the paratexts of the 'dyvers works' listed here. The 1473 *Recuyell,* with its well-known dedication to Margaret of Burgundy, appears to be framed as a foundational, programmatic enterprise. Although not directly pertaining to the 'history' category, Caxton's *Book of the Chess,* first produced in 1474 in Bruges, and dedicated to the Earl of Clarence, 'oldest broder of kynge Edward' (Caxton 1474: fol. 1ʳ), is related to the *Recueyll* through its Burgundian origins and its line of patronage.[7] In the prologue to the *Historie of Jason* (1477), Caxton explicitly refers readers to the *Recueyll* precedent, mentioning his first patron, Margaret of Burgundy, in the opening sentence, and framing the narrative as a continuation of this 'hystorye' (Caxton 1477: fol. 1ʳ). He establishes further textual and dynastic connections by noting that, while the original was presented to Philippe of Burgundy, the translation was composed under the 'protectyon' of King Edward – and then by dedicating it to the Prince of Wales (fol. 1ʳ⁻ᵛ). The reference to the Order of the Golden Fleece, of which Edward is presented as a most noble representative, similarly acts both as a thematic tie with the story of Jason, and as a reminder of the Burgundian alliance: Philippe of Burgundy, Charles the Bold and Louis de Bruges were all members of the Order.

The next title in Caxton's own paratextual catalogue, the *Myrrour of the Worlde* (1481) offers a comparable genealogy of translation. The provenance of the Middle French text is from Berri and Auvergne, as opposed to Burgundy; yet the textual and social trajectories drawn in the prologue closely match those outlined in the other translations. The text was drawn out of Latin into French, and then into English; and it was composed 'at the

---

[6] Note that Caxton himself highlights the intermeshing, or 'tissuing', of 'fable' and 'history' in the Prologue to his *Booke of Ovyde*: 'he [Ovid] had ordeyned hys sayenges some by fable & some by hystorye only. And otherwise tyssued & medled with fable and hystorye togidre' (fol. 13ᵛ). See on this Fumo 2011: 317.

[7] Caxton issued a new edition of the *Historie of Jason* in 1483, which is probably why the title is included in the list, by way of advertisement.

request of [...] Hugh Bryce [...] entendyng to present the same unto the vertious noble and puissaunt lord wyliiam lord hastynges lord Camberlayn unto the most Crysten kynge kynge Edward the fourthe' (Caxton 1481b: a2ᵛ). Caxton finally presents his 1481 *Godfrey of Boloyne*, 'translated [and] reduced out of ffrensshe in to englyshhe' as a chronicle, or history: 'hye couragyous faytee | And valyaunt actes of noble Illustruous and virtuous personnnes ben digne to be recounted | put in memorye | and wreton' (Caxton 1481a: a2ʳ). Again, the royal figure of Edward IV is presented as both 'protector' and dedicatee: 'under the shadow of whos noble protection | I hage achyeued this symple translacion [...] Thenne to hym my moost drad naturel and souerayn lord I adresse this symple and rude booke' (Caxton 1481a: a3ᵛ).

Scholars have long warned not to overemphasise the Burgundian element in Caxton's textual imports from the Continent (see Hellinga 1981; Blake 1991: 168; Goodman 2006: 109). Yet the *Booke of Ovyde*, as presented in the 1483 prologue to the *Golden Legend*, may still be read as part of a corpus of texts sharing, on the one hand, a mainly Burgundian textual lineage, and on the other, 'a system of a public legitimation through which Caxton can stage himself as counselor to his kings and dukes' (Adams 2006: 139). In that respect, it belongs to what Coldiron has identified as a programme of 'recursive engagement with the foreign past' (2015: 43), as well as a process of appropriation of the cultural capital represented by texts in the *histoire ancienne* tradition then produced on the Continent. Coldiron notes that the textual and political genealogies drawn in the prologues foreground the Burgundian line of transmission as 'an elegant, acceptable, comfortably francophone [...] source of advanced Continental culture' (2015: 44). This is not only true in terms of the dynastic and political aspects of Caxton's translations, but also in terms of their relationship to the English vernacular tradition. Caxton's imported 'historyes' are texts susceptible to being grafted onto an existing native tradition of 'books of Troy' – a tradition which Caxton is precisely in the process of shaping, through print, into an English literary canon.

Caxton's system of cross-references is particularly revealing in that respect. The political aspects of Caxton's mention of Lydgate's *Troy Book* in the *Recuyell* have often been commented upon: by establishing textual continuities between Bruges and England, Caxton is 'making matter of Troy into the matter of England' (Adams 2006: 139–40). Now, if we read the passage in terms of the emerging literary system, as it were, we can also see Caxton carving out a space for his translation, as an alternative, prose version to Lydgate's verse precedent:

And as for the thirde book whiche treteth of the generall & last destruccōn of Troye Hit nedeth not to translate hit in to englissh ffor as moche as that

worshifull & religyo[us] man dan Iohn lidgate monke of Burye dide translate
hit but late [...] But yet for as moche as I am bounde to contemplate my sayd
ladyes good grace and also that his werke is in ryme | And as ferre as I knowe hit
is not had in prose in our tonge | And also paraventure | he translated after
some other Auctor than this is | And yet for as moche as dyuerce men ben of
dyuerce desyres. Some to rede in Ryme and metre. and some in prose [...] I
have delibered in myself for the contemplacion of my sayd redoubtid lady to
take this laboure in hand. (Caxton 1473: Epilogue to Book II, fol. 252ʳ)

The prologue to the *Historie of Jason* equally situates the work in relation
to existing versions of the 'destruction of Troy'. Not only does Caxton
present his work as a sequel to the *Recuyell*, as noted above, but he also
points to the main sources for Troy material, namely, Dares and Guido
delle Colonne.[8] Considering that the latter was Lydgate's source, the
mention here again contributes to situating the new translated work within
the literary landscape familiar to Caxton's English readers.

Caxton's digressions and interpolations in Books XII and XIII of the *Booke
of Ovyde* may be read in a similar light. At the end of Book XIII, we find him
directly addressing his readers' previous knowledge of the Troy story, and
indirectly evoking their 'diverse desires' by pitching Lydgate's 'ballade'
against the prose of the *Recueyll*:

I can nomore saye but I shold telle you alle the battayle, which ye may wel
knowe of the monke of Bury in ballade and in the Recueil of troye whyche I
translated in prose al alonge. There ye may see how the cyté was taken,
betrayed, solde to the Grekes, and alle brente, destroyed & confounded. (fol.
131ʳ)

Likewise, Caxton's praise of Chaucer's *House of Fame* in the middle of the
Troy narrative in Book XII is instrumental in anchoring the French *Ovide
moralisé* to a vernacular English (verse) tradition:

Shortly, ther is nothing don in the worlde fere ne nygh, but that it torneth to
the place where as Dame Fame dwellith. Wel wryteth Geffrerey Chawcer that
noble man of the discripcion of this hows in hys booke named The Booke of
Fame. This Lady | Renomee or Fame lete the Troyans have knowledge of the
coming of the Grekes. (fols 87ᵛ–88ʳ)

While the interpolation may very well have been intended as a form of
advertisement – since Caxton's edition of the *House of Fame* was precisely

[8] Caxton mentions again the issue of the various sources for the Troy narrative (namely
Homer, Dares, and Dictys) in the final epilogue to the *Recuyell*, where he notes that
Dictys and Homer being Greek favoured that people, as opposed to Dares who had a
different perspective on the matter: '[...] ffor dictes & homerus as grekes sayn and
wryten fauorably for the grekes | and gyue to them more worship than to the troians |
And Dares wryteth otherwyse than they doo' (Caxton 1473: fol. 351ʳ).

printed in 1483 (see Moll 2013: 547) – it effectively connects the translated narrative to the major precedent established by Chaucer, 'that noble man', in English verse. Another interpolated passage in Book XI dealing with Iris has similarly been traced to Gower's *Confessio Amantis* (see Bennett 1950 and discussion in Moll 2013: 545). While it is likely, as Moll suggests, that the textual conflation was indeed caused by a difficulty in the French, with Caxton relying on Gower's poem to clarify his source, some of his readers may very well have caught the verbal echoes. This in turn would have encouraged them to identify Caxton's *Booke of Ovyde* as a prose alternative to Gower's response to the Ovidian source.

The fact that Gower's *Confessio* was also printed – together with Chaucer's *Troilus and Criseyde* – in that same year 1483 tends to reinforce such intertextual ties, at the same time as it confirms the 'recursive' pattern of Ovidian transmission at work in Caxton's translation and print activities. On the one hand, Caxton makes available in print the verse precedents from which his own version of *Ovyde* distinguishes itself, while relating to them more or less explicitly. On the other, his corpus of printed prose 'histories' contributes to creating a literary ground in which the new translations may be successfully transplanted. In fact, one could arguably extend the 'family' of texts surrounding the *Booke of Ovyde* to other English(ed) prose rewritings of *histoire ancienne* material also printed by Caxton at that time. These would include the *Chronicle of England*, issued in 1480 and again in 1482, with the myth of Brute famously extending the 'matter of Troy' to the history of England; and John of Trevisa's English version of the *Polychronicon* by Ranulf of Higden, printed in 1482 as a 'booke of stories' (Caxton 1482: 5ʳ). This tends to confirm Caxton's own framing of the *Booke of Ovyde* as part of a wide-ranging engagement with ancient material, in which highly desirable, imported Continental 'stories' coexist with native productions of a comparable kind.[9]

As noted above, the issue of prose represents an important theme in Caxton's staging of both his own productions and his readers' literary tastes. Another recurrent preoccupation is the variety of sources and competing narratives available to his audience. As Caxton notes in the epilogue to the *Recueyll*, 'dyuerce men haue made dyuerce bookes [...] whiche in all poyntes acorde not' (Caxton 1473: fol. 351ʳ). The *Recueyll* and *Jason* are thus presented as alternative, or complementary stories of Troy to those found in Homer or Guido, respectively. When referring his readers to Lydgate in the epilogue to Book II of the *Recueyll*, Caxton alerts his readers that 'he

---

[9]   Note that Goodman (2006: 109) suggests extending the family of texts to Malory's *Morte Dartur* (Caxton was working on it as early as 1481). As noted by Rutter (1987: 466), Caxton also advertised the 1483 *Golden Legend* as a chronical history and a devotional counterpart to the pagan *Polychronicon*.

translated after some other Auctor than this is' (Caxton 1473: fol. 252ᵛ). Discussions of parallel sources and divergent readings of the translated material crop up in other prologues by Caxton, revealing his keen awareness of contemporary reading habits that encouraged and savoured multiple narratives: 'for as moche as dyverce men ben of dyverce desyres' (Caxton 1473: fol. 252ᵛ; see on this Lyne 2002: 252; Hosington 2006: 45–46; Coldiron 2015: 65–66).

Naturally, Ovid offered a wonderful ground for such multiplicity, given the original poem's divergent design from the linear pattern of Virgilian epic, and its multi-layered textual and interpretive history in the *moralisé* tradition. The polyphonic aspects of the late-mediaeval Ovid are particularly salient in Caxton's major English precedents, with both Chaucer and Gower more or less explicitly and simultaneously engaging with epic sources, such as Virgil's *Aeneid*, and Ovidian counter-narratives in the *Metamorphoses*, the *Heroides*, and their mediaeval derivatives. One of the most evocative examples of this thickly layered reception is without doubt the Dido episode, with Ovid's own repeated accounts finding their ways into a variety of English and French vernacular works.[10] While the complex delineations of the Dido story in mediaeval literature have already been studied at length, a 'horizontal' approach to the corresponding passages in Caxton's *Booke of Ovyde* proves particularly useful. Indeed, source-oriented readings of Book XIV yield relatively little fruit: textual comparisons between Caxton's prose and French sources only confirm the hypothesis of a 'stencil' translation, with a few mistakes originating in scribal or interpretive errors (see Moll 2013: 554–55). Yet if one reads the passage in relation to the Anglo-French 'family of texts' outlined above, a much richer picture seems to emerge.

The version of the Dido *episode* in Book XIV of Ovid's *Metamorphoses* – and in the *Ovide moralisé en prose* translated by Caxton – clearly presents the queen of Carthage as a victim, not only of passionate love, but also of male treachery. The few lines devoted to the episode in Ovid's poem are actually expanded in all *moralisé* versions (whether in verse or in prose), in order to include a complaint by Dido mainly based on the *Heroides* (Possamaï-Pérez 2010). In Caxton's translation, Dido's status as a pitiful victim is unequivocal, as she exclaims: 'Alas [...] I have overmoche embraced the false traytoure' (fol. 154ᵛ). While scholars usually point out the *faux-ami* mistake (the French has 'et suis pour son amour embrasée', i.e. 'I am burned for his love', see Moll 2013: 555), I will focus instead on the 'false traytoure' characterization of Aeneas, an expansion of the original 'le faulz'. The interpretive framing of Aenas as 'false' follows Ovid's *Metamorphoses*, and

---

[10] See, among others, Leube 1969; Schmitz 1990; Desmond 1994; Baswell 1995; and for the French literary fortune of the Dido figure, Monfrin 1985 and 1986; Martin 1990; Possamaï-Pérez 2010, Berriot-Salvadore 2014.

perhaps more particularly, his *Heroides*.[11] It equally converges with the *Recueyll* portraiture of Aeneas, since the narrative follows Guido's *Historia destructionis Troiae* where Aeneas and Antenor are said to have betrayed Troy to the Greeks. In Caxton's 1474 translation, for instance, the corresponding heading in Book III reads: 'How Anthenor and Eneas spack to geder amonge them for to delyuere the cyte vnto the grekes by trayson. And dyde hit vnder symylacion of peas' (Caxton 1474: fol. 325ᵛ). This also the version underlying Lydgate's *Troy Book*, where Aeneas and Antenor 'would rather traitors be to Troy' (IV. 4548).

While Caxton's *Booke of Ovyde* thus aligns with other Troy narratives known (or available) to Caxton's readers, Dido's long complaint against Aeneas the 'false traytoure' would most importantly raise memories of Chaucer's *House of Fame* – especially after its overt advertisement in Book XII. Caxton's 1483 edition reads: 'he to her a traytour was | Wherfor she slowe her self alas'; and again: 'But lete vs speke of Eneas | How he betrayed her alas | And left her ful vnkyndly' (Caxton 1483: a5ᵛ). Similarly, the topic of the 'Legend of Dido' in the *Legend of Good Women* is immediately introduced as 'how Eneas to Dido was forsworn', with Chaucer further commenting on Aeneas's 'false tears' (lines 4 and 1301, respectively).[12] Caxton's readers were also likely to have been aware of Gower's treatment of the Dido episode in his *Confessio Amantis*. In this didactic poem, the queen of Carthage is a victim of Aeneas's 'laschesse', or sloth – a vice somewhat tainted with deceit: to quote from Caxton's 1483 edition of the *Confessio*, Aeneas is 'he who had his thoughtes feint | Towardes loue & ful of slouthe' (Gower 1483: 69ᵛ).

Dido's character was finally present in a previous publication by Caxton, namely Ranulf of Higden's *Polychronicon*, printed in the English translation of John of Trevisa, 'a little embellyshed' by Caxton (Higden 1482: Prologue). Her importance is made plain from the double entry (Dido/Elissa) in the index printed at the opening of Caxton's 1482 volume. The corresponding passages refer to two distinct moments in the story of Dido and its literary fortune. In Book I, Higden recounts Dido's foundation of Carthage; in Book II, he adopts the version of the 'chaste' Dido, according to which she committed suicide, not out of love for 'false Aeneas', but to avoid having to remarry. He further notes that it was historically impossible that Aeneas ever met her, since he died well before the

---

[11] In *Metamorphoses* XIV, Dido is portrayted as 'deceived' (decepta); *Heroides* 7 repeatedly associates Aeneas with the verb *fallere* ('altera Dido | iterum fallas'; 'fallor', 'falsa perjuria'; 'omnia mentiris; neque enim tua fallere lingua | incipit a nobis', etc.) (Goold and Showerman 2015).

[12] De Weever (1996) also notes that the mention of 'false Aeneas' appears at various points in *The Canterbury Tales*.

foundation of Carthage: 'Than is it truth that Eneas sawe neuer dydo the quene of cartage | For eneas was bifore and dyed thre honderd yere and more er cartage was buyld' (Higden 1482: 102ʳ). This 'chaste' version of the Dido story was to be made famous by Boccacio in the *Genealogia deorum*, the *De casibus*, and the *De mulieribus claris*.[13] In England, Lydgate's *Fall of Princes* immediately comes to mind. Notably enough, the re-telling of Boccacio's version in Book II is followed by a 'praise of Dido' by Lydgate, in which the translator self-consciously mentions the alternative story in which the Queen of Carthage did indeed meet Aeneas – before launching into a tongue-in-cheek envoy where he specifically directs widows not to follow the example of 'chaste' Dido.

Encountering Dido and Aeneas the 'false traytoure' in Book XIV of Caxton's *Ovyde* would have thus opened up a whole constellation of associations for readers who might be alert to the different versions of the story. Given his diligence in referring his readers to parallel sources (Chaucer, Gower, Lydgate), and in actually providing some of the corresponding textual material, Caxton proves consistent with his remarks on his readership's appetite for multiple retellings of the same ancient material. Such tastes can be documented for at least one of his intended readers, King Edward IV. While the manuscripts of the *Ovide moralisé en prose II* at the Bibliothèque nationale de France and the St Petersburg library are extant as stand-alone works, BL Royal MS 17 E IV offers instead a rich textual assemblage. Particularly notable among the Middle-French texts accompanying the *Ovide moralisé en prose* is Alain Chartier's *Complainte des ix malheureux et malheureuses*, including one by 'Dydo reine de Cartage'. The version of the story embraced by Chartier is here that of the 'chaste' Dido: 'Ores me faut pour garder mon veuvage | Par fer mouryr' (fol. 324ᵛ).[14] Another significant piece in the manuscript is Christine de Pizan's *Epistre Othea*, which in a way represents an offshoot of the *Ovide moralisé en prose*. Although it does not bear direct connexion with the Dido story, the presence of the *Epistre* in the compilation reflects the importance of Pizan both in the Ovidian tradition and in the *querelle*. As such, it even perhaps signals to her famous *Cité des dames*, where the queen of Carthage also appears twice: firstly as a founder, queen, and *virago*; and secondly, as a

---

[13] Although Boccacio echoed the Virgilian version in his *Amorosa visione* – one of Chaucer's direct sources for the complaint of Dido in the *House of Fame*. See on this Child 1895.

[14] Edward IV's library includes another manuscript (BL Royal MS 14 E II) containing Pizan's *Epistre Othea* and Chartier's *Complainte*, together with a French version of Ramon Lull's *Libre del Orde de cavayleria*– a work that Caxton was to translate and publish in 1484.

victim of her love for Aeneas.[15] Edward's library itself contained a manuscript of the *Cité des dames* most probably acquired by his father (BL Royal MS 19 A XIX). Certainly, one should not read too much into Caxton's dedicatory strategies: his mention of patrons and protectors is often virtual rather than real, and his readership was much wider and more diversified than Edward's court and nobility (see Rutter 1987). The collection, however, provides valuable insight into the kinds of literary assemblages that were familiar to Caxton's 'ideal' readers.

The multiple refractions of the Dido story contained in contemporary manuscript collections, and in Caxton's growing corpus of printed 'hystories', are best understood if we consider the character's central position in the ongoing *querelle des femmes*. As is well known, Chaucer's *Legend of Good Women* was framed as a response to the French *querelle de la rose* surrounding the misogynistic aspects of De Meun's *Roman*. Similarly, Lydgate's conflicting additions to Boccacio in the *Fall of Princes* – now a 'praise' of Dido's chastity; now an advice to widows with misogynistic overtones – fit the dual pattern of *querelle* disputes. Caxton's own positioning in the 'woman question' is notoriously ambiguous. As Brenda Hosington has remarked, he was aware of the topic's popularity as early as 1477 (2006: 45). In his epilogue to Woodville's translation of the *Dictes or Sayengs of the philosophers*, he restores the misogynistic material omitted in the translation, advertising the translator's assumed oversight, and offering as a tongue-in-cheek compensation a catalogue of the supposed virtues of English women: 'right good, wyse, playsant, humble, discrete, sobre, chast, obedient to their husbondis, trewe, secrete, stedfast, euer besy, & neuer ydle. Attemperat in speking, and vertuous in alle their werkis [...] or att leste sholde be soo' (quoted in Hosington 2006: 45). As Coldiron remarks, 'since the *Dictes*'s content is not primarily about gender, when Caxton highlights 'woman questions' so flamboyantly in the epilogue, he slants the overall character of the work, drawing on an existing readerly interest in gender issues' (2015: 68; see also Coldiron 2010: 61–65). Caxton's 1484 translation of the *Livre du chevalier de la Tour Landry* similarly combines a prologue in praise of the 'noble lady' who commissioned the work (supposedly Margaret Woodville, recently widowed from Edward IV), with the more controversial contents of the work, in which women are portrayed

---

[15]   Caxton's readers might also have been aware of Thomas Hoccleve's 1402 'Epistle to Cupid', based on Pizan's *Epistre au dieu d'amours* – although it was only to appear in print in the sixteenth century. While Hoccleve's translation has sometimes been characterized as misogynistic, it is of interest to us because it significantly expands Pizan's original mention of Dido, most probably in response to Chaucer. See on this Ellis 1996.

as bawdy and disobedient, and severely punished for being so (Hosington 2006: 44; Coldiron 2010: 66).

In her extensive study of Caxton's printed *querelle* material (including some of Pizan's own writings), Coldiron has equally noted the presence of 'discordant' paratextual elements (2015: 52).[16] This is particularly true of his positioning towards women in the *Recuyell*. There again, the dedication to Margaret of Burgundy stands in stark contrast with the depiction of Helen as an alluring temptress, and, most noticeably, with a violently misogynistic epigram placed at the end of Caxton's volume, with no equivalent in known French sources, rehearsing the *topos* that women are the source of all evil (Coldiron 2015: 56). Although certainly troubling, the conflicting paratextual discourse on women is perhaps less surprising if one considers the *disputatio* format that dominates the *querelle*, with its common juxtaposition of opposite narratives and arguments. As was already the case in the *Dictes,* the final misogynistic epigram could thus be read as a way of framing the *Recueyll*, post-facto, in terms of the popular debate on the worth – or unredeemable evil – of womankind.

The links thus established between Caxton's *histoire ancienne* translations and the *querelle* context – with Dido and Helen occupying comparable positions in the debate – may in turn shed new light one of Caxton's later 'recursive engagements' with the ancient past. The 1490 *Eneydos* translation presents a similar textual trajectory as those of the *Recueyll*, *Jason,* and to a certain extent, the *Booke of Ovyde*. All were translated from a French intermediary: Caxton's *Eneydos* is a close rendering of the *Livre des Eneydes* printed at Lyons by Guillaume Le Roy in 1483. All three belong to the 'histories of Troy' family: Caxton's dedication of the *Eneydos* is eloquent on that point: 'How after the generall destruccyon of the grete Troye, Eneas departed [...], wyth alle thystorye of his aduentures' (Caxton 1490: A1ʳ). Finally, they all represent textual composites. The *Recueyll,* for instance, compiled material from the *Histoire ancienne* with Guido's *Historia destructionis Troiae* (Le Corfec 2011: 2). Likewise, one of the most salient features of Le Roy's *Livre des Eneydes* – and therefore, of Caxton's *Eneydos* – is the double account it provides of the Dido episode, Boccacio's 'chaste' version being offered side by side with a much-enlarged rewriting of the Virgilian source.

Following the damning comment by the sixteenth-century translator, Gavin Douglas, that Caxton's translation bears no more resemblance to Virgil than 'the devil to Saint Augustine', scholars have routinely characterised the *Eneydos* as a 'bizarre' moment in the English Virgilian

---

[16] See also Coldiron 2006 and 2009 for other examples of Caxton's ambivalent position on the 'woman question'.

tradition (see e.g. Baswell 1995: 273).[17] Yet in the context I have sought to document so far, the presentation of two conflicting versions of the Dido story is instead quite congruent with reading and compiling habits associated to the *recueil* tradition, on the one hand, and to *querelle* material, on the other. Jacques Monfrin's analysis of the *Livre des Eneydes* is quite revealing here, since he shows that the French narrative is in fact a hybrid of the *Histoire ancienne jusqu'à César* and a *Livre de la reine Didon*, only surviving in fragmentary form, in which both versions of the story were presented side by side (Monfrin 1985, 1986). Monfrin identifies a trace of this collage in the framing of the Boccacio version, which reads very much like an opening: 'L'autrier en passant temps'.[18] I will add here that the passage presents unmistakeable features of *querelle* literature. Here it is in Caxton's translation:

> I was abasshed and had grete merueylle | how bochace whiche is an auctour so gretly renomed hath transposed or atte leste dyuersifyed the falle and caas otherwyse than vyrgyle hath in his fourth booke of Eneydos | In whiche he hath not rendred the reason | or made ony decysion to approue better the his than that other And yf ony wolde excuse hym and saye that he hadde doon hit for better to kepe thonour of wymmen. And wolde not treate ne saye thynge of theym dyshoneste. but that myghte be to theyr auaucemente ¶This reason hath noo place: For he hath putte in many places other grete falles ouermoche infamous of some quenes and ladyes | and hath not suffyced to hym to speke alle in generall. but hath made expresse chapytres | In blamynge the complexions of theym. (Caxton 1490: B7ᵛ)

Leroy is obviously addressing French arguments in the debate – and Pizan naturally comes to mind again, since her *Cité des dames* actively responds to Boccacio's precedent.[19] Yet the translated passage opens up additional dimensions for Caxton's English readership. The question of celebrating queens and ladies 'for beter to kepe thonour of wymmen' echoes Chaucer's prologue to the *Legend of Good Women*. Lydgate's *Fall of Princes*

[17] Douglas's remark is to be found in the prologue to his 1513 translation of the *Aeneid* into Middle-Scots, and has become a *topos* of scholarly discourse on Caxton's translation. See, however, Belle 2018 for a 'horizontal' analysis of Douglas's demarcation strategies, which involve, among others, the framing of Caxton's *Eneydos* as *querelle* literature.

[18] Quoted in Monfrin 1985: 216. The opening 'l'autrier' appears to be commonplace in dream visions, fabliaux and other poetic forms; it appears, among others, in *Le Parement et triomphe des dames*, composed in the early 1490s by the Burgundian rhétoriqueur, Olivier de la Marche (see Langfors 1917:195). Caxton's 1490 *Eneydos* has: 'That other daye in passing time'... Note also the chapter heading: 'Here bigynneth thistorye. how dydo departed from yᵉ coūtrey' (Caxton 1490: B7ʳ).

[19] See the seminal article by Jeanroy 1922, and more recently Desrosiers-Bonin 2008 and Johnston 2012.

had also already alerted readers to Boccacio's 'diversified' narrative, at the same time as it had 'transposed' the whole matter into a *querelle*-style debate on the exemplarity of Dido for English widows. If one is to read Caxton's *Eneydos* against the precedent established in the *Booke of Ovyde*, among other renderings of *histoire ancienne* material, these intertextual connections may be seen to play the same role as earlier references to Chaucer, Gower, or again, Lydgate. On the one hand, they help integrate the translated work into an existing corpus of English literature presumably familiar to Caxton's readership. On the other, they contribute to differentiating Caxton's prose romances from earlier literary responses to ancient history, especially in the popular forms of *querelle* literature.

The reception of the *Eneydos* seems to have followed Caxton's generic and intertextual indications, at least if one is to judge from the *Sammelbände* of his printed works first brought to light by Paul Needham. We thus find the translation bound together with Caxton's 1483 edition of the *Book of Fame* and various works by Lydgate also printed by Caxton in the same year, in volumes owned by the seventeenth-century Oxford scholar Nathaniel Crynes, and by the eighteen-century book collector Thomas Rawlinson (see Needham 1986: 77 and 74, respectively). More significant for us, however, is the collection assembled in 1510 by one R. Johnson, in which the *Eneydos* is bound with two other translations printed by Caxton, namely the 1481 *Godefrey of Boloyne*, and Christine de Pizan's *Fayts of Armes* (1489), as well as Chaucer's *House of Fame*.[20] The assemblage here effected suggests that at least one reader and book compiler did respond to Caxton's strategies, apparently internalising the three main textual and interpretive directions of Caxton's *histoire ancienne* translations. Together with the *Godefroy* and Pizan's *Fayts of Armes*, they may be read as books of chivalry; they evoke and respond to major English precedents, such as Chaucer; and finally, like Pizan's works and Chaucer's *House of Fame*, they invite readers to explore the complex, dialogic forms of the much-debated 'woman question'. Caxton's 1490 *Eneydos* translation is therefore not simply coherent with his last phase of Continental imports.[21] It also fits within a longer arc of engagement with the textual tradition of the *roman d'antiquité*

[20] Needham 1986: 80.

[21] As noted by Goodman (2006: 115). She particularly pairs Caxton's *Eneydos* with his translated romance, *Blanchardin and Eglantyne*. The plot of *Blanchardin* actually bears striking resemblances with that of *Aeneid* IV. Like Aeneas, Blanchardin is from Middle-Eastern Phrygia; like Dido, Eglantine is first presented as besieged by neighbouring suitors. Her falling in love with Blanchardyn closely echoes Virgil's treatment of Dido's passion, although the outcome, this time, is a happy one: the pair's wedding and the miraculous conversion of a pagan nation reads as a counterpart to Dido's suicide and her curse of an everlasting war between Rome and Carthage.

– of which the *Ovide moralisé en prose II*, with its blending of 'fable' and 'history', was clearly read as an example by Caxton and his contemporaries.

Although it remains uncertain whether it was printed or not, Caxton's *Booke of Ovyde* thus belongs to a wide-ranging network of textual transmission involving, on the one hand, the circulation of Middle-French literature through manuscript acquisition, production, and translation; and on the other, the development by Caxton of a corpus of English printed literature, in which translated prose narratives cohabit and interact with a canon of English authors in the making. It has been ten years since Christopher Martin (2009: 474) called for a re-assessment of Caxton's translation as 'a fascinating and still largely unappreciated portrait of cultural translation'. Indeed, once we step beyond the usual comparative methods that limit the *Booke of Ovyde* to an unoriginal, 'stencil' translation, the portrait that emerges is one of sizeable literary significance. The 'horizontal' approach embraced here has helped situate the *Ovyde* in relation to Caxton's wider practices of textual translation, intertextual allusion, and paratextual self-promotion. It has also revealed the multiple cultural, linguistic, literary and material mediations involved in the translation of *histoire ancienne* into the literary and cultural idioms of late fifteenth-century England. As such, the *Booke of Ovyde* offers a most evocative example of the 'recursive' patterns of transmission recently identified by Coldiron in Caxton's other translations. Finally, by tracing the textual, linguistic, and literary 'clusters' that relate Caxton's manuscript *Booke of Ovyde* to a host of interconnected, criss-crossing traditions – from the *roman d'antiquité* to the Chaucerian lyric, and from *querelle* literature to late-mediaeval mythography and romance – this study confirms the crucial importance of reading Caxton's seminal role in the making of English (printed) literature as part of an on-going, transnational cultural conversation between England and the Continent.

2

GENEVIEVE LIVELEY

OVID'S *METAMORPHOSIS* ENGLISHED:
SANDYS' EUROPEAN OVID

In 1621, George Sandys (1578–1644) published an English verse translation of the first five books of Ovid's *Metamorphoses*. A second edition would be released later that same year, and a third in 1623 – testament to the immediate appeal of Sandys' fresh vernacular rendering of Ovid's epic.[1] In the meantime, however, Sandys left England to sail for the New World and Jamestown where, under the auspices of The Virginia Company, he was to serve as inaugural treasurer and councillor for the new British colony. On the outward voyage he translated another two books of the *Metamorphoses* and, during the three turbulent years he was to spend in Jamestown, he found time to translate the remaining eight books. He returned to England in 1625 following a massacre at the Jamestown colony by native Americans and the Crown's formal dissolution of The Virginia Company. Almost immediately, he published his first full edition of *Ovid's Metamorphosis Englished*, presenting his translation of all fifteen books in a small folio imprint in 1626 (Sandys 1626).[2]

In a dedicatory epistle to this 1626 edition – addressed 'To the most High and Mightie Prince Charles, King of Great Britaine, France, and Ireland' – Sandys invites the King and his wider readership to regard the translation as: 'the first fruits of my Trauels, [...] limn'd by that vnperfect light which was snatcht from the houres of night and repose' during his time in Virginia (Sandys 1626: p. 1ʳ n. p.). Sandys offers a highly original form of classical *recusatio* in 'apologizing' that his translation therefore:

> needeth more then a single denization, being a double Stranger: Sprung from the Stocke of the ancient Romanes; but bred in the New-World, of the

---

[1] On the various editions of Sandys' Ovid see Davis 1941, Davis 1948, McManaway 1948. For an overview of the translation history and tradition of Ovid in translation see Martin 1998.

[2] On Sandys's Virginian adventure see Lyne 2001: 198–258. I have consulted a digital copy of the 1626 edition (STC, 2nd edition: 18964) held at the Ohio State University Library (Digitized): https://babel.hathitrust.org/cgi/pt?id=osu.32435018270405&view=1up&seq=8 [accessed 19 June 2019].

rudenesse whereof it cannot but participate; especially hauing Warres and Tumults to bring it to light in stead of the Muses. (Sandys 1626: p. 1ʳ n. p.)

'Warres and Tumults' and other calamities may have caused The Virginia Company to fail, but Sandys at least has this literary fruit to show for his time in Jamestown and to offer up to the greater glory of his King.

Indeed, as might be anticipated by the tenor of Sandys' *recusatio* here, there are no signs anywhere in the polished 1626 edition of any such alleged 'rudenesse' – unless, that is, we take this as an allusion to the absence therein of the translation notes and explanatory glosses that Sandys was already anticipating for his next edition of Ovid. If so, this 'rude' omission Sandys amends in the subsequent 1632 lavish folio edition of *Ovid Englished*, where he adds illustrations and commentaries to each book, and notes to the lightly revised text of his earlier 1626 translation, with the result that Ovid is not only *Englished* but also '*Mythologiz'd, and Represented in Figures*'.[3] Sandys further adds to this latest work, 'An Essay to the Translation of Virgil's Aeneis' – a translation of the first book of the *Aeneid* which, Sandys claims (in another modest note to his readers), is another rough effort, only included here 'in tender obedience to Soveraigne commaund' (Sandys 1632: 532).

The combined effect of this royal intervention and this Virgilian addition to the final few pages of the 1632 folio of Sandys' Ovid is to provide a balancing bookend to the material in the opening pages – both of which seek to support the reader's reception of the work as a product of the New World. For, as Sandys' Renaissance readers would have readily recognized, the story of Aeneas leaving Troy to build a new world empire in Italy provides a suggestive parallel for their own current efforts to colonize the New World. Thus, bookended by references to Sandys' own colonizing adventures in its opening pages and to Aeneas's adventures at its close, Sandys' *Metamorphosis* is explicitly advertised in its paratexts as a New World translation.[4]

---

[3] The 1632 edition proves that the 1626 translation was not so very 'rude' after all, as Sandys does not avail himself of the opportunity offered by the six-year hiatus between the 1626 and 1632 publications to make any significant changes. See Pearcy 1984: 79–99 on the minor variations between Sandys' different editions of his translation, which essentially include 'trivial refinements to spelling' and a few 'improvements based on new understanding of the Latin text or of Ovid's mythological allusions' (79). I have consulted a digital copy of the 1632 edition (STC, 2nd edition: 18966) held in the Boston Public Library (Rare Books Department) Digital Collections: https://archive.org/details/ovidsmetamorphos00ovid_0 [accessed 29 January 2019].

[4] On paratexts see Genette 1991 and 1997. See also Smith and Wilson 2011 on Renaissance paratexts; and Toledano-Buendía 2013 on the role of the translator's notes as paratexts.

Not surprisingly, then, it is this New World context in which *Ovid's Metamorphosis Englished* is usually received. Not without some degree of tension, Sandys' Ovid is celebrated as one of the first great works to champion the English vernacular, and as one of the first great works to come out of the New World – as American literature *avant le lettre*.[5] In this chapter, however, I propose a fresh evaluation of Sandys' 1632 *Ovid's Metamorphosis Englished* in terms of the mediating role that the 'Old World' of Europe plays in this supposedly 'New World' translation and its paratexts. Sandys' work, as we will see, represents a complex mosaic comprising snippets of material from a diverse range of European writers, set alongside first-person anecdotes and eye-witness accounts of strange phenomena from across both the Old and New World – but especially from Europe. In the preface to his 1632 work, Sandys registers his indebtedness to a host of European sources in inspiring his interpretation of the *Metamorphoses*, and across fifteen books of commentary and notes Sandys presents his translation of Ovid's *Metamorphoses* through a mediating prism which principally reflects the stories, ideas and writings not of New World Virginia but of Humanist Europe. Sandys' patchwork of translation, commentary, annotation, and anecdote thus presents *Ovid's Metamorphosis Englished* in a context that is self-consciously imbricated within a wider European no less than Virginian environment. In Sandys, as this chapter will demonstrate through analysis of selections from the 1632 edition of his translation, commentary, and notes, we find that *Ovid Englished* is also Ovid 'Europeaned'.

Sandys' New World Ovid?

We can charge Sandys' contemporary, the poet and critic Michael Drayton, for initiating the enduring reception of Sandys' *Ovid's Metamorphosis Englished* as a New World Ovid. In an elegy addressed 'To Master George Sandys, Treasurer for the English Colony in Virginia', Drayton encourages Sandys to continue with the translation project that he had started before his voyage to America. Drayton writes:

> And (worthy George) by industry and use,
> Let's see what lines Virginia will produce;
> Goe on with Ovid, as you have begunne,
> With the first five Bookes; let your numbers run
> Glib as the former, so shall it live long,
> And doe much honour to the English tongue:
> Intice the Muses thither to repaire,

---

[5] See, for example, Davis 1955 and Davies 1973: 13 (discussed below). See also Lyne 2001: 198–258 on Sandys's 'Virginian Ovid'.

Intreat them gently, trayne them to that ayre,
(Drayton, 'To Master George Sandys', lines 38–45)

Here the patriotic Drayton is eager to see Sandys' Ovid as bringing 'much honour to the English tongue'. And in an extension of that patriotism, is eager to see how Sandys's own physical 'translation' to the new English Colony in Virginia might influence and inspire Sandys's literary translation project: 'Let's see what lines Virginia will produce' – in other words, let's see how the Muses of the ancient world, who have already flourished in their transplantation into English soil, perform in a 'new' New World setting.

But in the event, there isn't very much to see. Books I–V had already been translated when Sandys set sail for Virginia in 1621 and Books VI and VII were translated during the voyage itself. In a Letter to Sir Samuel Wrote, dated 28th March 1623, Sandys writes:

Yet amongst the roreing of the seas, the rustling of the Shrowdes, and Clamour of Saylers, I translated two bookes, and will perhaps when the sweltring heat of the day confines me to my Chamber gain a further assaye. For which if I be taxt I have noe other excuse but that it was the recreacion of my idle howers. (Sandys in Kingsbury 1906–35: 66)

As remarkable as this insight is into the conditions under which Sandys produced his translation, both at sea and in Jamestown, these conditions leave no discernible trace upon the text. There are no distinguishing features of any kind in the translation to indicate that the second half of *Ovid Englished*, that is Books VIII–XV, was composed in the New World rather than the Old. There is nothing in the translation to indicate that it is – as Sandys describes the work in his dedication to King Charles – 'bred in the New-World'. Only in the notes and commentary do we find any evidence at all of Sandys drawing parallels between the ancient world of Ovid's *Metamorphoses* and his own experiences in the New World of colonial America – and this evidence is, at best, slight.[6] Commenting on the flood that Jupiter sends to destroy mankind after Lycaon's 'treachery' in Book I (I. 274–92), Sandys claims: 'There is no nation so barbarous, no not the saluage *Virginians*, but haue some notion of so great a ruine' (Sandys 1632:

[6] See also Lyne 2001: 236: 'When considering the translation, the evidence of an American influence is surprisingly exiguous'. Lyne 2002: 256 again observes that 'The interplay between a classical text and a New World does not result in any obvious or glib rapprochement'. Rubin 1985: 165 refers to Sandys's 'incorporation of data from the New World both from his personal experience in the Virginia Company and from his wide reading', somewhat obscuring the fact that Sandys' New World data comprises barely four separate entries and that the far greater wealth of material is garnered from European sources.

31). Commenting on the frogs into which the goddess Latona transforms a crowd of rude peasants in Book VI of the *Metamorphoses* (VI. 313–81), Sandys notes that such creatures: 'were sent as a plague to the *Aegyptians* [...and] these depopulated a Citty in France, and now not a little infest *Virginia* in Summer: called *Pohatans* hounds by the *English, of* their continuall yelping' (Sandys 1632: 295). Sandys appears to speak of these irritating Virginian frogs from his own first-hand experience here, and such is certainly the case in his comment on the transformation of Galanthis into a weasel in Book IX of the *Metamorphoses*: 'I haue seene [such] a Beast, which the *Indians* call a *Possoun*' (Sandys 1632: 441).[7] Similarly, we find Sandys drawing upon his own first-hand experience of the New World in a note to Pythagoras's speech in Book XV of the *Metamorphoses*, where Ovid catalogues a variety of transformations spontaneously occurring in the natural world. Sandys translates *Metamorphoses* XV. 262–65 as:

Where once was solid land, Seas have I scene;
And solid land, where once deepe Seas have beene.
Shels, far from Seas, like quarries in the ground;
And anchors have on mountain tops been found.
(Sandys 1632: 674)

In a marginal note to 'Shels', Sandys echoes Pythagoras in observing that: 'Such haue I seene in *America*'. However, this makes up the sum total of all the New World allusions drawn from his own first-hand experience to be found across Sandys's *Ovid Englished*. The translation and commentary may very well have been 'bred in the New-World' but there appears to be nothing of significance that materially distinguishes the new from the old in Sandys's translation or its paratexts. Each of Sandys's personalized New World observations emphasises continuity over change: the same strange people, animals, and landscapes endure – just as the same frogs that were once a plague to the ancient Egyptians, depopulated a city in old France, now infest New World Virginia.

Indeed, Sandys reminds his readers that old England itself once represented the New World. In his commentary upon Julius Caesar's apotheosis at the end of the fifteenth and final book of the *Metamorphoses* (XV. 745–842), Sandys describes the Roman 'conquest of our Britain' as a civilizing process, 'wherein the conquered were the gainers, hauing got thereby ciuility and letters, for a hardly won, nor a long detained dominion'

---

[7] Sandys consistently refers to the Native Americans as 'Indians': see his commentary to Book XI: 'Couetousnesse is Idolatry; and of this diuine verity the barbarous Indians had a naturall notion; who imagined that gold was the God of the Spaniards, in that they hunted after it so greedily' (Sandys 1632: 522). Non-American 'Indians' are always designated as East or West Indian.

(Sandys 1632: 526). It was, after all, through such conquest and colonization that Ovid's 'letters' were first carried over from Rome into New World Britain – although the suggested analogy with Britain's own attempts at conquest and colonization in the 'new' New World are not wholly positive here, particularly in the light of Sandys' own recent experiences of the 'saluage Virginians' in Jamestown.

Sandys' own paratextual directions to view his translation of Ovid as emerging from his experiences in the New World are far from straightforward, then. The evidence supplied by Sandys' translation, commentary, and notes certainly do not authorize the sorts of readings which propose that:

> His stay in Virginia had enabled him to translate the fantasies of an old world while he was surrounded by the marvels of a new, and in the act of translation he brought to a creative focus the parallel interests of literature and colonization. These comments scattered through the work are but graphic indications of his consciousness of the America which he had known. If American literature is a fusion of European intellect and American environment, Sandys's Ovid may well be included in it. (Davies 1973: 13)[8]

In fact, Sandys' comments regarding the British colonization of America are so sparsely 'scattered' across the work that the interpretation of his *Ovid Englished* as a product of that New World environment presents something of an elusive fantasy in itself. What we actually encounter in Sandys' Ovid is less a 'fusion' of European intellect and American environment and more a 'suffusion' of both European intellect and environment.

Sandys' European Ovid?

In terms of intellect, the paratexts to *Ovid's Metamorphosis Englished* locate Sandys' translation firmly within a familiar European classical tradition. In his preface to the 1632 edition of *Ovid Englished*, Sandys registers his indebtedness to a virtual encyclopaedia of post-classical pan-European sources: 'Of moderne writers, I have received the greatest light from Geraldus, Pontanus, Ficinus, Vives, Comes, Scaliger, Sabinus, Pierius, and the Crowne of the latter, the Vicount of St. Albans [Francis Bacon]' (Sandys 1632: 48). Sandys also acknowledges his use of the commentaries of 'Regius, Micyllus, Sabinus, and Pontanus; the mythographies of Comes, Cartams, and Giraldus; and the mythological dictionary of Stephanus' (Sandys 1632: 48). And, though he does not mention them by name in this prefatory roll-call, Sandys also engages with the ideas and writings of

---

[8]   For further criticisms of this approach see Lyne 2001: 255: 'It is difficult to trace with any confidence or clarity how the author's experience 'produced' the text, or how the Virginia colony acted as a suggestive space for reading the *Metamorphoses*'.

Erasmus, Lambinus, Sabaeus, Solinus, Bembo, Buchanon, and Alciatus in various of his commentary entries and notes.

In terms of environment, as we have seen, Sandys' New World adventure provides him with eye-witness testimony that helps him to comment upon a tiny handful of Ovidian myths – emphasising, like Ovid's own *Metamorphoses*, the aspect of continuity through change that essentially connects the ancient world with his own. But it is Sandys's adventures in and around continental Europe (and the eye-witness accounts of his Pan-European sources) that really shape and colour the commentary to *Ovid Englished*, lending his translation and its paratexts both authenticity and authority.[9]

Far more frequently than any American or Virginian references, parallels between Ovidian myths and European marvels appear in Sandys' commentary to every one of Ovid's fifteen books – and to the tales of strange creatures such as giants, werewolves, witches, mermaids and mermen found therein. Thus, querying the veracity of Ovid's gigantomachy (I. 151–76), Sandys notes that:

> *Scaliger* saw a Man at *Millan*, who hardly could lie on two beds, one set at the foot of another: and *Goropeus*, a Woman in the *Netherlands*, who exceeded ten feet. The Gyant of *Burdeux* (of the Guard to *Francis* the first) was so tall, that a man of indifferent stature might haue gon betweene his legges without stooping. (Sandys 1632: 27)

Commenting on the story of Lycaon (I. 199–243), Sandys draws a correlation between lycanthropy and 'what is so ordinarily said to be practised by the witches of *Germany*, who take and forsake the shapes of wolues at their pleasure, and for which they are daily executed' (Sandys 1632: 30). Even mermaids and mermen, the supposed source for Ovid's description of Neptune, have been reported by reliable European witnesses, according to Sandys. Accordingly:

> one Draconet Boniface of Naples, a souldier of much experience, report[s] in an honorable assembly, that in the warres of Spaine, he saw a sea monster with the face and body like a man, but below the belly like a fish, brought thither from the farthest shores of Mauritania. It had an old countenance; the haire and beard rough and shaggy, blew of colour, and high of stature, with finnes betweene the armes and the body. (Sandys 1632: 32)

Similarly validating the invulnerability of Cygnus (who the mighty Achilles cannot harm with his weapons) in Book XII (XII. 64–145), Sandys observes: 'Yet why not preserued from wounds by Enchantments? as many are said to be at this day in the Low Countries and *Germany*; some sticke-

---

[9] On the importance of 'seeing' to humanist discourse and inquiry in this context see Pearcy 1984: 37–70.

free, others shot-free' (Sandys 1632: 417). And in support of the traditional
story of Romulus and Remus suckled by a wolf, he further notes that:

> it is ordinary at this day in some parts of France for Goats to suckle the children
> of those poore women who either want milke; or haue other imploiments,
> which they doe with as great affection and sedulity, as if they were their owne
> Kids. (Sandys 1632: 486)

Sandys' European sources are also adduced to correct or explain some of
the more mundane of Ovid's stories from the *Metamorphoses*, especially
those dealing with the natural world and its phenomena. In the
commentary to Book I Sandys questions Ovid's view that only a narrow
temperate zone (coincidentally coterminous with the boundaries of the old
Augustan empire) is suitable for human habitation (I. 32–51). Sandys
disputes Ovid's view of the region around the equator as uninhabitable by
appealing to the modern authority of his own European peers. This region,
Sandys says, is 'found now by the Portugals and Spaniards not only
populous, but healthfull, pleasant' (Sandys 1632: 21). Similarly, the frozen
zone around the poles has now been found to be habitable by 'the
Hollanders, who have wintred neere unto that of the North' (Sandys 1632:
21). Sandys also appeals to his own first-hand experience of travels through
Europe to corroborate several of Ovid's myths, among them that of Echo
from Book III (III. 359–401):

> Now Eccho signifies a resounding which is only the repercussion of the voice,
> like the rebound of a ball, returning directly from whence it came: and that it
> reports not the whole sentence, is through the debility of the reuerberation. Yet
> in the garden of the Tuillereis in Paris, by an artificiall deuice vnder ground
> invented for musick, I haue heard an Eccho repeate a verse, not lowdly vttered,
> without failing in one sillable. (Sandys 1632: 103–04)

In comments such as these, which comprise a substantial part of the
commentary to *Ovid Englished*, Sandys likes to support the veracity of
Ovid's tales by telling us about the strange things he himself has seen or
heard about in his travels. We saw for ourselves one such example of this
arising from Sandys' travels to America, discussed above, but there are far
more examples in the commentary arising from Sandys' Grand Tour travels
around Europe. Indeed, Sandys had already published a travelogue detailing
this European tour in a 1615 book: *Relation of a Journey Begun Anno
Domini 1610*.[10] This journey took him through France, Italy, Cyprus,
Sicily, and the Holy Land, and the fragmentary translations that are
scattered throughout the text and its marginal notes indicate that Sandys

[10] I have consulted a digital copy of this edition (USTC: 3006492) held in the New York
Public Digital Collections: https://digitalcollections. nypl.org [accessed 29 January
2019].

was already translating Ovid during these travels in the early 1600s. The presentation of these early translations, interspersed between Sandys' first-person account of his adventures travelling through Europe and the Holy Land, and complemented by observations from various Classical and Humanist authorities, also anticipates the style and presentation of Sandys's subsequent full translation of the *Metamorphoses* in *Ovid Englished*. Here in the commentary and notes supporting the translation we encounter the same style of first-person anecdote based on direct experience, supported by the views of various authorities, and illustrated by snippets of classical poetry – all translated by Sandys himself – which we find in his earlier *Relation of a Journey Begun Anno Domini 1610*.[11]

Thus, commenting on the lethal mists of the river Styx (II. 31–48 – which Ovid's character, the god Sol, confesses he has himself 'never seen'), we find Sandys observing that: [such] 'exhalations I haue seene, in a dry and lightsome caue betweene *Naples* and *Putzoll*, to kill a dog in as short a time as I am in telling of it' (Sandys 1632: 65). Similarly appealing to his own European adventures as recorded in his *Relation of a Journey Begun Anno Domini 1610*, Sandys later affirms that 'I haue seene' a place in Italy that corresponds with Ovid's description of the Underworld in Book X of the *Metamorphoses* (X. 1–85), a place:

> which lies betweene *Naples* and *Puteoli*. A plaine inuironed with high chalky cliffes, out of which on euery side black and smoky exhalations ascend, of a sulphurous sauour. The Earth roareth vnder foot, and at diuers vents casts vp boyling water mingled with flames. (Sandys 1632: 358)

So obviously impressed was Sandys by the miraculous volcanic landscapes of Naples and Sicily as encountered on his Grand Tour that he seems to take any opportunity to drop in to his commentary such anecdotes arising from these European travels. Thus, to Pythagoras's account of natural wonders in Book XV (XV. 259–306), Sandys is prompted to add that: 'I haue seene a little Lake that would boyle an Egge as hard as a stone in an instant' (Sandys 1632: 516). The contrast between these colourful first-person reflections drawn from Sandys's European adventures and those plain annotations drawn from his American travels ('Such haue I seene in *America*') is stark – not only in number but in character.

The effect of these various European eye-witness observations is to bring the ancient world of Ovid's *Metamorphoses* that much closer to Sandys' own, to collapse the distance – both spatial and temporal – between them. As a consequence, Sandys presents much of Ovid's strange world as

---

[11] See Haynes 1980 and Ellison 2002 on the close affinities between *A Relation of a Journey Begun Anno Domini 1610* and *Ovid Englished*. See also Oakley-Brown 2006: 84 on 'The intertextual relationship between the Relation of a Journey and the *Metamorphosis*'.

strangely familiar. He posits himself, therefore, not as a tour-guide leading his readers through the foreign landscape of classical myth. Nor as a colonist, appropriating the classical world for the New. But as a translator 'carrying across' Ovid's *Metamorphoses* and relocating it in seventeenth-century Europe – much as Ovid himself had envisaged his own project as a kind of 'making new' (*in nova*), a translation of old myths into his 'own times' (*ad mea tempora*).[12]

Sandys' English Ovid?

If we acknowledge this overwhelming evidence that Sandys' European travels leave a far more significant trace upon his paratextual notes and commentary than those of his American travels, and if we accept that Old World European influences shape his encounter with Ovid to a far greater degree than his New World experiences, does this make any difference at all to our appreciation and understanding of Sandys' Englishing of the *Metamorphoses*?

In his prefatory address 'To the Reader', Sandys describes his undertaking, in part, as a patriotic attempt to demonstrate the power of the English language. One of his aims for the translation of the *Metamorphoses* is to prove that English is no less capable of conveying the substance of 'so excellent a Poem' than any other vernacular language. He writes:

> To the Translation I haue giuen what perfection my Pen could bestow [...] I haue also added Marginall notes for illustration and ease of the meere English Reader, since diuers places in our Author are otherwise impossible to be vnderstood but by those who are well versed in the ancient Poets and Historians [...] And for thy farther delight I haue contracted the substance of euery Booke into as many Figures [...] To this I was the rather induced, that so excellent a Poem might with the like Solemnity be entertained by vs, as it bath beene among other Nations: rendred in so many languages, illustrated by comments, and imbelished with Figures. (Sandys 1632: sig B ii[v])

In the dedicatory epistle to his 1626 stand-alone translation of the *Metamorphoses*, Sandys had already signalled the importance of the relationship between his translation and his notes, indicating some perceived potential deficiency in the translation itself. In the 1632 edition, he makes good this deficiency by adding to the translation, 'as the Mind to the Body, the History and Philosophicall sence of the Fables' (Sandys 1632: p. 2[r] n. p.) – that is, his extensive commentary and notes. By making these prose additions he can effectively translate his translation for 'the meere English Reader' in the margins and in the glosses between each book. And this

---

[12] Ovid outlines the project of his epic undertaking in the opening lines of the poem: *Metamorphoses* I. 1–4. See also Liveley 2011: 7–8.

proves (for the most part) an invaluable supplement to the main text of the translation – not only 'since diuers places in our Author are otherwise impossible to be vnderstood' but since there are numerous places in Sandys's translation which would also be obscurely incomprehensible if it were not for the supporting notes and commentary.[13] This is because Sandys's attempt to translate Ovid with due 'Solemnity' and to demonstrate the power of the English vernacular to vie with 'other Nations' in transforming the Latin of the *Metamorphoses* into an early modern European language is often achieved by resorting to a peculiarly and paradoxically Latinate form of English.

In his 1627 elegy on *Poets & Poesie*, Drayton had already celebrated Sandys's translation of the first five books of Ovid's epic for its 'Englishness'. According to Drayton:

> Then dainty Sands that hath to English done,
> Smooth sliding Ouid, and hath made him run
> With so much sweetnesse and vnusuall grace,
> As though the neatnesse of the English pace,
> Should tell the Ietting Lattine that it came
> But slowly after, as though stiff and lame.
>
> (Drayton, *Poets & Poesie*, lines 157–62)

Drayton, renowned for his own literary patriotism, approves Sandys' translation because of its supposed demonstration of what the English vernacular can achieve in poetry. He mentions it twice here to ensure we take the point of his praise. It is, indeed, not just Sandys' use of the English language that Drayton seems to have in mind here but his use of an English meter. Sandys has not just translated Ovid's Latin into English. He has translated Ovid's classical hexameter (its metrical feet figured here as belonging to an old man, stiff and lame) into English heroic couplets (its metrical feet figured as fresh and youthful, sweet and neat, full of grace and pace). So successful is Sandys' translation in Drayton's eyes that the original Latin poem now reads as if it were itself a clumsy translation (as if 'it came | [...] after'). For Drayton, Sandys' English translation reads as if it were itself the original. Sandys has taken on Ovid 'and hath made him run' in more than one sense.

However, Drayton's patriotic praise for Ovid thus Englished overlooks the fact that in order to make Ovid's Latin hexameters run so smoothly within the lines of his own English pentameter couplets Sandys' translation

---

[13] See Pearcy 1984: 89: 'His apparatus acquires an ambiguous status which he can exploit to expand the limits imposed by the need to keep his translation in due proportion with its original [...] Sandys can imitate Ovid's concise allusiveness, confident that his apparatus will save him from falling into obscurity'.

must heavily compress and contort the English.[14] The result is a form of English that is remarkably Latinate – both in terms of its vocabulary and its syntax.

Deborah Rubin's definitive study nicely illustrates the various strategies of 'gratuitous Latinity' that Sandys employs in his Englishing of Ovid, cataloguing Sandys' tendency to translate a Latin word or phrase with a false or imperfect English cognate, his fondness for adjectival forms, and for awkward ablative absolute constructions.[15] Indeed, we encounter a particularly egregious example of these devices pressed into service to help Sandys in his compressed translation of Ovid's first book, and the account there of Jupiter handing over bovine Io to his suspicious wife, Juno:

> Obtayn'd; not forth-with feare the Goddesse left;
> Distrusting Ioue, and iealous of his theft,
>
> (I.622–23: Sandys 1632: 14)

> Paelice donata non protinus exuit omnem
> diva metum timuitque Iovem et fuit anxia furti.
>   (Ovid, *Metamorphoses*, I. 622–23, Latin based on Miller's text)

> Though her rival had been handed over, the goddess did not immediately put away all of her suspicions; for she feared Jove and was worried about his tricks.
> (Ovid, *Metamorphoses*, I. 622–23, my own literal translation)

As the first line in this example amply demonstrates, 'at their worst, Sandys's attempts to be concise and to approximate Latin syntactical patterns are nearly unintelligible'.[16] And, unusually, there are no notes to help explain either the translation or the story to Sandys' 'meere English Reader' here. In this light, it is perhaps unsurprising that in the next generation of great Ovidian translators Dryden should complain that Sandys had 'evaporated' rather than translated Ovid's poetry, claiming that Sandys and his contemporary translators of Ovid: 'neither knew good Verse, nor lov'd it; they were Scholars 'tis true, but they were Pedants. And for a just Reward of their Pedantick pains, all their Translations want to be Translated, into *English*' (Dryden 1693 [2015]: 370).

---

[14] Oakley-Brown 2006: 81 points out that 'Sandys translates the 11,995 lines of the *Metamorphoses* into approximately 13,210 lines of English' – a testament to the remarkable compression achieved in this rendering of Ovid's inflected Latin hexameter into English pentameter.

[15] See Rubin 1985: 52–103 on Sandys' Latinity.

[16] Rubin 1985: 65 discussing Sandys' version of the battle between Perseus and Cepheus (Sandys 1632: 175).

Sandys's English vernacular is not as innovative – nor as 'English' – as Drayton's praise would have us believe, then.[17] It contains, moreover, nothing like the range and variety of Golding's earlier inventive expressions and vernacular translations for individual words.[18] Included in his cataloguing of the hounds who tear Actaeon to pieces in Book III, for example, Golding gave us 'Greedigut', 'Blab', 'Royster', and 'Jollyboy' in a packed list that perfectly captured the jostling pack of dogs in Ovid (III. 206–52). Sandys includes some of Golding's names in his own catalogue (among them, 'Blab', and 'Royster') but he complains in his notes that: 'The transposition of these names in divers places to sute with the numbers haue caused some to taxe there interpretations' (Sandys 1632: 85). The interpretations that Sandys himself puts upon these names are straight-forwardly, rather dully, literal: Ovid's *Oribasos* or 'Mountaineer' becomes 'Clime-cliffe'; *Nebrophonos* or 'Deerslayer' becomes 'Fawn-bane'; *Harpyia* or 'Snatcher' becomes 'Greedy'. The colour and vitality of Golding's exuberant English vernacular (in which *Harpyia* became 'Greedigut') is diluted in Sandys's far more literal, pedantic, translations.[19]

It was not only Ovid's Latin canines that Golding had transformed into a pack of good English 'houndes'. As Madeleine Forey summarises, Golding's Englishing of the word and the world of Ovid's *Metamorphoses* had transformed both into:

> a world of raspberries, hips and haws rather than mountain strawberries (1.119), crabs rather than octopuses (4.454), lapwings rather than hoopoes (6. 853). One encounters witches, pucks, elves and fairies not nymphs (*passim*) [...] Music is provided by pots and pans not clashing cymbals (3. 673, et al.), viols not lyres (5. 139 et al.), and shawms not flutes (14. 612). The dead are placed in coffins not urns (12. 682). (Forey 2002: 3)

One of the best, oft cited, examples of Golding's very English Ovid appears in the translation to Book I and the description Ovid gives there of the Golden Age, in which mankind: 'Did live by Raspis, heppes and hawes, by cornelles, plummes and cherries, | By sloes and apples, nuttes and peares,

---

[17] Rubin 1985: 59 stresses that what matters in this context 'is not the percentage of Latin words in Sandys's translation but their degree of Latinity – the degree to which they stand out in relief from the English, pointing to the original text and language'.

[18] On salient differences in the treatment of Ovid by Golding and Sandys see Lyne 1996, Oakley-Brown 2006: 78–81; Bloom 2001: 131–37; and Taylor 1986, for whom: 'Sandys's translation is 'urbane, elliptical, in controlled iambic pentameter', in contrast to Golding's which is couched in 'unsophisticated metaphrase, in trundling fourteeners' (Taylor 1986: 387).

[19] See also Lyne 2001: 204.

and lothsome bramble berries' (*Metamorphoses*, I. 104–05).[20] Sandys'
translation shows its indebtedness to Golding in rendering the same line (in
a similar, yet markedly more compressed style) as: 'They gather Wildings,
Strawb'ries of the Wood, | Sowre Cornels, what vpon the Bramble growes'
(Sandys 1632: 28). Although Sandys' translation is more muted than
Golding's in its Englishing of Ovid's original, Sandys nevertheless deems it
necessary to explain his vernacular choices: in a note he glosses 'Wildings' as
'*Arbuteos foetus* which I haue rather rendred in a familiar word, nor lesse
agreeable to the subiect' (Sandys 1632: 28).[21] Indeed, in the face of
Golding's abundant Anglicization of Ovid's Golden Age fruits, Sandys'
restraint no less than his explanation here seems almost apologetic.

Sandys' Ovid 'among other Nations'?

What are we to make of Sandys' Ovid thus 'Englished'? In comparison with
Golding, Sandys' Latinate English certainly achieves the 'Solemnity' he had
identified in his Dedication as the necessary quality that would enable the
Metamorphoses to be duly honoured 'by vs, as it bath beene among other
Nations' – that is, in other vernacular languages (such as French and
Italian). In line with his commentaries and notes, Sandys' Latinate English
certainly helps to bring the ancient world of Ovid's *Metamorphoses* that
much closer to Sandys' own, to present Ovid's strange world as strangely
familiar through the use of familiar yet unfamiliar Latin syntax and
etymological cognates. For Sandys' English does not, as Drayton claimed,
actually jettison the 'jetting Lattine' of Ovid's original but repeatedly
reminds us that English has Latin as one of its roots – that the English
vernacular, decidedly, 'came after'. And one effect of this is further to
remind us that English has much in common with those other vernacular
languages (such as French and Italian) into which Ovid was being translated
in this period – and with which Sandys has already invited comparison with
his own *Ovid Englished*.[22]

---

[20] See Lyne 2002: 253–54: 'These are English fruits, and this is an English *Metamorphoses*
[…] In the Preface Golding promises to deliver an Ovid who speaks English as if it were
his own tongue [… according to] the ambitions on behalf of their native tongue shared
by many renaissance writers'. Similarly, for Stanivukovic 2001: 5: 'Golding substitutes
English equivalents for the landscape, characters, and ideas of the Latin original, in effect
reinventing [… an] English Ovid [who] enabled Renaissance writers to treat his myths as
representative of their own nationhood'.

[21] See also Lyne 2001: 203.

[22] See Taylor 2017 on the late sixteenth and early seventeenth centuries as a period of rich
(and competitive) experimentation in French and Italian vernacular translations of
Ovid, both literal and allegorical. Sandys is likely to have known the recent French
translations of the *Metamorphoses* by Raimond and Charles Massac (1603) and by
Renouard (1606). Several Italian translations of Ovid were in circulation at this time,

This reminder brings with it some tension – particularly when we recall that Sandys dedicates both the 1626 and 1632 editions of *Ovid Englished* 'To the most High and Mightie Prince Charles, King of Great Britaine, France, and Ireland' (Sandys 1626: p. 1^r n. p.; Sandys 1632: p. 2^r n. p.). In the intervening years between these two editions, relationships between Britain and its neighbours in wider Europe were troubled – particularly between Britain and Spain, and between Britain and France. Outright and expensive war with both countries had ceased in 1630, but the negotiated peace remained uneasy. Political tensions between Britain and the rest of Europe, then, were high throughout the period in which Sandys was work-ing on the 1632 edition of his translation and commentary, and continued through the period of its printing and publication.[23] As a consequence, and as Liz Oakley-Brown points out, under Charles's autocratic rule 'vernacularity became an important political weapon' (2006: 81). English became the royally sanctioned language of Charles's court and French was banned: the King is even reported to have 'dismissed the Queen's French attendants [...] anxious to keep her and his own contacts with the French court to a minimum' (Sharpe 1987: 18).

Against this political backdrop, modern critics have tended to see in Sandys's vernacular Englishing of Ovid unambiguous evidence for his patriotism. In particular, they see his representation of other European nations (especially the French and Spanish) as cast in a distinctly negative light: the Spaniards, according to Lyne, are characterised by their avarice and their New World ventures deemed to be motivated by materialistic greed for gold;[24] and 'the French nation and its subjects are obviously disparaged' in Sandys' paratexts, according to Oakley-Brown.[25] Yet, for every example of such tacit or witty disparagement of his European peers to be found in Sandys's commentary, there are several more which cast them in a positive and amicable light. Spanish and Portuguese travellers and their reports of the wonders they have witnessed in the New World (especially in Peru and 'New Spain') are presented as Sandys' principal sources and authorities for his corroboration of Ovid's own wonder-tales. Certainly, in Sandys' paratexts '*Spaniards* bragge' (Sandys 1632: 198) and are renowned for their 'Couetousnesse' (Sandys 1632: 522), but stories of their strange

---

including the various medieval translations of Bonsignori (first printed 1497), Agostini (1522), and Dell'Anguillara (1561 and 1584). See Guthmüller 1981 on the Ovidian Italian canon and tradition. See also Part III and IV of this volume for an insight into French and Italian translations of the *Metamorphoses*.

[23] On the politics and conflicts of the period see Sharpe 1987 and James 2003.

[24] On Sandys' 'thinly veiled' criticisms of the Spanish (and Portuguese) see Lyne 2001: 238–39; see also Oakley-Brown 2006: 252.

[25] Oakley-Brown 2006: 85.

discoveries are 'credibly reported' (Sandys 1632: 265) and both Acosta (on Dionysian revels in the New World – Sandys 1632: 521) and '*Ferdinando Cortez*, the *Spaniard*' (on mounted conquistadors mistaken for centaurs by the Mexicans – Sandys 1632: 565) are respected as reliable sources.[26] The French may use goats as nursemaids (Sandys 1632: 486), practice witchcraft (Sandys 1632: 330), and tell tall tales (Sandys 1632: 393), yet they are among Sandys's most frequent interlocutors in the commentary.[27] Thus, in the gloss to Book XI we find Sandys reporting that:

> by a *French* Gentleman I was told a strange accident, which befell a brother of his: who saw on S. *Germans* bridge by the *Louure* a Gentlewoman of no meane beauty, sitting on the stones (there laid to finish that worke) and leaning on her elbow with a pensiue aspect. According to the *French* freedome he began to court her; whom shee intreated for that time to forbeare; yet told him if hee would bestow a visit on her at her lodging about eleuen of the clock, he should finde entertainement agreeable to his quality. He came, she receaued him and to bed they went; who found her touch too cold for her youth; when the morning discouered vnto him a Coarse by his side, forsaken by the soule the euening before: who halfe distracted ran out at the doore and carried with him a cure for his incontinency. Although this story haue no place in my beleife; yet is it not incredible that the Diuell can enter and actuate the dead by his spirits; as sufficiently appeares by that kinde of witchcraft, which giues answers by dead bodies, reported by diuers historians. (Sandys 1632: 393)

Sandys' wry observation of the '*French* freedome' and his comment that 'this story haue no place in my beleife' effects some distance between himself and both the credulous Frenchman and the hapless brother who provide the source for this tale. Yet Sandys retells the story with such relish and at such length that, as a result, he effectively closes that distance between Englishman and Frenchman. The setting for the encounter 'on S. *Germans* bridge by the *Louure*' implies familiarity with Parisian landmarks on the parts of both Sandys himself and his 'meere English Reader[s]'. What is more, by placing himself as the first-hand 'translator' of the tale – 'by a French gentleman I was told a strange accident' – Sandys' translation of this strange French narrative (to illustrate his translation of a strange Latin narrative) thereby draws our attention to his own close dialogue with this

---

[26] See his comment upon the tale of Midas (XI. 85–145), Sandys 1632: 522.

[27] In his comment upon the difficult birth of Hercules (IX. 273–323) – and including a rare instance of the French language in the paratexts of *Ovid Englished* – Sandys observes: 'Frenchmen at this day, by knitting a knot on a poynt, can disable the bride-groome from touching the Bride. In Gasconie called *Nověr l'eguillette*; and practised alwaies at the mariage: which is of no light regard, since by the Ciuill law it is punishable' (Sandys 1632: 330).

anonymous French interlocutor. Whether that exchange was originally in English or French, we can only wonder.

The cumulative effect of this rich paratextual dialogue between Sandys and his European sources – particularly seen against the backdrop of those European 'Warres and Tumults' during which *Ovid Englished* was produced – is to force us to rethink the identity and character of this work, and to look beyond narrow definitions of the translation and its apparatus as either patriotically 'English' or 'Virginian'. When Sandys describes his own work as needing 'more then a single denization, being a double Stranger' (Sandys 1626: p. 1ʳ n. p.), we should remember that *Ovid Englished* is also, in part, Ovid 'Europeaned'. In his role as a translator 'carrying across' Ovid's *Metamorphoses* and relocating it in seventeenth-century Europe, Sandys's paratexts reveal that he also envisions his endeavour as 'carrying across' the English vernacular to meet Europe's other national languages. After all, as Sandys observes of Ovid's Europa (II. 833–75), carried across the sea and to a new world: 'Of her name *our part of the world* was called *Europa*' (Sandys 1632: 79). And it is to this part of the world no less than to the New World that Sandys carries his European Ovid.

II

OVID IN THE IBERIAN PENINSULA

3

IRENE SALVO GARCÍA

THE LATIN COMMENTARY TRADITION AND
MEDIEVAL MYTHOGRAPHY: THE EXAMPLE OF THE
MYTH OF PERSEUS (*METAMORPHOSES* IV) IN SPANISH
AND FRENCH[1]

Due to the huge interest that Ovid's *Metamorphoses* aroused, vernacular translations flourished everywhere in Europe during the twelfth and the thirteenth centuries. Medieval readers of the original developed various techniques to explain a complex text, at either the narrative or the interpretative level, and produced extensive euhemeristic and allegoric commentaries. Ovid's poem was assimilated into a medieval literary canon, in which it was resemanticized. The collection of stories of metamorphosis was used to exemplify questionable human behaviours and tell the fundamental narratives of pagan Antiquity. Thanks to the euhemeristic interpretation, myths became history, and mythology was used as a source for Ancient Greek and Roman events that shared a common chronology with the Old Testament and the ancient history of the East.[2] Latin commentaries are fundamental to understanding the medieval transmission and reception of the *Metamorphoses*; they facilitated the difficult assimilation of the Ovidian myths into a Christian context. With exegetical glosses, the medieval commentaries also provided extensive mythographic contents. The *Metamorphoses* are characterized by an elliptical style, chronological jumps,

[1] This article was written as a part of the Marie Skłodowska-Curie project ROMAINE. Ovid as Historian. The reception of classical mythology in medieval France and Spain, ID: 705386 (2017-2019). I conducted a substantial part of this research as Visiting Research Fellow at King's College London, where I collaborated with the members of the project 'The Values of French Language and Literature', funded by an ERC-Advanced Grant. I thank Simon Gaunt and his team – Hannah Morcos, Maria Teresa Rachetta, Henry Ravenhall and Simone Ventura – for their warm wellcome during my stay in London. I would also like to thank Pablo Piqueras and Robin Wahlsten Böcker-man for their advice on the transcription and the translation of the fragments from the commentaries to Ovid's *Metamorphoses* and Prunelle Deleville on the *Ovide moralisé*.

[2] The reception of Ovid in the Middle Ages is the subject of many studies. For a recent survey, see J. G. Clark, F. T. Coulson and K. L. McKinley 2011.

embedded tales, and the synthesis of mythological cycles. Hence, many myths are hard to understand due to the lack of context. Medieval commentators tried to compensate for this difficulty by appealing to their own knowledge: to well-known mythographic manuals written in Late Antiquity such as those written by Servius, Fulgentius and indirectly also Hyginus, or to medieval compendiums like those of the anonymous Vatican Mythographers. Consequently, in the Romance translations, Ovid's original text was frequently diluted in a new narrative, and the Latin text and mythography were conveyed together with their medieval interpretations.

Medieval translators paid particular attention to a several myths narrated in the *Metamorphoses*. The literary works known as 'romans antiques' singled out and emphasized the success of the cycles relative to Thebes (Books III and IV) and Troy (Books XII and XIII).[3] The medieval re-writings of the Ovidian myths of Narcissus, Pyramus and Thisbe, and Philomela and Procne (Books III and IV) gave rise to original and independent literary creations that eventually replaced Ovid's *Metamorphoses* in the medieval transmission of these myths. Many characteristics of these medieval mythographic adaptations can be identified in the translation of certain myths, whose important role in the ancient cycles generated great interest among commentators, mythographers and translators.

One of these myths is the myth of Perseus, which is the object of the present article. The feats of the Argive hero were translated into Castilian from Ovid's *Metamorphoses* in the *General estoria* (*c.* 1270), and into Old French in the *Ovide moralisé* (*c.* 1320). In both these translations, the classical text was transformed into an autonomous mythographic narrative which displayed significant differences from Ovid's original text. After a brief presentation of the vernacular texts and their connections with Latin medieval commentaries, this article will address the changes made to the source by the authors of the *General estoria* and the *Ovide moralisé*. The goal is to identify the secondary sources that the translators used and to compare the features that characterize these two versions of Ovid's poem. As we shall see in the following analysis, the discrepancies between the French and the Castilian versions are due to the translators' reliance on different secondary sources, but also on their divergent interests. In addition to this, the similarities between these two versions show the existence of a shared mythographic tradition – in Latin or already in a vernacular language – that might have contained a story of Perseus very close to the one in both Romance works.

---

[3]   See, for example, the study by Marylène Possamaï-Pérez 2002 on the reception of the Roman de Thèbes in the *Ovide moralisé*.

The Spanish and the French translations of the *Metamorphoses* and the Latin commentary tradition

The *General estoria*[4] is an extensive universal history, a huge compilation comprising some 6700 pages in its modern edition, and includes one of the oldest translations of the *Metamorphoses*.[5] It was commissioned by Alfonso X (1221–1284), king of Castile and León, and was written in his *scriptorium* by a team of scholars known to modern critics as the Alfonsines. Alfonso commissioned it with the goal of compiling Biblical and pagan narratives in a single work. The king did not give priority to the Biblical narratives, and around 40% of the contents of the text are profane. The chronology of the *General estoria* is structured according to the Pentateuch. The compilers used the chronological framework given in the Bible, but they complemented it with Eusebius and Jerome's *Chronological canons*, Petrus Comestor's *Historia scholastica*, and Godfrey of Viterbo's *Pantheon*. When these structural sources mentioned a pagan feat, the Alfonsines turned to pagan sources to find missing information. One of the main sources used for Ancient Greek and Roman histories was Ovid. At least 22 mythological cycles were translated literally from the *Heroides* and the *Metamorphoses*.[6]

As the fragments taken from the Bible were compiled with the *Glossa ordinaria*, the translations from the *Metamorphoses* and the *Heroides* were accompanied by an extensive and complex gloss. Ancient commentaries of Classical mythology from Late Antiquity, such as the ones written by Servius or Lactantius had been copied together with more recent ones so as to form the complex commentaries of the thirteenth and fourteenth centuries. The Alfonsines probably started translating Ovid around 1270, a period in which the exegesis of Ovid was systematized and set.[7] The gloss in the *General estoria* is sometimes attributed to an anonymous 'freire' [monk], probably a minor brother or a preacher. In some other places, it is attributed to 'Johan el Anglés', better known as John of Garland, who is the author of an exegetic verse commentary to the *Metamorphoses* known as the *Integumenta Ovidii* (1220). Indeed, the glosses attributed to John of Garland coincide notably with the *Integumenta*; in some occurrences, the gloss

---

4 Today, there is only one complete edition of the *General estoria*: see Sánchez-Prieto Borja (dir.) 2009. All quotations in the article are taken from this edition.

5 Various partial translations of the *Metamorphoses* were written at the final years of the twelfth century and the beginning of the thirteenth. See Anna Cappellotto's article in this volume on Albrecht von Halberstadt's thirteenth-century translation of the *Metamorphoses* in Middle High German (Chapter 14).

6 For a survey of the reception of Ovid in the *General estoria*, see Brancaforte 1990 and Salvo García 2012a.

7 See the fundamental works by Ghisalberti 1932 and 1933b and, more recently, Coulson 1982, 1991 and 2015.

attributed to the 'freire' coincides with the gloss in Arnulf of Orleans'
Allegoriae (1190), which is one of the first systematic commentaries to the
Metamorphoses and the basis of later interpretations. However, some of these
correspondences were erroneous. Some of the attributions were reversed:
certain glosses attributed to the 'freire' are John of Garland's, and vice versa.
Sometimes, the gloss comes neither from the *Integumenta* nor from the
Allegoriae. Such imprecision is surprising: the Alfonsines' *modus operandi*
compelled the compilers to cite the authors of their sources whenever they
were able to identify them. Thus, the unidentified sources sometimes
suggest that the commentator was not reputed enough to be named, but
they also give information about the materiality of the Alfonsines' sources.
Indeed, the anonymity, content and location of the comments indicate that
in Alfonso's *scriptorium* there was a Latin manuscript of the *Metamorphoses*
transmitted with an extensive (and certainly anonymous) commentary located in the margins. One of the best-known examples of these commentaries
is the 'Vulgate commentary', written in France around 1250 and widely
distributed at the end of the thirteenth century.[8] The commentary used for
the *General estoria* was very likely similar to the Vulgate commentary.
However, one cannot claim that it was the only source, because it contained
interpretations possibly taken from commentaries other than those by John
of Garland and Arnulf of Orleans, such as the one transmitted in the
margins of the Vaticanus Latinus 1479 (*c.* 1300).[9]

Chronologically, the next extensive Romance version of the
Metamorphoses was the so-called *Ovide moralisé*, a complete translation
written in *langue d'oïl* around 1318-1320.[10] As in the Castilian text, Ovid
was not translated alone. A significant corpus of mythographical,
historiographical (*Historia scholastica*), religious (Old and New Testaments),
and literary texts (*Roman de Thèbes*) were added to the translation of myths
according to their chronological and thematic accuracy. Like the compilers
of the *General estoria*, the anonymous author of the *Ovide moralisé*
systematically inserted exegetic interpretations to the translation of each
myth.[11] The part devoted to the gloss was sometimes longer than the

---

[8]   On the Vulgate commentary see Coulson 1982 and 1991.

[9]   See Salvo García 2017: 200–20.

[10] There is only one complete modern edition of the *Ovide moralisé*, De Boer 1915–1938.
      More recently, the research group *Ovide en Français* (*OEF*) published a new edition of
      Book I: Baker et al. 2018. The bibliography on the *Ovide moralisé* is quite rich. For a
      survey, see the list of critical studies proposed by the group OeF: www.rose.uzh.ch/de/
      forschung/forschungamrose/projekte/oef/bibliographie.html [accessed 20 March 2020].

[11] On the relationship between Latin commentaries to the *Metamorphoses* and the *Ovide
      moralisé*, see the editions of Arnulf of Orleans, John of Garland, and the one, partial, of

translation of Ovid's text itself. The similarities between the *General estoria* and the *Ovide moralisé* are remarkable, because the fact that the reception of Ovid occurred in similar chronological contexts (only 30 or 40 years passed between the writing of the two texts) determined the type of material support on which Castilian and French authors read the *Metamorphoses*: a glossed manuscript with similar characteristics and contents.[12]

Structure and sources of the Perseus myth in the *General estoria* and the *Ovide moralisé*: the logic and chronology of medieval mythography

In Ovid's *Metamorphoses*, Perseus is the main character of the events narrated in Book IV (604–803: the myths of Atlas, Andromeda and Medusa) and Book V (1–249, his battle with Fineus during his wedding to Andromeda). A textual analysis reveals that although the French and Castilian translators had access to (and relied upon) a Latin original of the *Metamorphoses*, which at times they translated literally, in other cases they also extended, shortened, or even restructured certain episodes of Ovid's text. Table 1 presents an overview of the chapters in the *General estoria* and the *Ovide moralisé* in which Perseus is involved.[13] Only the underlined chapters correspond directly to the *Metamorphoses*. In the other chapters, additional mythographic information and a commentary are given. These additions are indicated in Table 1 with the word 'gloss'. Here, the word 'gloss' is used with a somewhat generic meaning: it is applied to any addition to the text of the *Metamorphoses*, whether it comes from another secondary source, or whether it was perhaps written in Alfonso's *scriptorium*.

Among the contents that did not come from the *Metamorphoses*, one can distinguish two types: 1) contents that were prompted by a short reference (one or two verses) in the *Metamorphoses*, and 2) contents that the translators considered to be related to Perseus, but were not mentioned at all in the principal source. The story of Danaë comes under the first heading, as it is connected to the narration of Perseus's conception and birth and is

---

the Ovidius moralizatus by F. Ghisalberti 1932–1933, Engels 1945, Demats 1973 and Salvo García 2018a: 193–210 and 2018c.

[12] On the relations between the *General estoria* and the *Ovide moralisé*, see the chapter 'Le frayre de la *General estoria* est-il l'auteur de l'*Ovide moralisé*?' in Engels 1945: 3–22, Solalinde 1921: 285–88, and Salvo García 2017 and 2018b: 235–58.

[13] For this study, I focus on the myths dealing with Perseus in Book IV of the *Metamorphoses*. The titles of the chapters devoted to the myth of Perseus in the *General estoria* are copied in italics.

Table 1

General estoria, II. 1. 375–407	Ovide moralisé, IV	Metamorphoses, IV
(1) Danaë and Jupiter: – Cap. 154 (De los fechos del rey Perseo e de Dane su madre) – Cap. 155 (Del liñaje de Dane e de Perseo) – Cap. 156 (De cómo entró Júpiter a Dane segunt dizen los auctores de los gentiles) Gloss: Cap. 157 (De lo que da a entender el grano de oro en que dizen los autores de los gentiles que se tornó Júpiter segunt unos lo esponen) – Cap. 158 (De cuemo fue echada Dane de so padre e fallada e casada)	(1) Danaë: OM, IV. 5332–5489 Gloss: lines 5490–5636:	(1) Met., IV. 604–621: Brief mentions of Danaë and Medusa
(2) Perseus and the Phorcydes (Graeae and Gorgons): – Cap. 159 (De la crianza de Perseo e cómo fue sabio e vino al rey Acrisio, su abuelo) – Cap. 160 (Del rey Forco e de so reino e de sus hijas) – Cap. 161 (De cómo venció Perseo a Medusa e a sus hermanas, e éll d'ellas ovo el reino) – Cap. 162 (<u>De lo que los autores de los gentiles dixieron de la batalla de Perseo e de las fijas del rey Forco</u>) Gloss: Cap. 163 (De lo que departen los nuestros sabios sobr'esto d'estos fechos de Perseo e de Medusa e de sus hermanas) Gloss: Cap. 164 (De lo que se entiende otrossí por Perseo)	(2) <u>Perseus, Graeae and Gorgons:</u> OM, IV. 5637–5713 Gloss: lines 5714–5891	(4) Met., IV. 771–803: The story of Graneae and Medusa told by Perseus in indirect speech
	(3) Bellerophon: OM, IV. 5892–5995; Gloss: lines 5996–6209	
(3) Perseus and Atlas: – Cap. 165 (De la contienda del rey Perseo e del rey Atlas de África segunt las estorias) – Cap. 166 (<u>De cómo cuentan d'otra guisa los auctores de los</u>	(4) <u>Perseus and Atlas:</u> OM, IV. 6210–6301 Gloss: lines 6302–6555	(2) Met., IV. 621–62: Perseus and Atlas

gentiles la contienda que ovo el
rey Perseo e el rey Atlant)
Gloss: Cap. 167 (De lo que
departen los sabios latinos sobre
lo que dixieron de Perseo e de
Atlas los gentiles)

(4) Perseus and Andromeda:	(5) Perseus and Andromeda:	(3) *Met.*, IV. 665–771:
– Cap. 168 (<u>Del rey Perseo e de</u>	*OM*, IV. <u>6586–6861</u>	Perseus and
<u>la infant Andromeda que</u>	Gloss: lines 6862–7185	Andromeda
<u>defendió éll, e fue ella su mugier</u>		
<u>después</u>)		
– Cap. 169 (<u>De las razones de</u>		
<u>Perseo e de los cavalleros de</u>		
<u>Cefea</u>)		

briefly told in the *Metamorphoses*. Ovid mentioned that Perseus was born to
Danaë and Jupiter under the form of golden rain (*Metamorphoses*, IV. 610–
11): 'neque enim Iouis esse putabat | Persea, quem pluuio Danaë conceperat
auro' [Nor did he admit that Perseus was son of Jove, whom Danaë had
conceived of a golden shower].[14] From these two Ovidian verses, both
Romance texts derived a detailed narrative on Danaë's story, which
comprised five chapters in the *General estoria* and nearly 300 verses in the
Ovide moralisé. For Danaë's story, the translators were guided by their usual
sources when completing Ovid's texts: mythographic glosses, usually taken
from the margins of the Latin manuscripts of the *Metamorphoses,* and the
mythographic compendiums themselves that told the tales integrally.
Because the marginal glosses and mythographic works are very often similar
in content, it is difficult to identify the specific type of source these texts
drew upon. For example, in the margins of the manuscript Vaticanus latinus
1479 one can read a gloss summarizing Danaë's story and its interpretation.
Here, Jupiter's metamorphosis is explained as follows: 'we say that Jupiter
was transformed into golden rain because the god bought Danaë's wardens
with money, so they would allow him to go to her.'[15] The same information

[14] All quotations from the *Metamorphoses* are taken from Tarrant (2004) and the
translations from Miller (1916).

[15] Here is the full gloss in Latin: 'Fabula talis est: Acrisius habuit unam filiam, Danem, de
qua audivit in responsis quod haberet filium qui illum a regno expelleret, unde inclusit
eam in turri. Iupiter in specie auri illam corrupit. [...] Rei veritas est talis: Perseus fuit
filius Danes. Quia Acrisius Danes audivit in responsis supradicta, inclusit filiam suam, id
est custodibus tradidit quos Iupiter auro corrupit, et sic genuit Persea qui per mare
missus fuit ad Gorgona destruendam', *Vat. lat. 1479*, fol. 85v (gloss to v. 604 and v.
614) [The fable says: Acrisius had a daughter, Danae. He heard from the oracle that she
would have a son who would expel him from his own kingdom. This is the reason he
locked her up in a tower. Jupiter, disguised as gold, raped her. [...] This is the truth of
the matter: Perseus was Danae's son. Since Acrisius heard from the oracle the

also appears in the mythographers such as Fulgentius (*Mythologiae* I, 9) and the Vatican Mythographer III (14, 1). In the autonomous commentaries, John of Garland transmitted a similar explanation, as we can see in Table 2.[16]

Table 2

Integumenta Ovidii, IV. 215-16	*General estoria*, II. 1. 378	*Ovide moralisé*, IV. 5490-5501
		Or vous dirai, selonc l'estoire | Comment la fable fet a croire | Dou dieu qui en la tour de pierre, | Ou Dané la bele iere en sierre, | Descendi comme pluie d'or. |
Iupiter est aurum cum Danem decipit auro Cuius custodes munere fallit amans.	Onde diz maestre Joán el Inglés esta palabra sobr'esta razón de Júpiter, que diz que se tornó oro porque dio mucho oro, ca envió donas e abtezas a aquellos e a aquellas que avién en guarda a Dane, e tantas dones les dio que todos los venció.	Cil rois de son riche tresor. | Pour acomplir sa volenté | De la pucele, a grant plenté, | Largement, comme s'il pleüst, | Dona dons, pour ce qu'il pleüst | A ceulz qui de la tour avoient | Les clez et garder la devoient.
[Jupiter is the gold when he deceives Danae with gold; whose guardians the lover deceives with bribes]	[On Jupiter's tale, John the Englishman says this word: he says he transformed himself into gold because he handed over much gold, since he sent gifts and wealth to those men and women who guarded Danae's confinement; and he gave so many gifts that he overcame everyone.]	[I am going to tell you something according to the history: how the fable makes us believe that a god descended like a golden rain and went into the stone tower where Danae was locked up. This king took advantage of his wealthy treasure to satisfy his desire of the maiden. He handed over many gifts, intensely as if it was raining, to soften those who guarded her and had the tower's key.]

Beginning with Perseus's conception meant going back to the natural order of events. Ovid deliberately altered the logical chronology, but he created narrative marks and had his characters tell their own story, in order to situate the different metamorphoses. This is what happened with the story of the Phorcydes (Medusa and her five sisters), which Perseus himself

---

aforementioned answers, he locked his daughter up, that is, he put guardians in charge of her. Jupiter bribed them with gold, and this is how Perseus was conceived. He was sent through the sea to destroy the Gorgon]. All the translations are by the author unless otherwise noted.

[16] All references to the *Integumenta* are taken from F. Ghisalberti's cited edition (1933b) and the translations from L. Born's translation (1929).

told during his wedding to Andromeda in the last tale of Book IV. Following the same objective of building a logical narrative, which included Danaë's tale, the medieval authors preferred to narrate these events in their chronological order, that is, before Atlas's story. Indeed, Atlas was metamorphosed into a mountain because he saw Medusa's head, which implies that Perseus was already holding it in his hand before he defied the giant. This modification can already be observed in Table 1: this episode appears at point (2) in the order given by medieval texts, while it is at point (4) in Ovid's poem.

The search for a fair, natural ordering in the different stories caused Danaë's myth to be inserted and Medusa's to be brought forward. However, one might wonder whether this new structure was an innovation on the part of the translators or whether it was already present in their sources. The Alfonsines explicitly wrote that the Phorcydes' story was the first one that they found written in their source: 'E contaremos primeramientre cómo venció a las fijas del rey Forco, *ca este es el primero fecho de aquellos que él fizo que fallamos escripto*' [First, we will tell how Perseus defeated Phorcys' daughters, because it is his first deed found in writing] (*General estoria*, II. 1. 382). In the *Ovide moralisé*, the order is the same, as we can see in the left-hand column of Table 1. A mythographic source may be the origin of this new order. This same structure also appears in the *Liber de natura deorum*, an anonymous twelfth-century text that contains some exclusive variants appearing in the *General estoria* and the *Ovide moralisé*.[17] The order of this myth in the *Liber de natura* is exactly the same as in the Romance works: 'De Danaë', 'De Perseo et Gorgone [Medusa]', 'De Atlante' and 'De Andromeda'. However, the Vatican Mythographers I, II and III – who are usually very close to the *General estoria* and the *Ovide moralisé* – differ from the Castilian and French translations and from the *Liber de natura*. Mythographer I (Ch. 72), for example, centres his narrative on Perseus and Andromeda; though some information can be found about Medusa and Atlas, they are in other parts of the text, and not always related to Perseus. Mythographer II (Ch. 133–37) follows the same order as the vernacular works for the beginning of the myth (Acrisius, the Gorgons, Atlas), but the narrative did not end with Andromeda. As for Mythographer III (Ch. 14),

---

[17] The anonymous work entitled *De natura deorum* (c. 1159–1179) is preserved in an early fourteenth-century manuscript, Oxford, Bodleian Library, Digby 221 (fols 100r–120v), edited and studied by Virginia Brown 1972: 1–70. See also Judson B. Allen 1970: 352–64. On the reception of the *Liber de natura deorum* in the *Ovide moralisé*, see also Salvo García 2018b. On its reception in the *General estoria*, see Saquero Suárez- Somonte and González Rolán 1993 and Salvo García 2012ab.

he begins the myth of Perseus with the story of Medusa, and then proceeds with three derived episodes: Pegasus, Bellerophon and the Chimera.[18]

Besides the order of the narrative, another feature suggests that the source for these sections was not just Ovidian. Both Romance texts offer confusing accounts of the Phorcydes. The name Phorcydes is a patronymic given to the daughters of Phorcys and Ceto, the Graeae (also known as the Grey Sisters) and the Gorgons (of which Medusa is the most famous). In Ovid's account of the story, the Graeae had only one eye in common, and Perseus stole it to escape them and reach the Gorgons. When he found himself in front of the Gorgons, Perseus managed to avoid Medusa's petrifying gaze and cut off her powerful head (*Metamorphoses*, IV. 772-78). Ovid clearly distinguished the Graeae from the Gorgons. In the vernacular translations, however, the Gorgons were described as the Graeae: they shared a single eye, which was stolen by Perseus before he beheaded one of them.[19] The overlapping of these two groups cannot be found in the gloss to the *Metamorphoses*. Arnulf, for example, did not mention the Graeae, nor their shared eye. John and the commentator of *Vat. Lat. 1479* interpreted the eye as a shared kingdom which was stolen by Perseus. These commentators did not state a name, and instead used the generic denomination 'filie Forci'. Rather than the commentators, the mythographers might have been a possible source for the Spanish and French translators. In fact, the same confusion between Graeae and Gorgons appears in Servius (*Comm. En.* VI, 289), Fulgentius (III, 1), in the Vatican Mythographers, and, again, in the *Liber de natura deorum*.

The Romance translators thus followed the same model, from which they inherited the new narrative structure of Danaë's and the Phorcydes' tales and also the confusion between the Grey sisters and the Gorgons. A mythographic compendium, belonging to the tradition related to the *Liber*

[18] For the Vatican Mythographers, the following editions are used: for Mythographer I: Nevio Zorzetti and Jacques Berlioz 1995; for Mythographer II: Péter Kúlsckar 1987 and for Mythographer III, Georg H. Bode 1834.

[19] In the *General estoria* (II. 1. 386) we read that 'E fallamos en el cuarto libro de Ovidio mayor que diz que estas fijas de Forco avién un ojo e non más con que veyén, e quel tomavan arrevezes el una del otra por veer. E que avién natura que todos aquellos, no los omnes tan solamientre, mas aun las vestias salvajes que ellas veyén con aquello ojo que todas se tornavan piedras' [In Ovid's major work, Book IV, we read that Phorcys' daughters had only one eye and that they took turns to see. And they had the power to transform into stone anyone they looked at with their single eye, not just mankind, but also wild animals]. In the *Ovide moralisé* (IV. 5659–64) we read that 'Un oeil avoient solement | Ces trois filles dont je vous parle. | L'une ert nomee Euriale ; | L'autres fu Staïnon nonmee ; | L'autre, qui plus fu renonmee, | Ot non Gorgon ou Medusa' [They only had one eye | the three daughters I am talking about | one of them was named Euriale; | the other one Staïnon; | and the last one, who was well-known | was Gorgon or Medusa].

de natura deorum and guided by the gloss of its manuscript of the *Metamorphoses*, may have been the source of the three modifications. Despite this model, and as in the case of other myths, the Romance translators differed in their treatment of the common episodes and in their selection of the various additions they made. They chose what they found most significant and most relevant, and built a new version of Ovid's text which corresponded to their interests.

The treatment of the additions to Ovid's text: Danaë and Medusa, the royal lineage, and the moral critique

One of the first differences we observe between the Castilian and the French texts is that Danaë's story is much longer in the *General estoria*. The central and salient part of this myth is when Danaë was imprisoned in a tower, where she conceives Perseus by Jupiter, who manifested himself in the form of golden rain. In the Castilian text, the Alfonsines developed this central narrative by adding details about the Danaë's sea voyage after her father discovered her pregnancy and sent her away. They wrote that Danaë, cast adrift in a wooden chest, eventually reached Italy. There, she was recovered by a fisherman and welcomed by the king, with whom she founded the town of Ardea (II. 1. 379-81). Among all the sources I have parsed, the *Liber de natura deorum* (Ch. XLVII) and the Vatican Mythographers I (154) and II (133) are the only ones to include this story, and their narrative is very close to the one in the *General estoria*.[20] All three texts share the basic elements of Danaë's trip and her arrival in Italy, although the details differ. According to the Vatican Mythographers, Perseus was born in Italy, while the *General estoria* and the *Liber de natura* claimed that he was born in the chest before reaching the shore. In contrast, the description of Turnus as the king (or an inhabitant) of Ardea shows a stronger relation with the Mythographers than with the *Liber de natura*.

Although the correspondences with the sources consulted are not exclusive, it appears that the Alfonsines extracted the whole narrative from a single work. This view is strengthened by the recurrent references to a single source: 'dize el autor', 'dize la estoria'. On other occasions, in fact, when

---

[20] Again, the source of the Vatican Mythographers seems to be Servius: 'Danaë, Acrisii regis Argivorum filia, postquam est a Iove vitiata, pater eam intra arcam inclusam praecipitavit in mare quae delata ad Italiam, inventa est a piscatore cum Perseo, quem illic enixa fuerat, et oblata regi, qui eam sibi fecit uxorem, cum qua etiam Ardeam condidit: a quibus Turnum vult originem ducere'. Maurus Servius Honoratus, Georgius Thilo (ed.) 1881, VII, 372 [After she was impregnated, Danae, the daughter of Acrisius, king of Argos, was locked up in a chest by her father and thrown into the sea. She arrived in Italy and was found by a fisherman together with Perseus, since she had given birth to him right there. And she was offered to the king, who made her his wife. He founded Ardea with her: from whom it is ckaimed Tumnus draws his origin].

there were several source texts, the Alfonsines wrote 'leemos en las estorias' or 'dizen los autores'. The absence of these elements in the gloss to the *Metamorphoses* suggests again that a mythographic compendium, an indirect heir of the traditions represented by the Vatican Mythographers and the *Liber de natura deorum*, was used to complete this part of the Castilian *estoria*, which was absent in Ovid as well as in the *Ovide moralisé*.

The use of anonymous mythographers and scattered glosses instead of a single and authorial *auctor* who must be followed word for word gave the Alfonsines freedom to update the narratives according to their own preferences, as happened with the Graeae's and Danaë's narrative summarized by Ovid in four verses. In the *General estoria*, the Alfonsines devoted a great deal of attention to the questions of lineage and inheritance. Many details show this thematic interest in the Castilian translation: for instance, Acrisius hid a document containing Danaë's lineage in the wooden chest in which she was cast away (II. 1. 380), so that whoever found her would quickly understand that she was the daughter of a king and treat her as such. The Graeae's common eye, as we have explained, was interpreted as the kingdom inherited from their father Phorcys.[21] According to the *General estoria*, in a kingdom, the change of sovereign and the transmission of power were dangerous moments because they weakened the hold on the territory and made it an easy prey for the enemy (II. 1. 385). This is indeed what happened in the Ovidian myth: Perseus stole the eye (i.e., the kingdom) when one of the sisters handed it to another (*Metamorphoses*, IV. 766–67). This event led to a long digression in which the Alfonsines explained that there must be only one heir, always the first-born male, if possible, or the eldest daughter; it was not desirable that siblings reigned together. We can read a similar statement in the *Partidas*, a detailed law book also commissioned by Alfonso X ('Cómo el fijo mayor ha adelantamiento et mayoria sobre los otros sus hermanos', Partida IIª, título XV, ley 2ª).

Unlike the *General estoria*, in the *Ovide moralisé* the stories of Danaë and the Phorcydes were used to criticize the character of women. Danaë was accused of selling herself for money (by means of the golden rain), and Medusa, in the euhemeristic interpretation, was defined as 'putain, sage et cavilleuse, | Decevable et mailicieuse' [a prostitute, wise and deceitful, deceptive and misleading]. The author accused Medusa of using her extraordinary beauty to rob the men she seduced (*Ovide moralisé*, IV. 5740–53). Therefore, both Danaë and Medusa were defined as covetous women who had no scruples about selling their charms for profit. Neither the gloss nor the mythographers gave these ideas, but there were elements in these

---

[21] See for example in the *Integumenta*: 'Unicus est oculus regimen quod tres habuere' (IV. 225). [The single eye is the realms which the three possess] (Born 1929: 137).

works that might spur the author of the *Ovide moralisé* towards a similar interpretation. Ovid, for example, described Medusa as a beautiful woman (*Metamorphoses*, v. 794–97). Servius (*Comm. En.* 6, 289) extended the Gorgon's beauty to her sisters – whom he confused with the Grey sisters, as noted above. Hence, beauty was shared by the three Gorgons, which explains why they looked through a single eye; he claimed that men were petrified by their beauty when they looked at them. John of Garland (*Integ.* I. 228-30) also adopted this last explanation, which can also be found in the *General estoria* and in the *Ovide moralisé*.[22] Building on these remarks, the French author used these characters to criticize female behaviour and added a mercantile element, both absent from the Latin sources and the Castilian translation. Denouncing prostitution through this type of interpretation of female characters was a leitmotiv in the *Ovide moralisé*. For instance, the author criticized Daphne and Io in Book I, Callisto in Book II, and Antea, Proetus's 'adulterous' wife, in Book IV. Criticism of female behaviour was part of the ongoing judgement of different social classes that was systematically inserted at the end of each myth of the *Ovide moralisé*, partly derived from the euhemeristic, allegoric and moral gloss.

The tale of Bellerophon and its sources: Vatican Mythographer III and the *Liber de natura deorum*

The second type of addition, as noted already, involves complete narratives, sometimes present in (only) one of the translations that were not included in the *Metamorphoses*. For example, in the *Ovide moralisé*, there is a long narrative digression focused on Bellerophon.[23] As we can see in Table 1, the French author placed the narration of this myth after the tale of Perseus and the Phorcydes (the Graeae and the Gorgons), while in the *Metamorphoses* it was not even mentioned. The link between Bellerophon and Perseus's

---

[22] 'Otros dizen que fue dicho por la fermosura que avién tan grant que cuantos las veyén que todos fincavan desmemoriados e como salidos de sentido' (*General estoria*, II. 1. 389). [Other people say it was told because of their beauty, because those who saw them became confused and, as it were, out of their wits]. 'Medusa fut de grant biauté, | Si sot trop de desloiauté. | Putain fu sage et cavilleuse, | Decevable et malicieuse. | [...] | Tuit convoitoient s'acointance, | Et cele, par sa decevance, | Les savoit atraire et chuer | Et de tous biens si desnuer, | Qu'el les lessoit nulz et despris, | Et cil estoient entrepris | Autresi come images mues: | Ensi les muoit en statues' (*Ovide moralisé*, IV. 5740–53) [Medusa was very beautiful, | but she also knew about disloyalty over-well. | She was clever and deceitful whore, | treacherous and spiteful. | Everybody wanted to know her well" | and she used tricks | to attract and flatter them | to deprive them of their possessions | to the point of leaving them naked and miserable, | and those were subjugated | as mute images | and thus she transmuted them into statues.]

[23] On the episode of Bellerophon and its meaning in the *Ovide moralisé*, see Jean-Yves Tilliette's analysis (2015).

adventures was established through Pegasus, the winged horse born from Medusa's blood, which helped Bellerophon to win the battle against the Chimera. Ovid mentioned Pegasus only briefly at the end of Book IV and at the beginning of Book V. However, due to the change in order that anticipated Medusa's story (V. 772–786) in the *Ovide moralisé*, the reference to Pegasus (V. 786) was brought forward and it came before the metamorphosis of Atlas. The new order of the French translation was thus: Danaë, Medusa, Pegasus, Bellerophon (see Table 1). Euhemeristic and allegorical explanations were intertwined in between.

Bellerophon's story begins after the gloss to Pegasus and it takes up no fewer than three hundred verses in Book IV (*Ovide moralisé*, IV. 5892–6209). These lines can be summarized as follows. The young Bellerophon was the son of Proetus. Proetus was the brother of Acrisius, who was Perseus's grandfather. Proetus's second wife Antea (or 'Cenole' in the French text, a name that might derive from the Latin 'Estenobee') fell desperately in love with Bellerophon, who rejected her. Antea took revenge on her stepson by claiming that he had attacked her. This false accusation spurred Proetus to punish Bellerophon by sending him to fight Chimera, the terrible threefold monster (with the body of a goat, the head of a lion, and the tail of a serpent).

The mythographers are, once again, the key for the insertion of this tale in the *Ovide moralisé*. The tale of Bellerophon tale appears in many Latin mythographers: Servius (*Comm. En.* V, 118), Fulgentius (III, 1), and the Vatican Mythographers (I, I, 70; III, 14, 4; *Vat. Myth.* I identified Perseus and Bellerophon). Paule Demats (1973: 75-77) has already shown that the version of Vatican Mythographer III is the closest to the *Ovide moralisé*. Three unique correspondences between these two texts support this claim: 1) the absence of the character Iobates, Proetus's brother-in-law, who instructed Bellerophon to kill the Chimera – in the *Ovide moralisé*, it is Proetus's initiative 2) the presence of Antea as a victim of an incestuous love; and 3) the euhemeristic interpretation of the Chimera, also given by Fulgentius and Servius, as a metaphor of a mountain which was home to the three beasts that composed its body, which represented different stages of the feeling of love.

Demats has argued that the tale of Bellerophon is not to be found in any of the texts she consulted apart from a marginal gloss in the commentary of the *Vat. Lat. 1479*. Here, the same events in Bellerophon's adventure were summarized, though more briefly than in Vatican Mythographer III and the *Ovide moralisé*. The gloss in the commentary *Vat. Lat. 1479* is situated in Book V (fol. 90ʳ), next to Ovid's verses about Pegasus (*Metamorphoses*, V. 256–59), a feature that would indicate a difference with respect to the source used in the *Ovide moralisé*, where the story of Bellerophon is inserted in Book IV. According to this material evidence, it is logical to agree with Demats that the insertion of Bellerophon's tale was spurred by a marginal gloss in the manuscript of the *Metamorphoses* used by the French author. However, for different reasons which will be explained below, this gloss was not necessarily the only source he used to build the story of Bellerophon.

There are two elements not mentioned by Demats that strongly suggest the use of a mythographic source (either beside or in lieu of a gloss). First, Vatican Mythographer III (14, 1–5) is the only one that follows the same structure as the *Ovide moralisé*: 1) Perseus and Medusa; gloss; 2) Pegasus; gloss; 3) Bellerophon; gloss; 4) interpretation of the Chimera. These four myths constitute a unitary group that is independent of the tale of Atlas and Andromeda, which belongs to the other parts of the compendium. Secondly, in the French translation Bellerophon was presented as Proetus's son. Although this genealogy strengthened the link between Bellerophon and Perseus (since Proetus was Perseus's great uncle) and this might have led the French author to innovate without a textual basis as a source, this version was also already present in mythographic sources. In this line of argument, Demats wondered whether the source of the *Ovide moralisé* already contained this relationship, which was far removed from the initial version of the myth. Among all the works of the mythographers I have consulted, the *Liber de natura deorum* is the only one that introduced Bellerophon as Proetus's son (Ch. XLV, 2). This exclusive correspondence supports the idea that the source of this passage of the *Ovide moralisé*, as well as a large part of the myths of Danaë and Medusa, refer to a mythographic compendium related to both Vatican Mythographer III and the *Liber de natura deorum*. The insertion of the two stories – Danaë's and Bellerophon's – at these particular points could indeed have been induced by a glossed manuscript similar to Vat. Lat. 1479, a commentary very close to the *Ovide moralisé* in many places, as was proven by Ghisalberti (1932, 1933b), Engels (1947), Demats (1973), and myself (Salvo García 2018a, b and c).

Direct translation of the glossed *Metamorphoses*: common model, diverse uses

The Romance translations share a common skeleton, given by Ovid and its gloss, which was fleshed out by contents pertaining to different traditions. However, as we observed in the narratives of Danaë and Medusa, the diversity of the two Romance versions is explained not only by the sources, but also by the treatment intentionally given to common contents. The same remark applies to the Ovidian contents (the original text and gloss) as well: they might have had the same sources, but they were treated differently.

The first common feature of this treatment is that when the source was Ovid directly, the translation is very literal, a characteristic found in other myths in both Romance texts. However, the Castilian and French translators did not always choose the same sections for this direct translation. The myths of Atlas and Andromeda offer a clear example. To tell Atlas's story, Ovid used one third of Perseus's myth, in which it was inserted. In the *General estoria* the metamorphosis of the giant into a mountain was described in detail. The Castilian translators did not change a single comma in the Latin text, and explained that Atlas's beard and hair became forests, his shoulders and hands became hills, his head was the mountain top and his bones became rocks. The only addition to the Latin text was the formula 'dizen los autores', which the Alfonsines usually quoted to point out an unusual element such as a supernatural physical transformation.

Quantus erat, mons factus Atlas; nam barba comaeque in siluas abeunt, iuga sunt umerique manusque, quod caput ante fuit, summo est in monte cacumen, ossa lapis fiunt 　　　　(*Metamorphoses*, IV. 657–60)	[Atlas] se fizo mont mayor […]. La barva e los cabellos *dizen los autores* ques fizieron selva; los hombros e las manos collados en ella; lo que era cabeça antes fincós assí por alteza e por cabeça en somo del mont; los huessos se tornaron piedras (*General estoria* II, 1: 395)
[Atlas transformed into a mountain huge, as the giant had been; his beard and hair were changed to trees, his shoulders and arms to spreading ridges; what had been his head was now the mountain's top, and his bones were changed to stones.]	[Atlas was transformed into a huge mountain. The authors say that his beard and hair were transformed into a forest; his shoulders and hands into hills; what was a head before, remained thus, as the height and the head, on the top of the mountain; his bones became stones.]

In the *Ovide moralisé*, by contrast, the metamorphosis was summarized in a single verse: '*Eu li muez en un grant mont*' (IV. 6286).

Later on, in the French poem, Andromeda's myth (IV. 6586–861) was translated more literally in the *Ovide moralisé* than in the *General estoria*. One can read, for instance, the detailed and expanded conversation between Perseus and the maid (IV. 6664–716), tied to a rock and exposed to a sea monster determined to devour her, which was summarized in the Castilian text. In fact, the Alfonsines were as concise as they could be: besides shortening this conversation, they ended the story after the death of the sea monster and excluded the story of the coral, which originated from the contact of Medusa's hair with algae. The *Ovide moralisé* included these elements, cleaving remarkably closely to its source.

Although the vernacular translations offered a very different treatment of individual passages in the Latin poem, their interpretation on these individual episodes is very similar and it refers to the usual commentators already mentioned: Arnulf of Orléans, John of Garland, and so on. As we can see in Table 3, the gloss about Atlas can be summed up as follows: Atlas was a wise astrologer, which is why the stars relied on him; he kept the knowledge in his garden or study, where a golden tree represented philosophy. We read similar interpretations in Arnulf's *Allegoriae*, in John of Garland's *Integumenta* and in the manuscript *Vat. Lat. 1479*.

Table 3

Allegoriae, IV. 19	*Integumenta Ovidii*, IV. 217–18	*General estoria*, II. 1. 397–98	*Ovide moralisé*, IV. 6302–17
Athlas in montem. [...] Vel quidam sapientissimus fuit qui in quodam monte studio vacans multum de ortu et occasu signorum comprehendit, et inde alios instruxit. Et hec est causa quare dicitur muta-tus in montem et celum sustinere.	Est Athlas doctor, ortus scola, pagina multa Virgultum pomum, clara sophia nitet.	(1) Dizen que este rey Atlas sabié de las estrellas e era grant maestro d'ellas e de todas las otras cosas del cielo. (2) E por los siete saberes del trivio e del cuadruvio dixeron árvoles que llevavan ramas e mançanas e fruta e fojas que eran d'oro, e estavan en aquella huerta como las artes de la filosofía. (3) E porque sopo Atlas toda la estrolomía e las naturas de todas las estrellas estudiando allí e creciera siempre en el saber dixeron que creciera aquel monte toda vía, e que tod el cielo con sus estrellas posaran en esse mont e folgara ý.	(1) (3) Athlas fu rois de grant noblesce	Et sorabondans en richesce.	Mestres fu de philozophie.	Tant sot de l'art d'astronomie,	Qu'il sot de tout le firmament	L'ordenance et le mouvement	Et des etoiles la nature	Et la chalour et la froidure	Et la cause dont ce venoit :	Por ce dist l'en qu'il soustenoit	Le firmament desor sa teste (2) Un vergier ot riche et honeste,	C'est son cuer ou ce sont si livre,	Ou plantee estoit a delivre	Tout l'art de philozophie,	Qui l'arbre doré signifie
[Atlas into a mountain [...]. Or read otherwise he was a wise man, who spent some time studying on a mountain and man-	[Atlas is the master; the garden is the school; shrubbery, books; and the fruit blooms forth as pure	[(1) They tell that King Atlas knew the stars and taught about them and about all the things related to the sky. (2) And they said that	[(1) (3) Atlas was a king of great nobility and boundless wealth. He taught philosophy. He knew so much of the art of astronomy that he knew all the

aged to comprehend the formation and the decline of con-stellations, and taught it to others. And this is the reason why it is said that he was transformed into a mountain and that he holds up the sky.]

philosophy.]

trees with golden branches, apples, fruit and leaves were the seven disciplines of the trivium and quadrivium and that they were in that orchard, just like the art of philosophy. (3) And, because Atlas studied and knew about astronomy and the nature of all the stars and his knowledge increased, they said that the mountain grew too and that all the sky with its stars laid on the top of that hill and there it rested.]

sky, its order and movement, and he knew the nature of stars, about heat and cold, and the cause of its origin. This is why it is said that he held the sky over his head. (2) An orchard had plenty of goods and wealth. It has its heart in its books, in which the art of philosophy (symbolised by the golden tree) was sown freely.]

In the case of Andromeda, explored in Table 4, both the Castilian and the French texts interpreted the maid as the human soul, abandoned to its death in the world, and a potential victim of a threatening monster. Perseus represented goodness, which prevented her from yielding to sin. Among all the consulted sources – the Vatican Mythographers, John of Garland, the commentary of *Vat. Lat. 1479* – Arnulf of Orleans (*Alleg.*, V. 1) and after him the Vulgate commentary are the only ones that transmitted both allegories. The Vulgate commentary also contains the etymology of Andromeda, derived from *andros*, man, which was included in the *General estoria*. Thus, the source for the interpretation of Andromeda's tale could be a commentary similar to the Vulgate commentary, though on the whole, the Romance translations bear a greater similarity to Arnulf in terms of both the content and the location of the gloss. Surprisingly, this interpretation of Andromeda's tale appears in Book V of the *Allegoriae*, and not in Book IV (as in Ovid's poem). In fact, both Romance texts followed the same structure, and inserted this specific allegory[24] as a closing of the translation of the verses corresponding to Perseus in Book V (*Ovide moralisé*, V. 1035-78, and *General estoria* II. 1. 407). In contrast, in the manuscript of the

---

[24] The *Ovide moralisé* also contains an interpretation of the myth of Andromeda in Book IV (v. 6886 sq.). However, it is slightly different from Arnulf's: Andromeda is human nature, a sinner as soon as the forbidden fruit was eaten. The monster is the Devil, who tempts her from then onwards. The fact that both glosses are copied in different books (IV and V) shows that for the author, the interpretations are complementary.

Table 4

Allegoriae, v. 1	*Vat. Lat. 1598*, fol. 44ᵛ	*General estoria*, II, 1. 405–06
Mostra maris interficit i. extirpat vicia. quibus extirpatis eam sibi coniugem assumsit. Anima enim a viciis liberata suo nubit creatori et coniugit.	Sic est mutata andromeda de ligata in solutam et est moralis ista mutatio quod ostendit allegorica historia que talis est: perseus enim interpretatur perfecte bonus unde per ipsum virtus accipitur. *andromede anima est que ab andros quod est uirile dicitur.* Hec est que ad cautes maris ligitur monstris exposita per quod intelligitur quod anima luteo corpori amixta uiciis exponitur	Por Andromeda departe que se da a entender el alma, onde dizen que este nombre Andromeda viene de otro nombre a que llaman los griegos *andros*, e quiere dezir en el nuestro lenguaje de Castiella tanto como 'varonil' o 'vertut', porque una de las mayores vertudes que nuestro señor dios fizo entre cuantas cosas crió e que éll más ama el alma del omne es.
[He kills the monsters of the sea, that is, he kills vice. With them removed, he took her as his wife, since the soul freed from vice marries its creator and joins him]	[And this is how Andromeda was transformed, from tied to untied, and this is a moral transformation because it shows an allegorical story, which is the following one: Perseus should be interpreted as someone good; this is the reason why he means virtue. Andromeda is the soul, which is named after 'andros', which means 'virile'. She is the one who is tied to the sea's rocks and exposed to monsters, meaning that the soul which is in a contemptible body is exposed to vice].	[[The commentator or the gloss] explains that Andromeda symbolises the soul and this is why her name comes from another Greek name, 'andros', which means in our Castilian language 'virile' or 'virtue', because one of the great virtues our lord made among the things he created and he loves is men's soul.]

Vulgate commentary consulted, the gloss is located in Book IV (*Vat. Lat. 1598*, fol. 44ᵛ), in the upper margin of the folio, where the story of the encounter of Perseus and Andromeda and their salvation is told.

As is evident from these examples, the presence of similar glosses of Atlas (Table 3) and Andromeda (Table 4) taken from the commentators already mentioned (among others, Arnulf of Orleans and John of Garland) shows that both the French and Castilian translators went back to their source manuscript as a support base for the original Latin text – a manuscript that brought common interpretations in these two vernacular versions. It also shows that text and gloss were treated as independent textual objects in the Romance translations.[25] The Castilian and the French authors did not hesitate to include long glosses about Andromeda and Atlas respectively, while they summed up their stories very briefly.

---

[25] For independence of text and gloss in vernacular compilations, see Salvo García 2014.

Conclusion

The comparative study of the French and Castilian translations of the myth of Perseus confirms the importance of the Latin models used by medieval authors at both the textual and the material level. As for other myths (see Book I and Books VII-VIII), the tradition of commentary that influenced the myth of Perseus shows striking similarities with a compendium collecting glosses by Arnulf of Orléans and John of Garland, the so-called Vulgate commentary, and a mixed commentary close to the one in the margins of the manuscript *Vat. Lat. 1479*. This study also shows the reception of mythographic notes that are often too long to have come from a marginal gloss. This is why we postulate the existence of narrative unities, following a new ordering and additions of contents inherited from sources other than Ovid that were transmitted together with mythology during the Middle Ages. The Vatican Mythographers (especially the Third, which is the most complete and the closest chronologically to both vernacular translators) and the tradition represented by the *Liber de natura deorum* explain some of the exclusive variants that we found in the additions to the myth of Perseus, such as the stories of Danaë in Castilian and of Bellerophon in French.

The common models were nevertheless adapted to the interests and needs of the translators, whose aims were to transmit not only Ovid's text, but also Ancient pagan history more generally. The author of the *Ovide moralisé* builds a continuous critique of the misconduct of contemporary society on the basis of a moral and Christian interpretation of the myths. The Alfonsines offer models of good or bad governance derived from errors in the transmission of a royal heritage.

Finally, the analysis shows that texts or mythographic additions, and interpretative glosses, do not have the same status for medieval authors. Although they are all merged in the final works, the methods of translation and compilations are different: the inclusion of an abridged version of a myth does not preclude the insertion of the complete gloss of the same myth. This *modus operandi* can be observed in the myths of Atlas in French and of Andromeda in Spanish. The contents are indeed different, but the practices of reading and commentary underlying the Romance texts refer to the same tradition. We see more common elements, beyond the shared sources, that create new tangible relations between the reception of the Classics in Spain and in France.

4

GEMMA PELLISSA PRADES

THE CATALAN MEDIEVAL COMMENTARY OF OVID'S
METAMORPHOSES: FRANCESC ALEGRE'S 'AL·LEGORIES
E MORALS EXPOSICIONS'[1]

This chapter deals with the reception of Ovid's *Metamorphoses* in Catalan in
the Crown of Aragon during the fourteenth and the fifteenth centuries. In
particular, it focuses on Francesc Alegre's *Transformacions*, a translation and
a commentary of the *Metamorphoses* written between 1472 and 1482 and
printed in Barcelona in 1494 with a print run of 1000 copies (Torró 1994,
Hernando i Delgado 2002: 514–16). I will argue that Alegre's commentary
is not merely a translation of Boccaccio's *Genealogia deorum gentilium*, as
had been assumed by critics, but a more complex work that draws on
different sources presented in a fictional framework in dialogue form. This
dialectical structure allows the narrator to represent himself as an equal to
Boccaccio and to nineteen other authors, all of whom appear as fictional
characters and discuss the myths translated in the first part of
Transformacions. This is a preliminary study based on the analysis of Alegre's
commentary of the first allegory in Ovid's Book I, which is transcribed,
translated and discussed in detail. I plan to publish the first modern edition
of Alegre's commentary in Classiques Garnier.

Ovid's *Metamorphoses* in the vernacular in the Crown of Aragon

In 1393, King John I of Aragon wrote a letter to his brother-in-law, the
Frenchman Henry of Bar, asking for a copy of 'Ovidi methamorfoseos
moralisat'. There are several theories regarding the exact kind of
moralisation the king was requesting. According to Antoni Rubió i Lluch
(1908–1921: I. 381), it was, in all probability, the *Ovide moralisé*. If this was

[1] This article has received the support of the Departament of Culture and the Secretary
for Universities and Research of the Ministry of Economy and Knowledge of the
Government of Catalonia (2014–2016 and 2017–2018) and the Ministry of Science
and Innovation of the Spanish government (2018–2020). I thank Martí Duran for his
collaboration in the edition of Francesc Alegre's *Transformacions*.

true, argues Lluís Cifuentes (2006: 183), it is possible that there was a
Catalan translation of the text already in existence. Thus, Cifuentes suggests
that the king's letter may actually have referred to Pierre Bersuire's *Ovidius
moralizatus* (*c.* 1342); there was a Spanish translation of this work, entitled
Morales de Ovidio, written before 1452, which seems in turn to be based on
a previous Catalan text that is now lost (Riera i Sans 1989: 708).
Furthermore, the inventory of the royal library on the death of King Martin
I (1396–1410) records a Latin commentary of Ovid's *Metamorphoses* as
'glosses de l'Ovidi Metamorfoseos' (Rubió i Lluch: 1908–1921, I). Pujol
(2011: 32–33) has identified it as a school commentary registered as n. 271
in the *Incipitarium Ovidianum* by Coulson and Roy (Pujol 2011: 32–33).
John I of Aragon was well connected with the French courts and, at the end
of the fourteenth century, French translations were often used at the Crown
of Aragon as a way to access classical works. After this time, however, the
Italian tradition started to play an important role in the translation of
classical works (Pujol 2004).

Giovanni Bonsignori's *Ovidio Metamorphoseos Vulgare* (*c.* 1375–1377),
an Italian translation based on Giovanni del Virgilio's *Expositio* and *Allegorie*
(1322–1323) in medieval Latin, was a pivotal reference point for fifteenth-
century Iberian translations of Ovid's *Metamorphoses*.[2] In the epilogue to his
Catalan translation of the *Metamorphoses*, Francesc Alegre refers to two
previous translations of Bonsignori's text. According to him, Francesc
Galceran de Pinós (1416–1475) translated some books from Ovid's poem
into Catalan through Bonsignori's translation. He also refers to a Spanish
translation but does not mention its authorship. Both translations are lost
and have not been documented anywhere else, but this information suggests
that before 1475 Bonsignori's work was known at the court of Prince Carlos
de Viana, son of King John II of Aragon and Queen Blanche I of Navarre.
Some time earlier, in the late 1450s, another Catalan author in the prince's
circles, Joan Roís de Corella, may have been influenced by Bonsignori's
translation, either directly or through another secondary source (Pellissa
Prades 2019: 25). Moreover, Corella also drew on Boccaccio's *Genealogia
deorum gentilium*, the main source of Alegre's commentary. Previously,
Bernat Metge used this work in *Lo somni* (1398–1399) as a complementary
source to tell the myth of Orpheus according to Ovid (Riquer 1959: 260,
276, Gómez 2002, Gómez 2009–2010).

---

[2] Nevertheless, no link has been established between the reception of Ovid's
Metamorphoses in Catalan and Simintendi's Italian translation of the poem (1330s), even
though the textual transmission of this text is related to Bonsignori's in manuscript form
(Bonsignori 2001: xxvii–xxxv).

Francesc Alegre's *Transformacions* is the last medieval translation of Ovid's *Metamorphoses* into Catalan and the only medieval Catalan commentary to the *Metamorphoses* that we know of. It was published in 1494 at Pere Miquel's press in Barcelona with a print run of 1000 copies (Hernando i Delgado 2002: 514–16). Manuel Peña Díaz (1997) has documented its existence in several libraries in the sixteenth century. This scholar also notes that some of the owners had a copy of Alegre's work together with a Latin edition of Ovid's *Metamorphoses*, which may suggest an interest, particularly, in Alegre's commentary.

Francesc Alegre's *Transformacions*: a preliminary analysis of the Catalan commentary

Francesc Alegre's work has survived in the form of nineteen incunabula preserved in European and North American libraries (*BITECA* Manid 1776). Alegre's *Transformacions* are composed of two parts, each one with its own prologue: 1) a translation of Ovid's poem in prose and 2) a commentary to the myths entitled 'Al·legories e morals exposicions' [Allegories and moral expositions]. (However, two of the existing incunabula do not contain the commentary.)[3] As far as the prose translation is concerned, although the Catalan translation is mainly based on a late Latin manuscript of the poem, Alegre takes into account other secondary sources, such as Bonsignori and Joan Roís de Corella (Alcina 1998, Pellissa Prades 2017 and 2019). With regard to the commentary, the 'Al·legories e morals exposicions' are based on Boccaccio's *Genealogia deorum gentilium*, which was used as a mythographic source (Farinelli 1929, Badia 1986).

Alegre's attitude towards his secondary sources differs in the prose translation and in the commentary. For example, he acknowledges his debt to Boccaccio in the 'Al·legories e morals exposicions' (Boccaccio's influence on the translation still needs to be examined in depth). In fact, in his commentary, Alegre represents himself in a fictional dialogue with Boccaccio and other authors in order to build *auctoritas* around his own interpretations of the myths, validated by the Italian author (Pellissa Prades 2020). In the prose translation, Alegre hides the dependence on Bonsignori as a complementary source in his translation. However, he explicitly refers to the Italian tradition as a precedent for his translation in the epilogue. He mentions in particular Giovanni del Virgilio and Bonsignori, although he emphasises the chronological distance with regard to these works from the

---

[3]   The two incunabula are in San Juan de Puerto Rico, Casa del Libro (Mérida Jiménez 2012) and in Barcelona, Biblioteca de Reserva de la Universitat de Barcelona, inc. 515, which shows marks of censorship (see *BITECA* copid 1164).

past. It is also significant that he does not mention the French tradition in the reception of the *Metamorphoses* (not even in his commentary):

> és ya trelladat lo libre de *Transformacions* en toscà, en castellà y en lengua catalana; e mostren no entendre los versos de Ovidi, los quals fins vuy no són vist trelladats en alguna vulgar lengua. Bé és ver que en temps passat un Johan Virgili, natural de Toscana, escriví en prosa latina, bé digne de aquells temps, la substància de les *Transformacions* del poeta Ovidi [...] ajustant lo dit toscà ab les faules de Ovidi, trocejades, moltes al·legories segons la fantasia. De aquest latí gros fon tret lo que és en toscà y del toscà, no sol lo castellà, mes uns quants libres en català traduïts del toscà en temps passat per lo noble don Francesch de Pinós. [...] E si pensàs no millorar-hi res, no y haguera tocat ni fora entrat en treball voluntari (Duran and Solervicens 1996: 39–40).[4]

> [The *Metamorphoses* have already been translated into Tuscan, Castilian and Catalan; and they show that Ovid's lines are not understood. Until today, they have not been translated into any vernacular. It is true that, in the past, a John Virgil from Tuscany wrote, in a Latin prose worthy of those times, the substance of Ovid's *Metamorphoses* [...]. The Tuscan writer mixed, together with Ovid's fables, fragmented, many allegories produced by imagination. From this vulgar Latin, the Tuscan rendering was composed and, from the Tuscan version, not only the Castilian one was written, but also some books in Catalan which the noble Francesc de Pinós translated in the past. [...] And if I thought I could not improve on these works at all, I would not have tried it nor volunteered to do it.][5]

In the same epilogue, Alegre also deals with the sources of his commentary by stating that 'los libres de Bocaci, sobre lo treball del qual se funda la part segona dels trenta libres meus, lo nom del qual Bocaci no és en mi callat' (Duran and Solervicens 1996: 41) [The second part of these thirty books of mine is based on Boccaccio's books. I do not hide Boccaccio's name]. In this case, Alegre does not feel any need to establish a chronological distance between his and Boccaccio's times, as he did with Giovanni del Virgilio and even with Francesc Galceran de Pinós. Indeed, he praises Boccaccio's work: 'lo treball de Bocaci, en aquest digne libre, lum de tots los poetes, on clarament per arbres ha tractat la genehologia de tots los déus antichs' [Boccaccio's work in this worthy book, which enlightens all the poets, deals with the genealogy of all the old gods in a clear way by means of family trees.]

---

[4] I have added a comma after *trocejades* that was not in Duran and Solervicens (1996). It is the book (Alegre's *Transformacions*) that talks in the epilogue; in this way, Alegre defends himself from potential criticism.

[5] All translations into English are my own.

In the epilogue Alegre claims the credit he feels he is due for his work: he has not merely translated Boccaccio's *Genealogia deorum gentilium*, but he has also selected only the myths that appear in the *Metamorphoses*, organised the allegories according to their order in Ovid's work, and completed the commentary with texts from the other authors featured in the dialogue (Pellissa Prades 2020). However, these other sources are still to be studied (as is Alegre's methodology in 'Al·legories e morals exposicions'). Further-more, as we will see, Alegre carefully designs the structure of the discourse by choosing the order in which the different authors participate in the discussion. Thus, he creates a whole new discourse in his commentary.

Regarding the circulation of the *Genealogia deorum gentilium* in the Crown of Aragon, Bernat Metge may have read Boccaccio (as well as other authors such as Petrarch) in a manuscript at the papal court at Avignon (Torró 2002: 107 and Cañigueral 2018: 17). As Gómez (2010) argued, Metge knew the *Genealogia deorum gentilium* in its integrity. In the fifteenth century, the influence of the *Genealogia deorum gentilium* is seen in works such as the anonymous chivalric romance *Curial e Güelfa* (*c.* 1440–1450) and Joan Roís de Corella (Badia and Torró 2011 and Martos 2001 respectively). Furthermore, there is a Catalan translation of Seneca's tragedies, written by an anonymous author in the late fourteenth century or the beginning of the fifteenth. In the tragedy of Medea, 'three manuscripts [...] supplement *Medea* with a fragment from Boccaccio's *Genealogia deorum gentilium* [...], which was probably already in the Latin exemplar used by the translator (Martínez Romero 1995: I. 34–35)' (Cabré, Coroleu, Ferrer, Lloret and Pujol 2018: 186).

In the prologue to 'Al·legories e morals exposicions', Alegre turns to Book XIV of the *Genealogia deorum gentilium* to insist that poetry conveys truth (Badia 1986). He then creates a fictional frame in which the author of the first part of *Transformacions* goes to Montjuïc, where he asks the Virgin for help to reveal the meaning of the myths he has translated.[6] Then, the narrator has a vision in which the Virgin sends Boccaccio and nineteen other authors who appear in the *Genealogia deorum gentilium* as an aid to interpret the *Metamorphoses*. Boccaccio will chair the discussion, narrated in a dialogue between an 'I' (Alegre's self-representation in the fictional frame) and the other twenty characters: Boccaccio, Lactantius, Augustine of Hippo, Eusebius of Caesarea, Fulgentius of Ruspe, Isidore of Seville, Rabanus Maurus, Leontius Pilatus, Theodontius, Barlaam of Seminara, Paulus Orosius, Pronapides, Huguccio, Macrobius, Paolo da Perugia, Pliny the

---

[6] For the sources of the prologue and its interpretation see Badia 1986 and also Bescós 2018. In addition, Bescós offers an edition of the prologue. See Pellissa Prades 2020 for an analysis of the way Alegre builds *auctoritas* in his commentary of Ovid's myths.

Elder, Pomponius Mela, Gaius Julius Solinus, Marcus Terentius Varro and Cicero (Fàbrega 1993: 89).

Fàbrega (1993: 89) identifies all the aforementioned authors. As he explains, Lucius Caecilius Firmianus Lactantius (*c. 250–c. 325*) was one of the Church Fathers. In the 'Al·legories e morals exposicions', he is mistaken for Lactantius Placidus, to whom the *Narrationes* and a commentary on Statius's *Thebaid* were attributed (see Tarrant 1995). Rabanus Maurus (*c. 780–856*) penned the treatise *De rerum naturis*. Leontius Pilatus (died 1366) taught Greek to Boccaccio. Theodontius was a Greek mythograph whose works have not survived. Boccaccio's quotations from him in the *Genealogia deorum gentilium* came from *Liber Collectionum*, a compilation of myths written in genealogical order by Paolo da Perugia (died 1348), King Robert of Anjou's librarian. Boccaccio already affirms that Paolo da Perugia's *Liber collectionum* was lost when he wrote the *Genealogia deorum gentilium*.[7] Barlaam of Seminara (*c. 1290–1348*) was a monk from Calabria and a master of Greek. Fàbrega (1993: 88) affirms that Paulus Orosius (*c. 375–418*) was not a Catalan historian, but was from Braga, in Portugal. The Athenian Pronapides was Homer's legendary teacher. Huguccio (died 1210) was a grammarian who wrote the *Liber derivationum*. Pomponius Mela (died 25 CE) penned *De chorographia*, a geographical treatise. Finally, Gaius Julius Solinus (third century CE) authored *Collectanea rerum memorabilium*, which circulated later as *De mirabilius mundi*.[8]

Next, I will transcribe for the first time the part of the commentary dealing with the first allegory of Alegre's translation of Ovid's Book I (the creation of the world) with footnotes in the Catalan text, and present it in English for the benefit of a wider audience of scholars.[9] Finally, I will discuss the challenges that arise from a preliminary analysis of the text. Thus, we

---

[7] For the possibility of Giovanni del Virgilio's influence on Paolo da Perugia and Boccaccio in Naples, see Ferretti (2007). Badia (1986) suggests there may be a connection between the Neapolitan manuscript transmitting Giovanni del Virgilio's *Allegorie* (Biblioteca Nazionale IV, F62) and a possible Hispanic reception of this work in the fifteenth century. Francesc Alegre does not seem to use Giovanni del Virgilio's *Expositio*, but he knows certain readings of the *Allegorie* that may come from marginal glosses in a manuscript containing Bonsignori's work (Pellissa Prades 2017). Ferretti (2007) notes that a study of the *Allegorie*'s manuscript tradition through marginal glosses is still needed.

[8] In this paragraph I have followed Fàbrega 1993 to explain the identity of the authors.

[9] The transcription of this text is part of the edition I am preparing of Alegre's *Transformacions* in two volumes. The second volume will be devoted to the 'Al·legories e morals exposicions'. In my edition, I maintain the original spelling, regularise the use of 'i'/'j' and 'u'/'v', develop the abbreviations, apply the rules of accentuation in modern Catalan, punctuate the text, and separate and unite words according to linguistic rules. I only use diacritics when they are necessary to understand the meaning of the word.

will be able to compare Alegre's own discussion of his methodology in the epilogue with a sample of the text. Bear in mind that Alegre writes in a learned style which flourished in the mid-fifteenth century and imitates classical authors (Ovid and Seneca's tragedies) and Boccaccio's hyperbolic style at the same time (Badia 2010: 189). Joan Roís de Corella is the best-known author who wrote in what was called *prosa d'art* or *valenciana prosa* (learned style).

Asseguts los venerables pares per orde entorn de mi, començà Johan Bocasi, tenint loch de promovedor, a parlar en tal forma:

—Desliberat és per aquests senyors, ans de res dir, veure lo que tu duptes; per què, dexades largues raons, digues què vols entendre de Ovidi e serà't satisfet.

E callant ell, yo responent diguí:

Acaba lo pròlech en las "Al·legorias e morals exposicions" del libre de *Transformacions* del poeta Ovidi. Comensa lo primer libre e capítol, tractant dues al·legorias, de Caos en espècies e dels quatre fills de Àuster en los vents principals

—Perquè desige lo meu entendre escrivint dir la causa per què, tractant en lo començ del libre seu Ovidi la creació del món, posà lo Cahos ("comfús", com dèyan los antichs)[10] transformat en espècia dels quatre elements, me plaurà de saber si sa intenció era creure-u así o, si és estat fengit, d'on ha agut començ aquesta fictió.

Passades entre ells aquelles cortesies que en los hòmens savis desijant la un altre honrar se acustumen, com a president d'aquell noble consell començà sanct Agustí a dir:

—Mon parer és, dexades totes altres serimònies, pus a Johan Bocasi à pres per acessor, començe aquell en cascun cap respondre, determenant de tots nosaltres vint los qui sobre lo demanat diguen lo lur parer, perquè la agudesa de son alevat e especulatiu entendre dignament tal càrrech li procura.

Loaren tots tal dir de sant Agustí e, obeint lo poeta toscà, feu començ a tals noves:

—Volent yo aplicar mon estudi en serca de la genologia dels déus antichs per condecendre als prechs de l'excel·lent rey de Xipre, primer me ocorregué aquell antich Demogorgon, falsament cregut déu, y ab ell, dos yguals en antiquitat, anomenats Eternitat y Caos.[11] Aquest és aquell de qui parla Ovidi, y açò, diversament segons diversos temps e diverses disposicions de enteniments, és estat per los passats [139r[137r]] cregut. E per donar a tu informació plena del

---

[10] The Vulgate Commentary contains the same definition: 'Chaos, that is to say, confusion' (Coulson 2015: 29, note to verse 7), which is often found in medieval glosses and commentaries.

[11] On Boccaccio and the Demogorgon, see Solomon 2012.

que desijant cerques, Theodonsi primer te recitarà d'on ni per qual raó en los antichs començà tal error. Aprés parlarà Tul·li per tots los philòsofs, dient lo que aquells han afermat del començ del món. E per lo alegant Lactanci Firmià seran ab forts arguments desfetes les falçes raons de la eternitat el món; en la fi declarant lo pare Agustí lo que fermament la Església creu.

E, callant ell, començà Teodonsi:[12]

—Causa de tan folla creença són los hòmens de Arcàdia, província situada luny de mar, dins la terra. A on, com vessen la terra per si produir arbres, plantes e flors de diverses natures, cregueren en ella haver alguna amagada deïtat; a la qual cosa cresqué fe sentir terratrèmol e lo bufar de furiosos vents.[13] Les quals coses, creent sol partir de la terra (e més perquè, entrant en les profundes coves, tant com més caminant dins se lunyaven de l'ús de la forana lum, sentien lur cor alterat tremolar, estimant tal moviment de por venir per alguna magestat en tal loch amagada), afermaren per cert en la terra habitar lo gran déu, nomenant-lo Demogorgon,[14] lo qual nom grech vol dir "déu de la terra," *quare* demon *grece idem est quod deus et* gorgon *terra*.[15]

» E perquè ab la rudesa de lurs grossos enginys comprengueren Déu dever ésser eternal, diguren la Eternitat, germana de Demogorgon, eternalment ésser ab ell

[12] As Boccaccio does in the third preface of his *Geneaogia deorum gentilium*, Alegre quotes Theodontius to explain the cause of the error by which the ancient authors thought Demogorgon was the creator of the world. Salvo Garcia (2012a: 246–47) argues that the *General estoria*, also studied in this volume, uses Theodontius as an intermediary source. In fact, she quotes Saquero Suárez-Somonte and González Rolán (1993: 100) to explain that the narrative on the Demogorgon in mythographic works comes from Theodontius and the works influenced by it, as is the case of the *Genealogia deorum gentilium*.

[13] 'Causa [...] vents': Alegre does not translate word by word in his commentary, nor from the other sources he draws on in the first part of *Transformacions*. In general, he summarises Boccaccio's text. Here, he does not translate the part I have marked in italics: 'Huius igitur inspide credulitatis causam dicit Theodontius non a studiosis hominibus habuisse principium, quin imo a vetustissimis Arcadum rusticis. Quim cum mediterranei essent homines atque montani et semisilvestres et viderent terram sponte sua, silvasque et arbusta queque producere, flores, fructus et semina emictere, *animalia alere cuncta et demum in se morientia queque suscipere, nec non et montes flammas evomere, ex duris silicibus ignes excuti, ex concavis locis* et vallibus exalare ventos [...]' (Boccaccio 2011: 32).

[14] 'e més [...] Demogorgon': summary of 'Cui errori auxit fidem apud rusticos antra ac profundissimos terrarum abditus intrasse non nunquam in quibus cum in processu languescente luce silentium augeri videatur, subintrare mentes cum nativo locorum horrore religio consuevit et ignaris presentie alicuius divinitatis suspicio quam a talibus suspicatam divinatem, non alterius quam Demogorgonis existimabant, eo quod eius mansio in terre visceribus crederetur ut dictum est (Boccaccio 2011: 34).

[15] 'lo qual [...] terra': Boccaccio also attributes the etymology to Theodontius, although it appears later in his preface, after he has quoted other authorities: 'Sonat igitur, ut reor, *Demogorgon* Grece, 'terre deus' Latine. Nam *demon* 'deus', ut ait Leontius, *gorgon* autem 'terra' interpretatur [...]' (Boccaccio 2011: 38).

estada.[16] E digueren aprés, continuant lur falç imaginar, Cahos ésser ab ells ensemps de ygual antiquitat; entenent sots aquest nom grech significant confusió[17] aquell confús ajustament dels elements y alementats cossos que posa Ovidi en lo primer capítol; del qual, com de matèria ha pres forma lo ésser de totes coses, estimant necessari que lo déu eternal tengués eternalment matèria disposta per a crear lo món.[18] Y d'ella diu Ovidi aprés, que ha posat repugnar en aquella les coses fredes a les caldes, les molles a les dures, les leugeres a les pesades. Aquesta qüestió lo alt Déu partí y a la natura donà millor ésser, com apar a la letra.[19] Totes aquestes coses axí grosament boscades, ab lo pinzell de lur avisat entendre han aprés apurades los philòsofs, com hoiràs del pare de eloqüència.

Tul·li: —Especulació de continuades vigílies e trebal diligent, cercant ab certesa de les coses duptoses poder determenar, han tant bé procurat in lo món que, sobre la agudesa dels primers enteniments, s'és aprés asentada la vertadera theogia. Los antichs filòsofs, investigant, vengueren a compendre que era de dar un principi per esquivar procés en infinit. Però no entengueren que fos lo món creat de no-res, ans lo gran fill de Nicòmaco,[20] mestre de veritat, lum de

---

[16] 'E perquè [...] estada': 'Sequitur de Eternitate, quam ideo veteres Demogorgoni sociam dedere, ut is qui nullus erat videretur eternus' (Boccaccio 2011: 40), from Book I, chapter 1, 'De Eternitate'. Alegre does not translate Boccaccio's rejection of Demogorgon's existence.

[17] 'entenent [...] confusió': It is not in Boccaccio, but it seems to appear in medieval glosses, as been explained above.

[18] 'Cahos ésser [...] món': 'Chaos, ur Ovidius in principio maioris sui voluminis asserit, fuit quedam omnium rerum creandarum inmixta et confusa materia [...] alias insigne phylosophi, sociam atque coeternam fuisse Demogorgoni, ut si quando in mentem illi venisset creaturas producere, non deesset materia, quasi non posset qui poterat rebus variis forman dare, materiam ex qua daret producere' (Boccaccio 2011: 44–46), from Book I, chapter 2, 'De Chaos'. Alegre turns to Boccaccio in search of mythological explanations and he summarises and re-organises this information in his commentary. One of the main topics discussed here is whether God created the world from nothing or using pre-existing matter. This idea appears in the *Ovide moralisé* (Book I, vv. 85–95) too, whereas Bonsignori (2001: 104–105) insists on the true God as the creator of the world.

[19] 'Y d'ella [...] letra': 'Patet igitur hoc ante alia fecisse, disgregasse scilicet que inter se erant elementa confusa, calida enim frigidis, sicca humidis, et levia gravidus repugnabant' (Boccaccio 2011: 52), from Book I, chapter 3, 'De Litigio primo Demogorgonis filio'. Salvo Garcia (2012a: 20) explains that the association between the creation of the world in the *Metamorphoses* and the Genesis started with Lactantius in order to argue that Ovid referred to only one god, linked to the Christian God.

[20] This passage refers to Aristotle (*Physics*, Book I, 8). Alegre also quotes Aristotle in Latin (*De generatione et corruptione*) in his original work in prose *Sermó d'amor*. *Sermó d'amor* is a theoretical discourse in defence of love in which Alegre uses quotations from Aristotle, the Bible and Petrarch (in the vernacular) and refers to Ovid and Pere Torroella. There is a new edition of this work in Bescós (2019: 222–233). His other sentimental works do not have direct quotations in Latin inside the text.

philosofia, té de ferm en lo primer dels *Phísichs*: "quod ex nichilo nihil fit". E seguint aquesta proposició, s'esforça provar en lo procés de la sua doctrina philosòphica ésser lo món eternal e no ésser creat ni haver may hagut començament. E dexant infinides raons sues, sol ne [139v[137v]] aportaré dues.

» La primera: en cascun instant ha principi e fi, per ço que si lo instant no havia principi e fi, no seria instant, mes seria eternal duració; lo que veem que no és, ans som forçats atorgar que té fi e principi qualsevulla instant. Y de açò resta que, si lo món és de nou creat, en lo instant que fon creat foren ensemps fi e principi, lo que és impossible; donchs lo món no és estat creat. La segona raó és: tota cosa que comença ha ésser, cové que per alguna mutació comence a ésser, pus sens mutació no poria passar de no ésser tal a ésser tal. Si, donchs, lo món à començat a ésser, per alguna mutació à començat: no mutació de si mateix en si mateix, que no seria dita mutació, mes per mutació de altre. Y axí, ans de l'ésser del món és necessari posar alguna permutasió, de la qual en si isqués en ésser, e ans de aquella, altre *et sic in infinitum*. E com no·s degue proseguir en infinit, segueix-se que lo món (o almenys la matèria per mutació de la qual ha rebut novell ésser) sia eternal. E confirmant aquestes raons, escrivint yo *De natura deorum*, diguí axí:

» Primerament, no és provable en alguna manera aquella matèria de qui totes coses són nades ésser estada feta per divina providència, mes tenir y haver hagut virtut per sa natura, que axí com lo artiste com ha hedificar no fa ell la matèria de què·s fa lo hedifici mes usa de aquella que té ja preparada, és estat necessari Déu haver hagut matèria per a crear lo món —no que la hage feta, mes eternalment preparada. E axí, si la matèria del món no és feta per Déu, segueix-se que la terra, l'aygua, lo ayra ne lo foch, ab les altres coses que ells quatre componen, no són fetes per Déu, mes eternalment de eterna matèria.[21] Y aquesta matèria à posada Ovidi sots fictió de Caos, falsament per los antichs imaginat.

Lectanci: —Primer, satisfent a les raons del philòsof en lo que és dit de l'instant que té fi e principi, dich que és ver e lo principi preceeix la fi en prioritat de natura e no de duració. Com instant sia un punt o part del temps indivisible, donchs no és impossible ne implica contradictió ésser en lo instant ensemps fi e principi. En la segona, quant és dit que tota cosa qui comença a ésser, per mutació comença a ésser, etc., dich que és ver en les coses fetes de prejassent matèria per los agents inferiors, mes no és ver en les coses fetes per lo agent superior qui és Déu, com clarament vull amostrar, desfent la falça conclusió de la eternitat del món escrita per Tul·li en lo libre *De natura deorum*.[22] Contra la

---

21 'Primerament [...] matèria': Argued through Cicero, *De natura deorum*, Book II, paragraphs 86–89 (Cicero 2003: 58–64). Alegre may have had access to a direct or indirect source on Cicero.

22 He contradicts Cicero in a dialogue in which different opinions are shared, even if there is a hierarchy in the order they are expressed. As Friedlein (2012) explains, although Plato and Cicero were models for the use of the dialogue form in the ancient times, in

qual, prengam per fonament que poder és tan gran e principal atribut en Déu, que sens ell no seria Déu. Lo home fa de so que és alguna altra cosa perquè per la mortalitat és inàbil, finida e de poca potestat; Déu, emperò, fa creant de açò que no és re u alguna cosa, perquè és eternal e de poder infinit. E, si alguna cosa era feta ans de Déu o sens Déu, perdria lo atribut de ésser omnipotent; lo qual, ell eternal, eternament conserve.[23] És veritat, [140r[138r]] açò?

—Sí —respòs Tul·li—, mes no diem la matèria ésser feta sens Déu o ans de Déu, mes negam totalment que sia estada feta, sinó que és eternalment ab Déu.

—De pus alt vos veig caure —dix en tal pas Lectanci—, donchs dieu dos cosas yguals seran eternalment sens destruir la una a la altra: Déu eternalment té poder; la primera matèria per si eternalment té poder, ¿com duraran aquestes potències eternas sens empatxar la una a l'altra? Da on apar que deu ésser una y simpla la natura del que és eternal, perquè d'ell, com de mena, préngan principi totes les altres coses. E axí, o Déu té dependència de la matèria o la matèria de

the Middle Ages Saint Augustine and Boethius' *De Consolatione Philosophiae* were clear references for Christian authors. In Catalan literature the dialogue form had a significant precedent: the fourteenth-century writer Bernat Metge penned *Apologia*, inspired by Petrarch's *Secretum*, and *Lo somni* (Badia 2014: 218–19).

[23] Whereas Cicero turns to Aristotle to argue that God is eternal, but that nothing can be created from nothing, Lactantius defends the position that God (an eternal being) *can* create from nothing and that this was how He created the world. The (direct or indirect, probably glossed) source of this argumentation comes from Lactantius' *Institutiones divinae*, Book II, chapter 2, 'De origine erroris'. Alegre quotes an excerpt from this work in Latin in the passage I have transcribed. In fact, the last paragraph in Cicero's speech ('Primerament [...] imaginat') already appears in the aforementioned passage by Lactantius, who criticises Cicero's thought. Alegre also quotes the example of the artist/builder from Lactantius. In fact, Alegre seems to know the contents of Lactantius' chapter well. Therefore, Lactantius' allusion to Cicero may have triggered Alegre's representation of a dialectical exchange between the two authors. Note that there is interaction between them. When, later, Alegre deals with the interpretation of the winds, he refers again to Lactantius' work through the *Genealogia deorum gentilium*. The exact quotation from Lactantius was already in Boccaccio. Alegre probably read Boccaccio's reference to Lactantius and decided to turn to this author to explain the origin of the world. Cabré, Coroleu, Ferrer, Lloret and Pujol (2018: 124), regarding notaries and lawyers in Barcelona, affirm: 'Detailed inventories of the holdings of several fifteenth-century private libraries, chiefly in Barcelona, give us a good idea of the breadth of their intellect. As the century advanced, these libraries grew considerably, both in size and in number. This change took place in the course of just three to four decades'. They explain that the library of Bernat d'Esplugues (died 1433) had copies of Livy, Quintilian, Pliny the Younger, Ovid, Virgil, Valerius Maximus, Lactantius and Augustine, among others, such as Boccaccio. Torró (1994) argued that Alegre may have started his translation in Palermo while he was studying Latin with the humanist Giacomo Mirabella. However, he probably returned to Barcelona during the civil war (1462–1472) and revised *Transformacions* before he printed it in Barcelona in 1494 (Bescós 2011: 4–24). In his prologue to the commentary, Alegre represents himself in Montjuïc (on the outskirts of Barcelona) when he received the Virgin's aid to write his commentary.

Déu. Qual de aquestes dos preposicions sia més ab lo ver concertada fàcilment se comprèn, perquè, sentiment de cosa insensada, raonable de irracional, impassible de passible, spiritual de corporal nunca hagué començ. No és Déu procehit de la matèria, ans lo contrari se amostre provable. Per ço que qualsevol cosa composta de espès e contractible cors pot rebre força e dan, lo qui reb dan se disol e mor, lo que mor és nat, lo que és nat té algun pare o principi de qui naix e, com la matèria sia tal, resta que de Déu ha hagut lo començ, pus en ell se troben sentiment, providència e infinit poder, coses necessàries a crear e dar principi.

» Per altra via se prova la matèria primera no ésser eternal, perquè a la cosa a qui manca principi és de necessitat que manque fi, com pus fàcil fos la cosa començada eternalment durar que no finar lo que no té començ. Que lo ésser de aquesta matèria hage hagut fi se prova axí. Tota cosa de què altre és feta, passant en lo ésser nou de la cosa feta, feneix lo ésser seu primer e axí, quant de aquesta matèria fon fet lo món, perquè passa en la substància de aquell, hagué fi lo seu ésser primer. Per on se prova, axí mateix, haver hagut començ *nam quod destruitur hedificatum; quod solvitur, alligatum, quod finitur, inceptum est.*[24]

» E per lo dit resta prou clarament provat la matèria primera e lo món haver hagut principi per acte de crear de aquella perfectíssima natura a qui per Déu honram. Lo qual, perquè de si mateix ha quant ha, és tal com lo ha plagut ésser: impassible, immutable, benuyrat y eternal. Aquest és lo que prehica y creu la militant Església, aquest és aquell que en la triumphant adóran los elets, aquest és per Ovidi nomenat sots scilenci quant diu, parlant de la Creació: "Quisquis fuit ille deorum";[25] en què mostra que no creya algú dels vanament exalçats ésser stat factor del món o creador segons la nostra fe.[26]

Agustí: —De les coses visibles, lo món és la major y Déu de les que no veem, però lo món ésser miram e creem Déu; mes haver Déu creat lo món no creem per algú sinó per Déu veritat infal·lible. E, en quin loch havem hoït a Déu dient ell haver creat lo món? Per cert, no en altre loch que en la Scriptura Santa, a on diu lo seu propheta: "In principio creavit Deus celum et ter-[140v[138v]]ram".[27] Donchs, que fon Moysès present quant Déu crèà la terra e

---

[24] Lactantius, *Institutiones divinae*, Book 2, 'De origine erroris'.

[25] Ovid, *Metamorphoses*, I. 32.

[26] Alegre draws on Lactantius, *Institutiones divinae*, Book II, 'De origine erroris', chapter 9.

[27] Genesis, 1. These Biblical references already appear in Saint Augustine's *City of God*. Alegre seems to know Augustine of Hippo's work well, although he may have obtained some of his quotations from indirect sources (for instance, all the quotations from Cicero in the interpretation of this myth were already in Boccaccio; this is not the case for Augustine). He may have used a copy of *City of God* with glosses. 'An apparatus combining [Thomas] Waley's commentary on books 1–10 and [Nicholas] Trivet's on books 11–22 is found in many extant manuscripts of Augustine's work (Smalley 1960: 58–65 and 88–100)' (Cabré, Coroleu, Ferrer, Lloret and Pujol 2018: 207). Alegre may have had access to a copy with these features. Moreover, there is a Catalan translation of

lo cel? No, mes fon-hi present la saviesa de Déu, per la qual són fetes totes coses; la qual se transfereix en les ànimes santes y los amichs de Déu constitueix prophetes; e narrant en aquells sens remor les grans obres de Déu, e més, que ab ells parlen los àngels de Déu, *qui semper vident faciem patris*,²⁸ e la voluntat sua revèlan als que és degut que sia revelada. Un de aquests axí inspirat fon lo propheta qui dix y scriví: "in principio creavit Deus celum et terram".²⁹ Per tal inspiració David prophetant, en molts lochs testifica aquesta veritat; en lo vuytèn psalm, quant dix: "videbo celos opera digitorum tuorum lunam et stellas qui tu fundasti",³⁰ y en setanta-tres: "Tu fecisti omnes terminos terre estantem et ver tu plasmasti",³¹ y a semblant propòsit, psalmo 88: "Orbem terre et plenitudinnem eius tu fundasti, Aquilonem et mare tu creasti",³² y en lo psalm següent: "Priusquam montes fierent, aut formaretur terra et orbis, a seculo et in seculum tu es",³³ *et* psalmo 94: "Ipsius est mare, et ipse fecit illud: et aridam fundaverunt manus eius",³⁴ e gloriosament conformant-se ab lo dir de Moysès, diu psalmo 101: "In initio tu, Domine, terram fundasti et opera manuum tuarum sunt celi".³⁵

» Lo gran savi Philon, per Déu il·luminat, confessa aquesta veritat en lo primer capítol del llibre *De saviesa*, dient: "Creavit Deus ut essent omnia et sanabiles fecit nationes orbis terrarum".³⁶ E Ysaÿes 66, parlant en persona de Déu, diu: "omnia hec manus mea fecit et facta sunt universa ista dicit Domunus".³⁷ E no sols los nostres prophetes, per Déu inspirats, an testificada aquesta veritat, mes la Sibil·la heritrea, singular entre totes, dix, segons és tret de grech en nostra lengua: "Deus solus unus eminentissimus, qui fecit celum solesque et estellas lunasque, fructiferam terram, aquam et humores ponti".³⁸ Per on clarament se mostre Déu eternal en lo principi haver creat la terra e lo cel —no en lo principi

---

City of God (books 2–10, 1383–early fifteenth century) that included Saint Augustine's text and Raoul de Presles' French commentary based on Trivet's (Cabré, Coroleu, Ferrer, Lloret and Pujol 2018: 207); however, Alegre quotes from a Latin source.

²⁸ Augustine of Hippo, *The City of God*, Book XI, chapter 4.

²⁹ 'De les coses visibles [...] terram': Alegre translates from *City of God* (Book XI, chapter 4). The quotation is from Genesis, 1.

³⁰ Psalm 8: 3.

³¹ Psalm 74: 17.

³² Psalm 89: 11–12.

³³ Psalm 90: 2.

³⁴ Psalm 95: 5.

³⁵ Psalm 102: 25.

³⁶ Wisdom 1: 14.

³⁷ Isaiah 66: 2.

³⁸ Excerpt attributed to the Erythraean Sybil in the *Sybilline Books*. Lactantius (*Institutiones divinae*, Book I, chapter 6) quotes it, as does Saint Augustine in *City of God* (Book XVIII) in Latin.

de la sua duració, la qual és eternal y sens començ, mes en lo principi del temps—, creant ensemps en un instant lo temps e lo món.[39] Per ço no haurà fi en algun temps; mes, acabada o cessant la mesura del moviment dels cels, *secundum prius et posterius*, serà acabat lo temps y lo món ensemps creat ab ell. E axí és stat creat lo món en lo primer instant del temps, com eternalment era per Déu previst.[40] De manera que, per haver creat en tal instant y no ans, no ha loch mutació en Déu, com conega reposant obrar y obrant reposar aquell qui la nova obra quant a nosaltres ordenà ab eternal voler, segons açò yo, quant pus pla he pogut, he tractat en los libres onze e dotze de *La ciutat de Déu*.[41]

» Dexa largues inquisicions, aderex ab lo Apòstol, dient: "Non plus sapere quam oportet sapere".[42] Per què, si és nodrit lo infant ygualant la porció de la virtut, nodrint ab la força del pacient, dispost aprofita y crex; si, emperò, lo nodriment passa los límits del poder del qu·és [141r[139r]] nodrit, ans de créxer és desfet.[43] Axí, lo nostre dèbil enteniment se empaxa en l'aspeculació de les coses sobranaturals y divines. Té per cert que lo corruptible cors dóna empaix a la ànima, no podent traure en acte la força de ses potències, essent vestida de aquesta grossa carn, e lo que ara ignores, procurant-ho los mèrits qui han causat ací nostra venguda, en la pàtria dels elets conexeràs *non per speculum in enigmate*,[44] mes faç a faç, contemplant los profundes secrets de la immensa e divina magestat, seguint la via del faro de la fe en lo baptisme donat a nostres ànimes, del qual diu lo propheta: "Signatum es super nos lumen vultus tui, Deus",[45] *psalmo quarto*.

» Creu fermament que la creació del món no és procehida del Cahos com ha posat Ovidi, ne ha tengut Déu matèria eternalment preparada, ans aquell que ha sabut y pogut de la matèria primera produir diversitat de formes, ha pogut e sabut crear aquella d'on les ha produhides. Si les forces de ton entendre no comprenen la manera, recort-te que Déu no seria infinit si per nostra finida conexença podia ésser comprès. E mira en lo primer capítol de Ovidi si duptes més en res, que, quant en aquest cap creure que est crestià, no·m consent en mes raons estendre per no dismininuir lo mèrit de la fe.

---

[39] 'Per on clarament [...] món': summary from Augustine of Hippo, *City of God*, Book XI, chapter 6.

[40] 'E axí [...] previst': Augustine of Hippo, *City of God*, Book XII, chapter 14.

[41] As Alegre explains in the epilogue, he does not just translate from Boccaccio, but also goes to the sources.

[42] Romans 12: 3.

[43] 'Perquè [...] desfet': As he does with Boccaccio's *Genealogy of the Pagan Gods*, Alegre re-organises the excerpts he translates from other sources. The simile comes from Augustine of Hippo, *City of God*, Book XII, end of chapter 15.

[44] 1 Corinthians 13: 12.

[45] Psalm 4: 6.

(Francesc Alegre, *Transformacions*, Barcelona, Biblioteca de Catalunya [Bon 10–VI–29], printed by Pere Miquel, 1494, fols 138ᵛ [136ʳ]–141ʳ[139ʳ]).

[The venerable masters sat in order around me; Giovanni Boccaccio, who was the moderator of the debate, spoke:

—It has been decided by these men that, before we say anything further, we want to see what you have doubts about. Therefore, without further ado, tell us what you want to know about Ovid and you will be satisfied.

Here the prologue of the 'Allegories and moral expositions' of Ovid's *Metamorphoses* concludes. The first book and chapter begin by dealing with two allegories, on Chaos in species and on the north wind's four sons in the main winds

—Because my understanding[46] wishes to write about the reason Ovid says in the beginning of his book (which addresses the creation of the world) that Chaos ('confusion', as the ancient writers referred to it) was transformed into four elements, I would like to know whether he wanted us to believe this as it is or, if it is a fiction, how it originated.

After they had exchanged all the usual pleasantries between wise men who want to honour each other, St Augustine, as the president of that admirable forum, began by saying:

—In my opinion, without further ado, since he has Giovanni Boccaccio as an adviser, he should answer as our moderator and decide who, among our forum of twenty, will express their views. It is the intelligence of his great and reflexive judgement that has procured him [Boccaccio] this position.

All of them praised St Augustine's words, and the Tuscan poet, obeying him, said:

—I wanted to devote my study to search the genealogy of the ancient gods to acquiesce to the request of the excellent king of Cyprus. First, I thought about that ancient Demogorgon, falsely believed a god and, together with him, about Eternity and Chaos, equal to him in age. Ovid refers to Chaos and this is what was believed by ancient men, with differences due to chronological differences and different minds. To offer you the full information of what you are looking for, first Theodontius will recite where and why this error began. Next, Cicero will speak for all the philosophers by explaining what they have stated on the beginning of the world. The discussant Firmianus Lactantius will defeat all the wrong statements on the eternity of the world by means of strong arguments. Finally, Saint Augustine will declare what the Church believes.

He said nothing else, and Theodontius began:

[46] As a faculty which deals with comprehension.

—The cause of this foolish belief is the people from Arcadia, a region located inland, far from the sea. Because they saw the earth growing trees, plants and different types of flowers, they believed there was a hidden divinity in her. They were even more convinced when they heard an earthquake and raging winds blowing. They thought all these things came from earth. And, what's more, they went into deep caves and the more they walked and moved away from external light, they felt their trembling hearts and thought that movement, sign of fear, came from a majesty who was hidden in that place. This is why they affirmed that a great god named Demogorgon lived in earth. This is a Greek name which means 'god of the earth', because *demon* in Greek means god and *gorgon*, earth.

And, because they understood, with the roughness of their common intelligence, that the god had to be eternal, they said Eternity, Demogorgon's sister, had been with him forever. Afterwards, led by their false imagination, they said Chaos was the same age as them. This Greek name means confusion, which refers to the way in which the elements and elemental bodies joined together, as Ovid explains in the first chapter. Since all the existing things took form from matter, they considered that the eternal god must eternally have had matter ready to create the world. Ovid then says that cold things repel hot ones, soft things repel hard ones, light things repel heavy ones. It was God Almighty who distributed these things and, as it says, He gave nature the best. All the matters that have been sketched out have been addressed in depth by philosophers by means of the paint brush of their wise judgement, as you will hear from the father of eloquence.

Cicero: —By seeking to determine the truth of uncertain things, the thoughts of continuous sleepless nights and diligent efforts have done so much good in the world that the true theosophy takes root in the wit of the first perceptions. The ancient philosophers understood, by researching, that there had to be a beginning in order to avoid an infinite process. However, they did not consider the world to be created from nothing, but Nicomachus' great son, master of the truth, light of philosophy, states in the first of the *Physics*: *from nothing comes nothing*. According to this proposition, he works to prove in his philosophy the eternity of the world, which was not created nor had a beginning. I will not elaborate on all his arguments, but I will explain two of them:

» The first one: each instant has a beginning and an end; if the instant did not have a beginning and an end, it would not be an instant but eternal duration, which we know it is not; thus, we are constrained to admit that any instant has a beginning and an end. It follows that, if the world was created from nothing, in the instant in which it would have been created its beginning and end would have been there at the same time, which is impossible; therefore, the world has not been created. The second argument is: every new thing needs a certain mutation in order to come into being, because if there is no mutation, it could not become to be something from not being anything. Thus, if the world has begun to be, this has to be due to a mutation: not a mutation from itself into itself, which would not be called a mutation, but because of the mutation of another thing. Therefore, it must have been an exchange of things before the world ever was. From this, the world became what it is and, before that mutation, there was another thing *and it goes on forever*. Since one cannot go on indefinitely, this means that the world (or, at least, the matter that gave it its new form through a mutation) is eternal. In support of these arguments I wrote *De natura deorum*, in which I affirm:

» First, it cannot be proved that the matter which originated all things was created by Divine Providence, but it must have and must have had power by its own nature, just as the artist who wants to build something does not put together the matter to construct the building himself, but it has already been prepared. Consequently, this means that God already had matter to create the world; he did not create the matter, but was eternally ready. Thus, if God did not create the matter that originated the world, it follows that He did not create soil, water, air or fire, together with all the things that are formed by the four elements but come from eternal matter. Ovid names this matter Chaos in his fable, as it was falsely imagined to be in ancient times.

Lactantius: —First, I will answer the philosopher's arguments on the instant having an end and a beginning. I confirm it is true, and the beginning precedes the end in priority of nature, but not in duration. Because an instant is a spot in or part of the indivisible time, it is not impossible or contradictory to have an end and a beginning in the same instant. Second, it has been said that every new thing needs a certain mutation to start being, etc. Although it is certainly true for things made of pre-existing matter by the inferior agents, it is not true for the things created by the superior agent, God, as I want to prove by undoing Cicero's false conclusion in the book *De natura deorum*, which defends the world's eternity. Against this conclusion, bear in mind that power is a primary and important attribute of God; without it, God would not be God. Human beings make something out of something because mortals are unqualified, finite and powerless. Nevertheless, God creates something out of nothing because He is eternal and has infinite power. If there were something made before God or without God, He would lose his attribute as an omnipotent being, but he is eternal and maintains His attribute forever. Is this true?

—Yes —answered Cicero—; however, we do not say that matter was made without God or before God, but deny absolutely that it had been created, as it was eternally with God.

—You are wrong, though —said Lactantius at this point—, as you argue that both will coexist forever without destroying one another: God has eternal power, primary matter has eternal power by itself, how will these eternal powers endure without disturbing each other? So it seems that there must be one simple nature of what it is eternal, because out of it, as its origin, all the other things will be born. Thus, either God is dependent on matter or matter is dependent on God. It is easy to understand which one of the two clauses is closer to the truth because no living thing has ever been made out of an inanimate thing, a rational thing out of an irrational one, a sensitive thing out of an insensitive one, a spiritual thing out of a corporal one. God does not originate in matter; in fact, the opposite can be proved. Everything with a thick and contractile body can receive force and damage. Damaged things dissolve and die. What is dead, was once born. If it was born, it has a father or a principle that gives birth to it. Because this is the case of matter, it follows that it had originated in God, who has the faculty to feel, providence and infinite power, all necessary things to create and to originate something.

» That primary matter is not eternal can be proved by other arguments. It is necessary that a thing that does not have a beginning lacks an end, as it is easier for something that has already started to be to last forever than for something with no beginning to finish. I will now prove that this matter has stopped being. When something comes out of another thing, it becomes a new being at the same time that its past being concludes. Thus, when this matter originated the world, as it became its substance, its past being disappeared. This means that matter also had a beginning, *as everything that is demolished, was previously built; everything being untied was first tied; all that finishes had a beginning.*

The aforementioned arguments clearly prove that both primary matter and the world had a beginning in the act of creation of the perfect nature we call God. As God has what he has only because of himself, He is as he wanted to be, impassive, immutable, blessed and eternal. The militant Church preaches about Him and believes in Him. He is adored by the chosen ones in all his glory. Ovid refers to him in silence when he says, regarding Creation: '*Whichever God he was*', by which he suggests that he did not believe that any of the vainly adored gods was the author of the world or its creator, according to our faith.

Augustine: —Among all the visible things, the world is the main one, as God is among the invisible ones; but we see the existence of the world and we believe in God. However, we do not believe in God's creation of the world because of somebody, but because of God, as an infallible truth. Where did we hear God saying He created the world? As a matter of fact, in the Holy Scriptures his prophet says: '*In the beginning, God created the heavens and the earth*'. Did Moses witness the creation of the heavens and the earth? He did not, but God's wisdom was there, as it is responsible for making everything. God's wisdom is transferred into the holy souls and, by it, the friends of God become prophets; and, in silence, it tells them the great deeds of God and, what is more, the angels of God, *who always see our Father's face*, talk to them. And they reveal His will to the ones to whom it needs to be revealed. The prophet who said and wrote as follows was inspired like this: '*In the beginning, God created the heavens and the earth*'. By this inspiration, David was a prophet. He testifies this truth in many places. In the eighth psalm, he says: '*When I look at your heavens, the work of your fingers, | the moon and the stars, which you have set in place*', and in psalm 73: '*You have fixed all the boundaries of the earth; | you have made summer and winter*', and in psalm 88: '*The heavens are yours; the earth is also yours; | the world and all that is in it, you have founded them. | The north and the south, you have created them*', and in the following psalm: '*Before the mountains were brought forth,* | *or ever you had formed the earth and the world,* | *from everlasting to everlasting you are God*', and psalm 94: '*The sea is his, for he made it,* | *and his hands formed the dry land*', and psalm 101, in perfect agreement with Moses: '*Of old you laid the foundation of the earth,* | *and the heavens are the work of your hands*'.

» The great wise man Philo, inspired by God, confesses this truth in the first book of *Book of Wisdom* by saying: '*For He created all things so that they might exist; the generative forces of the world are wholesome*'. And Isaiah 66, giving voice to God, says: '*Has not My hand made all these things? And so they came into being, declares the Lord*'. And not only our prophets, inspired by God, have testified this truth, but also the Erythraean Sybil, unique among all of them, said (according to what it has been translated from Greek into Latin): '*But there is one only God of pre-eminent power, who made the heaven, and sun, and stars, and moon, and fruitful earth, and waves of the water of the sea*'.[47] Which clearly proves that, by creating the earth and heaven in the beginning – not in the beginning of the existence of God, who is eternal and does not have a beginning, but in the beginning of time – God, who is eternal, created the time and the world at the same instant. This is the reason they will not stop existing: when, *according to priority and posteriority*, the measurement of the movement of the heavens stops, the time and the world (created together) will come to an end. And this is how the world was created in the first instant of time, as God had anticipated eternally. Therefore, there is no change in God due to the fact that He created at a certain instant and not before, because God, who started a new work with an eternal design, can act while He reposes and He can repose while He acts,[48] as I have explained, as clearly as I can, in books 11 and 12 of *The City of God*.

» Abstain from hazardous questions and obey the wholesome injunction of the apostle, who says: '*Do not think of yourself more highly than you ought*'. For if an infant receive nourishment suited to his strength, it becomes capable, as it grows, of taking more; but if its strength and capacity be overtaxed, it dwines away in place of growing.[49] Similarly, the speculation on supernatural and divine things fills up our weak understanding. Be assured that the soul is limited by our perishable body in a way that it [the soul] cannot channel the strength of its power as it is dressed of thick flesh. What you are ignorant of now, your achievements (which have led us here) allowing, you will know in the land of the chosen ones *not only as a reflection in a mirror*, but face to face,

---

[47] Trans. by Schaff (2017: 21).

[48] I have consulted Saint Augustine of Hippo's *City of God* (Book XII, chapter 14) in the online version, www.documenta-catholicaomnia.eu/ [accessed 5 May 2020] as an aid to translate this sentence.

[49] I also follow the aforementioned translation of Saint Augustine's work for the translation of this paragraph, with very small changes whenever Alegre summarises Saint Augustine.

fully knowing the deep secrets of the great and divine majesty. We will be following the path enlightened by the faith our souls were given in baptism, when the prophet says: '*Shine the Light of Your face upon us, O Lord*', *fourth psalm.*

» Firmly believe that Chaos did not originate the creation of the world, as Ovid says, and that God did not have matter eternally ready, but He who knew how and was able to create many forms out of primary matter, was also able to and knew how to create the matter to produce them. If your understanding does not comprehend how, let me remind you that God would not be infinite if it was possible for our finite knowledge to comprehend Him. And if you have any other doubt, look into Ovid's first chapter, because, as He is believed to be Christian, I cannot extend my arguments to avoid diminishing the importance of faith].[50]

Here Alegre closes the first 'allegory' or interpretation. After these explanations, the narrator is satisfied with the authority of the arguments. Because he wants to resolve doubts regarding other myths and does not wish to keep such prestigious authors for long, he then asks about the winds.

In conclusion, Alegre creates an original work by means of his commentary. The commentary agrees with his description of his own methodology in the paratextual materials (the epilogue). Firstly, the order of participation of the twenty authors in the dialogue (that is, its structure) is Alegre's work and it is not necessarily subject to Boccaccio's *Genealogia deorum gentilium*. The order is also relevant because it points to a certain hierarchy: the author who participates last has the chance to reject or validate the arguments of the prior discussants. In fact, in the interpretation of the first myth, it is Saint Augustine who plays this role, the same author who is represented as the president of the discussion.

Secondly, although Alegre acknowledges Boccaccio as his main source in the 'Al·legories e morals exposicions', he is not merely translating from the *Genealogia deorum gentilium*. Even when he draws on it, he summarises its content rather than translate Boccaccio closely. It is also relevant that Alegre completes the information he takes from this work, used as a mythographical encyclopaedia, with other authors already mentioned by Boccaccio. In the interpretation of the first myth of Alegre's commentary, Boccaccio, as the adviser to the fictional forum of twenty authors, introduces the order of speech of the *auctoritates* who take part in this particular discussion (which are not the twenty authors). The starting point for discussing the creation of the world is the Demogorgon, which Alegre

---

[50]   The italics in the English version are mine and mark Alegre's quotations in Latin. The quotations from the Bible are from *Online Bible Study Hub*, https://biblehub.com/ [accessed 5 May 2020].

borrows from *Genealogia deorum gentilium*, who is presented as the first god in Boccaccio's third preface. Then, Theodontius starts the discussion, but Alegre still depends on the *Genealogia deorum gentilium*. However, Alegre shows some knowledge of the content of the works of the other three authors participating in the debate (maybe Cicero and, particularly, Lactantius and Saint Augustine). He quotes their works in Latin; therefore, he does not seem to use the Catalan translation of *The City of God*.

There is an animated exchange between Cicero and Lactantius. The fact that Lactantius quotes Cicero in the *Institutiones Divinae* may have given Alegre the idea of representing a discussion between the two authors. We cannot affirm that Alegre had a copy of Cicero's *De natura deorum*, even though along with Seneca Cicero was the most renowned ancient philosopher at in the Crown of Aragon in the fourteenth and the fifteenth centuries, as Pujol (2014: 150) explains. Later, Alegre quotes other works penned by Cicero, such as *De natura deorum*. Nevertheless, he seems to have a sound knowledge of Lactantius' and Saint Augustine's work (probably in a glossed copy). The analysis of Alegre's use of sources in his commentary gives relevant information on the breadth of learning of this author, a citizen of Barcelona, consul in Palermo and the son of a merchant (see Torró 1994, Bescós 2011).

The fact that Alegre repeatedly transcribes quotations in Latin (not only from the Bible), suggests that the intended readers of 'Al·legories e morals exposicions' were able to understand them. As stated above, we know that some of the owners of *Transformacions* alo had copies of Ovid's *Metamorphoses* in Latin (Peña Díaz 1997). Nevertheless, the examination of the preserved incunabula of Alegre's work have few marginalia, and so we cannot speculate about the real interests of the readers. The lack of rich reading marks may point to a certain *auctoritas* conferred on the *Transformacions*. I have only identified two incunabula that link the Catalan translation with the Latin verses. In the margin of the Stuttgart incunabulum we read 'la terra, egualada ab sos pesos, no penjava' in folio 1^r[3^r], the Latin correspondence of Ovid's *Metamorphoses*, I. 12 and incunabulum 2435 in Biblioteca Nacional de España presents a correction: 'fins que lo alt Déu departí e a la natura donà millor ésser' with 'déu o millor natura dissolgué' (fol. 1^r[3^r]), which is a faithful translation of Ovid's verse 21 in Book I.[51]

Finally, in addition to the twenty authors who feature as characters in the dialogue with the narrator, Alegre uses at least one other source that he does not acknowledge, either in the prologue or within the text. This source is

---

[51] Stuttgart, Württembergische Landesbibliothek Stuttgart, Alte und wertvolle Drucke: Inc. fol. 12167 and Madrid, Biblioteca Nacional de España, INC/2435.

Bonsignori, whose influence can be seen in both the commentary and the translation; an example is the interpretation of the myth of Pyramus and Thisbe in Book IV in the 'Al·legories e morals exposicions', as argued in Pellissa Prades (2017).

The analysis of the direct and indirect sources in Alegre's commentary in full, together with the characteristics of the copies he used (glosses, paratextual materials), and the study of his creative role as an author (not only as a translator) are key to an assessment of the literary ambitions of 'Al·legories e morals exposicions'. In contrast with other vernacular versions of Ovid's *Metamorphoses* such as the *Ovide moralisé* and Bonsignori's *Ovidio Metamorphoseos Vulgare*, Alegre writes an autonomous commentary, with an original structure: a dialogue that takes place within a fictional framework in which the narrator is self-represented. Although Alegre prints the translation and the commentary together and refers to both parts in the paratextual materials accompanying the edition, the 'Al·legories e morals exposicions' are more ambitious, but also more demanding for their readers. Whereas in the translation of the Latin poem Alegre uses various techniques to make sure that the text (especially, its cultural references) is accessible to his readers (through vulgarisation, brief glosses, and so on), in the 'Al·legories e morals exposicions' there are many quotations in Latin which coexist with philosophical arguments. Alegre's knowledge of the prestigious authors he quotes is not limited to what Boccaccio gathers from them; sometimes, they engage with each other enthusiastically, as we have seen with Cicero and Lactantius. Furthermore, even though the prologue to the 'Al·legories e morals exposicions' may suggest that the narrator is adopting the role of the disciple, with Boccaccio's permission, at certain points in the commentary he feels free to participate in the exchange with original interpretations of his own (Pellissa Prades 2020). Alegre is, in fact, building his own *auctoritas* in a work in the vernacular under Boccaccio's eyes.

5

BARRY TAYLOR

ALLEGORICAL READINGS OF OVID'S
METAMORPHOSES IN GOLDEN AGE SPAIN

The year 1585 saw the first edition of Juan Pérez de Moya's *Philosofía secreta, donde debaxo de historias fabulosas, se contiene mucha doctrina, provechosa a todos estudios*. Pérez de Moya explains: 'De cinco modos se puede declarar una fábula, conviene a saber: literal, alegórico, anagógico, tropológico, y físico o natural' (Pérez de Moya 1995: 69) [A myth may be interpreted in five ways, namely: literal, allegorical, anagogical, tropological, and physical or natural].[1] In his influential *Ovid and the Renascence in Spain* of 1913 (reprinted as recently as 1995 and 2015), the eminent Hispanist Rudolph Schevill, co-editor of Cervantes, was explicit in his scorn for this example of the backwardness of Spanish culture: 'It seems incredible that this book of almost a thousand pages, attempting to interpret mythological names, chiefly from Ovid, in a traditional way, should have seen the light at so recent a date' (Schevill 1913: 14, n. 21).[2]

In 1613, in the *Carta en respuesta a la que le escribieron*, which many take as his poetic testament, Luis de Góngora argues that the *Metamorphoses* are obscure and present a superficial (i.e. literal) sense that must be pierced with effort:

> y si la obscuridad y estilo intrincado de Ovidio, que en lo *de Ponto* y en lo *de Tristibus* fue tan claro como se ve y tan obscuro en las *Transformaciones*, da causa a que vacilando el entendimiento, en fuerza de discurso trabajándolo (pues crece con cualquier acto de calor), alcance lo que así en la lectura superficial de sus versos no pudo entender luego, hase de confesar que tiene utilidad avivar el ingenio, y eso nació de la obscuridad del poeta. (Carreira 1990: 342)

> [Ovid is so clear in the *Tristia* and *Ex Ponto* and so obscure in the *Metamorphoses*.[3] The obscurity of Ovid causes the reader's understanding to attain what it could not immediately grasp literally. Obscurity does this by working

---

[1] All the translations are my own unless otherwise noted.

[2] Schevill was referring to the second edition, of 1599.

[3] The *Tristia* and *Ex Ponto* were more common than the *Metamorphoses* as school texts (for instance in the Jesuit *Ratio studiorum*: Gómez Rodeles 1901).

the understanding over and making it vacilate. The understanding grows by
being heated. Obscure poetry is useful because it awakens the reader's wit.]

He thus continues a manner of thinking which Schevill dismissed in Pérez
de Moya thirty years before.

Are these allegorical readings symptomatic of the cultural belatedness
which marked Spain out from the rest of Catholic Europe? In order to
attempt to answer this question I shall survey the history of Ovidian
allegoresis in Spain, putting it in the broader context of the reading of Ovid
in Italy and France. I shall also survey very briefly theories of fable in more
modern times and conclude with a few examples of Ovidian imitation.

My Spanish material includes translations of the *Metamorphoses*,
commentaries and editions, and imitations in longer narrative poems and
the drama. I shall not include the visual arts, as I feel the connections
between the sister arts are often exaggerated, and that art and literature, if
they develop together, do so at different speeds (Allen 2002). (Incidentally,
the two main Ovidian pictorial cycles of the Golden Age, the *poesie* painted
by Titian for Philip II and Rubens's paintings for the Torre de la Parada for
Philip IV, have left virtually no documents which might explain how
contemporaries 'read' them; Nash 1985, Alpers 1971.) Only two of the
Spanish Ovids I shall cite are illustrated. And as the reception of classical
myth, called 'fábula' in the Golden Age, was largely coterminous with that
of Ovid's *Metamorphoses*, I shall allow myself a certain licence in
understanding Spanish references to 'fábula' as being applicable to Ovid.

Theory of Fable

Most readings of myth, even modern ones, are broadly allegorical: that is, it
is axiomatic that it 'says one thing and means another' (Isidore, *Etymologiae*,
I. 37). Golden Age Spain inherited various classical and medieval interpretations of myth. For some, myths were the attempts of primitive man to
explain physical phenomena: 'limping Vulcan, because in nature fire never
goes straight' (Isidore, *Etymologiae*, I. 40). This goes back as far as Theagenes
of Rhegium (sixth century BC; Bulfinch 1993: 370), and Lucretius
(Morford and Lenardon 2003: 673), and as far forward as Max Müller
(1856; Morford and Lenardon 2003: 7).

According to the doctrine called Euhemerism, after Euhemerus of
Messene (*c.* 300 BC), the gods were originally humans. This was not a
Christian invention. It was influential on Augustine, *The City of God against
the Pagans*, VII. 18 (Morford and Lenardon 2003: 669). In this tradition is
Eusebius, who placed various mythical figures in his world chronology,
which he could only do on the assumption that they had actually existed as

persons. In Spain, the myths which Alfonso X takes from Ovid are placed in a chronological context (Brancaforte 1990).

A peculiarly medieval contribution to the reading of myth was the idea that pagan authors adumbrated the tenets of Christianity because they were privileged with an imperfect revelation of scripture: after all, Moses was earlier than Ovid. As part of this approach we find the application of the four senses of biblical exegesis: just as the Old Testament prefigured the New Testament, so pagan literature could prefigure Christianity, as Dante (1980: 64–69) argues in his comments on Orpheus in the *Convivio*. One feature of this was readings which made Orpheus or Narcissus figures of Christ (Moss 1982: 27).

An offshoot of the moral sense of myths is exemplarism, which treats the deeds of the gods as a repository of moral exempla, good and bad. This moralistic treatment of a text is certainly not exclusive to readings of myth: exemplarism has a much longer history, from antiquity to the present (Lyons 1989).

After 1700 the opinions of Fontenelle come as a blast of fresh air: writing in the 1690s but not published till 1724, he says: 'Those that made the fables were not the men to understand moral and physical nature, let alone discover the art of disguising such knowledge under borrowed images [...] So let us not look for anything in the fables except the history of the errors of the human mind' (Feldman and Richardson 1972: 18; Fontenelle 1932: 39). (In Spain, Feijoo was skeptical about Euhemerism and the relationship between the Bible and pagan myth, which he thought was only valid in a few cases (Trousson 1965–1966).)

Freud, *c.* 1900, returned to allegory. For him, myths are comparable with dreams because they 'reflect people's waking efforts to systematize the incoherent visions and impulses of their sleep world' (Morford and Lenardon 2003: 8).

Since Freud, interpretations have been less allegorical. For J. G. Frazer, 'Myth implies ritual, ritual implies myth' (Morford and Lenardon 2003: 11). The founder of this school is generally said to be W. Robertson Smith, *Lectures on the Religion of the Semites* (1894), for whom 'all myths were closely dependent on rituals [...] not entirely removed from savage ones' (Kirk 1974: 15). This link between myth and ritual is already in Ovid himself, in the *Fasti* (which Frazer edited for Loeb Classical Library in 1931). Malinowski (around the time of World War I) explains myths not in cosmic or mysterious terms, but as 'charters' of social customs and beliefs (Morford and Lenardon 2003: 11). Finally, Lévi-Strauss probably represents an extreme in the movement away from allegorism, being more concerned with the relation (usually binary) between the elements of myth: for him they do not mean something outside – in striking contrast to the medieval allegorists (Morford and Lenardon 2003: 12).

Readings of Fable in Spain and Elsewhere

This then is the range of possible readings of myth. I shall now proceed to a survey of actual readings. My interest is to a lesser extent when new ideas come in, and to a greater extent how long they survive. Taking my cue from the four scriptural senses, I shall distinguish between 'moral' and 'spiritual' allegories, the first of which tells us how to behave and the second addresses less day-to-day questions of the relationship between man and God.

Most of my examples are concerned with the myth of Acteon, beginning with Fulgentius, Bishop of Ruspe (d. 532).

> Fabula Acteonis. Curiositas semper periculorum germana: detrimenta suis amatoribus novit parturire, quam gaudia. Acteon denique venator Dianam lavantem vidisse dicitur: qui in cervum conversus a canibus suis non agnitus eorum morsibus devoratus est. Anasimenes: qui de picturis antiquis disseruit in libro .ii. ait venationem Acteonem dilexisse: qui cum ad maturam pervenisset aetatem desideratis venationum periculis .i. quasi nudam artis suae rationem videns timidus factus est: unde & cor cervi habere dicitur & Homerus ait […] .i. ebriose oculos canis habens & cor cervi. Sed dum periculum venandi fugeret: affectum tamen canum non dimisit: quos inaniter pascendo pene omnem substantiam perdidit: ob hanc rem a canibus suis devoratus dicitut [sic] esse. (1500?: fol. 4ᵛ)

> [Curiosity is the sister of dangers; it creates more harm than pleasure for its devotees. Acteon loved hunting, but when he came to maturity he saw the rationale of hunting nakedly for what it was and became timid like a stag. But he kept on his dogs, which consumed his finances, which is why he is said to have been eaten up by his dogs.]

We see that Fulgentius's interpretation is aimed at actually elucidating what he sees as the metaphorical language of the text, which he keeps in sight at all times. Although a Christian, he does not interpret the fable as referring to the Bible. We might also see his allegory as an explaining away of the text by treating it as metaphorical rather than literal.

A different tack is taken by the *Ovide moralisé* and a different work, the Latin *Ovidius moralizatus* of Pierre Bersuire (Berchorius). Both are of the fourteenth century. The French work need concern us less, as it was never printed in our period, although there was a manuscript Spanish translation (Carr 1992). Bersuire submits Ovid to the four biblical senses, which are summarized in the couplet:

Littera gesta docet; qui credas, allegoria;
moralis, quid agas; quo tendas, anagogia.

(Caplan 1929: 286)

[The literal teaches of things done [the story or history]; the allegorical is what you believe; what you do is the moral sense; and the anagogical is about your [eternal] destiny].

Bersuire's use of the techniques of biblical exegesis makes perfect sense when one recalls that the *Ovidius moralizatus* was intended as Book XV of the *Reductorium morale*, a larger work for preachers, Book XVI being the *Moralizationes Biblie*. Bersuire is not interested in the literal meaning of the myths, and his especial focus is on interpreting the various mythological characters as figures of Christ.

This type of allegory was mocked by reformers such as Luther (Seznec 1940: 87) and Erasmus (1986: 134, cited Moss 1982: 27), and after some two hundred years was also out of favour with the Catholic Church. In 1559 the *Index librorum prohibitorum* (Moss 1982: 27) prohibited 'In Ovidii Metamorphoseos libros Commentaria, sive Enarrationes allegoricae, vel tropologicae'. This I think explains why the copy of Francesc Alegre's translation of the *Metamorphoses* printed in 1494 with allegorical commentary (Pellissa 2017 and 2019) in Barcelona University Library has certain deletions removing the allegories (Badia 1986: 88). It is not entirely clear why the ban was introduced. Ann Moss (1982: 27) thinks the objection was not to the interpretations themselves, but to their unsystematic nature. I think the ban could also reflect a growing Counter-Reformation acceptance of Renaissance philology and a keener sense of the divisions between cultures, tied up with a growing sense of anachronism. Another factor must surely be the idea that Scripture has a special status and unique capacity for holding allegorical truths (Green 1957; Mölk 1966–1967: 424n), a medieval argument that resurfaced in the sixteenth and seventeenth centuries (Roses Lozano 1994: 102).

A particularly influential handbook in Spain was Boccaccio's *De genealogia deorum gentilium*, begun *c*. 1350, printed in Latin from 1472 to 1532 and in Italian till 1627. There was a Spanish translation for Santillana by Martín de Ávila, but this was never printed (Gómez Sánchez 2001). Boccaccio makes brief mention of three of the four biblical senses (Seznec 1940: 190), but generally his interpretations are spiritual without being Christ-centred.

The Italian translation of the *Metamorphoses* by Giovanni Bonsignori (Guthmüller 2008), written in the fourteenth century and printed up to 1520, uses a much narrower range of interpretative tools, relating the fables by reference to Ovid's life, or interpreting them as moral exempla:

Allegoria. Ovidio pose questa fabula che la dea fesse ingiustamente contra di
Ateon per exempio: {a} perciò che egli fu mandato in exilio da Octaviano
perche gli vide lo imperatore vituperosamente carnalmente peccare. {b} Overo
egli disse per che egli vide l' imperatrice nuda come nel exordio dinanci se
dichiara. {c} Questa fabula si espone in altra forma piu morale: cioe Ateon fu
uno anticho caciatore e fu maestro de le cacie: per la qual cosa essendo vivo li
caciatori lo adoraro per lo idio. {d} Ma advene chel cazare gli vene in odio e piu
non attendeva ala caza: impercio che vedeva esser cosa vana. E cio conoscendo
lasso l'arte dil cazare in tutto lo abandono. Ma i cani non lasso: anci li retenea
con seco che ne havea grande moltitudine. I quali cani per la molta spesa si lo
consumaro dogni havere impercio che non guardava nulla. Et perche Diana era
dea de li caciatori: dice Ovidio che Ateon vide Diana nuda cioe che poi che si
vide ogni cosa consumata vide Diana nuda: cioe vide che la caccia el tenere de
cani lhaviano denudato dogni havere & dogni suo thesoro: e dice che divento
cervo: vuol dire che lhuomo che viene di richeza in poverta diventa timido e
superbo, si come e el cervo. & non ardisse di apparere infra la gente, & cosi da
li altri ricchi è riputato come bestia. (Bonsignori 1520: fol. xvᵛ)

[Ovid put this fable in which the goddess acted unjustly against Acteon as an
example: {a} because Ovid was sent into exile by Octavian because he saw the
Emperor sinning carnally. {b} Or, he said that he saw the Empress naked. {c}
This fable is expounded more morally: that is, Acteon was an ancient huntsman
who was master of the chase, and therefore in his lifetime the hunters
worshipped him as a god. {d} But it happened that hunting became odious to
him. His dogs ate him out of house and home and he became a stag because the
man who comes from riches into poverty becomes unsociable and proud, like
the stag.]

Thus Bonsignori has two explanations which interpret the text in the light
of the life of the author {a, b}; and one which follows Fulgentius {d} with
the added element of Euhemerism {c}.

In France the printer-publisher Colard Mansion produced the *Bible des
poètes*, 'a French prose version of the *Metamorphoses* with allegorical
interpretations derived from Bersuire and the *Ovide moralisé* (Moss 1982:
23). Written in 1482, it was printed from 1484 to 1531. Both Mansion and
Bersuire ceased to be printed about the same time.

The Italian Raphael Regius produced what we might recognize as a
modern philological commentary on the *Metamorphoses*. His comments are
largely concerned with rhetorical features. The usefulness of his edition is
shown by its being in print for a hundred years (1493–1586) (Moss 1982:
28–31).

Petrus Lavinius, *Tropologicae enarrationes* on *Metamorphoses* I. 1–451, is a
late example of a critic who believed Ovid to have been divinely inspired.
First published in 1510, Lavinius was still in print in the 1570s in the
company of Regius (Moss 1982: 31–35).

A popular French translation, *Le Grand Olympe des hystoires poetiques*, is printed from 1532 to 1604 and has no allegories at all:

> [The French have translated Ovid into French] digne que tel livre soit par icelle [la langue françoise] leu selon le naturel du livre sans allegories; lesquelles mieulx que ailleurs sont traictees par Fulgence en ses Mithologies, lequel avec celeste faveur au premier jour parlera francoys. (*Le grand Olympe* 1537: fol. I')

> [The *Metamorphoses* are worthy to be read in French according to its literal sense without allegories, which are best discussed by Fulgentius, who will one day speak French.]

(Note that the translator has not omitted the allegories of Fulgentius because he is opposed to them.)

Lodovico Dolce's Italian translation (printed 1539–1570; Bucchi 2011), in thirty *canti*, has brief moralities which first appeared in Giolito's edition of 1561 (Dolce 1570: fol. 35'):

> Allegoria. Per Atheone trasformato per cagione di haver veduta Diana in cervo, e lacerato da propri cani, si dinota l'huomo profano che trascorso in qualche errore, ben che altra pena non gli segua, è molestato e traffito dalla propria coscienza.

> [Acteon means the profane man who, caught in some error, even though he suffers no other punishment, is troubled by his own conscience.]

Dolce's interpretation, unlike for example Fulgentius's, is little concerned with the text itself, and uses a broader interpretation of a type which will become more common. He was a best-seller, and was influential in Spain (on Pérez de Moya and Mey).[4]

With Jorge de Bustamante we come to the first Spanish translation of the *Metamorphoses*. The first edition is believed to be Salamanca 1536 (Ruiz Fidalgo 1994, n. 204), and it appears in the inventory of Fernando de Rojas in 1541 (Infantes 1998: 33). The first dated edition is 1542 and the last 1664. The translation is in prose, and there are no commentaries (until very late). However, Bustamante does set out some principles in a long prologue. The position he adopts recalls that of the earliest Christian writers for whom paganism was a living enemy:

> [I wish] con toda brevedad dezir quienes fueron algunos de los principales dioses de la ciega & vana gentilidad; y esto por que vean los que vieren esta obra quanta merced hizo Dios al que truxo a la religion christiana. (Bustamante 1546: fol. 2')

---

[4] For further insights into Dolce's translation see Giuseppe Capriotti's article in Chapter 10 of this volume.

[I wish to say with all brevity who were some of the principal gods of blind and vain paganism; and this so that those who see this work will see how great was God's mercy to him whom he brought to the Christian religion.]

He combines Euhemerism (citing 'Euchemero', fol. A3ʳ) with physical interpretations: he explains pagan gods originated as men who were set up as idols, such as Ninus; but also says the Romans called everything they feared 'gods' (fol. A5ʳ), and quotes the prophet, who says the pagan gods 'todos son demonios' [are all devils] (fol. A5ᵛ). With the coming of Jesus Christ the pagans saw the errors of their ways, 'como desto en nuestros tiempos tenemos experiencia en las Indias que agora cada dia se descubren que entrando en ellas el sanctissimo sacramento desapareciendo los demonios luego los indios conocen y menosprecian la vanidad de sus ydolos' (fols A5ᵛ–6ʳ) [as we have experience of this in our time in the Indies, which are discovered every day; for as the most holy sacrament enters there and the devils disappear, the Indians immediately know and despise the vanity of their idols]. To a degree Bustamante's pugnacious attitude to paganism can be attributed to the contemporary encounter between Europeans and Indians in the New World, but I wonder if he is also indebted to Augustine in *The City of God against the Pagans*.

His interpretations are moralizing: for him transformation into animals symbolizes moral degradation (fol. A7ʳ), and the ancient authors' purpose:

en inventar estas ficciones que no fue otro sino mostrar a los hombres muchos avisos y astucias para mas sabia y prudentemente vivir […] para que debaxo de la honesta recreacion de tan apazibles cuentos contados con alguna similitud de verdad poder induzir los curiosos lectores a muchas vezes leer su abscondida moralidad y que toda va fundada en manifestar las condiciones de los hombres […] sublimando las virtudes y vituperando los viciosos. (fol. A6ʳ)

[in inventing these fictions was none other than to show men many astute counsels to live more wisely and prudently, in order, under the decent recreation of such pleasant tales, told with a certain likeness to truth, to be able to induce the curious readers to often read their hidden morality, and all is founded on showing the conditions of men, praising virtues and blaming the vicious.]

So Bustamante has produced an entertaining prose narrative with a likeness of truth which teaches a lesson, like many another novel, romance or history (Coroleu 2006). His interpretations, brief and confined to his prefatory matter, are moral rather than spiritual.

Giovanni Andrea dell'Anguillara's Italian translation (printed 1561–1840; Cotugno 2007: 468–74; Bucchi 2011) appeared with the *argomenti* (one stanza per book) of Francesco Turchi; and *Annotationi* of Giuseppe Horologgi:

{a} Segue la favola di Atteone, ò per di meglio come vogliono alcuni l'historia scrivendo Fulgentio che Atteone fu uno che amò grandemente la caccia nella sua giovanezza, giunto poi nell'età matura, e considerando meglio i pericoli della caccia, che non faceva in quegli anni focosi non l'essercitava della maniera che era accostumato di fare[.] Nondimeno anchora che in quella età fuggisse il pericolo delle caccie, non però lasciò l'affettione smisurata a che portava a' cani; perche pascendone gran numero come facevan nel tempo che si serviva di loro consumò tutte le sue facoltà; onde venne a dar materia alla favola che narra ch'ei fu mangiato da' cani, {b} l'Allegoria è che quelli che si danno con ogni diligentia à considerare i misteriosi ordini de' cieli, e il variare della Luna, figurata per Diana, e trasmutato in cervo, stando nei boschi, e luoghi sollitarii tratto dalla curiosità di quella scientia, onde trovato poi delle proprie cure famigliari, che sono i cani, è divorato da esse, come quelle che non sopportano mai che l'huomo viva à se stesso, in questa favola descrive felicemente l'Anguillara la caccia del cervo come la fanno i gran Rè come è quella di Francia, cominciando nella stanza 'Acquista. (Anguillara 1637: fol. 37ʳ)

[{a} There follows the myth of Acteon, or rather as some would have it, the history: Fulgentius writes that Acteon was one who greatly loved hunting in his youth; then coming to maturity and being more aware of the dangers of the hunt which he no longer practised as had been his custom. However, although at that age he fled the dangers of the hunt, he did not lose his excessive affection for dogs; for by feeding a great number of them he consumed all his means; whence he came to give substance to the myth which tells he was eaten by his hounds.{b} The allegory is that those who scrutinize the mysterious order of the heavens, and the phases of the Moon (symbolized by Diana) are led by curiosity to haunt remote places and are found out by their family duties, which do not tolerate that a man should live just for himself.]

So the commentator of Anguillara's translation starts by following Fulgentius {a} and moves on to a more spiritual level {b}. Fulgentius's warning against curiosity is developed into a consideration of the tension between the melancholy scholar and society.

Anguillara was a source for Spanish painters of the Golden Age (López Torrijos 1985), and is by far the most common Italian Ovid found in modern-day Spanish libraries (see the Spanish union catalogue, *Catálogo colectivo del patrimonio bibliográfico español*). He is also quoted by Sánchez de Viana and Pérez Sigler in their Ovid translations.

The second Spanish Ovid is the verse of Antonio Pérez Sigler (printed 1580-1609). He has placed allegories at the end of each book, 'ayudandome en algunas dellas de las del Anguilara' [and turned to Anguilara's for some of them] (fol. ¶5ᵛ). We can see that his commentary on Acteon is lifted bodily from the Italian:

Anguillara: l'Allegoria è che quelli che si danno con ogni diligentia à considerare i misteriosi ordini de' cieli, e il variare della Luna, figurata per Diana, e trasmutato in cervo, stando nei boschi, e luoghi sollitarii tratto dalla curiosità di quella scientia, onde trovato poi delle proprie cure famigliari, che sono i cani, è divorato da esse, come quelle che non sopportano mai che l'huomo viva à se stesso. (Anguillara 1637: fol. 37ᵛ)

Pérez Sigler: Por Acteon … se entiende, que aquel que se da a considerar la mysteriosa orden de los cielos y el variar de la luna (que es Diana) es transformado en ciervo, andando en bosques y lugares solitarios: atraydo de la curiosidad de aquella sciencia, a donde hallado de los propios cuydados de su familia (que son los perros) es comido de ellos: como aquellos que no consienten que el hombre viva para si solo. (Pérez Sigler 1580: fols 75ᵛ–76ʳ)

In Antwerp in 1595 Bustamante's translation was re-issued with 175 pictures, and 'con las allegorias al fin dellos, y sus figuras, para provecho de los artifices' (fols 119–241) [with the allegories at the end, and their pictures, for the use of artists]. The allegories are copied from Pérez Sigler (Carrasco Reija 1997: 989); the woodcuts are by Virgil Solis, copying Bernard Salomon (López Torrijos 1985: 38). These embellishments are found only in this edition.[5]

The 1609 edition of Pérez Sigler ended with a *Diccionario Poetico, donde se contienen todos los nombres de personas, reynos, provincias, pueblos, rios, fuentes, montes, valles, arboles, animales, peces, y aves, y otras cosas de que haze mencion Ovidio en sus Metamorphoseos, y otros poetas, por el orden del A.B.C.* This is a translation of the *Dictionarium poeticum* of Charles Estienne (Starnes and Talbert 1955: 8). The dictionary is strictly concerned with the literal sense. Thus, in the 1609 edition a spiritual reading of the *Metamorphoses* coexists with a literal one. Cossío (1952: 45) notes Pérez Sigler's 'preocupación moralista, que por entonces casi era anacrónica' [moralizing preoccupations, which by then were almost anachronistic]. (Its anachronism I think is debatable.)

In 1585 there appeared the work which Schevill criticized so at the head of this article, Juan Pérez de Moya's *Philosofía secreta, donde debaxo de historias fabulosas, se contiene mucha doctrina, provechosa a todos estudios.* Pérez de Moya (1995: 68–69) explains why the ancients wrote fables: 1) to educate their children gently (he uses the commonplace of the golden pill, which contains medicine enclosed in an attractive covering); 2) to aid the memory; 3) because a lack of paper and the wherewithal for writing encouraged brevity; 4) 'Y también el no querer que sus secretos fuesen comunes a todos.' (1995: 68–69) [Because they did not want their secrets to

---

Schevill (1913: 163) thought more than one edition was affected: 'The commentary found at the close of editions printed in the latter half of the sixteenth century gives in detail the allegorical sense of the chief tales'. Only one British Library copy has these final allegories: Antwerp 1595 (shelfmark: 11388.aaa.9).

be common property]. So he is one of the few authors who refer to hermeticism.

He explains the biblical four senses:

> De cinco modos se puede declarar una fábula, conviene a saber: literal, alegórico, anagógico, tropológico, y físico o natural.

> Sentido literal, que por otro nombre dicen histórico o parabólico, es lo mismo que suena la letra de la tal fábula o escriptura.

> Sentido alegórico es un entendimiento diverso de lo que la fábula o escriptura literalmente dice.

> Anagógico se dice de *anagoge*, y *anagoge* se deriva de *ana*, que quiere decir 'arriba', y *goge*, 'guia', que quiere decir 'guiar hacia arriba', a cosas altas de Dios.

> Tropológico se dice de *tropos*, que es 'reversio', o 'conversación', y *logos*, que es 'palabra', o 'razón', o 'oración'; como quien dijese, 'palabra o oración convertible a informar el ánima a buenas costumbres'.

> Físico o natural es sentido que declara alguna obra de naturaleza.

> Ejemplo: Hércules, hijo de Júpiter (según fingimiento poético), concluidos sus trabajos vitorioso fue colocado en el cielo.

> Tomando esto según sentido literal, no se entiende otra cosa más de lo que la letra suena.

> Y según alegoría o moralidad, por Hércules es entendida la victoria contra los vicios.

> Y según sentido anagógico significa el levantamiento del ánima, que desprecia las cosas mundanas por las celestiales.

> Y según sentido tropológico, por Hércules se entiende un hombre fuerte, habituado en virtud y buenas costumbres.

> Y según sentido físico o natural, por Hércules se entiende el Sol, y por sus doce trabajos o hazañas, los doce signos del zodíaco, sobrepujados dél por pasar por ellos en un año.

> Y es de advertir que los tres sentidos últimos, puesto que sean nombrados por diversos nombres, todavía se puede llamar alegóricos, porque, como hemos dicho, alegoría dicen a lo que es diverso del sentido histórico o literal. Y los que es de estos sentidos es mi intento declarar en las fábulas es el sentido histórico, y el físico y natural. (Pérez de Moya 1995: 69)

[A myth may be interpreted in five ways, namely, literal, allegorical, anagogical, tropological, and physical or natural. Literal sense, alias historical or parabolic, is the same as the letter of a fable or tale. Allegorical sense is a meaning different from what the fable or tale literally says. Anagogical derives from *anagoge*, and *anagoge* derives from *ana*, which means 'upwards' and *goge* 'guide', meaning 'guide upwards' to the high things of God. Tropological derives from *tropos*, which is 'turn' or 'conversion' and *logos*, which is 'word, phrase or speech', as one might say 'word or speech which can be turned to instruct the soul in good words'. Physical or natural is the sense that explains some phenomenon of nature. For example: Hercules, son of Jupiter (according to poetic fiction), having completed his labours was placed in the heavens. Taking this in the literal sense, nothing is understood than the sound of the words. And according to the allegory or morality, by Hercules is understood victory over vices. And according to the anagogical sense it means the elevation of the soul, which despises worldly things in favour of the heavenly. And according to the natural or physical sense, by Hercules is understood the Sun, and by his twelve labours or feats, the twelve signs of the zodiac, overcome by it when it passes through these in a year. Note also that the last three senses, although called by different names, can still/regardless be called allegorical, because, as we have said, everything is called allegorical which is different from the historical or literal sense. And the senses which I intend to explain are the historical, and the physical and natural.]

His section (1995: 578–80) on Acteon is part Fulgentius, part Pérez Sigler:

Acteon: *Declaración moral*: Por Acteón podemos entender cualquier hombre de grande estado, que en lugar de darse a aprender buenas costumbres para hacerse apto de administrar bien su república se da a la caza … Este tal es comido y disipado de sus canes, porque lo echan a perder … Por Diana podemos entender la codicia de la caza [...]

Sentido histórico: San Fulgencio declara … que Acteón amó mucho la caza significada por Diana, y siguióla, y después de venido a edad cumplida, conoció ser cosa sin provecho, y no menos peligrosa que dañosa.... Ver a Diana desnuda es decir que entonces conoció Acteón a la clara y descubiertamente ser la caza cosa sin provecho … Viendo Acteón los daños y poco provecho de la caza, temió: y esto es tornarse en ciervo, que es animal temerosísimo, y apartóse de ella, mas tenía en tanto el amor de los perros y cazadores [*read* perros cazadores], que no los dejó, y como tenía muchos, por sustentarlos casi destruyó toda su hacienda. Y esto es decir que sus perros le mataron y comieron porque consumieron su haber …

Amonéstanos también esta fábula que evitemos saber secretos agenos.

En otro modo se puede entender que los que se dan con toda diligencia a considerar la misteriosa orden de los cielos y el variar de la Luna, figurada por Diana, es mudado en ciervo estando en los bosques y lugares solitarios, llevado de la curiosidad de aquella sciencia, donde hallado de los propios cuidados, familiares de su causa [*read* casa] (que son los perros), es comido de ellos, porque no consienten que el hombre viva para sí mismo.

[*Moral explanation*: By Acteon we may understand any man of great estate who instead of dedicating himself to learning good skills to enable him to administer his republic gives himself over to hunting. … He is consumed and dissipated by his dogs, because they ruin him … By Diana we may understand the desire of hunting

Historical sense: St Fulgentius declares … that Acteon greatly loved the hunt signified by Diana, and pursued it, and once he reached maturity he recognized that it was a worthless thing, and no less dangerous than harmful. … To see Diana naked means that Acteon then saw clearly and nakedly that hunting is a vain thing … Seeing the dangers and worthlessness of hunting, Acteon feared; and this is to be turned into a stag, which is a most timid beast; and he distanced himself from her, but he so kept his love for his hunting dogs that he did not give them up.   And as he had so many of them, to feed them he almost destroyed his estate, which is to say that his dogs killed and ate him because they consumed his household.

This myth also teaches us to avoid knowing other people's secrets.

In another way [following Pérez Sigler] it can be understood that he who diligently gives himself over to considering the mysterious order of the heavens and the phases of the moon, figured by Diana, is turned into a stag, haunting woods and lonely places, led by his curiosity for that knowledge, where, found out by his own cares, the members of his house (the dogs), he is eaten up by them, because they do not allow a man to live for himself alone.]

Was Schevill correct in calling Pérez de Moya archaic? First, he is backward-looking in naming the biblical senses, which had not been used in new works on the interpretation of myth since the 1530s. But he is not indicative the general 'belatedness' of Spain: this exegesis was out of fashion in Spain as well as the rest of Catholic Europe, so Pérez de Moya was unusual in both Spanish and European terms. Secondly, we might ask if he genuinely uses the four-fold exegesis he describes in his prologue. The exegetical terminology used in the body of the text is limited to 'sentido moral' and 'sentido histórico', and these are rare. It seems to me that in practice Pérez de Moya uses the rather timid allegoresis of Dolce, Anguillara and the earlier Spanish Ovids to read the *Metamorphoses* as a set of exempla. He does not use Christ-centred arguments.

In 1586 Felipe Mey published his verse translation *Del metamorphoseos de Ovidio en octava rima*. The translation is partial, as it only goes up to Book VII, and there was only one edition. Like Bustamante's, his text has no commentaries, but Mey promises 'hasta entanto, que llegando con el favor de Dios al fin de la segunda parte, demos una declaracion copiosa de todas las fabulas' (1586: fol. Dd7^v) [until such time as, reaching with God's favour the end of the second part, we will give a full explanation of the fables]. No edition is known of the commentary volume, but as Mey cites Dolce and Anguillara by name in his prologue, it is possible that he followed a moralizing tradition.

The third Spanish Ovid in a decade is Pedro Sánchez de Viana, *Las transformaciones de Ovidio: traduzidas del verso latino, en tercetos y octavas rimas ... con el comento, y explicacion de las fabulas: reduziendolas a philosophia natural, y moral, y astrologia, e historia* (Valladolid: Diego Fernández de Córdoba, 1589). There were only two editions in the Golden Age, of 1589 and 1679. Each book opens with a woodcut, taken from an edition of Anguillara (López Torrijos 1985: 38).

Sánchez de Viana's prologue is a sophisticated defence of poetry and the special nature of the poet. Addressing Hernando de Vega, he likens fables to the Silenus, an ugly statue of the drunken faun which opened to reveal a god, described by Erasmus (Adagia 3.3.1):

> Verdad natural y moral [...] estos Silenos de Alcibiades que encubren lo que los philosophos antiguos sintieron de la generacion del Mundo, elementos, animales, fuerças de naturaleza, divina providencia, premios, y penas, que despues de la muerte se proponen a cada uno (segun la vida passada) debaxo de su no muy tosca corteza. (Sánchez de Viana 1589: fol. 3ᵛ)

> [Natural and moral sense. These Silenuses of Alcibiades which enclose what the ancient philosophers opined of the generation of the world, elements, animals, forces of nature, divine providence, rewards and punishments which await one after death, according to his past life, beneath their far from rude integument.]

In his prologue 'A los lectores' (fols 4–8) he quotes Aristotle to the effect that the earliest poets were philosophers (fol. 2) and alludes to the poet's 'furor divino' (fols 2ᵛ–3ʳ) (Alcina 1999), quoting Ficino.

He does not believe that Ovid was vouchsafed a preview of Christian revelation:

> *A esto se allego que por el hado, | se acuerda verna tiempo que la llama | la tierra, mar, cielo avra quemado, etc.* Facilmente se persuadira qualquiera con estas palabras, a que nuestro Poeta tuvo noticia de la sagrada escriptura, pues conformandose con ella, parece tocar en ellas el juyzio final. Pero bien puede ser entendiesse esto de la doctrina de los Philosophos Stoycos. (Sánchez de Viana 1589: *Annotaciones*, fol. 26ʳ)

> [*To this was added that he remembers that, by fate, the time will come when flames will burn land, sea and heavens, etc.* [Ovid *Metamorphoses*, I. 256–58] Anyone will be easily persuaded by these words that our poet was aware of Holy Writ, as by conforming to it he seems to touch on the Last Judgment. But it may be that he knew about this from the teachings of the Stoics.]

But he is sure that Ovid had read Moses: '[Ovid] no solamente consta de sus transformaciones, aver leydo las obras excelentes de los Griegos, mas aun ser versado en las lenguas Hebrayca, y Caldea, de todas las quales compone su varia poesia' (fol. 7ᵛ) [Ovid shows in his *Metamorphoses* that he not only read the excellent works of the Greeks, but was versed in the Hebrew and Chaldean languages, from all of which he composes his varied poetry].

In the following example on Phaethon Sánchez de Viana's approach is Euhemeristic:

> Platon, sant Agustin, sant Fulgencio, Landino, y Natal Comite, Orologio aqui, que alega a Eusebio, y Orosio, y a Sanchez, dizen algunos que la historia sobre que se funda esta fabula: Fue que en Grecia acontecio [...] un grandissimo incendio, que parecio mas castigo del cielo por los insultos de la tierra, que causado por humana obra, al que llamaron el incendio de Phaeton. [...] No le pudo tener este fuego, hasta que las aguas del Otoño le apagaron. La cayda de Phaeton, y el llanto de sus hermanas, y conversion en arboles se funda en otra historia, que cuenta Zezes. Y fue que Phaeton fue hijo de un rey, el qual como corriese en un carro de quatro caballos a la orilla de Pado, rio de los Celtas, cayendo en el rio acabo la vida, cuya muerte lloraron con tanta amargura sus hermanas, que el dolor y sentimiento las bolvio stupidas: Y porque los tales parece que solo tienen vida vegetativa, como plantas, dixeron averse convertido en arboles. (Sánchez de Viana 1589: *Annotaciones*, fol. 50^r)

> [Plato, St Augustine, Landino, and Natale Conti and Giuseppe Horologi, who here cites Eusebius, Orosius and Sánchez [on Alciato], some say that the history on which this myth is based is this: in Greece a great fire occurred, which seemed rather a punishment sent by heaven for the insults of the earth than caused by human action, and this they called Phaethon's fire. This fire could not be contained until the autumn rains extinguished it. The fall of Phaethon, and his sisters' laments and transformation into trees, is based on another history, told by Johannes Tzetzes [allegorizer of Homer]. Phaethon was a king's son, who racing in his four-horse chariot on the banks of the Po, river of the Celts, falling into the river ended his life, whose death was lamented by his sisters so bitterly that the grief made them insensible. And because such people seem to have only vegetative life, like plants, they were said to have been turned into trees.]

Ulrich Mölk (1966–1967) argued that Góngora's reference to the 'obscuridad y estilo intrincado de Ovidio' cited at the beginning of this article derived from his reading of Sánchez de Viana.

The seventeenth century is much less productive of translations of the *Metamorphoses* into Italian or Spanish, so I shall briefly survey some French versions. Renouard's French translation (printed 1606–1661) is moralizing, with particular application to the courtier:

> Ce petit fils, premier sujet de ses plaintes, fut Acteon, lequel servit de proye aux chiens qu'il nourissoit, pour l'entretien de son plaisir. Ainsi bien souvent les flatteurs, que les Grands nourissent à leur table, afin d'ouyr d'eux quelque mot pour rire, sont les premiers prests à les mordre, & sans * respect deschirer cruellement les ingrats, apres avoir receu plusieurs bons offices d'un amy, au lieu de rechercher à se desgager des obligations qu'ils luy ont, se jetter pour

quelque legere occasion, du party de ses ennemis & plustot le ruiner, que luy
rendre un bien-fait reciproque. Ce sont chiens, qui mescognoissent ceux des-
quels ils ont receu toutes sortes de courtoisies, & par cette mescognoissance sont
attirez à des effects contraires aux services qu'ils doivent. Mais que nous
apprend l'occasion du changement & du desastre d'Acteon? Il meurt pour
avoir veu une Deesse dans le baing, n'est ce pas, docte Ariste, un advis qui nous
doit faire apprehender le danger qu'il y a d'approcher les Grands, & se glisser au
cabinet de leurs secrets? Quant à moy il me semble, ayant l'oeil sur le desastre
de ce nourriçon de Diane, voir Arate avec le poison dans le sein, cracher le sang
& dire en se plaignant de Philippe, voila le loyer de l'amitié des Roys: il n'est
pas | bon de les voir trop prés, ce sont des flames qui nous esclairent à la verité,
mais dangereuses si nous n'en sommes quelque peu esloignez. Notre Poëte l'a
espouué, l'orage de son banissement luy vint du feu de tels foudres, par la veuë
de quelques actions d'Auguste: aussi dedans les vers de son affliction
s'accompare-il soy mesme à cet infortuné chasseur. Vous avez raison, respondit
Ariste de quelque façon que ce soit tousjours les approches de Grands sont
perilleuses.

Marginal headings:

*Moralitez

¶ Periculosum Regum familiaritatem flammarum naturae compara, quae sicut
paululum à se remotae illuminant, ita satis admotae comburunt. Sidonius.
(Renouard 1638: second pagination, pp. 68–69)

[This grandson [of Cadmus], the first object of his lamentations, was Acteon,
who furnished the prey to the dogs which he fed, for the pursuit of his pleasure.
Thus very often flatterers whom the great feed at their table, in order to hear
from them some laughable word, are the first to bite them and without respect
cruelly and ungratefully tear them apart, after having received several good
turns from a friend, instead of seeking to repay their obligations to him, throw
themselves into the party of his enemies at some slight opportunity, and rather
ruin him than repay him some reciprocal good deed. These are dogs, who are
ungrateful to those from whom they have received all sorts of kindnesses, and
by this ingratitude are attracted to effects contrary to the services they owe. But
what does the case of the transformation and disaster of Acteon tell us? He dies
for having seen a goddess at her bath: is this not, learned Ariste, a warning
which must make us apprehend the danger of approaching the great, and slip
into the cabinet of their secrets? Looking on the disaster of this creature of
Diana, I seem to see Aratus with poison in his breast spitting blood and saying
complainingly of Philip, Behold the friendship of kings: it is not good to see
them at close quarters, these are the flames which light us to truth, but are
dangerous if we do not keep our distance. Our poet has experienced this, the
storm of his banishment came to him from the fire of such lightning, by way of
some actions of Augustus: so too in the verses on his affliction he compares

himself to this unfortunate huntsman. 'You are right,' replied Ariste, 'be what they may, approaches to the great are always dangerous.'

Marginal headings:

*Moralities

¶Compare the familiarity of kings to the nature of flames, which illuminate from a distance and burn up close. Sidonius Appolinaris, *Ep.* iii.]

The French translation of Thomas Corneille saw various editions between 1669 and 1698. It represents a format which is by now familiar: a prefatory statement that the ancient myths contain information on science, morality, physics and politics; yet in the text there is no commentary:

> Preface [the *Metamorphoses* are] un parfait modéle de tout ce qui est à imiter ou fuir dans la vie | humaine et dans la civile. Cela est si vray que si l'on examine bien les Fables, on reconnoistra qu'elles contiennent non seulement ce qu'il y a de plus excellent dans les plus nobles Sciences, mais encore les plus beaux secrets de la Morale, de la Physique, & mesme de la Politique. C'est ce qui a fait dire à Platon que les sages de l'antiquité avoient voulu qu'elles fussent le premier lait que l'on fist succer auz Hommes, qui devoient les considerer comme un aliment qui passe dans l'esprit sans peine, & qui l'entretenant agreablement, le rend enfin capable d'une plus solide nourriture. En effet quelles grandes utilitez ne tire-t'on pas de la connoissance de la Fable, qui nous donne de si belles instructions de Morale, en nous apprenant nous gouverner dans l'une & dans l'autre fortune, en détournant notre esprit des passions déreglés par les exemples qu'elle nous propose des malheurs arrivez à ceux qui s'y sont abandonnez, & en nous enseignant la crainte de Dieu, crainte salutaire, qui vaut seule toutes les vertus ensemble. (Corneille 1698: I, fol. *4ʳ)

> [The *Metamorphoses* are a perfect model of all that is to be imitated or fled in private and public life. This is so true that if one examines the myths correctly, one will recognize that they contain not only what is most excellent in the most noble sciences, but also the most beautiful secrets of morality, physics and even politics. This is what made Plato say that the sages of antiquity had wanted them to be the first milk that men were put to suck, as they must have considered them a food which enters the mind easily and which by entertaining it makes it finally capable of more solid nourishment. Indeed, what great utilities does one not derive from the knowledge of myth, which gives us such beautiful instruction in morality, teaching us to rule ourselves in good and bad fortune, turning our minds away from the unruly passions with examples which it shows us of bad ends which have befallen those who have abandoned themselves to them, and teaching us the fear of God, a salutary fear which is worth all the virtues together.]

Bellegarde's French translation (printed 1701–1716) uses the fables as material for moralizing:

Midas: Explication. Les avares ont en quelque maniere le pouvoir de convertir
tout en or; ils ont mille adresses & mille industries pour amasser des richesses
par leurs épargnes; ils n'osent ni boire ni manger de peur de faire de la dépense.
Ils sont mal logez, mal vêtus, ils ne se chaussent point pendant l'hyver: ils se
refusent toutes des commoditez & tous les agremens de la vie; ils sont pauvres
au milieu de l'abondance; ils respectent leur or comme une chose sacré à quoi
ils n'osent toucher. Midas vendoit toutes choses, même les plus necessaires pour
en faire de l'argent. Voilà pourquoi le Poëte a feint qu'il changeoit en or tout ce
qu'il touchoit: il fit diviser plusieurs canaux le Pactole pour arroser son pays, &
pour rendre ses terres plus fertiles. On regarde Midas comme le modèle des
Princes avares; l'avarice est une grande tache dans les personnes privées; mais
c'est un vice impardonnable dans les Princes qui sont faits pour l'utilité
publique. (Bellegarde 1716: vol. II, p. 9)

[Midas: Explanation. Misers have to some extent the power to convert
everything into gold; they have a thousand ways and means to amass riches by
their savings; they dare neither drink nor eat for fear of the expense. They are ill
housed, ill dressed, they wear no shoes in winter; they deny themselves all the
comforts and conveniences of life; they are poor in the midst of abundance;
they revere their gold as a sacred thing which they dare not touch. Midas sold
everything, even the most necessary, to make money from it. This is why the
poet has feigned that he changed to gold all he touched: he diverted several
channels of the Pactolus to water his country, and to make his lands more
fertile. One regards Midas as the model of miserly princes; avarice is a great
fault in private individuals, but it is an unpardonable vice in princes who are
made for the public utility.]

To return to Spain, in 1620 Fray Baltasar de Vitoria brought out part I
of his *Teatro de los dioses de la gentilidad*. Part II came out in 1623 and a
third part was added by Juan Bautista Aguilar in 1688. It was reprinted
until 1738. The approach of this dictionary as it stands is solidly literal, but
I suspect that Vitoria intended to include allegories in his third part which
was never printed. Part II is announced as a dispassionate description of
paganism on its own terms:

[...] lo que en estos treze libros se trata, es quien fue cada Dios, sus padres, y sus
hijos, sus metamorfoseos, conversiones, y ensayos. Los Templos que les fueron
consagrados, las Ciudades en que fueron adorados, y reverenciados [...]
Tambien se trata en estos libros de las aves, animales, arboles, y plantas, que à
cada Dios son dedicadas, con todas sus propriedades, essencias, y virtudes.
Fuera desto se trata de las imagines, pinturas, y estatuas levantadas, y
consagradas à estos Dioses, que es lectura muy curiosa, y entretenida, y aun
muy trabajada, porque para favorecer el intento, se han visto muchos libros [...]
Estos libros no sirven de mas, que de dàr mano, y aparejo à los que quieren
tratar de poesia. (Vitoria 1623: fol. A1ᵛ).

[What is set down in these thirteen books is: who was each god, his parents, and his children, his metamorphosis, conversions and ordeals. The temples which were sacred to them, the cities where they were worshipped and revered. There is also explanation in these books of the birds, animals, trees and plants which are dedicated to each god, with all their properties, essences and virtues. In addition, there is also explanation of the images, paintings and statues raised and dedicated to these gods, which makes for very curious reading, entertaining and the product of much labour, as many books have been consulted for this purpose. These books serve only to give support and material to those who wish to discuss poetry.]

My reason for thinking this is that in his prologue to Part I Vitoria argues that virtuous pagans like Varro (doubtless cited via Augustine, *The City of God against the Pagans*) invested the vain and dirty deities with symbolic meanings:

> Al lector. No es mi intento en este Prologo (curioso Lector) persuadir quan vana, y sin fundamento sea la pluralidad, y multitud de los Dioses, que la antigua Gentilidad adorava; cosa que tan doctamente confutaron el Angelico Doctor Santo Thomàs, y San Juan Damasceno; porque entre los Christianos (y aun entre los Hereges) nadie lo duda, y para los Gentiles era menester otro modo de proceder; solo pretendo mostrar al ignorante el desatino tan desigual, y la ceguera tan grande con que viviò siempre la antigua Gentilidad [...] Y assi Marco Varron y otros muchos Gentiles, viendo las imagenes de sus falsos Dioses, que representavan hombres, y mugeres de vida, y costumbres torpes, y sensuales (como Iupiter, Mercurio, Marte, Baco, y Venus, y otra semejante canalla) quisieron como hombres cuerdos transferirlos, y transformarlos con razones misticas, simbolicas, mitologicas, a las cosas naturales, y divinas, vencidos, y confusos de natural verguença de los que respetavan, y adoravan, pero ellos acudieron tarde; y porque no pareciesse novedad, y liviandad, y tambien por el peligro que corria | su autoridad, y su vida, se quedaron en su engañosa idolatria. (Vitoria 1620: fol. §2ʳ)

> [To the reader. It is not my intention in this prologue, curious reader, to persuade how vain, and unfounded is the plurality of gods which ancient paganism worshipped: a matter that was so learnedly refuted by the Angelic Doctor St Thomas, and St John Damascene: because among the Christians (and even among the heretics) nobody doubts it and the pagans had need of another way of proceeding: I wish only to show the ignorant the uneven confusion and great blindness in which ancient paganism always lived. And thus Marcus Varro and many other pagans, seeing the images of their false gods, which showed men and women of low and sensual life (such as Jupiter, Mercury, Mars, Bacchus, Venus and other such rabble) wished the wise men to transfer and transform them with mystical, symbolic and mythological arguments into things natural and divine, overcome and confounded with a natural shame of those they respected and adored, but they arrived too late; and

lest it should appear a novelty or whim, and for the danger which their
authority and lives ran they stayed in their deceitful idolatry.]

He also repeats that the poets were the ancient theologians, and that they
had read Moses:

Sabida cosa es, que los Filosofos, y Poetas antiguos, fueron los Theologos de la
antigua Gentilidad, como lo afirman Lactancio Firmiano, S. Agustin, y S.
Ambrosio, y assi los mas de los Poetas procuraron aprovecharse de los libros del
sapientissimo Moyses, y de los demàs que tocavan à la Sagrada Escritura,
sacandola de sus quicios para adorno de sus fabulas. Assi lo afirman S. Iustino
Martir, S. Theodoreto, y S. Clemente Alexandrino, por lo qual todas las fabulas
que compusieron, fue trasegandolas, y traduciendolas de las verdades
Catholicas, componiendolas, y enmascarandolas à su modo gentilico. (Vitoria
1620: 1)

[It is known that the ancient philosophers and poets were the theologians of
ancient paganism, as Fulgentius, St Augustine and St Ambrose affirm, and so
most of the poets wished to benefit from the books of the most wise Moses, and
the others who treated of Holy Writ, taking it out of its home to adorn their
myths. So affirm St Justin Martyr, St Theodoret and St Clement of Alexandria.
Thus all the myths which they composed was by transferring and translating
them from the Catholic truths, composing and disguising them in their pagan
fashion.]

However, in the body of the text his treatment of myth is literal:

De como la Diosa Diana convirtiò en ciervo à Acteon. [...] Tiene esta fabula
mucho de moralidad, y de historia, como dize San Fulgencio, y Natal Comite,
en las Mythologias, y lo màs desto lo remito para el Tratado ultimo de las
fabulas, donde se tratará largamente desto. (Vitoria 1623: 349)

[How the goddess Diana changed Acteon into a stag. [...] [Story as in Ovid et
al.] This myth has much of morality, and of history, as St Fulgentius and
Natale Conti in the *Mythologies* say, and the rest I reserve for the final treatise
on myths, where there will be longer discussion.]

Whatever Vitoria's attitude to the true meanings of pagan myth, he was at
least prepared to allow two volumes of his work to be published which
merely described classical culture on its own terms.

I close this survey of Ovidian translations with a late example of allegory.
Between 1727 and 1738 Diego Suárez de Figueroa, 'doctor en Sagrada
Teologia', and his nephew Ignacio published an edition of Ovid, with
Spanish translation, in 12 volumes. In volumes VII to X, dedicated to the
Metamorphoses, each fable ends with an allegorizing moralization. The
translators give six reasons for the utility of myth, picking up all the
arguments that had circulated since Antiquity, including allegory:

De aqui se sigue, que las doctrinas son utiles. Lo primero, por las verdades que tienen tomadas de los libros sagrados. Lo segundo, por sus mismos errores, pues en lo primero nos instruimos de lo que debemos hacer, en lo segundo de los que debemos huir. [...] Lo tercero, por las muchas sentencias, que Ovidio mezcla en sus fabulas, que instruyen en buenas acciones morales. Lo quarto, porque las acciones de un Hercules [...] encienden en los fuertes los animos à emprehender singulares proezas. Lo quinto, porque apenas ai Arte, ni Ciencia, que no pueda adelantarse en la leccion de estos eruditissimos libros: [...] las mas antiguas historias [...] la Astronomia [...] la Oratoria, y Retorica [...] la Cosmographia, y Geographia [...] el Arte Poetico [...] la Philosophia natural, y moral [..] y ultimamente [...] muy saludables doctrinas, disfrazadas en sus alegorias, tropologias, y metaforas, pues las mas de la transformaciones las escribieron con el fin, de que à vista de los castigos, evitassen los pecados, y fueron motivos de padecerlos. (Suárez de Figueroa 1735: 178)

[Hence it follows that these doctrines are useful. First, for the truths which they have taken from the Holy Books. Second, for their very errors, as in the first we are instructed in what we must do, and in the second in what we must flee. Third, for the many sententiae which Ovid mixes into his fables, which instruct in good moral actions. Fourth, because the actions of a Hercules kindle in the strong the desire to undertake singular deeds of prowess. Fifth, because there is scarcely an art or science that cannot be advanced by the reading of these most erudite books: the most ancient histories, astronomy, oratory and rhetoric, cosmography and geography, the art of poetry, natural and moral philosophy and finally very healthy doctrines, disguised in their allegories, tropologies, and metaphors, since most of the transformations were written with the purpose that in sight of punishments they should avoid sins, and were the reasons for suffering them.]

This is perhaps the place to point out that there is a lack of editions of the Latin *Metamorphoses* in Spain: in fact, there seems to have been only three before 1800. (It is an axiom that the Spanish book trade preferred importing Latin editions to printing them: Clavería 1995). The Salamanca incunable (1488) survives only as a fragment, but its layout suggests there was no commentary (Vindel 1946: 29–30, n. 19). The edition of Salamanca 1570 is a reprint of an edition printed at Lyons by Sebastian Gryphius between 1534 and 1559, which in turn derives from an Aldine edition of 1502.[6] The Salamanca edition has marginal headings indicating literal subject, rhetorical figures and textual variants, as well as a life of Ovid by Aldus Manutius. So we may say that the few Spanish editions of the Latin text make no room for allegory.

---

6   The poet Diego Hurtado de Mendoza owned a copy of Gryphius 1550 (Cossío 1952: 91).

Ovidian Writing in the Spanish Golden Age

I now turn briefly to imitations of Ovid in the Golden Age, to see how they compare with the translation and commentary traditions.

Cossío took account of 360 narrative poems on Ovidian themes for his magisterial book of 1952. From his study it emerges that very few Golden Age poets gave their Ovidian themes any form of explicit allegorical interpretation. A rare example is Castillejo's (d. 1550) *Fábula de Acteón*, which has 60 lines of narrative and 120 lines of moralization (Castillejo 1926–1928: II. 262–69).

In the drama the role of allegory is severely circumscribed. Calderón wrote about a dozen *comedias mitológicas* [mythological plays] between 1630 and 1670 (Páramo Pomareda 1957). It seems to me that they are not informed by the allegorical readings we have seen in translations and other works. Where Calderón does use allegory – indeed, four-fold biblical allegory – is in the ten *autos sacramentales* [allegorical plays] on mythological themes which he wrote over a similar period. The title of *El divino Orfeo* is sufficient indication that Orpheus is a figure of God, and Orfeo makes his appearance on stage singing:

> Pues mi voz, en el principio
> el cielo, la tierra, cria,
> despues del cielo, y la tierra
> hágasse, la luz, del dia.
>
> (Calderón 1952: III, 1820)

[Since my voice in the beginning | creates the heavens and the earth,/after heaven and earth | let there be the light of day.]

There is a tradition in Calderonian scholarship of applying the allegories of the *autos mitológicos* to the *comedias mitológicas*: this seems to originate with an article of Aubrun (1976) and has been worked on most insistently by Neumeister (2000). The argument is that Calderón was steeped in a culture of Christian (more specifically Jesuit) humanism which favoured such readings, but I think critics need to be able to point to specific verbal features of the texts which link them to traditions of allegoresis (Parker 1988).

Conclusions

Allegorical readings of the *Metamorphoses* in Spain were present throughout the Golden Age, to varying degrees. Although works of allegoresis were produced in greater numbers in the sixteenth century, their hardiness is shown by the fact that they continued to be reprinted throughout our period. One might discern a general movement away from allegorical and moralizing interpretations, but at different speeds in translation, commentary and imitation. In sixteenth-century translations and commentaries, allegory continues to the end of our period, with a general tendency for the multiple interpretations of the Middle Ages to be reduced to moralizing and exemplarism. Of the three sixteenth-century translators, by far the most popular was Bustamante, whose allegories do not interrupt the flow of his translation, being confined to his prefatory matter. Allegories were more prominent in the other translations of Pérez Sigler, Mey and Sánchez de Viana.

We may note a certain discrepancy between the authors' claims in their prologues and their practice. Bustamante confines his allegories to his prologue. Pérez de Moya's citation of the techniques of scriptural exegesis is indeed out of date, but his actual practice is not. Vitoria may have intended to allegorize his material but his practice in his extant work is antiquarian and literal.

Allegory rarely appears in the longer Spanish poems written in imitation of Ovid studied by Cossío and is lacking in the Latin editions produced in Spain. (There is little to be said of Spanish editors of Ovid at this date.)

And finally, what of the accusations of belatedness levelled at Pérez de Moya and Góngora? Neither Pérez de Moya in 1585 nor Góngora in 1613 were out of step with readers of Ovid in France and Italy: they formed part of a vigorous tradition which stretched back to Antiquity and was to survive to the beginning of the eighteenth century. Spain was neither ahead of nor behind the rest of Catholic Europe in its use of allegory, with one exception: the *auto sacramental* on Ovidian themes, which in the mid-seventeenth century revived the Christ-centred techniques of the 1300s.

III

OVID IN FRENCH

6

MATTIA CAVAGNA

THE *OVIDE MORALISÉ* BETWEEN
VERSE AND PROSE, TEXT AND GLOSS,
IN MANUSCRIPT AND PRINTED FORM

The *Ovide moralisé* offers a thrilling challenge to the medieval reader as well as to the modern scholar because of its hermeneutic richness. The international research group 'Ovid en Francais' (OEF) has launched a new series of studies dealing with the origin of the text, with its sources and with its medieval and early modern reception.[1] The first volume of our edition was recently published by the Société des Anciens Textes Français.[2] The more we work on the *Ovide moralisé*, the more we realize that, despite its richness, it must be considered as part of a network of texts and glosses, which further enrich its signification both in terms of its production and in terms of its reception.

Thanks to Fausto Ghisalberti (1932, 1933b and 1933c) and Frank Coulson (2015, 2016 and 2018), we know that the Latin *Metamorphoses* were commented on by medieval clerics. But many other texts also inspired our author. A simple survey of the sources of Book I (forty-three hundred verses) shows that only 37 % derives directly from Ovid's *Metamorphoses*. The rest comes from other sources and/or from the author's mind, heart and imagination. Several have been identified so far, both in Latin (mythographers and commentators, such as John of Garland, Arnulf of Orléans),[3] and in French (*Roman de la Rose*), but we suspect that the author also drew inspiration from vernacular sermons (Salvo García 2018a).

In terms of the reception of the text, it is possible to identify four large documentary series that bear witness to different stages of diffusion, namely: 1) a group of eighteen extant manuscripts of the *Ovide moralisé*; 2) an additional group of four manuscripts in which the versified text is

[1] See the OEF project (*Ovid in French: Genesis, Transformation, and Reception of the Ovide moralisé*) www.agence-nationale-recherche.fr/Project-ANR-12-FRAL-0001 [accessed 10 January 2020]. See also Mora, Possamaï-Pérez, Städtler and Trachsler 2011, and Cavagna, Graggero and Greub 2014.

[2] See Baker et al. 2018.

[3] It remains to be determined, however, if the author had direct or only indirect knowledge of these works.

accompanied by an important set of glosses; 3) two prose versions; 4) a series of printed editions, based on the second prose redaction. In reality, this typological overview only takes into consideration the format of the text. There are a large number of clues that inform us about reading practices, the public, the owners of the manuscripts and the printed editions. In this article, we will present some new perspectives on these questions, insisting, on the one hand, on recent and ongoing research dealing with the reception of the text and focusing, on the other hand, on one of the most innovative parts of the project: the study of the glosses.

Aspects of the Reception of the Text

The reception of the text is currently the object of an ongoing doctoral dissertation by Pauline Otzenberger.[4] As Marc-René Jung (1996a) has pointed out, each manuscript reveals an individual project: they can be considered as 'editions'. Let us focus on some manuscripts that reveal very different approaches to the text. For instance, the Lyon manuscript, owned by Jean de Berry, is an important example of 'lay reception'.[5] The scribe systematically eliminated the Christian, moral interpretations that followed the fables in his model. He only retains the euhemeristic, historical and naturalistic explanations.

Another group of manuscripts shows a peculiar program of illustrations. The manuscripts of the E group show some miniatures representing the gods.[6] They represent fifteen major deities and place one miniature at the beginning of each book. This choice must be linked to Pierre Bersuire who, in his *Ovidius moralizatus*, describes the fifteen main gods of the Greek pantheon in the same order: fol. 5 (Saturn), 28 (Jupiter), 56 (Juno), 72^v (Vulcan), 117 (Pluto), 133 (Athena), 156 (Diana), 176 (Bacchus), 199 (Hercules), 218^v (Venus), 241 (Mercury), 263 (Mars), 290 (Apollo), 315^v (Neptune), 353 (Pan). The same cycle inspired another copy: G^1.[7]

Finally, we have to mention the Copenhagen manuscript, which is certainly the richest and most luxurious codex.[8] This manuscript offers a French translation of another work by Pierre Bersuire, the *De formis deorum*, which is placed before the transcription of the *Ovide moralisé*. This beautiful

---

[4]   'Recherches sur la réception de l'*Ovide moralisé*' (unpublished doctoral dissertation, Université catholique de Louvain, ongoing).

[5]   Lyon, Bibliothèque municipale, MS 742, *c.* 1390.

[6] E^1: Geneva, Bibliothèque de Genève, MS français 176 (*c.* 1380); E^2: Vatican, Biblioteca Apostolica Vaticana, MS Reg. Lat. 1480 (*c.* 1380).

[7]   Paris, Bibliothèque nationale de France, MS français 373 (*c.* 1400).

[8]   Copenhagen, Det Kongelige Bibliotek, MS Thott 399 (*c.* 1480).

manuscript also presents an important number of glosses containing, among other things, citations of and allusions to other (biblical, patristic, classical) texts. We will return later to these.

As we can see, the *Ovide moralisé* participates in a network of texts. On the one hand, its author draws on a stock of allegorical interpretations offered by the Latin tradition, and his text can even enter into a sort of textual dialogue with later contributions to this same tradition, such as Pierre Bersuire's *De formis deorum*, in the Copenhagen manuscript. On the other hand, the material presentation of the text at times shows the influence of other texts and authors, namely, again, Pierre Bersuire, who influences the very structure of some manuscripts.

The Prose Versions

The transmission of the original, versified text of the *Ovide moralisé* developed over a short period of about one hundred and fifty years, from *c.* 1320 to 1470. At the end of this period, the versified text stopped being copied nor was it be printed. Instead, it was twice converted into prose. The 'prosification', or *mise en prose*, is typical of the late French Middle Ages. Versified texts were often replaced by prose versions, that were better aligned with aristocratic tastes in the second half of fifteenth century.[9] Finally, only the prose versions would be published at the end of fifteenth and over the course of the sixteenth centuries.

The first prose redaction, or Prose I, is conserved by only one extant manuscript now in the Vatican Library.[10] It was commissioned by René d'Anjou (1409–1480), king of Sicily, who was a very devout and cultivated man. The author of the prose redaction summarizes the text of the *Ovide moralisé* and specifically emphasizes the Christian explanations of the myths. Let us have a look at the prologue:

> mon tres redoubté seigneur René, par la grace de Dieu roy de Jherusalem et de Sicille, duc d'Anjou et de Bar [...], je, très humble clerc, serviteur et subgect d'icelluy très noble prince et demourant en sa ville d'Angiers, sans moy nommer pour vaine gloire eschiver, me suis mis à convertir de rime en prose françoise le grant livre d'Ovide nommé *Methamorphose*.[11]

---

[9] Prosification literally became a kind of fashion (see Colombo Timelli and others 2014). All the old chivalric romances and epics were put into prose. But other versified texts, some of which are even older than the *Ovide moralisé*, survive. We are thinking here about the *Romance of the Rose*, and even the *Pèlerinage de vie humaine* by Guillaume de Digulleville, a text that has strong moral religious and allegorical aspects, and that was printed during the sixteenth century.

[10] Vatican, Biblioteca Apostolica Vaticana, MS Reg. Lat., 1686 (after 1467).

[11] De Boer 1954: 42. All English translations of medieval French and Latin texts are mine.

[My very redoubtable lord, René, king of Jerusalem and Sicily, duke of Anjou and Bar by the grace of God; I, a very humble cleric, servant and subject of this noble prince, residing in his city of Angers, do not wish to name myself to avoid vainglory. I began to translate from rhymed verse to French prose Ovid's great book called *Metamorphoses*.]

This passage elicits at least two remarks. As one can see, the author names his patron, but not himself. Here, then, we have an example of the humility topos. At the end of the passage, however, the author claims to have translated Ovid's *Metamorphoses*. This is misleading, or at best ambiguous, of course, since he did not directly translate the Latin text, but simply put into prose the French *Ovide moralisé*. Although the secondary translator of Prose I professes his humility, he is in fact subtly undermining the primacy of Ovid by assuming that the *Ovide moralisé* and the Latin *Metamorphoses* are the same text, and by accessing the Latin text only through the French translation, which takes the role of the primary source text.[12]

The second passage we wish to analyze is also very interesting for several reasons. It deals with the myth of Pasiphae, the mother of the Minotaur and wife of Minos, king of Crete. Pasiphae, as is well known, fell in love with a bull and asked the architect Daedalus to construct a wooden cow in order to deceive the bull into loving and impregnating her. As an extreme case of sexual transgression, the myth offers ample inspiration for moralizing interpretation. In the spiritual allegory – the only type of moralizing allegory – Pasiphae is identified as the personification of lust and more specifically of the sin of bestiality.

As Renate Blumenfeld-Kosinski (1996) has pointed out, the myth of Pasiphae is a very good illustration of how the author of the *Ovide moralisé* takes inspiration from a large number of texts, namely other Ovidian texts – in this case, the *Ars amatoria* – as well as vernacular courtly romance. She suggests that the author here draws on the *Roman d'Enéas*, among other sources, and more particularly the scene where Lavinia falls in love with Enéas while observing him from the tower. She also reminds us that the myth is recalled several times in the *Metamorphoses*. Let us now turn to the version given in Anjou prose redaction. At the beginning of Book VIII, the text mentions a dialogue between Scylla and Minos:

Elle se print a injurier le roy Minos et luy reproucha ung horrible cas, dont il ne savoit encore riens, que Pasiphé sa femme avoit perpetré, comme cy après sera touchié en temps et en lieu le plus birefvement possible et couvertement que je pourray. Et qui plus au long le vouldroit veoir si le quière ou fueillés IIIIXXIX du livre rymé qui pour le convertir ycy en prose françoise m'a esté baillé. Car

---

[12] For the agonistic nature of medieval translations – and in particular of the *Ovide moralisé* – see Copeland 1991.

jamais je ne vouldroie occuper ma langue à reciter ne ma plume à escripre ung si vilain cas qu'il est. [...] Sa dicte femme, qui fut trop aise de son corps et trop oyseuse, conceut et enfanta par sa ribaudie durant l'absence de son dit mary ung monstre, qui fut demy homme et demy thoreau: Minotaurus, de l'engendrement duquel plus amplement declairer je me deporte pour l'orreur du cas.[13]

[She [Scylla] began to insult King Minos and reproached him for a horrible action, of which he was not yet aware, that Pasiphae, his wife, had committed, as will be recounted below, in due course, as briefly and allusively as I can. And whoever would like to know more, let him go and find the story on page 89 of the rhymed book that was given to me so that I can convert it into French prose, for I would never want to occupy my tongue to tell or my pen to write such an ugly affair. [...] His wife, who was too focused on lust and laziness, as a result of her adultery, during the absence of her husband, conceived and gave birth to a monster, which was half man and half bull: the Minotaur. I will try to talk about this one in more detail: it is a very horrible affair.]

The author refuses to relate the story and by doing so he gives us two crucial pieces of information: 1) he is very prude, and simply says: 'I don't want to pollute my tongue with such a disgusting story'; 2) he makes references to the manuscript he uses. He encourages the reader to read the story on his own, and provides precise indications for locating the myth in the other manuscript – obviously a witness containing an early redaction of the *Ovide moralisé*. Unfortunately, none of the twenty-one extant manuscripts begin the story of Pasiphae on folio 89.[14]

Let us consider another interesting passage, located in Book XV, the final book of the *Metamorphoses*, in which Ovid relates some aspects of Pythagoras's theory about the geometry of the cosmos. As Jean-Yves Tilliette (2009) has pointed out, Ovid surrenders his voice to the philosopher in order to allow him to recapitulate the whole text and give a kind of key to reading and interpreting the text. The author of the *Ovide moralisé*, on the other hand, insists on the fact that Pythagoras's words should not be taken 'literally', but should be subjected to the same allegorical interpretation as the other myths. He uses traditional hermeneutical vocabulary ('Mes sous la fable gist couverte | La sentence plus profitable', XV. 2536–37) and translates the whole discourse.[15] What does this complex and problematic text become in the hands of the author of the first prose redaction? Here is the passage concerning Pythagoras:

---

[13] De Boer 1954: 225–26.

[14] Cerrito notices that the manuscript must have been very dense (in Baker et al. 2018: I, 241–42).

[15] De Boer 1938: 256. 'But underneath the fable is hidden the most valuable teaching'.

Et moult d'autres exemples et raisons racompta Pittagoras, dont je me tays yci pour abregier, et mesmement pour ce que la saincte foy catholique de Jhesucrist dit le contraire, laquelle il fault croire soubz peine de dampnacion eternelle. (De Boer 1954: 380–81)

[And Pythagoras told many other exemplary stories and made other speeches, which I will not relate here because I have to shorten my text, and also because the holy Catholic faith of Jesus Christ says the opposite. And this [faith] must be believed under pain of eternal damnation.]

Once again, our author refuses to put this passage into prose because it contradicts catholic doctrine.

A superficial reading of the text might suggest that it is a poor and mutilated version of the *Ovide moralisé*. Several articles have repeatedly expressed such an opinion over the last years.[16] Recent research by Pauline Otzenberger (2018) tends to renew our knowledge of this version and offer a more positive view of this version and the work done by its author. In her ongoing doctoral dissertation, she shows that the author has a vast knowledge of mythology and inserts various glosses and explanations concerning several characters, taking his information from other passages of the *Ovide moralisé* or from other sources such as Boccaccio's *Genealogia deorum gentilium* (Zaccaria 1998).

The second prose version, Prose II, dated to *c.* 1470, is extant in three luxurious manuscripts.[17] Although the author doesn't name his patron, specialists consider it to have been executed for Louis of Bruges, a very important patron of the arts and a book collector (Jung 1997).

The Parisian manuscript, BnF fr. 137, opens with a very large miniature composed of two parts. On the left, one recognizes Ovid showing an egg which, as is well known, was linked to his name by a strong pseudo-etymological tradition (*Ovidius ab ovo*). The egg also has a pregnant symbolic value as an image of the universe, the cosmos, and also as an image of rebirth and new life. The egg is also an invitation to go beyond the surface – a mineral surface that encloses organic life. In short, this is a cogent symbol of the extraordinary hermeneutic richness of the text. On the right side of the illustration, one finds a representation of the Creation of the four elements: air, fire, water and earth, each of which the artist has filled with numerous animals.

As for the text, Prose II generally stays closer to the versified *Ovide moralisé* than does Prose I, but eliminates the Christian, moral allegories.

---

[16] Moreover, studies specifically devoted to this version are relatively rare. Among those that do exist, see in particular Capelli 2013.

[17] London, British Library, MS Royal, 17. E. IV; Paris, Bibliothèque Nationale de France, MS français 137; Saint Petersburg, National Library of Russia, MS F. v. XIV. 1.

The prosifier only reproduces the euhemerist, historical, and naturalistic explanations. While we have already encountered this phenomenon in the Lyon manuscript, it must be said that there seems to be no genetic link between these two versions of the text.

In order to compare the two prose versions, deviations in the treatment of the myth of Pasiphae are revealing. Firstly, the author of Prose II does not shy away from retelling the story. Moreover, one of the illuminators choses to illustrate a scene of seduction with clear erotic overtones. In manuscript Paris, BnF fr. 137, fol. 102ᵛ, a beautiful miniature shows Pasiphae in front of the bull. She is caressing him and the animal smiles at her with a mischievous look in its eyes; the lower part of the animal's body shows that he is clearly ready for more (the bull in fact has a strong erection). The text says:

> De male heure veit le tor ne sa beaulté; non pas le tor ne sa beaulté, mais le vit, car certes a ne l'eust amé se grant vit n'eust eu. Moult me poise et desplait quant tel lait et hontoyable nom m'en convient dire et nommer.[18]

> [It is by her misfortune that she saw the bull and his beauty. In fact, it was not the bull nor his beauty, but his pizzle, for she certainly wouldn't have fallen in love with him if he hadn't had such a big pizzle. It grieves and upsets me to be compelled to say such an ugly and shameful word.]

The text, even more explicit and insistent than the image, bluntly states: 'certainly, she would not have fallen in love with him if he weren't so well endowed'. At least, to put it politely, because the author in fact uses the word 'vit', which belongs to a much lower register: the author talks of the bull's 'big cock'. But immediately after this, he adds: 'I regret to be compelled to say such an ugly and shameful word'. This is clearly a fictitious regret, for he seems to be rather enjoying the interplay between different registers as he adds unnecessary but steamy details.

The Printed Editions

The printing history of the *Ovide moralisé* begins very early. As I mentioned earlier, the versified text never made it to print. The Prose II version, however, fared better. In 1484, Colard Mansion, a very well-known Belgian printer located in Bruges, printed a massive volume containing Prose II with slight modification of some linguistic features. He commissioned thirty-four wood engravings for this printing: seventeen large images, and seventeen smaller ones. In addition to the engravings, this copy, was illuminated by hand. It is a very large book, consisting of no less than three hundred and ninety-one folios, that is presented as follows:

[18] MS français 137, fol. 103rb.

Cy commence Ovide de Salmonnen son livre intitulé Methamorphose contenant XV livres particuliers, moralisié par maistre Thomas Waleys, docteur en theologie de l'ordre Sainct Dominique, translaté et compilé par Colard Mansion en la noble ville de Bruges.[19]

[Here begins Ovid of Sulmona, his work, *Metamorphoses*, containing 15 books, moralized by master Thomas Waleys, doctor of theology, friar of the order of St. Dominic, translated and compiled by Colard Mansion in the noble city of Bruges.]

This passage elicits at least three remarks. First of all, one may recall that 'Salmonnen' designates Ovid's birthplace: Sulmona, Italy. Secondly, the rather surprising mention of Thomas Waleys deserves a word of explanation. Thomas Waleys was a Dominican friar, master of theology at Oxford University, who in fact played no role in the moralizations printed by Mansion. There was, however, an erroneous tradition that attributed to him the Latin *Ovidius moralizatus* which, as we already pointed out, was written by Pierre Bersuire. Finally, we might underscore the fact that Colard Mansion affirms that he personally 'translated' and 'compiled' the *Metamorphoses*. Of course, Colard Mansion is a well-known translator, who translated various Latin texts into French. In this case, however, he simply uses the Prose II redaction, which was already written in French. So is the presentation of the book in the incipit deceitful?[20] Yes and no. The verb 'compile' used to describe part of the printer's activity is perfectly accurate, as is the mention of Thomas Waleys / Pierre Bersuire in relation to the moralizing of the text. Colard Mansion obviously took advantage of the existence of the text offered by Prose II, but it must be remembered that this redaction eliminates the moral, Christian interpretations. That is why Mansion decided to insert a new series of interpretations, which he actually wrote himself on the basis of Pierre de Bersuire's *Ovidius moralizatus*. So it must be recognized that in fact he did personally do some translating – if only of Bersuire – in compiling his new version of the *Metamorphoses*.

When narrating the mythological fables, Colard Mansion closely follows Prose II, with only minor modifications. Let's take another look at Pasiphae, to get a better idea:

---

[19] Publius Ovidius Naso, *Metamorphoses [French] Ovide ... son livre intitulé Metamorphose* (adapted by Colard Mansion, with a commentary) (Bruges: Colard Mansion, 1484), p. 7. USTC: 71418. I have consulted a copy held in Bibliothèque Royale de Belgique, Réserve Précieuse (shelfmark: INC C 367). Reproductions of the book are accessible online uurl.kbr.be/1621899 [accessed 20 January 2020].

[20] At the end of the book, however, he writes that he found (trouvé) the text of the *Metamorphoses* 'bien et tres congruement translaté par meilleurs clers et plus sages de moi' [well translated by better and wiser clercs than me], Ovidius, *Metamorphoses* (Bruges: Colard Mansion, 1484), p. 781.

De male heure veyst le thor ne sa beauté; non pas le tor ne sa beauté, mais le membre du thor! Car certes elle ne l'eust ja amé se grant membre n'eust porté. Moult me poise et desplaist quant tel lait vergoignable et honteable nom me convient dire et nommer ou tant de hommes nobles et meismement tant de nobles et chastes damoiselles me porront veoir et oÿr lire.[21]

[It is by her misfortune that she saw the bull and his beauty. In fact, it was not the bull and his beauty but his member, for she would certainly not have fallen in love with him if he had not had such a large member. It weighs on me and displeases me to have to utter and mention such a naughty and shameful word where many noble men and many noble and chaste damsels will see me and listen to my reading of the text.]

Colard Mansion changes the keyword 'vit' [pizzle] to the more neutral 'membre' [member]. However, he copies and amplifies the apology that follows, 'I regret to say such an ugly and shameful word', which is not particularly coherent. However, that apology gives him the opportunity to paint the social portrait of an aristocratic audience.

Nine years after 1484, the Parisian printer Antoine Vérard printed a new edition of Colard Mansion's book. He chose a different, and quite significant title: *La Bible des poëtes*. The choice is very interesting indeed, because it underscores the link between mythical fictions and the truth of the Holy Bible. Through his choice of title, Vérard suggests that the readers of Ovid will find therein the proper way to interpret myths. Let us read an extract from the *prologue*:

Parquoy je, vostre treshumble et obeissant serviteur, a l'ayde de Dieu mon pere createur, selon mon simple entendement ay vouloir aprés le commandement de vous, mon tres redoubté et souverain seigneur Charles huytiesme de ce nom, trescrestien Roy de France, vous faire nouvellement ce present livre intitulé Ovide de methamorphose et en exposer les fables litterallement, celles au moins que je verray les plus convenables, puys aprés selon les expositions allegoriques et moralles les reduyre a aucune verité. Car il me semble que ce ne soit point impertinent de faire et que Ovide Salomeuse, qui si grant poëte fut que son livre par anthonomasie et excellence est appellé la Bible des poëtes, n'y assembla point les fictions et fables qui y sont qu'elles ne fussent reductives à aucune verité, ainsi comme bien appert en son livre.[22]

[That is why I, your most humble and obedient servant, with the help of God, my Creator Father, according to my weak talent, have decided – according to

---

[21] Ovidius, *Metamorphoses* (Bruges: Colard Mansion, 1484), p. 399.

[22] Publius Ovidius Naso, *La Bible des poetes metamorphose* (Paris: Antoine Vérard, 1493/1494), p. 14. I have consulted a copy held at the Bibliothèque nationale de France, département Réserve des livres rares (shelfmark: VELINS-559). USTC: 37566. Also available on Gallica: gallica.bnf.fr/ark:/12148/btv1b8626777x/f14.item [accessed 17 January 2020].

your command, my most redoubtable lord and sovereign, Charles the Eighth, very Christian King of France – to translate anew this present book entitled Ovid of Metamorphosis and to expose literally its tales, at least those which I will consider the most appropriate, and then to draw from it the true teaching, according to the allegorical and moral expositions. For it seems to me that it is not out of place to do this, and I believe that Ovid of Sulmona, who was such a great poet that his book is called by antonomasia the Bible of Poets, did not collect the tales and fictions therein if they could not be reduced to moral truths, so as it appears in his book.]

Once again, the role played by the editor is not very clear. Vérard dedicates his book to the French king Charles VIII (1483–1498), saying that he wants to 'remake this book for you' (vous faire nouvellement ce present livre) – the formula is ambiguous. After that, he affirms that he will interpret at least those myths that he deems appropriate to explain.

Finally, he mentions the name of the author. In the curious adjective 'Salomeuse', one again recognizes a reference to the birthplace of Ovid, Sulmona. Vérard points out that the Latin poet 'would not have collected these myths if they didn't contain some hidden truth, some word of wisdom.'

This new version was printed for the first time in 1493, then reprinted in 1499 and 1503. The book survives in several copies that present important differences. Some are printed on paper, with wood engravings; some luxury copies are printed on parchment, without wood engravings, of course, but with a painted illustration instead. The text is nearly identical to that of Colard Mansion, and shows only minor modifications.

During this period, printers were merchants, and had no shame in appropriating others' texts. It is worth remembering that back then there was no law protecting authorship and intellectual property. Michel Le Noir noticed that Vérard's edition had enjoyed wide success, and decided to publish two small books, as a sort of byproduct: *Le Livre du vaillant Perseus, filz de Jupiter*, in 1510 and *Le Livre de Orpheus translaté de latin en françoys, ouquel y a plusieurs choses recreatives*, also printed around 1510.[23] Those books are in fact extracts from the *Bible des poëtes*, taken, respectively, from Books IV-VI and X-XI.

---

[23] *Le Livre du vaillant Perseus, filz de Jupiter* (Paris: Michel Le Noir, 1510). USTC: 55680. The only extant copy is held in London, British Library (shelfmark: 12510.c.6); *Le Livre de Orpheus translaté de latin en françoys, ouquel y a plusieurs choses recreatives* (Paris: Michel Le Noir, 1510(?)). Paris, Bibliothèque nationale de France, Réserve des livres rares (shelfmark: RESP-Z-421); see gallica.bnf.fr/ark:/ 12148/bpt6k994084c/f1.image [accessed 20 January 2020].

Philippe le Noir, the son of Michel, published the whole *Bible des poëtes* twice: the first edition in 1523, the second in 1531.[24] The 1531 edition is the last printing of the *Bible des poëtes*.

In 1532, the Lyon-based printer Romain Morin produced a new version of this work under the new and elegant title: *Le Grant Olympe des histoires poëtiques du prince des poëtes Ovide Naso en sa Methamorphose*.[25] This edition marks a turning point. It embodies a different editorial and intellectual project, as can be seen both in the text and in the material aspects of its presentation. The book is of a small format, an *in-octavo* of about 130 x 190 mm, but is rather thick, with its six hundred and nine pages, printed in humanistic characters. This is an original choice. Until then, the printer had used a letter type that imitated the Burgundian handwriting known as *bastarda*. In this case, however, Romain Morin used a letter type imitating the Italian *rotunda* or humanistic handwriting.

Pierre Bersuire's prologue is removed. And once again the interpretation of the myths changes. The new prologue declares that the ancient paradigm is no longer valid. The didactic value of the myths remains, but the key to discovering it no longer lies with the Bible or Thomas Waleys, but rather with the philosopher Plato:

> Le divin philosophe Platon étant malade, et voiant les limites de sa vie, commanda luy estre faict oreillier du livre de Sophron, poëte mimographe, estimant poësie estre parfonde philosophie couverte du rideau de infatigable delectation; et ayant la cognoissance de la vie de l'homme, que n'est que une fable, voulut mourir sur icelluy. (fol. 1ᵛ)

> [The divine philosopher Plato, being sick, and seeing death approaching, commanded that the book of Sophron, poet and mythographer, be given to him as a pillow, for he considered poetry to be a profound philosophy, covered with the veil of untiring delight; and having the knowledge of man's life, which is just a fable, wanted to die on that book.]

Let's leaf through to the fable of Pasiphae. The details concerning the bull's genitalia are omitted. This version just insists, as did previous texts, on the animal and the brutish character of a love that goes contrary to nature.

---

[24] *La Bible des poëtes, Methamorphoze. Nouvellement imprimé a Paris* (Paris: Philippe Le Noir, 1523). USTC: 64020. *La bible des poëtes de Ovide Methamorphose*. Translatee de latin en françoys. Nouvellement Imprimee a Paris (Paris: Philippe Le Noir, 1531) USTC: 47798.

[25] Ovid, *Le Grant Olympe des histoires poëtiques du prince des poëtes Ovide Naso en sa Methamorphose* (Lyon: Romain Morin, 1532). USTC: 49832. I have consulted a digitized copy held at the Bibliothèque nationale de France, Réserve des livres rares (shelfmark: RESP-YC-1627); see gallica.bnf.fr/ark:/12148/btv1b8600297j [accessed 20 January 2020].

Car ung jour estoit Pasiphe aux fenestres de son hault palais, si regarda vers la prarie et vit entre plusieurs vaches ung toreau fier et coraigeux, lequel elle avisa et choisit par dessus tous aultres, moult luy pleust sa beaulté et son fier contenement. Tant le regarda la desnaturee folle que son amour fut si esprinse envers la beste que maint souspir luy en fit faire et que moult la contraignit la bestialité qui en elle estoit. (fol. 42r)

[For one day Pasiphae stood at the windows of his high palace and looked out into the meadow and saw between several cows a proud and brave bull. She saw him and spotted him among the others. She greatly appreciated his beauty and his proud appearance. She looked at him so much, the crazy distorted one, that she fell so much in love with the beast that she sighed many times and the bestiality that was in her got the upper hand.]

Instead of celebrating the bull's attributes, the author focuses on the woman's reaction and the expression of her love through sighs (*maint souspir*).

The Latin Glosses

This final section offers an exploration of some aspects of the four glossed witnesses of the versified *Ovide moralisé*, namely manuscripts *A¹*, *G¹*, *G³* and *F*.[26] Jean-Baptiste Guillaumin (2018b) edited the glosses to Book I from the first three manuscripts.[27] After his edition, Laura Endress discovered a fourth glossed manuscript, which has been given the siglum *F*. She is currently preparing a study dealing with its position in the transmission of the text. Thibaut Radomme (2019) has recently finished his doctoral dissertation, devoted to an in-depth study of the glossed manuscripts. Based on his work, it is possible to establish a typology of these glosses, which are both in Latin and French. The analysis will focus on the myth of Apollo and Daphne, beginning with the Latin glosses.[28]

First of all, we have a group of moralizing glosses (accompanied, or not, by biblical quotations). For example, in the description of Daphne, the text reads: '*Elle avoit | Crins blons despigniez*' (Baker et al. 2018: 155, I. 2879–80). The gloss explains the iconic *topos* of blond hair, saying 'By "blond hair", the text means the pure passions of pious souls'. This is followed by a

---

[26]   *A¹*: Rouen, Bibliothèque Municipale, MS O.4 (c. 1320); *G¹*: MS fr. 373; *G³*: MS Thott 399 (*c.* 1480); the location and signature of *F* has not yet been revealed by Laura Endress, who discovered the manuscript.

[27]   See also Guillaumin 2018a.

[28]   We presented a first draft of this analysis at Western Michigan University, Kalamazoo: M. Cavagna and Th. Radomme, 'Ovide Moralized Twice: On Three Glossed Manuscript of the *Ovide Moralisé*', *52th International Medieval Congress, Kalamazoo* (Michigan), 11-14 May, 2017 (session 109).

reference to the Song of Songs (VII. 5): 'The hair of your head is like royal purple.'[29]

The second category presents glosses that simply quote various *auctoritates* without any further explanation. It is left to the reader to understand the meaningful parallel made by the commentator when he decides to quote the *auctoritas* – here the Bible, Song of Songs again – in front of this specific portion of text. In fact, the logic of the quoting mechanism is quite obvious: the commentator reacts to keywords which then lead to search for *auctoritates*: for example, in the following passage, 'bele' (beautiful) activates the biblical reminiscence of a passage containing the word *pulchra*. Sometimes, we can find a sequence of such glosses:

Gloss[30]	Text (*Ovide moralisé*, I. 2878–93)[31]
Cant. iº: Ecce tu PULCHRA es, amica mea; ecce tu pulchra, oculi tui columbarum etc.[32]	Phebus ne se puet saoler D'esgarder la BELE; elle avoit Crins blons despigniez: quant la voit, 'Diex, dist il, quel cheveleüre,
Cant. iiiiº: Vulnerasti cor meum, soror mea, sponsa mea, uulnerasti cor meum in uno OCULORUM tuorum, in uno crine colli tui etc.	S'el fust pignie a sa droiture!' Vis li est des vairs IEX rians Que sont estoiles flamboians.
Idem iº: OSCULETUR me osculo oris sui.	Il voit sa BOUCHE petitete Qui pour BESIER samble estre fete. Mes li vooirs ne souffist mie: Trop la vaudroit avoir BESIE; Voit la face blanche et rosine Qui samble rose et flour d'espine,
Idem: Pulchrae sunt genae tuae sicut turturis et COLLUM tuum sicut monilia.	Voit la potrine et voit le COL Qui sont fet pour amuser fol, Les lons dois et les blanches mains
[Song of Songs 1: How BEAUTIFUL you are, my darling! Oh, how beautiful! Your eyes are doves, etc. Song of Songs 4: You	[Phœbus can't get enough of looking at the BEAUTIFUL one; she's got her blond hair down. When he sees her, he says: 'My

---

[29] Gloss: 'Per crines aureos notari possunt purae affectationes animae sanctae. Cant. vii: *Capilli capitis tui sicut purpura regia etc.*'. See Guillaumin 2018b: 280.

[30] Guillaumin 2018b: 280–81.

[31] Baker et al. 2018: 155.

[32] The use of the abbreviation 'etc.' in medieval *glossae* is a very widespread and characteristic phenomenon that reveals a precise reading practice: the author of the gloss provides only the beginning of a biblical or patristic passage that the reader - commentator (often a cleric, a preacher) will be free to develop according to his own sensibility.

have stolen my heart, my sister, my bride; you have stolen my heart with one glance of your EYES, with one jewel of your necklace, etc. Idem 1: Let him KISS me with the kisses of his mouth. Idem: Your cheeks are beautiful like turtle doves, your NECK with strings of jewels.]

God, what hair, if only it were properly combed!'. Her blue EYES look like flaming stars to him. He sees her small MOUTH that seems made for KISSING. But the sight is not enough for him: he wants to KISS her too badly. He looks et her white and red face that looks like a rose or a hawthorn. He looks at her chest and her NECK which are made to drive anyone crazy, the long fingers and the white hands.]

It is quite easy to identify the words that triggered the biblical reminiscence: 'pulchra' echoes 'belle'; 'oculorum' corresponds to 'iex' [the eyes]; 'oris' and 'osculetur', to 'bouche' and 'besier' [the mouth] and [kiss]; 'collum', to 'col', [the neck].

Sometimes, glosses of type 1 and type 2 can be found together, in a 'cluster of glosses'. It is very important to note that these glosses could be helpful in improving our understanding of the text and of its manuscript tradition. Here is another interesting example of the second type.

Gloss[33]

Text
(*Ovide moralisé*, I. 3378–79)[34]

Prima ad Corinth. xiii°: Si linguis hominum loquar et angelorum, caritatem autem non habeam etc.

Quar Dieux meïsme est charité,
A tesmoing de l'auctorité

Aug.: Caritas est potus sitientibus, esurienti dulcedo his qui in amaritudine sunt, solacium uerum et gratum his qui in tristitia sunt, portus nauigantibus uel fluctantibus, uia itinerantibus, pax peregrinantibus etc. Tullius in libro de uera amicitia.

[*First Corinthians 13*: If I speak in human and angelic tongues but do not have charity etc., *Augustine*: Charity is a drink for the thirsty, it is sweetness for those who find themselves in bitterness, relief for those who are in pain, it is a port for mariners, a way for the itinerant travellers, it is peace for those who wander, etc. *Cicero, in Book on friendship*.]

[For God himself is charity, as evidenced by the authority.]

The text says 'auctorité', which is a singular form, certainly referring to the Holy Scripture. But while preparing our edition, we were very surprised to

[33] Guillaumin 2018b: 286.
[34] Baker et al. 2018: 179.

see that several copyists – which are not linked together in the *stemma codicum* – had changed this singular form into a plural: 'des auctorités'.[35] An enlightening explanation for this is suggested by the glosses to the passage. Indeed, next to this section of the text, the commentator aligned three references to different *auctores*: the Bible, of course (1 Corinthians 13.1); a Patristic author, Augustine (in reality pseudo-Augustine);[36] and a classical one, Cicero (*Laelius de amicitia*).

The third category presents numerous quotations of the *Metamorphoses*. In the first book, these glosses to the *Ovide moralisé* quote almost twenty percent of the corresponding book of the *Metamorphoses*. The quotations contribute to structuring the French text and suggest practices of parallel reading of the *Metamorphoses* and the *Ovide moralisé*.

Gloss[37]	Text (*Ovide moralisé*, I. 2898–99)[38]
Ouidius: Siqua latent meliora putat, etc.	Et plus est biaux, si comme il cuide, Li remanans qu'il ne voit mie
[(Ovid, *Metamorphoses*, I. 502). Ovid: he thinks that whatever lies under her clothes must be better.]	[And he thinks that what he doesn't see is even more beautiful.]

In Book I, there are 127 quotations of the *Metamorphoses*. This, of course, sheds a new light on the question of the clerical *versus* vernacular reception of the *Metamorphoses*, a thrilling question that is at the very center of Thibaut Radomme's thesis and forthcoming book.[39]

Finally, a last group of glosses establish links to Ovid's other works. Two glosses refer to the *Ars amandi* and another to the *Remedia amoris*. These glosses are particularly interesting, because they are not just some links to Ovidian intertext. The following example is taken from the myth of Io and Jupiter.

Gloss: [40]	Text (*Ovide moralisé*, I. 3892–93)[41]
Secundum hoc potest intelligi quod Ouidius dicit in Arte amatoria: Nec fuge niligenae nymphatica templa iuuencae | Yo facit multum, quod fuit ipsa Iovi.	Si mist sa cure et volt entendre As autres vendre et decevoir.

---

[35] [de l'auctorité] des auctorités $D^5G^2YZ^{12}$.

[36] The citation comes from a sermon by Césaire of Arles, wrongly attributed to Augustine.

[37] Guillaumin 2018b: 281.

[38] Baker et al. 2018: 156.

[39] The study will also provide new insights into the identity of the author.

[40] Guillaumin 2018: 295.

[41] Baker et al. 2018: 208.

[According to this, one may understand what Ovid says in the Art of love [Ovid, *Ars Amatoria*, i. 77–78]: Do not skip the temples of the Nilean Cow, who persuades so many women to play the part she [Io] played to Jupiter.]

[She puts all her energy into selling others (making them prostitute) and misleading them.]

Here the text gives the historical interpretation of Io: she was a 'maquerelle' (keeper of a brothel). The gloss says: 'According to this, one may understand what Ovid says in the *Art of Love*'. As one can see, what is most interesting is that the commentator claims that this passage of the *Ovide moralisé* can be used to better understand the *Ars amandi*.

In the second example, the commentator thinks that the same Ovidian passage can find another explanation when being read in relation to the *Ovide moralisé*:

Gloss[42]	Text (*Ovide moralisé*, I. 4027–29)[43]
Secundum hoc potest exponi aliter illud Ouidii in Arte: Nec fuge niligenae nymphatica temple Dyanae | Yo facit multas, quod fuit ipsa Ioui.	Qu'ele est honoree et servie Par tout le monde en sainte Iglise Et de mains pecheours requise.

[According to this, one may understand what Ovid says in the *Art of love* [Ovid, *Ars Amatoria*, i. 77–78]: Do not skip the temples of the Nilean Diane, who persuades so many women to play the part she [Io] played to Jupiter.]

[That she is honoured and prayed for by everyone in the church and invoked by many sinners.]

Here the text compares Io to Mary of Egypt, who used to be a prostitute, but who converted and became a saint. The gloss says: 'According to this, one may understand differently' the same passage of the *Art of Love*.

Thus, the Latin intertextual glosses create a dynamic interaction between texts, that enriches and deepens the medieval reader's understanding of Ovid's thought and works.

If we now turn to the marginal annotations in French, we first find a series of allegorical glosses. At the very beginning of the story of Daphne, the gloss gives a key to interpreting the myth, that links Daphne to virginity:

---

42   Guillaumin 2018: 295.
43   Baker et al. 2018: 215.

Gloss[44]	Text (*Ovide moralisé*, I. 2737–39)[45]
Note ci aprez que par Dané, qui fut muee en lorier, puet estre entendue chasteté ou virginité.	Se nulz quiert pour quoi ne comment Li loriers vint premierement Je le li dirai sans demour.
[Note below that Daphne, who has been transformed into a laurel tree, represents chastity or virginity.]	[If anyone wonders what the origin of the laurel is, I will tell him immediately.]

The beginning of this long gloss anticipates an explanation that will be given by the versified text much later (I. 3080–86). This is a very interesting aspect of the glosses that should be analyzed in the context of a performative reading. In front of a live audience, one can imagine that foreknowledge of the interpretation to come was useful to the reader as he began to recount the myth. The gloss is a very useful instrument, because it indicates alongside the text a series of key-words.

A second category of French glosses presents explanations or punctual commentaries on isolated words:

Gloss:[46]	Text (*Ovide moralisé*, I. 2620)[47]
C'est assavoir peché contre nature	Trop fet li pechiez a blasmer
[That is, sin against nature.]	[Sin must be severely blamed.]

The preceding example shows how important it is that the copyist transcribes the glosses next to the corresponding lines of the *Ovide moralisé*.

A large number of French glosses take the shape of rubric-like marginal notes, that indicate narrative contents. For example: 'La fable comment Dané aprez ce que elle ot faicte sa priere a son pere fut muee en lorier' [The fable that tells how Daphne, after she prayed her father, was turned into a laurel tree].[48] This kind of note functions like chapter titles or a table of contents.

The fourth and last type of French glosses give indications concerning the structure of the text, potentially allowing the reader to skip passages and jump to other sections of the text:

---

[44] Guillaumin 2018: 277.
[45] Baker et al. 2018: 146.
[46] Guillaumin 2018: 276.
[47] Baker et al. 2018: 139.
[48] Guillaumin 2018: 284.

> or retourne l'aucteur a la fable (Guillaumin 2018b: 257)
>
>> [now the author returns to the fable]
>
> encore exposition des fables (Guillaumin 2018b: 267)
>
>> [another explanation of the fables]
>
> exposition de la fable (Guillaumin 2018b: 275)
>
>> [explanation of the fable]
>
> autre exposition (Guillaumin 2018b: 295)
>
>> [another explanation]

These annotations often correspond to *lettrines*, paragraph marks, etc., in the French text.

But things are not as simple as they may appear, since the glosses are not exclusively linked to the versified French text. As Thibaut Radomme (in press: 291–312) has pointed out, glosses are also linked to one another, in a very significant system of internal relations. As he shows in his thesis and forthcoming book (Radomme 2019), the commentary apparatus is linked to the text of the *Ovide moralisé*, because it works horizontally, through a system of immediate interactions between the margin and the text: the glosses' main purpose is to comment upon and develop the ideas presented by the *Ovide moralisé*. But the commentary is also independent from the *Ovide moralisé*, since it also works vertically, through a system of internal references: the full meaning of the glosses can only be understood if one is aware of the ties that bind them together as the expression of a coherent idea.

Conclusions

To conclude, it will be useful to return to the concept of 'network'. Although the *Ovide moralisé* is a very long and complex poem in and of itself, the study of its manuscript, print and textual traditions shows that it was often 'accompanied' or 'surrounded' by other texts. A first conclusion that might be drawn is that the Latin hypotext of the *Metamorphoses* was never entirely 'replaced' by its French adaptation. Some glosses confirm that both texts were read in parallel, and we have reason to suspect that the Latin source also exerted an influence on the division into books in French manuscripts. Secondly, Pierre Bersuire's *Ovidius moralizatus* and *De formis deorum* also played a very important role in the late-medieval reception of our text, most notably in some iconographic cycles and in the 'compilated' version elaborated and printed by Colard Mansion.

Future research on the prose versions and on the glosses will certainly shed new light on the question of the relationship between lay and clerical culture. And it is a personal source of both pride and optimism that the most innovative aspects of research presented here are now being developed by some brilliant young scholars.

7

MARYLÈNE POSSAMAÏ-PÉREZ

THE *OVIDE MORALISÉ*: FROM THE TEXT AND GLOSSES OF OVID'S *METAMORPHOSES* TO THE TEXT OF MS ROUEN BM. O. 4.

In order to study how the fables of Ovid's *Metamorphoses* are reworked in the old French text transmitted in the manuscript of the *Ovide moralisé* Rouen Bm O.4 (copied at the beginning of the fourteenth century), it is necessary to examine the intermediary texts through which medieval readers accessed the Latin poem.[1] It is important to mention the glosses copied in the manuscripts of the *Metamorphoses* which circulated in the thirteenth and fourteenth centuries, and which transmitted 'in catena' previous commentaries, particularly Arnulf of Orleans's *Allegoriae* and John of Garland's *Integumenta*.[2] The manuscripts *Vaticanus Latinus 1479* and *Vaticanus Latinus 1598*, for example, present the Latin text of the *Metamorphoses* accompanied by glosses offering an example of the kind of source text that the anonymous author of the *Ovide moralisé* may have used.[3]

In this article, I take the fable of Callisto as a case study. In Book II of Ovid's *Metamorphoses*, this myth occupies verses 409 to 530. In the *Ovide moralisé*, it is narrated in verses 1365 to 1694, to which should be added verses 1695 to 2006 for moralizations, verses 2007 to 2057 for Juno's request to the god Ocean, and verses 2058 to 2120 for the interpretation of

---

[1]   For the Latin text, I will use Lafaye 1966. For the *Ovide moralisé* I will use De Boer 1915–38, which relies mainly on manuscript Rouen Bm O.4, from now on *Om*. The research group 'Ovide en Français' has so far only published the first book of the poem (Baker et al. 2018).

[2]   On the glosses of the *Metamorphoses*, see Coulson 2015 and Salvo-Garcia 2018a, 2018b, 2018c, 2018d and 2018e. For Arnulf of Orleans, see Ghisalberti 1932; for John of Garland, Ghisalberti 1933b.

[3]   See Coulson 1987: 154, 158, 163 and 1994. I am relying on the transcripts of Lisa Ciccone, whom I thank here. The translations of these transcripts are mine. I did all the translations from Latin, except most of those of the *Metamorphoses*. See Ciccone et al. 2020. I must also warmly thank Frank T. Coulson for giving me his transcripts of the glosses of *Vat. lat. 1598* to the fable of Callisto (verses 409–780). I have translated them. See Coulson et al. (2021). See also Possamaï-Pérez (2008) on the link between glosses and the *Om*.

this request. In total, the story covers 122 verses in Ovid's poem, while the Old French poem devotes 330 verses to the legend *stricto sensu* and 50 verses to Juno's journey to the gods of Ocean, which is an amplification of the source text.[4] Furthermore, the translator adds more than 300 verses of moralizations. While it was already important in the Latin hypotext,[5] the fable of Callisto thus takes on much greater proportions in the *Ovide moralisé*. In the following analysis, I will try to characterize the nature of this amplification.

Let us briefly recall the fable of the nymph Callisto, who was a companion of the goddess Diana, and therefore devoted to chastity. She was deceived by Jupiter, who took on Diana's form in order to rape her. Callisto conceived a child from this rape, and Diana, noticing her pregnancy, chased away the unfortunate nymph, who gave birth to a son, Arcas. Callisto suffered a double punishment when Juno, mad with jealousy, turned her into a bear. One day, the young Arcas, unaware of his mother's metamorphosis, was about to kill her in a hunt, but Jupiter finally took pity on Callisto and offered her and her son a second metamorphosis, more glorious than the first one. Mother and son became the constellation of the Big Dipper flanked by its keeper, the Artophylax.[6]

After translating the legend into Old French, the author of the *Ovide moralisé* offers his readers an explanation of this myth that would be acceptable to medieval mythographers and readers.[7] The characteristic of the interpreter of the *Ovide moralisé* (at least of the original poet of the *Ovide moralisé*) is the establishment of a double level of interpretation.[8] He

---

[4] The usual proportion of French translation is of two octosyllables for a Latin hexameter. So there is an amplification of about 150 verses. We will see on which points of the legend the emphasis is placed.

[5] For the terminology, see Genette 1982: 13 and 554–55.

[6] In French, the Big Dipper is 'Grande Ourse' (Great Bear). Regarding Callisto's story see *Metamorphoses*, I. 54, note 4. In the rest of the myth, Juno's vindictiveness then increases: she goes to the god Ocean to ask him not to allow the star to complete the end of its revolution in his waters. In the limited context of this article, I will leave aside this last episode of the legend and its interpretation by the author of the *Ovide moralisé*.

[7] I will use the term 'translation', but some remarks are in order. Although the anonymous fourteenth-century author knows Latin perfectly and shows himself capable of faithfully translating his source, the medieval concept of translation (*traductio*) differs from the modern one: that is, of a translation that respects not only the letter of the text, but tries to render its spirit. The medieval author does not hesitate to amplify or shorten his source, or to inflect it in order to justify his allegorical enterprise, which is based on the *similitudo* between fable and interpretation.

[8] Some later witnesses, such as ms *B* (Lyon, Bm 742) and ms *Z*³ (Paris, BnF fr. 870) and *Z*⁴ (Paris, BnF fr. 19121), remove the second level of allegory. On this issue, see Deleville's article (Chapter 8) in the present volume.

begins by introducing the interpretation that he calls 'senefiance' or 'sentence', which emulates the naturalist-type readings, themselves imitating the Stoic interpretations, and those he often calls 'estoire', of the euhemeristic type. The author reserves the term 'allegory' for the second level of reading. This is a spiritual interpretation that may recall the three meanings that the Fathers of the Church applied only to the Sacred Scriptures: 'quid credas' (typology), 'quid agas' (tropology) and 'quo tendas' (anagogia).[9] More often than not, the author of the *Ovide moralisé* is content with a first sense of a naturalistic and/or historical type, and a second sense, a spiritual one, to which he grants a meaning 'plus noble et de meillor sentence' [a superior one] (*Om*, III. 605).[10] Between the first and the second senses, the author carries out what Dahan (1999: 435) calls a 'hermeneutic leap'.[11] This device is also adopted in the moralization of the fable of Callisto. Verses 1695–1914 offer a reading that I could call 'historical-moral'. What follows is a second interpretation, allegorical first (typological) and then anagogical.[12]

In the following analysis, I would like to trace the path that leads from the Ovidian narrative to the 740 or so verses in Old French. I will separate the study of the fable from that of the moralizations. However, in the space allotted to this article, it will be impossible to examine the whole fable: I will therefore focus on the portrayal of Callisto and her transformation into a bear, before moving towards the analysis of the possible sources for the moralization proposed by the *Ovide moralisé*.

1. The translation of the fable: possible sources

1.1 Jupiter's *inamoramento* and the portrayal of Callisto

> dum redit itque frequens, in virgine Nonacrina
> haesit et accepti caluere sub ossibus ignes.
>
> (*Metamorphoses*, II. 409–10)

---

[9]   Cf. Lubac 1948.

[10]   Cf. the second typological interpretation of Adonis' legend, which is 'Mieudre et plus digne de savoir' than the first, of a naturalist type (*Om*, X. 3749). This hierarchy between interpretations is a novelty compared to the previous moralizations of the *Metamorphoses*, such as those of Arnulf of Orleans or John of Garland: on this point, see Blumenfeld-Kosinski 1997: 119–21.

[11]   On these points, see Possamaï-Pérez 2006: 363–74.

[12]   The interpretation of Juno's journey and her request to the gods of Ocean follows the same pattern. A first reading (II. 2058–87), of a naturalist type, explains the episode in terms of the immobility of the constellation of the 'Ourse' (verse 2058), also called for this reason 'char tardis' (II. 2083). A second reading, this time anagogical (as the future indicative shows), makes the sea the image of Hell, where Callisto-Judea will never fall.

[And as he came and went upon his tasks he chanced to see a certain Arcadian nymph, and straightway the fire he caught grew hot to his very marrow.]

In Ovid's *Metamorphoses*, Callisto is described by the adjective 'Nonacrina' (*Metamorphoses*, II. 409). This term denotes the origin of the nymph, since Nonacris is a mountain in Arcadia. The author of the *Ovide moralisé* avoids translating this complex adjective; in fact, he probably does not want to mislead his readers by multiplying scholarly or exotic terms (Possamaï-Pérez 2006: 182–83). Instead, he describes Callisto only as a 'lady of Arcadia', following verse 405 of the *Metamorphoses* which suggests that Jupiter was in Arcadia before encountering Callisto, and probably also the many mythographers who suggest that the nymph is in fact Arcadian.[13] Furthermore, the translator does not render the verb 'haesit' (*Metamorphoses*, II. 410) [he was hooked] with the same intensity as his source text. Instead, he chooses 'il vit' [he saw].

The manuscript of the *Metamorphoses* on which the translator worked probably contained glosses (in the *Ovide moralisé*, the anonymous translator admits to using glosses on various occasions).[14] Interestingly, both the translatorial details that I have discussed above are present in the summary of the fable that the glossator of *Vat. lat. 1479* places in the margin of verse 409: '(Fabula que hic tangitur talis est): vidit Calistonem, nimpham Archadie' [The fable we are talking about here is this: Jupiter saw Callisto, a nymph of Arcadia].[15] This kind of marginal remark may have been enough to guide his choice of translation. For its part, *Vat. lat. 1598* explains that 'Nonacrina[16] vocatur Archadia a 'nonos' quod est *novem* et 'acros' quod est mons quoniam novem est montibus circumdata.' [Arcadia is called Nonacris, from 'nonos' which means nine and 'acros' which is a mountain, because Arcadia is surrounded by nine mountains]. For 'haesit', he adds 'quia ubi amor ibi oculus' [where love is, there is the eye], which does not

---

[13] Thus Hygin, in his *Astronomia*, 4, recalls that the Big Dipper was Callisto, daughter of Lycaon, who reigned in Arcadia ('Callisto nomine, Lycaonis filiam, eius qui in Arcadia regnavit', Le Boeffle 1983): Lactantius, in the V-VI fables of his *Narrationes fabularum*, states that Jupiter was 'in the vicinity of Nonacris, Mountain of Arcadia' ('circa Nonacrinum montem Arcadiae', Magnus 1914a). The second Vatican mythographer (II. 58) speaks of 'Lycaon, tyrant of Arcadia' ('Lycaon, tyrannus Arcadiae', Kulcsár 1987), whose daughter was called Callisto ('ejus filiam Calliston', Kulcsár 1987). John of Garland, in his *Integumenta* (I. 129–34), calls Callisto 'the Lady of Arcadia', 'Arcadia domina Calisto' (Ghisalberti 1933b).

[14] Cf. *Om*, I. 330: 'La glose dist que…'. See Possamaï-Pérez 2008: 184.

[15] Ms. *Vat. lat. 1479*, fol. 66ʳ.

[16] Or 'Nonacria', according to a second hand which corrects the first, and which Frank T. Coulson calls 'V2'.

render any better the idea of attachment, almost of adherence, given by 'haesit'.

In verse 410, the translation again dulls the words of the Ovidian poem that describe Jupiter's *inamoramento*. Ovid claims that the fire that Jupiter caught grew hot in his bones, 'accepti caluere sub ossibus ignes' [the fire he caught grew hot to his very marrow] (*Metamorphoses*, II. 410). The translator merely repeats the metaphor, probably already well-worn, 'Il fu touz de s'amour espris' [he was aroused by his love] (*Om*, II, 202). It must be said that his intermediary sources do not offer him a very colourful image – they simply write that Jupiter 'fell in love', 'incidit amorem' in Lactantius (1914); 'in amorem ejus incidit' in the Second Vatican Mythographer (Kulcsár 1987),[17] or simply 'loved her'. *Vat. lat. 1479*, for example, in the marginal glosses for verses 409 and 417, uses the verb 'adamavit' and gives 'amores' as the equivalent of 'ignes' in the interlinear gloss for verse 410.[18] One could therefore say that the fourteenth-century translator is closer to the source poem than the mythographers who preceded him. Indeed, he is probably fascinated by the Latin poem and keeps it in mind when he translates.

As anticipated in the title of this section, another interesting passage of this myth and its Old French translation is offered by the portrayal of Callisto. In the Latin *Metamorphoses*, the narrator presents Callisto as a natural beauty unaccustomed to female activities:

> non erat huius opus lanam mollire trahendo
> nec positu variare comas; ubi fibula vestem,
> vitta coercuerat neglectos alba capillos.
> (*Metamorphoses*, II. 411–13)

[She had no need to spin soft wools nor to arrange her hair in studied elegance. A simple brooch fastened her gown and a white fillet held her loose-flowing hair.]

Unlike the Latin poem, the *Ovide moralisé* portrayal of Callisto is presented through Jupiter's eyes: 'De la bele s'est garde pris, | S'avisa son contenement' [He took a look at the beautiful girl; | he considered her demeanour] (*Om*, II. 1394–95). The different point of view might suggest that the translator wanted to compete with one of his narrative models, Chrétien de Troyes, who describes Soredamor through Alexander's eyes in *Cligès* (Possamaï-Pérez 2006: 239–50). The portrayal of Callisto is developed only in Ovid's

---

[17] Second Vatican Mythographer, loc. cit.

[18] *Vat. lat 1598* completes 'ignes' with the genitive 'amoris', 'the fires of love'. But he understands better than *Vat. lat. 1479* that 'sub ossibus' refers to the intensity of the feeling, since he writes in the margins: 'Notat amoris vehemenciam dicendo sub ossibus' [He notes the vehemence of love by saying 'under the bones'.]

poem and in his Old French translation; the earlier mythographers care little about describing the nymph and are content at best to say that she was beautiful.[19] Here the translator of the *Ovide moralisé* covers the task of the poet, and attempts to convey to his readers the freshness of the nymph:

> D'une frange acesmeement
> Avoit çainte sa vesteüre,
> Et sa blonde cheveleüre
> Bendee a un las tout entour,
> Sans cointerie et sans atour.
> Onc n'ot apris a soi vestir (*Om*, II. 1396–1401).

[She had elegantly girded her garment with a brooch and surrounded her blond hair with a lace, without artificial elegance and primping. She had never learnt how to dress.]

As emerges from this passage, Callisto's indifference regarding her appearance is subtly transformed in the Old French hypertext. The toilet is here described as simple and natural, yet also 'acesmee' [elegant]. The adverb 'acesmeement' conveys its elegance, the skill of the person who performs it, and implies that the simplicity of Callisto's appearance is calculated. Furthermore, the author of the *Ovide moralisé* does not translate 'non erat hujus opus', which conveys the idea that female care and duties were not her task or her concern. In the margins in front of verse 412, *Vat. lat. 1598* copies a comment that perhaps points in the direction of the inflection given by the fourteenth-century anonymous writer: 'Si hoc faceret non erat opus huius' [if she were to do this (i.e., if she had arranged her hair), it was not her task, her concern]. This may be a way of saying that she did this anyway.

Another interesting word in this translation is 'frange', which translates the Latin 'fibula' [clasp]. The translator chooses this rendering even if other intermediary sources, such as *Vat. lat. 1479*, propose in the interlinear gloss for verse 412 the Old French word 'contache', which is not found in any dictionary, but is probably a word from the family of 'attache' [clip]. The word 'frange' comes from 'fimbria' [end of the garment]. Given this particular choice of translation, we might also speculate that the copy of the *Metamorphoses* used by the fourteenth-century translator contained 'fimbria' instead of 'fibula', or that the word 'fibula' was poorly written, or abbreviated, and therefore confused with 'fimbria'.[20] The word 'vitta alba', a white strip with which the Latin nymph had carelessly knotted her hair

---

[19] Only Arnulf of Orleans specifies that Callisto was beautiful before her delivery, 'pulcra ante partum' (Ghisalberti 1932).

[20] *Vat. lat. 1598* gives the following comment: '*fibula* id est zona' [*fibula* i.e. the belt].

(coercuerat neglectos [...] capillos)[21] is rendered by the Old French translator with the simple 'las' [fillet, yaw]. The adjective 'alba' is perhaps transposed on the hair,[22] which is 'blonde'. The simplicity of the nymph is one of the reasons (or the main reason) why Jupiter fell in love with her at first sight. As Mora (1994: 169–89) recalls, Diana and her nymphs are beautiful and unwillingly stir up male desire. Finally, 'neglectos' (*Metamorphoses*, II. 412–13) is rendered by 'Sans cointerie et sans atour' [without coquetry and without primping]) (*Om*, II. 1396–1400), which perhaps diminishes the wildness of the Ovidian heroin. The following two verses (1401-02) may refer again to 'non erat hujus opus' [it was not her task], but the translator completely evades the idea of the wool work mentioned by Ovid: 'Onc n'ot apris a soi cointir | N'a soi mignotement vestir.' [She never learnt to primp herself | nor to dress nicely].

In any case, this portrayal seems to have no other sources than the desire of the fourteenth-century author to compete with both Ovid and the authors of the twelfth-century Romances, especially Chrétien de Troyes. Moreover, it is worth noting the amplification of the translation in relation to its source, since five verses are used to translate a few words ('nec positu variare comas' [she didn't mind varying the layout of her hairstyle], 'neglectos capillos' [neglected hair]). The amplification focuses on that natural simplicity.

1.2 Callisto's metamorphosis into a bear

> tendebat bracchia supplex:
> bracchia coeperunt nigris horrescere villis
> curvarique manus et aduncos crescere in unguis
> officioque pedum fungi laudataque quondam
> ora Iovi lato fieri deformia rictu.
> neve preces animos et verba precantia flectant,
> posse loqui eripitur: vox iracunda minaxque
> plenaque terroris rauco de gutture fertur;
> mens antiqua tamen facta quoque mansit in ursa,
> adsiduoque suos gemitu testata dolores
> qualescumque manus ad caelum et sidera tollit
> ingratumque Iovem, nequeat cum dicere, sentit.
> (*Metamorphoses*, II. 477–88)

[And when the girl stretched out her arms in prayer for mercy, her arms began to grow rough with black shaggy hair; her hands changed into feet tipped with sharp claws; and her lips, which but now Jove had praised, were changed to

---

[21] *Vat. lat. 1479* gives 'cohercebat positos sine lege'.

[22] *Vat. lat. 1598* opens the way to a moral comment, when it glosses 'vitta' (ribbon) with 'in signum castitatis' (as a sign of chastity).

broad, ugly jaws; and, that she might not move him with entreating prayers, her power of speech was taken from her, and only a harsh, terrifying growl came hoarsely from her throat. Still her human feelings remained, though she was now a bear; with constant moanings she shows her grief stretches up such hands as are left her to the heavens, and, though she cannot speak, still feels the ingratitude of Jove.]

The translator of the *Ovide moralisé* knows Latin well and he is able to translate his source text literally. However, he often decides to amplify his text of departure 'pour mieus acomplir (sa) matire' [to better accomplish his subject].[23] This is the case of Callisto's metamorphosis into a bear, which Ovid describes in just twelve verses (II. 477–88) and the *Ovide moralisé* in 36 (II. 1618–53).[24] No previous commentator has been able to inspire the translator, who relies only on his source text. The commentators of the *Metamorphoses* are not interested in the process of mutation, which in contrast fascinates both personas embodied by the fourteenth-century translator: the poet and the moralist.[25] In the *Ovide moralisé*, Callisto's movement before her metamorphosis ('tendebat bracchia supplex') is well rendered by the two octosyllables 'Cele li tendoit humblement | Ses bras, pour requerre merci' (*Om*, II. 1618-19) [She humbly extended her arms to her forward to appeal for sympathy]. Similarly the translator could not find in other sources than the *Metamorphoses* the indication of the arms that begin to bristle with black hair, which he translates as 'En brief temps furent tout nerci, | Et plain d'orible poil velu' (*Om*, II. 1620-22) [They quickly darkened and the skin was fully covered with an awful fur]. The glossed manuscripts of the *Metamorphoses* comment on this blackening. *Vat. lat. 1479*, for example, proposes an interlinear equivalent only for 'villis' (it gives 'pilis') and in the margin it offers a commentary on the darkness of the hair: "Nigris': he says 'black' because of Juno's reproaches and because of the characteristic of the bear'.[26] *Vat. lat. 1598*, in turn, comments on 'horrescere' ('horribilia fieri') and also gives the equivalent 'pilis' for 'villis'.

The translator, however, does not exactly respect the order of Ovid's description. Instead, he follows the descending order of medieval portraits –

---

[23] Cf. *Om*, IV. 3155, VII, 245, IX, 1454, 1764. See also Possamaï-Pérez (2008).

[24] The usual proportion, which would be 24 octosyllables per twelve hexameters, is therefore exceeded by one third, indicating that the phenomenon is of great interest to the translator.

[25] The metamorphosis represents the perpetual fluctuations of earthly life; particularly, the metamorphosis into animals are the concrete image of 'negative metamorphoses', associated with sin, which makes the soul look ugly (Possamaï-Pérez 2006: 495–511).

[26] *Vat. lat. 1479*, fol. 67ʳ: 'Nigris dicit propter vituperationes illius et propter proprietatem urse'.

which mirror God's creation of men and women – and begins with the head to end with the feet. After describing Callisto's arms raised in the air as a sign of supplication, the Old French poet focuses on the face. Ovid's words 'laudataque quondam | ora Iovi lato fieri deformia rictu' [her mouth, once admired by Jupiter, widens in the form of a hideous mouth] (*Metamorphoses*, II. 480–81) are rendered by five octosyllables, which constitutes a slight amplification:

> Le visage ot sale et pelu,
> Qui tant soloit estre agreables:
> Or est vilz et abhominables
> Et rechigniez a grans merveilles:
> Fendus jusques vers les oreilles (*Om*, II. 1622-26)

[Her face, that had once been so nice, was dirty and hairy. It is now horrible, abominable and scowling out of the ordinary, split up to the ears.]

The glossed manuscript he uses may not have been able to guide the translator: the *Vat. lat. 1479*, like *Vat. Lat. 1598*, describes a deformation that goes in the opposite direction, downwards: 'ora fuere deformia, deorsum a propria forma' [so her mouth was deformed ('deformia') downwards in relation to its own form], 'Quia Iupiter ora laudaverat et propter pulcritudinem adamaverat et sic dicit laudataque quondam' [Because Jupiter had praised her mouth and loved her for her beauty and so he said 'formerly admired']. The translator thus managed with the words offered to him by the old French language. In this passage, the term 'rechignié' is quite apt to translate 'deformia' ('scowling, snarky', but also has the meaning of 'grimacing', *ATILF*), *Vat. lat. 1479* and *1598* provide the simple 'turpia' in the interlinear gloss. At the same time, the idea of the face that cracked to the ears renders the Latin 'lato rictu' quite well.[27] Victor Hugo would have admired this description of a monstrous face, which foretells the way he described Gwynplaine, the hero of *L'homme qui rit*. A gloss transmitted in *Vat. Lat. 1598* allows us to understand the journey from the Latin 'rictus' to the Old French 'rechignié'. It says 'os est hominis, rictus animalis bruti' [the mouth belongs to man, the 'rictus' to the stupid animal]. 'Rictus' is the past participle of 'ringor', which means 'to growl by showing teeth', and 'rictus' has the meaning of 'gaping mouth', when talking about animals. It would therefore be the simple 'lato' that would be rendered by 'split to the ears'.

Another point emphasized by the Latin author as well as by his medieval French translator is the transformation of the upper limbs, which touch the ground, thus causing the human body to lose its standing posture and the

---

[27] *Vat. lat. 1479* gives 'ritu', which he glosses by 'per ritum'.

possibility to look up to its Creator. The downward movement of the portrait in the Old French version leads the translator to move from the face to the transformation of the hands, thus inverting Ovid's order of narration. In the *Ovide moralisé*, verse 1627 describes the nails. They are 'grans et agues' [long and pointed], and the hands 'corbes et crochues' [curled and hooked]. The use of the synonymic doublet is typical in Old French poetry, and the translator uses it to render Ovid's inchoative verbs: the passive 'curvari' [bending] and the verb with the suffix -sc, 'crescere'. Usually the translator strives to show the phenomenon of transformation in its progress. Here, however, by substituting Ovid's verbs he diminishes the power of Ovid's description. In the task of translating this metamorphosis, the translator is probably not supported by the glosses of his manuscript. The interlinear glosses of *Vat. Lat. 1479* or those of *1598* merely remind us that 'curvari' still depends on 'ceperunt' (i.e. 'coeperunt' [started]), and propose only 'curvato' [curved] or 'curvo' [curve] for 'aduncos'. But *Vat. lat. 1598* emphasizes the length and power of the claws of the bear (the gloss at 'crescere' explains that 'ungues ursorum nimis extenduntur extra carnem' [the bears' claws extend notably beyond the flesh]). Then the glossator relies on Bernard Silvester.[28] On the other hand, the transition from human posture to animal position is rendered by the same idea as in Latin. In the Old French version the hands 'dont elle vait en leu de piez' [with which she walks instead of feet] and in the Latin poem the hands 'officioque pedum fungi' [serve as feet]. *Vat. lat. 1479* explains 'officio' by 'servicio' and 'fungi' by 'uti'.

The Old French author adds then three verses that he does not find in Ovid, and which underline the contrast between the ugliness of the bear and Callisto's former beauty. These verses insist on the pathos of the transformation, on the irremediable loss suffered by the nymph: 'Vilment est ses biaus cors changiez: | Qui la verroit ne croiroit mie | C'onques a Jovis fust amie' [Her beautiful body has grown ugly. If anyone saw her, they would not believe she ever was Jupiter's lover] (*Om*, II. 1630-32). This addition testifies to the 'literary temptations' and poetic talent of the author. At the same time, it also prepares the introduction of his moralization, as always when the Old French text transforms its source.

At the very end of the metamorphosis into an animal there is a recurrent theme: the loss of the ability to use human language: 'posse loqui eripitur' [the power of speaking is taken away from her]. Once again, the Old French

---

[28] 'Hoc bene commemorat Bernardus dicens de proprietatibus animalium: substitit in pectus leo forcior, ursus in ungues, anguis atrox morsu, dente timendus aper.' [Bernard well reminds us of this when he talks about the properties of animals: the lion is stronger in the chest, the bear in the claws, the snake is cruel by its bite, the wild boar fearsome by its tooth] (Dronke 1978).

translator renders this trait faithfully, translating it as 'L'en li a le parler toloit' (*Om*, II. 1637). And this loss is explained, as in Ovid, by Juno's desire to prevent Callisto from obtaining pity through prayers: 'Pour ce qu'en aucune maniere | N'amoloiast, par sa priere, | Les cuers de ceulz qui la verroient, | Et qui ses complaintes orroient' [so that she could not in any way soften through her prayer the hearts of those who could see her and hear her complaints] (*Om*, II. 1633–35). The translation is faithful, and it may have been guided by glosses of the type that we can read in *Vat. Lat.1479*, fol. 67r, in the margins in front of verse 484 of the *Metamorphoses*: 'Nolebat Iuno quod preces Calistonis flecterent Iovem et propter hoc quod removerentur sibi verba constituit' [Juno did not want Callisto's prayers to turn Jupiter and because of this she decided that speech would be taken away from her].[29] In the interlinear gloss, 'Posse (loqui)' is glossed by 'loquela' and 'eripitur' by 'removetur'.

But Callisto's portrait as a bear has a specific trait: the description of the sound emitted by the animal: 'Vox iracunda | minaxque plenaque terroris rauco de gutture fertur' [from her husky throat comes out only an irritated, menacing voice, which spreads terror] (*Metamorphoses*, II. 483-484) The *Ovide moralisé* renders it as 'Donnoit un tres orible son, | Maneçable et plain de paour | Et d'abominable roour' (*Om*, II. 1640-42) [It emitted a horrible sound, threatening and full of fear and awful hoarseness]. The word 'minax' and 'plena terroris' are translated literally. The adjective 'rauco' is rendered by the noun 'roor', which is not attested in any dictionary, but is formed from the adjective 'roé', which is found in Chrétien de Troyes. The *FEW* points to a feminine noun 'roeure', dated about 1508, in the sense of hoarseness: here the fourteenth-century poet probably creates the masculine noun 'roor, roeur', to render faithfully the Latin term.[30] This is not the only example of his verbal creation. In this description of the bear's cry, indeed, he is probably not helped by the glosses of his manuscript of the *Metamorphoses* since *Vat. lat. 1479* wrote in the margins 'Vox etiam sua fuit valde turpis' [Indeed her voice was quite horrible] and its interlinear glosses provide no particular illumination.[31] *Vat. lat. 1598* is a little more loquacious, because it glosses 'minax' by 'minatoria que raucitate sua videtur minari gentibus et feris' [threatening, which seems to threaten people and beasts by its hoarseness]. 'Rauco' is glossed by 'rauce sonante', which is not of much help.

Like other characters of the *Metamorphoses*, such as Io or Actaeon, Callisto also continues to present human features after her metamorphosis

---

[29]   The ms. transmits 'Iovis' instead of 'Iovem'; I have corrected it.

[30]   Godefroy (1881–1902) also refers to the term 'roueure'.

[31]   'iracunda' is glossed by 'plena ire', 'minax' by 'plena minarum', 'terroris' by 'timoris'.

into an animal. This permanence of human traits in the metamorphosed
character is very often emphasized in the Latin text as well as in its Old
French translation. Duality is what makes the transformed entity a hybrid
being. It is precisely this tragic and pathetic plurality that transforms a
person into a 'monster'. Verse 485 of the Latin poem 'mens antiqua tamen
facta quoque mansit in ursa' [However, now a bear, she is still animated by
the same feelings as before] finds a fairly accurate correspondence in the
verses 1644-45 of the *Ovide moralisé*: 'De quanqu'ele ot premierement | Ne
li remest fors seulement | L'entendement et la pensee' [From what she once
had, she only kept reason and her thought].[32] The translator adds of his
own coinage a concluding verse (*Om*, II. 1646) 'Elle est en vilz ourse muee'
[She is transformed into a vile bear] before rendering the last verse of the
Ovidian description – 'adsiduoque suos gemitu testata dolores' [a
continuous groan attests to his pain] (*Metamorphoses*, II. 486) – as
'Assiduelment se doloit' [She continually mourned]. The translator develops
this pathetic description by adding also: 'si souspire et plaint, | Et dedens
son cuer se complaint' (*Om*, II. 1649–50) [She sighed and mourned, and
inside her heart she moaned].[33] 'qualescumque manus ad caelum et sidera
tollit' [she lifts her hands as they are to heaven and to the stars] (*Metamor-
phoses*, II. 487) is rendered as 'Teulz bras et teulz mains come avoit | Tant au
ciel' [She raised her arms and hands as they were towards the sky] (*Om*, II.
1648–49). On the other hand 'ingratumque Iovem [...] sentit' [she feels
Jupiter's ingratitude] (*Metamorphoses*, II. 488) seems not to be understood
by the translator, who mentions Callisto's complaints against 'celui qui l'a
deffloree, | Pour qu'ele est tant deshonoree | Qu'ele est vilz ourse devenue'
(*Om*, II. 1651–52) [the one who took her virginity, since she is so
dishonoured that she has been transformed into a bear]. However, as he
knows Latin well, one might also think that he is preparing the moralization
by suggesting the equivalence of being metamorphosed into a bear and
dishonour, and also by refusing to mention the ingratitude of the person to
whom he will give the equivalence of the Christian God.

In conclusion, the Old French translator knows how to translate the
Latin poem literally. In order to render it as closely as possible, he can only
rely on his own understanding of the Latin text of departure, since previous
commentators of the *Metamorphoses* do not detail the beauty of the nymph
or the stages of her transformation. As we have seen in this analysis, the
examples of glossed manuscripts of the Ovidian poem do not give any help

---

[32] These verses are close to those concerning Actaeon: 'Riens qu'il eüst, fors le corage | Et la
premeraine pensee, | Ne li est en lui demoree.' (*Om*, III. 468–70).

[33] *Vat. lat. 1479* glosses the verse 486 by 'et tamen ad maiorem dolorem illi atribuendum',
'and yet this must be attributed to a very great pain'.

– or at least any inspiration – to render the freshness of the young huntress or the repulsive and fascinating ugliness of the transformed body in Old French. The form taken by this fourteenth-century translation is the result of the poetic taste and talent for literary creation of the translator. Similarly, as we will see in the following section, the translator's inventiveness is also exercised in the second 'transposition' of the source text:[34] the interpretations he proposes in order to give the fable a meaning not only acceptable to reason, but also compatible with Christian thought.

2. Moralizations

The author of the *Ovide moralisé* begins his task as moraliser by delivering a first meaning of a concrete, sensitive type: this moralization can imitate the Stoics' interpretative gesture, by proposing a naturalistic explanation, or can take up Euhemerus's interpretation by making of the mythical story the transposition of a historical narrative. These two types of interpretation can have two functions. They impose on an improbable or obscene myth an acceptable literal meaning and they prepare readers for the hermeneutic leap towards the spiritual allegory (Possamaï-Pérez 2006: 365–66 and 374–79). As with the fable, I will only address the moralizations of the first part of the story and leave to one side those concerning Juno's request to the Gods of the sea, as stated above.

Callisto's legend is first interpreted in verses 1695–1914. This reading could be considered historical-moral. There is no obvious introductory formula to identify what the author proposes to do, but the verbs conjugated in the past suggest the historical narrative. Moreover, the passage contains a long moral verse that reveals the author's indignation towards those mothers who resort to abortion or who abandon their children (*Om*, II. 1706–1819).[35] Then, from verse 1820 the simple past and the imperfect tenses signal a shift back to a more historical narrative. In the manuscript Rouen Bm O.4, illuminations are used as transitions. At the top of this historical-moral interpretation of the fable, the illumination is divided into two parts, which illustrate the chronology of this morality: on the left, Callisto, still a virgin, is beautiful alongside Diana who 'note pureté [...] de

---

[34] After the linguistic transposition – the translation, moralization is an axiological transposition Genette (1982).

[35] In manuscripts Z^{34}, the moralist's indignation turns against the men who seduce these poor women and abandon them when they are pregnant. Deleville (2019, I. 194–95) argues that the author of these manuscripts 'brings guilt to the man who seduces the girl. [...] the verse 'Car vierge fu, or ne l'est mie' replaces 'Maintes sont qui en puterie' (*Om*, II. 1706). So any trace of judgment is mitigated. Finally, the reviser removes the long diatribe against abortion (*Om*, II. 1707–1819). He keeps only a pathetic description of Callisto becoming a bear, fleeing into the wild, abused by animals.'

virginité' [notes purity of virginity] (*Om*, II. 1697-98). On the right, the miniature depicts Callisto's decline after the loss of her virginity: she lives 'en puterie' [in vice] (*Om*, II. 1706) among the men who share her favours.

A second interpretation, again without an introductory formula, provides a series of equivalences between Callisto and Judea, Arcas and Christ. Callisto's refusal to bathe corresponds to Judea's refusal to be baptized in Christ; the arrow fired by Arcas at his mother corresponds to Christ's wrath against Judea, and Jupiter's intervention to save Callisto corresponds to God appeasing Christ's wrath and converting Judea. It is therefore an allegory in the strict sense of typology, except for the last stage (*Om*, II. 1995-2006), which is anagogy. Nonetheless, it is not separated from the typology by an introductory formula; only the future tense of the verbs, which has an eschatological sense, reveals the anagogical reading.[36] The illumination that introduces this spiritual interpretation depicts a Crib. The illustrator may have read the allegory a little quickly, which makes Callisto Judea's equivalent, instead of the Virgin, the Virgin and Christ being the 'boneüree lignie' [the blessed lineage] (*Om*, II. 1932).[37] The image of the Virgin lying down after giving birth and Joseph in the foreground, with the child Jesus warmed by the donkey and the ox in the background, is perhaps not entirely adequate. Nevertheless, it is true that the text insists on the fact that the Virgin 'Nasqui de Juda droitement' (*Om*, II. 1947) [was really born from Judea].

Does the fourteenth-century moralist have sources for these two interpretations? Among the Vatican Mythographers, the first one mentions Callisto's name in his chapter on Lycaon, of whom she is the daughter.[38] The mythographer summarizes the fable in broad strokes, without commenting on it. The second Vatican Mythographer develops the story further (without describing, however, either the nymph's beauty or her metamorphosis into a bear, as it has been said) and is content with a commentary on the planets that Callisto and her son Arcas were transformed into: 'Ille *Arcturus*, et alio nomine *Arctophylax* vocatur; illa Arctos μείζων, Latine *septentrio major* appellatur; quod signum loco non

---

[36] It is appropriate to correct 'donna' (*Om*, II. 2000): the manuscript Rouen Bm O.4 has 'donra', in future tense.

[37] On the illustrator, the Master of *Fauvel*, see Besseyre and Roucheron-Mouilleron (2008: I, 18). The Master of *Fauvel* also illustrated manuscript Ars. 5069, but there is no illustration of Callisto's allegory in this manuscript.

[38] Bode (1968: I, 17, p. 5, De Lycaone): 'Idem Lycaon habuerat filiam Callisto. Quam quum vidisset Juppiter, Junon eam in ursam convertit; postea Juppiter miseratus, in signum transtulit caeleste' [this Lycaon had a daughter, Callisto. As Jupiter had seen her, Juno turned her into a bear; Jupiter later took pity on her, and carried her to heaven in the form of a star].

movetur, nec hac, quam dicturus sum, causa mergitur' [This one (Arcas) is called *Arcturus*, and by another name *Arctophylax* (the constellation of the 'Bouvier'); this one (Callisto) is called the *Larger Bear*, in Latin *Great Septentrion*; this star knows no revolution, and does not sink into the Ocean for the cause I will say].[39] The *Liber de natura deorum*, an anonymous book that circulated in the twelfth century, comments only on the names given to the constellations of the Great and the Little Dipper too (Brown 1972: 18– 19). The author of the *Ovide moralisé* will use only the naturalistic explanation below, after the account of Juno's request to the gods of the sea to prevent the stars from setting in the sea: in verses 2058–20, the agreement of the sea gods is explained by the stillness of the constellation of the Dipper.

What are the possible sources of the historical-moral interpretation? Fulgentius, who proposes moral maxims in his *Mitologiae*, does not deal with the fable of Callisto. This moralization may have been inspired by comments such as Arnulf of Orleans' *Allegoriae*: 'Et eam que pulcra erat ante partum, per partum deturpavit. Unde fingitur eam mutasse in ursam que turpissima est' (Ghisalberti 1932: II. 5–6) [She, who was beautiful before giving birth, became ugly after this. For this reason it was invented that she had turned into a bear, which is very ugly]. An alternative source could also be John of Garland's *Integumenta*: 'Arcadie domina Calisto dicitur ursa | Nam gravidata Iovis semine turpis erat (Ghisalberti 1933b: I. 129–30) [The princess of Arcadia Callisto is called a bear, because, being pregnant by Jupiter's seed, she became ugly].[40] The manuscripts of the *Metamorphoses* copied in the thirteenth and fourteenth centuries wrote these two comments in tandem without distinguishing between them, in what Coulson (2001) calls the Vulgate Commentary. The two manuscripts that I took as examples of possible tools for the translation of the fable were also able to help the author of the *Ovide moralisé* as he embarked on his second

---

[39]   Bode (1968: II. 58 and 94). The mythographer then goes to chapter 59, on Thetis: 'Thetis enim, filia Nerei, uxor Oceani, nutrix Junonis fuit. Quam Juno indignata, pel-licem suam in caelum translatam, rogavit, ut propter affectum nutricis eam prohiberet in oceanum cadere', 'Thetis indeed, Nereus' daughter, Ocean's wife, was Juno's nurse. Indignant that her rival had been transported to heaven, Juno asked Thetis, by virtue of her affection as her nurse, to prevent the star from lying in the Ocean.'

[40]   In verses 131–34, he discusses the astrological aspect: 'Ursa tibi maior Elice dicitur et Artos, | Sed Cinosura sequens dicitur Ursa minor. | Plaustri languentis hec est auriga Bootes | Et custos matris est Cinosura sue' [The Big Dipper is said, you must know it, Helixe and Bear, but Cynosure who follows her is called Little Dipper. The Bouvier is the charioteer of the Languissant Chariot, and Cynosure is his mother's guardian]. The name 'Helike' is due to the fact that the seven stars ('septentrion') of the Big Dipper 'curl up' around the North Pole. The terms 'plaustri languens' may be the origin of the 'chars tardis' of the *Om* (II. 2083).

transposition, that is, the moralization. *Vat. lat. 1479* uses the term 'turpis' in its explanation 'according to the truth' ('Rei veritas'): Juno 'ipsam mutavit in ursam, quia tantum post deflorationem turpis fuit quod universi qui videbant putabant quod ursa propter turpitudinem erat.' [changed her into a bear because she was so ugly after her rape that everyone who saw her thought she was a bear because of her ugliness].[41] The allegory is based on the search for *similitudo*, and physical ugliness is assimilated to moral ugliness. In the Latin comments, the polysemy of the adjective 'turpis' may aid this assimilation.

In addition, *Vat. lat. 1479* took care to present, in the right margin of folio 66[v], in front of verse 429 of *Metamorphoses*, all the 'morality' of the fable:

> Moralitas talis est. Caliste fuit venatrix. Fuit etiam virgo, unde tantum[42] vacabat alicui bono quod non curabat de stupro et Venere, imo semper aliud boni faciebat iuxta dictum sapientis: "semper aliquid boni facito ne te dyabolus inveniat occiosum", sed tamen Iupiter, qui est planeta calida,[43] illam defloravit, quia ad ultimum per falsum predicatorem viciata fuit, unde dicitur quod per Iovem, quia mutatum in specie Dyane, quia falsus predicator pro bono serens et alliciens, secundario malo corrumpens, et sic imprenata fuit a Iove, quia ab introitu sapientis specie generavit Archada, quia filium, unde dicitur mutari in ursam, quia tantum penituit quod faciem suam denigravit exarando et per ieiunium pulcritudinem devastavit. Archas filius suus voluit illam occidere, quia dolens quod adulter erat; tamen noluit, quia Iupiter deus prohibuit ne aliquis matri noceret, unde, penitencia facta, ambos celo coronavit; sic potest dici de qualibet virgine. (Transcribed by Ciccone et al. 2020: 386–387)

> [The moral is this: Callisto was a hunter. She was a virgin, and only devoted her time to good deeds, since she was not interested in lust and love, but always did something good, in the words of the sage: 'Always do something good so that the Devil does not find you idle'. But Jupiter, which is a hot planet, deflowered her, because in the end she was corrupted by a false preacher; so it is said that it was by Jupiter, who had taken on Diana's appearance, since the false preacher makes sowing and attracts by forging the good one, but corrupts by the evil that comes second. And so she was fertilized by Jupiter, that is, under the guise of a wise man's arrival, she gave birth to Arcas, her son, from which it is said that she was turned into a bear, because she did so much penance that her face turned black by tearing herself, and that she destroyed her beauty by fasting. Her son Arcas wanted to kill her, that is, he suffered from knowing her adultery; but he did not, because Jupiter-God forbids anyone to kill his mother;

---

[41] Transcribed by Lisa Ciccone, my translation; fol. 66[v], right margin, in front of verse 447.

[42] The manuscript transmits *tantus*.

[43] 'Planeta' is no doubt considered as a feminine noun here.

so, after they had done penance, he crowned both of them in heaven; this is what can be said of any virgin.]

One must note that this moralization is not a possible model for the long passage (*Om*, II. 1695-1914) that constitutes the first interpretation of the fable of Callisto. At most, the words 'universi qui videbant putabant quod ursa propter turpitudinem erat' can be found in verses 1820-23: 'Calisto, par son avoultire, | Fu desprisie et diffamee | Et laidengie et mains amee | De tous ceulz qui la connoissoient' [Callisto, because she had committed adultery, was despised and slandered, and blamed and less loved by all the people that knew her]. With this exception, none of the sources I consulted is responsible for these 220 verses. The moralist distinguishes himself both by the way he takes the elements of the fable, establishing a historical narrative that follows the details of the legendary narrative, and using the terms of his translation to emphasize the *similitudo* and justify his enterprise. Let's take a few examples, following the course of the text. The Callisto of the first part of the episode, beloved by Diana, is the young virgin, because 'Dyane note pureté, | Ce m'est vis, de virginité' (*Om*, II. 1697-98) [Diana values purity, this is virginity in my opinion]. Diana's discovery of the loss of her companion's virginity is reflected in a fact of banal experience: 'Puis fu, par son ventre, seü | Qu'ele avoit o malle geü' (*Om*, II. 1703-04) [Then it was known, by her belly, that she had sex with a man]. However, the original intention – to provide a historical narrative parallel to the legendary narrative, in order to 'cleanse' the fable of its unlikely slags and set the stage for spiritual allegory – is quickly interrupted because of the moralist's emotion, that of a preacher.[44] The change in the verb tense to the present indicative from verse 1706 onwards reveals the influx of this emotion, which will provoke the long diatribe against women who abort (*Om*, II. 1706-86), and which can be seen thanks to the interventions of the narrator – the *correctio* (*Om*, II. 1713), the parenthesis (*Om*, II. 1722), the exclamatory tone (*Om*, II. 1725-34), the modality of duty (*Om*, II. 1732–33),[45] and the hypothetical mood to mark regret (*Om*, II. 1751– 72),[46] finally and above all the strength of vocabulary (the lexicon of death, the

---

[44] On the pastoral tone, see Possamaï-Pérez (2006: 717–23).

[45] 'Celes qui meres et amies | Deüssent estre' [These, who mothers and friends should be] (*Met.*, II. 1732-33). *Cf.* 'Nulz ne devroit tel feme amer' [Nobody should love such a woman] (*Metamorphoses*, II. 1735).

[46] 'S'el vausist celer son putage, | Alast s'ent em pelerinage [...] | Si lessast son enfançon vivre [...] Au mains le lessast, sans deffaire, | Et chiez son pere l'envoiast [...] | Ou [...] | Lessast le, [...], | Devant l'uis d'aucun hospital ...' [If she wanted to hide her vice, she would go on pilgrimage ..., but she should let her baby live ..., at least leave him, without killing him, and send him to his father, or leave him ... in front of a hospital door] (II. 1751–72).

death of infants which revolts the Christian thinker) (*Om*, II. 1724–25, 1728, 1739, 1766, 1776).[47] He does not have too strong a term to condemn those mothers who, in order to 'couvrir lor mauvestié'[48] [to cover their wickedness] (*Om*, II. 1720), show 'grant desloiauté' [great disloyalty] and 'orrible cruauté' [horrible cruelty] (*Om*, II. 1725-26), make themselves the 'morteulz anemies' [deadly enemies] (*Om*, II. 1731) of their own children, have 'le cuer plain d'amer, | de rage et de forsenerie' [the heart full of bitterness, rage and madness] (*Om*, II. 1736-37), are 'aspres et dures' [harsh and hard] (*Om*, II. 1779).

Quite original is the digression on Nature's role in human conception, and on the pleasure associated with carnal union, an invention of Nature to promote 'generacion' [reproduction], for without this pleasure the carnal act would seem too disgusting ('ors et vis' [dirty and vile], 'ordure' [dirt]) to be performed (*Om*, II. 1787-1801). And this originality is all the more noteworthy because this type of explanation is very unusual under the moralist's pen. In Book XI, for example, the account of the nuptials of Thetis and Peleus, though added by the translator to his hypotext, does not inspire him to interpret it (there is also a certain shortness of breath on the part of the exegete in Books XI and XII). In this episode, some typological verses end with an admission of impotence and the transition to a physical explanation introduced by the exclamation 'Que l'en nel tienne a vilonie' (*Om*, XI. 1356) [do not judge this as villainy], which the publisher De Boer attaches to the desire of 'making short' confessed in previous verses, but which we are tempted rather to attach to the somewhat scabrous explanation of the 'pit' in which Thetis and Peleus were united and where Achilles was conceived. The digression on the 'human generation' is in this place somewhat laborious, which makes the one contained in the historical-moral reading of Callisto's fable even more surprising. Nevertheless, the digression is justified in verses 1802–16 by the need to 'elect the fruit' and not 'the pleasure', to engage oneself in the carnal act only therefore to procreate: it is indeed a subject for a sermon.

The author shows, however, that he acknowledges that he has strayed from his subject and given too much room for his indignation in verses 1817-19: 'Mes or lessons ester ces meres, | Qui tant sont aspres et ameres, | Si reprenons nostre matire' [But now let us leave those mothers, who are rough and bitter, and return to our subject]. As always, he has a clear awareness of the content and construction of his thought. He therefore returns to the narrative in the past tense to take up again his interpretation,

---

[47] Some verses suggest that the moralist thinks of the massacre of the Innocent Saints.

[48] Under our author's pen, the 'mauvestié' indicates the sex crime (Possamaï-Pérez 2009: 173–74). See also Héritier (1996, 39–40).

which is based on the strict parallelism between the mythical narrative and the historical-moral equivalence. It is indeed the shift from physical to moral ugliness that makes it possible to understand the transformation from the portrait of the nymph as pure, fresh and natural to the monstrous animal represented by the bear. The same terms are to be taken in another direction, as specified by the determinative complements. Thus she 'devint aspre et pelue | De souffrete et de povreté'[49] [became rough and hairy because of suffering and poverty] (*Om*, II. 1838–39). The passage from the physical to the moral sense is noted by the participle 'deshonnorez' (*Om*, II. 1844). But, once again, the moralist's emotion carries him beyond the fable and the long description of the prostitutes' life does not seem free of compassion: 'Souvent maldit, triste, adolee | Celui qui l'ot despucelee' [She was sad and hurt and often cursed the one who had taken her virginity] (*Om*, II. 1845–46), 'Elle musoit sole, esperdue' [She often wandered lonely, and was often distraught] (*Om*, II. 1860), 'Elle fuioit les robeours, | Les murtriers, les concheours, | Pour ce qu'il la tirepeloient,[50] | Et ce qu'ele avoit li toloient.' [she was fleeing from thieves, murderers, deceivers, because they tore her and took all that she had] (*Om*, II. 1869–72). The correspondence with the roars of the bear and her complaints against Jupiter's ingratitude in *Metamorphoses*, II. 486–88 may not be enough to justify the development of this passage, which seems to respond, once again, to the author's desire to establish a climate of pathos.[51]

[49]   Bersuire takes up the idea of debasement due to poverty: 'Istud potest allegari contra aliquos qui de foemina in ursam, id est de alto in bassum, de divitibus in pauperes fortunae casibus transmutantur', [this can be alleged against persons who from women are turned into bears, that is to say pass from the top to the bottom, rich persons become poor ones, because of the vagaries of fortune]. 'Calisto enim sicut dictum est potest significare illos qui de statu prosperitatis casu fortunae veniunt ad paupertatem, et inter viles et ignobiles personas computantur', [As has been said, Callisto can mean those who, from a state of prosperity, fall into poverty by bad fortune, and are considered to belong to vile and low-extraction people] (Engels 1962, liber II, fabula XII).

[50]   The verb 'tirepeler' is probably one of the words created by the author of the *Ovide moralisé*: it is not found in the *ATILF* or in the *TL*. Only Godefroy (1881–1902) mentions it, with two examples both taken from two manuscripts of the *Ovide moralisé*: Ms BnF fr. 373 and Ms. Ars 5069. I first thought of a kind of double word associating 'tirer' and 'peler', but Godefroy also points to a word of the dialect of Lyons, 'tirpilli', which would signify 'tirailler' and apparently would be related, according to the *FEW*, to the Latin 'palus' ('stake').

[51]   *Metamorphoses*, II. 486–88: 'adsiduoque suos gemitu testata dolores | qualescumque manus ad caelum et sidera tollit | ingratumque Iovem, nequeat cum dicere, sentit.', [a continual groan proves her pain, she lifts her hands, such as they are, toward the sky and toward the stars, and, without being able to speak, she feels all Jupiter's ingratitude.] *Om*, II. 1647–53: 'Assiduelment se doloit | Teulz bras et teulz mains come avoit | Tant au ciel, si souspire et plaint, | Et dedens son cuer se complaint | De celui qui l'a defloree, | Pour qu'ele est tant deshonoree | Qu'ele est vilz ourse devenue', [She often

Nevertheless, if his originality is already felt at the first level of interpretation, it bursts forth on the second level, that of allegory. No earlier commentator proposes this equivalence between Callisto and Judea, who was first a friend of 'nostre Seignour' [our Lord] (*Om*, II. 1921) and a servant of the 'Trinité' [Trinity] (*Om*, II. 1925).[52] Spiritual allegory, like the historical-moral explanation, takes up every step of the fable. To link Callisto's loss of virginity to this interpretation by Judea, the author's brainwave is to focus on the episode of Diana's bath and her nymphs: so Callisto's refusal to bathe with Diana can become the equivalent of Judea's rejection of Christ's baptism (*Om*, II. 1964–74), and Diana's rejection corresponds to the loss of God's love (*Om*, II. 1974–76). The metamorphosis into a bear and the miserable life of the nymph in this form represent the life of the Jews in sin (*Om*, II. 1977–82). Arcas' attempt to kill the bear is an image of Christ's wrath against Judea (*Om*, II. 1987–94). Finally, Callisto's metamorphosis into a star foreshadows God's mercy at the time of the Last Judgment: as it is quite often the case, typological reading leads to an anagogical reading that the future tense of the verbs indicates:

> Mes Dieus, peres plains de pitié,
> Qui de s'ancïenne amistié
> Recors et souvenans sera,
> Vers Judaïme apaisera
> De son fil l'ire et la vengance.
> [...]
> Lors sera Judee honnoree.
>
> (*Om*, II. 1995–2005)

[But God, merciful father who will recall his old friendship will ease his son's wrath and desire for revenge against Judea [...] then Judea will be honoured.]

The moralist can then declare himself satisfied with the light he has shed on the fable: 'Ensi s'acorde au voir la fable' [So the fable agrees with the truth] (*Om*, II. 2006). Everything happens as if the first explanation, though already very personal, could not in his eyes be enough to 'bring' the mythological legend to the truth – the only Truth that exists for him, the Christian Revelation that he presents in his spiritual interpretations. In the

---

complains, stretches her arms and hands, as they were, towards the sky, sighing and moaning, and inside her heart she complains about the one who took her virginity because she has been so dishonoured that she became a horrible bear].

[52]   The equivalence between Diana and the Trinity is detailed in the allegory of Actaeon's fable: Diana, the goddess Trivia (both goddess of hunting, of the night and of the underworld, the 'triple Hecate'), whose hair is braided at the time of bathing - while in the *Metamorphoses* it is raised in a bun), is interpreted as the Trinity (Possamaï-Pérez 2004: 198–200).

fifteenth century, as Prunelle Deleville showed in her thesis, the rewriter of the *Z* family will challenge this conception of truth, and prefer to see in the fables veils of a concrete, immanent, historical reality. Perhaps we will find that, in doing so, he will be more timid and less original than the first author of the *Ovide moralisé*.

Conclusion

The originality of the author of the *Ovide moralisé* is fully unveiled when we take into account his double transposition of the fable of Callisto. In the linguistic transposition, the translation of the legend into Old French, his 'literary temptations' give his version its characteristic features. He becomes a poet by describing Callisto, as fresh as her Latin model, but perhaps of a slightly more calculated naturalness. He is a painter in his realistic description of the stages of the metamorphosis into a bear, which faithfully takes up the Ovidian passage, testifying to the same fascination-repulsion as the Augustan poet. As for the second type of transposition, the interpretations of the legend, they do not owe much to the earlier commentaries on Ovid's *Metamorphoses*, whether they are anonymous mythographers of the eleventh and twelfth centuries, Arnulf of Orleans in the twelfth century or John of Garland in the thirteenth century, or finally the manuscripts of the Ovidian poem glossed in the thirteenth and fourteenth centuries. Vague moral interpretations make the physical ugliness of the bear the image of the moral ugliness of a debauched woman, but none suggests our author's indignation at the infanticide perpetrated by women who want to hide their dishonour, or his compassion for the same women who drag their shame and misery without finding a cure, and whom this life of unhappiness engulfs to the point of making them look like wild beasts. No mythographer associates the legend of Callisto with the characteristics of human procreation, which joins pleasure to the sordid aspect of the carnal act. Finally, and above all, no commentator has the audacity to link the legend to the truth of Christianity, and the two successive metamorphoses to the history of the Jewish people, degraded by their refusal of Christ's baptism but who will receive God's forgiveness at the end of time.

This originality, this exegetical audacity, has no equivalent either before the fourteenth century or after. No doubt, these are some of the reasons for the disrepute of the original *Ovide moralisé*, since as early as the fifteenth century some handwritten witnesses of the text in verse, one of its two prose versions, and the versions printed by Colard Mansion and Antoine Vérard will abandon these exegeses. The original *Ovide moralisé* will take more than four hundred years to recover from this discredit. Fortunately, today this injustice is currently being repaired.[53]

---

[53] Notably thanks to the work of the international team 'Ovide en français', responsible for the critical edition mentioned above of the first book of the *Ovide moralisé*.

8

PRUNELLE DELEVILLE

FROM THE *OVIDE MORALISÉ*
TO THE OVIDE "RE-MORALISÉ"

The *Ovide moralisé* is well known, not just as the first French translation of Ovid's *Metamorphoses*, but also as an allegorical text in its own right. Its anonymous translator interprets the Latin poem by attributing to it a natural, euhemeristic, moral or spiritual meaning. The *Ovide moralisé* survived in 20 manuscripts composed between the early fourteenth and the late fifteenth century (Baker et al. 2018: 13–15). As proved by Jung (1994, 1996a and 2009), the textual tradition is irregular. A significant example of the diversity of these manuscripts are two late exemplars that do not contain the spiritual allegories: Paris, BnF, français 870 (Z^3) *c.* 1410; Paris, BnF, 19121 (Z^4) *c.* 1390–1410. These two manuscripts are the object of this article, which aims to reveal the particular ways in which the author of the text transmitted by Z^3 and Z^4 (to whom I will refer from now on as the 'rewriter' or as the 'new author') understood and interpreted the *Ovide moralisé*. This study explores the rewriter's ideology and the methods he used to convey his opinion of the original text. By focusing on a specific case study, the myth of Calisto, this article seeks to shed light on the different positions taken by the author of the *Ovide moralisé* and his rewriter on the question of the spiritual meaning of the *Metamorphoses*. It will also show the strategies through which the rewriter framed his authorial voice within the textual space of the *Ovide moralisé*.

Distinctive Features of the Rewriting in Z^3 and Z^4

The two *codices* Z^3 and Z^4 are unusual in the tradition of the *Ovide moralisé*. Even though for the most part the rewriter maintains the French translation and the concrete interpretations of the text, he is not consistent throughout his work; he modifies some passages of the *Ovide moralisé* and deletes all the spiritual interpretations, which constitute a major part of the original work.[1] Moreover, the author adds and develops historical explanations that are not

---

[1]   For the difference between the concrete meaning and the spiritual one, see Possamaï-Pérez 2006: 380 and 396.

in the *Ovide moralisé* and omits others that are transmitted by the rest of the manuscript tradition.[2] [In this case, according to the classical and medieval conception of history (Guenée 1980: 27), I use the term 'historical' to describe the interpretations dealing with history or social morality.] The new author even modifies the translation itself in certain passages and also expresses his disagreement over particular interpretations, as we will see later in the article. As Jung (1996b: 270) convincingly showed, while the distinguishing feature of the *Ovide moralisé* are its spiritual interpretations, in Z^3 and Z^4 the *Ovide moralisé* is changed into something new, a 'livre d'histoire' (a book of stories). Jung (1996b: 274) also demonstrated that the rewriter did not work with a manuscript of the Latin text of the *Metamorphoses* or other Latin texts but with the *Ovide moralisé* itself, together with other vernacular texts. In contrast to the 'original' French translation, the new author changes or deletes some difficult passages, and he also elaborates on specific topics such as love, expanding the interpretations of the love stories of Pyramus and Thisbe, Eurydice and Orpheus, and Mars and Venus. Furthermore, he develops the fables about love; in the story of Cephalus, for instance, he adds 60 verses on the protagonist's despair over the death of his wife. Some narratives are also expanded by the addition of verses from other medieval works. For example, the rewriter complements the story of Oedipus with episodes from the *Roman de Thèbes*. In Z^3 and Z^4, Book IX recounts the genealogy of Oedipus in a version that is inspired by the *Roman de Thèbes* (*Ovide re-moralisé*, IX. 1098–1299) (Deleville 2019: III. 272).

So, if we consider the changes made to the *Ovide moralisé* by the new author, we are justified in applying the term 'rewriting' to the text transmitted in Z^3 and Z^4. According to Genette (1982: 340) and Arrigo (2015: 299–301), a rewriting always changes the meaning of the hypotext. Thus, the author of Z^3 and Z^4 can be considered a rewriter, for he does not simply copy out the *Ovide moralisé* identically, but he changes the overall meaning of the text and alters its moral reach at the same time. This is the process that I allude to in the title of this paper through the use of the adjective 're-moralisé'. Moreover, following Jung (1996b: 274), I choose not to define the new writer as a 'translator' or a 're-translator', in order to stress the fact that the text of Z^3 and Z^4 is not a new translation of the Latin *Metamorphoses*.

---

[2]   For that matter, the author of the *Ovide moralisé* uses the word 'histoire' for the readings from both euhemeristic and social ethics standpoints (Possamaï-Pérez 2006: 383–96).

The Debate on the Spiritual Meaning of the Text

Jung (1996a: 92) has shown that the rewriter distances himself from the spiritual interpretations given in the *Ovide moralisé* by systematically omitting Christian allegories (i.e. the spiritual readings). He maintains the historical interpretations and sometimes also the moral ones, but only when they deal with social topics concerning life on earth, not the afterlife. For example, he maintains the moral-historical description of Bacchus, in which there is a strong condemnation of alcohol abuse: he even concludes this interpretation with ten appended lines emphasizing the social damage that alcohol causes (Deleville 2019: II. 339, *Om*, III. 2312–23).[3]

The rewriter avoids any references to the spiritual allegories or to Christian dogma. In the prologue to Z^3 and Z^4, for example, he replaces the reference to Christian truth with a reference to plural and human truths. For the new writer, the *Metamorphoses* holds 'mainte grant science notable, | Maint secret, mainte demoustrance' [Many great significant knowledge, | Many secrets, many demonstrations] (Deleville 2019: II. 19, *Om*, I. 102–03).[4] These lines replace a part of the prologue of the *Ovide moralisé* that was deleted by the new writer:

> Qui le sens en porroit savoir,
> La veritez seroit aperte,
> Qui souz les fables gist couverte.
> (Baker et al. 2018: II, 9, I. 45–47)

[The truth that lies hidden beneath the fables will be disclosed to one who can discern the meaning of them (Copeland: 1991, 109).]

In this passage, the hidden meaning of the *Metamorphoses* is defined as a Christian one. The noun group 'la veritez' [the truth] refers specifically to the Christian truth. Thus, by deleting the passage, the rewriter rejects the spiritual readings imposed on Ovid's poem.

At the end of the poem, the rewriter explains why he deletes the spiritual readings transmitted in the *Ovide moralisé*:

> En ce livre je n'ai mie
> Escripte nulle allegorie
> [...]
> Ovides mesmes, qui les fist,
> N'i entendi pas tel sens sans do[t]e

---

[3] All the references to Deleville 2019 refer to the manuscripts Z of the *Ovide moralisé* (*Om*).

[4] All quotations from these two manuscripts are taken from the critical edition in Deleville 2019. All the translations from Old French to English are mine, except when another author has already translated a part of the *Ovide moralisé*.

Com l'alegorie nous note.
(Deleville 2019: II. *Om*, XIV. 102–03)

[In this book I have not written any allegory. [...] Even Ovid, who wrote the fables, certainly did not intend this meaning, as the allegory shows.]

With this term, 'allegorie', the rewriter is probably referring to the spiritual interpretations given in the *Ovide moralisé*. Although in Old French the word does not always refer to Christian readings (Jung 1971: 12), it is the term used by the author of the *Ovide moralisé* to allude to the Christian and moral meanings of the text (Possamaï-Pérez 2006: 396). Indeed, the author of the *Ovide moralisé* explains the difference between the 'allegorie' (spiritual meaning) and the other interpretations ('sentence', 'glose' or 'sens') (Possamaï-Pérez 2006: 396). Following the *Ovide moralisé*, the author of Z^3 and Z^4 also understands the word 'allegorie' in a spiritual way. In fact, he deletes every interpretation dealing directly with Christ and Christian motifs, and even removes the moral expositions which refer to the Christian dogma.

The rejection of the spiritual meaning given to Ovid's poem is also suggested by certain expressions that introduce additions or developments. When the rewriter develops or adds a historical explanation, he always insists on the truth of his own interpretation of the text. For example, the *Ovide moralisé* does not provide a historical meaning for the myth of Pasiphae. The reasons for this decision are obvious: the tale of Pasiphae is considered real in the Middle Ages, because it is part of History according to euhemerism. In addition, for Blumenfeld-Kosinski (1996: 317), the author of the *Ovide moralisé* does not give an euhemeristic explanation of the myth because he intends to focus on the spiritual interpretation of Pasiphae's behaviour.[5] Unlike the *Ovide moralisé*, the rewriter provides another interpretation of the story. Pasiphae is depicted as a shameful young woman who falls in love with a good-looking man that she has just seen going to a house of ill repute. She confesses her love to the attractive man. Unfortunately, he rebuffs her advances. Despite the rejection, the girl seeks a way to enjoy a night with her love interest, and Dedalus suggests that she dresses up as a prostitute so she can satisfy her immoderate desire. The rewriter describes his interpretation as the 'droit sens' [the right meaning] of the tale (Deleville 2019: I. 216, *Om*, VIII. 805). Expressions such as 'droit sens', or 'vraie exposition' [true interpretation] are systematically used in the rewriter's own interpretations of the myths. These expressions suggest the

---

[5]   If he had rationalized it, there would be no 'contre-nature' behaviour which 'allows for the idea that human nature is perverted in its lack for God' (Blumenfeld-Kosinski 1996: 317).

existence of an implicit debate with the original text on the hidden meaning of the *Metamorphoses*.

Replacing the Author of the *Ovide moralisé*: The example of Callisto

In the rewriting, the debate about the true meaning of Ovid's poem is ingeniously distributed across different sections of the text. Particularly interesting, for example, is the use of the word 'translateur' [translator][6] in the rubrics of Z^3 and Z^4 to designate both the rewriter and the author of the *Ovide moralisé*, thus challenging the latter's primacy. Another compelling example is the superimposition of a new meaning on both the text and the interpretation of the myth of Callisto in the rewriting of the *Ovide moralisé*.

In the manuscripts Z^3 and Z^4, the rubrics introduce the content of each passage. Four of these rubrics contain the word 'translateur' (Jung 1996a: 90). The first two occurrences are connected to the historical interpretation given by the author of the *Ovide moralisé* to Jupiter's punishment of humankind: 'Translateur raconte de la Bible' [The translator discusses the Bible] (Deleville 2019: II. 68, *Om*, I. 1329rubr.) and 'Cy parle le translateur de ce livre de Nambrot et des Babiloniens' [Here, the translator of the book talks about Nimrod and Babylonians] (Deleville 2019: II, 70, *Om*, I. 1392rubr.). In both cases, the word 'translateur' refers to the author of the *Ovide moralisé*, who discusses passages from the Bible (considered in the Middle Ages to be History) in relation to the myth of Jupiter (also understood as a historical event).

The term 'translateur' also appears in the rubrics introducing passages in which the rewriter explains his own understanding of the *Metamorphoses*. On this occasion, however, the term is associated with the rewriter rather than with the author of the *Ovide moralisé*. The word 'translateur', for example, introduces the moral reading of the myth of Callisto (which is not told in the *Ovide moralisé*), and also introduces the verses that I have already quoted above (Deleville 2019: II, XIV. 102–03), in which the rewriter claims to have chosen not to write an 'allegorie'. Thus, the rewriter identifies himself as a 'translateur' in the same way as he previously referred to the author of the *Ovide moralisé*. He replaces the writer, and the word 'translateur' becomes polysemous.[7] In Z^3 and Z^4, the word is used to designate both the author and the rewriter, which suggests that the rewriter

---

[6] Even though the new writer claims to be the 'translateur' of the text, I will still use the word 'rewriter' for the reasons given earlier.

[7] The rubrics are 'Translateur enseignement' [Lesson by the translator] (Deleville 2019: II. 169, *Om*, II. 1113rubr.) and 'La fin du grant sermon Pitagoras. Translateur' [The end of Pythagoras' sermon. Translator] (BnF, français, 870, fol. 268v).

is taking on the identity of the author of the *Ovide moralisé* (Jung 1996a: 92). According to Jung, the rewriter uses this device to distance himself from certain interpretations of the *Ovide moralisé* (1996a: 92). The new author not only takes on the identity of the original author and conveys his own reading of the *Metamorphoses*, but he goes further by trying to replace the author and to impose his own reading. The rational explanation of Callisto's myth, introduced by the word 'translateur', is a good example of this skilful substitution.

Thanks to the work of Marylène Possamaï-Pérez (2006: 190–233), we know that the original author of the *Ovide moralisé* ingeniously adapts his translation in order to introduce his allegories to the myth. In other words, the author is 'preparing the ground for the first moralization' already within the narration of the myth by adding some motifs which do not appear in the Ovidian text and are used in the moralization (Griffin 2015: 39). The rewriter adopts the same strategy. Like the author of the *Ovide moralisé*, he modifies the narration of a myth to introduce and strengthen the interpretations he wants to impose on it. The myth of Callisto (also addressed in Possamaï-Pérez's contribution to this volume in Chapter 7), is a fine example of this practice.

The young nymph Callisto wanted to keep her virginity in order to be an honourable servant of the chaste Diana. However, one day, Jupiter fell in love with her and resolved to sleep with her. He changed his appearance to look like Diana so that he could approach Callisto, and finally he raped her. Callisto tried to hide her pregnancy from Diana, but one day her secret was uncovered; Diana immediately cast her out and Juno transformed her into a bear. Callisto eventually gave birth to a child who later would try to kill her. Fortunately, Jupiter managed to protect her and change her into a constellation.

In the *Ovide moralisé*, Diana is presented as Virginity and Callisto as a girl who lost Diana's company. The author condemns young women who surrender themselves to their lovers and then abort. In his version of the myth, the rewriter maintains the beginning of this explanation, but discards the diatribe against debauchery and abortion. He prefers to give a new interpretation of his own. For him, Jupiter represents the duplicitous men who prey on innocent girls and tell them that it is acceptable to love someone just to be able satisfy their desire.

Unlike the author of the *Ovide moralisé*, in his rewriting and the following interpretation of the myth the new author insists on the topic of deceitfulness. For example, in the 'original' *Ovide moralisé*, Jupiter, who is in love with the beautiful Callisto, says to himself that he wants to take the girl's virginity without being discovered by his wife:

> De ceste avrai le pucelage
> Que ja ma feme nel savra
> Ne ja ne s'en apercevra.
> (De Boer 1915–1938: I, 203, ll. 1452–54)

[I will take her virginity, so that my wife will never know it and will never notice it.]

This passage is slightly changed and expanded upon in the rewriting of the *Ovide moralisé*. Particularly important is the emphasis placed on deceit:

> De ceste aray le pucellage.
> Homs ne femme ne le saura,
> Ne nul ne s'en apercevra.
> Se je puis, ge la desevray
> Et tout mon bon d'elle feray.
> (Deleville 2019: II, 157, ll. 869–873)

[I will take her virginity. No man or woman will know it or will ever notice it. If I can, I will deceive her and I will satisfy my desire for her.]

The addition of the last two lines prepares the rewriter's exposition of the male capacity to deceive innocent young women. In his interpretation, in fact, the rewriter repeats the verb 'decevoir' [deceive], suggesting that the introduction of the same verb in the translation was intentional. He states that '[ce] sa propre forme eüst, | Jamais deceue ne l'eüst' [[Jupiter] would never have deceived her, if he had worn his proper form] (Deleville 2019: II, 169, ll. 1122–23). For the rewriter, these duped girls would have saved their honour if 'hommes ne les eussent deceues' [men had not deceived them] (Deleville 2019: II, 171, ll. 1169).[8] Furthermore, the new author declares that: 'c'est moult grant pechés [...] | A homme de decevoir femme' [it is a great sin for a man to deceive a woman] (Deleville 2019: II, 171, ll. 1172–73). This link between the modification in the translation and the main topic of the new interpretation suggests that the rewriter is intentionally transforming the text for his own purpose, as the author of the *Ovide moralisé* did with Ovid's poem.

There is another aspect in which the two texts differ. In the *Ovide moralisé*, Jupiter 'Si prent de Dyane erroment | La forme et le contenement' [quickly takes the form and the behaviour of Diana] (De Boer 1915–1938: vol 1 203, Book II: 1461–62). The author underlines the speed of the metamorphosis by the use of the adverb 'erroment' [quickly]. Unlike the earlier author, the rewriter insists on the perfection of the metamorphosis: 'De Diane prist proprement | La forme et le contenement' [he took exactly the form and the behaviour of Diana] (Deleville 2019: II, 160, ll. 879–81).

---

8   In Deleville 2019: I, 176–201 and 2020.

The use of the adverb 'proprement' (exactly, in a way that specifically refers to one's reality) is also mentioned in the rewriter's interpretation, according to which the myth deals with men who act like Jupiter, 'Qui sa propre forme deffist, | Car [ce] sa propre forme eüst, | Jamais deceue ne l'eüst' [who changes his own form, because if he had borne his own form, he would never have deceived her] (Deleville 2019: II, 169, II. 1121–22). Here, the adjective 'propre' (of one's own) echoes the adverb 'proprement' in the narration of the fable. This link creates a parallelism between the narration of the myth and its interpretation. Thus, the rewriter works in the same way as the author of the *Ovide moralisé*: just as the author of the *Ovide moralisé* transformed Ovid's poem to accord with his own view of the world, so the rewriter of the *Ovide moralisé* adapts the translation to his didactic purpose. However, while the first author stresses female duplicity, the rewriter underlines the duplicity of the male character. Therefore, this is a complete inversion of the interpretation of the myth, due to an ideological difference regarding women.

Unlike the author of the *Ovide moralisé*, the rewriter sometimes defends female characters. Eurydice, for example, is now not seen in a negative light. She is no longer 'celle qui trop s'esloigne folement | De raisonable entendement' [the one who madly falls away from reason], as suggested by the author of the *Ovide moralisé* (De Boer 1915–1938: vol 4 16, Book X: 232–33). On the contrary, she is the woman who 'deffent | S'amour pour estriver mout fort' [defends her love through much effort] (Deleville 2019: vol 3 331, Book X: 210–11). The rewriter also defends a number of forsaken wives, like Dido against Eneas or Medea against Jason (Deleville 2019: vol 1, Book XIV: 176–79). As shown in these examples, the rewriter takes the side of the women and also influences contemporary female writers. As I have argued elsewhere, Christine de Pizan – in *Le livre du duc des vrais amants* – partly draws on the rewriter's interpretation of Callisto (Deleville 2019: vol. 1 176–201 and 'Christine de Pizan, lectrice de l'*Ovide moralisé*, mais lequel?' (forthcoming)). Christine de Pizan knew of the rewriting of the *Ovide moralisé* and found in it some examples and arguments to defend her position against Jean de Meun in the early fifteenth-century debate on the *Roman de la Rose*.

What emerges from these examples is the idea that the rewriter imposes his point of view on his source text by drawing on the same strategies employed by the author of the *Ovide moralisé* in his translation of Ovid's poem. In his diatribe against abortion and female debauchery, the author of the *Ovide moralisé* conveys his disapproval by asserting that no one should trust a woman who has had an abortion, because she has committed murder before and may do so again:

> J'oseroie dire en apert
> Que, qui en tel feme se fie,
> Il est em peril de sa vie
> [...]
> Pour voir, ele l'empoisonera,
> Ou en dormant l'estoufera!
>> (De Boer 1915–1938: I, 209, ll. 1742–48)

[I would freely say that whoever trusts such a woman is in danger for his life [...]. To tell the truth, she will poison him and suffocate him when he sleeps!]

The rewriter of the *Ovide moralisé* is as eloquent as his model, but he uses the same emphatic tone to a different end: that is, to warn women against unfaithful lovers:

> Ja ne sera que je m'en taisse,
> Car se femme croit mon conseil,
> Je li lo et moult li conseil
> Qu'elle ne croye homme en tel cas.
> S'elle fait, ne s'en doubte pas,
> Que encore s'en repentira
> Amerement et maldira
> L'eure c'onques homme crut
> Ne que telle acointance eut.
>> (Deleville 2019: II, 172, ll. 1183–91)

[I will never stop talking about it, because if a woman believes my advice, I urge and strongly advise her not to believe men in this case. If she does so, it is sure that she will still bitterly reproach herself for it and will curse the day when she believed such a man and had such company.]

Both texts present the same subjectivity, the same use of the future tense, and the same fatal representations. Although the rewriter may offer the impression of taking the voice and identity of the author, he enacts a complete moral reversal. By assuming the status ('translateur') and the voice of the author, he manages to replace him and has the last word on the interpretation of the myth.

Possamaï-Pérez has shown that the original author is a preacher who tries to involve and move the reader by using the phatic and emotional functions of language (Possamaï-Pérez 2006: 717–18, referring to Pomel 2001: 145). The interpretation of Callisto may be a good example of this type of rhetoric. Both the author and the rewriter of the *Ovide moralisé* speak directly to the readers and try to scare them in order to convince them. The main aim of the original author is salvation in the afterlife; the rewriter, on the other hand, has no interest in the hereafter, focusing only on life on Earth and specifically on topics such as women's reputations and men's dishonesty. The voice of the rewriter is not that of a preacher, as it is in the case of the author of the *Ovide moralisé*; he draws on the first author's language but only to replace the topics and voice of the preacher with his own. He never defines his interpretations as 'allegories', but talks of 'enseignement' (lesson), a description that the first author does not use (Deleville 2019: ii, 169, II. 1113rubr.). By using the word 'enseignement', which in Old French generally refers to a moral lesson, the rewriter presents himself as a moralist. He also uses the expression 'moral sens' [moral meaning] (Deleville 2019: ii, 412, IV. 1705) to define one of his interpretations of the Ovidian myths. Thus, for the rewriter, replacing the author is a means of conveying not only his view on the *querelle* about women but also to offer insights into the true meaning of the *Metamorphoses*.

A New Truth

The rewriter does not conceal his disagreement with the spiritual manner in which the author of the *Ovide moralisé* allegorizes the Ovidian poem. He deletes all the references to Christian dogma and all spiritual allegories, but he develops the historical aspects and provides some new ones. Thus, he seems to think that the truth of the *Metamorphoses* must be concrete and human. He also suggests that the meaning of the text must conform to the Latin poem. This opinion is clearly defended when he states that Ovid could not have had the same intention as the author of the spiritual interpretation of the *Ovide moralisé*; he searches for the intention of Ovid behind the fable, instead of an image of the Christian religion. He defines the exposition as 'l'antante a quoy la fable acorde' [the intention the fable adheres to] (Deleville 2019: II, 290, III. 1007). The allegorical interpretation is known as a *similitudo* between a text and its explanation, its deep signification (Strubel 2002: 20). The author of the *Ovide moralisé* also shares this conception and tacitly defines the allegories as a *similitudo* (Possamaï-Pérez 2006: 330, referring to ix. 2709) considering them as 'acordable a voir' [compatible with truth]. Yet, the rewriter insists on this idea, and emphasizes it in his interpretation while trying to offer new elements that are closer to the narrative. For example, in the interpretation of Callisto he focuses on the changing form of Jupiter and gives an explanation for it; the author of the *Ovide moralisé*, on the other hand, concentrates on his criticism of abortion, which has no clear link to the Ovidian myth. So the rewriter suggests that the author of the *Ovide moralisé* does not interpret the Latin poem properly, because he gives a Christian explanation that is far removed from the true meaning of the text. For him, the truth of the text must be found in accordance with it. As Miranda Griffin (2015: 46) has shown, in the *Ovide moralisé*, 'the naked truth turns out to be another layer of integument and interpretation, exposing a

Christian truth which was always-already there, but which can only be expressed in veiled language'. In contrast, in the text transmitted in manuscripts Z^3 and Z^4, the Christian truth is not 'always-already there', because for the rewriter Ovid could not have known this truth.

To conclude, I would like to return to the pun in the title of this paper. By '*re-moralisé*', I mean that the rewriter of the manuscripts Z changes the meaning of the text. He keeps the naturalistic and historical explanations offered by the author of the *Ovide moralisé*, but he deletes the spiritual interpretations in order to put forward new material expressing his own moral perspective. With codices Z^3 and Z^4, the *Ovide moralisé* became an 'Ovide re-moralisé', an ideological and philosophical reflection on women and the truth hidden in the *Metamorphoses*. For this purpose, the rewriter cleverly supersedes the author of the *Ovide moralisé*. His own voice merges with the first author's voice, so much so that it eventually replaces it.

9

PABLO PIQUERAS YAGÜE

THE USE OF SECONDARY SOURCES IN THE *OVIDE MORALISÉ* AND IN BERSUIRE'S *OVIDIUS MORALIZATUS*: A PRELIMINARY COMPARISON[*]

The *Ovide moralisé* and the *Ovidius moralizatus* are two medieval allegorical commentaries on Ovid's *Metamorphoses*. Both texts re-elaborate, summarise and present in new forms their source text through the imitation of ancient and medieval intermediary sources. The aim of this article is to show the different ways in which these two medieval commentaries made reference to, and presented, some of their secondary sources. By doing so, the study broadens our understanding of the different functions of these two works in the Middle Ages, while also shedding light on the changing face of the reception of Ovid in those times.

On the one hand, the *Ovide moralisé* is an anonimous vernacular poem written in the first half of the fourteenth century, *c.* 1315–1325 (Trachsler 2018: 188). The author translated the myths of the *Metamorphoses* and added some allegorical commentaries to aid the interpretion of the Ovidian text.[1]

On the other hand, the *Ovidius moralizatus* is an allegorical commentary on Ovid's *Metamorphoses* in Latin prose, written by Pierre Bersuire *c.* 1340–1362 as part of his major encyclopedia the *Reductorium morale* (the *Ovidius moralizatus* would be the fifteenth book of this greater work). During the

6

[*] This article was written as part of the Proyecto de Investigación FFI2013-42671-P, financed by Programa Estatal de Fomento de la Investigación Científica y Técnica de Excelencia, Subprograma de Generación del Conocimiento del MINECO, from Spain. I have received funding by the Ministerio de Educación, Cultura y Deporte para la Formación de Profesorado Universitario: FPU15/05527. I thank Rosa Mª Iglesias, professor at the Universidad de Murcia, for her comments on this paper, and also Irene Salvo García for her comments and for the time spent in Odense at the Center of Medieval Literature of the SDU, which was a great inspiration for my research. I also thank Professor M. T. Kretschmer for his comments on this article and for letting me read his forthcoming publication 'L'*Ovide moralisé* comme source principale des ajouts de la version parisienne de l'*Ovidius moralizatus* de Pierre Bersuire', which has been very helpful for this article. Finally, I thank the reviewers of the first versions of the article for their suggestions and guidance.

[1] For a complete study of the *Ovide moralisé* and its interpretation, see Possamaï-Pérez 2006. For a general introduction to the work, see Baker et al. 2018.

course of the treatise, he summarises a series of myths and then presents his interpretation of them.[2] There are three different versions of the *Ovidius moralizatus* (Engels 1971: 21–22). Bersuire wrote the first two versions (named *A₁* and *A₂* by Engels because they were composed in Avignon) without having read the *Ovide moralisé*; and after reading it, he wrote his last version (called *P* because it was composed in Paris), adding information from the vernacular poem.[3] For the *P* version, the *Ovide moralisé* was the most important source after the *Metamorphoses*, but Bersuire had not read the vernacular poem when he started to write the *Ovidius moralizatus*.[4]

In terms of the disposition of the myths and their interpretations, the *Ovide moralisé* presents a translation of the greater part of Ovid's masterpiece. This translation is used as an *expositio* of the myths, which are then interpreted from a moral point of view. In the *Ovidius moralizatus*, Bersuire summarises the mythological stories before presenting his comments and allegories. Both differ from previous commentaries and literary works written in the tradition of the *Metamorphoses* because their authors not only included explanations of the myths according to what they read in the *Metamorphoses*, but they also extended, added, or eliminated myths to suit their own purposes.[5] We could say that the purpose of the *Ovide moralisé* is to present a very broad view of the classical mythography (Copeland 1991: 122), whereas Bersuire's intention is to moralise the pagan myths and to provide material that preachers might use in their sermons to convince their audiences; he begins practically every moralisation with 'Dic quod [...]' [Say that [...]] (see, *e.g.*, Van der Bijl 1971: 27).

The addition or elimination of myths and the use of secondary sources is a common feature of these two works. Bersuire stated it very clearly in the prologue of his treatise:

---

[2]   Ghisalberti 1933c was the first complete study of Bersuire's treatise. It was followed by Engels 1966 and 1971, and Kretschmer 2016.

[3]   For the Parisian version Bersuire also included information found in Ridewall's *Fulgentius metaforalis* (Engels 1971: 21). Each version can be read in several manuscripts (Van der Bijl 1971: 25).

[4]   For the relationship between the two works, see Engels (1945: 23–45) and Kretschmer (forthcoming).

[5]   Arnulf of Orléans' *Allegoriae super Ovidii Metamorphosin* (*c.* 1175), John of Garland's *Integumenta Ovidii* (*c.* 1234) and Giovanni del Virgilio's *Allegorie librorum Ovidii Metamorphoseos* (*c.* 1323) are the main works in the *Metamorphoses*' allegorical tradition. I select these three works as the tradition because they are the three independent writings that can be read without the text of the *Metamorphoses*. I do not include the marginal comments like the Vulgate (*c.* 1260) or the one by William of Thiegiis, in spite of their important influence on these works.

Distingam ergo istum tractatum in quindecim capitula secundum quindecim libros in predicto Ouidii uolumine contentos. Aliquas tamen in aliquibus adiungam fabulas quas in aliis locis repperi, aliquas etiam detraham et omittam quas non necessarias iudicaui. (*Ovidius moralizatus* 1.1)[6]

[I shall divide this little treatise into fifteen chapters, as the fifteen books which are contained in Ovid's aforementioned book. In addition, I shall add some stories I have found in other places, while some stories I shall pass over and omit, since I have judged them to be unnecessary.][7]

Previous scholars have investigated the relationship between the *Ovide moralisé* and the *Ovidius moralizatus* and their secondary sources.[8] The present article furthers our knowledge of this relationship by focusing on two source texts that have not received much attention in previous investigations: the medieval commentaries on the *Metamorphoses* and Ovid's *Heroides*. We know that the author of the vernacular poem introduced some passages from the *Heroides* (Barbieri 2011 and Salvo García 2018b) and he read and used some medieval commentaries on the *Metamorphoses* (Salvo García 2018a and Salvo García forthcoming). In the case of the *Ovidius moralizatus*, however, given that there is no proper critical edition at present, ascertaining Bersuire's use of these sources is an extremely difficult task. Therefore, the goal of this article is to show the different uses of some of the mythography that appears in both moralisations of Ovid's epic but not in the *Metamorphoses* themselves.

As case studies, we are going to focus on four different myths from the *Ovidius moralizatus*: two were taken from the *Metamorphoses*' medieval commentaries and do not appear in the *Ovide moralisé*; and two were taken from the *Heroides* and were changed by Bersuire for the second version, version *P*, of his *Ovidius moralizatus* after reading the *Ovide moralisé*.

The two myths from the medieval commentaries of the *Metamorphoses* are the stories of the Palici (V. 406) and Maera (VII. 362), and the two from the *Heroides* are the episodes of the Danaides (letter 14) and Hero and Leander (letters 18–19).

---

[6]   The texts of the *Ovidius moralizatus* are transcribed from Troyes, Bibliothèque Municipale, MS. 1627. This corresponds to fol. 2ʳ.

[7]   This version is based on the forthcoming translation by Frank Coulson and Justin Haynes of the *De formis figurisque deorum*. I thank them for letting me use excerpts from their translation of Bersuire's treatise.

[8]   For the sources of the *Ovide moralisé*, see Salvo García 2019. For the *Ovidius moralizatus*, previous studies are Ghisalberti 1933c, Reynolds 1990, Kretschmer 2016 and Piqueras Yagüe 2019.

Medieval Commentaries

In the fifth book of the *Metamorphoses*, Ovid tells the myth of the rape of
Proserpine, daughter of Ceres. While collecting flowers with some other
girls, Proserpine was seized by Pluto and taken to the Underworld. After
looking for her daughter and discovering that she was with Pluto, Ceres
begged Jupiter to intervene; Jupiter decided that Proserpine should live half
of the year with her mother and half of the year with her new husband.

In the account of the rape, Ovid mentions the swamp of the Palici,
through which Pluto's horses passed as their master led his chariot to the
Underworld. This is Ovid's description of the moment:

> raptor agit currus et nomine quemque uocando
> exhortatur equos, quorum per colla iubasque
> excutit obscura tinctas ferrugine habenas;
> perque lacus altos et olentia sulphure fertur
> stagna Palicorum rupta ferventia terra
> et qua Bacchiadae, bimari gens orta Corintho,
> inter inaequales posuerunt moenia portus.
>
> (Ovid, *Metamorphoses*, V. 402–08)

[Her captor sped his chariot and urged his horses onwards, calling each one by
name, and shaking the dark-dyed reins on their necks and manes. Through
deep lakes he galloped, through the pools of the Palici, reeking with sulphur
and boiling up from a crevice of the earth, and where the Bacchiadae, a race
sprung from Corinth between two seas, had built a city between two harbours
of unequal size.] (Miller 1916: 267)

This passage is translated in the *Ovide moralisé* as follows:

> Li rois emporte Proserpine,
> Si vait ses chevaux semonant
> Et les regnes abandonant.
> Les estans de souffre a passez
> Et mains autres malz pas assez.
>
> (De Boer 1920: 230)

[The king carries Proserpine with the force of his horses and they leave the
kingdoms. They go through a cloud of sulphur and a great many other evils.][9]

Although the author of the poem translates 'olentia sulphure [...] | stagna' as
'les estans de souffre' the French anonymous author did not mention the
Palici, probably because the reference is irrelevant to both his mythograph-

---

[9]   The translations of the *Ovide moralisé* are mine, with the help of Mª Consuelo Álvarez
Morán and Alessandra Dolce, of the Universidad de Murcia.

ical and his moral purpose.[10] However, Bersuire does include two stories
related to these brothers in the fifth book of the *Metamorphoses*:

> Palasci sicut ponit integumentator super Ouidii libro quinto fuerunt 2 fratres
> quos Iupiter in Henne generauit, sed cum Iuno Hennem praegnantem de Ioue
> uiro comperisset et ira et zelo commota eam persecuta que timens rogauit
> Iouem ut absorberetur a terra antequam in manibus timoris caderet, quod et
> factum est. Filii igitur in terra cum intra matris uterum partus tempus
> compleuissent et ibi perfecti et geniti tandem prodierunt. [...] Palasci erant filii
> Iouis quorum matre ab terra absorta dum esset praegnans ab ipsis terre
> uisceribus nati sunt qui hospites suos occidebant et humanum sacrificabant
> quos uidens Iupiter iniquos filios suos fulminauit et terram subiectam fulmine
> perforauit, de foramine uero unda statim exiuit que adhuc Rome fluminis
> fetorem sulphureum emittit. Et forte illa est lacus Siciliae de quo dicit Solinus
> quod turpi odore abiicit proximantes, et forte ad ipsius fontis ostendendam
> naturam hec fabula est conficta, unde Ouidius: Olentia sulphure fertur | stagna
> Paliscorum. (*Ovidius moralizatus* 6.11–12)[11]

> [The Palici were two brothers, the sons of Jupiter, as the interpreter of the fifth
> book of Ovid says, whom Jupiter begat by Hebe. But when Juno had
> discovered that Hebe was pregnant by her husband Jupiter, she was moved by
> anger and zeal to persecute her. Fearing Juno, Hebe asked Jupiter that she be
> absorbed by the Earth before she fell into Juno's hands. And so it was done.
> When the sons had come to term within the womb of their mother in the
> ground, they came forth new-born and fully formed. [...] The Palici were sons
> of Jupiter whose mother was absorbed by the Earth while she was pregnant, and
> they were born from the bowels of the Earth. They became great and killed
> their guests and sacrificed human blood. When Jupiter saw this, he struck his
> unjust sons with a lightning bolt and made a hole in the Earth below them.
> From that cavity, a wave immediately arose which still showers down the
> sulfurous stench of the river in Rome. Perhaps this is the Sicilian lake which,
> Solinus writes, casts a foul odour on those nearby. And perhaps this myth was
> created to show the nature of this spring. Hence Ovid: the pools of the Palici,
> they say, smelling of sulphur and bubbling up from the split earth.]

In this case, Bersuire is very clear about his sources and he admits having
gathered together the information from an 'integumentator super Ouidii

---

[10] According to Possamaï-Pérez (2006: 822–24), the topic chosen by the *Ovide moralisé*'s
author for development in book 5 is *pénitance*; he focused only on the main myths of
this book, leaving allusions of this kind aside.

[11] Troyes, Bibliothèque Municipale, 1627, fols 64v–65r. I transcribe the mythological
names as they appear in the manuscript, because there is no proper edition of the
Avignon version of the *Ovidius moralizatus*. The references for this version in the
manuscripts are part of my PhD research ('El *Ovidius moralizatus* de Pierre Bersuire y su
papel en la tradición de las alegorías medievales de las *Metamorfosis*'), currently under-
way at the University of Murcia, and which will be finished in 2020.

libro quinto'. This is the only time in the *Ovidius moralizatus* that Bersuire claims to follow an *integumentator*, i.e. a commentator, but we cannot be sure which commentator he used. Following are three well known medieval commentaries on the *Metamorphoses*:

Vulgate	Guillelmus de Thiegiis	*Vat. lat. 1479*, fol. 92r
Iupiter opressit Ethnam matrem Paliscorum quam <cum> consequeretur Iuno, implorauit auxilium terre et intra sinum eius est recepta. Peperit autem gemellos non tamen matura partu sed illos tam diu in gremio terre fouit quam diu lex uteri postulauit et nati sunt inde et dicti sunt Palisci quasi bis nati sed hos immites et humano gaudere sanguine narrat historia et ideo misit eos Iupiter apud inferos et ubi mersi sunt lacus est qui sulpureum habet odorem ex fulmine quo fulminati sunt et ideo dicit stagna olentia.	Palisci duo fratres fuerunt filii Iouis et Ethne. Ethna vero absorta fuit a terra et Palisci singulis diebus uno cubito crescebant et homines interficiebant unde Iupiter timens ne proicerent ipsum a regno ipsos detruxit in terris et fluxerunt in aquam sulphuream sicut sunt loca sulphurea apud sodomam et gommoram. Vel forsitan actor dicit de illo quod per illum locum sit descensus ad inferos.	Perque describit actor locum per quem Pluto rapuit Proserpinam. Palisci erant filii Iouis et Ethne qui totidem crescebant ad magnitudinem unius palme et hanelitu suo omnia corrumpebant Iupiter hoc uidens eos fulminauit et propter hoc olent campi in illis partibus et per illam partem descendit Pluto ad infernum.[12]
[Jupiter violated Etna, the mother of the Palici. When Juno persecuted her, she implored Earth for help and was received into her bosom. She gave birth to twins prematurely. The Earth nourished them in her bosom as long as the law of the womb demanded, and then she brought them forth. Thus they are called Palici, "twice-born." According to the story, they	[The Palici were two brothers, sons of Jupiter and Etna. Etna was absorbed by the Earth and the Palici grew a cubit everyday and killed men, thus Jupiter fearing to be ejected from his kingdom destroyed them and they submerged in sulphuric water, like the sulphuric places in Sodom and Gomorrah. Or maybe the author speaks about the place through which it is	[The author describes the place through which Pluto captures Proserpina. Palici were sons of Jupiter and Etna who grew the size of a handspan and with their breath they destroyed everything. When Jupiter saw this, he struck them and because of that the fields in those places smell and through this place Pluto descended to the underworld.][13]

---

[12] I thank Professor Frank T. Coulson for the transcription of these three commentaries. The first two are transcribed from Vatican, *Vat. lat. 1598*, fol. 51r and Paris, BnF lat. 8010, fol. 66r.

[13] The translation of the three excerpts of the commentaries is mine.

were savage and used to be appeased by human blood. Later they were pacified by certain sacred rites, and their sacrifices were changed.]

the descent to the underworld.]

All the commentaries describing the Palici are very similar and it is difficult to determine which one Bersuire is referring to: the Vulgate seems to be the closest source, but *Vat. Lat. 1479* also makes Jupiter responsible for their punishment, whereas Thiegiis has exactly the same beginning. What is clear is that for Bersuire this reference to the figure of the Palici was important in order for him to explain the poverty of certain people and the evil of some rulers with the moralisations of these stories.

The origin of the legend of the Palici can be found in Servius and later in the First and the Second Vatican Mythographers, which seem to be the sources for the aforementioned commentators on the *Metamorphoses*:[14]

Servius *Aeneid* 9.581	Myth. Vat. 1.187	Myth. Vat. 2.57
Sunt Palici dei, quorum talis est fabula: Aetnam nympham, vel, ut quidam volunt, Thaliam, Iuppiter cum vitiasset et fecisset gravidam, timens Iunonem, secundum alios ipsam puellam terrae commendavit, et illic enixa est: secundum alios partum eius. postea cum de terra erupissent duo pueri, Palici dicti sunt, quasi iterum venientes: nam πάλιν ἵκειν est iterum venire. hi primo humanis hostiis placabantur, postea quibusdam sacris mitigati sunt et eorum inmutata sacrificia. ideo ergo 'placabilis ara', quia mitigata sunt eorum numina. [...] (Thilo & Hagen 1884: 359)	Sunt Palici dei quorum talis est fabula: Ethnam nympham Iuppiter cum uiciasset et fecisset grauidam, timens Iunonem secundum quosdam Terre commendauit et illic enixa est, secundum alios postea partum eius. cum de Terra erupissent duo pueri, Palici dicti sunt quasi iterum uenientes. Hii primo humanis hostiis placabantur, postea quibusdam sacris mitigati sunt et eorum immutata sacrificia. Ideo autem ara placabilis quia eorum mitigata sunt numina. (Kulcsár 1987: 73–74)	Iuppiter Ethnam nimpham compressit et grauidam fecit, quam cum Iuno persequeretur, illa Terre implorauit auxilium et in cuius sinus recepta enixa est geminos nec dum partu maturo. Vel, ut alii dicunt, Iuppiter timens Iunonem Terre commendabat ipsam, secundum alios partum eius. Hos Terra intra gremium suum tam diu fouit quam diu lex uteri postulabat, posteaque enixa est, unde Palici, id est bis geniti, appellati sunt. Hos autem inmites fuisse et humano sanguine placari consuetos fabula disserente est firmatum. Postea quibusdam sacris mitigati sunt et eorum inmutata sacrificia. (Kulcsár 1987: 142)

[14] The myth is also transmitted by Macrobius (*sat.* 5.19.15–24), in a version similar to Servius's but which includes more information. However, Bersuire's tradition seems to have its origin in Servius, so we can leave this text aside here. For the connection between the Vatican Mythographers and the medieval commentaries on Ovid, see Salvo García 2019.

[They are the Palici, gods whose story is as follows: when Jupiter violated Aetna the nymph (or, as certain writers say, Thalia) and made her pregnant, according to others, he entrusted the girl to the Earth out of fear of Juno. Aetna brought forth her children there; according to others, Jupiter later entrusted her offspring to the Earth. Later when the two boys burst forth from the Earth, they were called Palici, as if to say, "coming a second time," thus πάλιν ἵκειν means "to come a second time." At first they were placated by human victims; later they were appeased by certain holy rites, and their sacrifices were altered. Moreover, their altar is "placatable" because their divinities were appeased.]

[Dwell the Palici, gods whose story is as follows: when Jupiter violated Aetna the nymph and made her pregnant, he entrusted the girl to the Earth out of fear of Juno. According to certain writers, Aetna brought forth her children there; according to others, Jupiter later entrusted her offspring to the Earth. When the two boys burst forth from the Earth, they were called Palici, as if to say, "coming a second time." At first they were placated by human victims; later they were appeased by certain holy rites, and their sacrifices were altered. Moreover, their altar is "placatable" because their divinites were appeased.]

[Jupiter had intercourse with Etna the nymph and made her pregnant. When Juno persecuted her, Etna implored the Earth for help and was received into her bosom. She gave birth to twins prematurely. Or, as some say, fearing Juno, Jupiter entrusted Etna to the Earth, and according to others, he entrusted her offspring. The Earth nourished them in her bosom as long as the law of the womb demanded, and then she brought them forth. Thus they are called Palici, "twice-born." According to the story, they were savage and used to be appeased by human blood. Later they were pacified by certain sacred rites, and their sacrifices were changed.][15]

We can observe how the commentators take the myth from the Vatican Mythographers, who summarise Servius's explanation. Furthermore, we can also note how Bersuire, following the commentators, reproduces the myth in order to give an interpretation. This is a subject matter that the author of the *Ovide moralisé* prefers to omit, probably because this myth is not very well known to his audience and it is not relevant to the main story.

A similar difference in the treatment of the myths alluded to in the *Metamorphoses* is found in Book VII, in Medea's flight from Iolcus to Corinth after she murdered Pelias (Ovid, *Metamorphoses*, VII. 350–93). When Ovid mentions the places that Medea passed through during her flight, he names some that are related to obscure myths: Cerambus, a petrified Dragon, an anonymous son of Bacchus, Corytus and his father, Maera, the Women of Cos, Telchines, Alcidamas, Phyllius and Cycnus, Combe, Menephron, Cephisus's Grandchild, and Eumelus and his son. We

---

[15]   The translation used for the Vatican Mythographers is Pepin (2008) and Servius's is also based on it.

will analyse the case of Maera (VII. 362): 'et quos Maera novo latratu terruit agros' [Maera spread terror through the fields by her strange barking].[16]

The writer of the *Ovide moralisé* does not translate this verse, or any other of the references to the mentioned myths. As we will see in the following section, he jumps from *Metamorphoses*, VII. 351 to VII. 394–97 (De Boer 1931: 11) and mixes the text from the Ovidian epic with the translation of letter 12 of the *Heroides* and other texts (Barbieri 2011: 254–65). The reason for this omission could be the same as in the story of the Palici: the elimination of myths that are not necessary to follow and understand the main one. The only reference to this flight found in the *Ovide moralisé* is:

> Medea s'est lors avancié.
> La teste emprist, si l'a lancié
> En l'eau chaude et tourne en fuite.
> Li dui dragon l'en ont conduite
> Par l'air volant à sauveté
> Ou char qu'il orent apresté. (De Boer 1931: 47)

[Medea leaves. She grabs his head, throws it into the hot water and flees. Two winged dragons carry her through the air flying to salvation in the chariot that has been prepared.]

Unlike the author of the *Ovide moralisé*, Bersuire moralises all the myths that Ovid alludes to (*Ovidius moralizatus* 8.9–21), probably because he is interested in all of them from the perspective of the moral and Christian interpretations for preaching. This is the text related to Maera:

> Cum Hercules filios occidisset pro eo quod Meram uxorem suam prostituerant Mera de hoc dolens mutata est in canem, quod factum expiari non potuit, victis Lacedemoniis Hercules templum fecit in quo nobiles iuvenes sacrificari statuit ad quod sorte ducta est Helena sed eam ne sacrificaret aquila rapuit et sic cognitum est quod Helena ueraciter filia Iouis fuit. (*Ovidius moralizatus*, 8.13)[17]

[After Hercules had killed his sons because they had prostituted his wife Maera, Maera grieved over it and was turned into a dog. This deed could not be

---

[16] The identification of this Maera that Ovid mentions has been discussed over the years by the scholars and we will not consider this issue here: we will merely consider the medieval interpretations of it.

[17] Troyes, Bibliothèque municipale, 1627, fol. 77ʳ. Bersuire repeated this myth in *Ovidius moralizatus* 13.8 (fol. 111ʳ): Helena restituta Menelao uiro suo post destructionem debuit immolari ad expiandum crimen uxoris Herculis, que cum filiis concubuerat, sed ipsam Iupiter rapuit et in celo in stellam pessimam transmutauit. [Helen, who had been restored to her husband Menelaus after the destruction of Troy, as we read elsewhere, should have been sacrificed to expiate the crime of Hercules's wife who had slept with her sons. But Jupiter in the guise of an eagle snatched her up and transformed her into that most baleful star which still threatens danger to sailors.]

expiated until, with the defeat of the Spartans, Hercules built a temple in which he decided to sacrifice the young men and women of the nobility. Helen was chosen for this by lot, but an eagle snatched her to spare her from sacrifice, and thus it was known that Helen was truly Jupiter's daughter.]

This information about Maera is not found in the works of the earlier allegorical tradition. Both Arnulf of Orléans (*c.* 1175) and Giovanni del Virgilio (*c.* 1323) include an allegory of Maera in their works, but they do not provide any relevant mythographic information on the character:

Arnulf's Allegoria 7.7	Giovanni's Allegoria 7.9
Mera quia diis conviciabatur mutata fuit in canem quod fingitur propter assiduum eius in conviciando latratum. (Ghisalberti 1932: 219)	Nona transmutatio est de Meera conversa in canem. Per quam intelligo maledicam mulierem, que dum delectatur in male dicendo et oblatrando dicitur converti in canem. (Ghisalberti 1933a: 77)
[Because she reviled the gods, Maera was transformed into a dog, what is interpreted due to her constant offensive barking].	[The ninth transformation is about Maera transformed into a dog. Through her I understand a scurrilous woman, who is said to be transformed into a dog because she delights in wickedness by her constant talking and yelping.][18]

Interestingly, however, the glosses of Arnulf to the *Metamorphoses* contain an explanation of Maera that is similar to the one we find in Bersuire, although we do not find the same information in his *Allegoriae*. Arnulf's gloss to VII. 362 reads as follows:

Mera conuiciata est diis, ideo mutata est in canem; uel de Hecuba matre Hectoris legatur que binomia fuit; uel de Mera quadam uxore Herculis potest legi quam duo filii eius patre absente prostituerunt. Hercules uero reuersus duos filios interfecit, mater quoque pre dolore mutata est in canem, hoc factum expiari non potuit quousque deuictis Lacedemoniis templum constituit et filias nobilium immolari fecit, denique Helena illuc sorte ducta uenit et aquila eam rapuit sicque probatum est deos posse placari et Helenam Iouis esse filiam per aquilam.

[Mera is a reviler against the gods, and so was transformed into a dog; or 'Mera' should be taken from Hecuba, the mother of Hector, who had two names; or it could be read from 'Mera', a certain wife of Hercules. Her two sons prostituted her when her father was away. When Hercules returned, he killed the two sons; the mother was also turned into a dog due to her grief. This action could not have been atoned for until he founded a temple after the Lacedaemonians were conquered, and caused the daughters of the nobility to be sacrificed. Finally,

---

[18]   The translation of these two excerpts of the allegorical works is mine.

Helen came there after she drew her lot, and the eagle snatched her away. And in this way it was proved that the gods were placated and Helen was Jove's daughter through the eagle.] (Gura 2010: 75–76 and 188)

Arnulf's source for Maera remains unclear. Gura (2010: 74–75) states that the primary mythographic sources for Arnulf's commentary are Hyginus and the Vatican Mythographers, but this information does not appear in their works. However, it does appear in the twelfth-century *Liber de natura deorum*:[19]

XCIII. De Maera

Maera genere et loco Lydia, quia deos contemnens eis inferebat convicia, sic punita fuit, quod a superis in canem est mutata. Secundum alios uxor fuit Herculis, quam absente marito suo Hercule filii sui prostituerunt. Quos reversus Hercules iusta concitus ira interfecit. Maera vero non leviter dolens mutata est in canem. Quod factum expiari non potuit donec victis Lacedaemoniis Hercules templum fecit, in quo nobilium virgines sacrificari statuit. Ad quod sorte ducta fuit Helena, sed eam, ne sacrificaretur, rapuit aquila. Unde cognitum est et deos posse placari et Helenam veraciter Iovis esse filiam. (Brown 1972: 38–39)

[Maera is a reviler against the gods, and so was transformed into a dog; or 'Maera' should be taken from Hecuba, the mother of Hector, who had two names; or it could be read from 'Mera,' a certain wife of Hercules. Her two sons prostituted her when her father was away. When Hercules returned, he killed the two sons; the mother was also turned into a dog due to her grief. This action could not have been atoned for until he founded a temple after the Lacedaemonians were conquered, and caused the daughters of the nobility to be sacrificed. Finally, Helen came there after she drew her lot, and the eagle snatched her away. And in this way it was proved that the gods were placated and Helen was Jove's daughter through the eagle.][20]

The narration of the myth is very similar to the one we find in Arnulf; it contains exactly the same information about Maera. Both Arnulf's commentary and the *Liber de natura deorum* were written in the twelfth century, which means that this story of Maera was known at that time and circulated quite widely. So, Bersuire uses the mythographic information found in a commentary like Arnulf's, or a mythographic source similar to the *Liber*, to explain the myth and allegorise it. In addition, he does not include any of the other different interpretations of Maera that can be read

[19] For the *Liber de natura deorum*, see Allen 1970 and Salvo García 2012a: 248; 2012b; and 2018b: 254–55). Salvo García links this work to the tradition of Alfonso X's *General Estoria* and the *Ovide moralisé*.

[20] The translation for the excerpt of the *Liber de natura deorum* is based on Gura's translation for Arnulf.

in Arnulf – he only chooses the one he thinks that would be most interesting to moralise. Unlike Bersuire, the poet of the *Ovide moralisé* omitted this myth (like the myth of the Palici), because he was more interested in the main myths than their 'side stories'.

Ovid's *Heroides*

As we have already anticipated, the narration of Medea's flight is omitted from the seventh book of the *Ovide moralisé*. At this point of the Ovidian poem, the anonymous author inserted the translation of the *Heroides*' letter 12, the one that Medea wrote to Jason after he left her for Creusa. It has been repeatedly proved that the author of the *Ovide moralisé* knew of these letters and used them in his work (Barbieri 2011: 238 and Salvo García 2018b: 238–56). However, Bersuire's direct access to the *Heroides* is less clear. It is debated whether Bersuire knew the *Heroides* prior to the first version of the *Ovidius*. In fact, he added two stories related to the epistolary work only after reading the *Ovide moralisé*: the Danaides (or Belides), and Hero and Leander.[21]

In the *Ovide moralisé*, the story of the Danaïdes is told in Book II (4582–795, followed by the moralisation 4796–936).[22] The fifty daughters of Danaus were supposed to marry the fifty sons of Aegyptus (Danaus's brother) and on their wedding night all but one, Hypermnestra, killed their husbands. Due to the murders they were condemned to spend eternity carrying water in a sieve. The beginning of the episode, in which the author explains that the story is not included in the *Metamorphoses* and says that he will tell it at the end of Book II, goes like this:[23]

> Pour mieux acomplir ma matire,
> Vous vaudrai raconter et dire
> Un dit, qui n'est pas en c'est livre,
> Sans l'ordre de l'auctor ensivre.
> Ou premier livre, vers la fin,
> Vous dis d'Epaphus, qui Menphin
> Fonda, le mestre chief d'Egipte.
> Encor retrait l'estoire escripte
> Qu'Epaphus fu peres Beli. […]
> Cil ot huit filz de grant renom. […]
> Egistus ot cinquante filz, […]

---

[21] See Barbieri 2011, especially for the influence of the *Heroides* in the *Ovide moralisé*, and Salvo García 2018a and 2019 for its sources in general.

[22] Ovid names them Belides after their grandfather Belus, and we will read this denomination in the *Ovidius moralizatus*.

[23] We do not reproduce the whole text of the episode for reasons of space.

Danaüs ot filles autant.

(De Boer 1915: 268–69)

[In order to better accomplish my work I would like to tell you a story that is not included in this book, without the order of the author. In the first book, towards the end, Epaphus is mentioned, who founded Memphis, and he was the great leader of Egypt. It still remains written the tale that Epaphus was the father of Belus. [...] He had eight famous sons. [...] Egistus had fifty sons, [...] Danaus had the same number of daughters.]

In the first version of the *Ovidius moralizatus*, written in Avignon (*c.* 1340) before the author read the *Ovide moralisé* in Paris (*c.* 1350), the only reference to the Danaïdes appears at the end of the prologue. It is just a brief mention of the myth:

Alia est pena Belidum que aquam in dolio sine fundo perpetuo fundunt ipsumque implere credunt nec possunt. [...] Quarta poena significat uicium auaricie. Auari enim illis Bellidibus sunt similes quia scilicet dolium cordis sui implere et saciare aquis deliciarum credunt sed quia fundo siue sufficientia caret immo nichil faciunt immo semper ipsum uacuum et insaciabilem inueniunt nec aqua diuitiarum sufficit quam infundunt. (*Ovidius moralizatus* 1.15)[24]

[Another is the punishment of the daughters of Danaus who forever pour water into a jar with no bottom and strive to fill it without success. [...] The fourth punishment signifies the vice of greed. For greedy men are like the daughters of Danaus because they attempt to fill up the jar of their heart and to satiate it with the waters of delights. But because it lacks a bottom and cannot be filled, they accomplish nothing but find it always empty and unable to be filled. Nor does the water of the riches that they pour suffice.]

However, after reading the *Ovide moralisé*, Bersuire expanded the story of the daughters of Danaus referring to the vernacular poem in his Parisian version. He added to his story the name of Epaphus's sons, the fight between Aegyptus and Danaus and the story of Hypermestra and Linceus:

Hic fit mentio de Belidibus in capitulo praecedenti. Quid autem istae fuerint, inveni sic in illo libro ubi fabulae in rithmis gallicis continentur. Dicit enim quod Epaphus filius Iovis fuit ille qui fundavit Memphis civitatem Aegypti, cuius filii fuerunt Ninus, Pretus, Abbas, Agenor, Belus, Danaus, Egistus et Acrisius, qui omnes reges fuerunt. Verumtamen Egistus et Danaus regnum unicum habuerunt in quo, cum quilibet vellet esse maior, semper in bello et discordia vixerunt. Verum quia Egistus habuit L filios, Danaus autem totidem filias, filios Egisti cum filiabus Danay pro pacis foedere coniunxerunt. Sed pater proditor taliter cum filiabus ordinavit quod in nocte nuptiarum viros suos ebrios occiderunt; una dumtaxat excepta, scilicet Ypermestra, quae Linum sponsum suum occidere noluit, sed fugiendi spatium sibi dedit. Propter quod a patre incarcerata et tandem exulata fuit, et ita Danaus occisis nepotibus et fugato patre solus regnavit. Verumtamen Linus congregato exercitu Danaum cito post vita et regno privavit, et sic mortem fratrum et patris exilium vindicavit. Dii autem istas filias quae viros occiderunt, incessabiliter damnaverunt et ipsas in inferno miserunt, ubi in poenam aeternam implent dolium sine fundo. (Engels 1966: 51–52)

[The daughters of Danaus are mentioned in the preceding section. I discovered who they were in that book in French verse where the myths are contained. For it says that Epaphus, the son of Jove, founded Memphis, a city in Egypt. His sons were Ninus, Pretus, Abbas, Agenor, Belus, Danaus, Aegyptus and Acrisius, all of whom were kings. Aegyptus and Danaus had a single kingdom in which, since each one wanted to be greater, they lived in war and discord. But since Aegyptus had fifty sons and Danaus the same number of daughters, they joined the sons of Aegyptus with the daughters of Danaus as a pledge of peace. But the treacherous father arranged with his daughters to kill their husbands as they lay drunk on their wedding night. Only one daughter, namely Hypermnestra, did not take part and refused to kill her husband Lynceus, but granted him time to flee. For this she was imprisoned and exiled by her father. Thus Danaus, with his nephews dead and their father put to flight, ruled alone. Lynceus, however, afterwards assembled an army and killed Danaus, depriving him of his kingdom and thus avenging the death of his brothers and the exile of his father. The gods moreover damned forever those daughters who had killed their husbands and sent them to Hell, where as punishment they filled for eternity a jar with no bottom.]

Thus, Bersuire reveals where he has read the episode and he claims that he found who the Belides were 'in illo libro ubi fabulae in rithmis gallicis continentur', that is, the *Ovide moralisé*, although he knew some storylines of the myth beforehand. He mentions this poem as his *auctoritas* and he does not refer to Ovid's letters – surprisingly, given that in medieval thinking a classical *auctoritas* was always the best source for information.

The case is similar to that of Hero and Leander,[25] two lovers who lived on either side of the Hellespont. Every night Leander swam across the strait to spend time with Hero and she lighted a lamp at the top of her tower to guide his way. But one night a storm appeared, blowing out Hero's light and leaving Leander shaken by the waves. Eventually, Leander drowned and when Hero saw his dead body, she threw herself from the tower and died immediately.

---

[25] For Hero and Leander in the *Ovide moralisé*, see Lechat 2002, Barbieri 2011: 239–44. The aforementioned forthcoming publication of Kretschmer will show the influence of the *Ovide moralisé* on the Parisian version of the *Ovidius moralizatus*, focusing on Book IV.

There is a reference to this story in the Vatican Mythographers (II. 262 and III. 4), and probably Bersuire also knew it through these works, but he did not include a moralised version of the story in his *Ovidius moralizatus* until he read the *Ovide moralisé*, where it appears in verses IV. 3150–731. The story of Hero and Leander follows the one of Phrixus and Helle in the French poem: the first verses concerning the two young lovers are:

> Sur cele mer qu'Hellès se nome
> Ot en Abidos un riche home,
> Poissant home et de haute gent.
> Cil avoit un fil bel et gent,
> Bien apert et bien afetié:
> C'iert Leander, qui s'amistié
> Avoit a bele Hero donee,
> Une pucele en Sexte nee.
>
> (De Boer 1920: 78)

[At the sea, whose name is Helles, a rich man lived in Abidos, a powerful man and from a noble lineage. He had a beautiful and gentle son, well amenable and good: his name was Leander, who has given his friendship to the beautiful Hero, a lady born in Sexte.]

As noted above, the story of Hero and Leander is not included in the Avignon version of the *Ovidius moralizatus*; it can only be read in the Paris version, which signals that Bersuire took it from the vernacular poem, although he did not mention the *liber ubi fabulae in rithmis gallicis continentur* this time. This is the transcription of the beginning of the story:

> Hic inueni aliam fabulam de Leandro et Hero. Erat enim Leander iuuenis pulcherrimus qui ab una parte Hellesponto in uilla Aludos morabatur. Hero domicella pulcherrima in opposito maris manebat littore in uilla que Sexta tunc temporis dicebatur. [...] (*Ovidius moralizatus* V. 10)[26]

[Here I discovered another story about Leander and Hero. Leander was a very handsome young man who lived on one side of the Hellespont, in the city of Aludos. The very beautiful young lady Hero stayed on the opposite of the sea, in the city that at that time was called Sexta.]

Although the reference is less direct than in the story of the Danaides, the position of this story in Book IV is closely related to its inclusion in *Ovide moralisé*'s Book IV and the beginning is very similar to the one in the

---

[26] For this transcription I have used Paris, BnF lat. 5703, fol. 186ʳ and Madrid, Biblioteca Nacional 3922, fols 75ᵛ–76ʳ. For the order of this chapter in the Parisian version, I follow Kretschmer (forthcoming).

Danaides' story (Hic inveni... | Hic fit mentio...), so that *hic* could refer to the vernacular poem.[27]

The reason why Bersuire added these two episodes to his latest version of the treatise seems to be clear. After reading the vernacular poem, he considered that they were usefull for his purpose (that is, to use some classical myths for moralisation and preaching). He cites the *Ovide moralisé* as the source and not Ovid's letters – perhaps because he had recently read the vernacular composition which served as the inspiration for the inclusion of the episodes.

Conclusion

The intentions of the authors of the *Ovide moralisé* and the *Ovidius moralizatus* are different, and they use the text of the *Metamorphoses* and its commentaries in very different ways. Possamaï-Pérez (2006: 803–31) explains how each of the books of the *Ovide moralisé* develops its own topic, and the author chooses the myths and their moral interpretations in accordance with this particular topic. Bersuire's intention seems to be to moralise the myths individually, without seeking a connection between them.[28] This may be the reason for the selection of the myths from the commentaries. It may explain why Bersuire focuses more on the myths only alluded to by Ovid and narrated in the earlier medieval commentaries, and also why the same myths are left out in the *Ovide moralisé*: that is to say, because they are irrelevant to the main moral topic of the book.

In addition, we have the myths from the *Heroides*. Did Bersuire know these letters? In the prologue, he stated that he included some stories that were not present in the *Metamorphoses*. Therefore, we can conclude that if there were any tales that interested him, he would have included them in his first version of the treatise.[29] However, it was not until he was able to read the *Ovide moralisé* that he included the stories of the Danaides and Hero and Leander. Perhaps the reason for this was that he found them interesting

---

[27] As Kretschmer (forthcoming) points out, explaining the Parisian version of the *Ovidius moralizatus*, 'après le prologue [...], Bersuire ne mentionne l'*Ovide moralisé* que deux fois: au début de la partie exégétique du deuxième chapitre ("iuxta expositionem quam inueni in rithmis Gallicis") et au début du sixième chapitre ("hic in libro Gallice lingue fit mentio de scuto Persei Christi")'.

[28] For example, the moral topic of Book V would be penitence, and all the episodes that the author included there are related to it (Possamaï-Pérez 2006: 822-24).

[29] *Vid. supra*: Aliquas tamen in aliquibus super hoc adiungam fabulas quas in aliis locis repperi, aliquas eciam detraham et omittam quas non necessarias iudicavi (*Ovidius moralizatus* 1.1). [In addition, I shall add some stories I have found in other places, while some stories I shall pass over and omit, since I have judged them to be unnecessary.]

only after reading their interpretation in the *Ovide moralisé*. It also seems reasonable to think that Bersuire's primary source for these myths was the vernacular French poem itself, since he mentions the *auctoritas* of the French work, and not that of Ovid, when he speaks of these tales, and in his Parisian version he uses the *Ovide moralisé* to extend his treatise.

IV

OVID IN ITALIAN

10

GIUSEPPE CAPRIOTTI

THE *TRASFORMATIONI* BY LODOVICO DOLCE AND GIOVANNI ANTONIO RUSCONI: THE PLACEMENT OF THE IMAGES AND THEIR RELATION TO THE TEXT

The aim of this paper is to analyse the criteria that guided the placement of the images in Lodovico Dolce's *Trasformationi*, a vernacular translation of Ovid's *Metamorphoses* first published by Gabriel Giolito de' Ferrari in 1553 and illustrated with xylographs by Giovanni Antonio Rusconi. In particular, I will analyse the positioning of three images that were repeated two or three times in the first edition of the book, to show how the publisher, probably with the help of the translator, arranged the images in relation to the adjacent text. To better understand why these xylographs were used repeatedly in the first edition, a short summary of the history of this editorial project will be required.

The first edition of the *Trasformationi* was printed in 1553, with a run of over 1800 copies that sold out in just four months. This success led its Venetian publisher, Giolito, to publish a second edition in the same year and to reprint the volume four more times in the following years (1555; 1557; 1558; 1561).[1] All six issues were edited by Dolce and illustrated with xylographs by the Venetian architect Rusconi.[2] Dolce and Rusconi worked simultaneously, but often from different points of view. Dolce translated the poem from Ovid's original Latin, although he also used some earlier vernacular editions.[3] Indeed, before his translation, two other important vernacular editions of Ovid's *Metamorphoses* had been published in Venice.

The first edition was the *Ovidio metamorphoseos vulgare* by Giovanni Bonsignori, published in 1497 by the typographer Giovanni Rosso from Vercelli and the Florentine publisher Lucantonio Giunta, who both worked

[1]   The number of copies sold was recorded by Gabriel Giolito in the letter *Ai nobili e sinceri lettori*, which follows the text of the second edition of 1553. See Dolce 1553b, unnumbered page in the final paratext. On the history of the book see Guthmüller 1997: 237–50; Capriotti 2013: 25–28. On the history of this edition see Bongi 2006: 395–401.

[2]   Giovanni Antonio Rusconi was identified as the creator of the images of the *Trasformationi* by Guthmüller 1997: 237-250. For an updated biography of Rusconi see Marchegiani 2017.

[3]   On Dolce's translation of Ovid's *Metamorphoses* see: Trebaiocchi 2016: 271-316; Bucchi 2011: 83-123.

in Venice (Guthmüller 2008: 62–114; 185–203). As we know, Bonsignori's text composed between 1375 and 1377 is not an accurate translation of Ovid's poem, because the author preferred to follow the texts of the explanations of the *Metamorphoses* given by Giovanni del Virgilio in a series of lectures in Bologna between 1322 and 1323 (Ardissino 1993 and Bonsignori 2001: 4–5). The text by Giovanni del Virgilio had a clear didactic aim and, in fact, it is divided in two parts – a paraphrase and a comment (*Expositio* and *Allegorie*) – in which an interpretation of a historical, natural and moral-philosophical approach prevails.[4] In order to make the Latin poem clear for his students, in his explanatory paraphrase Giovanni del Virgilio illustrates all Ovid's myths in detail, even those mentioned only briefly by the poet. The paraphrase of the university professor is thus much richer in myths than the Latin original. After attempting to translate the first book from Ovid's Latin version directly, from the second book onwards Bonsignori chooses to turn to the texts written by Giovanni del Virgilio, which he evidently finds easier and clearer (Guthmüller 2008: 62–86). This choice is also useful for his goal, that is, a translation that is more easily comprehensible for his readership; he no longer follows the original text and writes the paraphrase as well as the allegorical commentary of each episode one after the other, explaining all the mythological allusions in Ovid's text. In this way his translation, which centres exclusively on the content of the poem, is enriched with details that are not included in the Latin version of the *Metamorphoses*, thus becoming a proper manual of mythology in the vernacular, addressed to a public that would not have been able to fully understand the original poem (Guthmüller 2008: 62–86). As previously stated, in 1497, this text was chosen by the printers Rosso and Giunta for a luxury edition, decorated with an important set of xylographs conceived by a designer and several engraving artists.[5] Numerous details in the images show that these artists did

---

[4]   On the text by Giovanni del Virgilio see Marchesi 1909 (who even proposed to attribute the two parts to two different authors, based on the differences in time and manner of compilation); Ghisalberti 1933a; Huber-Rebenich 1997; Huber-Rebenich 1998; Huber-Rebenich 2009. Gerlinde Huber-Rebenich and Beatrice Wyss are preparing a critical edition of Giovanni del Virgilio's *Expositio*. As regards his allegorical comment, Giovanni del Virgilio refers to the exegesis by Alfonso d'Orléans, a university professor who had held courses on Ovid in the twelfth century, and to the *Integumenta Ovidii* by John of Garland, an allegorical commentary on the *Metamorphoses* dating back to the thirteenth century. See Ghisalberti 1932 and 1933b.

[5]   According to Giulio Pesavento (2018: 108), the scene drawings relating to the 52 woodcuts of the volume were conceived by the Paduan miniaturist Benedetto Bordon, probably assisted by the Second Master of the Canzoniere Grifo, while the wood carving was created by three different masters: Jacopo da Strasburgo, who signed 17 prints with the initials *ia* (Iacobus Argentoratensis); Master N, who signed five woodcuts with this

not use Ovid's original text to carry out their works but the vernacular version by Bonsignori, which they probably found easier to read (Hubert-Rebenich 1992).

The second vernacular version of Ovid's work was written by Niccolò degli Agostini and was published by Niccolò Zoppino in Venice in 1522 (and then in 1533, 1537, 1538, 1547, 1548) with the title *Tutti gli libri de Ovidio Metamorphoseos tradutti dal litteral in verso vulgar con le sue allegorie in prosa*. Even though the author stated that he translated from the Latin original, the text is actually a version of Bonsignori's translation written in ottava rima, based on the model of chivalric romances (Guthmüller 2008: 204–52). Starting from the very first edition, the volume was illustrated with a new series of woodcut prints (Huber-Rebenich, Lütkemeyer, Walter 2014: 73–81).

Unlike these two previous authors, Dolce translated the *Metamorphoses* starting from Ovid's Latin poem, even though sometimes he also followed the translation by Niccolò degli Agostini which he used to write some additions and to clarify some of the myths.[6] Apart from the Ovidian tradition, the other model that Dolce uses in his translation is Ludovico Ariosto's *Orlando furioso*. As a man of letters who had worked for many years in the printing house of Giolito (as a translator, as well as editor and author of various texts), Dolce, as an editor, had the opportunity to follow the publication of the *Orlando furioso* in 1542.[7] Not only did he use the ottava rima like Ariosto, he also transformed the 15 books of Ovid's *Metamorphoses* in the 30 cantos of his *Trasformationi*, reframing the structure of the poem completely to follow the model of the 46 cantos of the *Orlando furioso*. Always looking at Ariosto's example, in his *Trasformationi* Dolce sometimes splits the tale of an individual myth at the end and at the beginning of two different cantos and often introduces a short proem at the beginning of the canto.[8]

Even though the first privilege that Giolito requested from the Venetian Senate for the Ovidian translation dates back to 1548 (followed by the ones in 1550 and 1553), due to his numerous assignments in the publishing

---

letter; and finally an anonymous Florentine master, who can only be identified thanks to his particular style.

[6] See for example the case of the myth of Medea that I have studied in Capriotti 2013b.

[7] On the importance of Dolce in the Venetian book production and market see Trovato 1997: 209–40. On the relationship between Dolce and Giolito see Nuovo and Coppens 2015: 101–104. On the 1542 *Orlando furioso* see Nuovo and Coppens 2015: 222–225.

[8] On the importance of the *Orlando furioso* as a model for the *Trasformationi* see the entry by Andrea Torre in Bolzoni and Girotto (eds.) 2013: 52–54 and, more generally, Torre 2017: 283–309; Javitch 1981; Bucchi 2011: 88–99 and Bolzoni (eds.) 2017.

house Dolce was unable to start translating it before 1552.[9] Moreover, he carried out his task with great haste, to beat the initiative of a rival publisher who had announced the publication of the vulgarization by Giovanni Andrea dell'Anguillara, which finally came out in 1561 (Bucchi 2011). Because of this urgency, the publisher was probably forced to assign the task of conceiving the xylographs to Rusconi before Dolce's translation was ready. Therefore, the engraver was unable to work from Dolce's text and, finding the original Latin text too complicated, he used the two vernacular translations that were available in the Venetian book market: namely, the prose text by Bonsignori and the verse translation by Agostini. To sum up, Dolce translated starting from the Latin poem, while Rusconi conceived his xylographs by reading two authors who had supplemented their texts with a large number of myths that Ovid had mentioned only briefly, and embellished them with details which are missing from his original tales. This misalignment between Dolce and Rusconi not only generated the numerous discrepancies between the text and images in the book, but also (as we will see) led to the production of prints which had nothing to do with Dolce's words.[10] These discrepancies caused problems for the creator of the volume's layout. Since there were too few Ovidian prints, he was forced to reuse the same image several times or to insert biblical prints (starting from the second edition of the volume, the number of these prints was reduced to one).[11] By the second edition of 1553, the publisher made up for this by introducing four new Ovidian prints and changing the placement of several of the images (Capriotti 2017: 309–24). The final adjustments to the arrangement of the prints continued up to the very last edition of 1561.

By analysing the changes between the first and the second edition, it is possible to identify the key role of the prints (Calegari 2014: 584). Sometimes they act as an enjambment between one octave and the next, and sometimes they anticipate the narrative, introducing a myth; sometimes they replace the story of a myth, filling in for its absence. Through the analysis of significant shifts and relations to the octaves preceding and following the images, we can almost enter the workshop of the sixteenth-century Venetian printer, identifying the layout strategies Giolito

---

[9]   On the privileges see Bongi 2006: 395; Nuovo and Coppens 2005: 238–239.

[10] Guthmüller (1997: 237–250) was the first scholar to understand the numerous discrepancies between Dolce's text and Rusconi's images. For further studies of Rusconi's illustrations see Capriotti 2013 and Huber-Rebenich, Lütkemeyer and Walter 2014: 81-88.

[11] Capriotti 2013: 40–41. The Biblical insertions and repetitions were probably due to the lack of Ovidian illustrations. The artist had in fact provided several blocks for the first 23 *canti*, but he had then worked sparingly. From the *canto* XXIV onwards, the publisher could only use a single woodcut, placed at the beginning of the *canto*.

implemented to continually improve the editorial product. I am going to analyse the positioning of three of the images that were repeated two or three times in the first edition before being moved in the second and subsequent editions. These images are of Rhodope and Haemus, Priapus and Lotis, and Orpheus.

In the original Latin text, Ovid briefly mentioned the myth of Rhodope and Haemus three times: in the second book, describing the itinerary of Phaethon on his father Apollo's chariot, he simply quoted Mount Rhodope, which is located in Thrace and is never covered with snow (*Metamorphoses*, II. 222); in the sixth book, in the tapestry woven for her challenge against Arachne, Athena depicts Rhodope and Haemus as arrogant monarchs who dared to usurp the names of the gods, for which they were transformed into icy mountains (*Metamorphoses*, VI. 87, 589); in the tenth book Rhodope is mentioned a few times as a mountain in Thrace, in the backdrop to Orpheus's story (*Metamorphoses*, X. 11, 50, 77). Although Ovid and Dolce only ever alluded to the stories of Rhodope and Haemus, Rusconi decided to illustrate this myth because he was working from Bonsignori's vernacular translation, where the story was recounted in detail. In the sixth book Bonsignori explains that the king of Thrace, Haemus, after his marriage to Rhodope, obliged his people to venerate him as Jupiter and his wife as Juno; for this reason, Jupiter punished them on his chariot, transforming the couple into mountains (Bonsignori 1497: xliiii^r). This tale explains why Rusconi produced an image that bore no relation either to Ovid's classical version or to Dolce's translation: he represented the ongoing transformation of the king and queen into mountains, while a god on a chariot passes by in the sky (Figure 10.1). This anomaly was brilliantly explained by Bodo Guthmüller (1997: 269) from close inspection of Bonsignori's text. Bonsignori wrote that in her tapestry Athena depicts 'la victoria che hebe Iove nel carro de Rodope e Hemo' [Jupiter's victory in the chariot over Rhodope] (Bonsignori 1497: xliiii^v). The chariot, not normally associated with Jupiter, was drawn by Rusconi because he was following Bonsignori, who based his text on Giovanni del Virgilio's. Giovanni del Virgilio had in fact said, 'In primo angulo depinxit de victoria Iovis in eur(um) et rodopem';[12] Bonsignori interpreted 'in eur(um)' (a miswriting of 'in emum') as 'in currum' thus translating it as 'Jupiter in the chariot', which explains Rusconi's odd iconography. Although it is an illustration of a myth that Dolce hardly mentioned, the image was used three times.

---

[12] I quote Giovanni del Virgilio from Guthmüller 1997: 269. On the problem of this translation see also Bonsignori 2001: 295 and 329 (notes 15 and 16).

Figure 10.1. Giovanni Antonio Rusconi, *Rhodope and Haemus*, from *Le Trasformationi by Lodovico Dolce* (Venice: Gabriel Giolito de' Ferrari, 1553²), private collection.

The image is first seen at the start of Canto V, in the middle of the story of Apollo and Coronis: Canto IV ends with Apollo discovering Coronis's infidelity, Canto V begins with Apollo taking his revenge. According to the Ovidian myth (*Metamorphoses*, II. 531–632), Apollo was in love with Coronis and, since he had to leave on a journey, he asked the crow to watch over the girl. Coronis was unfaithful to him and when the crow informed Apollo of her infidelity, in anger the god killed her, even though she was pregnant with his child. In this context the image typologically represents the theme of revenge, which Dolce made explicit in the first octave of the canto:

> Ah quanto a grave error conduce l'ira
> L'huomo; se la ragion non è possente
> A spegner quel calor, che move e tira
> A vendetta crudel l'accesa mente (1553¹: 49)

[Anger leads man to commit grave errors, if reason is not able to extinguish the heat that drives the inflamed mind to cruel revenge.]¹³

Between text and image, the layout offers a comparison: just as Jupiter punishes Rhodope and Haemus in revenge, so Apollo avenges Coronis's infidelity. In the second edition of the *Metamorphosis* this print was substituted by a new, more appropriate one: Apollo and Coronis.

The print with Rhodope and Haemus is next used at the start of Canto XII, during Ceres' search for Proserpine. According to the tale in the

---

¹³ The translations from Dolce's texts are mine.

Metamorphoses (V. 341–437), Pluto kidnapped Proserpine in Sicily, carrying her off as his wife into Hades; Ceres, Proserpine's mother, was driven mad by her daughter's disappearance and took revenge on the Sicilian lands as she started to search for her. In the *Trasformationi*, the tale of this myth is split between the end and the beginning of two cantos. At the end of Canto XI, Ceres destroys all the island's crops. Dolce (1553[1]: 117) says that Ceres acts 'per vendetta di sue pene' [in vengeance for her suffering]. In the first octave of the following *canto*, immediately after the print, Dolce again reflects on the retribution of the powerful against those who offend them:

> O, quante volte e bene può far fede
> In ogni parte sua tutta la terra
> Una particolare offesa diede
> Alta cagion di porre il mondo in guerra:
> che, mentre volge a la vendetta il piede
> L'empio, che regge, ogni pietade atterra:
> Onde, per conseguire il suo disegno,
> Ogni ufficio crudel reputa degno. (1553[1]: 118)

[Many times, as has happened in many parts of the earth, a particular offence was the cause of a war, which leads the impious to revenge, banishes all pity and deems every cruel action worthy in order to achieve his design.]

The image, therefore, should be read in typological terms as both introduction and commentary on the episode of revenge told in the text, in which Ceres rides a chariot, just like Jupiter in Rusconi's image. From the second edition of the volume onwards, this print was replaced with a new image depicting Ceres and Arethusa.

In the final case the image is in the right place, following the octave in which Dolce briefly recounts the metamorphosis of the Thracian king and queen into mountains, depicted in a tapestry by Arachne (Dolce 1553[1]: 127). Here, accidentally, the detailed print makes up for the absence of narrative details in Dolce's text. The print continued to appear in this position in the second edition of the book.

In this case the discrepancy between text and illustration clearly testifies to the importance of earlier translations in making the *Trasformationi* a highly unusual book composed by many heterogeneous elements. Nevertheless, these discrepancies can also be interpreted positively: that is, as an implementation of the number of mythological tales to which the reader and viewer had access. For the moment we lack any documentation regarding the functionality and use of the book. However, it is possible that word and image might also have been enjoyed separately and that the iconographic programme of the book would envisage two independent readings from the beginning: one based on the text, and another on the flow of the images.

The myth of Priapus and Lotis is told in just two verses in the ninth book of Ovid's original text (*Metamorphoses*, IX. 347–48) as part of the narration of the myth of the nymph Dryope. This is the same in Dolce's text, who clearly states that he did not want to develop this myth further:

> E fu conversa in arbore, fuggendo
> Del lascivo Priapo, ond'era vinta,
> L'osceno assalto: in cui non mi distendo,
> Per esser d'altro a ragionar accinta. (1553[1]: 199)

[While fleeing, Lotis was transformed into a tree, to avoid being raped by the lascivious Priapus in an obscene assault, on which I will not dwell because my mind is intent on discussing other things.]

However, in Bonsignori's translation, which follows Giovanni del Virgilio's text, the myth of Priapus and Lotis is told in detail (Bonsignori 1497: lxxviii[v]–lxxviiii[r]): Lotis went outside the city walls to perform a sacrifice for Bacchus; Priapus, who had been expelled from the city by the women because his penis was as big as a donkey's, fell in love with Lotis, who rejected him; while she was asleep, Priapus tried to take advantage of the situation to rape her, but a donkey started to bray, waking up Lotis, who immediately started to run away; during her escape, thanks to divine intervention, she was transformed in a lotus tree.

Rusconi, working from the text and iconography of Bonsignori's 1497 edition, illustrated the episode with many extra details that are not included in Dolce's text (Figure 10.2).[14] On the left, Priapus is lifting Lotis's skirt while she sleeps. Meanwhile, a farmer's donkey in the centre of the image is braying so loudly that it wakes Lotis up, who tries to escape and is eventually turned into a tree. This illustration is only explained through Bonsignori's text, which included these details of the myth that Ovid had omitted. Despite its difference from Dolce's text, Rusconi's image was used twice in the first edition of the volume. In the first case, the print is in the Canto XIX, placed in the middle of the story of Dryope. According to the *Metamorphoses* (IX. 329–93), Dryope went to gather garlands of flowers for the nymphs of a lake where there was a lotus tree; when she picked a flower from this tree, which immediately started to bleed, she was unwittingly committing sacrilege, because the lotus tree was the transformed body of Lotis; for this reason Dryope too became a tree. Lotis' story occupies only two verses in the *Trasformationi*, but in the following octave Dolce describes Dryope's metamorphosis with words that could also apply to Lotis's transformation, illustrated by Rusconi:

---

[14] On the fortune and misfortune of this xylograph see: Capriotti (2021).

Ma volendo partirsi, è ritenuta

Da tenaci radici, e a forza resta.
Si scuote in vano, in vano ella s'aiuta
In van si duole, in van move la testa:
Ch'a poco a poco in arbore si muta;
Cresce la scorza, e le fa dura vesta.
Volle stracciar le belle chiome bionde;
Et ambedue le man s'empie di fronde.

(Dolce 1553[1]: 199)

[Although she wants to move away, Dryope is held back by tenacious roots. She shakes in vain, complains in vain and moves her head in vain. She slowly turns into a tree; the bark grows and becomes her dress; she would like to tear up her beautiful blond hair, but her hands fill with fronds.]

Figure 10.2. Giovanni Antonio Rusconi, Priapus and Lotis, from *Le Trasformationi* by Lodovico Dolce (Venice: Gabriel Giolito de' Ferrari, 15532), private collection.

The image thus shows Lotis's metamorphosis, but also evokes that of Dryope in the reader's mind, because of its proximity to the octave by Dolce. Something very similar happens in the second use of the image, in Canto XXI. The print is positioned before the account of Myrrha's escape from her father, who wants to kill her after discovering her incest and subsequent metamorphosis into a Myrrh tree. Once again, the description of Myrrha's metamorphosis is extraordinarily similar to that of Lotis represented in the image:

Fece, che i pie da una radice dura
Con subito rigor le furo intorti.
Il corpo in legno tronco si trasforma;
Preser le braccia di gran rami forma.

E così di minor preser le mani:
Si fe la pelle scorza, e l'ossa legno.
Il sangue succo, e di quei membri humani
Più non apparve, e non si vide segno.
L'arbore havea con suoi legami strani
Cinto il ventre di Mirrha, ch'era pregno,
E 'l petto, e cignea il collo: ond'ella presta
Nel legno, che crescea, chiuse la testa (1553[1]: 219)

[Myrrha's feet quickly turned into hard roots. Her body turns into a trunk, her arms into large branches and her hands into small branches. The skin becomes bark and the bones become wood. Blood becomes lymph and there is no trace left of the human body. The tree had encircled the chest, the neck and the womb of Myrrha who was pregnant. The growing wood finally covered her head.]

Even though between text and image the description is similar, in the new context of Myrrha's story the meaning is inverted: it is no longer an erotic chase, as in the case of Priapus's sexual advances on Lotis, but rather a murderous one, whose aim is the killing of a daughter by her father. In both cases, Lotis's metamorphosis anticipates the transformations of Myrrha and Dryope. From the second edition on, the image was removed from this position, probably because two images in Canto XXI were considered sufficient.

The myth of Orpheus and the heroes celebrated by his poetry take up most of the tenth book and the start of the eleventh in Ovid's original text. On the very day of his wedding with Eurydice, Orpheus lost his wife, killed by a snake bite. By means of his music he persuaded Pluto to allow him to bring his wife back from Hades, as long as he did not turn around to look at her face during the ascent toward the surface of the earth; because he did not respect the prohibition, he lost his wife forever. After this failure, Orpheus refused to have sex with women and started to sing his love for young boys, founding pederasty in Thrace. Dolce, who followed Ovid, begins Orpheus's story halfway through the Canto XX. The print with Orpheus singing in the forest (Figure 10.3), as the animals flock together to listen to him, is repeated three times. In the first case, the image is at the beginning of the Canto XX and breaks up the story of Byblis's incestuous love for her brother Caunus. According to the Ovidian myth (*Metamorphoses*, IX. 450–665), Byblis fell in love with her brother Caunus, who decided to escape, when his sister, revealing her love, tried to convince him; looking

Figure 10.3. Giovanni Antonio Rusconi, *Orpheus,* from *Le Trasformationi by Lodovico Dolce* (Venice: Gabriel Giolito de' Ferrari, 1553[2]), private collection.

for him continuously, Byblis wept until she became exhausted and was transformed into a spring. The print with Orpheus at this point creates a mirror between Byblis's despair for her unrequited love before metamorphosising into a spring, and the sad song of Orpheus who sings only of love for young boys following Eurydice's death. In his translation, of course, Dolce also expresses his opinion on Byblis's love:

> Scelerati desii ne' petti accende
> Questo crudel, che 'l mondo chiama Amore;
> Se avvien, che mente temeraria ascende
> Là, dove calca il debito e l'honore:
> M'assai più voi, Donne mie care offende,
> Poi ch'avete di noi forza minore. (1553[1]: 203)

[The cruel god of love kindles wicked loves in breasts, even in the reckless mind in which honour reigns. But most of all he offends women, who have less strength than men.]

Later in the same canto Dolce also voices his opinion on the love songs of Orpheus, declaring:

> Ch'introdusse in Thracia (e n'ebbe aspra ventura)
> L'iniqua usanza, scelerata e vile,
> D'amar contra le leggi di Natura
> I giovinetti ad uso femminile. (1553[1]: 209)

[Orpheus introduced in Thrace (and reaped the bitter consequences) the unfair, chosen and vile custom of loving young boys against nature, as if they were women.]

In Dolce's comments, Byblis's love is generated by a wicked desire that often burns in the hearts of women; in the same way the form of love that Orpheus sings about is wicked, unfair and vile, since it goes against nature. In the second edition the print maintains the same position, perhaps because Orpheus's wicked love is considered analogous to Byblis's. In this case the image serves as an enjambment between the two parts of Byblis's story. The same image with Orpheus singing is repeated in the middle of the canto, when Dolce describes the poet's descent to the underworld and his plea to Pluto. The association with the text in this case is extremely weak. In the second edition this image was replaced with a more appropriate one that depicts Orpheus and Eurydice carrying torches to Hymenaeus, Eurydice being bitten by a snake, and Orpheus at Hades' door (Figure 10.4). This latter image can actually be found in the first edition placed at the beginning of Canto XXVIII, after the ending of the story of Picus and Canens in Canto XXVII. According to Ovid's myth (*Metamorphoses*, XIV. 320–434), Picus was transformed into a woodpecker by Circe for rejecting her love, because he had married Canens, the only woman he loved. In Dolce's tale (very close to Ovid's story), Canens, after the transformation of Picus, desperately looks for her beloved at night, together with other people carrying torches:

> Per questo in compagnia de la citade;
> Che con accesi lumi corse ogn'uno;
> Cercando 'l già per l'intricate strade
> L'addolorata sposa a l'aer bruno. (1553[1]: 281)

[For this reason, in the company of the inhabitants of the city who flocked with bright lights, the sorrowful bride went looking for her beloved on the narrow winding streets.]

The torches carried by Orpheus and Eurydice on their way to honour Hymenaeus are here reinterpreted as the torches used to look for Picus. There is a further similarity: the burning city that is Orpheus's underworld becomes the same underworld from which Circe summons the infernal gods to turn Picus into a woodpecker. In both cases the placement offers an interpretation in typological terms: like Canens desperately trying to find Picus, Orpheus tries in vain to bring his lost Eurydice back to this world. The image with the sad story of Orpheus and Eurydice was used again in this position, in relation to Picus and Canens, in all the following editions of the *Trasformationi*.

Figure 10.4. Giovanni Antonio Rusconi, *Orpheus and Eurydice,* from *Le Trasformationi by Lodovico Dolce* (Venice: Gabriel Giolito de' Ferrari, 1553²), private collection.

The print with Orpheus singing was used the last time in the middle of Canto XX, after the octave in which Dolce described the death of Cyparissus's deer and when Orpheus starts singing about love for young boys (Dolce 1553¹: 210). In this case the image perfectly mirrors the text.

In conclusion, it is possible to see how the repetition of images or the bizarre positioning of some of the prints follows a sort of logic, based on a thematic correspondence between the octaves and the image selected. In this way the creator of the layout (probably the publisher with the help of the translator) tried to solve the problem of the lack of appropriate images. As we have seen in the examples analysed, the typological reading supports each choice: the myth of Rhodope and Haemus was used twice to express the theme of revenge; the myth of Priapus and Lotis was used twice to represent the similar metamorphoses, into trees, of Dryope and Myrrha; Orpheus was used to refer to the wickedness of love; at the same time the torches in the print with the wedding of Eurydice and Orpheus were employed to visualize the torches used in the search for Picus described in Dolce's octaves. These are not mistakes, but ingenious attempts to solve a problem. Thus, rather than talking about positioning errors, we should analyse each single use of the image case-by-case in order to understand the sometimes unusual choices made by the publisher, who probably created the layout of the volume under the watchful eye of the translator.

11

MARTA BALZI

GIOVANNI ANDREA DELL'ANGUILLARA'S *METAMORFOSI*: THE AUTHORISING FORCE OF THE TRANSLATOR-PORTRAIT[1]

Perseus and his Winged Horse

The painting *Andromeda* by Rutilio Manetti (*c.* 1612) illustrates an Ovidian myth that was particularly dear to sixteenth- and seventeenth-century artists (Figure 11.1). Andromeda was the princess of Ethiopia, and her attractiveness was such that her mother, Cassiopea, claimed that her daughter was more beautiful than the Nereids, the nymph-daughters of the sea god Nereus. Cassiopea's arrogant statement aroused the wrath of the gods, who sent the sea monster Cetus to ravage Ethiopia. On the advice of an Oracle, Andromeda was then offered in sacrifice to the monster in order to appease the gods, but just before the slaughter, Perseus happened upon Andromeda, naked and chained to a rock. Inflamed by her beauty, Perseus engaged in a battle with Cetus and rescued her from the monster's assault. In his painting, Manetti chose to represent the scene in which the myth reached its climax, picturing the moment at which Cetus approached Andromeda and Perseus descended from the sky to save her. The artist set Andromeda in the foreground, depicting her with both her wrists chained to the rock while she gazes in terror at the sea. Her posture makes her nudity strikingly visible to the beholder, highlighting the erotic connotations of the myth.

Andromeda conveys the rich eroticism and wittiness of Ovid's narration, but a closer look at this painting reveals that the Latin *Metamorphoses* was not Manetti's primary source of inspiration. Ovid had Perseus fly in winged sandals, and not on a winged horse:

[1] This article was originally part of my PhD dissertation (Balzi 2020). I would like to thank the South West and Wales Doctoral Training Partnership for offering financial support during my doctoral research. My warmest thanks must also go to my supervisor, Rhiannon Daniels, for the guidance and support she has provided throughout my doctoral studies, and to my viva examiners Guyda Armstrong and Carol O'Sullivan for offering advice on how to improve my thesis.

Figure 11.1. Rutilio Manetti, *Andromeda*, c. 1612, oil on canvas, 177 × 20, Galleria Borghese, Rome. Su concessione della Galleria Borghese / courtesy of Borghese Gallery, Rome.

pennis ligat ille resumptis
parte ab utraque pedes teloque accingitur unco
et liquidum motis talaribus aera findit.

(Ovid, *Metamorphoses*, IV. 665–67)[2]

[Then Perseus bound on both his feet the wings he had laid by, girt on his hooked sword, and soon in swift flight was cleaving the thin air]

The association of Perseus and Pegasus, the mythological winged horse, was not new, but it gained currency in the late medieval treatment of Andromeda's rescue, and it continued to be popular in early modern visual art and literature (Javitch 1978). By the time Manetti composed his painting, the popularity of this version was also intensified thanks to the work of Giovanni Andrea dell'Anguillara (1519–1569), the author of the sixteenth-century best-selling translation of Ovid's *Metamorphoses*.[3] This translation offered the same combination of Perseus and Pegasus:

Quando su'l pegaseo veloce ascese
Perseo, e per l'Etiopia il volo prese.

(Anguillara 1563, IV. 411. 7–8)[4]

[Perseus mounted the fast Pegasus, and took off towards Ethiopia.]

This excursus of Ovid's Perseus and Andromeda through the lens of Anguillara gives us a valuable starting point for our study. Anguillara's *Metamorfosi*, as shown in this example, is not a literal rendition of Ovid's source text. Anguillara's combination of Perseus and Pegasus, for instance, is the result of the mingling of the Ovidian myth with the tale of Ruggero and Angelica, narrated in one of the most popular sixteenth-century chivalric poems, the *Orlando furioso*, by Ludovico Ariosto (*OF*, X. 92–115) (Javitch 1991: 79). Anguillara radically transformed Ovid's *Metamorphoses* by supplementing the source text with mythological accounts that were taken from ancient and modern literary works, and that, as in the case of Manetti's *Andromeda*, were later disseminated through the visual arts.

Scholars have unpicked the breadth of secondary sources employed by Anguillara and have argued that his creative re-writing of Ovid was the primary feature that allowed this translation to become a reference point for

---

[2]   Throughout this article, quotations from the Latin text and the translation are taken from the Loeb edition, see Ovid [1916] 1977.

[3]   According to Claudio Mutini (1961), Anguillara was born in 1517 ('Giovanni Andrea dell'Anguillara', *DBI*, 1961, www.treccani.it/enciclopedia/giovanni-andrea-dell-anguillara_(Dizionario-Biografico)/ [accessed 16 February 2017]). Bucchi (2011: 321–34), however, referring to a notary document found in Sutri, claimed that the correct date would be 1519.

[4]   The text is taken from a digitised copy of Anguillara 1563 held at the British Library in London (shelfmark: Digital Store 833.g.37).

readers, writers and painters who sought access to the Ovidian myths. Maria
Moog-Grünewald (1979: 105–12), for example, has shed light on the
intertextual relations between Anguillara's translation and contemporary
vernacular literary works, such as Castiglione's *Il libro del cortegiano (Book of
the Courtier)* and Ariosto's *Orlando furioso*, showing how the translator
transformed the Latin poem into a text full of references that could meet the
expectations of an elitist public of Renaissance courtiers. Daniel Javitch
(1991: 71–80), in his land-mark study on the canonization of Ariosto's
chivalric poem, has investigated the role played by this translation in the
affiliation between Ovid's *Metamorphoses* and Ariosto's poem, pointing to
the textual analogies between these works. Finally, Gabriele Bucchi's
monograph on Anguillara's *Metamorfosi* enriched previous observations on
this matter by underscoring Anguillara's re-employment of themes and
episodes extrapolated from Latin epic poems (particularly Virgil's *Aeneid*
and Statius's *Thebaid*), from the genre of the *novella* and especially from
Ariosto's *Orlando furioso*, which constituted Anguillara's primary source of
inspiration (Bucchi 2011: 159–96; Moog-Grünewald 1979: 73–100).

The following article argues that the success of this translation in the
sixteenth century was also prompted by the paratext that accompanied
sixteenth-century printed editions of Anguillara's *Metamorfosi*.[5] The
publishing history of the *Metamorfosi* by Anguillara began with the
publication of a series of incomplete editions containing the first books of
Ovid's poem.[6] The *Metamorfosi* was printed for the first time in 1553 by
Giovanni Griffio in Venice, in an edition that included only the translation
of the first book of Ovid's *Metamorphoses*.[7] The *editio princeps* of
Anguillara's full text of the *Metamorfosi*, consisting of fifteen books, was
then printed in 1561 by Giovanni Griffio in Venice. A few years later, in
1563, Griffio printed another edition, but this time 'ad istanza di M.
Francesco Senese', to whom Anguillara had sold his printing privilege.[8]

---

[5] The studies dealing with the editorial history of Anguillara's *Metamorfosi* are Argelati
1767: III. 119–69; Cotugno 2007: 461–541; Bucchi 2011: 335–45; Balzi 2020: 146–
47.

[6] For a history of the first editions see Bucchi 2011: 128–29.

[7] This first book was then reprinted again, probably in Perugia, by Giacomo Cartolari. In
1554, André Wechel printed a new edition of Anguillara's *Metamorfosi* in Paris in an
expanded version that included a translation of the first three books of Ovid's
Metamorphoses. These three books were then printed twice in 1555, the first time by
Wechel in Paris, and the second time by Vincenzo Valgrisi in Venice. In 1558,
Francesco Marcolini printed another edition of Anguillara's three books in Venice
commissioned by Alberto di Gratia da Lucca, who was likely a *cantimbanca* and pedlar.

[8] There is a notarial act showing the change of ownership from Anguillara to Francesco
de' Franceschi Senese: see Bucchi 2011: 330.

After the translator's printing privilege was sold, various editors and printers published new editions of the *Metamorfosi* in turn, often supplying their readers with new paratextual material, such as commentaries, marginalia, dedicatory letters and portraits (Bucchi 2011: 299). The editions of the *Metamorfosi* printed in 1584 and 1592 by Bernardo Giunti were the richest in paratextual elements and the most lavishly decorated. Focusing on two specific paratextual elements printed in these two editions, the translator and author portraits, this chapter shows how printers, editors, illustrators and the other book agents co-operated to establish this translation as a new classic of the vernacular language by presenting the *Metamorfosi* as a canonical text comparable to other novelties of the vernacular literature (beginning with the *Orlando furioso*), and by presenting Anguillara as the new Ovid.

Translator- and Author-Portraits in Anguillara's *Metamorfosi*

The two sixteenth-century editions of the *Metamorfosi* printed by Giunti contain different portraits of Anguillara. The first portrait was made by the designer and engraver Giacomo Franco, and it was printed on the title page of the 1584 Giunti edition of the *Metamorfosi* (Figure 11.2).[9] In what follows, I will refer to this portrait as an 'individual portrait', which I define as the representation of a single individual in a single format. The second translator-portrait was printed in the border surrounding the illustrations of the 1592 edition of the *Metamorfosi* printed by Giunti in Venice, and it was accompanied by a portrait of Ovid (Figure 11.3).[10] This is a 'double portrait', which I define as the representation of two figures in the same portrait, or the co-existence of two individual portraits of different individuals in the same frame.

---

[9] For Giacomo Franco see Bury 2001: 226; Pasero 1935: 332–56.

[10] Among the editions of the *Metamorfosi* printed after the sixteenth century we can find another three portraits of Anguillara. The first seventeenth-century translator portrait is an imitation of the 1584 portrait and it was printed on the title page of the 1677 edition of the *Metamorfosi* (Anguillara 1677). In the eighteenth century, a double portrait of Anguillara and Ovid was printed in the *Metamorfosi* by Girolamo Dorigoni in Venice (Anguillara 1757). The last translator-portrait was designed by Giuseppe Benaglia and published in the 1805 edition of Anguillara's *Metamorfosi* printed in Milan by the Società tipografica de' classici italiani (Anguillara 1805). Cotugno (2007: 523–25, 538) mentioned only the 1584 portrait, the 1594 portrait on the border of the illustrations, and the 1805 portrait.

Figure 11.2. Giacomo Franco, Portrait of Giovanni Andrea dell'Anguillara. Anguillara 1584a, fol. †1r, Rome, Fondazione Marco Besso, BIBL G9 E 36. Courtesy of Fondazione Marco Besso, Rome.

My definition of double portrait differs slightly from the one given by Dena Woodall (2008: 15) in her study on double portraiture, which says that 'Double portraits are images in which two figures cohabitate in a single format, existing on the same visual field'. I believe that two portraits do not

Figure 11.3. Double portrait of Anguillara and Ovid.
Anguillara 1592, fol. †8ʳ, Rome, Biblioteca della Fondazione Marco Besso, BIBL.
G.9.E 4. Courtesy of Fondazione Marco Besso, Rome.

have to co-exist on the same visual field to form a double portrait. As will emerge from some examples addressed later in this study, in the case of book-portraits, there are instances in which, despite two individual portraits not being on the same page or on facing pages, readers/viewers contemplate them as part of the same reading experience. The book is like a frame, and by turning the pages, readers place the portraits in relation to one another as if they existed on the same visual plane.

Art historians working on the illustrations of the *Metamorfosi* by Anguillara have not discussed these translator-portraits. Francesca Casamassima (2001, 2015) addressed the series of woodcuts and copperplates representing the episodes narrated in the text of the *Metamorfosi* without dwelling on the illustrations pertinent to the paratext of the editions. The *Ovidius Pictus* project, which gathers the illustrated editions of Ovid's *Metamorphoses* (in Latin and in the vernaculars) printed between the fifteenth and the nineteenth centuries, offers a search engine that enables searches for portraits of Ovid, but not for portraits of the translators.[11] Among textual scholars, Cotugno (2007: 523–25) mentioned the portraits of Anguillara as proof of the recognition given to this translator in the sixteenth century. Building on Giuseppina Zappella's bibliographical study of printed portraits in the Italian sixteenth-century book, Cotugno claims that the translator-portrait is an unproblematic paratextual component common in the Renaissance, when the act of translation received a greater level of appraisal than today (Zappella 1998: I. 70, 123). Furthermore, he argues that the portrait of Anguillara was meant to celebrate and canonize the translator. By comparing the portraits of Anguillara with other sixteenth-century printed portraits, and studying the arrangement of the portraits inside the space of the book, the following analysis looks beneath the celebrative surface of the portrait to unveil a set of functions more complex than previously suggested. Anne Coldiron (2018: 51–74), in her recent publication on the translator portraits in the early printed book, argues that these visual paratexts are fundamental instruments to study the complex construction of authorship in the Early Modern Age. Title pages and portraits were becoming authorial spaces in early print culture and the translators' visibility in these parts of the book suggests the existence of a link between translation and authorship, which Coldiron calls 'transla[u]t[h]orship' or the translator-authorship.[12] Following Coldiron's approach to the study of the translator portrait, the following research focuses on how printer and editors used the printed portrait to construct the translator's authorship.

---

[11] 'Ovidius Pictus. Ovidian Digital Library: Ovid Illustrated Editions in Spanish Libraries (15th-19th centuries)', http://www.ovidiuspictus.es [accessed 23 March 2018].

[12] As noted by Coldiron (2018), the term 'transla[u]t[h]orship' was originally coined by Nathalie Hancisse and Stéphanie Vanasten as: 'Transl[a]ut[h]ors: Questions de traduction à l'écriture: Regards croisés sur la littérature et les échanges culturels entre le XVIème et le XXIème siècles', *International Conference held at the Université catholique de Louvain* (Louvain-la-Neuve, Belgium), 10 September 2015.

Portraits are visual elements that necessitate a close engagement with image-based disciplines. At the same time, these paratexts exist in the space of the book and should therefore be studied within the realm of book history. As will become clear in my study, the printed portrait is inextricable from the material structure of the book, which we could consider as the portrait's frame. The book-frame, as I propose to name it, is like a threshold that guides us towards the interpretation of the portrait: the collocation of the portrait in the book, its proximity to the text and its repetition inside the book are all elements that inform our understanding of the portrayal and its function inside the book. The union between printed portrait and book has not always been emphasised by previous scholars, who have often withdrawn the printed portrait from its original context of production. The digital platform *Bildarchiv Austria*, for example, allows one to look for the portraits of various notable characters simply by typing their name into the research engine.[13] The limit of this otherwise useful archive is that there is no bibliographical reference that links the portrait to its original provenance, despoiling it of its textual and material surroundings. Furthermore, in comparison with portraits in other branches of the visual arts, the printed portrait is subject to the social, economic and mechanical dynamics that comprise print culture. A single portrait is replicated multiple times, and its features change significantly depending on the public targeted by the printing house, and on the agents responsible for the material production of the book. The nature of the portrait and its meaning are determined by the relationship between the person portrayed and the agents (e.g. printer, editors and engravers) responsible for the making of a book.

The union of book and portraiture in the *Metamorfosi* allows us to reflect on the link between the emergence of the genre of portraiture in the fifteenth and sixteenth centuries and the rise of a sense of individualism. This connection was first drawn by Jacob Burckhardt (1911) in his famous praise of the civilization of the Italian Renaissance, and in recent years it has been the object of a lively debate.[14] The individual printed portrait, in fact, was often recycled in various books to represent different persons, underscoring the instability of the idea of individualism in the early modern period.[15] In his introduction to the special issue of *Word & Image* devoted to the influence of reproducible media on portraiture, Adrian Randolph (2003: 2) has shown how, due to the replicability of the book, the printed portrait

---

[13] 'Bildarchiv Austria', www.bildarchivaustria.at [accessed 24 April 2018].

[14] Pope-Hennessy 1966; Mann and Syson 1988. For some contrary views see Gentili, Morel and Cieri Via 1989–1993; Cranston 2000; and Randolph 2003.

[15] Issues of replicability are addressed in Randolph 2003: 1; Burke 1995: 147–57; and also Landau and Parshall 1994.

targeted a vast readership that was for the most part unacquainted with the true likeness of the person in the portrait. Because of the absence of familiarity between the person portrayed and the reader, the referential value of a portrait was not given by likeness per se, but it was achieved through the employment of visual conventions. Costume, symbols and textual elements were the features that shaped the character of the person portrayed connecting him/her to a professional, dynastic or social group. According to Zappella (2005), the portrait on the title page of an early modern book did not offer its viewers the real and unique character of the person that had been portrayed, but rather a 'paradigma ideale' of an individual.

While studying these portraits, I had to confront the challenge of the absence of an archive of printed portraits.[16] Some of the portraits in this study came to my attention while browsing through online databases of digitised books, and through the special collections of various libraries in Italy and England. I found other printed portraits in studies on the visual representation of single authors. Joseph B. Trapp (1955), for instance, published individual studies of visual representations of Ovid, and there are several individual studies on the portraits of modern authors such as Petrarch, Ariosto and Boccaccio.[17] The greatest and most varied repertoire of book-portraits, however, was offered by two bibliographical studies, authored respectively by Giuseppina Zappella (1988) and Ruth Mortimer (1996).[18] Both gather and describe a large number of printed portraits, and while distinguishing various typologies of portrait, they trace the evolution of the representation of individual characters during the Renaissance.

Individual Printed Portraits

The 1584 translator-portrait of Anguillara breaks with the tradition of author-portraits of the Italian and Latin *Metamorphoses* (Figure 11.2). The

---

[16] In a limited number of online catalogues, such as the ESTC, it is possible to search for the physical description 'portrait', which retrieves a number of books containing this paratextual feature. This methodology has been employed by Sarah Howe (2008) in her investigation into author portraits in Renaissance England. This methodology has its limits, since it is based on the assumption that the cataloguers have signalled the presence of the portrait among the physical features of the book. Nonetheless, this research engine allows one to gather a number of book-portraits. However, the USTC, Edit 16 and SBN do not allow one to search for the physical description of books in any detail. In Edit 16, for instance, it is possible to search for the physical description 'ritratto', but this operation only retrieves a 1536 edition of Ariosto's *Soppositi*.

[17] For the portraits of Ariosto see Dorigatti 2008. For the portraits of Petrarch and Laura see Trapp 2001. For Boccaccio see Kirkham 1999 and 2015.

[18] Ruth Mortimer (1989) has also published a study on the author-portrait in the French sixteenth-century book.

individual portrait of Ovid, in fact, was included in the majority of editions of this poem. The representation of ancient writers is often conventional since in many instances we lack an authentic image of the author. This is the case for Ovid, of whom we do not possess an authentic portrait or an ancient biography providing a description of his appearance (Trapp 1995: 254–55). The earliest examples of Ovid's portrait found in manuscripts date back to the beginning of the thirteenth century. In these first occurrences Ovid is always portrayed together with other authoritative writers. The individual portrait of Ovid makes its first appearance at the beginning of the fourteenth century.[19] These representations were seldom included in the Latin editions of his works, and were more frequent in the illuminated manuscripts of the vernacular adaptations of the *Metamorphoses*, such as the *Ovide moralisé* or the *Ovidius moralizatus* (Trapp 1995: 258–59).

The bond between translation and portrait was strong in the Italian tradition. Three manuscripts of Giovanni Bonsignori's *Ovidio metamorphoseos vulgare* (a fourteenth-century translation of the *Metamorphoses*) depict the author (Guthmüller 2008: 291–98). The first manuscript, dated to the beginning of the fifteenth century, has a full page portrait of Ovid (Figure 11.4).[20] A half-bust, set on a book with Ovid's name written on the fore-edge, represents Ovid with a doctor's ermine cope emphasising his wisdom.[21] The other two miniatures of Ovid can be found in fifteenth-century manuscripts. In both cases, the portrait of Ovid is contained in the space of an illuminated initial.[22] The addition of a portrait to the manuscript underlines the emerging desire to associate the text with an image of its author. The portrait, according to Roger Chartier (1992: 52), has the function of authenticating a text, and the high number of author-portraits in the adaptations of the *Metamorphoses* suggests that the desire for authentication was higher in this vernacular literary context, where translators, copyists or later compilers might have wanted to underscore the faithfulness of the translation to the source text.

[19] An example of early individual portrait is Stefano Degli Azzi's miniature of Ovid in the late fourteenth-century manuscript held in the Biblioteca Malatestiana (Cesena, Biblioteca Malatestiana, MS S.XXV.6). See Ghedini 2018: 238.

[20] Further studies on the portrait of Ovid in this manuscript can be found in Trapp 1995: 264; Guthmüller 2008: 293.

[21] Scholars have noticed that this portrait is similar to a representation of Dante, and they have suggested that both portraits (together with one of Boccaccio) could have been part of a repertoire of portraits of illustrious men. See Lazzi and Savino 1996: 74–75.

[22] Pavia, Biblioteca Universitaria, Fondo Ticinese, MS 545, f. 1ʳ; Rome, Biblioteca Corsiniana (Accademia dei Lincei), Fondo Niccolò Rossi, MS 377, f. 43ᵛ. See Guthmüller 2008: 294–95.

Figure 11.4. Portrait of Ovid. Florence, Biblioteca Riccardiana, MS Ricc. 1544, fol 5ᵛ, courtesy of Ministero della Cultura, Italy.

The author-portrait made its appearance also in early sixteenth-century printed editions of the vernacular *Metamorphoses*. In all the editions of the translation written by Niccolò degli Agostini (d. *c.* 1526) there is a portrait of a poet with the inscription 'Ovid' on the title page.[23] The 1522 portrait printed by Niccolò Zoppino, for example, imitates the famous portrait-type of Petrarch in his study complete with cat or dog.[24] The portrait in the studio underscores the intellectual and creative effort of the poet, and the presence of books elevates the writer by linking him with ancient culture.[25] The other two images are equally standardized. Both represent a poet holding a book, which symbolises the author's work (Zappella 1988: i. 54–55). As was the custom in the sixteenth century, all three portraits were probably recycled from previous editions (not necessarily of Ovid's works). The portrait of Ovid in the 1502 edition of Domenico da Montichiello's translation of Ovid's *Heroides*, for instance, was recycled from a portrait of Dante with the city of Florence at his back and Inferno on the side, depicted as a cave with flames and demons (Trapp 1995: 268).[26]

The portrait of Gabriello Simeoni printed on the title page of his *Metamorfoseo* marks a first step away from the tradition of author-portraits in the re-writings of Ovid's *Metamorphoses* in the Italian vernacular. Gabriello's oeuvre, printed in 1559 in Lyon by Jean de Tournes, belongs to a different literary tradition in comparison to the verse translation of Anguillara.[27] This work was inspired by one of the masterpieces of the French Renaissance, *La Métamorphose d'Ovide figurée*, printed in 1557 in Lyon by Jean de Tournes. The structure of Simeoni's work clearly recalls emblem books and illustrated Bibles, and it aims at a perfect equilibrium between text and images. The text, in addition, is not a translation of the fifteen books of Ovid's poem, but it is a synthesis of a selection of myths taken from the *Metamorphoses* and transformed in brief epigrams written in *ottava rima*.[28]

---

[23] Agostini's translation was printed several times during the first half of the sixteenth century (1522, 1533, 1537, 1538, 1547, 1548). For an analysis of these editions and their title pages see Guthmüller 2008: 204 and Balzi 2020: 135–38.

[24] For more information about the Petrarch portrait-type see Trapp 1995: 268–69.

[25] For information about the studio portrait see Zappella 1988: I. 45–50.

[26] The woodcut portrait of Dante pointing to the *Inferno* is, in turn, inspired by the famous painting by Castagno del Domenico, *Dante holding his Commedia*, Museo dell'Opera del Duomo, Florence (see Kirkham 1999: 95).

[27] There is also a second edition of Simeoni's work, which was printed in Lyon in 1584.

[28] For the relationship between Gabriello Simeoni's translation and *La Métamorphose d'Ovide figurée* see Guthmüller 1997: 213–50. Ilaria Andreoli (2013b) has also addressed the relationship between the series of illustrations in Simeoni's work and the French

The medallion portrait on the title page depicts Simeoni in profile dressed in classical attire. At the bottom of the medallion there is the Latin inscription 'spiritus astra super' [the soul beyond the stars]. The motto is visually represented within the portrait, where Simeoni's bust seems to fluctuate in the sky above gods and constellations. This short inscription is in all probability inspired by the epilogue of Ovid's poem, where the poet predicted his eternal survival through the re-telling of his poem: 'parte tamen meliore mei super alta perennis | astra ferar' [still in my better part I shall be borne immortal far beyond the lofty stars] (Ovid, *Metamorphoses*, XV. 875–76). By quoting this epilogue, Symeoni suggested that he would survive the passage of time and become immortal through his work, as happened to Ovid before him.

At the top of the medallion is another inscription: 'Par animus formae, dispar fortuna duobus' [His spirit is equal to his body, fate prevails on both].[29] The first half of this sentence is a quotation from Book XIV of Ovid's *Metamorphoses* (Ovid, *Metamorphoses*, XIV. 324). In that passage, Ovid claimed that Picus, a mythological character, was beautiful in the inner as well as the outer parts of his body. In Simeoni's portrait, these words probably hinted at the idea that the portrait, which represents the physical features of the writer, is also a faithful representation of his spirit. The second part of the Latin sentence is a reminder of the power of fate, which commands the destiny of soul and body. In the portrait, the mutability of all things and the passage of time are clearly evoked by the zodiacal symbols. Although the portrait of Simeoni substitutes the author-portrait, Ovid remains extremely visible in this illustration. The portrait is surrounded with Ovidian quotations, and addresses themes and topics that are central to Ovid's poetics, such as the survival of the soul, the mutability of all things and the passage of time. Simeoni, instead of presenting his individual self, employed his portrait to present himself as a new Ovid, and to link his own immortality to that of the Latin poet.

The translator-portrait of Anguillara in Giunti's 1584 edition of the *Metamorfosi* marks a shift away from the portrait of Simeoni and from the author-portraits in the translations of Ovid's poem. Anguillara's portraiture does not make any reference to the Latin author. On the contrary, it associates the translator with modern writers in the vernacular language, and in particular with Ariosto. What caused this break in the tradition of portraits of Ovid, and what strategies did printers and editors use to affiliate Ariosto and Anguillara's portraits?

---

tradition of emblem books. Elisa Modolo (2015: 1-71) has dedicated a chapter of her thesis to Simeoni's translation and his contribution to the creation of Baroque poetics.

[29] The translation is mine.

Looking more broadly at the paratext of other early modern verse translations, we can identify a general movement in the late sixteenth century towards the use of translator-portraits in place of author-portraits. The 1544 edition of *I sei primi libri dell'Eneide*, a translation of the first six books of the *Aeneid*, portrays Virgil at the beginning of each *libro*. The author-portrait, however, is replaced by the translator-portrait in later translations. There is a portrait of Ercole Udine in the front matter of the 1597 edition of his translation of Virgil's poem, for example, and there is a full-page copperplate portrait of Annibal Caro in the 1608 edition of his translation of the *Aeneid*. Looking at other works this transition is confirmed. The printer Noro Perugino, for instance, published a translation of Ovid's letters in 1541 with a portrait of the translator Vincenzo Menni in the front matter of the book (Zappella 1988: II, Tav. 234).[30] In 1573, Giolito printed Dolce's *Ulisse*, a translation of Homer's *Odyssey*, including the portrait of Dolce in the front matter of the book.[31]

The preference for the translator-portrait in the late sixteenth century results from a series of intertwined phenomena. The stability of the vernacular language and the international and national prestige acquired by Italian literature bolstered the confidence of the moderns, who presented themselves as equals to the classical authorities they translated (Dionisotti 1967: 132–33). The translator-portrait is telling of the prestige acquired by the vernacular language and of the rising ambition to compete with classical heritage. The book agents who authored the paratext of Giunti's 1584 *Metamorfosi* probably wanted to emphasise how Anguillara managed to carve out his own authorial space from a very well-known text, and celebrate his poetic success.

The visibility of Anguillara in the paratext of the *Metamorfosi* was also incentivized by the rising popularity of portraits of modern personalities in the visual arts (e.g. painting, coin manufacture and sculpture). The number of portraits of contemporary individuals soared significantly in the fifteenth century, when humanists aimed to embrace every aspect of the ancient lifestyle as it was expressed through old coins and sculptured busts. Reproducing these ancient artefacts with the likenesses of the moderns allowed humanists to link themselves to the ancients and gave them an artistic medium through which they could express and investigate their personality. In this field, Leon Battista Alberti provides an important reference point. He had a remarkable fascination with his intellectual self,

---

[30] For Vincenzo Menni's translation see the USTC 803867.

[31] For other examples of sixteenth-century translator-portraits see Zappella 1988: I. 70–73.

which he expressed in his writings as well as in his self-portraits.[32] Alberti was an avant-gardist who anticipated a new artistic time in which Renaissance medallists, painters, sculptors and engravers explored the depths and mobility of the human condition through the visual arts (Pope-Hennessy 1966: 103–54).

When portraits began to gravitate in the Gutenberg galaxy, the likeness of modern personalities became a promotional medium of unprecedented potential that 'heightened the recognition accorded to individual achievements' (Eisenstein 2005: 146).[33] Pietro Aretino perfectly understood this potentiality, and, working in close collaboration with his printers, he employed portraits to frame his authorial identity and orient the reading of his texts.[34] In one of his letters, Aretino even persuaded Pietro Bembo to include his portrait in the edition of the *Prose*:

> Ma perché l'effigie, con cui onorate il mondo e la natura, sia ogni or la medesima come tuttavia sarà la istessa la fama che avete, consentite con il presto venir qui, che se le cominci e fornisca la stampa, dove apparirete vero e vivo. E ciò fate, perché quei che nasceranno, s'innamorino de l'imagine di colui che gli terrà in continuo stupore con gli essempi de le cose scritte. (Aretino 1997: I. 1, 157–58, 6 Febbraio 1537)

> [In order for your semblance, with which you honour our world and nature, to always stay the same – as will the fame that you possess – accept our invitation to come here so that we can prepare a print in which you will seem true and alive. Do it, so that those who will come after us will fall in love with the image of the person who keeps them in constant amazement with his writing.][35]

The portrait guaranteed the persistent fame of the author, because the contemplation of a visual character, combined with his written words, provided a full representation of a person, with whom the reader could interact, and even fall in love. Jodi Cranston (2000: 1–14) has very meaningfully associated the individual Renaissance portrait with a written letter, because both involve the beholder/reader in an intimate dialogue. Petrarch himself, in the Familiares, blurred the distinction between writing and speaking, reading and seeing. Reading a letter from a friend, according to Petrarch, equalled the act of visualising his face:

---

[32] The two self-portraits of Alberti that survive today are bronze reliefs: see Pope-Hennessy 1966: 66–68.

[33] The phrase 'Gutenberg galaxy' refers to the pivotal study by Marshall McLuhan (2011) on the impact of the invention of the printing press on European culture.

[34] For an analysis of the portraits of Aretino see Mortimer 1996: 78–80. For a general study of the relationship between Aretino and the printing press see M. Bertolo 2003.

[35] The translation is mine.

Dulce michi colloquium tecum fuit, cupideque et quasi de industria protractum; vultum enim tuum retulit per tot terras et maria teque michi presentem fecit usque ad vesperam, cum matutino tempore calamum capissem. (Petrarca 1933-1942: I (1933), I, 1.47)

[This conversation with you was pleasant, and I prolonged it eagerly, as though by design. It brought back your face before me over so many lands and seas. It made you present before me from the morning, when I took the pen in my hands, until dusk.]

Therefore, the printed portrait, usually set in the front matter of the book, acted together with the dedicatory epistle as a paratextual tool that fully visualized the person portrayed, indicating his physical and intellectual idiosyncrasies.

Not all portraits, however, tried to convey the unique features of an individual. The way in which the printed portrait framed the identity of a person and made him or her familiar to the readers varied according to the agents in control of the material production of the book. Aretino, for example, had more than one portrait made specifically to accompany his texts.[36] In his *Stanze*, printed in 1537 in Venice by Francesco Marcolini, Aretino was portrayed by Titian in the guise of an adoring shepherd looking up at the apparition in the sky of his lover Angela Serena, depicted as a winged siren (Mortimer 1996: 78). According to Mortimer (1996: 79), Titian's representation of Aretino is a 'literary portrait' because it translates in images a specific passage of Aretino's *Stanze*. This illustration conveys not only a personal biographical information regarding the author, but it also gives visual presence to Aretino's poetic imagination. The resemblance of Aretino's portrait to his own persona depends on the close relationship he had with the printer Marcolini; a relationship, according to Amedeo Quondam (1980: 89–90), that almost dissolved the boundary between author-function and editor-function. The co-operation with Titian, one of Aretino's closest friends in Venice, was also important.[37]

When the person beheld was not involved in the material production of the book, there was no reason why a printer or editor would add his or her 'true' likeness to the paratext. The Venetian market of the printed book had a wide, international appeal, and the standard reader would be familiar with just a small number of public faces. Therefore, in order to convey a sense of familiarity and authority, it was sufficient for the printer to add a standard portrait representing the generic features of an author adorned with laurel

---

[36] Aretino also commissioned painted portraits of himself. He deemed his painted portrait by Titian a true likeness of himself that expressed his inner soul: see Woodall 2008: 12.

[37] Giuliano Innamorati, 'Pietro Aretino', *DBI*, www.treccani.it/ enciclopedia/pietro-aretino_(Dizionario-Biografico)/ [accessed 14 December 2019].

and toga. The situation was different in a smaller market. In Florence, for example, the book business had a regional reach, and the connection of the printing press with the Academy gave place to a familiar environment in which the roles of author, editor and printer were blurred (McGrath 2003). In this cultural setting, portraits were usually less conventional and type-centred, providing a true likeness of the person portrayed.

In Giunti's 1584 edition of Anguillara's *Metamorfosi*, editorial responsibility fell completely on the shoulders of editor, printer, illustrator and other book agents responsible for the material production of the book. Anguillara was already dead, and it is possible that the illustrator had never met him in person and that he or she had no access to another portrait of the translator. In any case, Giunti's aim was not to print a faithful representation of the translator, but to employ a standardised portrait of Anguillara that could authorise the printed text by affiliating it with the novelties of vernacular literature, and in particular with the *Orlando furioso*. The affiliation between Anguillara and Ariosto was favoured by the gradual standardisation of the portraits of the latter. After Ariosto's death, subsequent editors and printers lost interest in printing the likeness of this author, and adopted a symbolic illustration. In the following analysis, I will present the evolution of Ariosto's portraits in order to show how, by the end of the sixteenth century, they became the model for Anguillara's portrait.

The first portrait of Ariosto was included in the edition of the *Furioso* printed by Niccolò Zoppino in 1530 (Dorigatti 2008: 151–52; Mortimer 1996: 37). This edition was published without the consent and supervision of the author. The portrait, however, was realistic, portraying the author with the cap that (as Ariosto wrote in his *Satire*) he wore to cover his incipient baldness. There was only one symbolic element in this representation of Ariosto: the laurel branches in the background. The second portrait of Ariosto was added to the back matter of the 1532 edition of the *Furioso* printed in Ferrara by Francesco Rosso (Dorigatti 2008: 152; Mortimer 1996: 37–38). This portrait was engraved following the design made by Titian, and it was included in the book under the supervision of Ariosto, who personally sponsored this edition. This representation of Ariosto is free from all the symbolic elements characterising the standard author–portrait: book, laurel or Roman attire (Dorigatti 2008: 152–53; Andreoli 2006: Scheda 4). Instead, it is entirely focused on the humanity of the character, whose old age and weakness are not hidden but rather showcased as an emblematic mark of the individuality of the poet. This author-portrait was reproduced various times in the editions of Ariosto's works printed during the first half of the sixteenth century. In the 1535 edition of Ariosto's comedy *La Lena*, for instance, on the title page there is a reproduction of the 1532 portrait of Ariosto made according to Titian's design.[38]

The realistic 1532 portrait of Ariosto was gradually replaced by standardized ones. Giolito had a different portrait cut for his 1542 *Furioso*, which employed Titian's profile but transformed it into a classical bust with laurel wreath and toga (the garment worn by the citizens of ancient Rome) (Mortimer 1996: 38). Something similar happens to the author-portrait on the title page of the 1552 edition of Ariosto's *Rime*.[39] In both portraits, Ariosto's profile portrait is set in the oval space of the medallion, thus creating a connection with the classical coins, which implicitly elevated him to a higher level of authorial dignity.[40] The process of standardization increased in the 1556 edition of the *Furioso* printed by Valgrisi in Venice, where the author-portrait is set in a small medallion on top of the architectural border of the title page.[41] The portrait medallion is held by two flying amorini. This setting creates a connection with classical art, evoking Roman funerary monuments such as the Roman *Marble Sarcophagus with Flying Erotes Holding a Clipeus Portrait*.[42] In this edition, the portrait is small, and Ariosto's distinctive profile is less discernible, leaving the symbolic features of the portrait fully visible. The Valgrisi portrait is the model for the engraved title page of the *Furioso* printed in 1584 by Francesco de' Franceschi.[43] In this new edition, the artist Girolamo Porro refashioned the ornamentation of the border, and readjusted the space of the portrait on the title page, leaving untouched Ariosto's symbolic attire. In contrast with Titian's portrait, the following representations of Ariosto (1552; 1556; 1584) lost their individualizing function. In the hands of editors and printers, the portrait of Ariosto became a celebrative and marketing tool.

The 1584 portrait of Anguillara (Figure 11.2) is a conspicuous imitation of the portrait-type of Ariosto developed in the late sixteenth century

---

[38] Ludovico Ariosto, *La Lena: Comedia di Messer Lodovico Ariosto* (Venice: Nicolò d'Aristotile detto Zoppino, 1535).

[39] Ludovico Ariosto, *Rime* (Venice: [n. pub.], 1552).

[40] Claudia Cieri Via (1989: I, 60) has claimed that the imitation of classical coins in the Renaissance was meant to extol the virtues and the status of the person beheld in the portrait.

[41] For a study of the illustrations in Valgrisi's edition of the *Furioso* see Andreoli 2006: Scheda 4. For the portrait printed in this edition see Mortimer 1996: 38–39.

[42] Roman, *Sarcophagus with Flying Erotes Holding a Portrait Medallion*, c. A.D. 190–200, marble, 45.1 x 179.1 x 53.3 cm, Metropolitan Museum of Art, New York. Digitised: www.metmuseum.org/art/collection/ search/254855 [accessed 16 April 2018].

[43] For a study of de Franceschi's edition of the *Furioso*: see the edited volume Andreoli 2013a. For the portrait in this edition see also Mortimer 1996: 39.

(Mortimer 1996: 39–41). In de' Franceschi's *Furioso*, the title page presents a border with two flanking statues. The statue on the left is Mars and that on the right is Venus. On top of the frame there is the medallion portrait of Ariosto held by two angels. Giacomo Franco, the author of Anguillara's title page, recreated the same structure only with minor changes. The position of the statues, for example, is reversed. The statue on the right is Minerva, and it takes the stance of Porro's Mars in the 1584 *Furioso*. The statue on the left represents Mercury, who repeats the same gesture as Porro's Venus. As in Porro's title page, the medallion portrait stands over the title supported by two angels. The position of these portraits is highly symbolic (Cieri Via 1989: I. 52–54). In the Middle Ages and Renaissance, the likeness of political authorities was displayed at the entrance of institutional palaces and private villas to mark their political and ethical dominion.[44] The portrait of Anguillara and Ariosto brings the reader back to this ancient tradition and underlines the fact that beyond the title page there is a world that stands under the authority of the person portrayed at the entrance.

The link with Ariosto's portrait suggests that the function of Anguillara's representation is not merely to celebrate the translator. The title page of the *Metamorfosi* aims to communicate to the reader an affinity between a group of writers and a genre of texts rather than simply showcasing and celebrating an individual author.

Sharing Spaces: The Dynamics of Double Portraiture

The idea of doubling a portrait arose well before the Renaissance. Roman Antiquity provides similar examples in painted effigies, sarcophagi, death masks, sculpted figures, *imagines clipeatae*, gems and ancient coins (Woodall 2008: 38–60).[45] With the Renaissance revival of ancient art and culture, double portraiture spread in Europe, encompassing all branches of the visual arts. Southern European double portraits, however, remain largely unexplored in scholarship. This gap is due to the axiom that southern artists were not interested in this form of artistic expression (Woodall 2008: 30–37). Woodall is the first to argue against this accepted truth, bringing to critical attention numerous examples of Renaissance Italian double portraits taken from different branches of the visual arts. Thanks to her study, we can recognise double portraiture as a proper category within the genre of portraiture. In this study, I will use some of the double portraits discussed by Woodall, and I will also add eleven new examples taken from

---

[44] A good example is the Porta della Carta in Palazzo Ducale, Venice.

[45] *Imago clipeata* is an art term used in reference to the images of ancestors, famous people or the deceased produced on round shields (in Latin: *clipeus*).

manuscripts and early printed editions, including the double portrait of Ovid and Anguillara.

Books are rich repositories of double portraits. Within these material objects, the poet with his lady love is a well-known double portrait type (Woodall 2008: 215–20). The manuscripts of Petrarch's *Rerum vulgarium fragmenta* and *Trionfi* host numerous illuminations of the poet with Laura. In a late fifteenth-century manuscript of Petrarch's *Rime*, for instance, there is an illuminated initial with the portrait of a man and a woman facing each other in profile.[46] According to Trapp (2001: 69–71), this could either be a representation of the owners of the book, the bridal couple Corrado da Fogliano and Gabriella Gonzaga, or an illustration of Petrarch and Laura. The same formula of a pair of facing busts, which finds its model in Roman funerary reliefs, is reproduced multiple times in sixteenth-century editions of Petrarch's works. In 1547, Giolito printed in Venice a double portrait of Petrarch and Laura inside a funerary urn.[47] Set in the front matter of the book, this portrait is followed by a sonnet that explains how Petrarch and Laura will be eternally united and immortalised thanks to Petrarch's verses. The portrait is a symbol of the book itself, which is a sacred temple in which the spirit of Petrarch and Laura will rest forever. A different sort of double portrait of Petrarch and Laura was added to the 1549 edition of Petrarch's *Rime* printed in Venice by Nicolini da Sabbio. Two medallion portraits illustrate the facing busts of Petrarch and Laura with their names written in the medallion's frame.[48] The association in portraiture of Laura and Petrarch led also to the creation of another famous couple: Boccaccio and Fiammetta (Kirkham 1999: scheda 68, fig. 107). The relationship between the portrayed subjects in this case is complicated by the fact that Fiammetta is not only Boccaccio's love interest. In Boccaccio's *Elegia di Madonna Fiammetta* the female character is also the first person narrator.[49] Therefore, what is suggested in the double portrait is not only an amorous bond

[46] Berlin, Kupferstichkabinett der Staatlichen Museen zu Berlin, MS 78 C 22, fol. 1ʳ. See Trapp (2001: 69–71, fig. 43).

[47] Francesco Petrarca, Il Petrarcha, con l'espositione d'Alessandro Vellutello di novo ristampato con le figure ai Triomphi e con più cose utili in vari luoghi aggiunte (Venice: Gabriele Giolito dei Ferrari, 1547), fol. *2ᵛ. See Trapp 2001: 112, fig. 80; Woodall 2008: 669, fig. 3.24.

[48] Francesco Petrarca, Sonetti, canzoni e triomphi di M. Francesco Petrarca con la spositione di Bernardino Daniello da Lucca. Con privilegio del Italianissimo Senato Vinitiano (Venice: Pietro and Giovanni Maria Nicolini da Sabbio for Giovanni Battista Pederzano, 1549). See also Zappella 1988: II. 119.

[49] Armstrong (2013: 302-08) has studied Boccaccio's construction – on the Ovidian example – of Fiammetta's authorial voice in his *Elegia* and has shed light on the negotiation of Boccaccio's and Fiammetta's authority in the English translation of the *Elegia*, the *Amorous Fiammetta*.

between poet and muse, but also an interlocking of their authorial voices. The double portrait of Boccaccio and Fiammetta bridges the divide between the portrait of the poet and lady love and that of two narrating authorities, which we shall address in what follows with another example taken from Boccaccio's portraits.

The manuscript of a French *Decameron* shows in the same miniature two separate scenes involving Boccaccio and his translator, Laurent de Premierfait (d. 1418).[50] In the scene on the left, Laurent is in the foreground in the act of presenting his book. In the background, Boccaccio looks at the book presentation with approval, and holds a scroll in his hands to remind the readers of his status of *auctor*. In the scene on the right, Boccaccio and Laurent sit in front of a two-sided lectern, facing each other. As Coldiron (2018: 66) has proposed in her article on early printed portraits, the two-sided lectern can be seen as an 'image of the author-translator relation'. In the portrait of Margaret More Roper that Coldiron analyses, the female translator is sitting on one side of the lectern and the empty space on the other side invites us to infer the absent presence of the author. In Boccaccio's and Laurent de Premierfait's miniature, both author and translator are portrayed to manifest the existence of a multi-layered authorship. Both hold writing instruments and work on a book placed in front of them. The fact that they employ the same lectern communicates the idea that both played a part in the making of the French *Decameron*. Their collocation on different sides, however, underscores their use of different languages, and their belonging to different literary worlds.

In contrast with the portrait of the poet with his lover, the typology of author and translator entails a different relationship between the individuals portrayed. The persons beheld are usually of the same gender, and their unity under the book-frame is not due to a sentimental and poetical bond, but rather to a literary affinity and shared participation in the authorship of the text. The co-existence of these two writers in the same book, in addition, generates a power relationship, and the following analysis investigates the way in which this relationship is visualised in the double portrait of Ovid and Anguillara printed by Giunti in 1592.

The Latin and vernacular editions of Ovid's works offer various examples of the portrait-type of author and translator. The late fourteenth-century North Italian codex of the *Ovidius moralizatus* has a miniature with Ovid standing next to Thomas Waleys, the Dominican friar to whom this moralized adaptation of Ovid's *Metamorphoses* was for a long time

---

[50] Paris, Bibliothèque nationale de France, MS FR. 129, f. 4r. I consulted a digitised copy, http://gallica.bnf.fr/ark:/12148/btv1b9009540b [accessed 13 April 2018]. See also Kirkham (1999: 110–11, fig. 110).

attributed.[51] This trend continues in the first years after the invention of the printing press. The verso of a British Library vellum incunabulum of Vérard's *Bible des poètes*, for instance, shows a miniature of Ovid in the left-hand column, together with a miniature of the compiler standing in front of a lectern.[52] The plurality of personalities in the miniatures of manuscripts and early prints suggests that the meaning and unity of a text was not determined by an individual author. Multiple agents (author, copyist, commentator, translator and also the reader) oriented the meaning of a text, and their agency emerged in visual terms in the material space of the book. An example of this plurality is the large number of illuminations of Ovid expounding *ex cathedra* to a group of listeners, or the woodcuts representing Ovid together with his commentators.[53]

The 1592 double portrait of Ovid and Anguillara follows the tradition of collective and double portraiture already established in the Middle Ages in the field of Ovid's vernacular and Latin works (Figure 11.3). The half bust of Ovid and that of Anguillara are represented in different medallion frames. Their unity, however, is guaranteed by their coexistence inside the border that surrounds the illustration of the *Metamorfosi*. In this double portrait both author and translator are given visibility and authorial standing through their visual presentation. Anguillara, for example, wears a laurel wreath and although his portrait is slightly smaller compared to Ovid's, it holds a privileged position on the page at the top of the border. Furthermore, it is the only portrait in the book that is included inside each illustration-border printed in the book. Ovid wears a laurel wreath as well as a toga and his portrait is bigger and also closer to the centre of the page. Ovid's portrait, however, does not appear in each border, but it alternates with the portraits of Mercury and Mars. This disposition diminishes Ovid's visual presence, but it associates this classical author with deities, thus elevating his status. This complex presentation of the authority of translator and author, as I will show in the following analysis, was growing in popularity in the second half of the century. By comparing Ovid's and Anguillara's double portrait with other examples of early printed double

---

[51] Gotha, Forschungsbibliothek, MS membr. I.98, f. 1. I have not consulted this manuscript, and so rely upon the description made by Trapp 1995: 261.

[52] Ovid, *Cy commence Ouide de Salmonen̄ son liure jntitule Metamorphose* (Paris: Antoine Vérard, [1493]). For a description of this incunabulum see Trapp (1995: 264).

[53] Paris, Bibliothèque nationale de France, MS Français 137, f. 1ʳ. Digitised: http://gallica.bnf.fr/ark:/12148/btv1b105385281. In this illumination Ovid is holding out a large egg to his listeners. The name of Ovid was etymologized in the Middle Ages as 'ovi dividens'. This etymology was applied to Creation through the correspondence of the four elements of the earth with the four constitutive parts of an egg, see Trapp 1995: 259.

portraits, the following analysis aims to 1) show the visibility of translators in early printed books; 2) investigate how the translator's authority was presented in the paratext of early printed books; 3) clarify what was the function of the double portrait in Anguillara's *Metamorfosi*.

The earliest example available to me of author and translator printed portrait is set in the Sicilian-Latin dictionary written by the Italian lexicographer Lucio Cristoforo Scobare, printed in Venice in 1519 by Bernardino Benalio (Zappella 1988: ii, Tav. 244). The Sicilian part of the dictionary is a translation from the Spanish text of Antonio de Nebrija's *Dicionario latino-español* (1492). There is a woodcut on the title page, and thanks to the names printed on top of it, we can identify it as a double portrait of Scobare and de Nebrija. Although author and translator are sitting at the same writing table, their position and body language implies a hierarchy between the two. The author Antonio de Nebrija looks directly towards the reader/beholder and sits at the heraldic dexter, while the translator looks at the author's book, looking over to work from it. The different direction of sight of author and translator signals their different status. As in devotional painted portraits, or in printed portraits of author and commentator, the saint/divinity or the author are the only characters looking towards the beholder, while all the others are depicted in profile (Cieri Via 1989: I. 59–66). In addition, the translator is represented in the act of copying, implicitly suggesting his fidelity to Nebrija.

This sort of composition is hardly unique, and it recalls the portrait type of mentors and pupils (Woodall 2008: 425–30). The *Double portrait of Fra Luca Pacioli with pupil* (c. 1495) by Jacopo de' Barbari, for instance, shows a very similar disposition of the characters and balance of power (Figure 11.5).[54] As in the double portrait of Scobare and Nebrija, master and pupil are behind a table full of working instruments. The Franciscan friar and mathematician Luca Pacioli stands in a prominent position, occupying the centre of the painting and the heraldic dexter of the pupil. His gestures are reminiscent of those of Nebrija: his hand is set on a page of the book open in front of him, while the right holds a tool. Furthermore, in both illustrations, the pupil/translator plays a supportive role. He stands in a position that gives him visual access to the working material of the master/author, bolstering the higher status of the other figure in the portrait. Interestingly, the same portrait structure of the independently painted portrait of Pacioli with student influenced another woodcut of

---

[54] Jacopo de' Barbari, *Portrait of Fra Luca Pacioli and his pupil*, c. 1495, oil on panel, 99 x 120 cm, Museo e Gallerie di Capodimonte, Naples. It has also been attributed to Guidobaldo da Montefeltro (?-1495). The pupil has been thought to be Guidobaldo Duke of Urbino as well as Albrecht Dürer: see Woodall (2008: 425, n. 153).

master and pupil printed in the medicine handbook written by the Italian lecturer Alessandro Achillini (*c.* 1463-1512) and printed in Venice in 1521.[55] The connection between the author and translator and the mentor and pupil portrait-type implicitly suggests the lowly status of the translator at the beginning of the sixteenth century, when he was often associated with a pupil who is learning from a master.

Figure 11.5. Jacopo de' Barbari, *Portrait of Fra Luca Pacioli and his pupil*, c. 1495, oil on panel, 99 x 120 cm, Museo e Gallerie di Capodimonte, Naples. *Su concessione del Ministero della Cultura – Museo e Real Bosco di Capodimonte.*

The representation of Girolamo Malipiero and Petrarch in the 1536 *Petrarca spirituale* printed in Venice by Francesco Marcolini complicates the relationship between the authority of the translator and that of the author. In these illustrations and in the paratext that surrounds them, the translator is not represented as an inferior pupil, but as a secondary author legitimised by Petrarch himself. Malipiero is not a translator in the strict sense, because

---

[55] Alessandro Achillini, *Alexander Achillinus de humani corporis Anatomia* (Venice: Giovanni Antonio Nicolini da Sabbio and brothers, 1521), fol. a1[r].

his work is a moralized adaptation of Petrarch's *Rerum vulgarium frag-mentia.*[56] The first woodcut on the title page of the *Petrarca spirituale* is an individual portrait of Petrarch. Around the illustration there is an inscription in Latin and Greek saying 'this is the true face of Petrarch as it was in the past', a statement that refers to the physical features engraved in the woodcut, as well as to the text that follows, which is restored by Malipiero to Petrarch's true intention. Turning the page, there is another full page woodcut. This time Petrarch is portrayed as he speaks to Malipiero. This illustration is divided in two parts: on the right are Petrarch and Malipiero at the edge of a wood; on the left is an open landscape with a path leading up to a Church.

The double portrait of Petrarch and Malipiero translates in images the dialogue printed in the front matter of the *Petrarca spirituale*, where Malipiero described an imaginary conversation with Petrarch, who gave him a mandate to moralize his verse.[57] In the dialogue, Malipiero met Petrarch's soul as it was wondering in the woods close to Arquà, Petrarch's burial place, condemned to linger in a limbo until his amorous sonnets and canzoni were emended. In the dialogue, Petrarch claimed that the first sonnet in his *Canzoniere* revealed the unholy nature of the love that animated his youthful poetry, the 'primo giovenile errore' (*RVF*, I. 3), and the sinful desire of glory and fame that led him to write poetry. Desiring to atone for his sin, in the dialogue Petrarch asked Malipiero to correct his juvenile error by moralising his poetry. This exchange between Petrarch and Malipiero recalls Dante's first canto in the *Commedia*. At the beginning of their journey, in fact, both Malipiero and Dante encountered a poetic authority coming from the afterlife to lead them towards the right path. The affinity of Dante and Malipiero's moral mission is also emphasised by the double portrait, which mirrors the opening of the editions of the *Commedia*, where Dante and Virgil are portrayed as they meet for the first time in the 'selva oscura'.[58] The Church in the background of the illustration hints towards the final destination of Malipiero's journey, which is the salvation of Petrarch's soul.

If we consider these portraits together with the printed paratext that surrounds them, it emerges that Petrarch is portrayed as the primary author.

---

[56]   Girolamo Malipiero, *Il Petrarca spirituale* (Venice: Francesco Marcolini, 1536), fols *1ʳ-1ᵛ.

[57]   'Dialogo. Di Frate Hieronymo Maripetro venetiano del sacro ordine de minori di osservanza al Petrarcha theologo et spirituale introduttivo': see Malipiero (1536: fols A2ʳ-B4ʳ).

[58]   See for example the full-page woodcut facing the opening of Dante's *Commedia* in the edition printed by Francesco Marcolini in Venice in 1544. In this illustration (fol. CC10ᵛ) Dante meets Virgil at the edge of the 'selva'.

He is the only authority visualised on the title page. Furthermore, in the double portrait, Petrarch wears a laurel as a symbol of his poetic glory and he towers over a smaller Malipiero. Petrarch is portrayed speaking, suggesting that what is written in the *Petrarca spirituale* is his own and Malipiero is an intermediary between the poet and his readers. Although Petrarch's primacy is not challenged, the double portrait and the translatorial paratext frame the authority of the translator, who is presented as a poet chosen – and therefore legitimised – by Petrarch himself. In this case, the presence of the author guarantees the authority of the translator.

In the final part of this section I will address the double portraits printed in two translations of Ariosto's *Orlando furioso*: one in Castilian and one in English. In 1553, Giolito printed in Venice the *Furioso traduzido*, a Castilian translation of Ariosto's *Furioso* composed by Jerónimo Jiménez de Urrea.[59] This edition, according to Martínez, copied the printing style originally established by Giolito for his Italian *Furioso* (1542) and it bears witness to the international appeal of this epic and to the wide reach of the Venetian book trade (Martinez 2015: 89). An important novelty of the Spanish translation is the combination of two printed portraits: one of the translator and one of Ariosto. This double portrait has a celebrative function. The shape of the medallion establishes an immediate connection with the classical heritage of both writers. Furthermore, the portrait of de Urrea and that of Ariosto are followed by a laudatory composition: a sonnet in Castilian for the first one, and a brief letter in Italian for the second one. The combination of portrait and laudatory text emulates the function of the two faces of the ancient coin: the recto/portrait individualises the person, and the verso/text characterizes him/her, thus offering a complete representation of the person portrayed.[60] Although both portraits are celebrative, Ariosto's representation emphasizes his higher poetic status in presenting him with a symbolic laurel wreath and a Roman toga. De Urrea's modern attire, compared to Ariosto's, communicates to the reader his lower poetic rank. The different status of author and translator established through the clothing is also underscored by the placement of the portraits in the book. Although the first portrait that the reader encounters is that of de Urrea, the portrait of Ariosto faces the beginning of the text, which is the core of the book. Ariosto's portrait directly mirrors his own poem, suggesting to the readers his authority and primacy. This presentation of author and translator stresses the trustworthiness of De Urrea as a cultural

---

[59] Zappella (1988: I. 134) mentions this portrait in the section of her study that deals with double portraits.

[60] Cieri Via (1989: II. 9–29) has argued that the biography in the paratext of the books performs the role of the verso of the portrait, giving an idea of the character of the person described, while the portrait individualized him through his physical features.

mediator in the movement of the book and his primary author, Ariosto, across linguistic and national borders. De Urrea is portrayed as a modern poetic figure who is closer to the intended reading public and capable of facilitating the encounter with a foreign text and its author.

The last example that I address in this section is the most closely relatable to that of Ovid and Anguillara because of the disposition of the medallion portraits on the page. The double portrait in question represents author and translator on the title page of John Harington's English translation of Ariosto's *Orlando furioso* printed in 1591, 1607 and 1634. These editions are objects of particular interest for scholars in history of book design because two surviving autograph manuscripts of Harington's translation bear witness to the translator's keen interest in details of layout, ornament and typography and to the translator's instructions to his printer Richard Field on how to make the book.[61] As shown by Simon Cauchi (1986: 140), Harington formed his design-intentions by studying Italian printed editions. An especially influential one was the 1584 de' Franceschi edition of the *Furioso* with Porro's engravings, which – as we have seen in the previous section – was also the main model for the 1584 Giunti edition of Anguillara's *Metamorfosi* (Figure 11.2).[62] In both the Italian and the English *Furioso*, the portrait of Ariosto is set on top of the doorway in a medallion held by two angels, and at the sides of the border are the free standing figures of Mars and Venus with Cupid. The major change on Harington's title page is in the lower side of the title-border. At the bottom of the doorway, the engraver of the English *Furioso*, Thomas Cookson, set the portrait of Harington in the space that was previously occupied by the printer de' Franceschi's Peace device. According to Mortimer (1996: 39) and Coldiron (2018: 60), the disposition of the translator's portrait in a central-vertical-line relation to the author's portrait subtly unsettles the primacy of the author. In the portrait, Ariosto's elevated status as established poet is foregrounded by his classical attire and laurel wreath. The position at the top of the border, as we have seen in previous portraits, is an established authorial setting in the visual arts and it also repeats the vertical axis of translation from the Italian (which holds a higher status) to the English (Coldiron 2018: 60). Furthermore, the chained dog that is gazing at Harington from the corner of the border could symbolise the translator's fidelity to his source text. This notwithstanding, we must also recognise that Ariosto's portrait is small and it has suffered from copying (Mortimer 1996:

---

[61]   The extensive biography on Harington's skills as book designer includes Cauchi (1986); Scott-Warren (2001); Armstrong (2015: 98–102).

[62]   For a comparison between the 1584 *Furioso* and Harington's title page see also Mortimer (1996: 39-40).

39). Harington's portrait, on the contrary, is bigger than Ariosto's and it is full of details, from his clothing, the Elizabethan ruff and slashed doublet, to the compass open in front of him on a table. The visual focus shifts to the larger medallion thus awarding the translator 'the pride of place and centrality' (Coldiron 2018: 60).

As in the portrait of the *Orlando furioso* 'englished' by Harington, the double portrait of Anguillara and Ovid in the 1592 edition of the *Metamorfosi* places the translator in a central-vertical-line relationship with the author (Figure 11.3). The position of the translator at the top of the border suggests an inversion of the vertical axis of translation from hierarchical language (Latin) to the lowly vernacular. Overall, however, in the double portrait the visual emphasis is on Ovid's portrait, which is closer to the page's centre and is also considerably bigger. By comparing this portrait with other sixteenth-century double portraits, we can conclude that printers and editors of Anguillara's *Metamorfosi* used this paratext to convey the affinity between Ovid and Anguillara. The double portrait emphasizes the authenticity of this translation by associating it with two writers presented as established authors, one classical and the other modern. Chartier (1992: 26–59), in *The Order of Books*, has claimed that the emergence of the portrait of the author in the book is telling of the innate tendency in print culture to put the unity of a text in the person of the author. Whether the individual portrait endows the author (or the translator) with real or symbolic attributes, says Chartier, 'the function of the author's portrait is to reinforce the notion that the writing is the expression of an individuality that gives authenticity to the work' (Chartier 1992: 52). The example of the double portrait of Anguillara and Ovid allows us to reflect upon Chartier's definition, and argue that the function of the portrait in the early modern book was to express one or more individualities that could bestow authenticity to the work. The persistence of collective and double portraits lends support to the view that the creation of the modern author-function, i.e. the social discourse through which we put the unity and meaning of a written text in the individual figure of the author, was a gradual and intermittent process.

Conclusion

This article shows the pivotal role played by the translator portraits in the canonisation of this Renaissance translation. This visual paratext to the *Metamorfosi*, in fact, foregrounds the translator following three powerful strategies. The first is to centralise the translator and his text, as happens visually on the title page of the 1584 edition of the *Metamorfosi*, where the translator-portrait is placed at the top of the doorway on the title page, projecting the authority of the translator onto the translated text. The second strategy to foreground the translator is to associate him closely with established authors. The most obvious connection shaped in the *Metamorfosi* is that with Ariosto. The 1584 individual portrait of Anguillara, for example, was designed to recall the portrait of Ariosto on the title page of the *Orlando furioso* designed by Porro. The third strategy is to present Anguillara as a new, improved, Ovid. The 1592 double portrait illustrates author and translator within the same frame, communicating their affinity and their poetical link.

12

FRANCESCA CASAMASSIMA

TRANSLATING GIOVANNI ANDREA
DELL'ANGUILLARA'S *METAMORFOSI* IN IMAGES:
AN INVESTIGATION INTO GIACOMO FRANCO'S
TEXTUAL AND ICONOGRAPHIC SOURCES

The subject of this paper is the iconographic series that decorates the
vernacular translation of Ovid's *Metamorfosi* written by Giovanni Andrea
dell'Anguillara (1517–1569) and printed by Bernardo Giunti in 1584.[1] The
author of this series is the engraver Giacomo Franco (1550–1620), who
creates, for each one of Ovid's books, a full-page illustration representing
the myths recounted there. Attention will be paid to the additions made by
the engraver and the details that show inconsistencies with the Ovidian
original: the aim is to show that Franco used Anguillara's text as the main
source for his illustrations, and completely ignored the Latin version. When
Franco created these prints, more than 20 years had already passed since the
first publication of Anguillara's translation, which in the meantime had
become a best seller *ante litteram*. The engraver's decision to rely on
Anguillara's translation therefore bears witness to the desire of the public to
see a well-known text translated into images, but it also reveals Franco's
desire to exploit the text which had become, even among artists, the major
source for the dissemination of the Ovidian myths. In some cases, however,
these prints also testify to the undeniable originality and inventiveness of the
engraver. Franco, as I aim to demonstrate in this study, draws on an
extensive figurative background to produce new iconographic inventions
that had no connection with Anguillara's text. Franco's work is not a mere
transposition of the text into images, but a reworking filtered by personal
interpretations and judgments which influences not only on the ways in
which the individual myths are represented, but also the choice of whether
or not to depict specific episodes.

The first section of this article offers a brief overview of the history of the
illustrations of Ovid's *Metamorphoses* in printed editions. Following this

[1] I would like to thank most sincerely all the reviewers, whose comments and advice have
enabled me to introduce important improvements in the study.

review are two separate sections devoted to a description and analysis of Franco's *modus operandi*. First, I analyse cases in which the illustrations show the close relation between Franco's iconographic choices and Anguillara's translation. Many of Franco's prints contain iconographic details that are absent in the Latin text and can only be found in Anguillara's version. These details are crucial because they demonstrate that the engraver had read – and worked closely with – Anguillara's text before creating his images. Furthermore, these details provide us with evidence to understand the engraver's iconographic and textual sources, and they also shed light on the texts that make up Anguillara's cultural background. Secondly, I address cases in which Franco moved away from Anguillara: the engraver often represented the myths in a different order to Anguillara (and also to Ovid), and he used iconographies that do not correspond to Anguillara's poem. These practices indicate his intention of imprinting his personal interpretation on the text and his choice of following the iconographic tradition.

The History of the Illustrations of Ovid's *Metamorphoses* in the Fifteenth and Sixteenth Centuries

In 1497, the Venetian printer Lucantonio Giunta printed the first translation of Ovid's *Metamorphoses* in the Italian vernacular. This translation was not written specifically for this edition, but it was copied from a manuscript edition of a vernacular translation written by Giovanni Bonsignori (*c.* 1375–1377).[2] Giunta's printed edition was decorated with 52 illustrations placed at the beginning of some of the chapters into which Bonsignori had divided the fifteen Ovidian books. The scholar Giulio Pasavento (2018: 109) argues that the design for these engravings was made by the illuminator Benedetto Bordon (*c.* 1450–1530), possibly helped by the anonymous Secondo Maestro del Canzoniere Grifo (fl. 1470–1510). There were probably three engravers: Jacopo da Strasburgo, recognizable by his initials *ia*, Maestro N, who signed with this letter, and an anonymous Florence master.[3] The designer made considerable use of continuous narrative, illustrating each myth through the representation of several

---

[2]   There are four complete manuscripts of this translation. With regard to the existing manuscript versions, the text published in 1497 presents additions both in the translation and in the allegories. We do not know whether these alterations were made by the curator who prepared the text for printing or whether they were already present in the antigraph used. In any case, the printed edition is a text that has very little to do with the manuscript tradition. See Bonsignori 2001: xli-xlii.

[3]   On these illustrations see also: Diaz Platas 2012: 543–30; Blattner 1998; Huber-Rebenich, Lütkemeyer and Walter 2014: 32–42.

episodes placed in sequence in the same engraving.[4] In 1522, in Venice, Niccolò Zoppino printed a vernacular translation of Ovid's *Metamorphoses* written by Niccolò degli Agostini (?–c. 1526). Though written in the sixteenth century, this translation maintained significant links with Bonsignori's medieval re-writing of Ovid's poem. In fact, as Bodo Guthmüller (2008: 219) has extensively demonstrated, Agostini did not translate directly from Ovid's Latin but re-wrote Bonsignori's prose translation in *ottava rima*, a rhyming stanza in the Italian lyrical tradition. Zoppino's 1522 edition is decorated with 72 woodcuts placed at the beginning of some of the myths. A comprehensive examination of Zoppino's series shows that, for the most part, it was not innovative but was inspired by (and heavily based upon) the series printed in Giunta's 1497 edition of Bonsignori's translation.[5]

We may observe a leap in the quality of the images in the sophisticated illustrations that decorate the 1553 edition of Lodovico Dolce's vernacular translation of Ovid's *Metamorphoses* printed by Gabriele Giolito in Venice. Thanks to Guthmüller's research, we know that the engraver of this series was the architect Giovanni Antonio Rusconi (1520–1587).[6] Unlike previous engravers and illustrators, Rusconi reduced the use of the continuous narrative and created mainly illustrations of individual scenes. Despite Rusconi's innovative compositional strategies and his superior skill in comparison with his predecessors, the series of illustrations in Giolito's edition shows some similarities with the woodcuts accompanying the previous translations of Bonsignori and Agostini. These similarities, as shown by Guthmüller (1997: 255–74), are due to the fact that Giolito commissioned the illustrations to Rusconi before Dolce had finished his translation. Consequently, Rusconi was forced to work on his illustrations using a different text from the one that would accompany his woodcuts: that of Bonsignori (Guthmüller 1997: 251–75; Capriotti 2013: 43–71). Dolce's translation, thanks also to the beautiful series of illustrations that accompanied it, was extremely successful, so much so that it was re-printed several times in the sixteenth century.[7] However, its popularity declined

---

[4]   On Bonsignori and his translation see Guthmüller 2008: 62–203; Ballistreri 1970: 407–09.

[5]   On Agostini's translation see Guthmüller 1997: 194 and Guthmüller 2008: 97–123.

[6]   On Rusconi see Guthmüller 1983: 771-79; Temanza 1966: 362–69; Cellauro 2009: 224–37; Capriotti 2013: 31–32. For an analysis of Rusconi's work see also Chapter 10 in this volume.

[7]   It was reprinted twice by Giolito, in 1553 and again in 1555, 1557, 1558, 1561. It was then printed in Venice by Francesco Sansovino in 1568 and again in the same city by Domenico Farri in 1570. On these editions and on Dolce's translation see Guthmüller 1997: 251–74; Bongi 2006: 395–401; Capriotti 2013.

notably after the publication of Anguillara's translation of Ovid's *Metamorphoses*.

In 1561, in Venice, Giovanni Griffio printed the first complete edition of Anguillara's *Metamorfosi*.[8] After this publication, Dolce's and Giolito's *Trasformationi* went out of print, while Anguillara's translation enjoyed considerable success; his *Metamorfosi* (in its complete version) was printed 29 times during the sixteenth century (Cotugno 2007: 468). Looking closely at all these editions, we can recognize eight different illustration series (Casamassima 2017: 19). All these series contain fifteen woodcuts, one for each of the books in Ovid's *Metamorphoses*. Anguillara divided his translation in fifteen books as well, so the engravers prepared one illustration for the opening of each book of the poem. The first series of illustrations can be found in the 1561 edition of Anguillara's *Metamorfosi* printed by Giovanni Griffio. This first series was never used again in its entirety, but it was partly reworked for the second series of illustrations published in 1563 in Francesco de Franceschi's edition. De Franceschi, in fact, commissioned new woodcuts for the first seven books, but re-used the woodcuts from the 1561 series of Anguillara's *Metamorfosi* for the last eight. As shown in my publication, the first seven woodcuts of the 1561 series were not lost or destroyed but were either sold or lent to the printer Francesco Sansovino, who used them in his edition of Dolce's *Trasformationi* in 1568 (Casamassima 2017: 21–22).

The 1563 series of illustrations became a model for most of the subsequent series printed in Anguillara's translations in the sixteenth century. All these series merely refer to the iconographic and compositional scheme used by the engraver of the 1563 edition, simplifying the scenes in case of the smaller format illustrations (Casamassima 2017: 26–27). A significant exception is represented by the series of illustrations printed in Bernardo Giunti's 1584 edition of the *Metamorfosi*, made by the illustrator Giacomo Franco. Whereas previous engravers of the vernacular translations had only used small images, Franco's series contains fifteen full-page copper-plates. As such, this series of engravings represents a major innovation among the illustrated *Metamorphoses*, as Franco managed to fit almost all the myths in the book within a single illustration. By building a bird's eye view, the illustrator placed one of the first myths told by Anguillara right in the foreground and put all the other stories in the book across the background, in the order in which they appear in the text. Specifically, these scenes are organized in a zig-zag fashion, between the foreground and the background, gradually decreasing in size according to the perspective. In

---

[8] On this first edition see Gentilini 1993: 75; Cotugno 2007: 482; Bucchi 2011: 125–294.

Figure 12.1. Giacomo Franco, Opening print of Book X, from G. A. dell'Anguillara, *Le Metamorfosi di Ovidio* (Venice: Bernardo Giunti, 1584).

this way, the illustration achieved the effect of representing multiple scenes occurring simultaneously across a deep spatial focus. The move from previous small illustrations to Franco's full-page style was dictated by the desire to develop an iconographic system that allowed readers to browse the many episodes and characters of the Ovidian poem more easily. This purpose is achieved by creating a mnemonic system based on *loci* and *imagines* that help the reader to follow and memorize the rather complex narration.[9] Another novelty in Franco's series is the use of inscriptions that name all the characters depicted in the plate, an addition probably made to aid the memorization of the myths by creating a figurative index (Casamassima 2017: 430–35; Tomasi Velli 2007: 103–09).

In order to understand Franco's innovative and original approach to the illustrations of the *Metamorphoses*, it is not enough to dwell on his compositional choices; we must consider his iconographic and narrative choices as well.

From Giacomo Franco to Anguillara: Iconographic and Textual sources

In the print decorating Book X, the engraver illustrates Ganymede's abduction by Jupiter (Figure 12.1). In this scene, there are two figures looking up towards Ganymede and Jupiter with their arms raised to the sky.[10] The presence of these onlookers was not mentioned in Ovid's *Metamorphoses* (Ovid, *Metamorphoses*, X. 155–60), but was added by Anguillara in his translation (X. 60).[11] Anguillara was the only Renaissance translator of the *Metamorphoses* to speak of these spectators, but he did not invent this addition outright; rather, he recovered it from a section of Virgil's *Aeneid*. In Book V, while describing the garment that was given as a prize to Cloantus, Virgil tells the story of the kidnapping of Ganymede, adding the reaction of its witnesses: 'longaevi palmas nequiquam ad sidera tendunt custodes,| saevitque canum latratus in auras' [His aged guardians in vain stretch their hands to the stars, and the savage barking of dogs rises skyward] (Virgil 1999, V. 488–89).[12] Anguillara must have known the poem

---

9   On the relation between books illustrations and the art of memory see Tomasi Velli 2007: 107–09; Bolzoni 1995: 224.

10   On this print see also Casamassima 2018: 45–49.

11   Also, in the Ikonographisches Repertorium (Huber-Rebenich, Lütkemeyer and Walter 2014: 130), we read that the presence of the two characters could be related to Anguillara's translation.

12   On this passage from the *Aeneid* see Bucchi 2001: 163–64. On the epic texts that Anguillara used as a model see Bucchi 2001: 159–77.

very well, since he translated its first two books between 1561 and 1564 (Bucchi 2001: 159–77).

Several artistic creations bear witness to the iconographic popularity of Virgil's version of the myth of Ganymede. For instance, a fourth-century AD mosaic shows, in addition to the two protagonists Jupiter and Ganymede, a shepherd who sees the abduction (Figure 12.2; Foucher 1979: 14, 155–68).

Figure 12.2. *The rape of Ganymede*, 4th century AD,
Hatay Archaeology Museum, Antiochia.

Another example is the decoration of a capital of the Basilica of Saint Mary Magdalene in Vezelay, in France, where a male character, perhaps a servant, disconcertedly watches the kidnapping while raising his arms in the air (Figure 12.3; Forsyth 1976: 241–44). Again in the first half of the fifteenth century, a *cassone* decorated with paintings inspired by the *Aeneid* and produced by the workshop of Apollonio di Giovanni features two characters raising their arms to the sky, watching Ganymede being seized by Jupiter (Figure 12.4; Marongiu 2002: 21–22).[13] At the beginning of the sixteenth century, Giovanni Battista Palumba created a woodcut in which Jupiter and Ganymede are represented in the sky, illustrated in a composition symmetrical to the one used by Franco (Morganti 2005: 7–8; Piccininni 1981: 51; Marongiu 2005: 22). Below them, some naked men observe the abduction (Figure 12.5). Another image from the first half of

[13] On *cassoni* see Gombrich 1955: 6–34.

Figure 12.3. *The rape of Ganymede*, 1120–1138,
capital of the Basilica of Saint Mary Magdalen, Vezelay.

Figure 12.4. Apollonio di Giovanni (workshop of),
The Rape of Ganymede, 1416–1465, Museum of Fine Arts, Boston.

Figure 12.5. Giovan Battista Palumba, *The rape of Ganymede*, 1505–1515, Metropolitan Museum, New York.

the sixteenth century painted on a 1544 majolica shows three male figures beneath the representation of the rape of Ganymede: one pointing upwards, one raising his arms to the sky and another with his hands joined in prayer (Figure 12.6; Ravanelli Guidotti 1985: 148–49). The last example is the representation of the myth of Ganymede in the illustrated initial 'G' (Figure 12.7) featured in the 1562 Valgrisi edition of the *Orlando furioso*.[14] This illuminated initial is part of a series of woodcuts called 'iniziali parlanti' (speaking initials) which creates an intertextual reference with mythological events. In each letter the myth of a mythological character is represented whose name begins with the same initial: for example, in Valgrisi's edition the letter G illustrates Ganymede's story (Petrucci Nardelli 1991). Depicted in this letter are three men witnessing the abduction, with one of them raising his arm to the sky, pointing at the event.

Figure 12.6. Fontana d'Urbino (workshop of), *The Rape of Ganymede*, 1544, Civic Medieval Museum, Bologna.

---

[14] On carved initials in general see: Petrucci Nardelli 1991.

Figure 12.7. Engraver of 1556, *G: Ganymede*, print from Ludovico Ariosto, *Orlando Furioso* (Venice: Vincenzo Valgrisi, 1562).

As these examples show, the illustrative tradition deriving from Virgil's version of the myth is quite firmly established. We cannot be sure that Franco saw all these illustrations, but we can hypothesize that he would at least have observed the carved initials of Ganymede printed in the *Furioso*. In fact, although from an iconographic standpoint this image is quite different from Franco's, it is possible that the engraver had seen it; he had decorated the edition of Ariosto's *Cinque canti*, a continuation of the *Furioso*, printed in Venice by Francesco de Franceschi in 1584 (Pasero 1935: 332–56).Therefore, it is plausible that he would have referred to previous illustrated editions in order to devise his personal interpretation.

As such, it is interesting to note how the figurative tradition of this myth developed through two parallel models: one borrowing from Ovid's version of the story, and the other leaning more on Virgil's. Since an iconographic scheme can originate both from its textual source and from a comparison with previous graphic representations, the presence or absence of the aforementioned characters is not enough to establish the process behind it. Furthermore, on many occasions the choice is determined above all by compositional and spatial requirements or by the meaning that the artist

Figure 12.8. Giacomo Franco, Opening print of Book XII, from G. A. dell'Anguillara, *Le Metamorfosi di Ovidio* (Venice: Bernardo Giunti, 1584).

sought to convey through his image. Undoubtedly, a case-by-case study would be necessary to understand these images fully. However, in this context it is crucial to emphasize the distinction between the two models, since Ovid's and Virgil's versions necessarily converge in Anguillara's vernacular translation.

Book XII of Ovid's *Metamorphoses* is entirely dedicated to episodes of battle inspired by the Homeric poems. In his re-writing of this book, Aguillara expanded freely on Ovid's account by using intermediary sources. Similarly, in the case of Jupiter and Ganymede, Franco's illustration unveils Anguillara's borrowing from sources other than the Ovidian text (Figure 12.8).[15] In the foreground of this illustration is the sacrifice performed by the Spartans to placate the sea and to be allowed a safe voyage to Troy (Ovid, *Metamorphoses*, XII. 1–23). Anguillara lists Menelaus, Achilles and Ulysses as participants in the rite – the very same characters represented in the illustration, as the inscriptions to their side clearly explain (1584: 422). However, Ovid only speaks of the soothsayer Calchas, and none of the translators preceding Anguillara mentioned these three characters. As for the presence of Ulysses (whom Anguillara adds to the scene) the reference could pertain to the hero's account of the aforementioned sacrifice in the *Iliad*. Even though Homer never specified whether Achilles and Menelaus attended the sacrifice, this passage in the *Iliad* (Homer, II. 185–408) mentions both repeatedly. It is possible that the Homeric poem inspired Anguillara to include these characters by giving them a physical presence in the scene.

Another interesting image in this engraving is the fight between Hector and Ajax, placed at the centre of the illustration. This episode is left unmentioned by Ovid in Book XII, but it is narrated in Book XIII (82–90), while Anguillara refers to it in Books XII (1584: 34–35) and XIII (1584: 426). This print also offers another interesting scene. Returning to the subject of the Spartan sacrifice, Franco included Ulysses in the illustration of Iphigenia's sacrifice; Ovid does not mention this, as he devotes only a few verses to this episode (24–38). Meanwhile, Anguillara speaks of Ulysses being sent to talk to Clytemnestra, Iphigenia's mother, in order to persuade her to send her daughter to the battlefield (1584: 422).[16] In describing the moment of the sacrifice itself Anguillara does not mention Ulysses' presence, but it is possible that Franco includes him in order to recall his role in the story. The figure dressed in a long gown standing behind Iphigenia may be her mother, even though Anguillara specifies that Clytemnestra did not leave with Iphigenia (1584: 422). Ulysses seems to make a gesture with his hand, as if to dissuade her from approaching her daughter. It is also possible that the figure in the long dress in front of Ulysses is not a female character at all but Calchas, who is illustrated in a similar manner in the foreground; hence, it may be that Ulysses' gesture was not directed to Calchas, but

---

[15]   On this print see also Casamassima 2018: 49–52.

[16]   None of the other translators talk about this deceit.

Figure 12.9. Giacomo Franco, Opening print of Book VII,
from G. A. dell'Anguillara, *Le Metamorfosi di Ovidio* (Venice: Bernardo Giunti, 1584).

rather to the troops standing behind him. What is certain is that Ulysses'
presence in the engraving makes us wonder about the translator's sources.
Euripides is the first to mention Iphigenia's sacrifice (*Iphigenia in Aulide*, IV.
12). In his account Ulysses is sent to take the girl, who tells her mother to
remain at home. Thus, according to the Greek tragedian, the mother should

not be present at the sacrifice, and neither should Ulysses. The only character mentioned is, in fact, the soothsayer Calchas. Hence, this version of the myth does not accord with what we see in the print.

In 1551, Dolce wrote his tragedy *Ifigenia in Aulis*. Here as well the engraving does not match the text, which specifies that Clytemnestra was not present at the sacrifice; in fact, a servant told her about the event. Besides, no mention of Ulysses is made either (Dolce 1551: III, 19–30). Notwithstanding the fact that Anguillara never mentions Ulysses' presence, the most plausible hypothesis remains that Franco read his translation and added the hero on account of his role in the story. These iconographic details inserted by Franco not only help us to confirm that the engraver had read Anguillara's text, but also draw attention to the translator's own narrative choices and his alternative personal decisions.

When moving away from Ovid's Latin poem, Anguillara did not rely exclusively on ancient poems. He also used previous vernacular translations of 'modern' poems, such as (as we will see) the works of Boccaccio. Anguillara writes that Medea gave her children gifts to take to Creusa, Jason's new wife, and that one of these presents was a chest that when opened burst into flames and set fire to Creusa's house, killing her (Anguillara 1584, VII. 244). This version is substantially different from the one told by Ovid, who only writes that Jason's wife is burned by poisons from Colchis (*Metamorphoses*, VII. 394–95). Giovanni Boccaccio's version of this myth is the most similar to Anguillara's: in his *Genealogia deorum gentilium* Boccaccio wrote that Medea gave her children a trunk (*scrineolo*) to take to Creusa and when the latter opened it she was burnt, along with all her palace.[17] Giuseppe Betussi's vernacular translation of the *Genealogie*, which was first printed in 1547 and then republished several times, rewrote this passage faithfully, translating the word *scrineolo* first as a crate (*cassetta*) and then as a chest (*arca*), exactly the same word used by Anguillara:

> Il che sopportando Medea malamente si pensò una malitia, et mandò suoi figliuoli con alcuni doni rinchiusi in una cassetta a Cassandra, sotto fintione che placassero l'ira della madrigna. La qual arca non prima fu aperta da Cassandra che subito n'uscì una grandissima fiamma che volò per tutto il palazzo reale, et insieme con Creusa tutto l'arse. (Betussi 1547: 66ʳ)[18]

The main source for this myth is Euripides, who, in his tragedy dedicated to Medea, writes that she sent her children to Creusa with a

---

[17] 'Quod cum egerrime ferret, excogitata malitia, filios suos, quasi ad placandam sibi novercam, cum donis in scrineolo clausis misit, quod a Creusa non ante apertum est, quam per omnem regiam flamma evolaverit ingens, a qua cum ipsa Creusa regia omnis exusta est' (Boccaccio 1957: 277–78).

[18] On this translation see Bucchi 2001: 166.

poisoned *peplo* (garment) (*Medea*, 1132–203). Dolce, who, a few years before Anguillara's *Metamorfosi*, had translated Euripides' tragedy, followed the Greek model faithfully (Dolce 1560: 32^v–33). Ovid's other translators such as Bonsignori evoke Euripides' version and write that Medea sent Creusa a poisoned shirt that killed her; they never mention a chest, as Betussi does (Bonsignori 2001: 349).[19] So Anguillara's source is probably the vernacular translation of Boccaccio's *Genalogia* translated by Betussi.

In his illustration of this myth, Franco shows Medea's children taking Creusa an object that resembles a chest: so there can be no doubt that Franco took his inspiration from this version (Figure 12.9).

Franco's decision to rely on Anguillara's translation rather than the Ovidian version suggests that he studied very closely the translation he was decorating. It is understandable that he would have preferred to read a vernacular text rather than the Latin original, but it is less obvious why he should have chosen Anguillara's translation. The decision to rely on the text he was decorating may show that he was aware of the difference that separates Anguillara's version not only from the Latin one, but also from the previous translations.

New Connections, Famous Models and Ancient Iconographies: Cases in Which Franco Moves Away from Anguillara

Although for the most part Franco based his illustrations on Anguillara's translation, there are some instances in which he moved away from his main source text. In this section, I analyse three different examples of Franco's inventiveness: first, prints where the myths do not appear in the order in which Anguillara (and also Ovid) told them; second, illustrations featuring anomalous iconographic details or the omission of whole myths; and third, prints in which the engraver followed the iconographic tradition rather than Anguillara's text.

Book VIII of Ovid's *Metamorphoses* begins with the narration of the myth of Scylla and Minos (VIII. 1–151). In Franco's illustration of this book, however, he subverted the chronological order and placed this myth in the background. As we can see in Figure 12.10, Franco decided to foreground the encounter between Bacchus and Ariadne, which Ovid narrates after Scylla's myth.[20] The engraver's choice was probably dictated by questions of

[19] Agostini, recalling Bonsignori, tells this story in the *Allegoria delle cose dette*. See 1538: 77^r.

[20] The design of this scene is based on Tintoretto's painting *Nozze di Bacco e Arianna, c.* 1576-77, 146 x 167 cm, oil on canvas, Palazzo Ducale, Venice. See: Huber-Rebenich, Lütkemeyer and Walter 2014: 104.

space, since it would have proven difficult to feature a seascape in the foreground. This disposition also allowed the artist to create a thematic dialogue between foreground and background, since both episodes revolve around the abandonment of a female character by a man she loves: Scylla by Minos and Ariadne by Theseus.[21] Another significant element in Figure 12.10 is the precise moment in the story of Scylla that Franco chose to represent. Previous engravers had either depicted her surveying the enemy army from her tower or had portrayed the moment in which she gave Minos a lock of hair belonging to her father; this latter scene, for example, was chosen by Rusconi and the unknown engraver who decorated the 1561 edition of Anguillara's translation. Franco decided to illustrate the most tragic moment in the abandonment: when Scylla leaps into the sea in an attempt to reach her beloved. From this choice, we infer his desire to draw attention to the subject of abandonment in order to underscore the parallelism with the episode in the foreground.

The creation of parallelisms within an illustration is a feature of Franco's *modus operandi* that we also find in other prints. In Book IV, in the foreground he depicts the double suicide of two unfortunate lovers, Pyramus and Thisbe (Figure 12.11). In the background we see the double suicide of Ino, who threw herself and her son off a cliff in order to escape from her husband (Ovid, *Metamorphoses*, IV. 416–543). Though it is Minyas's three daughters (the Minyades) who tell the myth of Pyramus and Thisbe, they only appear in the background, to the right. The moving episode of the two unfortunate lovers is thus given centre stage, which also strengthens the connection with Ino's suicide. In this way, the terrace from where the Minyades tell their myths dominates the representation of the stories of Pyramus and Thisbe, the stories of Clytia and Leucothea and the union of Salmacis and Hermaphroditus.[22] Above all, Figure 12.11 emphasizes the engraver's attention not only to the compositional aspects of the image but also to the narrative ones, suggesting that Franco's work was not a mere transposition of myths, but involved much more critical attention. Franco rewrote and reworked the text that he was reading, thus creating new connections and meanings and overstepping the narrative sequence designed by Ovid and then by Anguillara.

---

[21] Claudia Cieri Via also highlighted this detail in her lecture at the international conference 'Galassia Ariosto: Il modello editoriale del *Furioso* dal libro illustrato al web' organized by the Scuola Normale Superiore di Pisa on 26 and 27 May 2016. See also Bondi 2017: 344.

[22] On the decision to place the Minyades in this part of the print see also Bondi 2017: 336.

Figure 12.10. Giacomo Franco, Opening print of Book VIII, from G. A. dell'Anguillara, *Le Metamorfosi di Ovidio* (Venice: Bernardo Giunti, 1584).

In Figure 12.11, the only myth missing among the ones told by the Minyades is the one concerning Mars and Venus, which was frequently depicted in the early modern age and in the previous editions of the *Metamorphoses*. This exclusion takes us to what is the second focus of this section, namely the cases in which the use of anomalous iconographic details and at times the omission of entire myths seem to indicate a willingness on the engraver's part to offer his personal interpretation or even his judgement on the story. Both the engravers who decorated Bonsignori's and Agostini's translations depict the scene in which Vulcan discovers that Venus was deceiving him with Mars and imprisons them both in a mesh. Anguillara dedicated great attention to this story, even more so than Ovid had done in his text. In

Figure 12.11. Giacomo Franco, Opening print of Book IV, from G. A. dell'Anguillara, *Le Metamorfosi di Ovidio* (Venice: Bernardo Giunti, 1584).

addition, Anguillara (1584: 117) charged the tale with erotic references, particularly the finale:

> 162
> E vi fu più d'un Dio giovane, e forte,
> Che de la ignuda Dea venne in desire'
> [...]
> 164
> À preghi d'ambedue Mercurio sciolse,
> Il ben disposto Dio, la bella Dea,
> E gran piacer di lei toccando tolse,
> Mentre la rete intorno le svolgea.
> Ella vergogna havea, pur gli occhi volse,
> Et al guardo, et al toccar, ch'egli facea,
> S'accorse (e piacer n'hebbe) del desio,
> Ch'era nato di lei ne l'altro Dio.

Franco may well have preferred to omit such a provocative episode, which required the representation of the naked bodies of the two gods: indeed, the depiction of nudity is something the engraver seems to avoid as much as possible.[23] For this passage, the translator summarized the *Ars amandi* (Ovid, *Metamorphoses*, II. 561–88), reproducing the most suggestive details – which may have increased the distaste of our 'chaste' artist still further (Bucchi 2001: 245).

In the print decorating the fourth book, Franco omitted other two frequently depicted episodes, both featuring Perseus as the protagonist: the fight against Medusa, and the rescue of Andromeda from the sea monster. Again, all the engravers who worked on previous illustrated editions had included both these episodes, with the sole exception of Rusconi. If in the case of Andromeda's scene perhaps one could attribute the omission to modesty on the engraver's part, it is harder to deduce why he also decided to leave out the killing of the Gorgon. In any case, it is interesting that these two tales, along with the story of Venus and Mars, were the ones that Rusconi omitted as well.

The second book features an image at the top showing Jupiter on his eagle while casting thunderbolts at Phaethon and letting him fall to his death (Figure 12.12). The eagle's head is turned towards its master, appearing to grasp his arm with its beak. As the myth never even mentions this creature, we know that the representation of the gesture did not

---

[23] On the moralizing intent conveyed by Franco in his representation of the myths, see also Bondi 2017: 340–44.

Figure 12.12. Giacomo Franco, Opening print of Book II,
from G. A. dell'Anguillara, *Le Metamorfosi di Ovidio* (Venice: Bernardo Giunti, 1584).

originate from Ovid.[24] More probably, the engraver produced an interpretation inspired by iconographic models that represent the eagle in profile, semi-turned towards Jupiter. For instance, this model can be found in Nicolas Beatrizet's engraving derived from a drawing made by Michelangelo for Tommaso de' Cavalieri (Hirst 1993: 155–58).[25] Nevertheless, in neither image does the eagle seem to want to grasp Jupiter's arm, as it appears to do in Franco's print. This might suggest the artist's desire either to mitigate or reprimand Jupiter's cruel action through the intervention of the eagle, but there is not enough substantiated evidence to back up this interpretation. What is certain is that this deviation from Michelangelo's model demonstrates that Franco felt free to reinvent his own models, introducing details deriving from his personal artistic sensitivity and not just from previous iconographic and textual models.

Another significant and interesting choice made by Franco is his decision to devote the illustration of Book IX entirely to Hercules' adventures, even though they are barely mentioned by Ovid and Anguillara (Figure 12.13). The clash between Hercules and Achelous to win Deianira's affection, exhaustively narrated by Ovid, appears in the foreground of Franco's illustration. Behind are scenes representing Hercules and Atlas, Hercules against Antaeus, and Hercules fighting the Hydra. These episodes, hardly mentioned by Anguillara, lack an iconographic tradition in the previous illustrated editions, where the engravers focused mainly on Deaianira's kidnapping by Nessus and on Hercules' fight with Antaeus. To illustrate this particular fight, Franco applied the same iconographic scheme used by the engraver of Bonsignori's translation to portray the fight between Hercules and Achelous. In the image, the hero raises the giant off the ground to prevent him touching the Earth from where he draws his energy (Figure 12.14).

Giving a wide 'narrative space' to Hercules allowed the engraver to exclude two myths which were extensively covered by Ovid and Anguillara, but which Franco may have considered indecent: the incestuous feelings of Byblis for her brother Caunus, resolved with her flight after her rejection by the young man (Ovid, *Metamorphoses*, IX. 442–665), and the story of the Sapphic love between Iphis and Ianthe, which concludes with the metamorphosis of Iphis from female to male (Ovid, *Metamorphoses*, IX.

---

[24] The eagle is not even mentioned in the text because in the *Metamorphoses* it represents only one of the possible transformations by Jupiter, not one of his attributes: therefore, the presence of the god excludes that of the bird.

[25] See Bianchi 1990: 2–9.

Figure 12.13. Giacomo Franco, Opening print of Book IX,
from G. A. dell'Anguillara, *Le Metamorfosi di Ovidio* (Venice: Bernardo Giunti, 1584).

Figure 12.14. Series of 1497, Hercules and Achelous, from G. Bonsignori, *Ovidio Metamorphosesos vulgare* (Venice: Lucantonio Giunta, 1497).

666–797).[26] This latter myth adds a further fascinating element to our investigation: not only is Anguillara's version of the story longer than Ovid's, but he made it far more lascivious, ending it with a description of Iphis and Ianthe's wedding night rather than stopping the tale at their marriage as does Ovid (1584, IX. 351).[27] As has already been demonstrated, Franco had certainly read Anguillara's translation;[28] perhaps he was reluctant to represent it visually. On the other hand, the myths of Byblis and Caunus and of Iphis and Ianthe rarely received visual interpretations. Iphis's myth is never represented in monumental art and Agostini's edition is the only one among the Italian translations of *Metamorphoses* that includes both these tales; but they figure inthe 1557 edition of the *Illustrations de La Métamorphose d'Ovide figure*, whose illustrations are also used in the epigrams by Gabriello Simeoni, published in 1559 (Capriotti, Casamassima 2020: 203-207).

---

[26] On the myths of Byblis and Iphis in general, see: Fletcher 2001: 18–9; Pintabone 2002: 253–85; Karmen 2012: 21–26.

[27] See Bucchi 2001: 247-48.

[28] The presence of the warrior at the left corner of the fence shows that Giacomo Franco read Anguillara. See: Huber-Rebenich, Lütkemeyer and Walter 2014: 118.

Figure 12.15. Giacomo Franco, Opening print of Book XIV,
from G. A. dell'Anguillara, *Le Metamorfosi di Ovidio* (Venice: Bernardo Giunti, 1584).

The last case concerns the prints in which the iconographic details find no precedent, either in the Ovidian story or in Anguillara's translation. An interesting example is found in the print at the opening of Book XIV (Figure 12.15). In the middle of this illustration we see Ulysses blinding the cyclops

Polyphemus. This mythological episode is not cited by Ovid and is given only three verses by Anguillara (1584: 65), even though it circulated widely in the illustrations of editions of the *Metamorphoses* after Bonsignori's (2001: 626–27). Agostini, who wrote his translation after Bonsignori, also decided to give space to this story (1522: XIV, c. xv). Dolce does not mention the episode, but it is represented by Rusconi. So, since Anguillara mentions it in passing, it is likely that Franco turned to the iconographic sequences decorating previous vernacular translations. We see a similar case in the print opening Book XIII, which depicts Ajax's suicide (Figure 12.16).

Figure 12.16. Giacomo Franco, Opening print of Book XIII, from G. A. dell'Anguillara, *Le Metamorfosi di Ovidio* (Venice: Bernardo Giunti, 1584).

In the background of this full-page illustration, the hero is seen throwing himself on his sword, which is inserted in the ground. Neither Ovid nor his Renaissance translators, including Anguillara, mention Ajax falling on his sword. The only uncertainty among the translators concerns Bonsignori, who tells the tragic end of the hero in a somewhat ambiguous way, saying that Ajax, trying to strike himself, 'Si ferì per superbia se stesso, ed andando um poco sì cadde' [He wounded himself out of pride, and upon stumbling slightly, eventually fell] (Bonsignori 2001: 584).[29] However, this verse does not explain the dynamic of the suicide in detail, so it is more likely that Franco's iconography originates from a different source. What emerged from my research is that all the engravers, including Franco, showed Ajax intentionally falling on his sword. Particularly, in the woodcut accompanying Agostini's translation (1522: XIII, TV), we specifically see the hero grasping the blade with one hand, in exactly the same way as in Franco's engraving (Figure 12.17). Is there any way of determining where this iconography originates? This is how Sophocles, in his tragedy *Ajax*, describes the hero committing suicide by throwing himself on his sword, rammed into the ground up to the hilt, the tip of the blade pointing upwards:

> a gift of Hector, the acquaintance I most hated, and whose sight I most detested; it stands in the enemy soil of Troy, newly sharpened with a whetstone that cuts away the iron, And I have planted it there with care, so that it may loyally help me to a speedy death [...] Ajax falls upon his sword. (Sophocles 1994, 107. 819–65)

Figure 12.17. Engraver of 1522, Ajax's suicide, print from Niccolo degli Agostini, *Tutti gli libri de Ovidio Metamorphoseos tradutti dal litteral in verso vulgar con le sue allegorie in prosa* (Venice: Niccolo Zoppino, 1522).

[29] Translated into English by the author.

The description matches our images. However, it seems unlikely that the engravers would have read Sophocles' tragedy: more probably, they drew their inspiration from an illustration of this text. In Ancient Greece and Etruria, for example, Ajax's suicide was a recurring visual theme (Touchefeu 1981: 335). The earliest evidence comes from a seventh-century BC carved stone, showing the hero throwing himself on his sword (Figure 12.18; Touchefeu 1981: 329). In Greece, we also find a metope of the Temple of Hera Argiva, by Paestum, where the hero's suicide is represented in the same way (Figure 12.19; Touchefeu 1981: 131).

Figure 12.18. Ajax's suicide, 7th century BC, carved stone, Metropolitan Museum of Art, New York.

Figure 12.19. Ajax's suicide, 6th century BC, metope, National Archaeological Museum, Paestum.

Other Greek examples include two vases that do not feature exactly the same iconography but clearly reflect the subject's popularity. The first one, an Attic amphora, depicts Ajax in the process of inserting the sword in the ground before using it to end his life (Figure 12.20; Touchefeu 1981: 329);

Figure 12.20. Exékias, Ajax's suicide, 540 BC, Attic amphora, Municipal Museum, Bologna.

in the second one, a *lekythos* from 460 BC, we see the hero kneeling in front of his weapon moments before his death (Figure 12.21; Touchefeu 1981: 329). The last Greek example is found in the detail of a terracotta altar, in which the traditional iconography returns: the hero immolates himself on his sword (Figure 12.22; Touchefeu 1981: 331). The last two artefacts we examined are Etruscan in origin: the oldest is a carved *kantharos* from the fifth century BC (Figure 12.23), the first of a series of gems depicting the subject of Ajax's suicide (Touchefeu 1981: 329). The other one is a fourth century BC krater, depicting the hero slumped over his sword as the weapon pierces his ribs from side to side (Figure 12.24) (Touchefeu 1981: 330). The compositional scheme of these testimonies, which is reflected in

Figure 12.21. Alkimachos Painter(?), Ajax's suicide, 460 BC, lekythos, Antikenmuseum, Basilea.

sixteenth-century engravings, suggests that this iconography survived
through the Middle Ages until the Renaissance. Revived by the engraver of
the translation of 1497, it gave rise to the iconographic formula used in
printed texts from then until the eighteenth century.

Figure 12.22. Ajax's suicide, 530 bc, terracotta altar, Ny Carlsberg Glypothek,
Copenhagen.

Figure 12.23. Ajax's suicide, 5th
century BC, beetle, British
Museum, London.

Figure 12.24. Ajax's suicide, 4th century BC,
crater, British Museum, London.

Conclusions

This cross-referenced and synchronous study of Anguillara's text and of its
decorative iconography sheds light both on Franco's *modus operandi* and on
his engagement with multiple secondary sources. Franco's relationship with
Anguillara's translation, in fact, although primary, was by no means

exclusive: Franco worked on Anguillara's text with considerable autonomy, distancing himself from it when he felt the need or desire to do so. The engraver demonstrates his familiarity with the iconographic tradition and with previous illustrations of Ovid's *Metamorphoses*; his depictions of the blinding of Polyphemus and Ajax's suicide, for example, are indebted to the illustrations printed in Bonsignori's translation. However, Franco seems in particular to have studied and rethought Rusconi's woodcut series: not so much in terms of the iconographic schemes that he reproduced in his copperplates, but in response to the decisions made by Rusconi on the choice of myths to represent. As we have seen, Franco omitted the same episodes that Rusconi had already avoided, such as Nessus and Deianira, Andromeda and Perseus, the killing of Medusa, Iphis and Ianthe, Byblis and Caunus. These choices suggest that although Dolce's translation may have quickly lost its appeal, the same cannot be said of its series of illustrations, whose influence endured beyond the translation's lifetime. In some of these cases, Franco may have also decided to ignore certain episodes for personal reasons, applying a sort of self-censorship of the stories he considered licentious or of those that would have required the representation of nudes. Franco also demonstrates that he relied on the iconographic tradition on the occasions in which it was most innovative, as in the case of Ajax's suicide – an extraordinary example of the rebirth of Antiquity through Ovidian prints. In any case, Franco looked critically at his own models, feeling free to modify them in accordance with his artistic sensitivity, as is the case of the representation of Jupiter and the eagle. In the end, then, we can say that Franco made a critical interpretation of Anguillara's text: just as the translator transformed Ovid's poem through his vernacular translation, so Franco renewed Anguillara's version through the reworking of secondary textual and iconographic sources.

13

ANDREA TORRE

THE IMITATION GAME:
THE TRANSLATION AND RE-USE OF OVIDIAN TEXTS
AND IMAGES IN THE SIXTEENTH CENTURY

> Some are transformed just once
> And live their whole lives after in that shape
> Others have a facility
> For changing themselves as they please.
>
> (Ted Hughes, *Tales from Ovid*)

Furious metamorphoses

How are the Italian vernacular translations of Ovid's *Metamorphoses* represented visually in the illustrations printed in sixteenth-century editions of these works? In the cases in which an iconographic apparatus was created *ex novo* for a printed edition, what kind of dialogue is established between the source text, the translated text and its translation into images? What were the criteria that presided over the appropriation of iconographic material from editions of Ludovico Ariosto's *Orlando furioso* and their re-use in illustrated editions of the vernacular *Metamorphoses*? More generally, is it possible to identify the elements through which the illustrations of *Orlando furioso* and the *Metamorphoses* were actually performed as iconographical models? And how do the memory of the images and the memory of Ariosto's poem interact?

By trying to answer these questions, this essay aims to investigate how and why Ariosto's *Orlando furioso* exerted a decisive influence on the Italian translations of Ovid's *Metamorphoses* during the sixteenth century, a time when both poems enjoyed great popularity and were widely read.[1]

---

[1]   In 1522, Nicolò degli Agostini's *Tutti gli libri de Ovidio Metamorphoseos* was published in Venice. Interestingly, the packaging of the volume bears a striking resemblance to the one used a few years later by the same publisher, Nicolò Zoppino, for the first complete illustrated edition of *Orlando furioso* in 46 cantos (1536). In 1530 Zoppino also printed an illustrated edition of the 40-canto version. In 1584, two Venetian printers published

The Renaissance genre theory attributed a great privileged *auctoritas* to Ariosto's poem: its romance elements and its literary features were praised by the scholars G. B. Pigna and G. B. Giraldi Cinzio, and the work was staunchly defended against accusations of being a failed attempt to reshape classical epics (Javitch 1991).[2] Taking inspiration from Ovid's technique of myth-making and storytelling, displayed by the Latin poet in his *Metamorphoses*, Ariosto learned to weave his own masterpiece of fictional realism. Consequently, *Orlando furioso* became a lens through which Ovid's poem necessarily had to be read (and seen).[3]

The enormous success of Ariosto's *Orlando furioso* from the moment of its first appearance in 1516 in Ferrara by the printer Giovanni Mazzocchi, and the general acclamation of its definitive version, published (also in Ferrara) in 1532 by Francesco Rosso of Valenza, profoundly affected the cultural life of the epoch. *Orlando furioso* was a 'bestseller' all over Europe (as is reflected in the speed with which it was translated into French by Jean Martin [1544], into Spanish by Jerónimo Urrea [1549-1550] and finally into English by John Harington [1591]), which went on to influence other literary and figurative traditions. Furthermore, over the centuries *Orlando furioso* has fostered a large and varied set of cultural practices, from refined literary elaborations and lavish entertainments for the courts of Europe (parties, ballets, games, melodramas) to expressions of 'popular' culture (poetry improvisations, public recitations, and the eternally popular puppet show). As happened with Tasso's *Gerusalemme liberata*, *Orlando furioso* rapidly passed beyond the literary confines of its genre; while it maintained an audience of cultivated readers who were captivated by its classical and rhetorical erudition, over the years and through many changes in taste it also attracted a broader public of less cultivated readers (Roggero 2006). For

---

both the last original illustrated edition of Ariosto's poem (De Franceschi) and the precious reprint of Giovanni Andrea dell'Anguillara's *Metamorfosi d'Ovidio* (Giunti). The two books feature the same type of iconographic apparatus: there are chalcographic plates which take up the whole page and represent the entire content of a canto through the laws of perspective. Lodovico Dolce's *Trasformationi* appeared between those two dates. First published in 1553, this work was reprinted six times by Gabriele Giolito de' Ferrari: the publisher had announced his forthcoming publication of a vernacular translation in *ottava rima* of Ovid's *Metamorphoses* as early as in his 1551 edition of *Orlando furioso*.

2   Daniel Javitch (1991) has demonstrated the importance of Ariosto's poem as a model for the translation into the vernacular of the classics. Furthermore, he has shown how translations of vernacular texts, Ovid's *Metamorphoses* in the first place, set in motion the process of *Orlando furioso*'s 'canonization'.

3   On the vernacular translations of Ovid in the sixteenth century and their relationships with Ariosto's *Orlando furioso* see: Guthmüller 1981, Looney 1996, Guthmüller 1997, Guthmüller 2009, Bucchi 2011.

instance, the popularity of the *Furioso* encouraged the publication of a vast number of illustrated editions. The series of illustrations eventually left the page to influence the visual and performing arts (Bolzoni 2014). The publication of the *Furioso* also sparked an intense theoretical debate over the literary canon of modernity and triggered renewed interest in the poem's medieval romance tradition (Rivoletti 2015). A series of *Furioso*'s sequels and spin-offs were published, and the work even exerted a significant influence, in terms of narrative and formal structure, on vernacular translations of ancient epic.

For example, every Italian translator of the *Metamorphoses* into the vernacular referred not only to the linguistic and stylistic pattern of Ariosto's poem, but also to its publishing pattern (Javitch 1991: 71-86). The print layout of the vernacular translations of Ovid usually resembles the format of chivalric poems, and their sets of illustrations also have much in common with those of chivalric poems, as they often echo the iconographic devices conceived to illustrate *Orlando furioso*.[4] In the workshops of different printers, a parallel history evolved showing a mirroring between the two works that sometimes is due only to principles of formal and typographical economy, but in some cases underlines (or reveals) a duplication of the narrative material between the *Furioso* and the vernacular editions of the *Metamorphoses*. Sometimes the two stories are illustrated in a sort of competitive mimesis of the narrative content; in other cases, a few episodes (or just one) have been selected in order to proleptically guide the reading and memorization of the text; finally, there is the suggestion that the printer decided not to create woodcuts *ex novo* to specifically represent a text but to reuse moulds created for iconographic sets of similar episodes. Investigating the ways in which the stories of Ovid's intricate plot were read, selected, and re-elaborated in their trans-codification in a new language and in the illustrative sets has proved vital to sketch not only the selection criteria and their ideological premises, but also the possible alterations of the narrative substance and their subtle meanings. In this way, the manners in which the poem's memory was conveyed through the illustrations can be appreciated. Every single image contained in a printed edition of the *Metamorphoses* had to be carefully analysed, and considered as a component of an articulate system made up of a number of paratextual components (prefatory letters, commentaries, allegories, tables of contents, indexes, etc.): by doing so, it would be possible to understand that those illustrations are not only a *narratio per figuras* of the fiction, but also a response by images to the

---

[4] On the illustrated editions of Ariosto's *Orlando furioso* see: Bolzoni 2010, 2014 and 2017; Rossi–Caracciolo 2014.

contemporary critical debate. In other words, the images looked at the words of the Poet and of the critic alike.

This article will thus analyse some significant visual specimens in order to illustrate the complex dialogue between the following elements: the Ovidian thematic and stylistic hypotext, Ariosto's reuses of Ovid's text (that is to say, Ariosto's Ovidian intertext), and finally, the hypertexts of the vernacular translations of Ovid modelled on Ariosto's *Orlando furioso*. Three paradigmatic examples will be given. The first one attests to the persistence of a specific iconographic pattern throughout the history of illustration of Ariosto's *Cinque canti* (i.e., Ariosto's sequel of *Orlando furioso*) and Ovid's poems; the second concerns the presence, both in *Metamorphoses* and in *Orlando furioso*, of some narrative themes paralleled by corresponding figurative motifs; the last one demonstrates that the Renaissance cultural model of book illustration (and specifically the model of *Furioso*) continued to exert a long-lasting influence in the following centuries.

The cutting of Erysichthon

The first example which will be examined shows how Ariosto's *Cinque canti* were translated into images in some illustrated editions across the centuries.[5] These editions are highly representative of Ovid's textual and iconographic influence on Ariosto's work as well as of Ariosto's influence on the vernacular translations of Ovid's great poem. The figurative apparatus of the second canto, for instance, is characterized by a recurring iconographic detail which clearly testifies to the persistence of a literary motif in both Ariosto and Ovid (and in other authors as well). In order to understand this, it is useful to look at the xylography printed in the first edition of the sequel published in 1548 by the Venetian printer Gabriele Giolito (Figure 13.1).

---

[5]   Over the years the interest of the scholars in Ariosto's *Cinque canti* focused mainly on its genealogical relationship with *Furioso* and underlined the strongly dramatic tone of the representation of the chivalric world offered by the *Five cantos* which is very far from that of *Orlando furioso*. Moreover, the status of the *Five cantos* was perceived as problematic soon after its *editio princeps* by the Venetian printer Aldo Manuzio (1546). Was it the draft of a new poem that was supposed to fill out and continue the story narrated in the *Furioso*? Was it conceived as poetic material that Ariosto would have placed here and there in the poem if he had had the time to do so? Was it a more or less cohesive and complete group of stanzas that was supposed to be attached at the end of *Furioso*? The debate is a lively one because the history of the *Five cantos* became not just a real editorial history, but also a history of book illustration. For a critical introduction to Ariosto's *Cinque Canti* see: Saccone 1965; Segre 1966: 121–77; Padoan 1975; Beer 1987: 141–67; Quint 1996; Zatti 1997; Sangirardi 2006: 218–29. On the illustrated editions of this work see Torre 2014.

PER LA RVBELLIONE ET MOVIMENTI DI TANTI PREN=
cipi contra Carlo comprendesi, che le piu uolte il 'ospetto è cagion di muouere altrui crudelissime guerre. Per Carlo, che uaa trouare i nimici nei ,pprij dominij, dimostr .si la prudenza di saggio Re;i quale, quanto puo, sempre tiè lontana la guerra dil ,pprio regno. Per Cano finalmête si dinotano le astutie degli inuidi & traditori.

CANTO SECONDO.

Figure 13.1. The defeat of the Longobard army in Mortara and Carlo Magno's cutting down of a sacred tree in the Bohemian forest. Ludovico Ariosto, Cinque canti II (Venice: Gabriele Giolito, 1550), fol. 277r, Ferrara, Biblioteca comunale Ariostea, E 3. 1.

This edition of Ariosto's *Cinque canti* is characterized by the same editorial pattern already adopted by Giolito as early as 1542, which is also the same editorial pattern reused in 1553 for Dolce's *Trasformationi*. Of the four images that accompany the canto, the second, third, and fourth ones already appeared in Luigi Pulci's *Morgante maggiore*, printed in Venice in 1546 by Comin da Trino. While in the *Morgante* the second engraving represented the episode of Canto XI in which Rinaldo, Orlando, and Ricciardetto (on the left side) save Astolfo from the gallows (on the right side), in the second of the *Cinque canti* the same image illustrates two different scenes of the narrative sequence. From left to right, we can see the depiction of the defeat of the Longobard army in Mortara, followed by Charlemagne's cutting down of a sacred tree in the Bohemian forest, which had been enchanted by evil powers so as to prevent the imperial army from passing through. The two parts of the illustration intend to celebrate Charlemagne by emphasizing both his ability to react promptly to the insubordination of the people and his Christian faith, which granted him immunity to any superstition or evil force.

Both the literary account of the episode of the Bohemian forest and its visual representation, made by the reuse of a typographic matrix taken from Pulci's *Morgante maggiore*, recall a passage in Book VIII of Ovid's *Metamorphoses*, in which Erysichthon profanes a place consecrated to Ceres and her nymphs:

Ille etiam Cereale nemus violasse securi
dicitur et lucos ferro temerasse vetustos.
Stabat in his ingens annoso robore quercus,
una nemus; vittae mediam memoresque tabellae
sertaque cingebant, voti argumenta potentis.
Saepe sub hac Dryades festas duxere choreas,
saepe etiam manibus nexis ex ordine trunci
circuiere modum [...]

(Ovid, *Metamorphoses*, VIII. 741–48)[6]

[He also is reported to have hewn in wicked wise | The grove of Ceres and to fell her holy woods, which aye | There stood in it a warry oak which was a wood alone. | Upon it round hung fillets, crowns and tables many one, | The vows of such as had obtained their heart's desire. Full oft | The woodnymphs underneath this tree did fetch their frisks aloft, | And often times with hand in hand they danced in a round | About the trunk.][7]

Né mai Diana, né mai ninfa alcuna,
né Pane mai, né satir, né Sileno
si venne a ricrear a l'ombra bruna
di questo bosco di spavento pieno;
ma scelerati spirti et importuna
religion quivi dominio avieno,
dove di sangue human a Dei non noti
si facean empi sacrifici e voti.

(Ariosto, *Cinque canti*, 1997 : II. 102)

[Nor did Diana, or any Nymph, or Pan, or Satyr, or Silenus ever come to play in the dark shadow of this fearful wood; but wicked spirits and ill-starred superstition had dominion there, where impious rites and sacrifices of human blood were made to gods unknown][8]

As we can read in *Metamorphoses*, Erysichthon unleashes his destructive fury on a huge oak, which is in fact a nymph metamorphosed. Afraid of committing sacrilege, Erysichthon's servants refuse to cut down the tree, while he starts to strike the trunk violently. Neither the complaints of the humanized oak nor the blood flowing from the wounds stop the fury of Erysichthon, who even cuts off the head of a servant unwilling to strike the sacred tree.

---

[6] Throughout the article, all the quotations from Ovid's *Metamorphoses* are taken from Pietro Bernardini Marzolla's edition (1979).

[7] Throughout the article, translations in English of Ovid's *Metamorphoses* are taken from the Penguin edition of Golding's sixteenth-century translation (Golding 2002, VIII. 927–35).

[8] Throughout the article, translations in English of Ariosto's *Cinque canti* are taken from Firpo's edition (Ariosto 1996, II. 102: 165).

The episode of Erysichthon is translated by the Venetian writer Lodovico Dolce in his *Trasformationi* (XVIII. 30–35). First published in 1553, this work was reprinted six times by Gabriele Giolito, who, already in his 1551 edition of the *Furioso*, was informing his readers of the forthcoming publication of a vernacular translation in *ottava rima* of Ovid's *Metamorphoses*:

> perché niuna cura è in noi maggior che di giovare alli studiosi delle buone lettere et a gli amatori della lingua volgare, speriamo di darvi similmente fra pochi mesi le dilettevoli Trasformationi d'Ovidio, tradotte dal sovradetto Dolce in questa ottava rima. (Ariosto 1555: 255ᵛ)

> since no care is greater in ourselves than that of pleasing the connoisseurs of literature and those who love the vernacular, we hope to provide you in like manner in the space of a few months Ovid's delightful *Transformatione*, translated by the abovementioned Dolce in the same *ottava rima*.

By mentioning 'a vernacular translation in *ottava rima*', Giolito reveals the literary and publishing project of embodying the formal, thematic, and functional characteristics of the highly esteemed epics of Antiquity, especially Ovid's masterpiece, in the modern poetry of *Furioso*. The literary style of Dolce's translation is in fact deeply grounded in the narrative and authorial solutions created by Ariosto. Therefore, in the vernacular version of Ovid, we again find the use of *entrelacement*, which transforms the 15 books of *Metamorphoses* into the 30 cantos of the *Trasformationi*; and we also find the imitation of Ariosto's pattern with the moralized beginning and the interruption at the end of each canto. The elevation of *Orlando furioso* to the rank of a classic and the fact that the vernacular translations of Ovid drew heavily on literary forms and functions typical of Ariosto's work help the Renaissance reader of Dolce's *Trasformationi* to accept without any qualms the anachronistic allusions to modern characters such as Orlando, Marfisa, and Bradamante in the Ovidian stories. We can find interesting examples in Canto V and XVI of the *Trasformationi*:

> Mentre [Cadmo] serba la via, ch'al fonte viene,
> Ne l'altro Canto ad ascoltar v'aspetto,
> Nel qual io vi verrò forse contando
> Prove, che tal mai ne fece Orlando
>
> (Dolce 1555, V. 82. 5–8)

> [While Cadmus walks the path that leads to the spring, I will wait for you to listen to me in the next canto, in which I will tell you of feats even greater than those accomplished by Orlando.][9]

> La qual non men gagliarda era che bella,

---

[9]   All translations of Dolce's *Trasformationi* are my own.

E forse può agguagliar la fama vostra,
Marfisa e Bradamante, onde si vanta
L'età di Carlo; e detta era Atalanta
(Dolce 1555, XVI. 24. 5–8)

[She was as strong as she was beautiful and her fame parallels that enjoyed by
Marfisa and Bradamante in the age of Carlo: her name was Atalanta.]

Dolce's version of Erysichthon's episode offers an interesting example of
textual and iconographic, stylistic and editorial 'dubbing'[10] of Ovid's poem
(i.e., a complex appropriation and re-elaboration of its content and its
narrative style) through the editorial model of *Orlando furioso*:

Sprezzator de gli dèi fu Erisittone
tanto, ch'a nessun Dio rendeva onore:
e mettendo da parte ogni ragione,
avea sì folle e temerario il core
che in un antico bosco il ferro pone
di Cerere, com'uom senza timore,
dove una quercia era d'estrema altezza,
e d'una incomparabile grossezza.

[…]

Era l'altezza sopra naturale,
che tanto soprastava a l'altre piante,
quanto a gli alberi l'erba è disuguale,
ma ciò non mosse l'empio et arrogante:
anzi, com'uom ch'avea l'animo quale
altro giamai non ebbe, o poscia od ante,
comanda che la taglino i suoi servi
sì che memoria più non se ne servi.
Ma vedendo, che quei n'avean risguardo,
giudicando tal opera profana:
"Poi che ciascun di voi trovo infingardo",
disse con mente temeraria e insana,
"voglio alquanto provar s'io son gagliardo,
o pur se la mia forza anco sia vana.
Così se Cerere in questa si trovasse,
ch'io farei che sozzopra ella n'andasse".
Stupiro i servi, e alcun prese ardimento
di chiamar l'opra iniqua e disonesta.
Ma il poverin, mentre a vietarla è intento,
fu colpito da l'empio ne la testa,
e cadde su 'l terren di vita spento.

---

[10]   On this theoretical approach to the phenomenon of rewriting see Conte 2012: 178.

Questo ritorna, e di colpir non resta,
quando una voce uscì del legno fuore,
che parole formò di tal tenore.

(Dolce 1561, XVIII. 30–35)

[Erysichthon despised the gods so much that he did not worship any of them: he was so brave and so foolish that, laying reason aside, he brandished his sword against an ancient wood sacred to Ceres, where there stood an oak of great height and exceptional size. // [...] It was of supernatural height, so much taller than the other trees as trees are if compared to grass. But that did not deter the arrogant and impious man: his soul was unlike that of any other man that ever existed or ever will exist, and so he ordered his servants to cut down the tree, so that its memory would be lost forever. // But seeing that they hesitated because they deemed the deed to be profane, the daring and insane man said: 'as I think that all of you are lazy, I will now prove my strength or show that my vigour is worthless. And so, if Ceres dwells in this oak, I will overcome her. [...] // His servants were astonished and one gathered the courage to denounce that act as unfair and dishonest. But while the poor man was still protesting, he was hit on the head by his impious master and fell lifeless on the ground. Erysichthon then smote the tree, when suddenly a voice came out of the trunk and spoke as follows.]

As I have already said, Dolce's *Trasformationi* has been produced with the same packaging used by Giolito for his fundamental 1542 edition of the *Furioso* (Javitch 1998; Capriotti 2013). The artist Giovanni Antonio Rusconi modelled the iconographic *apparatus* of the *Trasformationi* around the stylistic features of Giolito's *Furioso*. In the illustrations of the vernacular Ovid we therefore find the same pictorial effects, the same meaningful use of perspective, and also the same elegant and sentimental representation of landscapes and human beings which were already present in the images for Ariosto's poem.[11] In the illustration of Erysichthon's episode a further detail is worth noting (Figure 13.2): in the engraving which represents it, the cut on the trunk and the wound of the servant have the same inclination, as if the two blows delivered by Erysichthon were only one. Through this stylistic strategy the engraver Rusconi intended to condense two different narrative moments into one image (Tomasi Velli 2007: 101–18). The likeness between this image and the one from the *Cinque canti* underlines the similarity of the two literary episodes, and encourages us to consider the Ovidian passage as a source of Ariosto's scene. Charlemagne's remarkable resoluteness is comparable to that of Erysichthon, and so are the fears felt by the soldiers and the servants:

---

[11]   See Huber-Rebenich 1992 and Andreoli 2012.

Figure 13.2. Giovanni Antonio Rusconi, Erysichthon profanes a place consecrated to Ceres and her nymphs. Lodovico Dolce, *Trasformationi* (Venice: Gabriele Giolito, 1555), fol. 188, Reggio Emilia, Biblioteca Panizzi, 17.D.247.

> Non tamen idcirco ferrum Triopeïus illa
> abstinuit, famulosque iubet succidere sacrum
> robur; et ut iussos cunctari vidit, ab uno
> edidit haec rapta sceleratus verba securi:
> "Non dilectae deae solum, sed et ipsa licebit
> sit dea, iam tangent frondente cacumine terram"
> (Ovid, *Metamorphoses*, VIII. 751–56)

[Yet could not this move Triop's son his axe therefro to hold, | But bade his servants cut it down. And when he did behold | Them stinting at his hest, he snatched an axe with furious mood | From one of them and wickedly said thus: "Although this wood | Not only were the darling of the goddess but also | The goddess even herself, yet would I make it ere I go | To kiss the clowres with her top that pranks with branches so".] (Golding 2002, 938–44: 261)

> L'imperador commanda che dal piede
> taglin le piante a lor bisogno et uso:
> l'esercito non osa, perché crede,
> da lunga fama e vano error deluso,
> che chi ferro alza incontra il bosco, fiede
> sé stesso e more, e ne l'Inferno giuso
> visibilmente in carne e in ossa è tratto,
> o resta cieco o spiritato o attratto.
>
> Carlo, fatta cantar una solenne
> messa da l'arcivescovo Turpino,
> entra nel bosco, et alza una bipenne,
> e ne percuote un olmo più vicino […]

> Sotto il continuo suon di mille accette
> trema la terra, e par che 'l ciel rimbombi.
> (Ariosto, *Cinque canti*, II. 118–22)

[The Emperor commands his men to cut down the trees at their base for their need and use; the army does not dare because, deluded by old stories and foolish error, it believes that any man who raises his blade against that forest will strike himself and die and be dragged downward, visibly in his flesh and bone, to Hell, or be left blind or possessed by demons or paralyzed. // Charles, having had a solemn mass sung by Archbishop Turpin, goes into the forest, lifts a double-edged axe, and strikes the nearest elm with it… // The earth trembles under the continuous sound of a thousand hatchets, and the heavens seem to echo.] (Ariosto 1996: 173–75)

The condensation of the narrative content of the canto into the single image of Charlemagne striking the sacred tree becomes so iconic in the visual history of Ariosto's *Cinque canti* that the same image occurs once again in the last important illustrated edition of that work, published by the Venetian printer Orlandini in 1731 (Figure 13.3).

In this case, the image of the cutting down of a sacred tree and the motif of its human-like crying are also indebted to another textual as well as figurative source: Ariosto's scene of the Bohemian forest works as an archetypal situation in the episode of the enchanted forest of Saron narrated by Torquato Tasso in Canto XIII of his *Gerusalemme liberata*. Tasso's poem also has an interesting history of illustrated editions, which took its first step in 1590 at the workshop of Girolamo Bartoli in Genoa. The thirteenth engraving of this edition represents the episode in which Tancredi overcomes the fear that paralyses his comrades and manages to penetrate the enchanted forest of Saron, where he violently strikes a cypress (Figure 13.4).

This engraving is surprisingly similar in setting to the one printed in Orlandini's edition of the *Cinque canti*, and it amplifies the typological similarity between the two narrations. The fact that the author of the eighteenth-century illustration used that specific visual framework may certainly be due merely to his unconscious memory of the work of his predecessor, but it may also suggest that he deliberately intended to hint at a literary echo by means of a parallel visual one. Orlandini's illustration thus recalls Tasso's echo of the *Cinque canti* (and, implicitly of the *Metamorphoses*), exactly as Tasso had previously drawn on Ariosto and Ovid.

Figure 13.3. Carlo Magno's cutting down of a sacred tree in the Bohemian forest. Ludovico Ariosto, *Cinque canti* (Venice: Orlandini,1730), fol. 313^r, Parma, Biblioteca Palatina, PAL 8325.

The desperation of Alcyone

Our second example concerns Ariosto's allusive references to Ovid's mythological characters and narrative patterns. In a short passage from *Orlando furioso*, Bireno's desertion of Olympia is patently associated with

Figure 13.4. Tancredi strikes a cypress in the enchanted forest of Saron.
Torquato Tasso, *Gerusalemme liberata* (Genoa: Bartoli, 1590), fol. 247ʳ, Parma, Biblioteca
Palatina, PAL 09841.

the Ovidian narration of two myths dealing with love and abandonment, Ariadne and Theseus and Ceyx and Alcyone:

e s'udîr le Alcïone alla marina
de l'antico infortunio lamentarse.
Né desta né dormendo, ella la mano
per Bireno abbracciar stese, ma invano.
[...]
e corre al mar, graffiandosi le gote,
presaga e certa ormai di sua fortuna.
Si straccia i crini, e il petto si percuote,
e va guardando (che splendea la luna)
se veder cosa, fuor che 'l lito, puote;
[...]
Quivi surgea nel lito estremo un sasso,
Ch'aveano l'onde, col picchiar frequente,
cavo e ridutto a guisa d'arco al basso;
e stava sopra il mar curvo e pendente.
Olimpia in cima vi salí a gran passo
(così la facea l'animo possente),
e di lontano le gonfiate vele
vide fuggir del suo signor crudele:

vide lontano, o le parve vedere;
che l'aria chiara ancor non era molto.
Tutta tremante si lasciò cadere,
più bianca e più che nieve fredda in volto;
(Ariosto, *Orlando furioso*, X. 20–24)

[... and the halcyons could be heard over the water lamenting their age-old sorrows. Neither waking nor asleep, Olympia reached out to embrace Bireno, but in vain. [...] and run down to the sea, tearing her cheeks, full of forebodings, indeed past all doubt. She tore her hair and beat her breast and strained her eyes, the moon still being up, to see whether anything could be made out beyond the shore [...]. A rock rose by the water's edge, which the regular action of the waves had eaten away at the base so that it arched out over the sea. Olympia swiftly scaled it (for her agitation lent her strength) and she saw the billowing sails of her cruel lord receding into the distance: she saw them in the distance, or thought she did – for it was still but first light. She dropped to the ground trembling; her face was still but first light.] (Ariosto 1974: 95)

Ariosto's reuse of the myth of Ceyx and Alcyone is particularly significant for the purpose of this study. Ovid narrates that Ceyx abandons his wife Alcyone as he leaves for war, but his ship is caught in a storm and he dies in a shipwreck (*Metamorphoses*, XI. 410–43). In his vernacular translation of this Ovidian episode, Dolce alludes explicitly to Ariosto's account of Olympia and Bireno, thus underlining Ariosto's imitation of Ovid:

> Come'ella vide esser guernita, e quale
> A re si convenia, la nave in punto,
> Allor, come presaga del suo male,
> Le fu da estrema doglia il cor compunto:
> E poté a pena dir: "Ceice, vale,
> Da ch'esser dei da me così disgiunto";
> Né seguir puote a queste altre parole,
> E cadde, come corpo morto suole.
>
> Era il dì chiaro, et ella al lito scende
> Là, donde vide già scioglier la nave;
> E mentre col mirar più l'apre e fende
> La inconsolabil sua doglia sì grave,
> E che di qua di là l'occhio si stende,
> Un non so, che ne l'onde vedut'have.
> Dubita quel che sia: poi corpo umano
> Le sembra, benché fosse assai lontano.
> [...]
> V'era una mole, che rompeva a l'onde
> L'impeto primo; e fa riparo e schermo,
> (Che 'l mar non possa soverchiar le sponde)
> Contra la furia ad ogni tempo fermo.
> Questa però, che 'l corpo le nasconde,
> Sormonta, e non par ch'abbia il piede infermo
> La dolente Alcione: anzi mostrava
> Che vi volasse, e certo ella volava.
>
> (Dolce, *Trasformationi*, XXIII. 72. 3–7–8 and 74.1–2)

[As soon as she saw the ship prepared to set sail, equipped in such a way as was fit for a king, she was stricken with immense grief, as if she foresaw her future pain, and she could barely utter: 'Ceyx, farewell, since you and I must part'. She could speak no more and fell, like dead bodies do. // The day was bright when she walked to the shore, where she saw the ship set sail. That sight widened her wound and added to her overwhelming grief. Her eyes moved from side to side, as she saw something she could not recognise. She wondered what it was and then she seemed to discern a human body, although it was very far from her. [...] // There was a rock which broke the force of the waves and offered shelter and protection against bad weather (thus preventing the sea from flooding the shore). That rock hid the body from Alcyone's sight, but the distressed woman stared to climb it, and her steps were not unsteady: on the contrary, she seemed to be flying and indeed she was truly flying.] (The translation is mine)

CANTO DECIMO.

Figure 13.5. Bireno abandons Olympia. Ludovico Ariosto, *Orlando furioso* (Venice: Valvassori, 1553), fol. 147^r, Reggio Emilia, Biblioteca Panizzi, 17.C.53.

These textual recollections and this imitation game between Ovid, Ariosto and Dolce have a visual counterpart in an illustration indebted to the iconography of the Olympia episode, which was codified in the 1536 Zoppino edition of *Orlando furioso* and repeatedly drawn upon in the following illustrated editions of the Italian poem. In order to appreciate the similarities between the illustrations of the two episodes, it is useful to compare a xylography taken from the 1553 Valvassori edition of Ariosto with the image representing Alcyone's despair while watching the shipwreck from the shore. Special attention should be paid to the outline of the desperate woman running with open arms, a posture which almost prefigures her future metamorphosis into a bird (Figures 13.5-13.6). What is particularly interesting in this connection is that, as widely known and demonstrated by scholars, Ovid's *Metamorphoses* is one of the most relevant hypotexts of Ariosto's poem. More specifically, Ariosto's account of Olympia's desperation, among its many other sources, is patterned after Alcyone's sorrow. Thus, the figurative correspondence retraces the textual influence. Besides, a similar criss-cross influence concerns the literary relationship between the two texts: while Ovid was a model for Ariosto, Ariosto was a model for the metrical, rhetorical and stylistic strategies of translation adopted by Dolce in his *volgarizzamento*.

The strong resemblance between Ovid's tale and the episode in Ariosto's poem, highlighted by the iconographic similarity of the two engravings, was

Figure 13.6. Giovanni Antonio Rusconi, *Alcyone's desperation at the shipwreck of Ceyx.*
Lodovico Dolce, *Trasformationi* (Venice: Gabriele
Giolito, 1555), fol. 238, Reggio Emilia, Biblioteca Panizzi, 17.D.247.

also recognised in the seventeenth century by Francesco Bardi in his *Ovidio, istorico, politico e morale*, at once a moralizing summary and an emblematic rewriting of the *Metamorphoses*.[12] Each page of the text engages with a specific Ovidian myth and is devised as a kind of emblem: it features an *inscriptio* (i.e., a summary of Ovid's tale), a *pictura* (i.e., an image selected from the set of illustrations by Rusconi which decorate Dolce's *Trasformationi*), and a *subscriptio* (i.e., an explanation of the allegorical meaning of the myth). Bardi appropriates the engravings printed in Dolce's translation of Ovid in all the editions of his *Ovidio, Istorico, Politico e Morale*, except for a copy published in 1684 by the printer Stefano Cursi. In that copy, Bardi's text is accompanied by images which are not drawn from any previous Italian translation of Ovid, but rather from the illustrated editions of *Orlando furioso* published in 1542 by the printer Giolito, and in 1568 by the printer Varisco. There were obvious practical reasons which led the publishers to reuse the woodcuts (such as, in particular, their cost and the amount of work required in their manufacture), but the 1684 edition of Bardi's work also shows a notable exegetical competence in the arrangement of the reused engravings, if not, sometimes, a thorough understanding of the subtle intertextual relations between *Metamorphoses* and *Orlando furioso*. In this case, we can consider that every edition reveals a specific approach to the reuse of the woodcuts, and introduces its own way of adjusting the pre-existing images to the new text that they are meant to illustrate. The analysis

---

[12] See Guthmüller 1997: 213–36.

F A V O L A LXXIV.

CEice Rè di Theſſaglia figlio di Lucifero, non ſapendo noua di Dedalione ſuo fratello, (che precipitandoſi dal Parnaſo in mare, era ſtato tramutato in Auoltoio, perche la di lui figlia Chio ingrauidata da Mercurio, e da Apollo, era ſtata ſaettata da Diana con la quale hauea ardito contendere,) poſtoſi in mare contro il conſiglio della moglie per ricercarlo, naufragò. Del che auuiſata Alcione ſua moglie in ſogno da Giunone, correndo al mare, vedendo ſu l'onda il cadauere, mentre in quelle ſi precipitaua, fù lei con il marito trasformata in Alcioni: quali Vccelli, come ſcriue Ambrogio nell'Hexamerone, hanno forza di tranquillar il mare in tempo che couano l'Oua.

A L L E G O R I A.

E meglio ſeguir l'altrui conſiglio anco men vtile, che idolatrare le ſue riſolutioni, come fece Ceice. Alcioge poi auuiſata in ſogno, moſtra che il Cielo ſempre ci preſagiſſe gl'infauſti ſucceſſi. La morte di Ceice dinota, che il Cielo per ordinario ci leua le coſe più care, acciò non amiamo che Dio.

F. A.

Figure 13.7. Bireno abandons Olympia. Francesco Bardi, *Fauole d'Ouidio istorico, politico, morale, con le allegorie. Breuemente spiegato, e delineato con artificiose figure* (Venice: Curti, 1684), p. 74, Parma, Biblioteca Palatina, AA X.24370.

of these materials highlights the importance of considering that the editors working for Renaissance printers did not all have the same grasp of the narrative and figurative material they were going to deal with; hence the more or less sophisticated and intriguing solutions, and the rough or refined iconographic reuses. It is no coincidence, for instance, that the printer appropriates the illustration of the desertion of Olympia to illustrate the tragic separation between Alcyon and Ceyx summarized in the short allegorical text of Bardi's work (Figure 13.7).

The other complete Italian translation of Ovid's *Metamorphoses* in the sixteenth century – Giovanni Andrea dell'Anguillara's *Metamorfosi d'Ovidio* – also displays a similar iconography of female sorrow.[13] There are two illustrated editions of this work and eight series of illustrations (Casamassima 2017). The first one was published by the printer Francesco de Franceschi in 1563 and is characterized by the fact that each book opens with a small engraving which illustrates the first mythological tale narrated in it. These illustrations are generally simpler and less accurate than the set of woodcuts in Dolce's *Trasformationi*. The second original series of illustrations to Anguillara's *Metamorfosi* was published by the Venetian printer Giunti in 1584, and the multiple narrative structure of his full-page plates reproduces the one adopted in the illustrated edition of Ariosto's *Orlando furioso* printed by de Franceschi in the same year (Bondi 2017). The illustrations of the edition of Ariosto's poem, created by the artist Girolamo Porro, and those of Anguillara's work, devised by his apprentice Giacomo Franco, both take up the whole page, and the sharp precision of the copper engraving technique enables the artists to represent a large number of episodes, drawn from each book, organized on different planes of perspective. Just as Anguillara's extraordinarily successful *volgarizzamento* of the Ovidian masterpiece is strongly influenced, at both structural and formal level, by the innovative poetic procedures of Ariosto's *Furioso*, Franco's set of illustrations seeks to imitate the Ariostan operation of his master Porro, giving at the same time a personal reading of Anguillara's narrative. To a certain extent, Franco reproduces Anguillara's taste for erotic transgression, anachronism, tragic and emphatic effects, but the boundaries imposed by the *triumphans* Counter-Reformation on his expressive code force him to mask, conceal, or attenuate some problematic traits of the text.

In the eighth plate we can see, for example, the *Pathosformel* of the desperate woman, which, in this case, illustrates not the story of Ceyx and Alcyon but

---

[13] For further details on Anguillara's work see: Cotugno 2007; Bucchi 2011.

the lament of Scylla abandoned by Minos (Figure 13.8).[14] That Ovidian tale is the explicit source of Ariosto's episode of Olympia and Bireno, and Anguillara's translation of Ovid highlights the stylistic and thematic elements of Ariosto's imitation of his classical source. In Anguillara's work, the iconographic reproduction of the illustrations originally designed for the *Orlando furioso* is paralleled by his rewriting of those stanzas of Ariosto's poems which are deeply informed by the recollection of Ovid's *Metamorphoses*. In the plate where Scylla's desertion is depicted, a similar subject is represented in the foreground: the meeting between Bacchus and Ariadne, just abandoned by Theseus. The upper portion of the plate is thus thematically related to the lower one, and the suggested relationship between the two episodes stands out as a meaningful element: through the same narrative situation the illustrator creates an interesting contrast between the representation of the failure of a lustful marriage and a betrothal scene; in doing so he clearly alludes to the Counter-Reformation ideology, which celebrated the triumph of institutional marriage over the dangerous enticements of erotic love. In this regard, the placement of images at the beginning of each book of the illustrated poem is very significant, because it represents a common book illustration strategy of mnemonic prolepsis and control of the act of reading that invites or encourages the reader to search for that part of the text that best corresponds to the scenes depicted at the start. From this point of view, the work of art has to be considered not as an inert object, but as a living element that takes shape through processes similar to those of a performance and exerts specific effects on the reader-spectator, thus placing itself at the juncture between expectations, constrictions, categories of interpretation, and mental and cognitive schemes.

In the illustration we trust

The last textual and visual example offered here shows another interesting instance of the reuse of engravings designed to add to the enjoyment of reading a translation of Ovid. In this case, we are dealing with the translation of the first book of Ovid's *Metamorphoses* written by Francesco Pona (1594–1655) and printed in 1618 by the Veronese printer Bartolomeo Merlo. Within the Venetian 'Academia degli Incogniti', the physician and writer Pona stands out for his rich literary production, which includes lyric poetry, short stories, sacred and profane theatre, chivalric poems, medical treatises, and literary translations (Buccini 2013). As far as

---

[14] On this illustration, please see also the essay by Francesca Casamassima in this volume (Chapter 12).

Figure 13.8. Giacomo Franco, Girolamo Porro. *Baccus and Ariadne. Giovanni Andrea dell'Anguillara, Metamorfosi d'Ovidio* (Venice: Giunta, 1584) Parma, Biblioteca Palatina, PAL 11005.

this last genre is concerned, the *Trasformazione del primo libro delle Metamorfosi d'Ovidio* gives important evidence of the evolution of prose as a literary medium, one which was often preferred to poetry, and especially to the *ottava rima*. Pona's vernacular translation was originally published without a set of illustrations; however, I was able to find and buy a copy in the collectors' market which is richly decorated with images taken from previous illustrated editions of Ovid, as well as from chivalric poems and books of emblems. The general intent of this figurative patchwork is merely decorative, but in a few cases the choice of images implies a close relationship with the text.

Let us take, for instance, a passage from Pona's translation in which the divine origins of the Cosmos and the creation of the humankind are described. A former owner of the book inserted some engravings on these subjects taken from the second great illustrated translation of Ovid into the vernacular, i.e., *Tutti gli libri de Ovidio Metamorphoseos tradutti dal litteral in verso vulgar* by Nicolò degli Agostini (Venice: Zoppino, 1522) (Figure 13.9).

These illustrations are characterized by a Christian reinterpretation of the Ovidian *incipit*, as is undoubtedly consistent with the religious beliefs of Pona, who lived during the Counter-Reformation. Pona's defensive foreword is, in this regard, very clear:

> Dove il lettore udirà mentovar un Giove, un Cupido o altre tale Dio sappia ch'io ho favoleggiato col mio Poeta, professando di non voler né qui né altrove dilungarmi [...] da' Catolici dogmi Romani.

> [Please be warned that if I allude to Jove, or Cupid, or any other God, it is just because I have told fairy tales, as I am always very deferential to [...] the Catholic dogmas.] (The translation is mine)

On some occasions, the illustrations do not represent the content of the myth specifically, but are thematically related to it. This is the case, for instance, of the episode of Deucalion and Pyrrha's consultation of the oracle. While there is no illustration of the story in the principal sixteenth-century edition or Italian translation of the *Metamorphoses*,[15] the anonymous designer of this unusual edition of Pona's work decided to represent it by employing an engraving thematically akin to it: the one depicting the sorceress Medea dealing in magic (Figure 13.10).

---

[15] However, the illustration of Deucalion and Pyrrha at the temple can be found in sixteenth-century editions. For example, it can be found in Bernard Salomon's 1557 illustrations and in Gabriello Simeoni's 1558 adaptation of the *Metamorphoses*.

Figure 13.9. The divine origins of the Cosmos.
Francesco Pona, *Trasformazione del primo libro delle Metamorfosi d'Ovidio* (Verona: Merlo, 1618), p. 48, Piacenza, Private collection.

Figure 13.10. Medea. Francesco Pona, *Trasformazione del primo libro delle Metamorfosi d'Ovidio* (Verona: Merlo, 1618), p. 94, Piacenza, Private collection.

Figure 13.11. Perseus and Andromeda. Francesco Pona, *Trasformazione del primo libro delle Metamorfosi d'Ovidio* (Verona: Merlo, 1618), p. 176, Piacenza, Private collection

The long description of Syrinx's female body sleeping under the lustful gaze of Pan has been analogously associated with the illustration of another famous scene where female beauty is exhibited: that is, the moment when Perseus sees the beautiful naked body of Andromeda chained to the rock and threatened by the monster. Because of the hero's lust, the image is here partially censored (Figure 13.11).

Pona's book thus reveals a specific approach to the reuse of the woodcuts, and introduces its own way of arranging the pre-existing images to the new text to be illustrated. The Renaissance tradition of illustrated translations of Ovid seems to have been too influential to be ignored, even by a private collector.

Conclusion

By studying the illustrations produced (or simply readapted) for printed editions of Ariosto's *Orlando furioso* and for Italian vernacular translations of Ovid's *Metamorphoses,* I have tried to address the question of the relationship between words and images within the body of a book, and to answer certain theoretical questions regarding the comparison between the verbal and the iconic codes: the ways in which the poetic content is selected to form the figurative material; the semiotic and perceptual mechanisms that determine the deciphering of the elements of the illustration, considered in themselves and in relation to the text; and the possible interaction of the illustrations with other paratexts, and with possible annotations and comments (or with material interventions on the physical status of the book, as was the case with the aforementioned edition of Pona's translation). These represent three different routes through which the experiences of transition from text to image, or vice versa, can investigate the relationship between the intention of an author and the reception of his work, between a text and its imitations or re-writings.

.

V

OVID IN GERMAN AND DUTCH

14

ANNA CAPPELLOTTO

RECASTING OVID IN MEDIEVAL GERMANY: ALBRECHT VON HALBERSTADT'S *METAMORPHOSES*

This paper will focus on the first extant rendering of Ovid's *Metamorphoses* in the German vernacular. This translation was allegedly written by a Saxon cleric named Albrecht von Halberstadt between the end of the twelfth and the beginning of the thirteenth century in Thuringia. The text survives only in a few fragments belonging to a thirteenth-century Oldenburg manuscript that transmit Albrecht's Middle High German adaptation of some myths in *Metamorphoses* VI (fragment A), XI (fragment B), and XIV (fragment C).[1] An idea of the style and content of the remaining parts of Albrecht's translation is given to us by an early modern adaptation of Ovid's *Metamorphoses* by Jörg Wickram (*c.* 1505-before 1562), who claimed to have translated from Albrecht's medieval version. Wickram's edition was published in Mainz at Ivo Schöffer's printing house in 1545.[2]

Despite the relevance of this Albrecht's work for the study of Ovid's medieval reception, little scholarship considering both Albrecht's and Wickram's renderings is available, except for Rücker's study (1997), which includes a synoptic transcription of the fragments (based on previous editions), together with the Latin text by Ovid, and the early modern German.[3] A complete new edition of the Middle High German fragments

---

[1] The first German editions of the fragments are the following: fragment B (Staatsbibliothek zu Berlin, Preußischer Kulturbesitz, Ms. germ. fol. 831) = Leverkus (1859); fragment A (Oldenburg, Staatsarchiv, lost) = Lübben (1865) both reprinted also in Bolte (1905–1906); fragments C+D+E (Niedersächsisches Landesarchiv, Standort Oldenburg, NLA OL, Slg 10 [Best. 297] E 22) = Last (1966). The letters referring to the fragments (A, B, C, D, E) are numbered according to the sequence of the fabulae in the *Metamorphoses*. Fragments D and E cannot be taken into consideration for the purpose of text analysis since they are only a few parchment strips preserving the very beginning or end of some verses. Modern editions of Wickram's adaptation are Bolte 1905-1906 and Roloff 1990.

[2] Jörg Wickram, P. Ouidij Nasonis deß aller sinnreichsten Poeten Metamorphosis, Das ist von der wunderbarlichen Verenderung der Gestalten der Menschen, Thier vnd anderer Creaturen (Mainz: Ivo Schöffer, 1545). USTC 681909.

[3] The first thorough investigations of Albrecht's work are in Bartsch 1965; Runge 1908; Ludwig 1912. A common methodological problem of these analyses is that they tend to

along with an Italian translation has been published by the author of this article (Cappellotto 2019), whereas at the moment of writing no other translations either of the fragments or of Wickram's edition exist. This is the reason why the text is still not accessible to many scholars and, as a consequence, overall assessments of Ovid's influence in European vernaculars tend to neglect it, which ends up significantly altering the picture of the medieval reception of the *Metamorphoses*.[4]

This contribution will undertake to fill this research gap or *desideratum*: a brief introduction about the forms of reception of Ovid in the German area during the Middle Ages will lead into an analysis of Albrecht's translation.[5] After a survey on the extant tradition, Albrecht's Middle High German text will be analysed along with the Latin and the early modern German counterparts. Because Albrecht's translation is not derived from any intermediate source, it also qualifies as a good test-bed to detect translation strategies through a close analysis of selected *loci paralleli*. To do this, fixed categories identifying typical Ovidian devices will be considered, i.e. narratological phenomena such as passages connecting myths, proper nouns and epithets, time and place expressions, and in general the treatment of *realia*.[6]

demonstrate Albrecht's translation strategies by providing evidence from Wickram's edition. Neumann (1955) wrote a long article where he investigated and compared the fragments with their counterparts in Ovid and Wickram. Heinzmann (1969) authored a comparative study of Albrecht and Wickram. However, none of the above-mentioned analyses could take into consideration all the fragments, as the last one (C) was found in 1966. Rücker's dissertation (1997) deals with the fragments along with a study of Wickram. In a recent study Behmenburg (2009) discussed the myth of Philomena in the French and German medieval tradition from a comparative perspective. Other analyses of single myths or specific aspects concerning the Middle High German fragments are Kern (2003), Klein (2008), Saibene (2018a, 1998, 1988) and Cappellotto (2019, 2016, 2014). Toepfer recently focused on the adaptation of the myth of Philomela in Wickram and other early modern sources (2018b) and on the reception of Ovid and Homer in early modern times (2018a).

[4] Such as in the major publication *Ovid in the Middle Ages* (Clark, Coulson, McKinley 2011), which does not mention Albrecht von Halberstadt, but also in more recent works like Rehm (2018), focused on the medieval reception of mythology. Ralph J. Hexter (2007: 1318-20) introduces Albrecht's and Wickram's undertakings in a survey about Ovid in translation in the vernaculars.

[5] Both the terms *translation* and *adaptation* are deliberately used here, as it is difficult to define their boundaries when it comes to medieval literature. For a discussion on this topic see, among others, Copeland 1991.

[6] According to Vlahov and Florin's classical definition *realia* are works expressing objects, concepts and phenomena related to a specific people which do not have exact equivalents in other languages (Vlahov and Florin 1970).

It is not possible to identify with precision the manuscript of Ovid's poem used by Albrecht. However, a brief comparison with the *Narrationes fabularum ovidianarum* and Arnulf d'Orléans's glosses and allegoriae[7] shows that a number of additions or variants in the target text are not necessarily to be considered an innovation and that they might actually derive from a glossed or commented Latin manuscript used by the translator.[8] The data collected through the analysis will try to demonstrate that translating Ovid's mythological work at a rather early stage did not necessarily mean unveiling a Christian truth behind the pagan fables, an interpretative practice which was common within the Medieval Latin and Romance tradition. Albrecht adheres to the source text and adapts it to the taste and skills of his expected audience: the outcome is not a *verbatim* rendering, but it cannot be defined as a free adaptation of the *Metamorphoses* either, as relevant examples will try to show.

On a broader perspective, this analysis is a means of reassessing the significance of Middle High German literature within the study of the medieval reception of Ovid. In so doing and together with the other contributions in this volume it will hopefully outline a more comprehensive overview of the *aetas ovidiana* in the European vernaculars.

Forms of Ovidian reception in Middle High German literature

Within an attempt to trace the history of Ovid in the Middle Ages, a look at his influence on German vernacular literature can help to shape an overview of forms and models of reception. It is a way of reconstructing what Ralph J. Hexter calls the other 'half of the story', that is, Ovid's indirect tradition:

> Students of Ovid's impact both in the Middle Ages and Renaissance who only focus on the transmission and study of the original text miss at least half of the story, for however great the impact was on medieval and Renaissance readers and writers of Latin, many more diverse audiences [...] were delighted, instructed and titillated by Ovid in their own languages. (Hexter 2007: 1310)

---

[7] Arnulf's glosses and *Allegoriae super Ovidii Metamorphosin* (*c.* 1175) are partially edited by Ghisalberti (1932) and by David T. Gura (2010, dissertation). The *Narrationes* are edited by Magnus (1914b). As regards the Latin source text that Albrecht could have used, see Bolte (1905–1906: xix); Bartsch (1861: cxlii–clxv); Runge (1908: 87–96).

[8] A similar thesis is at the core of a recent article by Pellissa Prades (forthcoming): by means of relevant examples she provides evidence that some readings shared by medieval vernacular versions of the Metamorphoses – the *Ovide moralisé*, the Italian translation by Arrigo Simintendi (1330s), Giovanni del Virgilio's *Expositio* and *Allegorie* (1322–1323), Bonsignori's translation of Simintendi (*c.* 1375-1377), and the *Transformacions* by Francesc Alegre (*c.* 1472–1482) – might be handed down by late Ovidian manuscripts.

The picture resulting from adopting this more encompassing perspective is both fascinating and complex, as it shows an Ovid who was 'incorrigibly plural' (Clark 2011: 16). Such a plurality was not only due to the existence and circulation of Latin and vernacular texts but was rather an inherent feature of each considered tradition, which enacted different ways and strategies of cultural and linguistic transfer.

The medieval recasting of ancient stories revolving around the matter of Rome, Alexander the Great, Apollonius of Tyre, or mythological tales is labelled 'reception of Antiquity' (*Antikerezeption*), a phenomenon of adaptation of these subjects to fit in the medieval social and cultural context, where they were influenced by Christian belief (Lienert 2001: 13). Through literature the ancient past could provide the rising courtly society with a form of self-representation: the concepts of *translatio studii et imperii*, rooted back to the Carolingian age, conveyed the idea of a transfer of power and knowledge from the Greek East to the Latin West and through this to European vernaculars. Literary subjects derived from classical sources, including mythological ones, functioned as a key for representing and understanding reality in various ways and contexts. They could become positive or negative *exempla*, as in the case of Alexander the Great, who was praised for his royal virtues and at the same time was morally condemned because of his excessive pride. Widely circulating Ovidian tales such as Pyramus and Thisbe or Hero and Leander allowed a double key to reading: a story of unending love to recover and imitate as a paramount example from the past and at the same time a warning against the consequences of love.[9]

Medieval German literature offers various forms of Ovidian reception, such as adaptations of a single myth and a number of allusions to Ovidian stories placed within other works and subjects. Heinrich von Veldeke's *Eneit* (before 1174 – completed after 1184), for instance, combines his source text with Ovidian reminiscences; in Herbort von Fritzlar's *Liet von Troye* (1190-1200) or in Konrad von Würzburg's *Trojanerkrieg* (1287, incomplete) the primary source texts are blended with Ovid and other materials. French literature certainly played a prominent role in the circulation of *materia antiqua* in the German speaking Middle Ages and functioned as a 'donor literature': this means that it provided poets with high standard literary models and sources which had already undergone cultural transfer and

---

[9]   The myth of Pyramus and Thisbe circulated first in Medieval Latin as a text employed in the classroom and in the European vernaculars: for a survey on the Middle Latin, French, German and Dutch versions see Pratt 2017, whose interesting contribution is aimed at analysing the adaptations together within their material context. For an analysis of Hero and Leander in different vernacular literary traditions see Murdoch 1977 and Gärtner 2009; Toepfer 2016 has recently focused on early modern German renderings.

recodification (Kern and Ebenbauer 2003: xxx). Such a process is to be recognized in Veldeke's *Eneit*, translated from the anonymous old French *Roman d'Eneas* (*c.* 1160) or in Herbort's *Liet von Troye*, adapted from the old French *Roman de Troie* assigned to Benoît de Sainte-Maure (1160-1170).[10]

Ovid was first of all a *praeceptor amoris*, so his influence is clearly visible in courtly poetry, such as Heinrich von Morungen's work, where the myths of Philomela and Narcissus are rehashed.[11] Also in Gottfried von Straßburg's *Tristan*, the famous love cave (*minnegrotte*) scene is endowed with references probably derived both from the *Metamorphoses* and the *Heroides*.[12] The latter is a case of the so-called *Anspielungrezeption* (allusive reception), that is, the re-use of mythological plots, single scenes, or even just intensive 'name dropping' (Kern and Ebenbauer 2003: xxviii): the references to Ovid are usually employed to either reinforce an argument or to make it clearer and the allusive way of citing him suggests that an amount of mythological knowledge was shared among learned audiences. In other instances, mythological tales can be extracted from the context where they belonged and can be rewritten as if they were independent stories: this happened especially with a number of Ovidian tales such as Pyramus and Thisbe from the *Metamorphoses* or Hero and Leander from the *Heroides*.[13] A

[10] Due to the presence of intermediate vernacular models it is not easy to identify innovations introduced by German poets. As for the German rewriting of Virgil's *Aeneid* by Veldeke, for instance, the presence of Ovid is also visible in the old French *Roman d'Eneas*; a comparative analysis is offered by Kistler 1993.

[11] In the poem *Mir ist geschehen als einem kindelîne* [It happened to me the same as to a child] Heinrich von Morungen does not refer explicitly to Narcissus – addressed only as a 'kint' (child) – nor does he in the poem *Ez ist site der nahtegal* [It is habit of the nightingale], which alludes to the myth of Procne and Philomela through the reference to a 'nahtegal' [nightingale] and to 'eine swal' [swallow]. See Tervooren 1975: 48–49; 130–31; for a thorough analysis of the Narcissus poem, see Kern, Edwards and Huber-Rebenich 2015. Unless otherwise indicated translations in English are those of the author.

[12] Here Tristan and Isolde spend part of their time telling each other some ancient stories of love-pain (*senemære*) including the tragic destinies of Dido, Phyllis, Canace and Byblis. Gottfried concentrates the references to the agonizing stories in a handful of verses (*Tristan*, 17186–203), but except for Dido the others are minor characters in the Ovidian works to which they belong. According to Cipolla (2014: 166-67) the author might have had a repertoire similar to Hyginus's *Genealogiae* (first century BC- first century AD) at his disposal, where the love heroines are to be found in exactly the same order. Within the Tristan narration, they could 'function as a comparison between modernity and Antiquity, a sort of *translatio amoris*' (Kern and Ebenbauer 2003: li). Concerning Ovidian influences in Gottfried see Usener 1999.

[13] An adaptation of the fable of Pyramus and Thisbe possibly dating back to the middle of the fourteenth century can be found in the following miscellany manuscripts: Vienna, Österreichische Nationalbibliothek, Cod. 2885 (fols 19ᵛ–24ʳ, 1393) and in Innsbruck,

further way of integrating Ovidian works within the German literary culture was enacted by means of full interlinguistic translations and adaptations, as in the case-study which will be examined in the next section.

The tradition of the German *Metamorphoses*

The documents passing on the first rewriting of the *Metamorphoses* that we have evidence of are a few fragments belonging to a single parchment manuscript dating back to the second half of the thirteenth century and connected with the lineage of Oldenburg (Last 1966: 47). Fragment B was discovered by Leverkus who later donated it to the State Library of Berlin where it is currently preserved (Staatsbibliothek zu Berlin, Preußischer Kulturbesitz, Ms. germ. fol. 831, 279 verses). B is a parchment *bifolium* which at some point, presumably around the beginning of the seventeenth century, had been removed from its material context and had been used as a cover of a governmental *regesta*. The status of preservation of the document is decent, even though time and usage have caused the partial removal of ink, which makes the reading of some passages at times difficult. The text, handwritten in a calligraphic *textura* (Leverkus 1859: 359; Last 1966: 44), displays the short and rhymed couplets in a two-column layout where the verses are alternately indented and start with small majuscules. B contains two blue and red sorts of filigree-decorated initials: an A at fragment B 72 'Als ich han gesprochen' [As I said before] and a V at B126 'Vernemet iz gescach alsus' [Listen! It happened that] and the only surviving rubric in the whole tradition between fragment B, 71–72 'Wie Laomedon mein eide wart' [How Laomedon became a perjurer].[14] This might derive from the Latin source text the translator was using, possibly a commented Ovidian manuscript which circulated at that time in Germany.[15] The practice of adding titles to Ovidian myths dates back to the *Narrationes fabularum ovidianarum*, where summaries of the tales are preceded by a brief content list in the form of titles. Arnulf's work was probably influenced by it and shows an analogous structure, as short titles summing up the content of the

---

Tiroler Landesmuseum Ferdinandeum, Cod. FB32001 (fols 14ᵛ–17ʳ, 1456). The tale is edited by Grubmüller 1996: 337–63. See Plotke 2013; Klein 2017. A rendering of the tragic fate of Hero and Leander can be found in Karlsruhe, Landesbibliothek, Cod. Donaueschingen 104, first half of the fifteenth century (fols 46ʳ–49ʳ). This is edited by Schulz-Grobert 2006: 114–41.

[14] Albrecht von Halberstadt's fragment are quoted in this article according to my own edition (Cappellotto 2019).

[15] The oldest comment to the *Metamorphoses* comes from the south of Germany (Munich, Staatsbibliothek, Clm 4610) and it is edited by Meiser 1885. On this topic see Coulson 2011: 48, especially footnote 4.

fabulae are to be found before the *allegoriae*.[16] Fragment B is important because it bears the only sequence of myths we have got at our disposal, which are derived from *Metamorphoses*, XI. 156–290: Phoebus and Pan, Laomedon, Peleus and Thetis, Daedalion and Chione.[17]

The second fragment, named A, was found some years later in Oldenburg by Lübben (Oldenburg, Staatsarchiv, lost, ed. Lübben 1865, 144 verses). Unfortunately, it went lost some time after its publication, so there is no facsimile left and the analysis must be based on Lübben's edition. Fragment A hands down the initial part of the myth about Tereus, Procne and Philomela derived from *Metamorphoses*, VI. 440–79.

The last fragments (C+D+E, in Niedersächsisches Landesarchiv, Standort Oldenburg, NLA OL, Slg 10 [Best. 297] E 22) were found and published by Last (1966).[18] The state of preservation of C, a parchment leaf, is worse than B: after the codex was dismembered, the page was used for binding purposes (as the marginal annotation 'Polizey Ordnungh' on the bottom of fol. 1ʳ indicates). For this reason, the ink faded in the middle of the page length, where it was folded. The most serious damage, however, can be seen on the sides of the page, which have been cut out. On the upper left side, the shape of the cut is square-like, which might suggest that an illumination had been removed, as often happened with these kinds of artifacts. C hands down two *fabulae* from *Metamorphoses*, XIV. 685–758: the frame myth about Vertumnus and Pomona and the tale of Iphis and Anaxarete, which is told by Vertumnus under false pretenses as a persuasive argument to convince Pomona to exchange his love. Fragment C contains another inset majuscule placed at a relevant point of the narration: 'Vrouwe dich maget du hast den sige' (fragment C, 68) [Be pleased, maiden! You have the victory]. This is very similar to the one in B, even though there it marked the beginning of two myths.[19]

Despite its extant fragmentary condition, in all probability Albrecht's text was originally a complete translation of the fifteen books of Ovid's poem. This hypothesis is upheld by the fact that the fragments narrate myths that were told one after the other in the source text, and also by the

---

[16] See Ghisalberti 1932.

[17] Though the first one is acephalous and the last one preserves only the background story of Peleus's arrival at Trachis.

[18] As mentioned before, fragments C+D are not useful for our purposes due to their state of preservation. Fragment D has been identified with Ovid, *Metamorphoses*, XI. 708–27; 772–95 whereas fragment E with *Metamorphoses*, XIII. 245–82; 350–69. See Last 1966.

[19] Respectively, Laomedon and Peleus and Thetis. Marginal notes on the parchment in fragment A suggested that the manuscript had to be gathered into quaternions, which makes the hypothesis that the documents were part of a longer codex sounder (Lübben 1865: 237).

circumstance that the early modern German version by Wickram, which is based on Albrecht's, is almost complete. In one of the dedications placed at the beginning of his edition, Wickram explains that he had no knowledge of Latin, and therefore chose to rely on the medieval German version by Albrecht.[20] This statement, however, should not be taken at face value. Indeed, scholarship demonstrated that Wickram was also occasionally using the Latin version of Ovid's *Metamorphoses* as well as other sources.[21]

The *editio princeps* of Wickram's translation was published in 1545 and it successfully adapted Albrecht's work to the style and taste of an early modern audience.[22] The edition included Albrecht's allegedly original Middle High German prologue, which provided relevant information about the political and cultural context for Albrecht's medieval translation (see Figure 14.1). These opening verses, for example, locate Albrecht's undertaking at the court of Hermann I (1155-1217), the most prominent literary *milieu* for the reception of classical Antiquity.[23] However, unlike

---

[20] See Wickram's dedication to Wilhelm Böckle in Roloff (1990: 5, line 24): 'daß ich deß Lateins gar unkundig binn' [because I am totally ignorant of Latin].

[21] For a survey see Heinzmann (1969: 38–87). For instance, Wickram used Boccaccio's the *De claris mulieribus* in the translation of Heinrich Steinhöwel (1541); *De casibus virorum illustrium* in the German version by Hieronymus Ziegler (1545); Christoph Bruno's prose adaptations of some *fabulae* of the *Metamorphoses* (1541); Polydore Vergil of Urbino's *De inventoribus rerum* (in the German edition of 1537 by the Swiss humanist Marcus Tatius); Simon Schaidenreisser's early modern rendering of the *Odyssey* (1537); Thomas Murner's translation of Vergil's *Aeneid* (1515). There is also evidence that he employed Sebastian Brandt's *Narrenschiff* (1494); Hans Sachs's master songs based on Ovid's *Metamorphoses* (1545), as well as a number of further sources which have not been identified so far (Heinzmann 1969: 88–116).

[22] Later printings of the same work date back to 1551 (Mainz, by Ivo Schöffer); 1581 (Frankfurt am Main, by Sigmund Feyerabend); 1609 (Frankfurt am Main, by Johann Saurn); 1631 (Frankfurt am Main, Gottfried Tampach). Bolte reminds the reader of other three editions presumably published in Frankfurt am Main in 1551, 1625, 1641. The first was probably mixed up with the Mainz edition; the other two have never been found and no record of them has been found in the Frankfurt fair catalogues. See Bolte 1905–1906: v-xi.

[23] The dating of the work is ambiguously inferred from the Prologue (ed. Roloff 1990: 7–10), lines 80–89 (especially 84–85): 'Zwelff hundert jor | Und zehene bevorn' [twelve hundred years | and ten before]. Most scholars, including Wickram, hypothesize 1210 as a possible date of composition, but the text shows archaistic traits which lead other scholars to prefer the hypothesis of 1190. For a summary of this scholarly discussion see Rücker (1997: 32–40). Regarding the commissioner of the work, see Prologue (ed. Roloff 1990: 9), lines 89–93: 'Bei eynes Fursten zeiten | Der inn allen Landen weiten | Daß was der Vogt von Türingen Lant | Von seiner Tugent wol bekant | der Lantgrafe Herman' [In the age of a prince | who was known in all lands. | It was the reeve of Thuringia, | well known for his virtue: | the landgrave Hermann]. For a thorough

Prologus.

Von Gott dem vatter gesant
Von eyner iunckfrawen geboren
Darzů sunderlich auserkoren/
Darnach über lange zeit
Als ich euch jetz bedeut
Auch da setz zů vor
Zwelff hundert jor
Vnd zehene beuorn
Seit vnser Herr ward geporn
Ergangen an die stund
Daß ich das Bůch begund
Bei eynes Fursten zeiten
Der inn allen Landen weiten
Daß was der Vogt von Türingen lant
Von seiner Tugent wol bekant
Der Lantgrafe Herman
Ich han billichen daran
Dem Fursten zů hand
Wan diß Bůch in seinem Landt
Auff eynem Berg wolbekandt
Er ist Zechenbuch genant
Wardt in dichten gedacht
Begunnen vnd vollenbracht:

Nota, Solang ists das diß Bůch erstlich verteutscht, nemlich 355 iar.

Finis.

Freündtlicher lieber Leser/ ich bitte mit allem fleiß/ wöllest mir nit zů argem ermessen daß ich obgemelte (Meister Albrecht Vorred im Ingang diß büchs gestelt) dann das auß keyner verachtnuß geschehen/ sunder alleyn darum/ das du magst erkennen/ wo dise bücher solcher gestalt getruckt weren worden/ das sie mit schwerem verstand hetten mügen gefaßt werden/ wie dañ die alten reimė gemeinlich mit schwerem verstand außgetruckt seindt. Bitt auch hiemit/ sampt vnd sunders wo ich inn meinen reimen zů litzel oder vil daran gethon/ mir die gütlich corrigieren/ auch meinem vnuerstande zů geben: So weit mir aber müglich/ hab ich mich geflissen meine reimen zů verstentlichsten zů machen/ auch hierin alle vnzucht vermittė/ damit diß bůch von jungen vnd alten Frawen vnd Junckfrawen/ sunder allen anstos gelesen werden. Nun ist fürnemlich zů mercken/ das diser zierlich Poet alles (so er schreibt) in lauter Fablen verwendet/ wiewol solche Fablen jren vrsprung auß den waren Historijs haben: Dan als er schreibt von der Jo / oder Jsidis/ wie die inn eyn Ků verwender/ ist der warheyt nit gar vngleich/ dann Jupiter hatt dise Junckfraw auff eynem schiff (an weliches Segel eyn Ků gemolt) hinweg gefürt. Er meldet auch von der Europa/ welche Jupiter / als
er sich

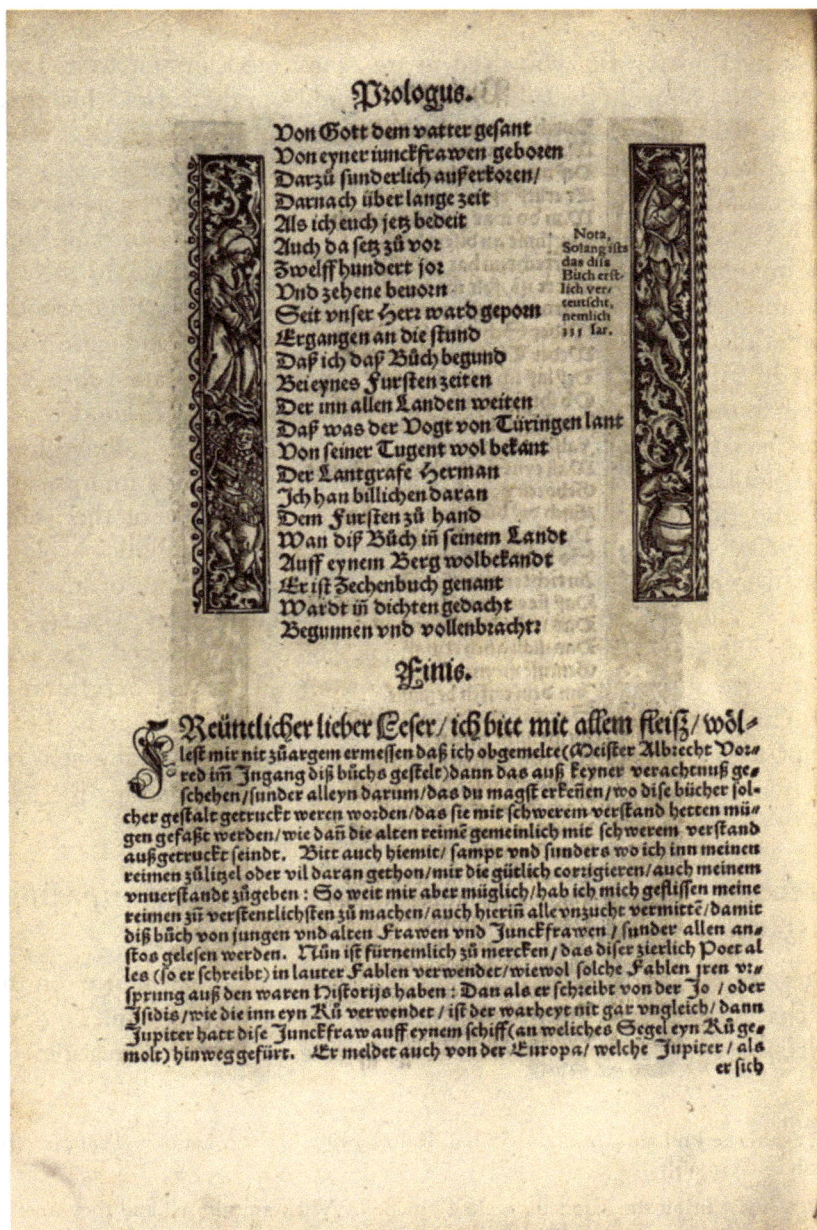

Figure 14.1. Prologue. Jörg Wickram, *P. Ouidij Nasonis deß aller sinnreichsten Poeten Metamorphosis, Das ist von der wunderbarlichen Verenderung der Gestalten der Menschen, Thier vnd anderer Creaturen* (Mainz: Ivo Schöffer, 1545), fol. a3[v], München, Bayerische Staatsbibliothek, 2.A.gr.b.1037#Beibd.1.

analysis of the prologue see Rücker (1997: 29–53); among the attempts at reconstructing its original form see Kralik (1928).

other coeval poets who who used to translate into German from French source-texts, Albrecht declared he had worked from the Latin, which makes his undertaking particularly interesting.[24]

Wickram's edition is a complex multimodal enterprise: each book displays subdivisions, which lead the reader into the development of the plot. An analogous orientation function is played by the *maniculae* located at the margin of the main text pointing at relevant passages in the story. Wickram's adaptation, moreover, is endowed with beautiful woodcuts placed at the beginning and in various parts of the books (see Figure 14.2).[25] Myths are also provided with summarizing titles, similar to the rubric which can be found in B, which were probably written on the model of the *Narrationes fabularum ovidianarum*, but they could as well derive from a model similar to Arnulf's commentary. Gerhard Lorichius's interpretations (*Außlegungen*) accompany the text as well: at the request of the Mainzer printer Ivo Schöffer, Lorichius (1485-before 1553), a Catholic theologian, prepared moralizing comments to be added at the end of the myth sequences, though they are not inserted in a systematic way. Usually, after summarizing the contents of the book to be interpreted, he added authoritative supporting arguments, e.g. from the Sacred Scriptures and other Christian sources. His undertaking is noteworthy as it is the first attempt to moralize the *Metamorphoses* in the German speaking area more than two centuries after the paramount French undertaking, the *Ovide moralisé* (1309-1320).[26]

Albrecht von Halberstadt and Jörg Wickram: comparing translation strategies

A look into some translation strategies will provide evidence on how Albrecht and Wickram recast Ovid's *Metamorphoses* in German. To do this a selection of examples grouped according to fixed categories and

---

[24] See again the Prologue, lines 54–55 (ed. Roloff 1990: 8): 'von Latin zu Teütsche' [from Latin to German].

[25] In the first edition the woodcuts were 47 made by Wickram himself and they were later substituted with a series of 178 woodcuts created by the Nuremberg master Virgil Solis. A digital facsimile of the *editio princeps* is available on the website of the Bavarian State library: <http://mdz-nbn-resolving.de/urn:nbn:de:bvb:12-bsb10139926-7> [accessed 9 December 2019]. For an analysis of the iconographic apparatus see Huber-Rebenich, Lütkemeyer, Hermann 2004 and Blattner 1998.

[26] By the decision of the first modern editors, these comments were excluded from the first modern edition (Bolte 1905–1906: xxxiv). Stackmann (1966) managed to bring scholars' attention back to them, so they have been included in the latest modern edition of Wickram's *Metamorphoses* edited by Roloff (1990).

corresponding to specific features will be considered: transitions between tales, nouns and epithets, time and place expressions and finally *realia*.

a. Transitions between myths

It is well-known that Ovid's style is characterized by quick passages between the narrations – realized by means of one verse or even one word only – which result in an apparent dissimulation of the solid structure of the carmen perpetuum (Albrecht 2009: 131). The fine interconnections among the fables, however, are visible in the architecture of the books and, on a more enlarged perspective, in the whole work which follows both a chronological and a genealogical development.

The only fragment of the German *Metamorphoses* in which we can observe the narrative transition from one myth to the other is B. In Ovid the passage from the tale of Phoebus and Pan to the story of Laomedon is achieved as follows: 'Ultus abit Tmolo liquidumque per aera vectus | [...] | Laomedonteis Latoius adstitit arvis (Ovid, *Metamorphoses*, XI. 194–96) [His vengeance now complete, Latona's son retires from Tmolus and [...] he came to earth in the country of Laomedon].[27] Phoebus had turned Midas's ears in those of a donkey because, during the music competition against Pan, the king disagreed with Tmolus's verdict: the god's vengeance is expressed here only by the participle 'ultus' and Ovid refers to him with the matronimic 'Latoius', that is Latona's son. This is a good example of the stylistic virtuosity characterizing Ovid's writing, which Albrecht does not imitate. On the contrary he alters the text with the purpose to make it more explicit, first by transforming the participle into a full sentence and then by avoiding the matronimic: 'Als ich han gesprochen, | hete sich gerochen | Phebus (fragment B, 72-74) [As I said | Phoebus had taken revenge | and went away]. The passage is rendered unambiguous by Wickram too, who prefers to repeat the name 'Midas' to avoid any confusion: 'Phebus der hatt gerochen sich | An Mida gantz gewaltigklich' (Wickram, *Metamorphosen*, xi. 349-50) [Phoebus, he took revenge | against Midas in such a violent way].[28]

---

[27] The quotations and translations from the *Metamorphoses* are derived from Miller's bilingual edition 1966–1968.

[28] Wickram's *Metamorphosen* are quoted according to the critical edition published by Roloff 1990.

Das Sechste büch Ouidij.

Inhalt der dritten Figur des sechsten buchs Ouidij von verenderung der Gestalten.

Tereus fart inn Thraciam
Philomela begert über Meer
Tereus brint inn liebe hert
Philomele wirt jr Zung abgeschnitten
Progne zu jrer schwester kam
Jr eigen kinde tödet sie gar
Sie gwinnen all drey Vogels gstalt
Fürt Orithyam hin mit gwalt

Philomela auch inn den Saal kam
Jr vatter darumb trawret seh:
Von seinen Schweher wirt er gewert
Bachis fast hale man mit unsitten
Wirt jrem man Tereo gram
Philomela mit dem haupt kumpt dar
Boreas inn grosse lieb falt

Tereus schneit Philomele die Zungen ab damit sie semlichen zwanck sal nit von jm auß bring left sie ellend vnd betrüpt inn der wüste allein / fart mit seinem Schiff wider daruon. xvij.

Er trawen jm sein hertz erschreckt
So ward er auch aus zorn bwegt
Das er inn groß verzweifflung kam
Von jrm golfarben hor er nam
Daraus macht er eyn starck gebend
Vnd band die zarten weissen hend
Der Philomela an den rucken
Thet demnach bhende eyn messerzucken
Davon die trawrig junckfraw jung
Empfohen thet grosse hoffnung
Vermeinet der schalck wird sie tödten
Damit jr gholffen würd auß nöten

* Philomela wirt mit jrem hor gebunden.

* Philomela freut sich des Tods.

Den hals reck sie jm willig dar
Vnd thet jhn erst bschelten gar
Domit er sie an als mitleiden
Mit seinem messer thet durchschneiden
Er aber mit eyner Eyßnen zangen
Jr Zungen riß aus jren wangen
Vnd schneid jr die ab mit dem schwert
Zu sterben sie er erst begert
Zu sein Schiff gieng der schalckhafft ge-
Vn für dohin mit schnelle wind schwind
Heim inn sein stat zu seiner Frawen
Heimlich hat im deß mordts gerawen
Wiewol er nie der gleichen thet
Darzu kein wort nie dauon redt
Bald er zu Progne sein weib kam
Vnd aber sie gar nicht vernam
Wie es doch vmb jr schwester stünd
Do fragt sie jren man geschwind
Erdochte antwurt er jr bode
Vnd sagt sie wer vor langem tode

Doch

Figure 14.2. Illustration to Book VI. (Procne and Philomena). Jörg Wickram, *P. Ouidij Nasonis deß aller sinnreichsten Poeten Metamorphosis, Das ist von der wunderbarlichen Verenderung der Gestalten der Menschen, Thier vnd anderer Creaturen* (Mainz: Ivo Schöffer, 1545), fol. s1ᵛ, München, Bayerische Staatsbibliothek, 2.A.gr.b.1037#Beibd.1

Similar strategies may be observed throughout the text, for instance at the end of a tale belonging to the Trojan cycle of the *Metamorphoses*: Apollo and Neptune volunteered to help Laomedon build the walls of Troy, but the king did not honour his promise and did not reward the gods. In anger, Neptune flooded the land and wanted to sacrifice Laomedon's daughter Hesione to a sea monster. Hercules freed her, but Laomedon refused to reward him with the horses he promised: as a consequence, Hercules campaigned against Troy with the help of Telamon, to whom Hesione is eventually given as a reward. Telamon is mentioned only to introduce his brother Peleus and his wife Thetis who are the protagonists of the following myth. Thetis is referred to as 'goddess' and 'wife': 'siquidem Iovis esse nepoti | contigit haut uni, coniunx dea contigit uni' (Ovid, *Metamorphoses*, XI. 219–20) [since it had fallen to not one alone to be grandson of Jove, but to him alone had it fallen to have a goddess for his wife]. In both German versions the translators prefer to explicitly mention her name, so that the reader can easily connect this tale with the following one, where she is the protagonist. Moreover, whereas in the Latin version Thetis is simply described as a goddess, the German texts add the epithet 'dame' and a periphrastic verse explaining that she is the sea queen: 'vrowe Thetis […] | des meres koniginne' (fragment B, 124–25) [lady Thetis, | queen of the sea]. It is likely that the translator wanted to anticipate the 'viriginis […] marinae' to be read later (Ovid, *Metamorphoses*, XI. 228) and to provide his reader with all the necessary information about the character he had just introduced. Albrecht's strategy is perfectly replicated by Wickram, whose version is also aimed at helping the reader by means of the removal of ambiguity in a passage which would probably be difficult to interpret: 'Fraw Thetis | deß Meers königin zart' (Wickram, *Metamorphosen*, XI. 396) [when lady Thetis, the sweet queen of the sea].

The shift from the third to the fourth myth, that is from the love story of Peleus and Thetis to the tale of Daedalion and Chione, is achieved by means of a character who is absent in both stories (*transitio per rem absentem*). In *Metamorphoses* XI Ovid narrates that the hero Peleus killed his brother Phocus, and that he is consequently forced to leave his land and seek shelter with king Ceyx, in Trachis. Given that Phocus is neither part of the third nor of the fourth myth, the reference to him in the Latin text has the sole function of leading the reader into the next fable.

> Felix et nato, felix et coniuge Peleus,
> et cui, si demas iugulati crimina Phoci,
> omnia contigerant: fraterno sanguine sontem
> expulsumque domo patria Trachinia tellus
> accipit.
>
> (Ovid, *Metamorphoses*, XI. 266–70)

[Peleus was blessed in his son, blessed in his wife, and to him only good befell, if you except the crime of the murdered Phocus. Driven from his father's house with his brother's blood upon his hands, he found asylum in the land of Trachin.]

The German translator adds more information concerning the reason why Peleus had killed his brother, that it is a disagreement ('durch ein zetrage*n*' fragment B, 233), but it is also plausible that the verse has the function of helping the poet build the couplet (fragment B, 232–33 'erslagen' : 'zetrage*n*'). Moreover, the translator clarifies the connection between the Peleus and Phocus, which in the Latin text is realized by means of the sole expression 'fraternal blood'. Wickram aligns with Albrecht, even though he does not mention any reason for the fratricide. It is worth noting that Albrecht also tries to reproduce some stylistic devices used by Ovid: the repetitions in 'felix et nato, felix et coniuge Peleus', indeed, are rendered in the verses 'an wibe, an kinde, Peleus' (fragment B, 229) [in his wife and in his son, Peleus], but they are lost in Wickram. Albrecht's translation, moreover, appears to have a mistake: instead of 'Trachinia tellus' (Ovid, *Metamorphoses*, XI. 269) [the land of Trachin], the text witnesses 'zeinem koning in Tracyam' (fragment B, 237) [to a king in Thrace], which could be either a scribal misreading of the passage in the source text or derive from the model he was using:[29]

> Unde wart ein selech man alsus
> an wibe, an kinde, Peleus,
> unde heter aller selden teil,
> gebrech im et ein unheil.
> Er hete Focum erslagen,
> den brûder sin, durch ein zetragen.
>
> (fragment B, 228–33)

[He became blessed then, | Peleus, in his wife and in his son | and he had all the joys, | if only a misfortune did not damage him. | He had killed Focum, | his brother, for a disagreement.]

> Peleus der ward eyn selig man
> Dann im an keynem glück zerran
> Biß das es sich hinach zu trug
> Sein eygnen bruder er erschlug
>
> (Wickram, *Metamorphosen*, XI. 493–96)

[Peleus was a happy man | and he did not miss any luck | until it happened | that he killed his own brother.]

---

[29] Magnus's (1914b: 693) apparatus, for instance, records *tracia* in M (= Cod. Marciano florentino 225, tenth-twefth century) and *trachiam* in N (= Cod. Neapolitano IV F 3, eleventh century).

As one can infer from these examples, the Middle High German texts displays a regular removal of ambiguities in the quick and implicit passages between the tales, to make it easier for his reader to establish connections. It is also noteworthy that Albrecht to some extent tried to reproduce Ovid's stylistic devices. In this regard, Wickram's attitude looks less regular: he sometimes accepts Albrecht's innovations such as the alterations in myth transitions, sometimes not, as in the case of style imitation.

b. Onomastic variance

Another phenomenon to consider is onomastic variance: as already mentioned in the previous section Ovid often refers to characters by means of patronimics, matronimics, or characterising epithets. Albrecht instead chooses to employ a single name variant, which he occasionally substitutes with conventional epithets. For instance, where Ovid uses 'Apollo', 'Phoebus', 'Delius', and the matronimic 'Latoius' to identify the god of music, both German versions witness a single form, 'Phoebus'.[30]

Beyond the recurring tendency of simplifying Ovidian proper nouns, an interesting phenomenon related to onomastic variation is to be seen in the myth of Procne and Philomela in fragment A (Ovid, *Metamorphoses*, VI). It narrates that Procne asks her husband Tereus to go visit her father Pandion to convince him to bring Philomela (Procne's sister) back to her. Albrecht's text begins with Philomela's request and is interrupted at Tereus's reaction at the sight of the woman. Albrecht employs the form 'Philomena' instead of 'Philomela': to some scholars the variant used by Albrecht might derive from a corrupted form and might also be a sign that the German translator had made use of a French source text.[31] The variant 'Philomena' is actually found in both Latin and vernacular sources and it is attested for example in Arnulf's glosses or in the Old French version of the myth assigned to Chrétien de Troyes, which is handed down only in the *Ovide moralisé*.[32] However, a first text comparison between the Middle High German and the Old French version of the tale showed substantial differences, which weakens the hypothesis that the German translator had employed a French model.[33]

---

[30] See fragment B, 19; 29 and Wickram, *Metamorphosen*, XI. 272; 275; 294; 305; 349.

[31] Neumann (1955: 352) considers it an erroneous variant. See also Saibene 2018b: 186.

[32] In Arnulf's glosses: 'Philomena in luciniam. Thereus in hupupam. Progne in hirundinem. Itis in fasianum' [Philomena in a nightingale, Thereus in a hoopoe, Progne in a swallow, Itis in a pheasant]. Ghisalberti 1932: 215. In the Prologue of his *Cligés*, Chrétien de Troyes refers to his adaptation of the myth in Old French, which has been identified with the one embedded in the French *Ovide moralisé* (first edited by De Boer in 1909 and included in the latest edition of Chrétien's œuvres by Poirion 1994).

[33] See Behmenburg 2009; Cappellotto 2019: 155–70.

Fragment C, preserving the story of Iphis and Anaxarete, witnesses another kind of translation strategy concerning nouns. At the very beginning of fragment C Vertumnus, in the guise of an old lady, tries to convince Pomona to return his love. To that end, Ovid mentions Venus and Nemesis: the former is hidden behind the epithet 'Idalia', standing for Idalio, and is in Cyprus, a place of worship dedicated to her, while the latter has the epithet 'Rhamnousia', that is the goddess of Rhamnous, an ancient Greek city in Attica: 'Ultoresque deos et pectora dura perosam | Idalien memoremque time Rhamnusidis iram!' (Ovid, *Metamorphoses*, XIV. 693–94) [And have a thought for the avenging gods and the Idalian goddess who detests the hard of heart, and the unforgetting wrath of Nemesis!]. Albrecht and Wickram render unambiguous the reference to Venus, whereas the one to Nemesis is avoided in both German references: 'Ouc]h vurchte du der gote zorn | un]de Veneris ze vorn (fragment C, 14–15) [And be afraid of the gods' anger, | above all of Venus]; 'Veneris | der Gœttin' (Wickram, *Metamorphosen*, xiv. 811) [Venus the goddess]. Simplification seems to be the guiding principle of the German translators, who decided either to unveil Ovid's variations or omit them, to make the audience easily find its way within the onomastic tangle characterizing the Latin text.

Another interesting translation strategy regarding nouns can be found in the third myth handed down in fragment B. In the Latin source text the character is described as 'senex [...] Proteus' (Ovid, *Metamorphoses*, XI. 221) [the old [...] Proteus] and later as 'Carpathius [...] vates' (Ovid, *Metamorphoses*, XI. 249) [Carpathian [...] seer].[34] In the Middle High German translation he first appears as 'der manechvalde' (fragment B, 127) [the manifold], then as 'der wissage' (fragment B, 190) [the seer]. Proteus's capability to transform himself in this tale as it is told by Ovid, *Metamorphoses*, XI is not relevant at all here, given that the only one who changes her appearance is Thetis. Hence, either the translator had a model that contained this specific reference (in the form of a gloss for instance) or he could remember this detail from another passage of the Latin source where Proteus was actually described as the one who could 'transire figuras' (Ovid, *Metamorphoses*, VIII. 730) [to assume many forms]. It might be that the translator considered it a detail that was worth adding, because it anticipated Thetis's ability of transformation narrated throughout the myth.

Further, in the source text dealing with the same myth Jove is assigned the epithet 'Aeaciden' (Ovid, *Metamorphoses*, XI. 227) [the son of Aeacus], which is used to define Eacus's descendants, whereas Peleus appears as 'nepotem' [grandchild]: 'In suaque Aeaciden succedere vota nepotem | iussit et amplexus in virginis ire marinae' (Ovid, *Metamorphoses*, XI. 227–28) [and

---

[34] 'Carpathius' refers to the island of Carpathus, where Proteus comes from.

bade his grandson, the son of Aeacus, assume the place of lover in his stead, and seek a union with this virgin of the deep]. Both German versions omit Jove's epithet, which is not relevant at all for narrative purposes, whereas Albrecht turns the Latin noun 'nepotem' into a more general 'kunne' [relative]: 'Dez hiez er daz sin kunne | sie neme, Peleus, vor in | unde minnete die gottin (fragment B, 143–45) [he decided that his relative | Peleus, had to take her instead of him | so he loved the goddess]. The reference to a 'nephew' or to a 'relative' is rendered totally unambiguous in the early modern text, which reads 'Peleus' instead: 'Dann er | der gröst | So jemals war | Umb solchs Peleus thet kummen dar' (Wickram, *Metamorphosen*, xi. 415–16) [Then he, the great, made Peleus come to this purpose].

As one can see from these few examples, onomastic analysis is certainly relevant in at least two ways: it reveals a translation pattern according to which names are regularly simplified in the target text, where they appear in a single form without any variance. A look at nouns, however, is relevant also to detect plausible models used by the translator. Besides, sometimes epithets undergo a process of transformation, which suggest that the translator was familiar enough with the source text and with mythology to be able to move them according to his needs. In Wickram's translation there is a general tendency to comply with the Middle High German text, however with some deviations such as in the case of Philomela, which is not necessarily an innovation of the early modern German translator but might be related to the source text he used.

c. Place and time expressions

Place and time references are other interesting points to consider in the detection of translation strategies which are similar to the ones observed so far. It is well known that Ovid's stylistic virtuosity is characterized by a wide use of periphrastic expressions, above all when it comes to descriptions of places and time references. The first example chosen can be found at the beginning of the tale about Peleus and Thetis. In the Latin source text the description of the setting is very detailed:

> Est sinus Haemoniae curvos falcatus in arcus,
> bracchia procurrunt: ubi, si foret altior unda,
> portus erat; summis inductum est aequor harenis;
> litus habet solidum, quod nec vestigia servet
> nec remoretur iter nec opertum pendeat alga;
>
> (Ovid, *Metamorphoses*, XI. 229–33)

[There is a bay on the Thessalian coast, curved like a sickle into two bays with arms running out; it would be a safe port for ships if the water were deeper. The

sea spreads smooth over the sandy bottom; the shore is firm, such as leaves no
trace of feet, delays no journey, is free from seaweed]

Albrecht simplifies the Latin and substitutes the word 'falcatus' [curved like
a sickle] with 'die krumbe' [inlet], defining in more general terms the place
where the story is set. The rest of the description is quite close to the source
text, even though the impression is that the effort to render the content in
detail somehow affects the stylistic quality of the target text:

> In Emonyen an einer stat
> hat daz mere sinen stad
> also nidere daz die unden
> scupphen under stunden
> dar uf an ungeverte
> und ist sin sant so herte
> daz er trites nicht gevazzet
> noch vûzes nicht ne lazzet.
>
> (fragment B, 150–57)

[In a place in Haemonia | the sea has its shore, | so low that the waves | often
shattered | there onto the savage place. | And its sand is so hard | that neither
footstep is impressed | nor foot is restrained.]

For the sake of comparison, it is worth noting that the same verses are
densely glossed by Arnulf d'Orléans: 'est sinus id est angulus, describit
locum ubi capta fuit Thetis. falcatus ad modum falcis curuatur' (Gura 2010:
248) [*est sinus* that is a gulf, it describes the place where Thetis was captured;
falcatus curved in the guise of a sickle]. The early modern version at the
corresponding place substitutes the general reference employed by Albrecht
with the phrase 'geformet wie eyn sichel' [in the shape of a sickle], that is
perfectly overlapping the 'falcatus sinus' to be found in Ovid and it is
evidence that here Wickram probably could rely on the Latin source:

> Inn Emonien an eynem ort
> Hatt das Meer so eyn nider port
> Das die wallen zu zeiten groß
> Das port bedecken [...]
> [...] so ist der sandt
> So hart | so man schon darinn dritt
> Thut man keyn huffschlag sehen nitt
> Darzu so ist der stad all rumb
> Geformet wie eyn sichel krumb
>
> (Wickram, *Metamorphosen*, XI. 419–28)

[In a place in Haemonia | the sea has such a low shore | that the waves that
sometimes were big | covered the shore [...] | [...] so the sand is so hard that

when one steps on it | you cannot see any footstep. | Moreover, the shore all around | has the shape of a curved sickle.]

This is an example showing that the early modern version sometimes disregards the Middle High German text, when it oversimplifies Ovid; however, this attitude is not at all consistent. In the myth of Procne and Philomela, for instance, Ovid describes in geographical detail Tereus's departure from the Cecropian harbour towards the shores of the Piraeus, where King Pandion is located: 'iubet ille carinas | in freta deduci veloque et remige portus | Cecropios intrat Piraeaque litora tangit' (Ovid, Metamorphoses, vi. 444–46) [Tereus accordingly bade them to launch his ship, and plying oar and sail, he entered the Cecropian harbour and came to land on the shores of Piraeus]. Albrecht substitutes the detailed place reference with the adverb 'dare' [there]: 'Ou]ch stunt der wint dare wart, | dar] der koning wolde vare, | de]s quam er vil schiere dare' (fragment A, 20–22) [The wind was also favourable, | when the king wanted to leave, | so they arrived there quickly]. This time, the same reading is accepted in the early modern text: 'Der wind im auch gantz glücklich wardt | Zů seinem fürgenomnem far | Darum kam er kürtzlichen dar' (Wickram, Metamorphosen, VI. 925–27) [The wind became also very favourable to him | to his undertaken journey | so he arrived quickly].

Both German poets might have thought that the Latin text would be too difficult for their audience to understand and not relevant enough for the narrative development of the tale. For the same reasons, in the description of the areas Phoebus flies over before chancing upon the sight of Laomedon building the walls of Troy (that is at the beginning of the second myth handed down in fragment B), the German translators omit the references to 'the narrow sea of Helle, daughter of Nephele' as well as to 'the Sigean and the Rhoethean promontories' and to the 'Panomphaean Thunderer' to be read in Ovid ('angustum citra pontum Nepheleidos Helles | [...] | dextera Sigei, Rhoetei laeva profundi | ara Panomphaeo vetus est sacrata Tonanti': Ovid, Metamorphoses, XI. 195–98). In fact, both turn these periphrastic geographic expressions into a very much vaguer place indication: 'von der luft, da er swanch' (fragment B, 76) [from the air, where he soared]; 'Biß er von dem Lufft sehen kundt' (Wickram, Metamorphosen, XI. 352) [until he could see from the air].

Time references are often reduced as well, as one can see in the story of Peleus trying to seduce Thetis. After receiving Proteus's advice on the strategy to adopt to overpower Thetis, Peleus comes back to the usual place where the goddess rests with the aim of catching her during the afternoon. The time reference in the Latin source is a long periphrastic expression conveying the information that the action took place in the afternoon: 'Pronus erat Titan inclinatoque tenebat | Hesperium temone fretum, cum pulchra relecto | Nereis ingreditur consueta cubilia saxo' (Ovid, *Metamorphoses*, XI. 257–59) [Now Titan was sinking low and kept the western sea beneath his down-sloping chariot, when the fair Nereid, seeking again the grot, lay down upon her accustomed couch]. Both vernacular versions reject this exquisitely Ovidian time reference, as it was probably too difficult to understand for an audience which was not strong enough in mythology, and make it unambiguous: 'Diu sunne ie zů ze tale schoz | Vergangen war der mitter tach' (fragment B, 203–04) [The sun came down to the valley | midday had passed]; 'Die Sunn jetzundt ab zu thal schoß | Vergangen was der mitte tag' (Wickram, *Metamorphosen*, XI. 472–73) [The sun now came down to the valley | midday had passed]. Interestingly, the same passage seems in need of further explanation also in Arnulf's glosses, so it is possible that the translator employed a similar source text while translating from the Latin: '*pronus erat Titan* descriptio est serotini temporis' (Gura 2010: 257) [*pronus erat Titan* this is the description of the evening time].

Such a pattern is recognizable in fragment B. In the tale of Phoebus and Pan: after the servant whispered into a hole that Midas had donkey-like ears, he covered the secret so that no-one else would know it and went away. Ovid describes the passing of time by means of the following expression: 'creber harundinibus tremulis ibi surgere lucus | coepit et, ut primum pleno maturuit anno, | prodidit agricolam (Ovid, *Metamorphoses*, XI. 190–92) [but a thick growth of whispering reeds began to spring up there, and these, when at the year's end they came to their full size, betrayed the sower]. In contrast to Ovid, the earlier vernacular version avoids giving any time information, whereas the early modern version sums it up with the adverb 'bald' [soon]: 'Seht wie roren da entsprungen, | die riefen unde sungen (fragment B, 64–65) [see how reeds grew there, | that called and sang]; 'Bald darnach wuchsen rhor sehr groß' (Wickram, *Metamorphosen*, XI. 338) [Soon after big reeds grew].[35]

d. Realia

In addition to translation phenomena concerning nouns or the rendering of time and place expressions, significant changes involve translating other kinds of *realia*. To this purpose, it is worth considering the description of

[35] It is worth noting that Albrecht provides an additional piece of information, which is rejected by Wickram: 'Daz stopphen was in unplech' (fragment B, 63 the coverage [of the hole in the ground] was abandoned). The detail is relevant, as it creates a cause-effect relation between the fact that the servant did not look after the evidence that he buried in the ground and the growth of the singing reeds. In other words, this verse allows the reader to trace connections within the narration and, in this way, it makes it easier to follow.

Philomela. In Ovid the immense beauty of the young woman is described in four verses where she is compared to nymphs such as Naiads and Dryads: 'quales audire solemus | naidas et dryadas mediis incedere silvis' (Ovid, *Metamorphoses*, VI. 452–53) [such as we are wont to hear the naiads described, and dryads when they move about in the deep woods]. Albrecht describes her as more wonderful than all the other women on earth, and to outline her beauty he makes use of several associations: the Roman empresses, the morning star, a divine miracle, a gemstone, the flower of May (fragment A, 43–81), and finally 'Ein]er wilden feyen' (fragment A, 80) [a wild fairy]. This last association is quite unusual: it certainly helps the translator to adapt the classical mythological reference (to the naiads and the dryads) into Germanic lower mythology that his reader would have been more familiar with.[36] Another explanation for adding this witty comparison is to show that Philomena, beyond being a pure chaste being, also has an uncanny appeal. This can somehow differently distribute the responsibility of the violence described in the Latin source text, induced not so much by the native attitude of Thracian people to lust, as described in Ovid (*Metamorphoses* VI. 455–60), but rather by the seductive appearance of the woman and by the destructive power of the *minne*.[37] Diversely, Wickram's early modern adaptation reminds the reader that Philomela's beauty is connected to her chastity, as it is clear from the celestial description provided in his rendering: 'Gleich imm Meyen die blůmlin reyn'; 'Philomela der Jungfrawen zart' (Wickram, *Metamorphosen*, VI. 977; 981) [like the pure flower of May; Philomena, the sweet maiden]. The quality of the maiden disappears in Wickram's text, whereas Albrecht's translation emphasizes it: none of the German versions seem to adhere to the source text in both form and style, even though the substance of the story is kept unaltered. The need to turn the portrayal of Philomela into a *descriptio puellae* can be also explained by the attempt to align to coeval literature and to the literary taste of the addressed audience.[38]

Another example is to be found in the tale revolving around the love story between Peleus and Thetis. In Ovid Thetis is described as a beautiful Nereid: 'pulchra [...] Nereis' (Ovid, *Metamorphoses*, XI. 258–59), whereas Albrecht assigns to her the typical and less characterizing female attribute

---

[36] Similar renderings for Phoebus: 'deum pecoris' (Ovid, *Metamorphoses*, XI. 160) [shepherd-god] turned into 'got der twerge' (fragment B, 25) [god of the dwarfs].

[37] See in particular Ovid, *Metamorphoses*, VI. 460, explaining the connection of Thereus attitude through his genealogy: 'flagrat vitio gentisque suoque' [his own fire and his nation's burnt in him].

[38] See for instance the Camilla's portray in Heinrich von Veldeke, *Eneit*, 5142–85 (Kartschoke 2010).

'wonderful' (fragment B, 206 'die wunderen scone Thetis').[39] Thetis used to rest in a grotto after riding her dolphin naked: 'quo saepe venire | frenato delphine sedens, Theti, nuda solebas' (Ovid, *Metamorphoses*, XI. 236–37) [to this grot oftentimes, riding thy bridled dolphin, O Thetis, naked wast thou wont to come]. For Albrecht the Nereid is 'naked on her dolphin' and soon 'naked and ready' (fragment B, 163 'nacket uf ir delphin'; 165 'nacket und also bereit'), two expressions which are maintained in Wickram (*Metamorphosen*, XI. 433 'Nackent saß sie uff irn Delphin' [naked she sat on her dolphin]; 437 'Das sie Peleus gantz nackent fandt' [that Peleus found her completely naked]). The Ovidian source emphasizes the nakedness as well, but by repeating the adjective twice within to verses the Middle High German version seems to disclose a moral judgment and conveys the idea that because Thetis is naked she is ready to be possessed by Peleus. The suspicion here is that the verse might derive from another gloss, but it might be also an innovation by the translator who wants to wink at a Christian audience, as happens with Tereus, who is defined as 'des tiubels genoz' (fragment A, 107) [the devil's companion].

The first time Peleus tries to assault Thetis, the maiden manages to escape the abuse by turning into different forms: a bird, a tree and finally a tiger. It is surely remarkable that at this point the Latin and early modern versions correspond whereas the Middle High German text displays a variant, since the tiger is substituted with a bison: 'Tertia forma fuit maculosae tigridis' (Ovid, *Metamorphoses*, XI. 245) [the third disguise was a spotted tigress' form]; 'Als ein wisent vreisam' (fragment B, 182) [a cruel bison]; 'Ward sie inn eyn groß Tiger thier' (Wickram, *Metamorphosen*, XI. 451) [she turned into a big tiger]. It might be that the translator wanted to choose an animal his audience could be more familiar with, but this variant was already present in the Latin source, as the *fabula* shows a certain amount of fluidity within its transmission (Galasso, Paduano, and Perutelli 2000: 1357).

Another interesting *locus* of comparison regarding *realia* is to be found again in fragment B (Phoebus and Pan). The competition is assessed by the judge/mount Tmolus, whose sentence is favourable to the god Apollo: all creatures agree with Tmolus's decision, except for Midas, whose ears are turned into donkey's ears as a punishment for questioning Tmolus's authority. In the Latin source text Midas hides his ears under a 'purpureis [...] tiaris' (Ovid, *Metamorphoses*, XI. 181) [a purple [...] turban], whereas the old German version changes it into 'Eine huben von zindale' (fragment B, 40) [a silk bonnet], an object which was more fashionable in the target-

---

[39] At the end of the first myth she was called 'des meres koniginne' (fragment B, 125) [the sea queen].

culture. This change is maintained also in Wickram's version, which reads 'Eyn haub gemacht von Zendel rich' (Wickram, *Metamorphosen*, xi. 315) [a bonnet made of fine silk]. Ovid specifies that Apollo (i.e. 'Delius') out of anger decides to turn Midas's ears into donkey ears: 'cetera sunt hominis, partem damnatur in unam | induiturque aures lente gradientis aselli' (Ovid, *Metamorphoses*, XI. 178–79) [Human in all else, in this one feature was he punished, and wore the ears of a slow-moving ass]. In this case Albrecht gives the reader a further help in understanding the metamorphosis by explaining that the ass, like Midas, is unintelligent (literally slow in understanding), an addition which is maintained also in Wickram:

> Phebus schůf den einen teil,
> der die richte solde horen,
> daz waren des mannes oren,
> der daz urteil beschalt,
> als eines eseles gestalt.
> Der ist ouch von tragen sinnen.
>
> (fragment B, 29–34)

[Phoebus transformed the part | that should have heard the fair, | it was ears of the man, | who criticized the judgement, | in the form of those of a donkey. | It is also slow in understanding.]

> Phebus schuff bald Mida zwen ohren
> Die wolgezimpten eynem thoren
> Die hatten eynes Esels gstalt
> Umb das er solche urtheyl schalt
> Der Esel was von tregen sinnen.
>
> (Wickram, *Metamorphosen*, XI. 305–09)

[Phoebus soon turned Midas's two ears | that suit well to a stupid | They had the shape of a donkey | because he criticized that verdict. | The donkey was of slow understanding.]

This verse looks like a gloss probably taken from the model the translator was working with. In fact, right at this point, Arnulf writes in his *Allegoriae*: 'de contentione satiri i. insipientis et Apollinis i. sapientis iniuste iudicavit, aures asininas habere meruit. *Asinorum siquidem est esse stultos*' (Ghisalberti 1932: 224) [on the controversy between the satyr (that is, the ignorant) and Apollo (that is, the wise), he judged wrongly and deserved to have the ears of a donkey. *Because it is in the nature of donkeys to be stupid*].[40] As one can see, the similarity is striking and lends support to the view that medieval commentaries served as an intermediary source text for the composition of the German translation. However, it is important to underline that only

---

[40] The emphasis is mine.

further analysis can ascertain if Arnulf's *Allegoriae* was the commentary employed by the translator.

Another example of transformation of *realia* can be found in fragment C, narrating the story of Iphis and Anaxarete. According to the version of the myth given by Ovid (*Metamorphoses*, XIV. 699–771), the shepherd Iphis was in love with princess Anaxarete, who harshly refused his advances and mocked his feelings. Despairing after this refusal, Iphis asked them not to forget his story and killed himself. After his death, Iphis's mother led the corpse of her dead son around the town towards the funeral pyre: 'funera ducebat mediam lacrimosa per urbem | luridaque arsuro portabat membra feretro' (Ovid, *Metamorphoses*, XIV. 746–47) [through the midst of the city she led his tearful funeral and bore the pale corpse on a bier to the funeral pyre]. Unlike Ovid, Albrecht describes how Iphis's corpse is put into a coffin, and how it is carried through the town: 'Den toten baret men un*de* tr[uc | gebaret durch die stat hin' (fragment C, 124–25) [the corpse was put into a coffin and brought | in the coffin through the town]. This omission of the pyre and the emphasis on the coffin – the corresponding German verb 'baren' [put into a coffin] is repeated twice – could be another attempt to update the source text, as during the Christian Middle Ages cremation wasn't practiced. Instead of accepting one of the two options, Wickram rejects both and writes a general reference to Iphis's funeral cortège: 'Man den jüngling zustundt rumb trug | Mit grosem klagen durch die statt (Wickram, *Metamorphosen*, XI. 909–10) [the young man was then brought around | through the town with great mourning]. As one can see, Wickram shows an inconsistent attitude towards Albrecht and Ovid, and it is often not possible to predict his strategies.

The analysis of *realia* makes clear that Albrecht intervenes quite often: no matter if the source text is about Midas's headgear, the animals Peleus has to face, or Iphis's funeral, in all cases the medieval translator feels the need to update the text and transform specific elements to fit them into his own target culture.

Conclusion

This paper has tried to convey an idea of how the reception of Ovid developed in the German realm throughout the Middle Ages. Albrecht of Halberstadt, the author of the first vernacular translation of the *Metamorphoses* we have knowledge of, translated directly from the Latin text in a readable and enjoyable way for his audience. Where he modifies the source, such as in the case of nouns, time and place expressions, or *realia*, clear translation patterns can be recognized. His guiding principles seem to be simplification and cultural transformation; nonetheless, the substance of the narration remained unaltered and it is also possible to single out attempts to imitate some Ovidian stylistic devices. A close analysis of the text has shown that at times the translator endows the source texts with moral judgment, probably to better fit into the receiving Christian culture.

As for Wickram's later undertaking, despite recognisable but irregular attempts to go back to Ovid, text comparison has shown that the early modern rendering of the *Metamorphoses* is less consistent. This might be partly due to the fact that Wickram, next to the Middle High German text, makes use of Ovid and a number of other Latin and vernacular sources, which ended up preventing the reader tracking regular translation patterns.

Textual evidence also supports the hypothesis that Albrecht might have employed medieval commentaries to the *Metamorphoses*, which probably looked similar to the *Narrationes fabularum ovidianarum* or to Arnulf d'Orléans's *glosulae* and *allegoriae*. However, the tradition of the Middle High German text is too scarce to draw definitive conclusions and Wickram is not reliable enough to allow any further evidence-based assumption.

Lastly, the German tradition of the *Metamorphoses* can contribute to reconstructing the modes of circulation and reception of both the vernacular and Latin Ovid during the Middle Ages and it proves that the *Metamorphoses* were suitable for appreciation in different forms, languages, and cultures. The resulting picture looks complex and plural and only interdisciplinary research on this topic can produce an accurate global assessment.

15

JOHN THOLEN

FRAMING THE VERNACULAR OVID:
THE PARATEXTUAL INFRASTRUCTURE OF
THE FIRST DUTCH TRANSLATION (1552–1650)
OF OVID'S *METAMORPHOSES*

In 1558, the artist Pieter Bruegel the Elder finished a painting that is known under the name *Landscape with the Fall of Icarus*, now held in the Royal Museums of Fine Arts in Brussels.[1] The scene of Icarus falling into the water is shown as a detail in the landscape, just beneath the ship in the background. It displays the tragic death of Icarus, who ignored the parental advice not to fly too high in the sky so that the sun would not melt the wax between the feathers of his wings. It is the landscape in this painting, however, that directly connects Bruegel's scene to Ovid's version of this story. The painting refers to particular verse lines in Ovid's *Metamorphoses*, showing that it was specifically inspired by the ancient author's narrative. On Icarus's ill-fated flight, Ovid wrote:

> Hos aliquis tremula dum captat harundine pisces,
> aut pastor baculo stivave innixus arator
> vidit et obstipuit, quique aethera carpere possent,
> credidit esse deos.
> (Ovid, *Metamorphoses*, VIII. 217-20, Tarrant 2004)

[Now some fisherman spies them, angling for fish with his flexible rod, or a shepherd, leaning upon his crook, or a plowman, on his plow-handles – spies them and stands stupefied, and believes them to be gods that they could fly through the air.] (Miller 2004)

The fisherman, the shepherd, and the ploughman: all three are present in Bruegel's painting (although they do not seem stupefied by the scene, but rather are focused on their respective tasks). Through this visual citation, it can be assumed with some certainty that Ovid's text inspired Bruegel in painting his work of art.[2]

---

[1] On the name of this painting see Yeazell 2015: 97–109.

[2] See Nuechterlein 2017 on Bruegel's painting as a work of classical reception.

In 1552, a couple of years before Bruegel had finished the painting, the first Dutch translation of Ovid's text was published (USTC 408777, Tholen O 16). It recounts the Icarus scene, quite literally translated from Ovid's Latin:

> Dit vliegen siende eenen visscher die metter engel roeden by d'water lach, een herderken by sijn schaepkens, ende eenen ackerman aen zijnen ploech, werde*n*der grootelijc inne verwondert, en*de* dachten dattet niet moghelijc en ware yemant inde locht te vliegen te*n* moest eenen godt wesen.[3]

> [The sight of this flight greatly amazed a fisherman who was lying near the water with his fishing-rod, a shepherd with his sheep, and a plough-man to his plough, and they thought nobody but a god was able to fly in the sky.]

I will argue that this first Dutch translation of the *Metamorphoses* intended to convince artists such as Pieter Bruegel and his contemporaries to buy the book as a helpful tool to their work. I use 'paratextual infrastructure' as a key concept to explain this process of cultural appropriation, denoting the interaction of textual and material elements within the translated edition that guide the interpretation of the source text. In doing so, I investigate how the paratextual environment of Ovid's *Metamorphoses* played a fundamental role in its early modern reception.

The paratextual infrastructure as a transformative manifestation

My investigation of the reception of Ovid's *Metamorphoses* in the Low Countries combines two crucial insights. Firstly, translations in particular have been identified as methods for re-contextualizing texts (Barker and Hosington 2013: xviii–xxi; Belle and Hosington 2018: 5–9). Therefore, a translation cannot be defined as merely the transfer of content from one language to another: translation alters the cultural frame of reference. In this process of re-contextualisation, transformations necessarily occur (Stockhorst 2010: 23).[4] Important transformations in my case study concern the material context of book editions. Secondly, therefore, it is important to notice that the concept of an abstract text as we know it today had not yet developed in the medieval and early modern periods.[5] In general, texts were

---

[3] This is a translation by Florianus, taken from a 1615 edition (USTC 1001871; Tholen O 42): fols Q3v–4r; all the translations of early modern sources are my own.

[4] The translator played a crucial role in such processes, as Rizzi (2017) demonstrates.

[5] For example, Cerquiglini (1989) argues that medieval texts lacked a fixed, authorial status, and instead characterised by a high degree of 'variance'. Johns (1998) argues that early modern texts are fluid because their printed form provides ample opportunities for change.

fluid manifestations, depending on their particular material contexts: paratextual aspects importantly influenced the reading experience of Ovid's *Metamorphoses* within the material context of a book. Early modern text and paratext could not be identified as separate categories within their material contexts, but functioned as a highly entwined synthesis.[6]

Proceeding from these views, I approach the material editions of Ovid's *Metamorphoses* as transformative manifestations: the edition's paratextual elements, such as the title page, preface, and index, functioned as important mechanisms of transfer. Analysis of these paratexts will show how they were part of an interactive construct: this paratextual infrastructure foregrounds the cluster of various paratextual elements within the edition as a consistent paratextual design by its book producers.[7]

The first Dutch translation: an Antwerp project

From 1552 onwards, such a standardised paratextual infrastructure accompanied Florianus's translation of the *Metamorphoses*; for almost a century, these paratexts were the traditional elements that provided access to the translation, and guided readers in their reception of Ovid. The paratexts enabled a meaningful transfer of the *Metamorphoses* into the urban cultural contexts of Antwerp and Amsterdam: they provided the translation of a clear, local frame.

The first edition of this Dutch translation of Ovid's *Metamorphoses* was an Antwerp project: its translator Johannes Florianus was head of the local Antwerp Latin school, its printer Hans de Laet had his workshop in the city, its dedicatee Nicolaes de Schermer was an Antwerp politician, and its intended readers were the members of the local Saint Lucas guild, with which all the artists, poets, and also printers in the city were associated.[8] Judging from the prompt succession of reprints, the project was a successful Antwerp printing concept: from its initial publication in 1552, no less than sixteen reprints up through the seventeenth century were printed, mostly in Antwerp and Amsterdam.[9] The concept was even transferred from the

---

[6] This contrasts Gérard Genette's (1997) hierarchical definition of paratextuality, in which paratexts function as subordinate texts to frame the main text. In his emphasis on the contrast with Genette's approach of modern paratext, Enenkel (2015: 7) considers the construct of early modern text and paratext 'ein miteinander unauflöslich verflochtenes Ganzes' (a deeply intertwined whole). Cf. Tholen (in press).

[7] I introduced this concept as a method to study paratext in my doctoral thesis (Tholen 2019). Cf. Tholen (in press).

[8] On the Antwerp Saint Lucas guild: Lampo 2017: 65-102; Peeters 2009.

[9] This translation was printed by De Laet in Antwerp (Florianus 1552 and 1566), and by Harmen Jansz. Muller and his heirs in Amsterdam (1588, 1599, 1609, and 1621); by Peeter (I) Beelaert and his widow in Antwerp (1595, 1608, and 1631); by Jan van

southern to the northern Low Countries: in 1588, the Amsterdam book producer Harmen Jansz. Muller almost exactly copied it. He only altered the dedicatee, resulting in a different, local group of intended readers, as I will explain later on. This continuous availability of the translation in print made Florianus's version of the *Metamorphoses* an influential factor in the early modern reception of Ovid in the Low Countries: only almost a century later, a second translation was printed.[10]

For the most part, De Laet adopted the elements of his paratextual infrastructure from Antwerp editions with Ovid's Latin text printed from the beginning of the sixteenth century.[11] He only introduced two elements that had not yet been provided in Antwerp editions of the *Metamorphoses*, but were nonetheless common in publications of Latin works: a dedication and a Latin preface. These two additional paratexts were particularly instrumental to De Laet's framing of the text. It shows how this middleman consciously constructed his paratextual infrastructure to appropriate Ovid's text for his intended cause to sell his books to the members of the Saint Lucas guild.

Clear messages from the title page

One of the first places of the paratextual infrastructure where book producers encountered their potential readers was the title page. Therefore, it was an important paratext to present books to customers commercially (Wagner 2008: 143–6; Smith 2000: 91–108). The experienced overload of printed information supported a straightforward typographical identification of the product for sale; booksellers even used the page as an advertising poster.[12]

Waesberge in Rotterdam (1615); by Gheleyn Jansens in Antwerp (1608 and 1615); by Willem Lesteens in Antwerp (1619); by Pieter van Waesberge in Rotterdam (*c.* 1635), and about the same time again; and once again in Pieter van Waesberge's 1637 edition containing Antonio Tempesta's engravings; Peeter (II) Beelaert printed two final Antwerp editions in 1650. Only the editions from 1637 onwards slightly deviate from the traditional paratextual infrastructure that had accompanied the translation since 1552. Although all these editions were part of my PhD research, my thesis has not investigated their paratextual infrastructure as a case study in particular (Tholen 2019). For references, surviving copies, and early modern ownership of these editions, see: Tholen (in press).

[10] In 1643, five book producers in Amsterdam simultaneously printed an identical edition with an anonymous translation: only the respective title pages differed (USTC 1019443, 1013754, 1013755, 10137556, and 1029288; Tholen O 61–65).

[11] The earliest Antwerp edition of Ovid's *Metamorphoses* in Latin was printed in 1529 by Govaert van der Haeghen as part of an *opera* edition (USTC 410235; Tholen O 9).

[12] On the early modern information overload, see Blair 2010; title pages as advertising posters: Shevlin 1999: 48–9.

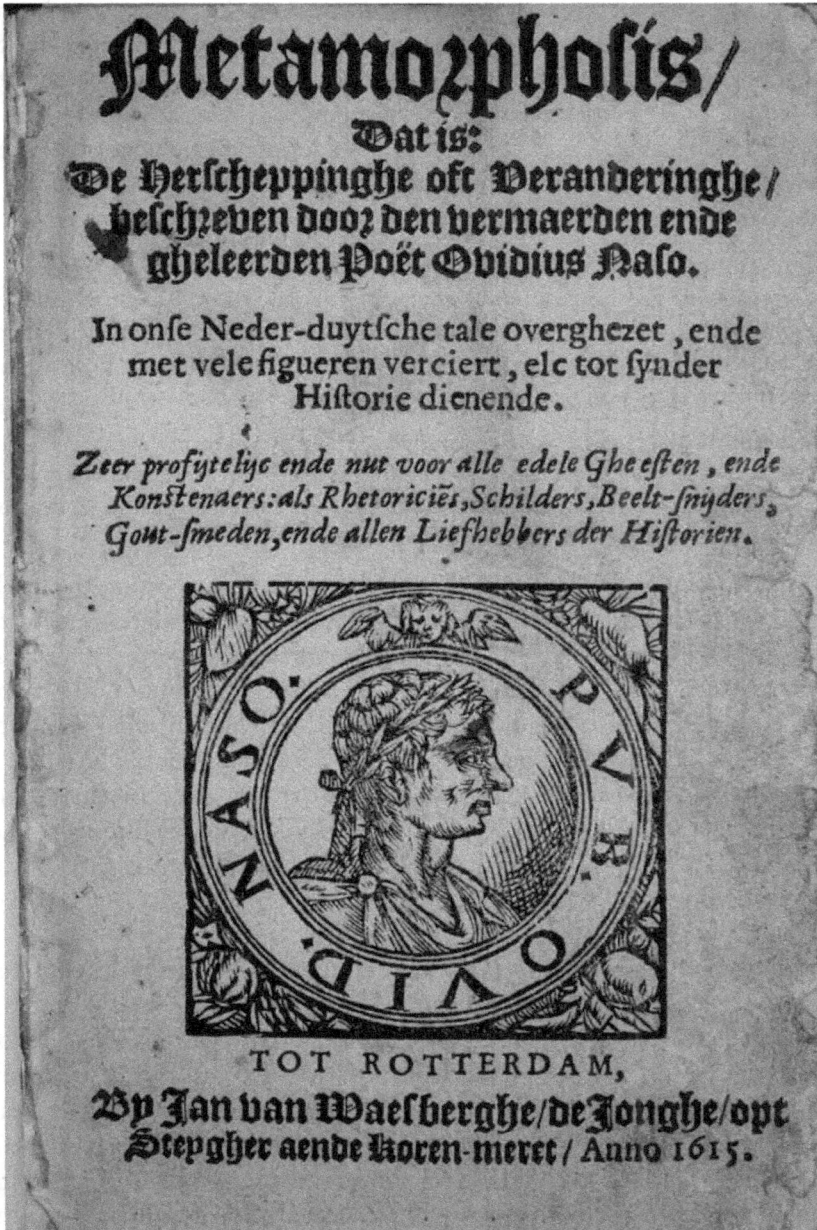

Metamorphosis/

Dat is:
De Herscheppinghe oft Veranderinghe/ beschreven door den vermaerden ende gheleerden Poët Ovidius Naso.

In onse Neder-duytsche tale overghezet, ende met vele figueren verciert, elc tot synder Historie dienende.

Zeer profytelijc ende nut voor alle edele Gheesten, ende Konstenaers: als Rhetoriciës, Schilders, Beelt-snyders, Gout-smeden, ende allen Liefhebbers der Historien.

TOT ROTTERDAM,
By Jan van Waesberghe/de Jonghe/opt Stepgher aende Koren-meret/ Anno 1615.

Figure 15.1. Title page of a reprint of Florianus's translation. Ovidius, *Metamorphosis, dat is: De herscheppinghe oft veranderinghe* (Rotterdam: Jan III van Waesberge; [Antwerpen, typ. Hendrik Swingen], 1615). Bibliotheek Rotterdam, 26 E 8; USTC 1022737; Tholen O 42.

The coherent design of the 1552 title page to Florianus's translation functions as a clear message on its intended use. As a first step, the title page clearly singles out the book's content: 'Metamorphosis', printed in the largest font on top of the page, unmistakably acknowledged the ancient text. Furthermore, the unprecedented vernacular of this Ovidian edition provoked an identification of the intended reader, who might not have been self-evident. The title formula suggests that Hans de Laet wanted to be crystal clear on this:

> Metamorphosis dat is, Die herscheppinghe oft veranderinghe, beschreuen int Latijn vanden vermaerden en*de* gheleerden Poeet Ouidius: En*de* nu eerst overghesedt in onsen duytsche: seer ghenuechlijc en*de* oock profijtelijck voor alle edele gheesten, ende constenaers, als Rhetoriciens, Schilders, Beeltsnijders, Goutsmede*n*, etc. (USTC 408777: fol. A1ʳ)

> [Metamorphoses, that is, the Recreations, or Transformations, written in Latin by the famous and learned poet Ovid. Now for the first time translated to our Dutch language. Very pleasurable and helpful to all noble minds, and artists, such as rhetoricians, painters, sculptors, goldsmiths, et cetera.]

This title formula devotes considerable attention to explaining the book's contents: a translation of a famous Latin poem on transformations. De Laet even provided two synonyms of the title: the vernacular words 'recreations' and 'transformations' explain what is meant by the Latin word 'metamorphoses'. This suggests readers who are not familiar with the classics, although they are generally acknowledged as 'noble minds'. In particular, however, the title addressed 'artists': this is a specifically defined group by four particular artistries, but at the same time it concerns an all-inclusive category by an additional 'et cetera'. In doing so, the printer-publisher commercially presented the text to an audience as broad as possible.

Apart from the message on the intended use of the book, the title page points to the credibility of the edition.[13] Underneath the title formula, a portrait of Ovid strengthens the claim on the ancient author as a 'famous and learned poet': the large woodcut prominently displays a bust of a traditional *poeta laureatus*.[14] The austere Ovid is depicted as a conventional Roman nobleman, wearing a toga and a laurel wreath. These visual and textual representations of Ovid as a sincere Roman author framed the edition as a reliable and eminent source, suitable for professional use. From the fifteenth century onwards, authenticity increasingly became an important aspect of the author's portrait, that no longer represented a rather

---

[13] Johns (1998) pointed to the high level of general mistrust towards the book world.

[14] On the tradition of depicting ancient poets as poeta laureatus: Enenkel 2015: 336–38.

generic figure.[15] Therefore humanists were in search for sources that could provide information on the ancient authors' appearances. Such a source on Ovid was presented by the Ovid commentator Hercules Ciofanus, who owned an ancient sculpture discovered in Ovid's birthplace Sulmona.[16] From the sixteenth century onwards, this sculpture provided the traditional model for representations of Ovid.

Apart from Ovid, also the book producer had a role in the creation of the edition's commercial credibility. An additional strategy to convince readers of the book's reliability concerns the imprint, the textual information on the lower part of the title page provided by book producers to represent themselves as the publishers. In the sixteenth century, its level of information increased and the imprint became an invitation to readers for visiting the print shop. This local rhetoric was especially relevant if the place sold books (Maclean 2012: 129; Smith 2014: 23; Meeus 2018: 81). The imprint on the 1552 title page clearly functions as such a navigational tool for customers: they can find the shop 'in de Camerstrate inden Salm', providing a specific location by identifying a street name and a shop sign. No matter whether customers actually accepted this invitation, De Laet created the impression of transparency.

At the bottom of the title page yet another paratext supports the edition's credibility as a reliable and useful source. It notes: 'Met gratie ende previlegie' (with approval and privilege). Such a statement on the protected status of an edition, granted by religious or legislative authorities, benefitted the edition in two ways. In the first place, it warned other book producers not to reproduce the edition without the printer's consent. In this way, printers protected their investments against the wide-spread and common practice of unauthorised copying and piracy in the book world. Secondly, such a privilege showed that the book producer presented an original product that he considered worth the high costs for applying an official privilege, that may have taken considerable time to receive. Thus, it promotes the special identity of the edition.[17]

The dedication as an address to intended readers

The front matter interacts with this title page: the edition's dedication introduces a specific group of artists as the intended readers of the translation. In doing so, it strengthens the title page claim on the edition's usability.

---

[15] See Fowler 2017: 25–27, who discusses this in the context of portraits on engraved title pages.

[16] Trapp (1995: 256, 267–68) investigates the role of this model for early modern representations of Ovid.

[17] On the practice of privileges; see: Mclean 2012: 134–70.

The front matter had a fundamental role within the construct of early modern books: prefaces and dedications were not subsidiary elements, but functioned as mediators that introduced a book and its identity to readers (Enekel 2008: 40–41 and 2015; Schitzgebel 1996). This becomes clear from my current case study. Hans de Laet included a dedication in his edition that supports the frame of this book as an indispensable tool for every kind of artist. The dedication echoes the title page statement, claiming that the translation is 'most necessary for all artists and noble minds' ['voor alle constenaren ende edel gheesten grootelijck is van noode', STCN 399363025, fol. A3ᵛ]. The dedicatee Nicolaes de Schermer in particular authorizes and specifies this claim. De Schermer was a local politician, but in the context of this book foremost important as the chairman of the Saint Lucas guild, as De Laet states in his dedicatory text. By addressing him, De Laet places the *Metamorphoses* within the specific context of the guild: the dedication designates the general group of 'artists' from the title page as the members of the local guild. In this way, De Laet created his own, specific market for the translation.[18]

The dedication also explains why the translation is useful. It poses a rhetorical question: who, nowadays, can understand painting, rhetoric, sculpture, et cetera without a knowledge of ancient mythology?[19] Thereby, Ovid's contents are presented as inevitable information for artists to do their work. De Laet presents this as self-evident: according to the dedication, the intended readers themselves had even requested the translation. As the guild members would easily have been able to disprove this statement, there is probably some truth in it: at least, most painters and rhetoricians did not master the Latin language (Van Dixhoorn, Mareel, and Ramakers 2018: 17).[20]

The Amsterdam editions of the translation used the dedication to modify the edition to the specific Amsterdam cultural context. Printer Herman Jansz. Muller reused De Laet's dedicatory letter with some minor adjustments. He replaced the Antwerp dedicatee's name in favour of the Amsterdam chamber of rhetoric De Eglantier. Thus, Muller claimed that the translation was of great importance for the chamber's members who had

---

[18] In the sixteenth century, membership of the guild significantly increased in numbers, corresponding Antwerp's 'Golden Age' of economic growth (Martens and Peeters 2006). This helps to explain De Laet's specific focus.

[19] STCN 399363025, fol. A3ʳ: 'Want wie can hedensdaechs eenighe schriften, schilderijen, ghesneden oft ghegoten werck, oft yet dat vander ouder tijdt is, verstaen: oft wie can hem in de conste van rhetorica yet vermeten, hij en moet kennisse van Poeterijen hebben?'.

[20] The painter Peter Paul Rubens forms an exception: he consulted Ovid's Latin (McGrath 2015: 160, 164-5).

repeatedly requested the edition. It established an exclusive link between the edition and Muller's intended customers.

The navigational infrastructure: a tool for artists

After having persuaded the intended readers to use the edition, the paratextual infrastructure also guides them in doing so. Three paratexts in particular show how this guidance functioned: the index, marginalia, and illustrations together present readers a navigational infrastructure that guides them to the most useful elements of Ovid's text.

An index always selects what contents it includes, and thus it influences the level of access that readers have to this contents. Therefore, the index is never an unbiased search tool (Cevolini 2014; Gilmont and Vanautgaerden 2001).[21] Early modern book producers pinpointed their indices as unique selling points of their editions. The index title in the first Dutch translation especially foregrounds the alphabetical order of the entries: although alphabetical indices were composed from the thirteenth century onwards, this was not common until the second half of the sixteenth century.[22] The title is clear about the purpose of the index: it intends to enable readers to find 'all the stories in this book' ['Een Register bij a.b.c. gereet om te vinden alle Historien van desen Boecke', STCN 843234997, fol. 2h1ʳ]. It uses the Dutch word 'Historien' (histories); in contrast to the Latin word 'historiae', the vernacular interpretation context of the word 'historien' particularly included stage performances and pictorial compositions. In this way, it alludes to a more poetical or artistic context of interpretation, instead of a historical account (Bietenholz 1994: 149). In this way, the index title foregrounds the usability of the book for its specific groups of intended readers, such as stage performers and painters.

The selection criteria of this index importantly narrowed the readers' access to Ovid's text to well-known transformations. The index foremost includes entries of the rather basic formula 'A into B', presenting Ovid's text as a source on mythological transformations, for example: 'Aglauros into a stone', or 'Jupiter into a bull'. The latter, for example, refers to the story of Jupiter falling in love with the girl Europa, transforming himself into a beautiful bull in order to kidnap her. The background story is kept out of the index: it presents the transformation as the key element in the story. Furthermore, in contrast to the title's claim to present 'all the stories', the index mainly includes the stories that have the most verse lines.

---

[21] This has been argued for religious contexts in particular: Visser 2011.

[22] On the development of the index; see Rouse and Rouse 1989: 102-04; on alphabetical indices in the early modern period: Blair 2010: 142 and Wall 2014: 170.

The index entries are only one part of the edition's navigational infrastructure, which also includes marginal notes and illustrations. Together, these paratexts guide readers to specific parts of Ovid's text. Each index entry refers to a page where a marginal annotation guides readers to a specific place in the mythological story. In the case of Aglauros, the margin notes: 'Aglauros transformed into a black stone'.[23] A reader who wanted to know the cause of this transformation is guided by another marginal note on the previous page, indicating where the story begins. Also many illustrations display scenes of transformation. Starting from the second edition in 1566, the woodcut series printed with Florianus's translation are copies of Virgil Solis's 1563 series.[24] The woodcut to the Aglauros story, for example, shows the very moment of transformation: Mercury transforms the girl, pinned to the floor, into a stone. In these ways, the core elements of the book's navigational infrastructure (the index, page numbers, marginal notes, and illustrations) guide the reader's attention to Ovid's transformations in particular. This focus supported rhetoricians and painters, who could easily find these topics as Ovid's most interesting narratives for their art works.

Persuasion of scholarly readers

As I have argued, all the paratextual elements in my discussion prominently pinpoint the artist communities in early modern Antwerp and Amsterdam in particular. There is, however, one paradoxical exception: Florianus himself wrote a humanistic preface to the reader in Latin, which was included in all the editions of his Dutch translation. The claim of the dedication that the intended readers repeatedly requested a Dutch translation implies that these readers were not proficient in Latin, and therefore unable to read the Latin preface. Therefore, the translator's Latin preface makes clear that the intended readership of the book was not limited to artists: it addresses a second group of intended readers.

The preface claims that the translation was a product of humanistic activity, and therefore also suitable to a more scholarly reader. Florianus's use of the Latin language itself suggests a context of scholarly reading (Waquet 2002: 87). The Dutch dedication presented mythology as a valuable means of education and explained the reasons for reading Ovid,

[23] STCN 843234997, fol. 33ᵛ: 'Aglauros in eenen swerten steen verandert'.

[24] The first 1552 edition was printed without illustrations; see Sluijter 2000: 194-5 for an overview of the illustrated editions printed in the Low Countries. One edition with Florianus's translation (USTC 1030028; Tholen O 57, printed in 1637) includes copies of Antonio Tempesta's engravings. Jörg Wickram's German adaptation of Ovid's work in 1545 was accompanied by forty-seven illustrations of his own authorship, later substituted by Virgil Solis's (Cappellotto 2013: 86–87).

but the Latin preface foremost exhibits classical erudition. Florianus also invites members of the Republic of Letters to make improvements to his translation. These were common elements for prefaces to humanistic publications that were used for scholarly purposes. By adding this humanistic paratext to a vernacular book, the publisher created a broader market for his edition. It echoes the 'noble minds' that were addressed by the title page: also educated readers were persuaded to buy this book.

The cultural context of vernacular Humanism

At first sight, the combination of a Dutch dedication and a Latin preface is paradoxical. It perfectly fits, however, the contemporary cultural context of vernacular Humanism: early modern cultural life in the Low Countries was deeply related to the humanistic world. Therefore, it is not surprising that the first translation of the *Metamorphoses* was brought out in Antwerp in 1552, followed by a reprint in Amsterdam only in 1588, and that it was printed by De Laet and Muller in particular. A vogue of vernacular Humanism, to which De Laet and Muller contributed as printers, created the intellectual climate that made it possible for Florianus's translation to become a successful printing product. This climate provided an important stimulus for the publication of the Dutch translation.

All over Europe, late Renaissance Humanism introduced the vernacular languages in an educational, intellectual, and political context as compelling and valuable extensions of the Latin language. A boost of vernacular printing took place in the second half of the sixteenth century, along with the infiltration of the vernacular in universities (Boutcher 1996: 193–94; Waquet 2002: 81-82; Van de Haar 2018: 122). During the sixteenth century, there was a growing interest in humanistic literary vernacular activity in the Low Countries, instigated by Italian and French examples such as Petrarch and the French Pléiade as well as by a growing national identity related to the Spanish-Dutch war. This resulted in a transfer of the ancient ideals of literary activity to Dutch poetry. Especially rhetoricians, groups of poets and stage performers, were aiming to dignify and exalt the Dutch language (Van Dixhoorn 2009: 268); Porteman and Smits-Veldt 2013: 40 and 155); Van de Haar 2018: 137). Local cultural entrepreneurs engaged in the transfer of humanistic knowledge to vernacular culture. Translations of classical literature, important sources for all cultural activities, fit within the first stage of these developments, and it is feasible that there was a growing demand for classics in translation. This demand perfectly corresponds De Laet's claim of frequent requests to provide Ovid in translation: at least, such a claim would not have surprised his intended readers.

In the printing capitals of the Low Countries – at first Antwerp and, after the Dutch Revolt and the Fall of Antwerp, Amsterdam – printers actively participated in local networks involved in vernacular Humanism and upgrading the Dutch language. These printer's alliances with the vernacular vogue in the Low Countries were clearly reflected in their printing activities: the Antwerp printers Hans de Laet and Christopher Plantin, for example, supported a standardised Dutch language, with a uniform and institutionalised vocabulary and spelling. De Laet published *Het tresoor der Duytscher talen* (The treasure of the Dutch language) in 1553 to introduce a new, understandable juridical vocabulary. Plantin printed the world's first vernacular dictionary in 1573, after years of research and compiling activities by his editors.[25] In another publication by the Plantin company, the editor Cornelis Kilianus even explicitly stated that he 'hoped to enhance the language of the homeland' ['in patrio sermone excolendo'; *Etymologicum* (1599), fol. [*2]ʳ, cited from Langereis (2014: 373, n. 9)].

At the same time in Amsterdam, Harmen Jansz. Muller – in the early 1580s the city's only printer – still was primarily occupied with printing traditional devotional texts in Latin. The migration of many printers from the Spanish southern Netherlands to the proclaimed Dutch Republic in the late sixteenth century, however, was an important stimulus to such a widespread vernacular enhancement in the north. Dirck Coornhert became an influential apostle of the Dutch language in the northern Netherlands, and Muller printed some of his works. Also the members of the Amsterdam chamber De Eglantier started to be actively involved in publications concerning the development of Dutch as a cultural and scholarly language (Van de Haar 2018: 121–3). Coornhert moulded a wide network of humanistic intellectuals as well as rhetoricians from the literary chambers of rhetoric around him, which clearly shows the interactivity between these two domains within early modern Dutch society. A standardised Dutch language was Coornhert's means to reach his main goal: the moral elevation of society. Coornhert's 1561 translations of *De officiis* and the *Odyssey*, the first Dutch translations of works by Cicero and Homer, are clear contributions to this objective. The subtitle to Cicero's work, probably invented by Coornhert himself, is unambiguous: 'teaching what everyone should do in every condition'. Karel van Mander, himself a Flemish immigrant, was another influential pivot in this cultural-scholarly network (Van Dixhoorn 2009: 276–9). He was the author of the first Dutch commentary to the *Metamorphoses* (*Wtlegghingh op den Metamorphosis*, published in 1604 as a supplement to his *Schilder-boeck*). It shows that there existed a special interest in Ovid within the vernacular-humanistic context.

[25] *Thesaurus* (1573); see Langereis (2014: 72–75).

This was the context in which also Florianus's translation of the *Metamorphoses* was printed. The publication of translations of classical texts perfectly fits the activities to enhance the position of Dutch language: Florianus's translation, for example, offered general inspiration as well as specific themes and rhetorical examples, through which members of the Saint Lucas guild and De Eglantier could upgrade their vernacular literary work with humanistic elements. The paratextual construct of this translation included both humanistic and vernacular aspects, and thereby it is a signal expression of its contemporary intellectual climate.

Conclusion: Bruegel as the ideal reader

The first Dutch translation of Ovid's *Metamorphoses* was introduced to the book market as an intricate paratextual construct. In 1552, the Antwerp printer Hans de Laet presented a printing concept that situated the *Metamorphoses* within the local Antwerp vernacular-humanistic, cultural community. Within the paratextual infrastructure of the edition, all the paratexts together functioned to frame Ovid's text as an indispensable and necessary tool for a particular group of readers. The title page addressed all kinds of artists; the dedication acknowledged their common ground; the preface foremost represented their humanist identity; the marginalia and index supported their actual use of the book: it guided them to particular scenes of the best known stories as an inspiration for their work.[26]

The printing concept turned out to be a successful example of cultural transfer, by which ancient mythology was appropriated in an early modern context. Many reprints were produced, and the concept was copied and brought to Amsterdam. In this way, Florianus's translation became widely known and available as the most common vernacular access to Ovid's *Metamorphoses*.

At last, once more back to Bruegel, with whom we started. Little is known about Bruegel's actual life.[27] He is supposed to have been acquainted with the humanist circles of his time. In 1551 he became a member of the Antwerp Saint Lucas guild.[28] Around this time, Hans de Laet framed Florianus's version of Ovid's *Metamorphoses* into the direct artistic context in which Bruegel became an active member. Some years later, he even

---

[26] Unfortunately, all the copies I have consulted do not provide sufficient reader traces (such as written marginalia) to inform about actual use of the books.

[27] See Huet 2016 for a recent biography.

[28] Karel van Mander notes in his *Schilder-boeck* (1604: fol. 233ʳ): 'Hy vercoos en nam zijn wooninghe t'Antwerpen, en quam aldaer in het Gildt oft Schilders-camer, in't Iaer ons Heeren 1551.' [He chose to live in Antwerp, and became a member of the local painters guild, in the year 1551 AD.]

finished a painting that refers to Ovid's *Metamorphoses*. Although it is, of course, purely speculative whether Bruegel bought a copy of Florianus's translation, the paratextual infrastructure in these editions indicates men like him as their ideal reader.

VI

OVID IN GREEK

16

ANDREAS N. MICHALOPOULOS

IOANNIS MAKOLAS'S GREEK VERNACULAR TRANSLATION OF OVID'S *METAMORPHOSES* (VENICE, 1686)

In this chapter I will discuss and evaluate Ioannis Makolas's prose translation (1686) of eleven stories from Ovid's *Metamorphoses*.[1] Makolas's translation of the *Metamorphoses* is the first in the Greek vernacular and at the same time 'the oldest translation of the *Metamorphoses* in the post-Byzantine Greek world' (Nikitas 2012: 112).[2] It was followed by the vernacular prose translations by Kaisarios Dapontes (*c.* 1737–1750) and Spyridon Vlantis (1798).[3] In Byzantine times, the most famous and complete translation of Ovid's *Metamorphoses* was the one by the monk and scholar Maximus Planoudes (1255–1305) during the so-called aetas

---

[1] Makolas's Ovidian translation has gone largely unnoticed so far. A notable exception is Nikitas 2012.

[2] For the post-Byzantine Latinitas of Greek scholars see Nikitas 2001 and 2002-2003.

[3] Dapontes's translation is based on an Italian translation of the *Metamorphoses* as a go-between text, still to be identified. On Dapontes's translation, see Kechagioglou 1978: 14–17 and 249–50; 1986: 36–41 and 2001: I, 566–68; Nikitas 2012: 110–112. Dapontes translated 44 'μύθους' [myths] from the *Metamorphoses* and attached to them their allegorical interpretation (Ὀβιδίου μῦθοι καὶ ἀλληγορίαι ἀπὸ τὸ ἰταλικὸν μεταφρασθέντες παρὰ Καισαρίου Δαπόντε). Vlantis, the last director of the Flanginian School of Venice, translated the fifteen books of the *Metamorphoses*. Before each story he provided a short summary (ὑπόθεσις) and after each story, an allegorical interpretation and commentary (ἀλληγορία). On Vlantis's translation, see Karathanassis 1979, Nikitas (1998). Ioannis Frangopoulos also translated the *Metamorphoses* into the Greek vernacular (*c.* 1770), but most probably his translation was never published: see Nikitas 2012: 109, n. 21. Frangopoulos did not translate the text from the Latin poem but used a French translation written by Pierre du Ruyer (1680). Philippos Ioannou, the first Professor of Philosophy at the Ottonian University of Athens (now the 'National and Kapodistrian University of Athens'), later translated the first five books of the *Metamorphoses* in ancient Greek dactylic hexameters (1874), along with a translation of Ovid's *Heroides* 1 and 7 (see A. N. Michalopoulos 2015). In 1908 A. S. Kasdaglis produced a verse translation of the *Metamorphoses*: see C. N. Michalopoulos 2015.

ovidiana (twelfth and thirteenth centuries).[4] Makolas's prose translation of
Ovid, as well as being in the Greek vernacular of his time rather than in
ancient Greek, does not seem to have been influenced by Planoudes'
translation; nor does Makolas make the slightest reference to Planoudes or
to any other previous Greek translation of the *Metamorphoses*.

Makolas's work

The biographical information available about Ioannis Makolas is scarce.[5]
Born in 1661, he was a merchant from Athens whose translation was
published in Venice in 1686 by Michelangelo Barboni.[6] After the fall of
Constantinople and the subjugation of the Greek world to the Ottomans, a
great many scholars from Byzantium fled to Venice. As a result, Venice
became the successor of the Byzantine world ('Venetiae quasi alterum
Byzantium', in the words of Bessarion, Archbishop of Nicaea and
subsequently Cardinal of the Roman Church, in his letter to the Doge of
Venice, 1468) and one of the most important intellectual and cultural
centres of the free Greeks.[7] Thanks to the generous financial support of rich
merchants of the Greek diaspora, a large number of books were published in
Venice by its thriving Greek community.[8] The main destinations for these
books were the scattered Greek communities of Europe and the Ottoman-

---

[4] On Maximus Planoudes's life, career, and literary production, see among others Wendel
1950, Schmitt 1968, Fisher 1990, Papathomopoulos and Tsavari 2002, Michalopoulos
2002–2003 and 2003, Tzamos 2002–2003. Planoudes's translation of the
Metamorphoses is *ad verbum* and remains very close to the Latin source text. For Greek
translations of Latin works between the thirteenth and the fifteenth centuries, see
Salanitro 1991.

[5] Nikitas (2012: 116–20) has meticulously gathered information on Makolas's family and
their activities in Padua and Venice.

[6] On Michelangelo Barboni's publishing house, see Legrand 1994: 430.

[7] For the Greek community of Venice see, among others, Veloudos 1893;
Giannakopoulos 1965; Geanakoplos 1966; Fedalto 1967; Manussacas 1973, 1980 and
1989; Karathanassis 1975 and 2010; Xanthopoulou-Kyriakou 1978; Mavroidi 1989;
D'Antiga 1993; Tsiknakis 1993; Imhaus 1997: 288–302; Maltezou 1999a and 1999b.

[8] On the publication of Greek books in Venice after the fall of Constantinople, see most
recently Ploumidis (2018), who notes that the production of Greek books in Venice
during the fifteenth and sixteenth centuries was dominated by humanistic works, but
soon gave way to scholastic-ecclesiastical books. He further points out that the real
expansion of production of Greek books occurred in the late seventeenth century, when
the publishing houses passed into the hands of wealthy merchants. See also
Contossopoulos 1954; Ploumidis 1971 and 2002; Veloudis 1974 and 1989; Iliou 1975;
Follieri 1977; Liata 1977; Politis 1977; Vranoussis 1977; Manussacas – Staikos 1986;
Vlassi-Sponza 1989; Layton 1994, and Maltezou 2001.

occupied or Venetian-occupied East. Greek traders were responsible for their dissemination over the various regions (Liata 1977: 1–2).

The first reference to Ioannis Makolas and his work is found in the journal Ἑρμῆς ὁ Λόγιος (vol. 8, issue 2, 15 January 1818, p. 30):

Ἰωάννης ὁ Μάκολας ἐγεννήθη κατὰ τὸ 1661 ἔτος ἐν Ἀθήναις· ἦτον ἔμπορος κατὰ τὸ ἐπάγγελμα· μετέφρασεν ἐκ τοῦ Λατινικοῦ, ἐκτὸς τῆς ῥηθείσης Ἱστορίας, καὶ τοῦ Ὀβιδίου τὰς μεταμορφώσεις καὶ ἐξέδωκεν ἐν Βενετίᾳ κατὰ τὸ 1686 παρὰ τῷ Μ. Ἀγγέλῳ τῷ Βαρβωνίῳ· ἦτον δέ, ὅτε ταῦτα μετέφρασεν, 25 ἐτῶν. Πότε ἀπέθανε, καὶ ἂν μετέφρασε καὶ ἄλλα ἢ συνέγραψεν, ἀγνοοῦμεν

[Ioannis Makolas was born in Athens in 1661. He was a merchant. Apart from the aforementioned Histories, he translated Ovid's *Metamorphoses* from Latin and published his translation in Venice, in 1686, at the publishing house of Michelangelo Barboni; he was 25 years old at the time. We do not know when he died or whether he translated or wrote any other works.][9]

The full title of Makolas's book is:

ΒΙΒΛΙΟΝ ΙΣΤΟΡΙΚΟΝ ΚΑΛΟΥΜΕΝΟΝ ΙΟΥΣΤΙΓΝΟΣ, ΜΕΤΑΦΡΑΣΘΕΝ. Ἐκ τῆς Λατινίδος φωνῆς εἰς ἁπλῆν φράσιν παρὰ Ἰωάννου Μάκολα τοῦ Ἀθηναίου, προσέτι δὲ καί τινες μῦθοι μεταφρασθέντες καὶ αὐτοὶ ἐκ τῆς Λατινίδος φωνῆς εἰς τὴν κοινὴν γλῶσσαν παρ' αὐτοῦ διὰ δὲ δαπάνης καὶ συνδρομῆς τοῦ πανευγενεστάτου Κυρίου ΜΗΧΑΗΛ τοῦ ΠΕΡΟΥΛΗ τοῦ ἐξ Ἀθηνῶν ἐτυπώθη εἰς κοινὴν ὠφέλειαν τῶν φιλομαθῶν, διορθωθὲν μετὰ πλείστης ἐπιμελείας. Ἐν δὲ τῷ τέλει τῆς αὐτῆς βίβλου τυγχάνει καί τις διδασκαλία Χριστιανική, ἀναγκαιοτάτη εἰς καθ' ἕνα. [...]. Παρὰ Μιχαὴλ Ἀγγέλῳ τῷ Βαρβωνίῳ

[History book called 'Ιουστίνος' translated from Latin into simple language by Ioannis Makolas from Athens. Furthermore, some myths also translated from Latin into the vernacular by the same man, thanks to the funding and help of the most gentle Mr Michael Peroulis from Athens. The book was printed for the common benefit of the studious and corrected with the utmost diligence. At the end of this book there is a Christian teaching, most necessary to everybody. [...] Printed by Michelangelo Barboni.][10]

As stated in the title, Makolas's book is divided into three parts: the first and longest part is a prose translation in the Greek vernacular of the

9 The same information is later repeated by Sathas (1868: 411); Dimitrakopoulos (1871: 72), and Zaviras (1872: 368). See Nikitas 2012: 113, n. 34. The Greek translations are mine unless otherwise stated.

10 I retain Makolas's spelling throughout my citations. Unlike Makolas, however, I capitalize the first letter of proper names. See Nikitas 2012: 113, n. 39 for the libraries with copies of the book. Makolas's book is available online through the Digital Library of Modern Greek Studies 'Anemi': https://anemi.lib.uoc.gr/metadata/8/8/a/metadata-165-0000018.tkl [accessed 26 April 2020].

epitome of *Pompeius Trogus's Historiae Philippicae* written by M. Iunian(i)us Iustinus in the fourth century AD. The second part contains the translation of twelve 'μῦθοι', that is, twelve stories from Ovid's *Metamorphoses* – or more precisely eleven, since the last story, that of Iphigenia, does not belong to *Metamorphoses*. The Iphigenia story translated by Makolas covers the plot of Euripides' *Iphigenia in Aulis* and *Iphigenia in Tauris*. The third part of the book (pp. 365–82) is a 'Χριστιανικὴ διδασκαλία' [Christian teaching], a dialogue between an anonymous teacher and an anonymous student on the subject of the Christian faith.[11]

Immediately after the title of the book comes a dedicatory letter from Makolas to his sponsor and fellow Athenian, Michael Peroulis, and a letter addressed to his readers (τοῖς ἐντευξομένοις).[12] The contents of the book are listed after these two letters (Πίναξ τῶν ἐξαιρέτων Ἱστοριῶν τῶνδ' ἐν τῇ παρούσῃ βίβλῳ περιεχομένων) [Table showing the wonderful stories included in this book]. The stories of the first historiographical part of the book are listed in alphabetical order, whereas the 'μῦθοι', on which I will focus in this chapter, are presented in order of appearance. The myths are the following: Pyramus and Thisbe ('Μῦθος τῆς Θίσβης καὶ τοῦ Πυράμου', pp. 308–11); Daphne ('Μῦθος τῆς Δάφνης', pp. 311–14); Phaethon ('Μῦθος τοῦ Φαέθοντος', pp. 315–24); Phaethon's sisters ('Μῦθος τῶν ἀδελφῶν τοῦ Φαέθοντος', pp. 325–26); Cycnus ('Μῦθος τοῦ Κύκνου', pp. 326–27); Narcissus ('Μῦθος τοῦ Ναρκίσσου', pp. 327–30); Arachne and Minerva ('Μῦθος τῆς Ἀράχνης καὶ τῆς Ἀθηνᾶς', pp. 331–34); Niobe ('Μῦθος τῆς Νιόβης', pp. 334-39); Procne and Philomela ('Μῦθος τῆς Πρόκνης καὶ τῆς Φιλομέλης', pp. 339–46); Orpheus ('Μῦθος τοῦ Ὀρφέως', pp. 346–48); Ajax and Ulysses ('Μῦθος τῆς διχονοίας τοῦ Αἴαντος καὶ Ὀδυσέως', pp. 349–60) and Iphigenia ('Μῦθος τῆς Ἰφιγενείας', pp. 360–64).

Makolas refers to Ovid as the author of these myths only once, in his letter to Michael Peroulis, the sponsor and dedicatee of the book. Ovid's work is not mentioned anywhere else:

διαλαμβάνει [ἡ παροῦσα βίβλος] καὶ μερικοὺς μύθους πάνυ ὠφελίμους καὶ τερπνούς, δώδεκα εἰς τὸν ἀριθμόν. Μεταφρασθέντες καὶ αὐτοὶ παρ' ἐμοῦ ἐκ τῆς λατινίδος φωνῆς ἀπὸ τὸν Ὀβίδιον, οἱ ὁποῖοι συμβάλλουσι πολλὰ εἰς τὸ

---

[11] Both the first and the third part of Makolas's book have generally been neglected by scholars. Again, the notable exception is Nikitas (2012).

[12] Michael Peroulis (1622–1707) was an Athenian merchant, a prominent and wealthy member of the Greek community of Venice. In fact, he served as president of the community for four years (1683, 1694, 1697, 1706). For Peroulis and his distinguished family see Veloudos 1893: 187; Koukou 1965: 72, n. 68; Karathanassis 1975: 109, n. 5; Liata (1977: 2). See also Nikitas 2012: 120–23 on the relationship between Makolas and Peroulis and Makolas's encomium for his patron and sponsor.

νὰ τοὺς ξεύρῃ καθ᾽ ἕκαστος, ἐπειδὴ καὶ δι᾽ αὐτῶν δύναται μεγάλως νὰ στολίσῃ τὸν ἑαυτόν του᾽ (p. 2 of his letter to Peroulis)

[[This book] also includes some very useful and pleasant myths, twelve in number. These too have been translated by me from Latin and from Ovid. They contribute a great deal to everyone's knowledge, because with them everyone can surely adorn themselves.]

Makolas declares that the purpose of his book is the pleasure and benefit of his readers and Greek compatriots, who are in great need of useful books. He bestows a clearly national dimension on this work. In his own words: 'τὸ δεδοξασμένον καὶ πεφημισμένον γένος τῶν Ἑλλήνων τὴν σήμερον εὑρίσκεται εἰς μεγάλην ἔνδειαν ἀπὸ τοιαῦτα βιβλία ὠφέλιμα' (p. 2 of his letter to Peroulis) [The glorious and famous nation of the Greeks today shows a considerable lack of such useful books]. He repeatedly refers to his translation as 'ὠφέλιμον' [useful] or even 'ὠφελιμοτάτη[ν] βίβλο[ν]' [most useful book] (Nikitas 2012: 126–29; Michalopoulos 2015: 301 and Pappas 2015: 260).

The second part of Makolas's book, which includes translations of stories from Ovid's *Metamorphoses*, begins on page 308. The translator introduces this section as follows: 'προσετέθησαν δὲ ἐνταῦθα, καίτινες μῦθοι ὠφέλιμοι, χάριν τῶν φιλομαθῶν ἀνθρώπων' [I have added here some useful myths too for the sake of the studious men]. As in the title of the book, there is no reference to Ovid and the *Metamorphoses*. Because of this recurrent omission of the name of the author, the reader might mistakenly conclude that these myths are the work of an anonymous author. Also missing from the book is any reference to the Latin text that Makolas used for his translation. However, an educated guess would be that Makolas used the edition of Ovid's works by N. Heinsius, which was very influential in its time.[13] He may also have had at his disposal a collection of various myths, a florilegium of sorts. The adoption of a similar source text would explain the inclusion of the myth of Iphigenia along with the myths from the *Metamorphoses*, and it would also explain the differences in the order of appearance of Ovid's myths in Makolas's book: for example, in Makolas the story of Pyramus and Thisbe comes first, followed by the story of Daphne.

The titles that Makolas gives to each story are not uniform. Two of them are as short as they could possibly be (Μῦθος τῆς Δάφνης, [myth of Daphne], p. 311, Μῦθος τοῦ κύκνου, [myth of Cycnus], p. 326), while the rest briefly foretell the outcome of each story without referring to the 'crime'

---

[13] Nicolaus Heinsius, *P. Ovidii Nasonis opera omnia in tres tomos divisa*, Amstelodami apud Waesbergios, Boom & Goethals (1651¹, 1658-61²). See Nikitas 2012: 126, n. 90, although he later seems doubtful (137): 'we are in the dark as regards the Latin text used by Makolas'.

or the fault committed by the protagonists.[14] The translation of the story of Pyramus and Thisbe is introduced by a brief announcement of the content and the outcome of the story. No such announcement features in the Latin original, but is added by Makolas for the sake of his readers. The translation begins with the phrase 'καθὼς γοῦν μυθολογοῦσιν οἱ ποιηταί' [as the poets narrate], which does not feature in the source text either. In fact, the majority of the stories that Makolas translates begin with the same (or a similar) phrase.[15] This opening is puzzling because, on the one hand, these 'ποιηταί' are not named, and on the other hand because Makolas knows very well – as is obvious from his dedicatory letter to Peroulis – who the author of these 'μῦθοι' is (Ovid). One would normally expect the phrase 'καθὼς γοῦν μυθολογεῖ ὁ Ὀβίδιος' [as Ovid narrates] instead.

The translation

Makolas's prose translation is in the Greek vernacular of his time, free from archaisms and obscure words. Although it sounds outdated to our ears, we can safely assume that Makolas's language would have been easily

---

[14]   Pyramus and Thisbe (p. 308): 'καὶ πρῶτον εἶναι ὁ μῦθος τῆς Μαύρης συκαμινιαίας, ἡ ὁποία ἐκοκίνησεν τοὺς καρποὺς της ἀπὸ τὸ αἷμα τοῦ Πυράμου καὶ Θίσβης, ὡς φαίνεται κάτωθεν ὁ μῦθος τῶν αὐτῶν ὁποῦ ἀδίκως ἐφονεύθησαν.' [and first is the myth of the black mulberry tree whose fruits became red from the blood of Pyramus and Thisbe, as shown by the following myth about those who were killed unjustly]; Phaethon (p. 315): 'Μύθος τοῦ Φαέθοντος ὁποῦ ἐγκρεμμίσθη ἀπὸ τὸν οὐρανὸν μὲ τὰ πατρικά του ἀμάξια.' [The myth of Phaethon who was thrown down from the sky with his father's chariot]; Phaethon's sisters (p. 325): 'Μύθος τῶν ἀδελφῶν τοῦ Φαέθοντος, ὁποῦ ἐμεταβάλθησαν εἰς δένδρον." [The myth of Phaethon's sisters, who were turned into trees]; Narcissus and Echo (p. 327): 'Μύθος τοῦ Ναρκίσσου ὁποῦ ἔγεινεν εἰς ζερμεκαμπέ καὶ τῆς Ἠχὼ εἰς φωνήν.' [The myth of Narcissus who became a flower and Echo who became a voice]; Arachne (p. 331): "Ὁ μῦθος τῆς Ἀράχνης καὶ τῆς Ἀθηνᾶς ὁποῦ ἀνάμεσόν τους ἐπολέμησαν ἀπάνω εἰς τὴν ἀνυφαντικήν καὶ ἐνίκησεν ἡ Ἀθηνᾶ.' [The myth of Arachne and Athena, who competed against each other in weaving and Athena won]; Niobe (p. 334): 'Ὁ μῦθος τῆς Νιόβης ὁποῦ ἐμεταβάλθη εἰς μάρμαρον.' [The myth of Niobe who was turned into marble]; Procne, Philomela, Tereus, Itys (p. 339): 'Ὁ μῦθος τῆς Πρόκνης, καὶ Φιλομέλης καὶ τοῦ Τυρέως, καὶ τοῦ Ἴτης, ὁποῦ ἐμεταβάλθησαν εἰς πουλιά.' [The myth of Procne and Philomela and Tereus and Itys, who were turned into birds]; Orpheus, Zeus-Ganymede, Apollo-Hyacinth (p. 346): 'Ὁ μῦθος τοῦ Ὀρφέως, καὶ τοῦ Διὸς ὁποῦ ἔγεινεν ἀετὸς καὶ ἅρπαξεν τὸν Γανηημίδην ὁμοίως καὶ τοῦ ἄνθους τοῦ Ἰακίνθου. [The myth of Orpheus and of Zeus who became an eagle and ravished Ganymede; also the myth of Hyacinth's flower]; Ὅπλων κρίσις between Ajax and Odysseus (p. 349): 'Μύθος τῆς διχονοίας ὁποῦ ἐστάθη ἀναμεταξὺ εἰς τὸν Αἴαντα καὶ τὸν Ὀδυσέα ἀπάνω διὰ τὰ ἄρματα τοῦ μεγάλου καὶ θαυμαστοῦ Ἀχιλέως καὶ ἐνίκησεν ὁ Ὀδυσεὺς μὲ τὴν μεγάλην του εὐγλωττίαν.' [The myth of the strife arisen between Ajax and Odysseus over the weapons of the great and admirable Achilles. Odysseus won thanks to his great eloquence.]

[15]   The only exceptions are the myths of Daphne, Phaethon's sisters and Niobe.

understood by his contemporaries and that it would arouse their interest in the source text. Makolas adheres to both the letter and the spirit of the Latin original, but avoids the logic of an ad verbum translation. His translation reveals his sound knowledge of both Latin and Greek, even though in his letter to the readers he humbly calls himself a beginner and inexperienced in Latin ('μάλιστα ἀρχάριος καὶ ὀλίγον ἔμπειρος εἰς τὴν λατινικὴν φωνὴν', p. 3 of the letter).

In what follows I will discuss some telling passages from Makolas's translation which present certain particularities and problems. I will divide these into the following groups: a) additions of words, phrases or entire sentences that do not exist in the Latin text; b) omissions of words, phrases or entire sentences of the source text; c) misinterpretations of the Latin original and translation mistakes. Since it is virtually impossible to discuss the whole of Makolas's translation in this chapter, I examine extracts drawn from the following three stories: i) the story of Pyramus and Thisbe; ii) the story of Daphne and Apollo; and iii) the myth of Procne, Philomela and Tereus, because of its great length and its particular association with Athens.[16] Here is a synopsis of each story as narrated by Ovid:

i) The myth of Pyramus and Thisbe was set in ancient Babylon. The two protagonists were in love and could communicate only through a crack in the wall. Their parents, in fact, did not allow their union. In order to consummate their love, they agreed to meet in the middle of the night under a mulberry tree. Thisbe arrived first, but saw a lioness and hid in a cave. The beast found the veil Thisbe had left behind and tore it to pieces with its bloody jaws. When Pyramus came by the tree and saw the bloody veil, he thought that Thisbe had been devoured by the lioness and killed himself. Later, Thisbe found him mortally wounded under the mulberry tree and put an end to her life. The fruit of the mulberry, previously white, turned dark red due to the lovers' blood.

ii) Engrossed by his military successes, Apollo laughed at the god Cupid for using a bow, a weapon that is unsuited for the games of love. To punish Apollo, Cupid shot him with a golden-tipped arrow and made him fall in love with Daphne, the daughter of the river Peneus. Daphne, however, was shot by an arrow with an opposite effect. She rejected Apollo and started running away from him. As Apollo was about to catch her, however, Daphne – by divine intercession – was transformed into a laurel tree. Apollo made the laurel his sacred tree.

iii) Tereus, the king of Thrace, married Procne, the daughter of the king of Athens, Pandion. After five years of marriage, Procne begged Tereus to bring her sister Philomela to her. In Athens, however, Tereus lusted after

[16] On Makolas's pride in his Athenian origin, see Nikitas 2012: 117–18.

Philomela and raped her upon their return to Thrace. To prevent her from revealing what had happened, Tereus cut out Philomela's tongue, but the heroine wove Tereus's crime into a tapestry and sent it to Procne. To avenge themselves, the two sisters slayed Procne's and Thereus's only child and served him as a meal to his father. Upon discovering the murder, Tereus started chasing the two sisters with the aim of killing them. During the chase, however, Tereus was transformed into a hoopoe, while Procne and Philomela were turned into a swallow and a nightingale respectively.

1. Additions

In this section I will explain and exemplify the type of additions that Makolas makes in his translation. These can be grouped into three main categories: a) mythological information one would find in a mythological dictionary or a mythographic work, b) additions aiming to facilitate the readers' understanding of the text, and c) sentimental amplifications.

a) In his translation, Makolas often offers additional information to make the classical references accessible to his readers. In the following examples we see that the translator concentrates in particular on geographical references. For instance, he translates 'Semiramis urbem' (Ovid, *Metamorphoses*, IV. 58) [the city of Seminaris] as 'εἰς τὴν χώραν τὴν περίφημον τῆς Βαβυλῶνας, ποῦ τὴν ἔκτισεν ἡ βασίλισσα ἡ Σεμήραμις' (p. 308) [In the renowned land of Babylon, the city built by the queen Semiramis.] This kind of addition is reminiscent of the interpretative glosses usually found in the margins of medieval manuscripts. Likewise, when Pyramus and Thisbe agree to meet at the tomb of Ninus (Ovid, *Metamorphoses*, IV. 88: 'ad busta Nini'), Makolas adds a comment on Ninus's reign: 'ὁ ὁποῖος ἐβασίλευσεν εἰς τὴν Βαβυλῶναν καὶ Συρίαν' (p. 309) [who was king in Babylon and Syria.] By the same token, in the translation of the myth of Procne and Philomela, the Athenian Makolas specifies that Pandion was 'ὁ βασιλεὺς τῆς Ἀθήνας' (p. 339) [the king of Athens].[17] In the same myth, Tereus's arrival at Piraeus (Ovid, *Metamorphoses*, VI. 445–46) is rendered by Makolas as an arrival at Athens ('ἔφθασεν εἰς τὰς 'Αθήνας', p. 340).

More substantial additions may be related to glosses and mythographic works. At the ending of the story of Tereus, Procne, and Philomela, Makolas adds the transformation of Tereus's son into a pheasant. This detail is missing from Ovid's account but was current in the mythological

---

[17] All translations of Ovid's *Metamorphoses* are by A. S. Kline (with slight adaptations). This translation is available online at: https://ovid.lib.virginia.edu/trans/Ovhome.htm [accessed 8 March 2020]

tradition and the mythological dictionaries of the time:[18] 'ὁμοίως καὶ τὸ παιδὶ του ὁ Ἴτης ἔγεινεν ἀφασιανός, ὁ ὁποῖος ἀκόμη ἔχει τὸ σημεῖον εἰς τὸν λεμόν του, ὁποῦ ἔκοψεν τὸ κεφάλη του ἡ Φιλομέλη.' (p. 346) [Likewise, his child, Itys, became a pheasant, and still has the mark on his neck where Philomela cut off his head.]

Similarly, at the end of the story of Daphne and Apollo Makolas provides some interesting information of unknown origin, which is absent from the Latin text: namely that the laurel in which Daphne has been transformed will be safe from Zeus's thunderbolts ('καὶ ἀκόμη εὑρισκόμενον τὸ αὐτὸ δένδρον ἀναμεταξὺ εἰς τὰ ἄλλα δένδρα νὰ εἶναι ἄβλαβον ἀπὸ τὰ ἀστροπελέκια τοῦ πατρός μου τοῦ Διός', p. 314) [What's more, this tree standing among other trees will not be harmed by the thunderbolts of my father, Zeus.][19]

b) Makolas feels the need to add words or sentences to his translation in order to make Ovid's text clearer. In *Metamorphoses* I. 472–73 Amor shoots Daphne and Apollo with two different types of arrows: 'hoc deus in nympha Peneide fixit, at illo | laesit Apollineas traiecta per ossa medullas' [With the second arrow he transfixed Peneus's daughter, but with the first he wounded Apollo piercing him to the marrow of his bones.] To spell out Amor's reason for doing so, Makolas adds: 'διὰ νὰ ἀνάψῃ ἡ καρδία του ἀπὸ τὸν ἔρωτα' (p. 312, for Apollo) [So as to light up his heart with love] and 'διὰ νὰ μὴν ἀγαπήσῃ τὸν Ἀπόλλωνα' (p. 312, for Daphne) [So that she does not love Apollo.] In Daphne's request to her father Peneus to allow her never to marry, Makolas omits the details of her embrace of her father (Ovid, *Metamorphoses*, I. 485: 'inque patris blandis haerens cervice lacertis' [And clinging to her father's neck with coaxing arms]). Instead, he expands on Ovid's lines: '"da mihi perpetua, genitor carissime," dixit | "virginitate frui!"' (Ovid, *Metamorphoses*, I. 491–92) [She said: "Dearest father, let me be a virgin forever!"] becomes 'πάτερ μου, παρακαλῶ σε ἄφησέ με νὰ χαρῶ αἰωνίως τὴν παρθενίαν μου, μὴ μὲ ὑστερήσεις λέγω, ἐκλαμπρώτατε πατέρα μου, ἀπὸ τὴν μοναδικὴν ζωήν' (p. 312) [My father, please allow me to enjoy my virginity in eternity, do not deny me, I say, my most brilliant father, the chance to live on my own.][20] Without the limitations of the verse, the translator shows an interest in style. In fact, he extends Daphne's speech by using rhetorical devices.

---

18 See, for instance, Nathan Bailey's Ovid's Metamorphoses, in Fifteen Books: With the Notes of John Minellius, and Others, in English (London, 1741³).

19 Makolas may be confusing the laurel with the oak, Zeus's sacred tree.

20 Notice the use in the same passage of both the ancient Greek vocative 'πάτερ' and the vernacular form 'πατέρα'.

Another notable case of addition occurs in Makolas's translation of Procne's lament for Philomela's alleged death (Ovid, *Metamorphoses*, VI. 569–70): 'falsisque piacula manibus infert | et luget non sic lugendae fata sororis' [And mistakenly brought offerings, and lamented the fate of a sister, not yet due to be lamented in that way.] In this passage Makolas intervenes. He assumes the role of the narrator and anticipates to his readers the actual reason why Procne should be sorry for her sister: 'ἡ ὁποῖα δὲν ἔπρεπεν εἰς τοιοῦτον τρόπον νὰ κλέγῃ τὴν ἀδελφήν της ὡς ἀποθαμένην, ἀλλὰ νὰ λυπᾶται διατὶ ὁ Τηρεὺς τῆς ἔκαμεν τέτοιαν ἐντροπὴν ἀνυπόφορον' (p. 343) [Who should not lament her sister in this way, as if she were dead, but she should be sorry for the fact that Tereus caused her such unbearable shame.]

Makolas also makes sure that his linguistic choices are understood by his potential readers. An indicative case is the rendering of *Metamorphoses* I. 533 'ut canis' [Like a hound] as 'καὶ καθὼς ὁ κύων, ἤγουν ὁ σκύλος' (p. 314) [And like the κύων, I mean the dog ('σκύλος')]. While first using the ancient Greek word 'κύων' to render canis, Makolas immediately glosses it with the contemporary vernacular word for 'dog' (σκύλος).

Furthermore, Makolas adds sentences in transitional points, such as the beginning or the end of a speech, a common practice in prose versions of poetic sources. For instance, after the end of Apollo's speech to Daphne (Ovid, *Metamorphoses*, I. 524) he adds: 'ἐτοῦτα καὶ ἄλλα ὅμοια ἔλεγεν ὁ λαμπρὸς 'Απόλλων πρὸς τὴν Δάφνην' (p. 313) [The brilliant Apollo told these and similar things to Daphne]. Similarly, before translating Pandion's words to Tereus, he announces their contents to his readers: 'ὡς γοῦν ἦλθεν ἡ ἡμέρα ἄρχησεν ὁ Πανδίων καὶ ἀγγάλιαζεν τὸν γαμπρὸν του καὶ μὲ μεγάλους ἀναστεναγμοὺς καὶ δάκρυα τὸν ἐπαρακάλει διὰ νὰ ἔχῃ τὴν εὔνοιαν τῆς Φιλομέλης εἰς κάθε πρᾶγμα' (p. 341) [So when the day came, Pandion embraced his son-in-law and with great sighs and tears begged him to take care of Philomela in every respect.]

c) Sentimental amplifications are frequent in Makolas's translation. For instance, he expands on Pyramus's lament while the latter holds Thisbe's blood-stained veil. The dramatic address to the veil 'ὦ μανδύλιον τῆς ἀγαπημένης μου Θίσβης' (p. 310) [Oh veil of my beloved Thisbe] and the phrase 'διατὶ χωρὶς τὴν Θίσβην δὲν εἶναι δυνατὸν νὰ ἔχω ζωὴν εἰς τὸν Κόσμον' (p. 310) [Because without Thisbe I cannot be alive in this world] are missing from Ovid's text, but add pathos to Makolas's translation. In the same way, in order to achieve a more dramatic effect, Makolas adds the reason for the change of colour of the mulberries from white to dark red: 'ἀπὸ τὴν θλίψιν τους' [Out of grief]. This explanation is not found in the Latin text (Ovid, *Metamorphoses*, IV. 125–26: 'arborei fetus adspergine caedis in atram | vertuntur faciem' [Sprinkled with blood, the tree's fruit turned a deep blackish-red]). What is more, Makolas adds the emotionally charged 'τοῦ ἀθλίου Πυράμου' ('of the wretched Pyramus', p. 310) to the translation of 'sanguine' in line 4.126. Then, by analogy to 'ἄθλιος Πύραμος', he renders Ovid's 'illa' (4.129) as 'ἡ κακορίζηκη Θίσβη' ('the unfortunate Thisbe', p. 310), to stir the readers' sympathy for the ill-fated couple.

2. Omissions – Untranslated passages

Among the common features of Makolas's translation are the omissions of certain parts of Ovid's text, usually short passages: a single line, or a couple of lines. He may have felt that the meaning of the text would not be affected by these omissions. A symptomatic case occurs in the translation of *Metamorphoses* VI. 486–87. Ovid's brilliant poetic image of the end of the day ('iam labor exiguus Phoebo restabat, equique | pulsabant pedibus spatium declivis Olympi' [Now little was left of Phoebus's daily labour, and his horses were treading the spaces of the western sky]) is condensed by Makolas into the rather unpoetic and otiose λοιπὸν καθὼς ἐβράδιασεν ['so, when the night arrived'], which nonetheless does not affect the sense.

Occasionally, however, these omissions do change the meaning. For instance, in the story of Pyramus and Thisbe, the omission of 'sed vetuere patres' (Ovid, *Metamorphoses*, IV. 61) [But their parents prevented it] and its replacement by the vague 'μὴν ἠμπορῶντας νὰ φανερώσουσι τὴν ἀγάπην τους' (p. 308) [Not being able to reveal their love] leaves the reader wondering why Pyramus and Thisbe could not meet, since their houses were next to each other.

Makolas also leaves untranslated the reason for Apollo's pride at the beginning of Daphne's story just before he meets Cupid. In Book I, Ovid explains that Apollo was proud to have exterminated Python (Ovid, *Metamorphoses*, I. 454: 'victa serpente superbus' [Exulting at his victory over the serpent]); Makolas merely translates 'ὁ ὑπερήφανος καὶ λαμπρὸς Ἀπόλλων' (p. 311) [The proud and brilliant Apollo], probably wishing to avoid any connection with the previous story in the *Metamorphoses*, which he did not translate. Similarly, Makolas does not translate 'suaque illum oracula fallunt' (Ovid, *Metamorphoses*, I. 491) [but his own oracular powers fail him], or the beautiful Ovidian detail that Apollo felt Daphne's heart still beating under the trunk that covered her body (Ovid, *Metamorphoses*, I. 554: 'sentit adhuc trepidare novo sub cortice pectus' [he felt her heart still quivering under the new bark]).

Even more significant are Makolas's choices when he translates Apollo's declaration of Daphne's future use under her new form. Ovid's Apollo famously declares that the laurel will crown the Roman leaders in their triumphs and adorn the gates of Augustus's residence with its branches and foliage (Ovid, *Metamorphoses*, I. 560–64): 'tu ducibus Latiis aderis, cum laeta Triumphum vox canet et visent longas Capitolia pompas; | postibus Augustis eadem fidissima custos | ante fores stabis mediamque tuebere quercum' [You will go with the Roman generals when joyful voices acclaim their triumph, and the Capitol witnesses their long processions. You will stand outside Augustus's doorposts, a faithful guardian, and keep watch over the crown of oak between them]. Makolas removes all the Roman and Augustan references of the Latin original from his translation, apparently assuming that they mean nothing for his contemporary readers. He does not mention Augustus and only writes about kings and palaces in general ('ἀκόμη καὶ ὅσοι βασιλεῖς καὶ γενναῖοι ἄνδρες κάμνουσι κανένα θρίαμβον θέλω νὰ εἶναι καὶ αὐτοὶ στεφανωμένοι ἀπὸ τὸ αὐτὸ δένδρον.'Ἀκόμη καὶ ὅλα τὰ ἀρχοντικὰ καὶ βασιλικὰ παλάτια θέλω νὰ εἶναι στολισμένα ἀπὸ τοὺς κλάδους τοῦ αὐτοῦ', p. 314) [When kings and brave men celebrate a triumph, I want them to be crowned with leaves from this tree. And I want all the mansions and royal palaces to be decorated with branches from this tree]. Instead of Roman generals, those who will be crowned with laurel branches are those who 'πέζουσι, παλεύουσι ἢ τραγουδοῦσι' (p. 314) ['dance, wrestle or sing'].

3. Misinterpretations

Of all the divergences between Ovid's Latin poem and Makolas's translation, perhaps the most noteworthy are those caused by misinterpretations of the Latin text. Although Makolas seems to have had a good knowledge of Latin and as a rule renders Ovid's text accurately, his translation is not without misinterpretations.

One such case occurs in the translation of Peneus's response to Daphne (Ovid, *Metamorphoses*, I. 487–88): 'ille quidem obsequitur, sed te decor iste quod optas | esse vetat, votoque tuo tua forma repugnat' [He yields to that plea, but your beauty itself, Daphne, prevents your wish, and your loveliness opposes your prayer]. Makolas attributes to Peneus the words that the narrator himself addressed to Daphne. In fact, Makolas translates the verb obsequitur ('he yields to that plea') as 'ἀπεκρίθη' (p. 312) ['he replied']. As a result, he takes everything that follows in Ovid as Peneus's response to his daughter (p. 312):[21]

---

[21] Ovid *Metamorphoses*, I. 490–8: 'Phoebus amat visaeque cupit conubia Daphnes, / quodque cupit, sperat, suaque illum oracula fallunt, / utque leves stipulae demptis adolentur aristis, / ut facibus saepes ardent, quas forte viator / vel nimis admovit vel iam sub luce reliquit, / sic deus in flammas abiit, sic pectore toto / uritur et sterilem sperando nutrit amorem. / spectat inornatos collo pendere capillos / et 'quid, si comantur?' ait [Phoebus loves her at first sight, and desires to wed her, and hopes for what he desires, but his own oracular powers fail him. As the light stubble of an empty cornfield blazes;

ἀλήθεια λέγεις ὦ θύγατέρ μου, μ' ὅλον τοῦτο ἡ εὐγένεια ἡ ἐδική σου ἀδύνατον εἶναι νὰ σοῦ ἐμποδίσῃ τὴν ὑπανδρίαν, ἤξευρε πῶς ἐσένα σὲ ἀγαπᾷ ὁ λαμπρὸς Ἀπόλλων, καὶ ἐπιθυμᾷ καταπολλὰ νὰ σὲ πάρῃ διὰ γυναῖκα του. Καὶ ἐκεῖνο ὁποῦ ἐπιθυμᾷ ἐλπίζει βέβαια νὰ τὸ ἀπολαύσῃ. Καὶ καθὼς τὰ ξηρότατα χόρτα, καὶ ἄχερα, ἂν ἴσως καὶ τινὰς ῥίψῃ εἰς ἐκεῖνα φωτία, μεγάλως μαραίνωνται, καὶ κατακαίωνται, τέτοιας λογῆς καὶ ὁ Ἀπόλλων, καταφλογίζεται, καὶ ταλεπωρᾶται ἀπὸ τὴν ἐδικὴν σου ἀγάπην. Βλέπωντας τὰ μαλία σου τὰ εὐγενικά, τὰ ὁποῖα ἂν ἴσως καὶ τῶρα ὁποῦ δὲν τὰ ἔχεις εὐτρεπισμένα εἶναι πολλὰ ὡραῖα, ἀμὴ ὡσὰν τὰ εὐπρεπήσεις τὶ λογῆς εὐμορφίαν ἔχουν νὰ φανερώσουν·

[You speak the truth, my daughter, however your beauty is impossible to prevent you from marriage. Know that the bright Apollo loves you and eagerly desires to make you his wife. And he hopes to enjoy the thing he desires. And as the dry weeds and the stubble, if by chance someone throws fire at them, wither and get burned, so Apollo is on fire and is tortured by his love for you. Your beautiful hair, which is very fine even though it is disordered, what beauty will it have if you dress it properly?'.]

This is why Makolas feels the need to add the phrase 'ἤξευρε πῶς' ['know that']. He is also forced to add the sentence 'τέτοια λόγια εἶπεν ὁ Πενεὸς πρὸς τὴν θυγατέρα του τὴν Δάφνην' (p. 312) [Such words did Peneus tell to his daughter, Daphne] after *Metamorphoses*, I. 498 ('quid, si comantur?' ait ["What if it were properly dressed?", he says]), assuming that the subject of ait is Peneus and not Apollo.

Another example of a misinterpretation of the Latin text is the translation of "aspera, qua properas, loca sunt" (Ovid, *Metamorphoses*, I. 510) [These are rough places you run through], which Makolas translates as: 'ὦ κατὰ πολλὰ σκληρὴ διατὶ μὲ φεύγῃς;' (p. 313) [Oh, all too cruel, why are you running away from me?], because he apparently assumes that the adjective *aspera* modifies Daphne and takes it as a vocative. In fact, the adjective *aspera* is nominative plural and identifies the noun *loca*; Apollo warns Daphne that there is rough ground (*aspera loca*) nearby.

A slightly more demanding passage, *Metamorphoses*, I. 519–20 ('certa quidem nostra est, nostra tamen una sagitta | certior, in vacuo quae vulnera pectore fecit!') [My aim is certain, but an arrow truer than mine has wounded my free heart!], is simplified by Makolas, who merely renders the general meaning: 'ἐγὼ ὁποῦ εἶμαι τοσοῦτον θαυμαστὸς τὴν σήμερον καταφλογίζομαι δυνατὰ ἀπὸ μίαν φαρμακερὴν σαγήτα τοῦ ἔρωτος' (p. 313) [I, the admirable one, am burning strongly today by a poisonous arrow

---

as sparks fire a hedge when a traveller, by mischance, lets them get too close, or forgets them in the morning; so the god was altered by the flames, and all his heart burned, feeding his useless desire with hope. He sees her disordered hair hanging about her neck and sighs 'What if it were properly dressed?']

of love]. It would seem that Makolas failed to discern the difference between the two nostra in the Latin text: the first nostra is nominative and defines the noun sagitta that is to be understood, while the second one is ablative and defines the sagitta in the text, which is also ablative. What's more, Makolas transforms the wounds of love (vulnera) into flames ('καταφλογίζομαι', p. 313).

A similar misinterpretation leads to Makolas's unfortunate translation of *Metamorphoses*, VI. 581–83: 'evolvit vestes saevi matrona tyranni | germanaeque suae fatum miserabile legit | et (mirum potuisse) silet' [The wife of the savage king unrolls the cloth, and reads her sister's terrible fate, and by a miracle keeps silent]. To Ovid's amazement, when Procne sees Philomela's embroidery and realizes what has happened, she somehow finds the power to stifle her surprise and anger and to remain silent (mirum potuisse). Makolas misinterprets Ovid's parenthetical comment and thinks that Procne wondered how her husband could have committed such a crime: 'καὶ ἐθαύμασεν εἰς τὸν ἄνδρα της ὁποῦ ἔκαμεν τέτοιαν παρανομίαν' (p. 343) [And she was amazed that her husband committed such a crime].

Finally, in *Metamorphoses*, VI. 519–20 ('iamque iter effectum, iamque in sua litora fessis | puppibus exierant' [Now they had completed their journey, and disembarked from the wave-worn ship, on the shores of his country]), Ovid narrates Tereus's and Philomela's arrival at Thrace and her subsequent rape. There is a problem, however: if, as Ovid has it, Tereus and Philomela actually reached their final destination, how could Tereus possibly abduct and rape Philomela without anybody (especially Procne) noticing? It seems that Makolas realized the problem and tried to 'correct' Ovid. In his translation the rape does not take place at Tereus's final destination, but during a short stop of the fleet at a place 'near' ('σιμά') Thrace: 'ἐφθάσασιν εἰς ἕνα λιμένα σιμὰ εἰς τὸ μέρος τῆς Θράκης καὶ παρευθὺς εὐγῆκαν ἔξω ἀποκαμωμένοι διὰ νὰ ἡσυχάσουν ὀλίγον' (p. 342) [They arrived at a port near Thrace and immediately went outside, tired, to get some rest].

Conclusions

My goal in this chapter was to present the 1686 Greek vernacular translation of Ovid's *Metamorphoses* by Ioannis Makolas. Makolas's translation does not follow the word-for-word logic followed by Planoudes in his medieval translation. However, it remains close to the Latin original. The translator omits parts of the Latin original, misinterprets certain passages, and even adds phrases that are not in the source text in order to help his readers understand the text better. Although I have pointed out a number of such cases, Makolas's translation should not be considered as unsuccessful or/and inaccurate. On the contrary, his translation is to be commended and does justice to the source text: his style is flowing, lively, and attractive, and his language is simple and easily comprehensible. Makolas's translation can be read as a stand-alone text, as an appealing narrative. Although information on the dissemination of this translation and its commercial success is lacking, it is a most welcome contribution to the development of Greek vernacular literature and definitely ranks among the best Greek vernacular translations of Latin literature in the post-Byzantine era.

BIBLIOGRAPHY

Primary sources

Manuscripts cited

Berlin, Staatsbibliothek zu Berlin, Preußischer Kulturbesitz, MS germ. fol. 831),
thirteenth century (fragment B, Albrecht von Halberstadt)
Berne, Burgerbibliothek, MS 10, after 1456 (Z^1)
Bruxelles, Bibliothèque royale de Belgique, MS 9639, c. 1430–1440 (D^1)
Cambrai, Bibliothèque municipale, MS 973, last third of the fifteenth century (c. 1470
?) (D^2)
Cesena, Biblioteca Malatestiana, MS S.XXV.6, late fourteenth century
Copenhagen, Det Kongelige Bibliotek, MS Thott 388, 1480
Copenhagen, Det Kongelige Bibliotek, MS Thott 399, c. 1480 (G^3)
Genève, Bibliothèque de Genève, MS fr. 176, c. 1380 (E^1)
Gotha, Forschungsbibliothek, MS membr. I.98, late fourteenth century
Innsbruck, Tiroler Landesmuseum Ferdinandeum, Cod. FB32001, 1456
London, British Library, Add. MS 10324, c. 1400 (Y^5)
London, British Library, Royal MS 19 A XIX, second quarter of the fifteenth century
London, British Library, Royal MS 14 E II, 1473–1483
London, British Library, Royal MS 17 E IV, last quarter of the fifteenth century
Lyon, Bibliothèque municipale, MS 742, c. 1390 (B)
Madrid, Biblioteca Nacional, 3922
Munich, Staatsbibliothek, Clm 4610
New York, Pierpont Morgan Library, M. 443, c. 1410 (D^4)
Naples, Biblioteca Nazionale, MS IV F 3, late eleventh century
Niedersächsisches Landesarchiv, Standort Oldenburg, NLA OL, Slg 10 [Best. 297] E
22, thirteenth century (fragments C + D+ E, Albrecht von Halberstadt)
Oldenburg, Staatsarchiv, lost, thirteenth century (fragment A, Albrecht von
Halberstadt)
Paris, Bibliothèque de l'Arsenal, MS 5069, c. 1330-1335 (G^2)
Paris, Bibliothèque nationale de France, lat. 8010, early fourteenth century
Paris, Bibliothèque nationale de France, MS français 24305, 1356 (D^5)
Paris, Bibliothèque nationale de France, MS français 24306, third quarter of the
fourteenth century (D^3)
Paris, Bibliothèque nationale de France, MS français 871, last third of the fourteen
century (c. 1380 ?) (Y^1)
Paris, Bibliothèque nationale de France, MS français 872, last third of the fourteen
century (c. 1370-1380 ?) (Y^2)
Paris, Bibliothèque nationale de France, MS français 373, c. 1400 (G^1)
Paris, Bibliothèque nationale de France (BnF), MS 19121 (Z^4), c. 1390–1410
Paris, Bibliothèque nationale de France (BnF), MS français 870, c. 1410 (Z^3)
Paris, Bibliothèque nationale de France, MS fonds français 137, 1470–1480
Paris, Bibliothèque nationale de France, MS français 374, 1456 (Z^2)
Paris, Bibliothèque nationale de France, lat. 5703, fifteenth century
Paris, Bibliothèque nationale de France, MS FR. 129, fifteenth century
Pavia, Biblioteca Universitaria, Fondo Ticinese, MS 545, fifteenth century
Rome, Biblioteca Corsiniana (Accademia dei Lincei), Fondo Niccolò Rossi, MS 377,
fifteenth century

Rouen, Bibliothèque municipale, MS O. 4, *c.* 1325 (fol. 3–15) and *c.* 1315–1320 (*A¹*)
Rouen, Bibliothèque municipale, MS O. 11bis, last third of the fifteen century (*c.* 1475 ?) (*A²*)
Saint Petersburg, National Library of Russia, MS F. v. XIV. 1, 1310–1320
Troyes, Bibliothèque Municipale, MS 1627
Vatican, Biblioteca Apostolica Vaticana, MS Vaticanus Latinus 1598, thirteenth century
Vatican, Biblioteca Apostolica Vaticana, MS Vaticanus Latinus 1479, *c.* 1300
Vatican, Biblioteca Apostolica Vaticana, MS Reg. Lat. 1480, *c.* 1380 (*E²*)
Vatican, Bibioteca Apostolica Vaticana, MS Reg. Lat. 1686, after 1467

Vienna, Österreichische Nationalbibliothek, Cod. 2885, 1393

Printed works

Achillini, Alessandro. 1521. *Alexander Achillinus de humani corposis Anatomia* (Venice: Giovanni Antonio Nicolini da Sabbio and brothers)
Agostini, Niccolò (trans.). 1522. *Tutti gli libri de Ouidio Metamorphoseos tradutti dal litteral al verso vulgare con le sue allegorie in prosa* (Venice: Niccolò Zoppino)
Alegre, Francesc (trans.). 1494. *Transformacions* (Barcelona: Pere Miquel). Biblioteca de Catalunya, Bon 10–vi–29; Madrid, Biblioteca Nacional de España, INC/2435; Stuttgart, Württembergische Landesbibliothek Stuttgart, Alte und wertvolle Drucke: Inc. fol. 12167
Anguillara, Giovanni Andrea dell' (trans.). 1561. *Le Metamorfosi d'Ovidio al christianissimo re di Francia Henrico Secondo di Giovanni Andrea dell'Anguillara* (Venice: Giovanni Griffio)
— 1563. *Le Metamorfosi di Ovidio ridotte da Giovanni Andrea dell'Anguillara in ottava rima, al christianissimo re di Francia Henrico Secondo, di nuovo dal proprio auttore rivedute, et corrette; con le annotationi di M. Gioseppe Horologgi. Con Privilegii* (Venice: Giovanni Griffio for Francesco de' Franceschi Senese)
— 1584. *Le Metamorfosi ridotte in ottava rima* (Venice: B. Giunti)
— 1592. *Le Metamorfosi d'Ovidio, ridotte da Gio. Andrea dell'Anguillara in ottava rima, Al christianissimo re di Francia, Henrico Secondo. Nuovamente di bellissime e vaghe figure adornate, et diligentemente corrette. Con l'annotationi di M. Gioseppe Horologgi, et con nuove postille, et argomenti a ciascun libro, di M. Francesco Turchi. Con privilegio* (Venice: Bernardo Giunti)
— 1637. *Le Metamorfosi ... ridotte da Giouanni Andrea dall'Anguillara in ottaua rima. Con l'annotationi di M. Gioseppe Horologgi, et con gli argomenti di M. Francesco Turchi. Di nuouo in questa nostra vltima impressione con somma diligenza ricorrette, & di vaghe figure adornate* (Venice: Gio. Antonio & Gio. Maria Misserini Fratelli) (British Library, 1607/1488)
— 1677. *Le Metamorfosi di Ovidio ridotte da Gio. Andrea dell'Anguillara in ottava rima con le annotationi di M. Gioseppe Horologgi e gli argomenti di M. Francesco Turchi in questa nuova impressione di vaghe figure adornate* (Venice: Zaccaria Conzavi)
— 1757. *Le Metamorfosi di Ovidio, ridotte da Gio. Andrea dell'Anguillara in ottava rima. Con l'Annotationi di M. Gioseppe Horologgi, e con gli argomenti di M.*

Francesco Turchi dedicate a sua eccellenza la N.D. Catterina Segredo Barbarigo. Tomo primo. (Venice: Girolamo Dorigoni)

— 1805. *Le Metamorfosi d'Ovidio ridotte da Giovanni Andrea dell'Anguillara in ottava rima. Volume primo* (Milan: Società tipografica de' classici italiani)

Aretino, Pietro. 1997. *Lettere*, ed. by Paolo Procaccioli (Rome: Salerno Editrice)

Argelati, Filippo. 1767. *Biblioteca degli volgarizzatori, o sia notizia dall'opere volgarizzate d'autori, che scrissero in lingue morte prima del secolo xv. Opera postuma del segretario Filippo Argelati bolognese. Tomi iv. Coll'addizioni, e correzioni di Angelo Teodoro Villa*. 4 vols (Milan: Federico Agnelli Regio Stampatore)

Ariosto, Ludovico. 1535. *La Lena: Comedia di Messer Lodovico Ariosto* (Venice: Nicolò d'Aristotile detto Zoppino)

— 1552. *Rime* (Venice: [n. pub.])

— 1974. *Orlando furioso*, trans. by Guido Waldman (Oxford: Oxford University Press)

— 1996. *Cinque Canti - Five Cantos*, trans. by Alexander Sheers and David Quint (Berkeley: University of California Press)

Augustine. *City of God*, in Documenta Catholica Omnia, Multilingual Catholic e-Books Database: www.documenta-catholicaomnia.eu [accessed 05 May 2020]

Badia, Lola and Jaume Torró (eds). 2011. *Curial e Güelfa* (Barcelona: Quaderns Crema)

Baker, Craig, Marianne Besseyre, Mattia Cavagna, Stefania Cerrito, Olivier Collet, Massimiliano Gaggero, Yan Greub, Jean-Baptiste Guillaumin, Marylène Possamaï-Pérez, Véronique Rouchon, Irene Salvo, Thomas Städtler, and Richard Trachsler (eds). 2018. *Ovide moralisé. Livre I*, 2 vols (Paris: Société des Anciens Textes Français)

Bartsch, Karl (ed.). 1861. *Albrecht von Halberstadt und Ovid im Mittelalter* (Quedlinburg: Basse)

Bellegarde, Jean Baptiste (trans.). 1716. *Les Metamorphoses d'Ovide, avec des explications ... Traduction nouvelle par M. l'Abbé de Bellegarde*, 2nd corrected edn (Amsterdam: E. Roger). British Library, 11355.a.17

Bescós, Pere (ed.). 2011. *Francesc Alegre: La primera guerra púnica, 1472. Estudi i edició crítica* (doctoral thesis, Universitat Pompeu Fabra) < www.tdx.cat/handle/10803/31878#page=1> [accessed 05 May 2020]

— 2019. Francesc Alegre, *Obres menors* (Santa Barbara: Publications of *eHumanista*) <https://www.ehumanista.ucsb.edu/sites/default/files/sitefiles/publications/monogr aphs/BescosObresMenorsAlegre.pdf> [accessed 05 May 2020]

Betussi, M. Giovanni (trans.). 1547. *Della geneologia de gli dei di M. Giovanni Boccaccio Libri quindeci* (Venice: Del Pozzo)

Boccaccio, Giovanni. 1951, *Genealogie deorum gentilium libri*, ed. by Vincenzo Romano (Bari: Laterza)

— 2011. *Genealogy of the Pagan Gods*, ed. and trans. by Jon Solomon, 3 vols (Cambridge MA: Harvard University Press)

Bolte, Johannes (ed.). 1905–1906. *Georg Wickrams Werke*, Siebenter Band (*Ovids Metamorphosen: Buch 1–8*, 1905), Achter Band (*Ovids Metamorphosen: Buch 9–15*, 1906) (Tübingen: Litterarischer Verein in Stuttgart)

Bonsignori, Giovanni (trans.). 1497. *Ovidio Metamorphoseos Vulgare* (Venice: Giovanni Rosso & Lucantonio Giunta)

— 1520. *P. Ovidio Metamorphoseos vulgare. Novamente stampato. Diligentemente correcto & historiato* (Milan: per Rocho & Fratello da Valle) (BL, C.39.i.18)

— 2001. *Ovidio Metamorphoseos Vulgare*, ed. by Erminia Ardissino (Bologna: Comissione per i testi di lingua)

Born, Lester K. (ed. and trans.). 1929. *The Integumenta on the Metamorphoses of Ovid by John Garland* (unpublished doctoral thesis, University of Chicago)

Brown, Virginia (ed.). 1972. 'An edition of an anonymous twelfth-century *Liber de natura deorum*', *Medieval Studies*, 34: 1–70

Bruni, Leonardo. 2004. *Sulla perfetta traduzione*, ed. by Paolo Viti (Naples: Liguori)

Bustamante, Jorge de. 1536?. *Libro de metamorphoseos y fabulas del excelente poeta y philosofo Ovidio noble cavallero patricio romano* (Salamanca: Pedro de Castro)

Calderón de la Barca, Pedro. 1952. *Obras completas*, III, *Autos sacramentales*, ed. by Àngel Valbuena Prat (Madrid: Aguilar)

Cappellotto, Anna (ed.). 2019. *Metamorfosi delle 'Metamorfosi' di Ovidio: la traduzione in altotedesco medio di Albrecht von Halberstadt* (Alessandria: Dell'Orso)

Castillejo, Cristóbal de. 1926–28. *Obras*, ed. by J. Domínguez Bordona, Clásicos castellanos (Madrid: La Lectura)

Caxton, William (trans.) *c.* 1473. *hEre begynneth the volume intituled and named the recuyell of the historyes of Troye, composed and drawen out of dyuerce bookes of latyn in to frensshe by the ryght venerable persone and worshipfull man. Raoul le ffeure* (Bruges: William Caxton) Henry E. Huntington Library and Art Gallery, STC 15375

— 1477a. *For as moche as late by the comau[n]dement of the right hye [and] noble princesse my right redoubted lady my lady Margarete by the grace of god Duchesse of Bourgoyne Brabant [et]c. [...] as to the historie of Iason* (Westminster: William Caxton) British Library, STC 15383

— 1481a. *Here begynneth the boke intituled Eracles, and also of Godefrey of Boloyne the whiche speketh of the conquest of the holy londe of Iherusalem* (Westminster: William Caxton, 1481) British Library, STC 13175

— 1481b. *Hier begynneth the book callid the myrrour of the worlde* (Westminster: William Caxton) British Library, STC 24762

— 1483. *Legenda aurea sanctorum, sive, Lombardica historia* (Westminster: William Caxton) Cambridge University Library, STC 24873

— 1490. *Here fynyssheth the boke yf [sic] Eneydos, compyled by Vyrgyle, which hathe be translated oute of latyne in to frenshe, and oute of frenshe reduced in to Englysshe by me wyll[ia]m Caxton* (Westminster: William Caxton) British Library, STC 24796

— 2011. *The Middle English Text of Caxton's Ovid, Book I [...] With a Parallel Text of the Ovide Moralisé en Prose II*, ed. by Diana Rumrich (Heidelberg: Winter)

— 2013. *The Book of Ovyde Named Methamorphose*, ed. by Richard J. Moll (Toronto: Pontifical Institute of Medieval Studies)

— 2016. *The Middle English Text of Caxton's Ovid, Books II-III [...] With a Parallel Text of the Ovide Moralisé en Prose II*, ed. by Wolfgang Mager (Heidelberg: Winter)

Chaucer, Geoffrey. 1483. *The book of fame made by Gefferey Chaucer* (Westminster: William Caxton) British Library, STC 5087

— 1483b. *Troilus and Criseyde* (Westminster: William Caxton) British Library, STC 5084

Cicero. 2003. *La naturalesa dels déus*, ed. and trans. by Juan Manuel del Pozo, ii (Barcelona: Fundació Bernat Metge)

Coornhert, Dirck. (trans.). 1561. *Deerste twaelf boecken van Odysseae, dat is de dolinghe van Ulysse* (Haarlem: J. van Zuren, 1561) STCN 830112502

— 1561. *Officia Ciceronis, leerende wat yeghelǐck in allen staten behoort te doen*, trans. by Dirck Coornhert (Haarlem: J. van Zuren) STCN 830083707

Corneille, Thomas (trans.). 1698. *Les Metamorphoses d'Ovide mises en vers françois*, 3 vols (Liege: Broncart) British Library, 11352.aa.4

Cotugno, Alessio (ed.) 2019. *Giovanni Andrea Dell'Anguillara, Le metamorfosi d'Ovidio; con le Annotazioni di Giuseppe Orologi; e gli Argomenti di Francesco Turchi* (Manziana: Vecchiarelli)

Coulson, Frank T. (ed. and trans.). 2015. *The Vulgate Commentary on Ovid's Metamorphoses: Book One* (Kalamazoo, MI: Western Michigan University)

Coulson et al. 2021. *Commentaire Vulgate des* Métamorphoses *d'Ovide. Livres I-V* (Paris: Garnier)

Dante. 1544. *Commedia* (Venice: Francesco Marcolini)

— 1980. *Convivio*, ed. by Piero Cudini (Milan: Garzanti)

De Boer, Cornelis (ed.). 1909. *Philomena. Conte raconté d'après Ovide par Chretien de Troyes, publié d'après tous les manuscrits de l'"Ovide moralisé" avec introduction, notes index de toutes le formes et III appendices* (Paris: Geuthner)

— 1915–38. *Ovide Moralisé: poème du commencement du XIVe siècle, publié d'après tous les manuscrits connus*, 5 vols (Amsterdam: Afdeeling Letterkunde)

— 1954. *Ovide moralisé en prose (texte du XVe siècle), édition critique* (Amsterdam: North-Holland Publishing Company)

Deleville, Prunelle. 2019. *Metamorphosis of Metamorphoses: a critical edition and literary study of manuscripts of the Z family of the Ovide moralisé* (edition of the first twelve books, unpublished doctoral thesis, University of Lumière-Lyon 2)

Dolce, Lodovico (trans.). 1539. *Il primo libro delle Trasformationi d'Ovidio da M. Lodouico Dolce in volgare tradotto* (Venice: Francesco Bindoni & Maffeo Pasini)

— 1553. *All'invittissimo e gloriosissimo Imperatore Carlo Quinto. Le Trasformationi di M. Lodovico Dolce. Con privilegii* (Venice: Gabriele Giolito dei Ferrari and brothers)

— 1553². *Le Trasformationi di M. Lodovico Dolce. Di nuovo ristampate, e da lui ricorrette, et in diversi luoghi ampliate. Con la tavola delle favole. Con privilegi* (Venice: Gabriele Giolito dei Ferrari and brothers, 1553)

— 1551. *Ifigenia* (Venice: Gabriel Giolito de' Ferrari)

— 1555. *Le Trasformationi di M. Lodovico Dolce. In questa terza impressione di nuovo da lui riviste et emendate con la tavola delle favole. Con privilegi* (Venice: Gabriele Giolito dei Ferrari) Reggio Emilia, Biblioteca Panizzi, 17.D.247

— 1560. *La Medea* (Venice: Gabriel Giolito de' Ferrari)

— 1570. *Le Trasformationi di M. Lodovico Dolce tratte da Ovidio. Con gli argomenti et allegorie al principio, et al fine di ciascun canto. E con la giunta della vita d'Ovidio. Di nuovo rivedute, corrette, et di molte figure adornate a suoi luoghi* (Venice: Domenico Farri) British Library, C.81.b.11

— 2015. Lettere, ed. by Paolo Procaccioli (Rome: Vecchiarelli)

Drayton, Michael. 1931–41. *The Works of Michael Drayton*, ed. by J. William Hebel, 5 vols (Oxford: Basil Blackwell)

Douglas, Gavin (trans.). 1513 [1957]. *Virgil's Aeneid Translated into Scottish Verse: by Gavin Douglas*, ed. by David. F. C. Coldwell, 2 vols (Edinburgh: Blackwood)

Dronke, Peter (ed.). 1978. Bernardus Silvestris, *Cosmographia* (Leiden: Brill)

Dryden, John. 2015. 'Dedication to *Examen Poeticum*', in *The Works of John Dryden: Vol. 4, Poems 1693-1696*, ed. by A. B. Chambers and William Frost (Berkeley: University of California Press), pp. 362–75

Engels, Joseph (ed.). 1966. *Petrus Berchorius. Reductorium morale. Liber XV: Ovidius moralizatus, cap. i: De formis figurisque deorum. Textus e codice Brux., Bibl. Reg. 863-9 critice editus*. (Utrecht: Rijksuniversiteit, Instituut voor Laat)

Erasmus, Desiderius. 1986. 'Praise of Folly', in *Collected Works of Erasmus*, 27, ed. By Anthony Herbert Tigar Levi (Toronto: University of Toronto Press), pp. 77–153

Etymologicum Teutonicae linguae [...]. 1599. (Antwerp: Johannes Moretus)

Florianus, Johannes (trans.). 1552. *Metamorphosis, dat is die herscheppinghe oft veranderinghe* (Antwerpen: Hans de Laet) USTC 408777

— 1566. *Metamorphosis dat is de herscheppinge* (Antwerpen: Hans de Laet) 8o. STCN 399363025

— 1588. *Metamorphosis dat is, die herscheppinge oft veranderinge* (Amsterdam: Harmen Jansz Muller) USTC 422638

— 1595. *Metamorphosis dat is, die herscheppinghe oft veranderinge* (Antwerpen: typis Andreas Bax ten huyse Peeter Beelaert) USTC 413158

— 1599. *Metamorphosis dat is, De heerscheppinghe*[!] *oft ververanderinge* (Amsterdam: Harmen Jansz Muller) USTC 424307

— 1608a. *Metamorphosis dat is: Die herscheppinge oft veranderinghe* (Antwerpen: widow of Petrus I Bellerus and heirs of Petrus I Bellerus; [Andreas I Bacx]) USTC 1001926

— 1608b. *Metamorphosis dat is: Die herscheppinge oft veranderinghe*, (Antwerpen: Gheleyn Janssens; [Andreas I Bacx])

— 1609. *Metamorphosis dat is, Die herscheppinge oft veranderinge* (Amsterdam: Harmen Jansz Muller) USTC 1012642

— 1615a. *Metamorphosis dat is: Die herscheppinghe oft veranderinghe* (Antwerpen: Gheleyn Janssens; [Hendrik Swingen]) USTC 1001871

— 1615b. *Metamorphosis, dat is: De herscheppinghe oft veranderinghe* (Rotterdam: Jan III van Waesberge; [Antwerpen, typ. Hendrik Swingen]) USTC 1022737

— 1619. *Metamorphosis dat is: Die herscheppinge oft veranderinghe* (Antwerpen: Andreas I Bacx, for Guillaume Lesteens) USTC 1035461

— 1621. *Metamorphosis: Dat is, De herscheppinghe oft veranderinghe* (Amsterdam: heirs of Harmen Jansz Muller) USTC 1016552

— 1631. *Metamorphosis, dat is: Die herscheppinghe oft veranderinghe* (Antwerpen: Joannes II Bellerus and widow of Petrus II Bellerus) USTC 1007018

— c. 1635. *Den metamorphosis ofte herscheppinghe* (Rotterdam: Pieter I van Waesberge) USTC 1007223

— 1637. *Metamorphosis, dat is: De her-scheppinghe ofte verânderinghe* (Rotterdam: Pieter I van Waesberge [Den Haag, Isaac Burchoorn]) USTC 1030028

— 1650a. *Metamorphosis dat is: Die herscheppinghe oft veranderinghe* (Antwerpen: Peeter III Beelaert; Leiden: sold by Jacob Roels) USTC 1001406

— 1650b. *Metamorphosis dat is: Die herscheppinghe oft veranderinghe* (Antwerpen: Peeter III Beelaert; Rotterdam: sold by Pieter van I Waesberge) USTC 1011209

Forey, Madeleine (ed.). 2002. *The Metamorphoses* (Harmondsworth: Penguin)

Fulgentius. 1500?. *Enarrationes allegoricae fabularum Fulgentii Placiadis* (Venice: Bernardinum de Vitalibus?) British Library, 166.f.22(1)

Galasso, Luigi, Guido Paduano and Alessandro Perutelli (eds). 2000. *Ovidio, Le metamorfosi* (Turin: Einaudi)

Ghisalberti, Fausto (ed.). 1932. *Arnolfo d'Orléans. Un cultore di Ovidio nel secolo XII* (Milan: Hoepli)

— 1933a. 'Giovanni del Virgilio espositore delle "Metamorfosi"', *Giornale dantesco*, 34: 3–110

— 1933b. Giovanni di Garlandia, *Integumenta Ovidii: poemetto inedito del secolo XIII* (Messina-Milan: Principato)

— 1933c. 'L'*Ovidius moralizatus* di Pierre Bersuire,' *Studi Romanzi*, 23: 5–136

Golding, Arthur (trans.) 2002. *Ovid's Metamorphoses Translated by Arthur Golding*, ed. by Madaleine Foreley (London: Penguin)

Goold, George Patrick and Grant Showerman (eds). 2015. Ovid, *Heroides; Amores*, The Loeb Classical Library, vol. 41 (Cambridge, MA: Harvard University Press)

Gómez Rodeles, C. et al. (ed.). 1901. *Monumenta paedogogica Societatis Jesu quae primam rationem Studiorum anno 1586 praecessere*, (Matriti: typis Augustini Avrial)

Góngora, Luis de. 1990. *Antología poética*, ed. by Antonio Carreira, Castalia didáctica, 13, 3rd edn (Madrid: Castalia)

Gower, John. 1483. *tHis book is intituled confessio amantis, that is to saye in englysshe the confessyon of the louer maad and compyled by Iohan Gower squyer* (Westminster: William Caxton) British Library, STC 12142

Guillaumin, Jean-Baptiste. 2018b. 'Édition des gloses', in *Ovide moralisé. Livre I*, ed. by Craig Baker et al., ii (Paris, Société des Anciens Textes Français), pp. 231–307

Gura, David T. (ed.) 2010. *A critical edition and study of Arnulf of Orléans' philological commentary to Ovid's Metamorphoses* (unpublished doctoral thesis, Ohio State University)

Higden, Ranulf, 1482. *Prolicionycion [sic]*, trans. by John of Trevisa (Westminster: William Caxton) British Library, STC 13438

Homer. 1561. *Deerste twaelf boecken van Odysseae, dat is de dolinghe van Ulysse*, trans. by Dirck Coornhert (Haarlem: J. van Zuren, 1561) STCN 830112502

Kartschoke, Dieter (ed.). 2010. *Heinrich von Veldeke, 'Eneasroman', Mittelhochdeutsch/Neuhochdeutsch, nach dem Text von Ludwig Ettmüller ins Neuhochdeutsche übersetzt, mit einem Stellenkommentar und einem Nachwort von Dieter Kartschoke* (Stuttgart: Reclam)

Kingsbury, Susan Myra (ed.). 1906–35. *The Records of the Virginia Company of London*, 4 vols (Washington: United States Government Printing Office)

Kulcsár, Péter (ed.). 1987. *Mythographi Vaticani I et II* (Turnhout: Brepols)

Lafaye, Georges (trans.). 1966. *Ovide, Les Métamorphoses* (Paris: Les Belles Lettres)

Le Bœuffle, André (ed. and trans.). 1983. Hygin, *L'astronomie* (Paris: Les Belles Lettres)

Le Livre de Orpheus translaté de latin en françoys, ouquel y a plusieurs choses recreatives. 1510 ? (Paris: Michel Le Noir). Paris, Bibliothèque nationale de France, Réserve des livres rares. RESP-Z-421).

Le libre du vaillant Perseus, filz de Jupiter. 1510. (Paris: Michel Le Noir) USTC: 55680. British Library, 12510.c.6

Lydgate, John. 1923. *Lydgate's Fall of Princes, Part I*, ed. by H. Bergen (Washington: The Carnegie Institute)

Makolas, Iovannis. 1686. Βιβλίον ιστορικόν καλούμενον Ιουστίνος (Venice: Michael Angelos Varvonios)

Malipiero, Girolamo. 1536. *Il Petrarca spirituale* (Venice: Francesco Marcolini)

Magnus, Hugo (ed.). 1914a. *Lactanti Placidi qui dicitur narrationes fabularum ovidianarum* (Berlin: Weidmann)

— 1914b. *P. Ovidi Nasonis Metamorphoseon libri 15: lactanti placidi qui dicitur narrationes fabularum ovidianarum* (Berlin: Weidmann)

Mander, Karel van. 1604. *Het schilder-boeck* [including: *Wtlegghingh op den Metamorphosis Pub. Ouidij Nasonis*] (Haarlem: Paschier van Westbusch); www.dbnl.org/tekst/mand001schi01_01/> [accessed 05 October 2020]

Martínez Romero (ed.). 1995. *Sèneca, Tragèdies: traducció catalana medieval amb comentaris del segle XIV de Nicolau Trevet*, 2 vols (Barcelona, Barcino)

Marzolla, Piero Bernardini (ed.). 1979. Ovid, *Metamorfosi* (Turin: Einaudi)

Massac, Raimond, and Charles Massac (trans.). 1603. *Les Métamorphoses d'Ovide mises en vers françois par Raimond et Charles de Massac, père et fils* (Paris: A. l'Angelier)

Mey, Felipe. 1586. *Del metamorphoseos de Ovidio en octava rima* (Tarragona: Felipe Mey)

Ovid. 1493–1494. *La Bible des poetes metamorphose* (Paris: Antoine Vérard)

— 1484. *Metamorphoses [French] Ovide ... son livre intitulé Metamorphose*, adapted by Colard Mansion, with a commentary (Bruges: Colard Mansion)

— 1523. *La bible des poëtes, Methamorphoze. Nouvellement imprimé a Paris* (Paris: Philippe Le Noir)

— 1529. *Opera* (Antwerpen: [Merten de Keyser] apud Govaert van der Haeghen, 1529)

— 1531. *La bible des poëtes de Ovide Methamorphose. Translatee de latin en françoys. Nouvellement Imprimee a Paris* (Paris: Philippe Le Noir)

— 1532. *Le Grant Olympe des histoires poëtiques du prince des poëtes Ovide Naso en sa Methamorphose* (Lyon: Romain Morin)

— 1537. *Le grand Olympe des hystoires poetiques* (Paris: E. Caveiller)

— 1643a. *Metamorphosis, dat is verandering of herschepping*, anonymous translation (Amsterdam: for Jan van Hilten)

— 1643b. *Metamorphosis, dat is verandering, of herschepping*, anonymous translation (Amsterdam: for Pieter Robijn)

— 1643c. *Metamorphosis, dat is verandering, of herschepping*, anonymous translation (Amsterdam: for Jodocus Janssonius, 1643)

— 1643d. *Metamorphosis, dat is verandering, of herschepping*, anonymous translation (Amsterdam: for Dirck Cornelisz Houthaeck)

— 1643e [1693]. *Metamorphosus* [!], *dat is verandering, of herschepping*, anonymous translation (Amsterdam: for Jan Jacobsz Schipper)

— 1916 [1966-1968, 2014]. *Metamorphoses*, trans. by Frank J. Miller, rev. by G. P. Goold, The Loeb Classical Library, vols 42–43 (Cambridge, Massachusetts: Harvard University Press, rev. 1977)

Pepin, R. E. 2008. *The Vatican Mythographers* (New York: Fordham University Press)

Pérez de Moya, Juan. 1995. *Philosofía secreta*, ed. by Carlos Clavería, Letras hispánicas, 404 (Madrid: Cátedra)

Pérez Sigler, Antonio (trans.). 1580. *Los quinze libros de los metamorphoseos de el excellente poeta latino Ovidio. Traduzidos en verso suelto y octava rima por Antonio Perez con sus alegorias al fin de cada libro* (Salamanca: Juan Perier) British Library, 1068.g.36

Petrarca, Francesco. 1547. *Il Petrarcha, con l'espositione d'Alessandro Vellutello di novo ristampato con le figure ai Triomphi e con più cose utili in vari luoghi aggiunte* (Venice: Gabriele Giolito dei Ferrari)

— 1549. *Sonetti, canzoni e triomphi di M. Francesco Petrarca con la spositione di Bernardino Daniello da Lucca. Con privilegio del Italianissimo Senato Vinitiano* (Venice: Pietro & Giovanni Maria Nicolini da Sabbio for Giovanni Battista Pederzano)

— 1933–42. *Le Familiari*, ed. by. Vittorio Rossi, 4 vols (Florence: G. C. Sansoni)

Piccolomini, Alessandro (trans.). 1540. *Il sesto di Vergilio tradotto dal S. Stordito Intronato in lingua toscana, in versi sciolti da rima. Le due orationi le quali sono nel terzodecimo libro delle Metamorfosi d'Ovidio tradotte parimente dal medesimo S. Stordito* (Venice: Andrea Arrivabene)

Poirion, Daniel. (ed.) 1994. *Chrétien de Troyes, Œuvres completes, Trad. de l'ancien français par Anne Berthelot, Peter F. Dembowski, Daniel Poirion et Philippe Walter* (Paris: Gallimard)

Renouard, Nicolas (trans.). 1606. *Les Métamorphoses d'Ovide traduites en prose françoise avec XV discours contenant l'explication morale et historique des fables* (Paris: M. Guillemot)

— 1638. *Les Metamorphoses d'Ovide traduites en prose françoise ... et enrichies de figures à chacune fable. Avec XV. discours contenans l'explication morale et historique* (Rouen: Antoine de Quay) British Library, 11375.a.6

Roloff, Hans-Gert (ed.). 1990. *Georg Wickram. Sämtliche Werke*. Band 13/Teil 1 *Ovids 'Metamorphosen'* i-viii, Band 13/Teil 2 *Ovids 'Metamorphosen'* ix-xv (Berlin–Boston: De Gruyter)

Sánchez de Viana, Pedro (trans.). 1589. *Las transformaciones de Ovidio: traduzidas del verso latino, en tercetos y octavas rimas ... con el comento, y explicacion de las fabulas: reduziendolas a philosophia natural, y moral, y astrologia, e historia* (Valladolid: Diego Fernández de Córdoba) British Library, 1461.h.7

Sánchez-Prieto Borja, Pedro (ed.). 2009. *Alfonso el Sabio, 'General estoria'*, 6 vols (Madrid: Fundación Castro)

Sandys, George. 1615. *A Relation Of a Journey Begun Anno Domini 161: Foure Bookes. Containing a Description of the Turkish Empire, of Aegypt, of the Holy Land, of the Remote Parts of Italy, and Ilands Adjoyning* (London: W. Barrett)

Sandys, George (trans.). 1626. *Ovid's Metamorphosis Englished by G. S.* (London: William Stansby) (*STC,* 2nd edition: 18964).

— 1632. *Ovid's Metamorphosis Englished, Mythologiz'd, and Represented in Figures: An essay to the Translation of Virgil's Aeneis by G.S.* (Oxford: John Lichfield) STC 18966.

Simeoni, Grabriello (trans.). 1559. *La vita et Metamorfoseo d'Ovidio. Figurato e abbreviato in forma di epigrammi da M. Gabriello Symeoni. Con altre stanze sopra gli effetti della luna, il ritratto di una fontana d'Overnia, e una apologia generale ella fine del libro* (Lyon: Jean de Tournes)

Sirena, Pietro (trans.). 1556. *Il primo libro delle Metamorfosi tradotto da Pietro Sirena* (Venice: [n. pub.])

Sophocles. 1994. *Ajax. Electra. Oedipus Tyrannus*, ed. and trans. by Hug Lloyd-Jones (Cambridge, London: Harvard University Press)

Suárez de Figueroa, Diego and Ignacio (trans.). 1735-37. *P. Ovidio Nason, Metamorphoseos,* 4 vols (Madrid: Herederos de Francisco del Hierro)

Tarrant, Richard J. (ed.). 2004. *Ovid: Metamorphoses* (Oxford: Oxford University Press)

Tervooren, Helmut (ed). 1975. *Heinrich von Morungen, Lieder, Mittelhochdeutsch und Neuhochdeutsch* (Stuttgart: Reclam)

Thesaurus theutonicae linguae. Schat der Neder-duytscher spraken. 1573. (Antwerp: Christopher Plantin) USTC 59661

Thilo, Georgius (ed.). 1881. *Servii Grammatici qui feruntur in Vergilii carmina commentarii; recensuerunt Georgius Thilo et Hermannus Hagen,* vol. 7 (Leipzig: B. G. Teubner)

Thilo, Georgius and Hermann Hagen (eds). 1884. *Servii grammatici qui feruntur in Vergilii carmina commentarii, Vol. 2. Aeneidos Librorum VI-XII commentarii* (Lipsiae: Teubner)

Virgil. 1999. *Aeneid,* ed. by G.P. Goold and trans. by H. Ruschton Fairlough (Cambridge & London: Harvard University Press)

Vitoria, Fr. Baltasar de. 1623. *Teatro de los dioses de la gentilidad,* 2 vols (Madrid: Imprenta Real)

Wickram, Jörg (trans.). 1545. *P. Ouidij Nasonis deß aller sinnreichsten Poeten Metamorphosis, Das ist von der wunderbarlichen Verenderung der Gestalten der Menschen, Thier vnd anderer Creaturen* (Mainz: Ivo Schöffer). USTC 681909 (reprint 1551, Mainz: Ivo Schöffer; 1581 Frankfurt am Main: Johann Saurn; 1631 Frankfurt am Main: Gottfried Tampach)

Zaccaria, Vittorio (ed.). 1998. Giovanni Boccaccio, *Genealogia deorum gentilium.* 2 vols (Milan: Mondadori)

Zorzetti, Nevio, and Jacques Berlioz (ed. and tr.). 1995. *Le premier mythographe du Vatican (texte et traduction)* (Paris: Belles Lettres)

Secondary Works

Adams, Jenny. 2006. *Power Play: The Literature and Politics of Chess in the Late Middle-Ages* (Philadelphia: University of Pennsylvania Press)

Albrecht, Michael von. 2003 [2009]. *Ovid: eine Einführung* (Stuttgart: Reclam)

Alcina, Juan F. 1998. 'El poeta como Dios: la poética de Landino en España (de Francesc Alegre a Alfonso de Carvallo)', *Salina*, 12: 40–49

— 1999. 'The Poet as God: Landino's poetics in Spain: from Francesc Alegre to Alfonso de Carvalho', in *Latin and Vernacular in Renaissance Spain*, ed. by Barry Taylor and Alejandro Coroleu (Manchester: Manchester Spanish & Portuguese Studies), pp. 131–45

Allen, Judson B. 1970. 'An anonymous Twelfth-Century *de Natura deorum* in the Bodleian Library', *Traditio*, 26: 352–64

Alpers, Svetlana. 1971. *Corpus Rubenianum Ludwig Burchard: Part 9 The Decoration of the Torre de la Parada* (London & New York: Phaidon)

Andreoli, Ilaria. 2006. 'Ex officina Erasmiana: Vincenzo Valgrisi e l'illustrazione del libro tra Venezia e Lione nella metà del '500' (unpublished doctoral thesis, Università Ca' Foscari Venezia – Université Lumière Lyon 2)

— 2012. '"Fabulae artificialiter pictae": illustrazione del libro e decorazione ceramica nel Rinascimento', in *Fabulae pictae: miti e storie nelle maioliche del Rinascimento* (Florence: Giunti), pp. 110–25

— 2013a. *Exercices furieux: a partir de l'édition de l'Orlando furioso De Franceschi (Venise, 1584)* (Bern: Peter Lang)

— 2013b. 'Ovid's "Meta-Metamorphoses": Book Illustration and the Circulation of Erotic Iconographical Patters', in *Shakespeare's Erotic Mythology and Ovidian Renaissance Art*, ed. by Agnès Lafont (Farnham: Ashgate), pp. 19–39

Anselmi, Gian Mario and Marta Guerra (eds). 2006. *Le Metamorfosi di Ovidio nella letteratura tra Medioevo e Rinascimento* (Bologna: Gedit)

Armstrong, Guyda. 2013. 'The Framing of Fiammetta: Gender, Authorship, and Voice in and Elizabethan Translation of Boccaccio', in *Elizabethan Translation and Literary Culture*, ed. by Gabriela Schmidt (Berlin: De Gruyter), pp. 299–339

— 2015. 'Coding Continental: Information Design in Sixteenth-Century English Vernacular Language Manuals and Translations', *Renaissance Studies*, 29.1: 78–102

— 2016. 'Response by Armstrong to "Translation and the materialities of communication"', *Translation Studies*, 9.1: 102–06

— 2020. 'Media and Materiality', in *Routledge Encyclopedia of Translation Studies*, ed. by Mona Baker and Gabriela Saldanha, 3rd edn (London: Routledge), pp. 310–15

Arrigo, Nicolas. 2015. 'La réécriture française: quelques éléments pour un état des recherches', in *Réécritures: Regards nouveaux sur la reprise et le remaniement de textes, dans la littérature française et au-delà, du Moyen Âge à la Renaissance*, ed. by Dorothea Kullmann and Shaun Lalonde (Toronto: Pontifical Institute of Medieval Studies), pp. 299–318

ATILF. 2015. *Dictionnaire du Moyen Français en ligne*, www.atilf.fr/dmf/> [13 March 2020]

Aubrun, Charles V. 1976. 'Estructura y significación de las comedias mitológicas de Calderón', *Hacia Calderón, tercer coloquio anglogermano* (Berlin: de Gruyter), pp. 148–55

Badia, Lola. 1986. 'Per la presència d'Ovidi a l'Edat Mitjana, amb notes sobre les traduccions de les "Heroides" i de les "Metamorfosis" al vulgar', in *Studia in honorem prof. M. de Riquer*, 4 vols (Barcelona: Quaderns Crema), i. 39–71

— 2010. '"Volent escriure a vostra consolació e plaer". Metge, Corella i altres mestres de la prosa catalana dels segles XIV i XV', *Catalan Historical Review*, 3: 185–89

— 2014. 'Bernat Metge', in *Història de la literatura catalana. Literatura medieval (II). Segles XIV-XV*, dir. by Lola Badia (Barcelona, Enciclopèdia Catalana, Editorial Barcino & Ajuntament de Barcelona), pp. 185–238

Baker, Patrick. 2015. *Italian Renaissance Humanism in the Mirror* (Cambridge: Cambridge University Press)

Barker, Sara K., and Brenda M. Hosington (eds). 2013. *Renaissance Cultural Crossroads: Translation, Print and Culture in Britain, 1473-1640* (Leiden & Boston: Brill)

Balzi, Marta. 2020. 'Transforming Ovid's *Metamorphoses*: Vernacular Translation and Print Culture in Renaissance Italy' (unpublished doctoral thesis, University of Bristol)

Ballistreri, Gianni. 1970. 'Bonsignori, Giovanni de', in *Dizionario Biografico degli Italiani* (Rome: Istituto dell'Enciclopedia Italiana), *ad vocem*, xii. 407–09

Barbieri, L. 2011. 'Les *Heroïdes* dans l'*Ovide moralisé*: Léandre-Héro, Pâris-Hélène, Jason-Médée', in *Les translations d'Ovide au Moyen Âge*, ed. by A. Faems, V. Minet-Mahy, and C. Van Coolput-Storms (Louvain-la-Neuve: Publications de l'Institut d'Études Médiévales de l'Université Catholiqué de Louvain), pp. 235–68

Bassnett, Susan and André Lefevere (eds). 1990. *Translation, History and Culture* (London: Pinter)

Baswell, Christopher. 1995. *Virgil in Medieval England: Figuring the Aeneid from the Twelfth Century to Chaucer* (Cambridge: Cambridge University Press)

Behmenburg, Lena. 2009. *Philomela: Metamorphosen eines Mythos in der deutschen und französischen Literatur des Mittelalters* (Berlin & Boston: De Gruyter)

Belle, Marie-Alice. 2018. 'Knights, Schoolmasters and 'Lusty Ladies White': Addressing Readers in the Paratexts to Gavin Douglas's Fourth Book of *Eneados* (1513-1553)', in *Thresholds of Translation: Paratexts, Print, and Cultural Exchange in Early Modern Britain*, ed. by Marie-Alice Belle and Brenda M. Hosington (London: Palgrave Macmillan), pp. 139–59

Belle, Marie-Alice and Brenda M. Hosington (eds). 2018. *Thresholds of Translation. Paratext, Print, and Cultural Exchange in Early Modern Britain (1473–1660)* (Cham: Palgrave Macmillan)

Bennett, J. 1950. 'Caxton and Gower'. *Modern Language Review*, 45: 215–16

Berriot-Salvadore, Evelyne (ed.). 2014. *Les figures de Didon: de l'épopée antique au théâtre de la Renaissance*, www.ircl.cnrs.fr/francais/actes%20didon.htm> [accessed 10 July 2019]

Bertolo, M. 2003. *Aretino e la stampa. Strategie di autoproduzione a Venezia nel Cinquecento* (Rome: Salerno Editrice)

Bescós, Pere. 2018. '"E davellant murs, habitar les ciutats" (Al·legories, I.5): Montjuïc como espacio simbólico en las alegorías ovidianas de Francesc Alegre', in *Espacios en la Edad Media y el Renacimiento*, ed. by María Morrás Ruiz-Falcó (Salamanca: Universidad de Salamanca and Sociedad de Estudios Medievales y Renacentistas), pp. 383–96

Besseyre, Marianne and Véronique Rouchon-Mouilleron. 2018. 'Introduction', in *Ovide Moralisé. Livre I*, edited by Baker et al. (Paris, Société des Anciens Textes Français), i. 13–121

Bianchi, Silvia. 1990. 'Nicolas Béatrizet', *Grafica d'arte*, 4: 2–9

Bietenholz, Peter G. 1994. *'Historia' and 'Fabula'. Myths and Legends in Historical Thought from Antiquity to the Modern Age* (Leiden: Brill)

Bijl, M. van der. 1971. 'Petrus Berchorius, *Reductorium morale*, liber XV: *Ovidius moralizatus*, cap. ii', *Vivarium*, 9: 25–48

Bistué, Belén. 2013. *Collaborative Translation and Multi-Version Texts in Early Modern Europe* (Farnham: Ashgate)

BITECA. (1997–). *Bibliografia de textos antics catalans, valencians i balears*, Philobiblon, dir. by Vicenç Beltran, Gemma Avenoza and Lourdes Soriano (Berkeley: University of California) http://bancroft.berkeley.edu/philobiblon/ [accessed 05 May 2020]

Black, Robert. 2001. *Humanism and Education in Medieval and Renaissance Italy: Tradition and Innovation in Latin Schools from the Twelfth to the Fifteenth Century* (Cambridge: Cambridge University Press)

— 2011. 'Ovid in Medieval Italy', in *Ovid in the Middle Ages*, ed. by James G. Clark, Frank T. Coulson and Kathryn L. McKinley (Cambridge: Cambridge University Press), pp. 123–42

Blair, Ann. 2010. *Too Much to Know. Managing Scholarly Information before the Modern Age* (New Haven & London: Yale University Press)

Blake, Norman F. 1991. *William Caxton and English Literary Culture* (London: Hambledon Press)

Blattner, Evamarie. 1998. *Holzschnittfolgen zu den Metamorphosen des Ovid: Venedig 1497 und Mainz 1545* (München: Scaneg)

Bloom, Gina. 2001. 'Localizing Disembodied Voice in Sandys's Englished "Narcissus and Echo"', in *Ovid and the Renaissance Body*, ed. by G.V. Stanivukovic (Toronto: University of Toronto Press), pp. 129–54

Blumenfeld-Kosinski, Renate. 1996. 'The Scandal of Pasiphae: Narration and Interpretation in the *Ovide moralisé*', *Modern Philology*, 93/3: 307–26

— 1997. *Reading Myth: Classical Mythology and its Interpretations in Medieval French Literature* (Stanford: Stanford University Press California)

Bode, Georg H. (ed.). 1834 [1968]. *Scriptores rerum mythicarum Latini tres Romae nuper reperti*, 2 vols (Cellis: Impens E. H. C. Schulze, reprint Hildeshen: Georg Olms Verlag)

Bondi, Fabrizio. 2017. 'Cadmo e il serpente. Le *Metamorfosi* di Anguillara illustrate da Giacomo Franco', in *Galassia Ariosto: il modello editoriale dell'Orlando Furioso, dal libro illustrato al web*, ed. by Lina Bolzoni (Rome: Donzelli), pp. 325–52

Bongi, Salvatore. 2006. *Annali di Gabriel Giolito de' Ferrari da Trino di Monferrato, stampatore in Venezia* (Mansfield: Martino Publishing)

Bolte, Johannes (ed.). 1905–1906. *Georg Wickrams Werke*, Siebenter Band (*Ovids Metamorphosen: Buch 1–8*, 1905), Achter Band (*Ovids Metamorphosen: Buch 9–15*, 1906) (Tübingen: Litterarischer Verein in Stuttgart)

Bolzoni, Lina (ed.). 2014. *L'Orlando furioso nello specchio delle immagini* (Rome: Istituto della Enciclopedia Italiana)

— 2017. *Galassia Ariosto. Il modello editoriale del Furioso dal libro illustrato al web* (Rome: Donzelli)

Bolzoni, Lina and Carlo Alberto Girotto (eds.). 2013. *Donne cavalieri incanti follia. Viaggio attraverso le immagini dell'Orlando furioso* (Lucca: Maria Pacini Fazi)

Bolzoni, Lina, S. Pezzini, and G. Rizzarelli (eds). 2010. *'Tra mille carte vive ancora'. Ricezione del Furioso tra immagini e parole* (Rome: Donzelli)

Bondi, Fabrizio. 2017. 'Cadmo e il serpente. Le *Metamorfosi* di Anguillara illustrate da Giacomo Franco', in *Galassia Ariosto. Il modello editoriale del Furioso dal libro illustrato al web*, ed. by Lina Bolzoni (Rome: Donzelli), pp. 325–52

Botley, Paul. 2004. *Latin Translation in the Renaissance: The Theory and Practice of Leonardo Bruni, Giannozzo Manetti, and Desiderius Erasmus* (Cambridge: Cambridge University Press)

Boutcher, Warren. 1996. 'Vernacular Humanism in the Sixteenth Century', in *The Cambridge Companion to Renaissance Humanism*, ed. by Jill Kraye (Cambridge: Cambridge University Press), pp. 189–202

Brancaforte, Benito (ed.). 1990. *Las 'Metamorfosis' y las 'Heroidas' de Ovidio en la 'General estoria' de Alfonso el Sabio* (Madison: Hispanic Seminary of Medieval Studies)

Bucchi, Gabriele. 2011. *"Meraviglioso diletto": la traduzione poetica del Cinquecento e le Metamorfosi d'Ovidio di Giovanni Andrea dell'Anguillara* (Pisa: ETS)

Buccini, Stefania. 2013. *Francesco Pona. L'ozio lecito della scrittura* (Florence: Olschki)

Bulfinch, Thomas. 1993. *The Golden Age of Myth & Legend* (Ware: Wordsworth)

Burckhardt, Jacob. 1911. 'Das Porträt in der Italienischen Malerei', in *Beiträge zur Kunstgeschichte von Italien*, 2nd edn (Berlin: W. Speemann)

Burke, Peter. 2000. 'Early Modern Venice as a Center of Information and Communication', in *Venice Reconsidered: The History and Civilization of an Italian City–State, 1297–1797*, ed. by John Martin and Dennis Romano (Baltimore: Johns Hopkins University Press), pp. 388–419

— 1995. 'The Renaissance, Individualism and the Portrait', *History of European Ideas*, 21: 147–57

Buttenwieser, Hilda. 1940. 'Manuscripts of Ovid's *Fasti*: the Ovidian Tradition in the Middle Ages', *Transactions and Proceedings of the American Philological Association*, 71: 45–51

Bury, M. 2001. *The Print in Italy 1550-1625* (London: British Museum Press)

Cabré, Lluís, Alejandro Coroleu, Montserrat Ferrer, Albert Lloret and Josep Pujol. 2018. *The Classical Tradition in Medieval Catalan 1300-1500* (Woodbridge, Tamesis)

Calegari, Chiara. 2014. 'Le trasformazioni di Lodovico Dolce', *Nuova informazione bibliografica*, 2: 383–87

Cañigueral, Pau. 2018. *La influencia de Boccaccio en la literatura catalana medieval (1390–1495). Un estudio de la imitación literaria en Bernat Metge, Bernat Hug de Rocabertí y Joan Roís de Corella* (unpublihed doctoral thesis, University of Massachusetts, Amherst).

Capelli, Roberta. 2013. 'Il mecenate nel testo: l'ombra della committenza nell'*Ovide moralisé* in prosa', in *Da Ovidio a Ovidio? L'"Ovide moralisé" in prosa*, ed. by Anna Maria Babbi (Verona: Fiorini), pp. 1–27

Caplan, Harry. 1929. 'The Four Senses of Scriptural Interpretation and the Mediaeval Theory of Preaching', *Speculum*, 4: 282–90

Cappellotto, Anna. 2013. 'Le Metamorfosi di Albrecht von Halberstadt sull'esempio del mito di Filomela', in *Da Ovidio a Ovidio? L'Ovide moralisé in prosa*, ed. by Anna Maria Babbi (Verona: Fiorini), pp. 77–102

— 2016. 'Il mito di Apollo e Pan nelle *Metamorfosi* di Albrecht von Halberstadt', *Filologia Germanica / Germanic Philology*, 8: 1–20

Capriotti, Giuseppe. 2013. *Le* Trasformationi *di Lodovico Dolce. Il Rinascimento ovidiano di Giovanni Antonio Rusconi. Ristampa anastatica della prima edizione delle* Trasformationi (Ancona: Affinità elettive)

— 2017. 'Il tempo delle trasformazioni. Le quattro stampe di Giovanni Antonio Rusconi aggiunte alla seconda edizione del 1553 delle *Trasformationi* di Lodovico Dolce', in *Galassia Ariosto. Il modello editoriale dell'Orlando Furioso dal libro illustrato al web*, ed. by Lina Bolzoni (Rome: Donzelli), pp. 309–24

— 2021. 'Eroticism under a Watchful Eye. Censorship and Alteration of Xylographs in Ovid's *Metamorphoses* between the Fifteenth and the Sixteenth Centuries', in *The Reception of the Printed Image in the* Fifteenth and the Sixteenth *Centuries: Multiplied & Modified*, ed. by Grażyna Jurkowlaniec and Magdalena Herman (London: Routledge), 117–133.

Capriotti, Giuseppe, Casamassima, Francesca. 2020. 'Hermaphroditus and Iphis: Texts and Images from two Ovidian Myths to Visualize Sexual Ambiguity in the Early Modern Age', *Ikon*, 13: 199–212

Carnelos, Laura. 2016. 'Words on the Street: Selling Small Printed "Things" in Sixteenth– and Seventeenth–Century Venice', in *News Networks in Early Modern Europe*, ed. by Raymond Joad and Noah Moxham (Leiden: Brill), pp. 739–55

Carrasco Reija, Leticia. 1997. 'La traducción de las *Metamorfosis* de Ovidio por Jorge de Bustamante', in *Humanismo y pervivencia del mundo clásico: homenaje al profesor Luis Gil*, ed. by José María Maestre Maestre, Sandra Inés Ramos Maldonado, Manuel Antonio Díaz Gito, María Violeta Pérez Custodio, Bartolomé Pozuelo Calero and Antonio Serrano Cueto (Cadiz: Excmo Ayuntamiento de Alcaniz), II: 2, 987–94

Casamassima, Francesca. 2015. 'L'apparato decorativo delle *Metamorfosi* di Giovanni Andrea dell'Anguillara. Le serie iconografiche cinquecentesche.', *Il capitale culturale: Studies on the Value of Cultural Heritage*, 11: 424–46

— 2017. *Immagini delle Metamorfosi di Giovanni Andrea dell'Anguillara: catalogo delle serie iconografiche del 1563 e del 1584* (Ancona: Affinità elettive)

Casamassima, Francesca. 2018. 'Fetonte, Ganimede e il vello d'oro: alcune anomalie rivelatrici. Immagini e testo nelle *Metamorfosi* di Giovanni Andrea dell'Anguillara', in *'Le forme in novi corpi trasformati'. Mito e Metamorfosi tra arte e letteratura*, ed. by Valeria Merola (Ancona: Affinità elettive) pp. 25–55

Catálogo colectivo del patrimonio bibliográfico español. http://catalogos.mecd.es/CCPB/ccpbopac/ [accessed 06 October 2020]

Cauchi, Simon. 1986. 'The "Setting Forth" of Harington's Ariosto', *Studies in Bibliography*, 36: 137–68

Cavagna, Anna G. 1981. *Libri e tipografi a Pavia nel Cinquecento* (Milano: La Galiardica)

Cavagna, Mattia, Massimiliano Gaggero and Yan Greub. 2014. 'La tradition manuscrite de l'*Ovide moralisé*: prolégomènes à une nouvelle édition', *Romania*, 132: 176–213

Cellauro, Louis. 2009. 'La biblioteca di un architetto del Rinascimento: la raccolta di libri di Giovanni Antonio Rusconi', *Arte Veneta*, 58: 224–37

Cerquiglini, Bernard. 1989. *Éloge de la variante. Histoire critique de la philology* (Paris: Editions du Sueil)

Cerrito, Stefania. 2010. 'L'*Ovide moralisé* mis en prose à la cour de Bourgogne', in *Mettre en prose aux XIVᵉ–XVIᵉ siècles. Approches linguistiques, philologiques, littéraires* (Turnhout: Brepols), pp. 109–117

— 2012. 'Entre Ovide et *Ovide moralisé*: la variance des traductions des *Métamorphoses* au Moyen Âge', *Le texte médiéval. De la variante à la recréation*: 159–172

Cevolini, Alberto. 2014. 'Indexing as Preadaptive Advance: A Socio-Evolutionary Perspective', *The Indexer*, 32.2: 50–57

Chartier, Roger. 1992. *The Order of Books: Readers, Authors, and Libraries in Europe between the Fourteenth and Eighteenth Centuries*, trans. by Lydia G. Cochrane (Stanford: Stanford University Press)

Ciccone, et al. 2020. *Ovide 'entre les mains'. Commentaire aux* Métamorphoses, *Vaticanus Latinus 1479, Livres I–V* (Paris, Garnier, Textes Littéraires du Moyen Âge, 56)

Cieri Via, Claudia. 1989. 'L'immagine del ritratto. Considerazioni sull'origine del genere e la sua evoluzione dal Quattrocento al Cinquecento', in *Il ritratto e la memoria: materiali*, ed. by A. Gentili, 2 vols (Rome: Bulzoni), i. 45–91

Cifuentes, Lluís. 2006. *La ciència en català a l'Edat Mitjana i el Renaixement* (Barcelona: Publicacions i Edicions de la Universitat de Barcelona & Universitat de les Illes Balears)

Cipolla, Maria Adele. 2014. *Gli amanti nella selva. 'Herr Tristrant'. BSB Cgm 51* (Verona: Fiorini)

Clark, James G. 2011. 'Introduction', in *Ovid in the Middle Ages*, ed. by James G. Clark, Frank T. Coulson and Kathryn L. McKinley (Cambridge: Cambridge University Press), pp. 1–25

Clark, James, Frank T. Coulson and Kathryn L. McKinley (eds). 2011. *Ovid in the Middle Ages* (Cambridge: Cambridge University Press)

Clavería, Carlos. 1995. 'Quintiliano, Virgilio y Horacio no son negocio: la imprenta española en el siglo XVI', *Criticón*, 65: 5–15

Chaucer, Geoffrey. 2008. *The Riverside Chaucer*, ed. by Larry D. Benson, 3rd edn (Oxford: Oxford University Press)

Child, C. G. 1895. 'Chaucer's *House of Fame* and Boccaccio's *Amorosa Visione*', *Modern Language Notes*, 10.6: 190–92

Coldiron, Anne E. B. 2006. 'Taking Advice from a Frenchwoman: Caxton, Pynson, and Christine de Pizan's *Moral Proverbs*', in *Caxton's Trace. Studies in the History of*

English Printing, ed. by William Kuskin (Notre Dame: University of Notre Dame Press), pp. 127–66

—— 2009. *English Printing, Verse Translation, and the Battle of the Sexes, 1476-1557* (Aldershot: Ashgate)

—— 2015. *Printers Without Borders. Translation and Textuality in the Renaissance* (Cambridge: Cambridge University Press)

—— 2016. 'Response by Coldiron to "Translation and the Materialities of Communication"', *Translation Studies*, 9.1: 96–102

— 2018. 'The Translator's Visibility in Early Printed Portrait-Images and the Ambiguous Example of Margaret More Roper', in *Threshold of Translation: Paratexts, Print, and Cultural Exchange in Early Modern Britain (1473-1660)*, ed. by Marie Alice Belle and Brenda M. Hosington (Basingstoke: Palgrave Macmillan), pp. 51–74

Colombo Timelli, Maria, Barbara Ferrari, Anne Schoysman and François Suard (eds). 2014. *Nouveau Répertoire de mises en prose (xive-xvie siècle)* (Paris: Garnier)

Conklin Akbari, Susanne. 2007. 'Metaphor and Metamorphosis in the *Ovide moralisé* and Christine de Pizan's *Mutacion de Fortune*', in *Metamorphosis: The Changing Face of Ovid in Medieval and Early Modern Europe*, ed. by Alison Keith and Stephen James Rupp (Toronto: CRRS), pp. 77–90

Conte, Gian Biagio. 2012. *Memoria dei poeti e sistema letterario* (Palermo: Sellerio)

Copeland, Rita. 1991. *Rhetoric, Hermeneutics and Translation in the Middle Ages: Academic Traditions and Vernacular Texts* (Cambridge: Cambridge University Press)

Cornish, Alison. 2011. *Vernacular Translation in Dante's Italy: Illiterate Literature* (Cambridge: Cambridge University Press)

Coroleu, Alejandro. 2006. 'History into Fiction: Sixteenth-century Spanish Translations of Classical Prose Narratives', in *Latin and Vernacular in Renaissance Iberia, II: Translations and Adaptations*, ed. Barry Taylor and Alejandro Coroleu (Manchester: Dept of Hispanic Studies), pp. 13–22

Cossío, José María de. 1952. *Fábulas mitológicas en España* (Madrid: Espasa-Calpe)

Cotugno, Alessio. 2006. 'Piccolomini e Castelvetro traduttori della Poetica', *Studi di lessicografia italiana*, 23: 113–219

— 2007. 'Le "Metamorfosi" di Ovidio "ridotte" in ottava rima da Giovanni Andrea Dell'Anguillara: tradizione e fortuna editoriale di un best-seller cinquecentesco', *Atti dell'Istituto Veneto di Scienze, Lettere ed Arte: Classe di Scienze Morali, Lettere ed Arti*, 165. 3/4: 461–541

— 2009. 'Tra fuso e telaio: la terminologia di Anguillara traduttore delle *Metamorfosi* ovidiane negli episodi delle Minieidi e di Aracne', in *Lessico colto, lessico popolare*, ed. by Carla Marcato (Alessandria: Edizioni dell'Orso), pp. 1–37

— 2010. 'Filatura e tessitura: un banco di prova terminologico per i traduttori cinquecenteschi delle "Metamorfosi" ovidiane', *Studi di lessicografia italiana*, 27: 15–89

— 2015. 'Le annotazioni di Piccolomini e la *Poetica* di Castelvetro a confronto: tecnica argomentativa, vocabolario critico, dispositivi esegetici', in *Forms of Conflicts and Rivalries in Renaissance Europe* ed. by David A. Lines, Marc Laureys and Jill Kraye (Göttingen: V&R unipress, Bonn University Press), pp. 161–206

Coulson, Frank T., 1982. *A study of the 'Vulgate' commentary on Ovid's 'Metamorphoses' and a critical edition of the glosses to Book One* (unpublished doctoral thesis, University of Toronto)

— 1987. 'Hitherto Unedited Medieval and Renaissance Lives of Ovid (I)', *Mediaeval Studies*, 49: 152–207

— 1991. *The 'Vulgate' Commentary in Ovid's Metamorphoses: The Story of Creation and Orpheus and Eurydice* (Toronto: Toronto Medieval Latin Texts)

— 1994. 'A Bibliographical Update and corrigenda minora to Munari's Catalogues of the Manuscripts of Ovid's 'Metamorphoses'', *Manuscripta. A Journal for Manuscript Research*, 38: 3–28

— 2011. 'Ovid's *Metamorphoses* in the School Tradition of France, 1180-1400: Texts, Manuscript Tradition, Manuscript Settings', in *Ovid in the Middle Ages*, ed. by James G. Clark, Frank T. Coulson and Kathryn L. McKinley (Cambridge: Cambridge University Press), pp. 48–82

— 2016. 'Myth and Allegory in the Vulgate Commentary on Ovid's Metamorphoses', in *Lire les mythes. Formes, usages et visées des pratiques mythographiques de l'Antiquité à la Renaissance*, ed. by A. Zucker, J. Fabre-Serris, J.-Y. Tilliette and G. Besson (Lille: Septentrion), pp. 199–224

— 2018. 'The Allegories in the Vulgate Commentary', in *Ovidius explanatus. Traduire et commenter les Métamorphoses au Moyen Âge*, ed. by S. Biancardi, P. Deleville, F. Montorsi and M. Possamaï-Pérez (Paris: Garnier), pp. 23–38

Coulson, F. T. and B. Roy. 2000. *Incipitarium Ovidianum: A Finding Guide for Texts Related to the Study of Ovid in the Middle Ages and the Renaissance* (Turnhout: Brepols)

Cranston, Jodi. 2000. *The Poetics of Portraiture in the Italian Renaissance* (Cambridge: Cambridge University Press)

Cristóbal, Vicente. 2011. 'Ovid in Medieval Spain', in *Ovid in the Middle Ages*, ed. by James G. Clark, Frank T. Coulson and Kathryn L. McKinley (Cambridge: Cambridge University Press), pp. 231–56

Cronin, Michael. 2003. *Translation and Globalization* (London: Routledge)

Dahan, Gilbert. 1999. *Exégèse chrétienne de la Bible en Occident médiéval, xii⁰–xiii⁰ siècle* (Paris: Cerf)

Davis, Richard. 1941. 'Early Editions of George Sandys's "Ovid": The Circumstances of Production', *The Papers of the Bibliographical Society of America*, 35: 255–80

—. 1948. 'George Sandys v. William Stansby: The 1632 Edition of Ovid's *Metamorphosis*', *The Library*, s5-III (3): 193–212.

—. 1955. *George Sandys, Poet-Adventurer; A Study in Anglo-American Culture in the Seventeenth Century* (London: The Bodley Head)

—. 1973. *Literature and Society in Early Virginia 1608-1640* (Baton Rouge: University of Louisiana Press)

Davoli, Zeno. 2000. 'Dibattito su un incisore: Giacomo Franco', *Grafica d'arte*, 11: 3–7

Demats, Paule. 1973. *Fabula. Trois études de mythographie antique et médiévale* (Genève: Droz)

Deleville, Prunelle. Forthcoming. 'Christine de Pizan, lectrice de l'*Ovide moralisé*, mais lequel?', *Postérités de l'"Ovide moralisé'*, ed. by Catherine Gaullier-Bougass and Marylène Possamaï-Pérez (Paris: Garnier)

De Weever, Jacqueline. 1996. *Chaucer Name Dictionary. A Guide to Astrological, Biblical, Historical, Literary, and Mythological Names in the Works of Geoffrey Chaucer* (New York/London: Garland) www.columbia.edu/dlc/garland/deweever/menu.htm [accessed 10 July 2019]

Desmond, Marylin R. 1987. 'Introduction', in *Ovid in Medieval Culture*, ed. by Marilynn R. Desmond, Special issue of *Mediaevalia*, 13: 1–8

— 1994. *Reading Dido. Gender, Textuality, and the Medieval Aeneid* (Minneapolis: University of Minessota Press)

— 2011. 'Gender and Desire in Medieval French Translations of Ovid's Amatory Works', in *Ovid in the Middle Ages*, ed. by James G. Clark, Frank T. Coulson and Kathryn L. McKinley (Cambridge: Cambridge University Press), pp. 108–22

Desrosiers-Bonin, Diane. 2008. 'De l'exemplum antique à l'exemplar vivant dans la *Cité des dames* de Christine de Pizan', in *Les Femmes et l'écriture de l'histoire*, ed. by Sylvie Steinberg and Jean-Claude Arnould (Mont Saint-Aignan: Presses de l'Université de Rouen et du Havre), pp. 299–308

Díez Platas, Fátima. 2012. 'Una presencia excepcional de Ovidio en Mondoñedo: la edición de Parma 1505', *Estudios Mindonicenses*, 28: 543–60

Dimmick, Jeremy. 2002. 'Ovid in the Middle Ages: Authority and Poetry', in *The Cambridge Companion to Ovid*, ed. by Philip Hardie (Cambridge: Cambridge University Press), pp. 264–87

Dionisotti, Carlo. 1967. *Geografia e storia della letteratura italiana*, 2nd edn (Turin: Einaudi)

Dixhoorn, Arjan van. 2009. *Lustige geesten. Rederijkers in de Noordelijke Nederlanden (1480-1650)* (Amsterdam: Amsterdam University Press)

Dixhoorn, Arjan van, S. Mareel, and B. Ramakers. 2018. 'The Relevance of the Netherlandish Rhetoricians', *Renaissance Studies*, 32.1: 8–22

Dorigatti, Marco. 2008. 'Il volto dell'Ariosto nella letteratura e nell'arte del Rinascimento', *Italianistica*, 37: 147–57

Dulac, Liliane. 2002. 'Le chevalier Hercule de l'*Ovide moralisé* au *Livre de la mutacion de fortune* de Christine de Pizan', *Cahiers de recherches médiévales*, 9: 115–30 < https://journals.openedition.org/crm/68> [accessed 10 July 2019]

Eisenstein, Elizabeth. 1979. *The Printing Press as an Agent of Change. Communication and Cultural Transformations in Early Modern Europe,* 2 vols (Cambridge: Cambridge University Press)

— 2005. *The Printing Revolution in Early Modern Europe*, 2nd edn (Cambridge: Cambridge University Press)

Ellis, Roger. 1996. 'Chaucer, Christine de Pizan, and Hoccleve: "The Letter of Cupid"', in *Essays on Thomas Hoccleve*, ed. by Catherine Batt (Turnhout: Brepols), pp. 29–54

Ellison, James. 2002. *George Sandys. Travel, Colonialism and Tolerance in the Seventeenth Century* (Cambridge & Rochester, NY: D.S. Brewer)

Enenkel, Karl A. E. 2008. 'Reciprocal Authorisation: The Function of Dedications and Dedicatory Prefaces in the 15th- and 16th-Century "Artes Antiquitatis"', in *'Cui*

Dono Lepidum Novum Libellum?' Dedicating Latin Works and Motets in the Sixteenth Century, ed. by Ignace Bossuyt et al. (Leuven: Leuven University Press), pp. 35–47

—— 2015. *Die Stiftung von Autorschaft in der neulateinischen Literatur (ca. 1350–ca. 1650). Zur autorisierenden und wissensvermittelnden Funktion von Widmungen, Vorworttexten, Autorporträts und Dedikationsbildern* (Leiden & Boston: Brill)

Engelbrecht, Wilken. 2003. *Filologie in de Derdiente eeuw: De Bursarii super Ovidios van Magister Willem van Orléans (fl. 1200 ad): inleading, editie en commentaar* (Olomouc: Palacký Universiteit te Olomouc)

Engels, Joseph. 1945. *Études sur l'"Ovide Moralisé'* (Groningen-Batavia: J.B. Wolters)

—— 1971. 'L'edition critique de l'*Ovidius moralizatus* de Bersuire,' *Vivarium*, 9: 19–24

Fàbrega, Valentí. 1993. 'Les Transformacions del poeta Ovidi segons la versió de Francesc Alegre: el mite de Pigmalió', *Zeitschrift für Katalanistik*, 6: 73–96

Farinelli, Arturo. 1929. *Italia e Spagna* (Turin, Fratelli Bocca)

Feldman, Burton and Robert D. Richardson. 1972. *The Rise of Modern Mythology 1680–1860* (Bloomington: Indiana UP)

Ferretti, Matteo. 2007. 'Paolo da Perugia e i commentari ovidiani di Giovanni del Virgilio', in *Studi sul Boccaccio*, 35: 85–110

FEW. 2003. Walther von Wartburg, *Französisches Etymologisches Wörterbuch* (2003). https://apps.atilf.fr/lecteurFEW/ [accessed 06 November 2020]

Fielding, Ian. 2014. 'A Poet between Two Worlds: Ovid in Late Antiquity', in *A Handbook to the Reception of Ovid*, ed. by John F. Miller and Carol E. Newlands (Chichester-Malden: Wiley Blackwell), pp. 100–13

Folena, Gianfranco. 1991. *Volgarizzare e tradurre*, 2nd edn (Turin: Einaudi)

Fontenelle, Bernard. 1932. *De l'origine des fables (1724)*, ed. by J.-R. Carré (Paris: Alcan)

Forsyth, Ilene. 1976. 'The Ganymede Capital in Vezèlay', *Gesta*, 15: 241–46

Foucher, Louis. 1979. 'L'enlèvement de Ganymèd figuré sur les mosaïques', *Antiquités Africaines*, 14: 155–68

Fowler, Alastair. 2017. *The Mind of the Book. Pictorial Title Pages* (Oxford: Oxford University Press)

Friedlein, Roger. 2012. *El diàleg en Ramon Llull. L'expressió literària com a estratègia apologètica* (Barcelona: Publicacions i Edicions de la Universitat de Barcelona)

Fumo, Jamie. 2004.'Thinking upon the Crow: The "Manciple's Tale" and Ovidian Mythography', *The Chaucer Review*, 38.4: 355–75

—— 2011. 'Ovid's New Clothes: Text and Image in Caxton's "Booke of Ouyde" (1480) and Contemporary Prose Moralizations of the Metamorphoses', in *Vehicles of Transmission, Translation, and Transformation in Medieval Textual Culture*, ed. by Robert Wisnovsky, Faith Wallis, Jamie C. Fumo, and Carlos Fraenkel (Turnhout: Brepols Press), pp. 313–33

——2017. 'Ovid in the Middle Ages', *Oxford Bibliographies* <https://dx.doi.org/10.1093/obo/9780195396584-0224> [accessed 10 July 2019]

García Sanz, Oscar. 1993. 'Herencia y originalidad en la obra de dos humanistas: Pérez de Moya y Fray Baltasar de Vitoria. En torno a Baco', in *Humanismo y pervivencia del mundo clásico: actas del I Simposio sobre Humanismo y pervivencia del mundo clásico (Alcañiz, 8 al 11 de mayo de 1990)*, ed. by José Mª Maestre Maestre and Joaquin Pascual Barea (Cadiz: Instituto de Estudios Turolenses), i. 467–82

García Solalinde, Antonio. 1921. 'La fecha del *Ovide moralisé*', *Revista de Filología Española*, 8: 285–88

Gärtner, Thomas. 2009. 'Wer löscht das Feuer? Zur Rezeption der Hero-und-Leander-Sage in Mittelalter, Renaissance und Neuzeit', *Orbis Litterarum*, 64, 4: 263–82

Genette, Gérard. 1982. *Palimpsestes. La littérature au second degré* (Paris, Seuil)

— 1991. 'Introduction to the Paratext', *New Literary History*, 22: 261–72

— 1997. *Paratexts: Thresholds of interpretation* (Cambridge: Cambridge University Press)

Gentili, Augusto, Philippe Morel, and Claudia Cieri Via (eds). 1989–93. *Il ritratto e la memoria*, 2 vols (Rome: Bulzoni)

Gentilini, Anna R. 1993. 'Edizioni della Storia Romana di Tito Livio e delle Metamorfosi di Ovidio', in *L'Istoriato: libri a stampa e maioliche italiane del Cinquecento. Salone Sistino, 12 giugno-26 settembre '93* (Faenza: Gruppo editoriale FA), pp. 52–85

Ghedini, Francesca (ed.). 2018. *Ovidio: amori, miti e altre storie* (Naples: Arte'm)

Gilmont, Jean-François and Alexandre Vanautgaerden (eds). 2001. *Circuler et naviguer ou les index à l'époque humaniste* (Brussels: Musée de la Maison d'Érasme)

Godefroy, Frédéric. 1881–1902. *Dictionnaire de l'ancienne langue française et de tous ses dialectes du 9e au 15e siècles*, 10 vols (Paris: F. Vieweg)

Gombrich, Ernst. 1955. 'Apollonio di Giovanni: a florentin cassone workshop seen through the eyes of a humanist poet', *Journal of the Warburg and Courtauld Institutes*, 18: 6–34

Gómez, Francesc J. 2002. 'L'ofici del poeta segons Orfeu: una clau hermenèutica per a *Lo somni* de Metge, in *Literatura i cultura a la Corona d'Aragó*, ed. by Lola Badia, Miriam Cabré and Sadurní Martí (Barcelona: Curial and Publicacions de l'Abadia de Montserrat), pp. 63–85

— 2009–2010. 'Revelació i testimoniatge en *Lo somni*: models sacres i proemials', *Boletín de la Real Academia de Buenas Letras de Barcelona*, 52: 21–50

Gómez Sánchez, Esperanza Macarena. 2001. 'Boccaccio en España: la traducción castellana de *Genealogie Deorum* por Martín de Ávila: edición crítica, edición, estudio y notas mitológicas' (unpublished doctoral thesis, Universidad Complutense de Madrid)

Goodman, Jennifer. 2006. 'Caxton's Continent', in *Caxton's Trace. Studies in the History of English Printing*, ed. by William Kuskin (Notre Dame: University of Notre Dame Press), pp. 101–23

Green, R. H. 1957. 'Dante's "Allegory of Poets" and the Mediaeval Theory of Poetic Fiction', *Comparative Literature*, 9: 118–28

Griffin, Miranda. 2012. 'Translation and Transformation in the *Ovide moralisé*', in *Rethinking Medieval Translation: Ethics, Politics, Theory*, ed. by Emma Campbell and Robert Mills (Woodbridge: Boydell and Brewer), pp. 41–60

— 2015. *Transforming Tales. Rewriting Metamorphoses in Medieval French Literature* (Oxford: Oxford University Press)

Grubmüller, Klaus (ed.). 1996. *Novellistik des Mittelalters: Märendichtung* (Frankfurt am Main: Deutscher KlassikerVerlag), pp. 337–63

Guillaumin, Jean-Baptiste. 2018a. 'Cosmologie et représentations du monde dans les gloses latines du premier livre de l'*Ovide moralisé*', in *Ovidius explanatus. Traduire et commenter les Métamorphoses au Moyen Âge*, ed. by S. Biancardi, P. Deleville, F. Montorsi and M. Possamaï–Pérez (Paris: Garnier), pp. 99–138

Guenée, Bernard. 1989. *Histoire et culture historique dans l'Occident médiéval* (Paris: Aubier)

Guthmüller, Bodo. 1981 [2008]. *Ovidio metamorphoseos vulgare. Formen und Funktionen der*
Volkssprachlichen Wiedergabe klassischer Dichtung inder italienischen Renaissance
(Boppard am Rhein: Harald BoldtVerlag) [Trans. by Paola Picchioni (Fiesole: Cadmo) 2008]

— 1983. 'Nota su Giovanni Antonio Rusconi illustratore delle Trasformazioni del Dolce', in *Miscellanea di studi in onore di Vittore Branca. Vol. 3: Umanesimo e Rinascimento a Florence e a Venezia* (Florence: Olschki), pp. 771–79

— 1997. *Mito, Poesia, Arte. Saggi sulla tradizione ovidiana nel Rinascimento* (Rome: Bulzoni)

— 2009. *Mito e metamorfosi nella letteratura italiana. Da Dante al Rinascimento* (Rome: Carocci)

Haar, Alisa van de. 2018. 'Every Language Has Its Laws. Rhetoricians and the Study of the Dutch Vernacular', *Renaissance Studies*, 32.1: 121–39

Hardie, Philip. 1999. 'Absent Presences in the *Metamorphoses* and Petrarch's *Rime Sparse*', in *Ovidian Transformations: Essays on the Metamorphoses and Its Reception*, ed. by Philip Hardie, Alessandro Barchiesi and Stephen Hinds (Cambridge: Cambridge Philological Society), pp. 254–70

— 2002. 'Introduction', in *The Cambridge Companion to Ovid*, ed. by Philip Hardie (Cambridge: Cambridge University Press), pp. 1–10

Hardie, Philip, Barchiesi, Alessandro, and Stephen Hinds (eds). 1999. *Ovidian Transformations: Essays on the Metamorphoses and Its Reception*, ed. by (Cambridge: Cambridge Philological Society)

Haynes, Jonathan. 1980. *George Sandys's 'Relation of a Journey Begun An. Dom. 1610': The Humanist As Traveller* (unpublished doctoral thesis, University of Urbana, Illinois)

Heinzmann, Günther. 1969. 'Albrecht von Halberstadt und Jörg Wickram: Studien zu einer Rekonstruktion von Albrechts *Metamorphosen*' (unpublished doctoral thesis, Ludwig Maximilian Universität München)

Hellinga, Lotte. 1981. 'Caxton and the Bibliophiles', *Actes du XIe Congres International de Bibliophilie, Bruxelles 1979 (Brussels, 1982)*, pp. 11–38

Héritier, Françoise. 1996. 'Réflexions pour nourrir la reflexion', in *De la violence*, dir. by Françoise Héritier (Paris, Odile Jacob), pp. 11–53

Hernando i Delgado, Josep. 2002. 'Del llibre manuscrit al llibre imprès. La confecció del llibre a Barcelona durant el segle XV. Documentació notarial', *Arxiu de textos catalans antics*, 21: 257–603

Hexter, Ralph J. 2002. 'Ovid in the Middle Ages: Exile, Mythographer, and Lover', in *Brill's Companion to Ovid*, ed. by Barbara Weiden Boyd (Leiden: Brill), pp. 413–42

— 2007. 'Ovid in Translation in Medieval Europe', in *Übersetzung – Translation – Traduction. Ein internationales Handbuch zur Übersetzungsforschung / An International Encyclopedia of Translation Studies / Encyclopédie internationale de la recherche sur la traduction*, ed. by Harald Kittel et al. (Berlin & New York: De Gruyter), pp. 1311–28

— 2011. 'Shades of Ovid: Pseudo- (and para-) Ovidiana in the Middle Ages', in *Ovid in the Middle Ages*, ed. by James G. Clark, Frank T. Coulson and Kathryn L. McKinley (Cambridge: Cambridge University Press), pp. 284–309

Hirst, Michael. 1993. *Michelangelo, i disegni* (Turin: Einaudi)

Hosington, Brenda M. 2007. 'Translation, Early Printing, and Gender in England, 1484–1535', *Florilegium*, 23.1: 41–67

— 2015. 'Introduction: Translation and Print Culture in Early Modern Europe', Special issue of *Renaissance Studies*, 29.1: 5–18

Howe, Sarah. 2008. 'The Authority of Presence: The Development of the English Author Portrait, 1500–1640', *The Papers of the Bibliographical Society of America*, 102.4: 465–99

Huber-Rebenich, Gerlinde. 1992. 'L'iconografia della mitologia antica tra Quattro e Cinquecento. Edizioni illustrate delle Metamorfosi di Ovidio', *Studi umanistici piceni*, 13: 123–33

— 2009. 'A Lecture with Consequences: Tracing a Trecento Commentary on the Metamorphoses', in *Images of the Pagan Gods. Papers of a Conference in Memory of Jean Seznec*, ed. by Rembrandt Duits and François Quiviger (London & Torino: The Warburg Institute & Nino Aragno), pp. 177–98

Huber-Rebenich, Gerlinde, Sabine Lütkemeyer and Hermann Walter. 2014. *Ikonographisches Repertorium zu den Metamorphosen des Ovid. Die textbegleitende Druckgraphik. Bd. I.1: Narrative Darstellungen. Textteil; Bd. I.1: Narrative Darstellungen. Bildteil* (Berlin: Mann)

Huet, Leen. 2016. *Pieter Bruegel. De biografie* (Antwerp: Polis)

Infantes, Víctor. 1998. 'Los libros "traydos y viejos y algunos rotos" que tuvo el bachiller Fernando de Rojas, nombrado autor de la obra llamada *Celestina*', *Bulletin Hispanique*, 100: 7–51

Infelise, Mario. 2013. 'Book Publishing and the Circulation of Information', in *A Companion to Venetian History, 1400–1797* (Leiden, Boston: Brill), pp. 651–74

Ingham, Patricia. 2006. 'Losing French. Vernacularity, Nation, and Caxton's English Statutes', in *Caxton's Trace. Studies in the History of English Printing*, ed. by William Kuskin (Notre Dame: University of Notre Dame Press), pp. 275–98

Innamorati, Giuliano. 'Pietro Aretino', *DBI* www.treccani.it/enciclopedia/pietro-aretino_(Dizionario-Biografico)/ [accessed 14 December 2019]

Iser, Wolfgang. 1978. *The Act of Reading: A Theory of Aesthetic Response* (London: Routledge)

James, Heather. 2003. 'Ovid and the Question of Politics in Early Modern England', *English Literary History*, 70: 343–73

Jauss, Hans Robert. 1982. *Toward an Aesthetic of Reception* (Minneapolis: University of Minnesota Press)

Javitch, Daniel. 1978. 'Rescuing Ovid from the Allegorizers', in *Comparative Literature*, 30: 97–107

— 1991. *Proclaiming a Classic: The Canonization of Orlando furioso* (Princeton: Princeton University Press)

— 1998. 'The Emergence of Poetic Genre Theory in the Sixteenth Century', *Modern Language Quarterly*, 59: 139–69

Jeanroy, Alfred. 1922. 'Boccace et Christine de Pisan: le *De claris mulieribus*, principale source du *Livre de la Cité des Dames*', *Romania*, 48.189: 93–105

Johns, Adrian. 1998. *The Nature of the Book. Print and Knowledge in the Making* (Chicago & London: University of Chicago Press)

Johnston, Hope. 2012. 'Redressing the Virago in Christine de Pizan's *Livre de la cité des dames*', *Cahiers de recherches médiévales et humanistes*, 24: 439–60

Jung, Marc–René. 1971. *Étude sur le poème allégorique en France au Moyen Âge* (Berne: Francke)

— 1996a. 'Les éditions manuscrites de l'*Ovide moralisé*', *Romanistische Zeitschrift für Literaturgeschichte / Cahiers d'histoire des littératures romanes*, 20: 251–74

—1996b. '"Ovide, texte, translateur" et gloses dans les manuscrits de l'"Ovide moralisé", in *The Medieval Opus. Imitation, Rewriting, and Transmission in the French Tradition*, ed by Douglas Kelly (Amsterdam: Rodopi), pp. 75–98

— 1997. 'Ovide Metamorphose en prose (Bruges, vers 1475)', in *'A l'heure encore de mon escrire'. Aspects de la littérature de Bourgogne sous Philippe le Bon et Charles le Téméraire*, ed. by Claude Thiry, Special issue of *Lettres romanes*, pp. 99–115

— 2009. 'L'*Ovide moralisé*: de l'expérience de mes lectures à quelques propositions de lecture actuelle', in *Ovide metamorphosé: les lecteurs médiévaux d'Ovide*, ed. by Laurence Harf-Lancner, Laurence Mathey-Maille and Michelle Szkilnik (Paris: Presses de la Sorbonne Nouvelle), pp. 107–22

Karmen, Deborah. 2012. 'Naturalized Desires and the Metamorphosis of Iphis', *Helios*, 39: 21–36

Keith, Allison. 2014. 'Poetae Ovidiani: Ovid's *Metamorphoses* in Imperial Roman Epic', in *A Handbook to the Reception of Ovid*, ed. by John F. Miller and Carol E. Newlands (Chichester-Malden: Wiley Blackwell), pp. 70–85

Keith, Allison, and Stephen Rupp. 2007. 'After Ovid: Classical, Medieval, and Early Modern Reception of the *Metamorphoses*', in *Metamorphoses: The Changing Face of Ovid in Medieval and Early Modern Europe*, ed. by Allison Keith and Stephen Rupp (Toronto: Centre for the Reformation and Renaissance Studies), pp. 1–15

Kenney, E. J. 1962. 'The manuscript tradition of Ovid's *Amores, Ars amatoria*, and *Remedia Amoris*', *Classical Quarterly*, 12: 1–31

Kern, Manfred, Cyril W. Edwards, and Christoph Huber (eds). 2015. *Das Narzisslied Heinrichs von Morungen: Zur Mittelalterlichen Liebeslyrik Und Ihrer Philologischen Erschliessung* (Heidelberg: Winter)

Kern, Manfred and Alfred Ebenbauer (eds). 2003. *Lexikon der antiken Gestalten in den deutschen Texten des Mittelalters* (Berlin [u.a.]: De Gruyter)

Kern, Peter. 2003. 'Zur *Metamorphosen*-Rezeption in der deutschen Dichtung des 13. Jahrhunderts', in *Eine Epoche im Umbruch: Volkssprachliche Literalität 1200-1300.*

Cambridger Symposium 2001, ed. by Christa Bertelsmeier-Kierst, and Christopher J. Young (Tübingen: Niemeyer), pp. 175–94

Kistler, Renate. 1993. *Heinrich von Veldeke Und Ovid* (Tübingen: Niemeyer)

Kirk, G. S. 1974. *The Nature of Greek Myths* (Harmondsworth: Pelican)

Kirkham, Victoria. 2015. 'Le Tre Corone e l'iconografia di Boccaccio', in *Atti del convegno internazionale Firenze - Certaldo, 10-12 Ottobre 2013*, ed. by Michaelangiola Marchiaro and Stefano Zamponi (Florence: Accademia della Crusca), pp. 453–84

— 1999. 'L'immagine del Boccaccio nella memoria tardo-gotica e rinascimentale', in *Boccaccio visualizzato: narrare per parole e per immagini fra Medioevo e Rinascimento*, ed. by Vittore Branca, 3 vols (Turin: Einaudi), pp. 85–133

Klein, Dorothea. 2008. 'Metamorphosen eines Dichters. Zur Ovid-Rezeption im deutschen Mittelalter', in *Das diskursive Erbe Europas: Antike und Antikerezeption*, ed. by Dorothea Klein and Lutz Käppel (Frankfurt a. M. [u.a.]: Peter Lang), pp. 159–78

— 2017. 'Tragische Minne? Die Geschichte von Pyramus und Thisbe und ihre mittelalterlichen Bearbeitungen', in *Tragik und Minne*, ed. by Regina Toepfer (Heidelberg: Winter), pp. 85–108

Kralik, Dietrich. 1928. 'Der Prolog zur Ovidverdeutschung Albrechts von Halberstadt', in *Festschrift Max H. Jellinek zum 29. Mai 1928 dargebracht. Österreichischer Bundesverlag für Unterricht, Wissenschaft und Kunst, Wien 1928* (Wien, Leipzig: Österreichischer Bundesverlag), pp. 22–50

Kretschmer, M. 2016. 'L'*Ovidius moralizatus* de Pierre Bersuire: Essai de mise au point', *Interfaces: A Journal of Medieval European Literatures*, 3: 221–44

— Forthcoming. 'L'*Ovide moralisé* comme source principale des ajouts de la version parisienne de l'*Ovidius moralizatus* de Pierre Bersuire', in *Réécritures et adaptations de l'Ovide moralisé (XIVe – XVIIe siècle)*, ed. by C. Gaullier-Bougassas & M. Possamaï-Pérez (éds.), Brepols, Turnhout

Kuhiwczak, Piotr and Karin Littau (eds). 2007. *A Companion to Translation Studies* (Clevedon: Multilingual Matters)

Lampo, Jan. 2017. *Gelukkige stad. De gouden jaren van Antwerpen (1485–1585)* (Amsterdam: Amsterdam University Press)

Landau, David, and Peter Parshall. 1994. *The Renaissance Print, 1470-1550* (New Haven and London: Yale University Press)

Langereis, Sandra. 2014. *De woordenaar. Christoffel Plantijn: 's werelds grootste drukker en uitgever, 1520–1589* (Amsterdam: Balans)

Last, Martin. 1966. 'Neue Oldenburger Fragmente der *Metamorphosen*-Übertragung des Albrecht von Halberstadt', *Oldenbruger Jahrbuch*, 65: 41–60

Lazzi, Giovanna, and Giancarlo Savino (eds). 1996. *I Danti ricciardiani. Parole e figure* (Florence: Polistampa)

Lechat, D. 2002. 'Héro et Léandre dans l'*Ovide moralisé*', *Cahiers de Recherches Médiévales*, 9: 25–37

Le Corfec, Delphine. 2011. 'La question du sacré dans le Recueil des Histoires de Troie', *Camenulae*, 7; https://lettres.sorbonne-universite.fr/sites/default/files/media/2020-06/corfec-2.pdf [accessed 10 July 2019]

Lerer, Seth. 1999. 'William Caxton', in *The Cambridge History of Medieval English Literature*, ed. by David Wallace (Cambridge: Cambridge University Press), pp. 720–38

Leube, Eberhard. 1969. *Fortuna in Karthago: die Aeneas-Dido-Mythe Vergils in den romanischen Literaturen vom 14. bis zum 16. Jahrhundert* (Heidelberg: Winter)

Leverkus, Wilhelm. 1859. 'Aus Albrechts von Halberstadt Übersetzung der *Metamorphosen* Ovids', *Zeitschrift für deutsches Altertum und deutsche Literatur*, 11: 358–74

Lienert, Elisabeth. 2001. *Deutsche Antikenromane des Mittelalters* (Berlin: Erich Schmidt)

Littau, Karin. 2016. 'Translation and the Materialities of Communication', *Translation Studies*, 9.1: 82–96

Liveley, Genevieve. 2011. *Ovid's Metamorphoses: A Reader's Guide* (London: Blackwells)

Looney, Dennis. 1996. *Compromising the Classics. Romance Epic Narrative in the Italian Renaissance* (Detroit: Wayne State University Press)

López Torrijos, Rosa. 1985. *La mitología en la pintura española del Siglo de Oro* (Madrid: Cátedra)

Lowry, Martin. 1992. 'Magni nominis umbra? L'editoria classica da Aldo Manuzio Vecchio ad Aldo Giovane', in *La stampa in Italia nel Cinquecento, I, Atti del convegno Roma, 17–21 ottobre 1989*, ed. by Marco Santoro (Rome: Bulzoni), pp. 237–53

Lubac, Henri de. 1948. 'Sur un vieux distique. La doctrine du 'quadruple sens'', in *Mélanges Ferdinand Cavallera* (Toulouse: Bibliothèque de l'Institut Catholique), pp. 347–66

Lübben, August. 1865. 'Neues Bruchstück von Albrecht von Halberstadt', *Germania*, 10: 237–45

Ludwig, Karl. 1915. *Untersuchungen zur Chronologie Albrechts von Halberstadt* (Heidelberg: Winter)

Lyne, Raphael. 1996. 'Golding's Englished Metamorphoses', *Translation in Literature*, 5: 183–200

— 2001. *Ovid's Changing Worlds: English Metamorphoses, 1567–1632* (Oxford: Oxford University Press)

— 2002. 'Ovid in English Translation', in *The Cambridge Companion to Ovid*, ed. by Philip Hardie (Cambridge: Cambridge University Press), pp. 249–63

Lyons, John D. 1989. *Exemplum: The Rhetoric of Example in Early Modern France and Italy* (Princeton: UP)

Maclean, Ian. 2012. *Scholarship, Commerce, Religion. The Learned Book in the Age of Confessions, 1560-1630* (Cambridge, Massachusetts & London: Harvard University Press)

McGrath, Elizabeth. 2015. 'Rubens and Ovid', *The Afterlife of Ovid*, ed. by Peter Mack and John North (London: Institute of Classical Studies, School of Advanced Study, University of London), pp. 159–79

Mager, Wolfgang. 2016. 'Introduction', in *The Middle English Text of Caxton's Ovid, Books II-III [...] With a Parallel Text of the Ovide Moralisé en Prose II...*, ed. by Wolfgang Mager (Heidelberg: Winter)

Mann, Nicholas and Luke Syson (eds). 1988. *The Image of the Individual: Portraits in the Renaissance* (London: British Museum Press)

Marchegiani, Cristiano. 2017. 'Rusconi, Giovanni Antonio', *Dizionario Biografico degli Italiani* (Rome: Istituto dell'Enciclopedia Italiana), lxxxix: 298–300

Marongiu, Marcella. 2002. *Il mito di Ganimede: prima e dopo Michelangelo* (Florence: Mandragora)

Martens, Maximiliaan P.J. and Natasja Peeters. 2006. 'Artists by Numbers: Quantifying Artists' Trades in Sixteenth-Century Antwerp', in *Making and Marketing: Studies of the Painting Process in Fifteenth- and Sixteenth-Century Netherlandish Workshops*, ed. by Mollie Faries (Turnhout: Brepols), pp. 211–22

Martin, Christopher. 1998. *Ovid in English* (London: Penguin)

— 2009. 'Translating Ovid', in *A Companion to Ovid*, ed. by Peter E. Knox (London: Blackwell)

Martin, René (ed). *Enée et Didon: naissance, fonctionnement et survie d'un mythe* (Paris: CNRS)

Martindale, Charles (ed). 1988 [1990]. *Ovid Renewed: Ovidian Influences on Literature and Art from the Middle Ages to the Twentieth Century* (Cambridge: Cambridge University Press)

Martinez, Miguel. 2015. 'The Heroes in the World's Marketplace: Translating and Printing Epic in Renaissance Antwerp', in *Translation and the Book Trade in Early Modern Europe*, ed. by José María Pérez Fernández and Edward Wilson–Lee (Cambridge: Cambridge University Press), pp. 81–106

Martos, Josep Lluís. 2001. 'Boccaccio y Joan Roís de Corella: las *Genealogiae deorum*', Special issue of *Cuadernos de Filología Italiana* (Madrid, Universidad Complutense de Madrid), pp. 535–57

McGrath, Thomas. 2003. 'Facing the Text: Author Portraits in Florentine Printed Books, 1545-1585', *Word & Image*, 19: 74–85

McLaughlin, Martin. 1995. *Literary Imitation in the Italian Renaissance: The Theory and Practice of Literary Imitation in Italy from Dante to Bembo* (Oxford: Clarendon Press)

McLuhan, Marshall. 2011. *The Gutenberg Galaxy: The Making of Typographic Man* (Toronto: Toronto University Press)

McManaway, James G. 1948. 'The First Five Books of Ovid's Metamorphosis, 1621, Englished by Master George Sandys', *Papers of the Bibliographical Society of the University of Virginia*, 1: 71–82

McNeill, William. 1974. 'Venice as a Marginal Polity: 1481–1669', in *Venice: The Hinge of Europe, 1081–1797* (Chicago: University of Chicago Press), pp. 123–54

Meeus, Hubert. 2018. 'From Nameplate to Emblem. The Evolution of the Printer's Device in the Southern Low Countries up to 1600', in *Typographorum emblemata. The Printer's Mark in the Context of Early Modern Culture*, ed. by Anja Wolkenhauer and Bernhard F. Scholz (Berlin & Boston: De Gruyter), pp. 77–100

Meiser, Karl. 1885. 'Über einen Kommentar zu den *Metamorphosen* des Ovid', in *Sitzungsbericht der philosophisch-philologischen Classe der k. b. Akademie der Wissenschaften* (München: Franz in Komm.), pp. 47–58

Mérida Jiménez, Rafael M. 2012. 'L'exemplar incunable de les *Transformacions* d'Ovidi en versió de Francesc Alegre (Barcelona, Pere Miquel, 1494) a "La Casa del Libro" de San Juan de Puerto Rico', *Tirant*, 15: 171–74

Mitchell, Christine. 2010. 'Translation and Materiality: The Paradox of Visible Translation', *Translating Media*, 30.1: 23–29

Modolo, Elisa. 2015. 'Metamorphosis of the *Metamorphoses*: Italian Re-writings of Ovid between Renaissance and Baroque' (unpublished doctoral thesis, University of Pennsylvania)

Mölk, Ulrich. 1966-67. 'Góngora und der 'dunkle' Ovid', *Archiv für das Studium der Neueren Sprachen und Literaturen*, 203: 415–27

Moll, Richard. 2013. 'Introduction', in *The Book of Ovyde Named Methamorphose*, ed. by Richard J. Moll (Toronto: Pontifical Institute of Medieval Studies)

Monfrin, Jacques. 1985. 'Les translations vernaculaires de Virgile au Moyen Âge', in *Lectures médiévales de Virgile. Actes du colloque de Rome (25-28 octobre 1982)* (Rome: École Française de Rome), pp. 189–249

—— 1986. 'L'histoire de Didon et Énée au XVe siècle', *Études littéraires sur le XVe siècle, Actes du Ve colloque international sur le moyen français, Milan 6-8 mai 1985* (Milan: Università Cattolica), iii.161–97

Moog-Grünewald, Maria. 1979. *Metamorphosen der 'Metamorphosen'. Rezeptionsarten der Ovidschen Verwandlungsgeschichten in Italien und Frankreich im XVI. und XVII. Jahrhundert* (Heidelberg: Carl Winter)

Mora-Lebrun, Francine. 1994. 'L'ombre mythique de Diane dans le *Roman d'Eneas*', *Bien dire et bien aprandre*, Special issue 'Fées, dieux et déesses au Moyen Âge', 12: 169–89

Mora-Lebrun, Francine, Marylène Possamaï-Pérez, Thomas Städtler and Richard Trachsler. 2011. '*Ab ovo*. Les manuscrits de l'*Ovide moralisé*: naissance et survie d'un texte', *Romance Philology*, 65/1: 121–42

Morford, Mark P. O. and Robert J. Lenardon. 2003. *Classical Mythology*, 7th edn (Oxford: Oxford University Press)

Morganti, Carol. 2005. 'Il mito di Ganimede nei disegni e nelle incisioni del Rinascimento', *Grafica d'arte*, 16.12: 4–15

Mortimer, Ruth. 1989. *A Portrait of the Author in Sixteenth-Century France: A Paper Presented on the Occasion of the Fiftieth Anniversary of the Hanes Foundation for the Study of the Origin and Development of the Book* (Chapel Hill: Hanes Foundation, Rare Book Collection, Academic Affairs Library, University of North Carolina at Chapel Hill)

— 1996. 'The Author's Image: Italian Sixteenth-Century Printed Portraits', *Harvard Library Bulletin*, 7.2: 7–87

Moss, Ann. 1982. *Ovid in Renaissance France: A Survey of the Latin Editions of Ovid and Commentaries Printed before 1600*, Warburg Institute Surveys, 8 (London: The Warburg Institute)

Murdoch, Brian O. 1977. 'Die Bearbeitungen des Hero-und-Leander-Stoffes. Zur literarischen Ovid-Rezeption im späten Mittelalter', *Studi medievali*, 3, 18: 231–47

Nash, Jane C. 1985. *Veiled Images: Titian's Mythological Paintings for Philip II* (London: Associated University Presses)

Needham, Paul. 1986. *The Printer and the Pardoner. An unrecorded indulgence printed by William Caxton for the Hospital of St. Mary Rounceval, Charing Cross* (Washington: Library of Congress)

Neumann, Friedrich. 1955. 'Meister Albrechts und Jörg Wickrams Ovid auf Deutsch', *Beiträge zur Geschichte der deutschen Sprache und Literatur*, 76: 321–87

Neumeister, Sebastian. 2000. *Mito clásico y ostentación: los dramas mitológicos de Calderón* (Kassel: Reichenberger)

Nuechterlein, Jeanne. 2017. 'Pieter Bruegel The Elder's *Landscape with the Fall of Icarus*', *A Handbook to the Reception of Classical Mythology*, ed. by Vanda Zajko and Helena Hoyle (Malden, Massachusetts & Oxford: Wiley Blackwell), pp. 379–90

Nuovo, Angela and Christian Coppens. 2005. *I Giolito e la stampa nell'Italia del XVI secolo* (Geneva: Librairie Droz), pp. 67–101

Oakley-Brown, Liz. 2006 [2016]. *Ovid and the Cultural Politics of Translation in Early Modern England* (London: Routledge)

Online Bible Study Hub. 2004–2020. https://biblehub.com/ [accessed 05 May 2020]

O'Sullivan, Carol. 2012. 'Introduction: Rethinking Methods in Translation History', Special issue of *Translation Studies*, 5.2: 131–38

Otzenberger, Pauline. Ongoing. 'Recherches sur la réception de l'*Ovide moralisé*' (unpublished doctoral dissertation, Université catholique de Louvain)

Pairet, Ana. 2011. 'Recasting the *Metamorphoses* in Fourteenth–Century France: The Challenge of the *Ovide moralisé*', in *Ovid in the Middle Ages*, ed. by James G. Clark, Frank T. Coulson and Kathryn L. McKinley (Cambridge: Cambridge University Press), pp. 83–107

Páramo Pomareda, Jorge. 1957. 'Consideraciones sobre los "autos mitológicos" de Calderón de la Barca', *Thesaurus*, 12: 51–80

Parker, Alexander A. 1988. *The Mind and Art of Calderón: Essays on the 'Comedias'* (Cambridge: Cambridge University Press)

Parussa, Gabriela, 2008. 'Introduction', in Christine de Pizan, *Epistre Othea*, ed. by Gabriela Parussa (Geneva: Droz)

Pasero, Carlo. 1935. 'Giacomo Franco, editore, incisore, calcografo nei secoli XVI e XVII', *La Bibliofilia*, 37: 332–56

Pastorello, Ester. 1924. *Tipografi, editori, librai a Venezia nel secolo XVI* (Florence: Olschki)

Pearcy, L. T. 1984. *The Mediated Muse: English Translations of Ovid, 1560–1700* (Connecticut: Archon Books)

Peeters, Natasja. 2009. 'The Guild of Saint Luke and the Painter's Profession in Antwerp between c. 1560 and 1585: Some Social and Economic Insights', *Nederlandsch kunsthistorisch jaarboek*, 59.1: 136–63

Pellissa Prades, Gemma. 2017. 'The Italian Sources of the Catalan Translation of Ovid's Metamorphoses by Francesc Alegre (15th c.)', *Zeitschrift für romanische Philologie*, 133.2: 443–71

— 2019. 'Algunes dades sobre la influència de les proses mitològiques de Corella a les Transformacions de Francesc Alegre', *Caplletra*, 66: 15–32

— 2020. 'Innovation, Auctoritas and Tradition in the Medieval versions of Ovid's Metamorphoses', in *Traire du latin et espondre. Études de la réception médiévale d'Ovide*, ed. by Craig Baker, Mattia Cavagna and Elisa Guadagnini (Paris: Classiques Garnier), pp. 133-148

Peña Díaz, Manuel. (1997). *Libro y lectura en Barcelona, 1473-1600* (unpublished doctoral thesis, Universitat Autònoma de Barcelona)

Pérez Fernández, José María and Edward Wilson-Lee. 2015. 'Introduction', in *Translation and the Book Trade in Early Modern Europe*, ed. by José María Pérez Fernández and Edward Wilson-Lee (Cambridge: Cambridge University Press), pp. 1–21

Pesavento, Giulio. 2018. *Alle origini dell'illustrazione xilografica delle Metamorfosi: l'Ovidio Metamorphoseos vulgare (Venezia 1497)*, in *Ovidio. Amori, miti e altre storie*, ed. by Francesca Ghedini (Naples: Arte'm)

Petrucci Nardelli, Franca. 1991. *La lettera e l'immagine. Le iniziali 'parlanti' nella tipografia italiana (secc. XVI-XVIII)* (Florence: Olschki)

Pettas, William A. 2005. *A History and Bibliography of the Giunti (Junta) Printing Family in Spain 1526–1628* (New Castle: Oak Knoll Press)

Piccininni, Renata. 1981. 'Il mito di Ganimede in ambiente veneto tra '400 e '500', in *Giorgione e la cultura veneta tra '400 e '500: mito, allegoria, analisi iconologica* (Rome: De Luca), pp. 149–54

Pintabone, Diane T. 2002. 'Ovid's Iphis and Ianthe. When girls wont't be girls', in *Among women: from the homosocial to the homoerotic in the Ancient World*, ed. by Nancy Sorkin Rabinowitz and Lisa Auanger (Austin: University of Texas Pres), pp. 256–85

Piqueras Yagüe, Pablo. 2019. 'Three notes on the first book of the *Ovidius moralizatus*', in *Approaches to Greek and Latin Language: History and Literature: Κατὰ σχολήν*, ed. by Gréta Kádas, Sara Macías Otero and Sandra Rodríguez Piedrabuena (Newcastle upon Tyne: Cambridge Scholars Publishing), pp. 239–56

Plotke, Seraina. 2013. 'Verfahren der inventio im spätmittelalterlichen märe. "Von Pyramo und Thisbe, den zwein lieben geschah vil wê"', in *Carmen Perpetuum. Ovids Metamorphosen in Der Weltliteratur*, ed. by Henriette Harich-Schwarzbauer and Alexander Honold (Basel: Schwabe), pp. 111–28

Pomel, Fabienne. 2001. *Les voies de l'au-delà et l'essor de l'allégorie au Moyen Âge* (Paris: Honoré Champion)

Pope-Hennessy, John. 1966. *The Portrait in the Renaissance* (London and New York: Pantheon)

Porteman, Karel, and Mieke B. Smits-Veldt. 2013. *Een nieuw vaderland voor de muzen. Geschiedenis van de Nederlandse literatuur 1560-1700* (Amsterdam: Bert Bakker)

Possamaï–Pérez, Marylène. 2002. 'La légende thébaine dans l'*Ovide moralisé*. Un exemple de contamination des sources', in *Ce est li fruis selonc la letre. Mélanges offerts à Charles Méla*, ed. by Olivier Collet, Yasmina Foehr-Janssens et Sylviane Messerli (Paris & Geneva: Champion & Slatkine), pp. 527–45

— 2004. 'Comment Actéon devint le Christ', in *Textes et Cultures: réception, modèles, interférences: Réception de l'Antiquité*, i, ed. by Pierre Nobel (Besançon: Presses Universitaires de Franche–Comté), pp. 187–210

— 2006. *L'Ovide moralisé: Essai d'interprétation* (Paris: Champion)

— 2008. 'L'Ovide moralisé, ou la "bonne glose" des *Métamorphoses* d'Ovide, Regards croisés sur la glose', *Cahiers d'Études Hispaniques Médiévales*, 38: 181–206

— 2009. 'Mythologie antique et amours incestueuses: le regard d'un clerc du Moyen Âge', *Anabases*, 9: 171–82

— 2010. 'La figure d'Énée dans l'*Ovide moralisé*', HALSHS https://halshs.archives-ouvertes.fr/halshs-00548076/document [accessed 10 July 2019]

Pratt, Karen. 2017. 'The Dynamics of the European Short Narrative in Its Manuscript Context: The Case of Pyramus and Thisbe', in *The Dynamics of the Medieval Manuscript*, ed. by Karen Pratt and Hannah Morcos (Göttingen: Vandenhoeck & Ruprecht), pp. 257–85

Premoli, Beatrice. 2005. *Giovanni Andrea dell'Anguillara. Accademico sdegnato ed etereo* (Rome: Fondazione Marco Besso)

Pujol, Josep. 2004. 'El ámbito de la cultura catalana', in *Historia de la traducción en España*, ed. by Francisco Lafarga and Luís Pegenaute (Salamanca: Ambos Mundos), pp. 623–719

— 2011. 'The Hispanic Vernacular Reception of William of Orléans' *Bursarii ovidianorum*: The Translations of Ovid's *Heroides*', *Journal of Medieval Latin*, 21: 17–34.

— 2014. 'Traduccions i traductors', in *Història de la literatura catalana. Literatura medieval (II). Segles XIV-XV*, dir. by Lola Badia (Barcelona: Enciclopèdia Catalana, Editorial Barcino & Ajuntament de Barcelona), 141–46

Quint, David. 1996. 'Introduction', in Ludovico Ariosto, *Five cantos*, ed. by David Quint and Alexander Sheers (Los Angeles: University of California Press), pp. 1–44

Quondam, Amedeo. 1980. 'Nel giardino di Marcolini: un editore veneziano tra Aretino e Doni', *Giornale storico della letteratura italiana*, 157: 75–116

Radomme, Thibaut. 2019. 'La résistance des clercs. Enjeux du bilinguisme dans le Roman de Fauvel remanié et dans les gloses à l'*Ovide moralisé*' (unpublished doctoral thesis, Université catholique de Louvain & Université de Lausanne)

—In press. 'Lycaon, le loup et l'agneau. La satire dans l'*Ovide moralisé* et l'éclairage des gloses franco-latines', in *'Traire du latin et espondre'. Études sur la réception médiévale d'Ovide*, ed. by Craig Baker, Mattia Cavagna and Elisa Guadagnini, with the assistance of P. Otzenberger (Paris: Garnier)

Randolph, Adrian W. B. 2003. 'Introduction: The Authority of Likeness', *Word & Image*, 19: 1–5

Ravanelli Guidotti, Carmen (ed.). 1985. *Ceramiche occidentali del Museo Civico Medievale di Bologna* (Bologna: Grafis)

Rehm, Ulrich (ed.). 2018. *Mittelalterliche Mythenrezeption: Paradigmen und Paradigmenwechsel* (Köln: Böhlau)

Reynolds, W. D. 1990. 'Sources, Nature, and Influence of the *Ovidius moralizatus* of Pierre Bersuire', in *The Mythographic Art: Classical Fable and the Rise of the Vernacular in Early France and England*, ed. by J. Chance (Gainesville: University of Florida Press), pp. 83–99

Ricca, Alfonso. 2013. 'Giunta, Bernardo junior', in *Dizionario degli editori, tipografi, librai itineranti in Italia tra Quattrocento e Seicento*, coordinated by Marco Santoro, ed. by Rosa M. Borraccini, Giuseppe Lipari, Carmela Reale, Marco Santoro and Giancarlo Volpato (Pisa & Rome: Fabrizio Serra Editore), i. 500–01

Richardson, Brian. 1994. *Print Culture in Renaissance Italy: The Editor and the Vernacular Text 1470–1600* (Cambridge: Cambridge University Press), pp. 1–18

Richmond, John. 2002. 'Manuscript Traditions and the Transmission of Ovid's Works', in *Brill's Companion to Ovid*, ed. by Barbara Weiden Boyd, 2nd edn (Leiden: Brill), pp. 443–83

Riera i Sans, Jaume. 1989. 'Catàleg d'obres en català traduïdes en castellà durant els segles XIV i XV', in *Segon Congrés Internacional de la Llengua Catalana*, ed. by Antoni Ferrando (Valencia: Institut Interuniversitari de Filologia Valenciana), viii. 699–710

Riquer, Martí de. 1959. *Obras de Bernat Metge* (Barcelona: Universitat de Barcelona)

Rivoletti, Christian. 2015. *Ariosto e l'ironia della finzione. La ricezione letteraria e figurativa dell'"Orlando Furioso" in Francia, Germania e Italia* (Venice: Marsilio)

Rizzi, Andrea. 2017. *Vernacular Translators in Quattrocento Italy: Scribal Culture, Authority, and Agency* (Turnhout: Brepols)

Roggero, Marina. 2006. *Le carte piene di sogni. Testi e lettori in età moderna* (Bologna: Il Mulino)

Roses Lozano, Joaquín. 1994. *Una poética de la oscuridad: la recepción crítica de las 'Soledades' en el siglo XVII* (London: Tamesis)

Rossi, M., and D. Caracciolo (eds). 2014. *Le sorti d'Orlando. Il Furioso tra parole e immagini* (Lucca: Maria Pacini Fazzi)

Rouse, Mary A., and Richard H. Rouse. 1989. 'La naissance des index', *Histoire de l'édition française. Le livre conquérant Du Moyen Age au milieu du XVIIe siècle*, ed. by Roger Chartier and Henri-Jean Martin (Paris: Fayard & Cercle de la Librairie), pp. 95–108

Rubin, Deborah. 1985. *Ovid's Metamorphoses Englished: George Sandys as Translator and Mythographer* (London: Taylor & Francis)

Rubió i Lluch, Antoni. 1908–1921. *Documents per a la història de la cultura catalana mig-eval*, i (Barcelona: Institut d'Estudis Catalans)

Rücker, Brigitte. 1997. *Die Bearbeitung von Ovids 'Metamorphosen' durch Albrecht von Halberstadt und Jörg Wickram und ihre Kommentierung durch Gerhard Lorichius* (Göppingen: Kümmerle)

Ruiz Fidalgo, Lorenzo. 1994. *La imprenta en Salamanca 1501-1600*, 3 vols (Madrid: Arco)

Rumrich, Diana. 2011. 'Introduction', in *The Middle English Text of Caxton's Ovid, Book I [...] With a Parallel Text of the Ovide Moralisé en Prose II...*, ed. by Diana Rumrich (Heidelberg: Winter)

Runge, Otto. 1908. *Die 'Metamorphosen'-Verdeutschung Albrechts von Halberstadt* (Berlin: Mayer & Müller)

Rutter, Russell. 1987. 'William Caxton and Literary Patronage'. *Studies in Philology*, 84. 4: 440–70

Saccone, Eduardo. 1965. 'Appunti per una definizione dei *Cinque canti*', *Belfagor*, 20: 381–410

Saibene, Maria Grazia. 2018. 'Miti e metamorfosi. Ovidio nella riscrittura di Albrecht von Halberstadt', in *Tradurre. Un viaggio nel tempo*, ed. by Maria Grazia Cammarota (Venice: Ca' Foscari University press), pp. 175–206

— 1988a. 'La vicenda di Iphis e Anaxarete nella traduzione di Albrecht von Halberstadt', *Romanobarbarica*, 10: 367–81

— 1998b. 'Le Metamorfosi di Ovidio nella traduzione di Albrecht von Halberstadt, in *L'antichità nella cultura europea del medioevo = L'antiquité dans la culture européenne du Moyen âge: Ergebnisse der internationalen Tagung in Padua, 27.09.-01.10.1997*, ed. by Rosanna Brusegan and Alessandro Zironi (Greifswald: Reineke), pp. 21–30

Salvo García, Irene. 2012a. *Ovidio en la 'General estoria' de Alfonso X* (unpublished doctoral thesis, Universidad Autónoma de Madrid & École normale supérieure de Lyon)

— 2012b. 'El mito de Icario en la *General estoria* de Alfonso X', *Memorabilia*, 14: 145–160

— 2014. 'Ovidio y la compilación de la 'General estoria', *Cahiers d'études hispaniques médiévales*, 37: 45–61

— 2017. 'L'Ovide connu par Alphonse X (1221-1284)', *Interfaces. A Journal of Medieval European Literatures*, 3: 200–20

— 2018a. 'Introduction aux sources de l'*Ovide moralisé I*', in *Ovide moralisé, Livre I*, ed. by Craig Baker, Marianne Besseyre, Mattia Cavagna, Stefania Cerrito, Olivier Collet, Massimiliano Gaggero, Yan Greub, Jean-Baptiste Guillaumin, Marylène Possamaï-Pérez, Véronique Rouchon, Irene Salvo García, Thomas Städtler and Richard Trachsler (Paris: SATF), pp. 193–210

2018b. 'Les *Métamorphoses* et l'histoire ancienne en France et en Espagne (XIIIᵉ-XIVᵉ s.): l'exemple des légendes crétoises (Mét. VII-VIII)', in *Ovidius explanatus. Traduire et commenter les Métamorphoses au Moyen Âge*, ed. by S. Biancardi, P. Deleville, F. Montorsi and M. Possamaï-Pérez (Paris: Garnier), pp. 235–58

— 2018c. 'Les sources de l'*Ovide moralisé I*: types et traitement', *Le Moyen Âge, Revue d'histoire et de philologie*, 124.2: 307–36

—2018d. 'Mujeres sabias en la historiografía alfonsí. La infanta Medea', in *Histoires, femmes, pouvoirs. Mélanges offerts au Professeur Georges Martin*, ed. by Jean-Pierre Jardin, Patricia Rochwert-Zuili and Hélène Thieulin-Pardo (Paris : Classiques Garnier), "Rencontres", 368, pp. 339–65

— 2018e. '"Que l'en seult balaine clamer". Commentaire linguistique et traduction au Moyen Âge (XIIIe-XIVe siècles, Espagne, France)', *Médiévales*, 75: 97–116

Salzberg, Rosa. 2014. *Ephemeral City: Cheap Print and Urban Culture in Renaissance Venice* (Manchester: Manchester University Press)

Sangirardi, Giuseppe. 2006. *Ludovico Ariosto* (Florence: Le Monnier)

Saquero Suárez-Somonte, Pilar and Tomás González Rolán (1993). 'Aproximación a la fuente latina del *Libro de las generaciones de los dioses de los gentiles* utilizada en la *General estoria* de Alfonso X el Sabio', *Cuadernos de filología clásica: Estudios latinos*, 4: 93–112

Schaff, Philip. 2017. *Ante-Nicene Fathers: Volume 7. Fathers of the Third and Fourth Centuries: Lactantius, Venantius, Asterius, Victorinus, Dionysius, Apostolic Teaching and Constitutions, Homily*, in Documenta Catholica Omnia, *Multilingual Catholic e-Books Database* <https://www.documentacatholicaomnia.eu/> [05 May 2020]

Schevill, Rudolph. 1913. *Ovid and the Renaissance in Spain* (Berkeley: University of California Publications in Modern Philology)

— 1995 [2014]. 'Ovid and the Renascence in Spain and Italy', in *Ovid: The Classical Heritage*, ed. by William S. Anderson (London: Garland, reprint Abingdon: Garland), pp. 119–41

Schmitz, Götz. 1990. *The Fall of Women in Early English Narrative Verse* (Cambridge: Cambridge University Press)

Schulz-Grobert, Jürgen (ed.). 2006. *Kleinere mittelhochdeutsche Verserzählungen. Mittelhochdeutsch/Neuhochdeutsch. Ausgewählt, übersetzt und kommentiert* (Stuttgart: Reclam)

Schwitzgebel, Bärbel. 1996. *Noch nicht genug der Vorrede. Zur Vorrede volkssprachiger Sammlungen von Exempeln, Fabeln, Sprichwörtern und Schwänken des 16. Jahrhunderts* (Tübingen: Max Niemeyer Verlag)

Scott–Warren, Jason. 2001. *Sir John Harington and the Book as Gift* (Oxford: Oxford University Press)

Segre, Cesare. 1966. *Esperienze ariostesche* (Pisa: Nistri Lischi)

— 1996. *Volgarizzamenti del Due e Trecento*, 2nd edn (Turin: UTET)

Seznec, Jean, 1940. *La Survivance des dieux antiques: essai sur le rôle de la tradition mythologique dans l'Humanisme et dans l'art de la Renaissance* (London: The Warburg Institute)

Sharpe, Kevin. 1987. *Criticism and Compliment: The Politics of Literature in the England of Charles I* (Cambridge: Cambridge University Press)

Shevlin, Eleanor F. 1999. '"To Reconcile Book and Title, and Make 'em Kin to One Another": The Evolution of the Title's Contractual Functions', *Book History*, 2: 42–77

STCN, *Short Title Catalogue Netherlands*, www.stcn.nl [accessed 06 October 2020]

STCV, *Short Title Catalogue Vlaanderen*, www.stcv.be [accessed 06 October 2020]

USTC, *Universal Short Title Catalogue*, www.ustc.ac.uk [accessed 06 October 2020]

Sluijter, Eric Jan. 2000. *De 'heydensche fabulen' in de schilderkunst van de Gouden Eeuw: schilderijen met verhalende onderwerpen uit de klassieke mythologie in de Noordelijke Nederlanden, circa 1590–1670* (Leiden: Primavera Pers)

Smalley, Beryl. 1960. *English Friars and Antiquity in the Early Fourteenth Century* (Oxford: Blackwell)

Smith, Helen. 2014. 'Reading Early Modern Imprints', in *Renaissance Paratexts*, ed. by Helen Smith and Louise Wilson (Cambridge: Cambridge University Press), pp. 17–33

Smith, Helen and Louise Wilson (eds). 2011. *Renaissance Paratexts* (Cambridge: Cambridge University Press)

Smith, Margaret M. 2000. *The Title Page. Its Early Development, 1460–1510* (London: The British Library Publishing)

Snell–Hornby, Mary, Franz Pöchhacker and Klaus Kaindl (eds). 1994. *Translation Studies: An Interdiscipline* (Amsterdam: John Benjamins)

Solomon, Jon. 2012. 'Boccaccio and the Ineffable, Aniconic God Demogorgon', *International Journal of the Classical Tradition*, 19.1: 31–62

Stackmann, Karl. 1966. 'Die Auslegungen des Gerhard Lorichius zur *Metamorphosen*-Nachdichtung Jörg Wickrams. Beschreibung eines deutschen Ovid-Kommentars aus der Reformationszeit', *Zeitschrift für deutsche Philologie*, 86: 120–60

Stanivukovic, G.V. (ed.). 2001. *Ovid and the Renaissance Body* (Toronto: University of Toronto Press)

Starnes, DeWitt T. and Ernest William Talbert. 1955. *Classical Myth and Legend in Renaissance Dictionaries* (Chapel Hill: University of North Carolina Press)

Stefani, Chiara. 1993. 'Giacomo Franco', *Print Quarterly*, 10.3: 269–73

—— 1998. 'Franco, Giacomo', in *Dizionario Biografico degli Italiani*, 50 (Rome: Istituto dell'Enciclopedia Italiana), *ad vocem*, pp. 180–84

Stockhorst, Stefanie. 2010. 'Introduction. Cultural Transfer Through Translation: A Current Perspective in Enlightment Studies', in *Cultural Transfer Through Translation. The Circulation of Enlightened Thought in Europe by Means of Translation*, ed. by Stefanie Stockhorst (Amsterdam & New York: Rodopi)

Strubel, Armand. 2002. *'Grant senefiance a': Allégorie et littérature au Moyen Âge* (Paris: Honoré Champion)

Tarrant, Richard J. 1983. 'Ovid, *Amores, Ars amatoria, Remedia amoris*', in *Texts and Transmission*, ed. by L. D. Reynolds (Oxford: Clarendon Press), pp. 259–62

—— 1995. 'The Narrationes of 'Lactantius' and the Transmission of Ovid's Metamorphoses', in *Formative Stages of Classical Traditions: Latin Texts from Antiquity to the Renaissance*, ed. Oronzo Pecere and Michael D. Reeve (Spoleto: Centro Italiano di Studi sull'Alto Medioevo), pp. 83–115

Taylor, Anthony. 1986. 'George Sandys and Arthur Golding', *Notes and Queries*, 33: 387–91

Taylor, Helena. 2017. *The Lives of Ovid in Seventeenth-Century French Culture* (Oxford: Oxford University Press)

Temanza, Tommaso, and L. Grassi. 1966. *Vite dei più celebri architetti e scultori veneziani che fiorirono nel secolo decimosesto* (Milan: Edizioni Labor Riproduzioni e documentazioni)

Tholen, John. 2019. 'Ovidian Paratexts. Guiding the Reader to the *Metamorphoses* in the Low Countries' (unpublished doctoral thesis, Utrecht University)

——. In press. *Producing Ovid's 'Metamorphoses' in the Early Modern Low Countries. Paratexts, Publishers, Editors, Readers* (Leiden/Boston: Brill)

Tilliette, Jean-Yves. 2015. 'Pourquoi Bellérophon? Le sens et la composition du livre 4 de l'*Ovide moralisé*', in *Sens, Rhétorique et Musique. Études réunies en hommage à Jacqueline Cerquiglini-Toulet*, ed. by Sophie Albert, Mireille Demaules, Estelle Doudet, Sylvie Lefèfvre, Christopher Lucken and Agathe Sultan (Paris: Champion), pp. 149-66

TL. 1925. Peter Blumenthal and Achim Stein (eds.). *Tobler-Lommatzsch: Altfranzösisches Wörterbuch* (Stuttgart: Franz Steiner Verlag Wiesbaden gmbh)

Toepfer, Regina. 2016. 'Tragödientheorie und Narratologie. Die anonyme mittelhochdeutsche Versnovelle Hero und Leander', Mythos, 4: 187–201

—— 2018a. 'Ovid and Homer in "German Rhymes" (Ovid Und Homer in "Teutschen Reymen")', *Daphnis*, 46.1/2: 85–111

— 2018b. 'Veranschaulichungspoetik in der frühneuhochdeutschen Ovid-Rezeption. Philomelas Metamorphosen bei Wickram, Spreng und Posthius', in *Humanistische Antikenübersetzung und frühneuzeitliche Poetik in Deutschland (1450–1620)*, ed. by Regina Toepfer, Johannes K. Kipf and Jorg Robert (Berlin & Boston: De Gruyter), pp. 383–407

Toledano-Buendía, María Carmen. 2013. 'Listening to the Voice of the Translator: A Description of Translator's Notes as Paratextual Elements', *Translation & Interpreting*, 5.2: 149–62

Tomasi Velli, Silvia. 2007. *Le immagini e il tempo. Narrazione visiva, storia e allegoria tra Cinque e Seicento* (Pisa: Edizioni della Normale)

Torre, Andrea. 2014. 'Illustrando i Cinque canti', in *L'Orlando furioso nello specchio delle immagini*, ed. by Lina Bolzoni (Rome: Istituto della Enciclopedia Italiana), pp. 227–62

— 2017. 'Ovidio dopo Ariosto. Doppiaggi testuali e iconografici in edizioni illustrate del Cinquecento', in *Galassia Ariosto. Il modello editoriale del Furioso dal libro illustrato al web*, ed Lina Bolzoni (Rome: Donzelli), pp. 283–309

Torró, Jaume. 1994. '"Officium poetae est fingere": Francesc Alegre i la *Faula de Neptuno i Dyana*', in *Intel·lectuals i escriptors a la Baixa Edat Mitjana*, ed. by Lola Badia and Albert Soler (Barcelona: Curial & Publicacions de l'Abadia de Montserrat), pp. 221–42

— 2002. 'Bernat Metge i Avinyó', in *Llengua i cultura a la Corona d'Aragó, segles XIII–XV*, ed. by Lola Badia, Miriam Cabré and Sadurní Martí (Barcelona: Publicacions de l'Abadia de Montserrat)

Touchefeu, Odette. 1981. 'Aias I', in *Lexicon Iconographicum Mythologiae Classicae 1.1* (Zurich-Munich: Artemis), pp. 312–36

Trachsler, Richard. 2018. 'Auteur, milieu et date', in *Ovide moralisé. Livre 1. Tome 1*, ed. by C. Baker and others (Paris: Société des Anciens Textes Français), pp. 182–92

Trapp, Joseph Burney. 1995. 'Portraits of Ovid in the Middle Ages and Renaissance', in *Die Rezeption der 'Metamorphosen' des Ovid in der Neuzeit. Der Antike Mythos in Text und Bild: Internationales Simposium*, ed. by Hermann Waler and Hans Juegern Horn (Berlin: G. Mann), pp. 252–78

— 2001. 'Petrarch's Laura: The Portraiture of an Imaginary Beloved', *Journal of the Warburg and Courtauld Institutes*, 64: 55–192

Trebaiocchi, Chiara. 2016. '«Il letterato buono a tutto». Lodovico Dolce traduttore delle *Metamorfosi*', in *Per Lodovico Dolce. Miscellanea di studi. i. Passioni e competenze del letterato*, ed. by Paolo Marini and Paolo Procaccioli (Manziana: Vecchiarelli), pp. 271–316

Trousson, R. 1965-66. 'Feijoo, crítico de la exégesis mitológica', *NRFH*, 18: 453–61

Trovato, Paolo. 1991. *Con ogni diligenza corretto: la stampa e le revisioni editoriali dei testi letterari italiani, 1470–1570* (Bologna: Il Mulino)

— 1994. *Storia della lingua italiana: il primo Cinquecento* (Bologna: Il Mulino)

Tymcozko, Maria. 2007. *Enlarging Translation, Empowering Translators* (Manchester: St Jerome)

Usener, Knut. 1999. 'Verhinderte Liebschaft: zur Ovidrezeption bei Gottfried von Strassburg', in *Tristan und Isolt im Spätmittelalter. Vorträge eines interdisziplinären Symposiums vom 3. bis 8. Juni 1996 an der Justus-Liebig-Universität Giessen*, ed. by Xenja von Ertzdorff (Rodopi: Brill), pp. 219–45

Veilleux, Christian. 2017. 'Narcisse chasseur: jeu d'échos du motif cynégétique dans l'*Epistre Othea* de Christine de Pizan', *Memini*, 21 <https://journals.openedition.org/memini/90> [accessed 10 July 2019]

Vindel, Francisco. 1946. *El arte tipográfico en España durante el siglo XV, II: Salamanca, Zamora, Coria y Reino de Galicia* (Madrid: Dirección General de Relaciones Culturales)

Visser, Arnoud S. Q. 2011. *Reading Augustine in the Reformation. The Flexibility of Intellectual Authority in Europe, 1500-1620* (Oxford: Oxford University Press)

Vlahov, Sergej, and Sider Florin. 1970. 'Neperovodimoe v perevode. Realii', *Masterstvo perevoda*, 6: 432–56

Wagner, Bettina. 2008. 'An der Wiege des Paratexts. Formen der Kommunikation zwischen Druckern, Herausgebern und Lesern im 15. Jahrhundert', *Die Pluralisierung des Paratextes in der Frühen Neuzeit. Theorie, Formen, Funktionen*, ed. by Frieder von Ammon and Herfried Vögel (Berlin: LIT Verlag), pp. 133–55

Wall, Wendy. 2014. 'Reading the Home: The Case of *The English Housewife*', *Renaissance Paratexts*, ed. by Helen Smith and Louise Wilson (Cambridge: Cambridge University Press), pp. 165–84

Waquet, Françoise. 2002. *Latin or the Empire of a Sign. From the Sixteenth to the Twentieth Century*, trans. by John Howe (London & New York: Verso)

Wittgenstein, Ludwig. 1953 [1958], *Philosophische Untersuchungen* (*Philosophical Investigations*), trans. by G. E. M. Anscombe (New York: Macmillan)

Woodall, Dena Marie. 2008. 'Sharing Spaces: Double Portrait in Renaissance Italy' (unpublished doctoral thesis, Case Western Reserve University)

Wyatt, Michael. 2014. 'Renaissances', in *The Cambridge Companion to the Italian Renaissance*, ed. by Michael Wyatt (Cambridge: Cambridge University Press), pp. 1–16

Yeazell, Ruth B. 2015. *Picture Titles. How and Why Western Paintings Acquired Their Names* (Princeton & Oxford: Princeton University Press)

Zappella, Giuseppina. 1988. *Il ritratto nel libro italiano del Rinascimento*, 2 vols (Milan: Editrice Bibliografica)

— 2005. 'L'immagine frontispiziale', in *I dintorni del testo. Approcci alle periferie del libro*, ed. by M. Santoro and M. Tavoni (Rome: Edizioni dell'Ateneo), pp. 167–88

Zatti, Sergio. 1997. 'Introduzione', in Ludovico Ariosto, *Orlando Furioso e Cinque canti*, ed. by Remo Ceserani and Sergio Zatti (Turin: Utet), pp. 1633–51

LIST OF MANUSCRIPTS AND EDITIONS

a) Ovid's *Metamorphoses*

Title	Location	Date
San Marco 225 (*M*)	Florence, Biblioteca Medicea Laurenziana	10th-12th c.
IV.F.3 (*N*)	Naples, Biblioteca Nazionale	11th c.
Commentarium in Ovidii Nasonis Metamorphoseon libros (*Vaticanus Latinus 1479*)	Vatican, Biblioteca Apostolica Vaticana	*c.* 1300
Metamorphoses (*Vaticanus Latinus 1598*)	Vatican, Biblioteca Apostolica Vaticana	*c.* 1250

Pyramus and Thisbe in German manuscripts

	Vienna, Österreichische Nationalbibliothek, Cod. 2885 (fols 19^v–24^r)	22. April - 4. July 1393
	Innsbruck, Tiroler Landesmuseum Ferdinandeum, Cod. FB32001 (fols 14^v–17^r)	1456

Hero and Leander in German manuscripts

	Karlsruhe, Landesbibliothek, Cod. Donaueschingen 104 (fols 46^r–49^r)	first half of the 15th century

b) i. *Ovide moralisé*: manuscripts listed in chronological order

Ovide moralisé (A^1)	Rouen, Bibliothèque Municipale, MS O.4	*c.* 1320
Ovide moralisé (E^1)	Geneva, Bibliothèque de Genève, MS fr. 176	*c.* 1380
Ovide moralisé (E^2)	Vatican, Biblioteca Apostolica Vaticana, MS Reg. Lat. 1480	*c.* 1380
Ovide moralisé, owned by Jean de Berry	Lyon, Bibliothèque municipale, MS 742	*c.* 1390
Ovide moralisé, G^1	Paris, Bibliothèque nationale de France, MS fr. 373	*c.* 1400
Ovide moralisé G^3, copied with Pierre Bersuire's *De formis deorum*	Copenhagen, Kongelige Biblioteket, MS Thott 399	*c.* 1480

Ovide moralisé, Prose I	Vatican, Biblioteca Apostolica Vaticana, MS Reg. Lat., 1686	-?
Ovide moralisé, Prose II	London, British Library, Royal, MS 17. E. IV	Last quarter of the 15th century
Ovide moralisé, Prose II	Paris, Bibliothèque nationale de France, MS Français 137	*c.* 1470-1480
Ovide moralisé, Prose II	Saint Petersburg, National Library of Russia, MS F. v. XIV. 1	-?

b) ii. Pierre Bersuire

De formis deorum, copied with the Ovide moralisé	Copenhagen, Kongelige biblioteket, Thott 399	*c.* 1480

c) German: manuscripts transmitting the preserved fragments

Fragment A	Oldenburg, Staatsarchiv, lost	13th century
Fragment B	Staatsbibliothek zu Berlin, Preußischer Kulturbesitz, Ms. germ. fol. 831	13th century
Fragments C, D, E	Niedersächsisches Landesarchiv, Standort Oldenburg, NLA OL, Slg 10 [Best. 297] E 22)	13th century

d) Early Printed Books of Ovid's translations listed in chronological order

USTC

Ovid. 1484. *Metamorphoses [French] Ovide ... son livre intitulé Metamorphose (adapted by Colard Mansion, with a commentary)* (Bruges: Colard Mansion)   765551

— 1493/1494. *La Bible des poetes metamorphose* (Paris: Antoine Vérard)   37566

—1484. *Metamorphoses [French] Ovide ... son livre intitulé Metamorphose*, adapted by Colard Mansion, with a commentary (Bruges: Colard Mansion)   71418

—1494. Francesc Alegre (trans.). *Transformacions* (Barcelona: Pere Miquel)   333329

—1497. Giovanni Bonsignori (trans.). *Ovidio Metamorphoseos Vulgare* (Venice: Lucantonio Giunta)

—1510(?). *Le Livre de Orpheus translaté de latin en françoys, ouquel y a plusieurs choses recreatives* (Paris: Michel Le Noir)

— 1510. *Le Livre du vaillant Perseus, filz de Jupiter* (Paris: Philippe Le Noir)   55680

—1522. Niccolò degli Agostini (trans.). *Tutti gli libri de Ovidio Metamorphoseos tradutti dal litteral in verso vulgar* (Venice: Niccolò Zoppino)

—1523. *La bible des poëtes, Methamorphoze. Nouvellement imprimé a Paris* (Paris: Philippe Le Noir)   64020

—1529. *Opera* (Antwerpen: [Merten de Keyser] apud Govaert van der Haeghen, 1529) 8o. A-B8 a-i8 K8 l-z8. ff. [16] 183 [1]   410235

—1531. *La bible des poëtes de Ovide Methamorphose. Translatee de latin en françoys. Nouvellement Imprimee a Paris (Paris: Philippe Le Noir)*   47798

—1532. *Le Grant Olympe des histoires poëtiques du prince des poëtes Ovide Naso en sa Methamorphose* (Lyon: Romain Morin)   49832

—1536? Bustamante, Jorge de. *Libro de metamorphoseos y fabulas del excelente poeta y philosofo Ovidio noble cavallero patricio romano* (Salamanca: Pedro de Castro)

— 1537. *Le grand Olympe des hystoires poetiques* (Paris: E. Caveiller)   1019443

— 1539. Dolce, Lodovico. *Il primo libro delle Trasformationi d'Ovidio da M. Lodouico Dolce in volgare tradotto* (Venice: Francesco Bindoni & Maffeo Pasini)   845742

—1545. Jörg Wickram (trans.). *P. Ouidij Nasonis deß aller sinnreichsten Poeten Metamorphosis, Das ist von der wunderbarlichen Verenderung der Gestalten der Menschen, Thier vnd anderer Creaturen* (Mainz: Ivo Schöffer)   681909

—1551. Jörg Wickram (trans.). Ovidius Naso, Publius, *Metamorphosis das ist von der wunderbarlicher verenderung der gestalten der menschen thier und anderer creaturen...* (Meintz: Ivo Schöffer)   681908

—1553a. Lodovico Dolce (trans.). *Le Trasformationi* (Venice: Gabriele Giolito De Ferrari)   845802

—1553b. *Lodovico Dolce (trans.). Le Trasformationi di M. Lodovico Dolce. Di nuovo ristampate, e da lui ricorrette, et in diversi luoghi ampliate. Con la tavola delle favole. Con privilegi* (Venice: Gabriele Giolito dei Ferrari and brothers)   845803

—1555. Lodovico Dolce (trans.), *Trasformationi* (Venice: Giolito)   845810

—1561. Giovanni Andrea dell'Anguillara (trans.). *Le Metamorfosi di Ovidio* (Venice: Giovanni Griffio)   845828

—1563. Giovanni Andrea dell'Anguillara (trans.). *Le Metamorfosi di* *Ovidio ridotte da Giovanni Andrea dell'Anguillara in ottava* *rima, al christianissimo re di Francia Henrico Secondo, di* *nuovo dal proprio auttore rivedute, et corrette; con le* *annotationi di M. Gioseppe Horologgi.* Con Privilegii (Venice: Giovanni Griffio for Francesco de' Franceschi Senese)   845835

—1570. Lodovico Dolce (trans.). *Le Trasformationi di M. Lodovico* *Dolce tratte da Ovidio. Con gli argomenti et allegorie al* *principio, et al fine di ciascun canto. E con la giunta della vita* *d'Ovidio. Di nuovo rivedute, corrette, et di molte figure* *adornate a suoi luoghi* (Venice: Domenico Farri) British Library, C.81.b.11   845857

—1580. Antonio Pérez Sigler (trans.). *Los quinze libros de los* *metamorphoseos de el excellente poeta latino Ovidio. Traduzidos* *en verso suelto y octava rima por Antonio Perez con sus alegorias* *al fin de cada libro* (Salamanca: Juan Perier) British Library, 1068.g.36   340437

—1581. Jörg Wickram (trans.). *Metamorphosis, oder: wunderbarliche* *unnd seltzame beschreibung von der menschen, thiern und* *anderer creaturen veränderung, auch von dem wandeln der* *götter...* (Frankfurt am Mayn: bey Johann Feyerabendt, in Verlegung Sigmund Feyerabendts)   681915

—1584. Giovanni Andrea dell'Anguillara (trans.), *Metamorfosi* *d'Ovidio* (Venice: Giunti)   845904

—1586. Felipe Mei (trans.). *Del metamorphoseos de Ovidio en octava* *rima* (Tarragona: Felipe Mey)   340432

—1589. Pedro Sánchez de Viana. *Las transformaciones de Ovidio:* *traduzidas del verso latino, en tercetos y octavas rimas ... con el* *comento, y explicacion de las fabulas: reduziendolas a* *philosophia natural, y moral, y astrologia, e historia* (Valladolid: Diego Fernández de Córdoba)   340434

—1592. Giovanni Andrea dell'Anguillara (trans.). *Le Metamorfosi* *d'Ovidio, ridotte da Gio. Andrea dell'Anguillara in ottava rima,* *Al christianissimo re di Francia, Henrico Secondo. Nuovamente* *di bellissime e vaghe figure adornate, et diligentemente corrette.* *Con l'annotationi di M. Gioseppe Horologgi, et con nuove* *postille, et argomenti a ciascun libro, di M. Francesco Turchi.* *Con privilegio* (Venice: Bernardo Giunti)   845937

—1609. Jörg Wickram (trans.). *P. Ovidii Metamorphosis, oder, Wunderbarliche und seltzame Beschreibung von der Menschen, Thiern, unnd anderer Creaturen Verduderung, auch von dem Wandeln, Leben und Thaten der Götter Martis, Veneris, Mercury, etc. ...* (Frankfurt am Mayn: bey Johann Saurn, in Verlegung Francisci Nicolai Rothen)

—1618. Francesco Pona (trans.), *Trasformazione del primo libro delle Metamorfosi d'Ovidio* (Verona: Merlo)   4028469

—1626. George Sandys (trans.). *Ovid's Metamorphosis Englished by G. S.* (London: W. Stansby)

—1631. Jörg Wickram (trans.). *P. Ovidii Metamorphosis, Oder: Wunderbarliche und seltzame Beschreibung von der Menschen, Thieren und anderer Creaturen Veränderung, auch von den Wandeln, Leben und Thaten der Götter, Martis, Veneris, Mercurii etc. ...* (Franckfurt am Mayn: durch Gottfried Tampach, Truckts Caspar Rötel)

—1632. George Sandys (trans.). *Ovid's Metamorphosis Englished, Mythologiz'd, and Represented in Figures: An essay to the Translation of Virgil's Aeneis by G.S.* (Oxford: John Lichfield)

—1637. Giovanni Andrea dell'Anguillara (trans.). *Le Metamorfosi ... ridotte da Giouanni Andrea dall'Anguillara in ottaua rima. Con l'annotationi di M. Gioseppe Horologgi, et con gli argomenti di M. Francesco Turchi. Di nuouo in questa nostra vltima impressione con somma diligenza ricorrette, & di vaghe figure adornate* (Venice: Gio. Antonio & Gio. Maria Misserini Fratelli) (British Library, 1607/1488)   4012478

—1638. Nicolas Renouard (trans.). *Les Metamorphoses d'Ovide traduites en prose françoise ... et enrichies de figures à chacune fable. Avec XV. discours contenans l'explication morale et historique* (Rouen: Antoine de Quay)   6813473

—1643a. *Metamorphosis, dat is verandering of herschepping*, anonymous translation (Amsterdam: for Jan van Hilten) USTC 1019443   1019443

—1643b. *Metamorphosis, dat is verandering, of herschepping*, anonymous translation (Amsterdam: for Pieter Robijn)   1013756

—1643c. *Metamorphosis, dat is verandering, of herschepping*, anonymous translation (Amsterdam: for Jodocus Janssonius, 1643)   1013755

—1643d. *Metamorphosis, dat is verandering, of herschepping*, anonymous translation (Amsterdam: for Dirck Cornelisz Houthaeck)   1013754

—1643e [1693]. *Metamorphosus* [!], *dat is verandering, of herschepping*, anonymous translation (Amsterdam: for Jan Jacobsz Schipper)   1029288

—1677. Giovanni Andrea dell'Anguillara (trans.). *Le Metamorfosi di Ovidio ridotte da Gio. Andrea dell'Anguillara in ottava rima con le annotationi di M. Gioseppe Horologgi e gli argomenti di M. Francesco Turchi in questa nuova impressione di vaghe figure adornate* (Venice: Zaccaria Conzavi)

—1686. Ioannis Makolas (trans.). Βιβλίον ἱστορικὸν καλούμενον Ἰουστῖνος (Venice: Michael Angelos Varvonios)

— 1698. Thomas Corneille (trans.). *Les Metamorphoses d'Ovide mises en vers françois*, 3 vols (Liege: Broncart) British Library, 11352.aa.4

—1716. Jean Baptiste Bellegarde (trans.). *Les Metamorphoses d'Ovide, avec des explications ... Traduction nouvelle par M. l'Abbé de Bellegarde*, 2nd corrected edn (Amsterdam: E. Roger)

—1735–1737. Diego and Ignacio Suárez de Figueroa (trans.). *P. Ovidio Nason, Metamorphoseos*, 4 vols (Madrid: Herederos de Francisco del Hierro)

—1757. Giovanni Andrea dell'Anguillara (trans.). *Le Metamorfosi di Ovidio, ridotte da Gio. Andrea dell'Anguillara in ottava rima. Con l'Annotationi di M. Gioseppe Horologgi, e con gli argomenti di M. Francesco Turchi dedicate a sua eccellenza la N.D. Catterina Segredo Barbarigo. Tomo primo.* (Venice: Girolamo Dorigoni)

—1805. Giovanni Andrea dell'Anguillara (trans.). *Le Metamorfosi d'Ovidio ridotte da Giovanni Andrea dell'Anguillara in ottava rima. Volume primo* (Milan: Società tipografica de' classici italiani)

INDEX OF AUTHORS AND WORKS

SUBJECT INDEX